Oracle Database 12c Performance Tuning Recipes

A Problem-Solution Approach

Sam R. Alapati
Darl Kuhn
Bill Padfield

Oracle Database 12c Performance Tuning Recipes: A Problem-Solution Approach

ISBN-13 (pbk): 978-1-4302-6187-2

ISBN-13 (electronic): 978-1-4302-6188-9

President and Publisher: Paul Manning
Lead Editor: Jonathan Gennick
Technical Reviewer: Stéphane Faroult and Arup Nanda
Editorial Board: Steve Anglin, Ewan Buckingham, Gary Cornell, Louise Corrigan, James DeWolf,
    Jonathan Gennick, Jonathan Hassell, Robert Hutchinson, Michelle Lowman, James Markham,
    Matthew Moodie, Jeff Olson, Jeffrey Pepper, Douglas Pundick, Ben Renow-Clarke, Dominic Shakeshaft,
    Gwenan Spearing, Matt Wade, Steve Weiss, Tom Welsh
Coordinating Editor: Kevin Shea
Copy Editors: Angie Wood and Kim Wimpsett
Compositor: SPi Global
Indexer: SPi Global
Artist: SPi Global
Cover Designer: Anna Ishchenko

Distributed to the book trade worldwide by Springer Science+Business Media New York, 233 Spring Street, 6th Floor, New York, NY 10013. Phone 1-800-SPRINGER, fax (201) 348-4505, e-mail orders-ny@springer-sbm.com, or visit www.springeronline.com.

For information on translations, please e-mail rights@apress.com, or visit www.apress.com.

Apress and friends of ED books may be purchased in bulk for academic, corporate, or promotional use. eBook versions and licenses are also available for most titles. For more information, reference our Special Bulk Sales–eBook Licensing web page at www.apress.com/bulk-sales.

Any source code or other supplementary materials referenced by the author in this text is available to readers at www.apress.com. For detailed information about how to locate your book's source code, go to www.apress.com/source-code.

To Dale, Shawn, and Keith, with love and affection.

—Sam Alapati

To Lisa, Heidi, and Brandi.

—Darl Kuhn

With love to Oyuna, Evan, and my family.

—Bill Padfield

Contents at a Glance

About the Authors xlv

About the Technical Reviewers xlvii

Acknowledgments xlix

Introduction li

■Chapter 1: Optimizing Table Performance 1

■Chapter 2: Choosing and Optimizing Indexes 51

■Chapter 3: Optimizing Instance Memory 95

■Chapter 4: Monitoring System Performance 125

■Chapter 5: Minimizing System Contention 157

■Chapter 6: Analyzing Operating System Performance 193

■Chapter 7: Troubleshooting the Database 217

■Chapter 8: Creating Efficient SQL 259

■Chapter 9: Manually Tuning SQL 307

■Chapter 10: Tracing SQL Execution 335

■Chapter 11: Automated SQL Tuning 375

■Chapter 12: Execution Plan Optimization and Consistency 415

■Chapter 13: Configuring the Optimizer 457

■Chapter 14: Implementing Query Hints 501

■Chapter 15: Executing SQL in Parallel 537

Index 569

Contents

About the Authors... xlv

About the Technical Reviewers xlvii

Acknowledgments... xlix

Introduction li

■Chapter 1: Optimizing Table Performance 1

1-1. Building a Database That Maximizes Performance 2

Problem 2

Solution 3

How It Works 6

1-2. Creating Tablespaces to Maximize Performance 7

Problem 7

Solution 7

How It Works 8

1-3. Matching Table Types to Business Requirements 8

Problem 8

Solution 9

How It Works 9

1-4. Choosing Table Features for Performance 10

Problem 10

Solution 10

How It Works 11

1-5. Selecting Data Types Appropriately 12

Problem 12

Solution 12

How It Works 13

1-6. Avoiding Extent Allocation Delays When Creating Tables.............................16

Problem 16

Solution 16

How It Works 17

1-7. Maximizing Data-Loading Speeds 18

Problem 18

Solution 18

How It Works 19

1-8. Efficiently Removing Table Data...20

Problem 20

Solution 20

How It Works 21

1-9. Displaying Automated Segment Advisor Advice 23

Problem 23

Solution 23

How It Works 24

1-10. Manually Generating Segment Advisor Advice 26

Problem 26

Solution 26

How It Works 28

1-11. Automatically E-mailing Segment Advisor Output 29

Problem 29

Solution 29

How It Works 30

1-12. Rebuilding Rows Spanning Multiple Blocks 31

Problem 31

Solution 31

How It Works 34

1-13. Detecting Row Chaining and Row Migration 35

Problem 35

Solution 35

How It Works 36

1-14. Differentiating Between Row Migration and Row Chaining 36

Problem 36

Solution 37

How It Works 37

1-15. Proactively Preventing Row Migration/Chaining 37

Problem 37

Solution 37

How It Works 38

1-16. Detecting Unused Space in a Table 38

Problem 38

Solution 38

How It Works 39

1-17. Tracing to Detect Space Below the High-Water Mark 40

Problem 40

Solution 40

How It Works 41

1-18. Using DBMS_SPACE to Detect Space Below the High-Water Mark 41

Problem 41

Solution 41

How It Works 42

1-19. Freeing Unused Table Space 42

Problem 42

Solution 42

How It Works 43

1-20. Compressing Data for Direct Path Loading 44

Problem 44

Solution 44

How It Works 45

1-21. Compressing Data for All DML 46

Problem 46

Solution 46

How It Works 47

1-22. Compressing Data at the Column Level 48

Problem 48

Solution 48

How It Works 49

■Chapter 2: Choosing and Optimizing Indexes 51

2-1. Understanding B-tree Indexes 53

Problem 53

Solution 53

How It Works 59

2-2. Deciding Which Columns to Index 60

Problem 60

Solution 60

How It Works 62

2-3. Creating a Primary Key Constraint and Index 63

Problem 63

Solution 63

How It Works 64

2-4. Ensuring Unique Column Values 65

Problem 65

Solution..65

How It Works...66

2-5. Indexing Foreign Key Columns 68

Problem 68

Solution..68

How It Works...69

2-6. Deciding When to Use a Concatenated Index 72

Problem 72

Solution..72

How It Works...73

2-7. Reducing Index Size Through Compression...74

Problem 74

Solution..75

How It Works...75

2-8. Implementing a Function-Based Index 76

Problem 76

Solution..76

How It Works...77

2-9. Indexing a Virtual Column 78

Problem 78

Solution..78

How It Works...78

2-10. Limiting Index Contention when Several Processes Insert in Parallel 79

Problem 79

Solution..79

How It Works...80

2-11. Toggling the Visibility of an Index to the Optimizer 80
Problem 80
Solution 81
How It Works 81

2-12. Creating a Bitmap Index in Support of a Star Schema 82
Problem 82
Solution 82
How It Works 83

2-13. Creating a Bitmap Join Index 85
Problem 85
Solution 85
How It Works 86

2-14. Creating an Index-Organized Table 86
Problem 86
Solution 86
How It Works 87

2-15. Monitoring Index Usage 88
Problem 88
Solution 88
How It Works 89

2-16. Maximizing Index Creation Speed 89
Problem 89
Solution 89
How It Works 90

2-17. Reclaiming Unused Index Space 91
Problem 91
Solution 92
How It Works 92

■Chapter 3: Optimizing Instance Memory 95

3-1. Automating Memory Management 95
Problem 95
Solution 95
How It Works 96

3-2. Managing Multiple Buffer Pools 98
Problem 98
Solution 99
How It Works 99

3-3. Setting Minimum Values for Memory 100
Problem 100
Solution 100
How It Works 101

3-4. Monitoring Memory Resizing Operations 101
Problem 101
Solution 101
How It Works 102

3-5. Optimizing Memory Usage 103
Problem 103
Solution 103
How It Works 103

3-6. Tuning PGA Memory Allocation 104
Problem 104
Solution 104
How It Works 104

3-7. Configuring the Server Query Cache 107
Problem 107
Solution 107
How It Works 108

3-8. Managing the Server Result Cache 109

Problem 109

Solution 109

How It Works 111

3-9. Caching SQL Query Results 111

Problem 111

Solution 112

How It Works 112

3-10. Caching Client Result Sets 115

Problem 115

Solution 115

How It Works 116

3-11. Caching PL/SQL Function Results 117

Problem 117

Solution 117

How It Works 118

3-12. Configuring the Oracle Database Smart Flash Cache 120

Problem 120

Solution 120

How It Works 121

3-13. Tuning the Redo Log Buffer 122

Problem 122

Solution 122

How It Works 122

3-14. Limiting PGA Memory Allocation 123

Problem 123

Solution 123

How It Works 124

■**Chapter 4: Monitoring System Performance** **125**

4-1. Implementing Automatic Workload Repository (AWR) **125**

Problem 125

Solution..126

How It Works...126

4-2. Modifying the Statistics Interval and Retention Periods **128**

Problem 128

Solution..128

How It Works...129

4-3. Generating an AWR Report Manually **129**

Problem 129

Solution..129

How It Works...131

4-4. Generating an AWR Report via Enterprise Manager..**133**

Problem 133

Solution..133

How It Works...134

4-5. Generating an AWR Report for a Single SQL Statement..**135**

Problem 135

Solution..135

How It Works...136

4-6. Creating a Statistical Baseline for Your Database..**136**

Problem 136

Solution..136

How It Works...138

4-7. Managing AWR Baselines via Enterprise Manager **140**

Problem 140

Solution..140

How It Works...141

4-8. Managing AWR Statistics Repository 142

Problem 142

Solution 142

How It Works 142

4-9. Creating AWR Baselines Automatically 144

Problem 144

Solution 144

How It Works 145

4-10. Quickly Analyzing AWR Output 145

Problem 145

Solution 145

How It Works 147

4-11. Manually Getting Active Session Information 147

Problem 147

Solution 147

How It Works 151

4-12. Getting ASH Information from Enterprise Manager 152

Problem 152

Solution 152

How It Works 153

4-13. Getting ASH Information from the Data Dictionary 154

Problem 154

Solution 154

How It Works 155

■Chapter 5: Minimizing System Contention 157

5-1. Understanding Response Time 157

Problem 157

Solution 157

How It Works 158

5-2. Identifying SQL Statements with the Most Waits 159

Problem 159

Solution 160

How It Works 160

5-3. Analyzing Wait Events 160

Problem 160

Solution 161

How It Works 161

5-4. Understanding Wait Class Events 162

Problem 162

Solution 162

How It Works 163

5-5. Examining Session Waits 163

Problem 163

Solution 163

How It Works 164

5-6. Examining Wait Events by Class 164

Problem 164

Solution 165

How It Works 167

5-7. Resolving Buffer Busy Waits 167

Problem 167

Solution 167

How It Works 168

5-8. Resolving Log File Sync Waits 169

Problem 169

Solution 169

How It Works 169

5-9. Minimizing Read by Other Session Wait Events 170

Problem 170

Solution 170

How It Works 171

5-10. Reducing Direct Path Read Wait Events 171

Problem 171

Solution 172

How It Works 173

5-11. Minimizing Recovery Writer Waits 173

Problem 173

Solution 173

How It Works 174

5-12. Finding Out Who's Holding a Blocking Lock 174

Problem 174

Solution 174

How It Works 175

5-13. Identifying Blocked and Blocking Sessions 176

Problem 176

Solution 176

How It Works 177

5-14. Dealing with a Blocking Lock 177

Problem 177

Solution 177

How It Works 178

5-15. Identifying a Locked Object 179

Problem 179

Solution 179

How It Works 179

5-16. Resolving enq: TM Lock Contention 180

    Problem 180

    Solution 180

    How It Works 180

5-17. Identifying Recently Locked Sessions 182

    Problem 182

    Solution 182

    How It Works 182

5-18. Analyzing Recent Wait Events in a Database 185

    Problem 185

    Solution 185

    How It Works 186

5-19. Identifying Time Spent Waiting Because of Locking 186

    Problem 186

    Solution 186

    How It Works 186

5-20. Minimizing Latch Contention 188

    Problem 188

    Solution 189

    How It Works 190

■Chapter 6: Analyzing Operating System Performance 193

6-1. Detecting Disk Space Issues 195

    Problem 195

    Solution 195

    How It Works 196

6-2. Identifying System Bottlenecks 198

    Problem 198

    Solution 198

    How It Works 199

6-3. Determining Top System-Resource-Consuming Processes 200

Problem 200

Solution 200

How It Works..201

6-4. Detecting CPU Bottlenecks 202

Problem 202

Solution 203

How It Works..203

6-5. Identifying Processes Consuming CPU and Memory 204

Problem 204

Solution 204

How It Works..204

6-6. Determining I/O Bottlenecks 205

Problem 205

Solution 205

How It Works..207

6-7. Detecting Network-Intensive Processes 208

Problem 208

Solution 208

How It Works..209

6-8. Mapping a Resource-Intensive Process to a Database Process 210

Problem 210

Solution 210

How It Works..212

6-9. Terminating a Resource-Intensive Process 213

Problem 213

Solution 213

How It Works..215

■Chapter 7: Troubleshooting the Database...**217**

7-1. Determining the Optimal Undo Retention Period 217

Problem 217

Solution 217

How It Works 219

7-2. Finding What's Consuming the Most Undo 222

Problem 222

Solution 222

How It Works 223

7-3. Resolving an ORA-01555 Error 223

Problem 223

Solution 223

How It Works 224

7-4. Monitoring Temporary Tablespace Usage 225

Problem 225

Solution 225

How It Works 226

7-5. Identifying Who Is Using the Temporary Tablespace 226

Problem 226

Solution 226

How It Works 227

7-6. Resolving the "Unable to Extend Temp Segment" Error 228

Problem 228

Solution 228

How It Works 228

7-7. Resolving Open Cursor Errors 230

Problem 230

Solution 230

How It Works 231

7-8. Resolving a Hung Database 232
Problem 232
Solution 232
How It Works 234

7-9. Invoking the Automatic Diagnostic Repository Command Interpreter 236
Problem 236
Solution 236
How It Works 238

7-10. Viewing an Alert Log from ADRCI 240
Problem 240
Solution 240
How It Works 241

7-11. Viewing Incidents with ADRCI 242
Problem 242
Solution 242
How It Works 243

7-12. Packaging Incidents for Oracle Support 244
Problem 244
Solution 244
How It Works 245

7-13. Running a Database Health Check...245
Problem 245
Solution 246
How It Works 246

7-14. Creating a SQL Test Case 247
Problem 247
Solution 247
How It Works 249

7-15. Generating an AWR Report 250

Problem 250

Solution.. 250

How It Works.. 252

7-16. Comparing Database Performance Between Two Periods..................................253

Problem 253

Solution.. 253

How It Works.. 254

7-17. Analyzing an AWR Report..255

Problem 255

Solution.. 255

How It Works.. 258

■Chapter 8: Creating Efficient SQL 259

8-1. Retrieving All Rows from a Table 260

Problem 260

Solution.. 260

How It Works.. 261

8-2. Retrieve a Subset of Rows from a Table 261

Problem 261

Solution.. 261

How It Works.. 262

8-3. Joining Tables with Corresponding Rows 263

Problem 263

Solution.. 263

How It Works.. 264

8-4. Joining Tables When Corresponding Rows May Be Missing...............................266

Problem 266

Solution.. 266

How It Works.. 268

8-5. Constructing Simple Subqueries 269

Problem 269

Solution 270

How It Works 270

8-6. Constructing Correlated Subqueries 274

Problem 274

Solution 274

How It Works 274

8-7. Comparing Two Tables to Find Missing Rows 276

Problem 276

Solution 276

How It Works 277

8-8. Comparing Two Tables to Find Matching Rows 278

Problem 278

Solution 278

How It Works 278

8-9. Combining Results from Similar SELECT Statements 279

Problem 279

Solution 279

How It Works 279

8-10. Searching for a Range of Values 281

Problem 281

Solution 281

How It Works 282

8-11. Handling Null Values 285

Problem 285

Solution 285

How It Works 287

8-12. Searching for Partial Column Values 288

    Problem 288

    Solution 288

    How It Works 289

8-13. Re-using SQL Statements Within the Shared Pool 292

    Problem 292

    Solution 292

    How It Works 293

8-14. Avoiding Accidental Full Table Scans 296

    Problem 296

    Solution 296

    How It Works 297

8-15. Creating Efficient Temporary Views 298

    Problem 298

    Solution 298

    How It Works 299

8-16. Avoiding the NOT Clause 301

    Problem 301

    Solution 301

    How It Works 302

8-17. Controlling Transaction Sizes 303

    Problem 303

    Solution 303

    How It Works 304

■Chapter 9: Manually Tuning SQL 307

9-1. Displaying an Execution Plan for a Query 308

    Problem 308

    Solution 308

    How It Works 309

9-2. Customizing Execution Plan Output 310

Problem 310

Solution 311

How It Works 312

9-3. Graphically Displaying an Execution Plan 314

Problem 314

Solution 314

How It Works 315

9-4. Reading an Execution Plan 315

Problem 315

Solution 315

How It Works 316

9-5. Monitoring Long-Running SQL Statements 317

Problem 317

Solution 318

How It Works 318

9-6. Identifying Resource-Consuming SQL Statements That Are Currently Executing 318

Problem 318

Solution 319

How It Works 319

9-7. Seeing Execution Statistics for Currently Running SQL 320

Problem 320

Solution 320

How It Works 321

9-8. Monitoring Progress of a SQL Execution Plan 323

Problem 323

Solution 323

How It Works 325

9-9. Identifying Resource-Consuming SQL Statements That Have Executed in the Past...........326

    Problem 326

    Solution...327

    How It Works..327

Comparing SQL Performance After a System Change...328

    Problem 328

    Solution...328

    How It Works..333

■Chapter 10: Tracing SQL Execution...335

10-1. Preparing Your Environment 335

    Problem 335

    Solution...335

    How It Works..336

10-2. Tracing a Specific SQL Statement...338

    Problem 338

    Solution...338

    How It Works..339

10-3. Enabling Tracing in Your Own Session 340

    Problem 340

    Solution...340

    How It Works..340

10-4. Finding the Trace Files 340

    Problem 340

    Solution...340

    How It Works..341

10-5. Examining a Raw SQL Trace File...342

    Problem 342

    Solution...342

    How It Works..342

10-6. Analyzing Oracle Trace Files 343

Problem 343

Solution 343

How It Works 343

10-7. Formatting Trace Files with TKPROF 344

Problem 344

Solution 344

How It Works 344

10-8. Analyzing TKPROF Output 345

Problem 345

Solution 345

How It Works 345

10-9. Analyzing Trace Files with Oracle Trace Analyzer 348

Problem 348

Solution 348

How It Works 350

10-10. Tracing a Parallel Query 351

Problem 351

Solution 351

How It Works 352

10-11. Tracing Specific Parallel Query Processes 353

Problem 353

Solution 353

How It Works 353

10-12. Tracing Parallel Queries in a RAC System 353

Problem 353

Solution 353

How It Works 354

10-13. Consolidating Multiple Trace Files 354

    Problem 354

    Solution..354

    How It Works...355

10-14. Finding the Correct Session for Tracing..355

    Problem 355

    Solution..355

    How It Works...356

10-15. Tracing a SQL Session...356

    Problem 356

    Solution..356

    How It Works...357

10-16. Tracing a Session by Process ID 358

    Problem 358

    Solution..358

    How It Works...359

10-17. Tracing Multiple Sessions 359

    Problem 359

    Solution..359

    How It Works...359

10-18. Tracing an Instance or a Database..360

    Problem 360

    Solution..360

    How It Works...360

10-19. Generating an Event 10046 Trace for a Session 361

    Problem 361

    Solution..361

    How It Works...361

10-20. Generating an Event 10046 Trace for an Instance 363
Problem 363
Solution 363
How It Works 363

10-21. Setting a Trace in a Running Session 363
Problem 363
Solution 364
How It Works 364

10-22. Enabling Tracing in a Session After a Login 364
Problem 364
Solution 364
How It Works 365

10-23. Tracing the Optimizer's Execution Path 365
Problem 365
Solution 365
How It Works 366

10-24. Generating Automatic Oracle Error Traces 368
Problem 368
Solution 368
How It Works 369

10-25. Tracing a Background Process 369
Problem 369
Solution 369
How It Works 370

10-26. Enabling Oracle Listener Tracing 370
Problem 370
Solution 370
How It Works 371

10-27. Setting Archive Tracing for Data Guard 372

Problem 372

Solution 372

How It Works 372

Chapter 11: Automated SQL Tuning 375

11-1. Displaying Automatic SQL Tuning Job Details 377

Problem 377

Solution 378

How It Works 378

11-2. Displaying Automatic SQL Tuning Advisor Advice 379

Problem 379

Solution 379

How It Works 381

11-3. Generating a SQL Script to Implement Automatic Tuning Advice 383

Problem 383

Solution 383

How It Works 384

11-4. Modifying Automatic SQL Tuning Features 384

Problem 384

Solution 384

How It Works 385

11-5. Disabling and Enabling Automatic SQL Tuning 386

Problem 386

Solution 386

How It Works 387

11-6. Modifying Maintenance Window Attributes 388

Problem 388

Solution 388

How It Works 389

11-7. Creating a SQL Tuning Set Object 390
Problem 390
Solution 390
How It Works 390

11-8. Viewing Resource-Intensive SQL in the AWR 390
Problem 390
Solution 390
How It Works 391

11-9. Populating a SQL Tuning Set from High-Resource SQL in AWR 393
Problem 393
Solution 393
How It Works 394

11-10. Viewing Resource-Intensive SQL in Memory 394
Problem 394
Solution 395
How It Works 395

11-11. Populating a SQL Tuning Set from Resource-Consuming SQL in Memory 396
Problem 396
Solution 396
How It Works 397

11-12. Populating a SQL Tuning Set With All SQL in Memory 397
Problem 397
Solution 398
How It Works 398

11-13. Displaying the Contents of a SQL Tuning Set 399
Problem 399
Solution 399
How It Works 400

11-14. Selectively Deleting Statements from a SQL Tuning Set...401

Problem 401

Solution...401

How It Works...401

11-15. Transporting a SQL Tuning Set...402

Problem 402

Solution...402

How It Works...404

11-16. Creating a Tuning Task..404

Problem 404

Solution...405

How It Works...407

11-17. Running the SQL Tuning Advisor 407

Problem 407

Solution...408

How It Works...410

11-18. Generating SQL Tuning Advice from the Automatic Database Diagnostic Monitor 411

Problem 411

Solution...411

How It Works...414

■Chapter 12: Execution Plan Optimization and Consistency 415

Background 416

Seeing the Big Picture..417

12-1. Creating and Accepting a SQL Profile 420

Problem 420

Solution...420

How It Works...423

12-2. Determining if a Query is Using a SQL Profile..424

Problem 424

Solution...424

How It Works...425

12-3. Automatically Accepting SQL Profiles 425

Problem 425

Solution 426

How It Works 426

12-4. Displaying SQL Profile Information 428

Problem 428

Solution 428

How It Works 428

12-5. Selectively Testing a SQL Profile 429

Problem 429

Solution 429

How It Works 430

12-6. Transporting a SQL Profile to a Different Database 430

Problem 430

Solution 431

How It Works 432

12-7. Disabling a SQL Profile 433

Problem 433

Solution 433

How It Works 433

12-8. Dropping a SQL Profile 434

Problem 434

Solution 434

How It Works 434

12-9. Creating a Plan Baseline for a SQL Statement in Memory 435

Problem 435

Solution 435

How It Works 436

12-10. Creating Plan Baselines for SQL Contained in SQL Tuning Set..438

    Problem 438

    Solution...438

    How It Works..440

12-11. Automatically Adding Plan Baselines...440

    Problem 440

    Solution...440

    How It Works..441

12-12. Altering a Plan Baseline 442

    Problem 442

    Solution...442

    How It Works..442

12-13. Determining If Plan Baselines Exist 443

    Problem 443

    Solution...443

    How It Works..444

12-14. Determining if a Query is Using a Plan Baseline..445

    Problem 445

    Solution...446

    How It Works..446

12-15. Displaying Plan Baseline Execution Plans 447

    Problem 447

    Solution...447

    How It Works..447

12-16. Manually Adding a New Execution Plan to Plan Baseline (Evolving).............................448

    Problem 448

    Solution...448

    How It Works..450

12-17. Toggling the Automatic Acceptance of New Low-Cost Execution Plans 451

Problem 451

Solution 451

How It Works 451

12-18. Disabling Plan Baselines 451

Problem 451

Solution 452

How It Works 452

12-19. Removing Plan Baseline Information 452

Problem 452

Solution 452

How It Works 453

12-20. Transporting Plan Baselines 454

Problem 454

Solution 454

How It Works 455

■Chapter 13: Configuring the Optimizer 457

13-1. Choosing an Optimizer Goal 457

Problem 457

Solution 457

How It Works 458

13-2. Enabling Automatic Statistics Gathering 458

Problem 458

Solution 458

How It Works 459

13-3. Setting Preferences for Statistics Collection 460

Problem 460

Solution 461

How It Works 461

13-4. Manually Generating Statistics 466
Problem 466
Solution 466
How It Works 467

13-5. Locking Statistics 467
Problem 467
Solution 468
How It Works 468

13-6. Handling Missing Statistics 469
Problem 469
Solution 469
How It Works 469

13-7. Exporting Statistics 471
Problem 471
Solution 471
How It Works 472

13-8. Restoring Previous Versions of Statistics 472
Problem 472
Solution 472
How It Works 473

13-9. Gathering System Statistics 473
Problem 473
Solution 474
How It Works 475

13-10. Validating New Statistics 477
Problem 477
Solution 477
How It Works 478

13-11. Forcing the Optimizer to Use an Index 479

Problem 479

Solution 479

How It Works 479

13-12. Enabling Query Optimizer Features 480

Problem 480

Solution 480

How It Works 481

13-13. Keeping the Database from Creating Histograms 482

Problem 482

Solution 482

How It Works 482

13-14. Improving Performance When Not Using Bind Variables 483

Problem 483

Solution 483

How It Works 483

13-15. Understanding Adaptive Cursor Sharing 485

Problem 485

Solution 485

How It Works 486

13-16. Creating Statistics on Expressions 491

Problem 491

Solution 491

How It Works 491

13-17. Creating Statistics for Related Columns 492

Problem 492

Solution 492

How It Works 493

13-18. Automatically Creating Column Groups 493

    Problem 493

    Solution...493

    How It Works...494

13-19. Maintaining Statistics on Partitioned Tables...494

    Problem 494

    Solution...495

    How It Works...495

13-20. Concurrent Statistics Collection for Large Tables 496

    Problem 496

    Solution...496

    How It Works...496

13-21. Determining When Statistics Are Stale 498

    Problem 498

    Solution...498

    How It Works...498

13-22. Previewing Statistics Gathering Targets 499

    Problem 499

    Solution...499

    How It Works...500

Chapter 14: Implementing Query Hints 501

14-1. Writing a Hint 501

    Problem 501

    Solution...501

    How It Works...502

14-2. Changing the Access Path 503

    Problem 503

    Solution...503

    How It Works...504

14-3. Changing the Join Order 507

Problem 507

Solution 507

How It Works 508

14-4. Changing the Join Method 508

Problem 508

Solution 509

How It Works 511

14-5. Changing the Optimizer Version 511

Problem 511

Solution 512

How It Works 512

14-6. Choosing Between a Fast Response and Overall Optimization 513

Problem 513

Solution 513

How It Works 515

14-7. Performing a Direct-Path Insert 515

Problem 515

Solution 516

How It Works 517

14-8. Placing Hints in Views 519

Problem 519

Solution 519

How It Works 521

14-9. Caching Query Results 521

Problem 521

Solution 522

How It Works 524

14-10. Directing a Distributed Query to a Specific Database..525

Problem 525

Solution..526

How It Works..526

14-11. Gathering Extended Query Execution Statistics..529

Problem 529

Solution..530

How It Works..531

14-12. Enabling Query Rewrite 531

Problem 531

Solution..531

How It Works..532

14-13. Improving Star Schema Query Performance 533

Problem 533

Solution..533

How It Works..535

■Chapter 15: Executing SQL in Parallel 537

15-1. Enabling Parallelism for a Specific Query...537

Problem 537

Solution..537

How It Works..538

15-2. Enabling Parallelism at Object Creation..541

Problem 541

Solution..542

How It Works..542

15-3. Enabling Parallelism for an Existing Object 543

Problem 543

Solution..543

How It Works..544

15-4. Implementing Parallel DML 544
Problem 544
Solution 544
How It Works 545

15-5. Creating Tables in Parallel 547
Problem 547
Solution 547
How It Works 547

15-6. Creating Indexes in Parallel 549
Problem 549
Solution 550
How It Works 550

15-7. Rebuilding Indexes in Parallel 550
Problem 550
Solution 551
How It Works 551

15-8. Moving Partitions in Parallel 553
Problem 553
Solution 553
How It Works 553

15-9. Splitting Partitions in Parallel 555
Problem 555
Solution 555
How It Works 555

15-10. Enabling Automatic Degree of Parallelism 556
Problem 556
Solution 556
How It Works 558

15-11. Examining Parallel Explain Plans 559
Problem 559
Solution 560
How It Works 561

15-12. Monitoring Parallel Operations 562
Problem 562
Solution 562
How It Works 564

15-13. Finding Bottlenecks in Parallel Processes 564
Problem 564
Solution 564
How It Works 565

15-14. Getting Detailed Information on Parallel Sessions 566
Problem 566
Solution 566
How It Works 567

Index 569

About the Authors

Sam R. Alapati is a senior database architect at Cash America International in Fort Worth, Texas. Sam is an Oracle OCP 12c certification holder. Earlier, Sam worked as an Oracle DBA at AT&T, Boy Scouts of America, and Oracle Corporation. Sam has published several Oracle Database and middleware administration–related books, including forthcoming books such as *Oracle WebLogic Server 12c Administration Handbook and OCP Oracle Database 12c New Features for Administrators Exam Guide.*

Darl Kuhn is currently a DBA working for Oracle. He has written books on a variety of IT topics including SQL, performance tuning, Linux, backup and recovery, RMAN, and database administration. Darl also teaches Oracle classes for Regis University and does volunteer DBA work for the Rocky Mountain Oracle Users Group.

Bill Padfield is an Oracle Certified Professional, working for a large telecommunications company in Denver, Colorado, as a senior database administrator. Bill helps administer and manage a large data warehouse environment consisting of more than 100 databases. Bill has been an Oracle Database administrator for more than 16 years and has been in the IT industry since 1985. Bill also teaches graduate database courses at Regis University and currently resides in Aurora, Colorado, with his wife, Oyuna, and son, Evan.

About the Technical Reviewers

Stéphane Faroult is a French consultant who first discovered relational databases and the SQL language 30 years ago. Stéphane joined Oracle France in its early days (after a brief spell with IBM and a period of time teaching at the University of Ottawa) and developed an interest in performance and tuning topics, on which he soon started writing training courses. After leaving Oracle in 1988, Stéphane briefly tried going straight and did a bit of operational research, but after only a year, he succumbed again to the allure of relational databases. For his sins, Stéphane has been performing database consultancy continuously ever since and founded RoughSea Ltd in 1998. In recent years, Stéphane has had a growing interest in education, which has taken various forms, including books (*The Art of SQL,* soon followed by *Refactoring SQL Applications,* both published by O'Reilly) and more recently a textbook (*SQL Success,* published by RoughSea), a series of seminars in Asia, and video tutorials (`www.youtube.com/user/roughsealtd`).

 Arup Nanda has been an Oracle DBA for more than 18 years (and counting) working on all aspects of Oracle Database from modeling, performance tuning, backup, disaster recovery, security, and, more recently, Exadata. Currently he is the global database lead at a major multinational corporation near New York, managing, among other things, several Exadata installations. Arup has coauthored five books; published more than 500 articles in Oracle Magazine, OTN, and other publications; presented about 300 sessions at various Oracle technology conferences all over the world; and delivered 30 Oracle Celebrity Seminar series courses. He is an editor for SELECT Journal, the IOUG publication; a member of the board of directors of the Exadata SIG; an Oracle ACE director; and a member of the Oak Table Network. Acknowledging his professional expertise and involvement in the user community, Oracle awarded him the DBA of the Year title in 2003 and Architect of the Year in 2012.

Acknowledgments

Thanks to fellow coauthors Sam Alapati and Bill Padfield and also thanks to the numerous DBAs and developers who I've learned performance tuning techniques from over the years: Dave Jennings, Scott Schulze, Bob Suehrstedt, Pete Mullineaux, Janet Bacon, Sue Wagner, Mohan Koneru, Arup Nanda, Charles Kim, Bernard Lopuz, Barb Sannwald, Tim Gorman, Shawn Heisdorffer, Doug Davis, Sujit Pattanaik, Sudeep Pattanaik, Ken Roberts, Roger Murphy, Mehran Sowdaey, Kevin Bayer, Dan Fink, Guido Handley, Nehru Kaja, Tim Colbert, Glenn Balanoff, Bob Mason, Brad Blake, Cathy Wilson, Ravi Narayanaswamy, Abdul Ebadi, Kevin Hoyt, Trent Sherman, Sandra Montijo, Jim Secor, Maureen Frazzini, Sean Best, Stephan Haisley, Geoff Strebel, Patrick Gates, Buzzy Cheadle, Mark Blair, Karen Kappler, Mike Hutchinson, Liz Brill, Ennio Murroni, John Phillips, Mike O'Neill, Jack Donnelly, Beth Loker, Mike Eason, Greg Roberts, Debbie Earman, Bob Sell, Tom Wheltle, Chad Heckman, Ken Toney, Gabor Gyurovszky, Scott Norris, Joey Canlas, Eric Wendelin, Gary Smith, Mark Lutze, Kevin Quinlivan, Dean Price, Dave Bourque, Roy Backstrom, John Lilly, Valerie Eipper, Steve Buckmelter, John DiVirgilio, John Goggin, Simon Ip, Pascal Ledru, Kevin O'Grady, Peter Schow, Todd Sherman, Mike Tanaka, Doug Cushing, Will Thornburg, Steve Roughton, Sudha Verma, Christian Hessler, Tae Kim, Margaret Carson, Jed Summerton, Lea Wang, Ambereen Pasha, Dinesh Neelay, Kye Bae, Thom Chumley, Jeff Sherard, Erik Jasiak, Aaron Isom, Kristi Jackson, Karolyn Vowles, Britni Barovick, Amin Jiwani, Laurie Bourgeois, Vasanthan Dasan, Todd Wichers, Venkatesh Ranganathan, Dave Wood, Jeff Shoup, Brett Guy, and Jim Stark.

—Darl Kuhn

I'd like to thank Sam Alapati and Darl Kuhn for all of their help and support. Thanks to my managers over the years in helping me in my career. This includes but is not limited to Bob Ranncy, Beth Bowen, Larry Wyzgala, John Zlamal, Billie Ortega, Linda Scheldrup, Amy Neff, and Maureen Frazzini. I'd like to thank my current DBA team, for their great support and friendship. This includes Dave Carter, Debbie Fitzgerald, Sandy Hass, Pankaj Guleria, Brent Wagner, Kevin Tomimatsu, and John Townley. Over the years, I've learned an awful lot from the following folks, who have always been generous with their time and help and have been patient with my questions. I have to thank the Oracle architect at our company, Roby Sherman, for all his support and help over the years. There are a myriad of developers, testers, system administrators, and other folks who have been a tremendous help in my career. This includes Mark Nold, Mick McMahon, Sandra Montijo, Jerry Sanderson, Glen Sanderson, Jose Fernandez, Mike Hammontre, Pat Cain, Dave Steep, Gary Whiting, Ron Fullmer, Becky Enter, John Weber, Tony Romo, Avanish Gupta, Scott Bunker, Paul Mayes, Bill Read, Rod Ermish, Rick Barry, Sun Yang, Sue Wagner, John Saxe, Glenn Balanoff, Linda Lee Burau, Deborah Lieou-McCall, Bob Zumpf, Pete Sardaczuk, Kristi Sargent, George Huner, Pad Kail, Curtis Gay, Ross Bartholomay, Carol Rosenow, Scott Richards, Sheryl Gross, Lachelle Shambe, John Piel, Rob Grote, Rex Ellis, Zane Warton, Steve Pearson, Kim Lake, Jim Barclay, Jason Hermstad, Shari Plantz-Masters, Denise Duncan, Bob Mason, Brad Blake, Mike Nims, Cathie Wilson, Rob Coates, Shirley Amend, Rob Bushlack, Cindy Patterson, Debbie Chartier, Blair Christensen, Meera Ganesan, Kedar Panda, Srivatsan Muralidaran, Tony Arlt, Atul Shirke, Deb Kingsley, Brenda Carney, Paul Obering, Don Miller, Ned Ashby, Pat Wuller, and Adric Norris.

—Bill Padfield

Introduction

Oracle Database 12c Performance Tuning Recipes is a book of solutions—a *crib sheet* of sorts. Database performance problems often rear themselves suddenly, and with that suddenness comes great pressure from management and users to somehow work magic and get response time back under control. Everyone is in a panic. Everyone is upset (except idealy you!). Such is no time for a leisurely read of a book. This book is written with that pressure in mind. It is chock-full of prewritten queries and other solutions that you can immediately apply and get results.

Of course, you should not wait until the last minute. Take the time now when you're not in crisis mode to get familiar with the content in this book. Try the solutions for monitoring and analyzing. See what you can learn about your current database performance levels. Then take action to set some benchmarks and work on improvements so as to become practiced for when a crisis eventually hits. Or better yet, maybe you can avoid a crisis altogether.

Who This Book Is For

Oracle Database 12c Performance Tuning Recipes was written primarily for database administrators who manage Oracle Database environments. The book is especially useful to those administrators involved in tackling performance optimization problems. Serious SQL developers will also find the book useful, especially the chapters on aspects of SQL.

How This Book Is Structured

Solutions in this book are grouped into categories by chapter. Each chapter is composed of a number of recipes relating to the chapter's topic. Each recipe takes the following form:

Problem: A succinct description of the problem solved by the recipe

Solution: A terse and to-the-point presentation of queries and commands to execute in order to accomplish the task described in the recipe's problem statement

How It Works: A longer discourse on the solution and how and why it works, for those who are interested in a deeper understanding of the material

The book's structure allows you to open it to a chapter relating to a problem you are trying to solve. Then find a recipe in the chapter that solves the problem or that can be adapted to solve the problem. Read the solution. Read the "How It Works" description to fully understand the solution. Then apply the solution to your real-world problem.

Downloading the Code

The authors have made a zip file available with the queries and scripts from the recipe solutions. To download the zip file, first visit the book's catalog page on the Apress.com web site. The URL is as follows:

```
http://www.apress.com/9781430261872
```

Then scroll down the page and look for a tabbed section. Click the Source Code/Downloads tab, and download the zip file of examples using the provided link.

■ ■ ■

## CHAPTER 1

Optimizing Table Performance

This chapter details database features that impact the performance of storing and retrieving data within a table. Table performance is partially determined by database characteristics implemented prior to creating tables. For example, the physical storage features implemented when first creating a database and associated tablespaces subsequently influence the performance of tables. Similarly, performance is also impacted by your choice of initial physical features such as table types and data types. Therefore implementing practical database, tablespace, and table creation standards (with performance in mind) forms the foundation for optimizing data availability and scalability.

An Oracle database is comprised of the physical structures used to store, manage, secure, and retrieve data. When first building a database, there are several performance-related features that you can implement at the time of database creation. For example, the initial layout of the datafiles and the type of tablespace management are specified upon creation. Architectural decisions taken at this point often have long-lasting implications.

■ **Tip**   An Oracle instance is defined to be the memory structures and background processes. Whereas an Oracle database consists of physical files—namely, data files, control files, and online redo log files.

As depicted in Figure 1-1, a tablespace is the logical structure that allows you to manage a group of datafiles. Datafiles are the physical datafiles on disk. When configuring tablespaces, there are several features to be aware of that can have far-reaching performance implications, namely locally managed tablespaces and automatic segment storage managed (ASSM) tablespaces. When you reasonably implement these features, you maximize your ability to obtain acceptable future table performance.

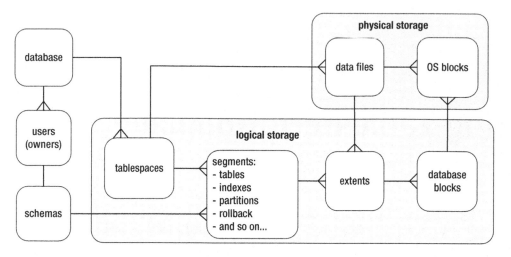

Figure 1-1. *Relationships of logical and physical storage*

The table is the object that stores data in a database. One measure of database performance is the speed at which an application is able to insert, update, delete, and select data. Therefore it's appropriate that we begin this book with recipes that provide solutions regarding problems related to table performance.

We start by describing aspects of database and tablespace creation that impact table performance. We next move on to topics such as choosing table types and data types that meet performance-related business requirements. Later topics include managing the physical implementation of tablespace usage. We detail issues such as detecting table fragmentation, dealing with free space under the high-water mark, row migration/chaining, and compressing data. Also described is the Oracle Segment Advisor. This handy tool helps you with automating the detection and resolution of table fragmentation and unused space.

1-1. Building a Database That Maximizes Performance
Problem

You realize when initially creating a database that some features (when enabled) have long-lasting implications for table performance and availability. Specifically, when creating the database, you want to do the following:

- Enforce that every tablespace ever created in the database must be locally managed. Locally managed tablespaces deliver better performance than the obsolete dictionary-managed technology.

- Ensure users are automatically assigned a default permanent tablespace. This guarantees that when users are created they are assigned a default tablespace other than SYSTEM. With the deferred segment feature (more on this later), if a user has the CREATE TABLE privilege, then it is possible for that user to create objects in the SYSTEM tablespace even without having a space quota on the SYSTEM tablespace. This is undesirable. It's true they won't be able to insert data into tables without appropriate space quotas, but they can create objects, and thus inadvertently clutter up the SYSTEM tablespace.

- Ensure users are automatically assigned a default temporary tablespace. This guarantees that when users are created they are assigned the correct temporary tablespace when no default is explicitly provided.

Solution

There are two different tools that you can use to create an Oracle database:

- SQL*Plus using the CREATE DATABASE statement
- Database Configuration Assistant (dbca)

These techniques are described in the following subsections.

SQL*Plus

Use a script such as the following to create a database that adheres to reasonable standards that set the foundation for a well-performing database:

```
CREATE DATABASE O12C
   MAXLOGFILES 16
   MAXLOGMEMBERS 4
   MAXDATAFILES 1024
   MAXINSTANCES 1
   MAXLOGHISTORY 680
   CHARACTER SET AL32UTF8
DATAFILE
'/u01/dbfile/O12C/system01.dbf'
   SIZE 500M REUSE
   EXTENT MANAGEMENT LOCAL
UNDO TABLESPACE undotbs1 DATAFILE
'/u02/dbfile/O12C/undotbs01.dbf'
   SIZE 800M
SYSAUX DATAFILE
'/u01/dbfile/O12C/sysaux01.dbf'
   SIZE 500M
DEFAULT TEMPORARY TABLESPACE TEMP TEMPFILE
'/u02/dbfile/O12C/temp01.dbf'
   SIZE 500M
DEFAULT TABLESPACE USERS DATAFILE
'/u01/dbfile/O12C/users01.dbf'
   SIZE 50M
LOGFILE GROUP 1
       ('/u01/oraredo/O12C/redo01a.rdo',
        '/u02/oraredo/O12C/redo01b.rdo') SIZE 200M,
       GROUP 2
       ('/u01/oraredo/O12C/redo02a.rdo',
        '/u02/oraredo/O12C/redo02b.rdo') SIZE 200M,
       GROUP 3
       ('/u01/oraredo/O12C/redo03a.rdo',
        '/u02/oraredo/O12C/redo03b.rdo') SIZE 200M
USER sys    IDENTIFIED BY f0obar
USER system IDENTIFIED BY f0obar;
```

The prior CREATE DATABASE script helps establish a good foundation for performance by enabling features such as the following:

- Defines the SYSTEM tablespace as locally managed via the EXTENT MANAGEMENT LOCAL clause; this ensures that all tablespaces ever created in database are locally managed. Starting with Oracle Database 12c, the SYSTEM tablespace is always created as locally managed.

- Defines a default tablespace named USERS for any user created without an explicitly defined default tablespace; this helps prevent users from being assigned the SYSTEM tablespace as the default.

- Defines a default temporary tablespace named TEMP for all users; this helps prevent users from being assigned the SYSTEM tablespace as the default temporary tablespace. Users created with a default temporary tablespace of SYSTEM can have an adverse impact on performance, as this will cause contention for resources in the SYSTEM tablespace.

Solid performance starts with a correctly configured database. The prior recommendations help you create a reliable infrastructure for your table data.

dbca

Oracle's dbca utility has a graphical interface and a command line mode from which you can configure and create databases. The visual tool is easy to use and has a very intuitive interface. In Linux/Unix environments to use the dbca in graphical mode, ensure you have the proper X software installed, then issue the xhost + command, and make certain your DISPLAY variable is set; for example:

```
$ xhost +
$ echo $DISPLAY
:0.0

$ xhost +
$ echo $DISPLAY
:0.0
```

The dbca is invoked from the operating system as follows:

```
$ dbca
```

You'll be presented with a series of screens that allow you to make choices on the configuration. You can choose the "Advanced Mode" option which gives you more control on aspects such as file placement and multiplexing of the online redo logs.

By default, the dbca creates a database with the following characteristics:

- Defines the SYSTEM tablespace as locally managed.

- Defines a default tablespace named USERS for any user created without an explicitly defined default tablespace.

- Defines a default temporary tablespace named TEMP for all users.

Like the SQL*Plus approach, these are all desirable features that provide a good foundation to build applications on.

The dbca utility also allows you to create a database in silent mode, without the graphical component. Using dbca in silent mode with a response file is an efficient way to create databases in a consistent and repeatable manner. This approach also works well when you're installing on remote servers, which could have a slow network connection or not have the appropriate X software installed.

You can also run the dbca in silent mode with a response file. In some situations, using dbca in graphical mode isn't feasible. This may be due to slow networks or the unavailability of X software. To create a database, using dbca in silent mode, perform the following steps:

1. Locate the dbca.rsp file.

2. Make a copy of the dbca.rsp file.

3. Modify the copy of the dbca.rsp file for your environment.

4. Run the dbca utility in silent mode.

First, navigate to the location in which you copied the Oracle database installation software, and use the find command to locate dbca.rsp:

```
$ find . -name dbca.rsp
./12.1.0.1/database/response/dbca.rsp
```

Copy the file so that you're not modifying the original (in this way, you'll always have a good, original file):

```
$ cp dbca.rsp mydb.rsp
```

Now, edit the mydb.rsp file. Minimally, you need to modify the following parameters: GDBNAME, SID, SYSPASSWORD, SYSTEMPASSWORD, SYSMANPASSWORD, DBSNMPPASSWORD, DATAFILEDESTINATION, STORAGETYPE, CHARACTERSET, and NATIONALCHARACTERSET. Following is an example of modified values in the mydb.rsp file:

```
[CREATEDATABASE]
GDBNAME = "O12C"
SID = "O12C"
TEMPLATENAME = "General_Purpose.dbc"
SYSPASSWORD = "f00bar"
SYSTEMPASSWORD = "f00bar"
SYSMANPASSWORD = "f00bar"
DBSNMPPASSWORD = "f00bar"
DATAFILEDESTINATION ="/u01/dbfile"
STORAGETYPE="FS"
CHARACTERSET = "AL32UTF8"
NATIONALCHARACTERSET= "UTF8"
```

Next, run the dbca utility in silent mode, using a response file:

```
$ dbca -silent -responseFile /home/oracle/orainst/mydb.rsp
```

You should see output such as

```
Copying database files
1% complete
...
Creating and starting Oracle instance
...
62% complete
Completing Database Creation
...
100% complete
Look at the log file ... for further details.
```

If you look in the log files, note that the dbca utility uses the rman utility to restore the data files used for the database. Then, it creates the instance and performs post-installation steps. On a Linux server you should also have an entry in the /etc/oratab file for your new database.

Many DBAs launch dbca and configure databases in the graphical mode, but a few exploit the options available to them using the response file. With effective utilization of the response file, you can consistently automate the database creation process. You can modify the response file to build databases on ASM and even create RAC databases. In addition, you can control just about every aspect of the response file, similar to launching the dbca in graphical mode.

■ **Tip** You can view all options of the dbca via the help parameter: dbca -help

---

How It Works

A properly configured and created database will help ensure that your database performs well. It is true that you can modify features after the database is created. However, often a poorly crafted CREATE DATABASE script leads to a permanent handicap on performance. In production database environments, it's sometimes difficult to get the downtime that might be required to reconfigure an improperly configured database. If possible, think about performance at every step in creating an environment, starting with how you create the database.

When creating a database, you should also consider features that affect maintainability. A sustainable database results in more uptime, which is part of the overall performance equation. The CREATE DATABASE statement in the "Solution" section also factors in the following sustainability features:

- Creates an automatic UNDO tablespace (automatic undo management is enabled by setting the UNDO_MANAGEMENT and UNDO_TABLESPACE initialization parameters); this allows Oracle to automatically manage the rollback segments. This relieves you of having to regularly monitor and tweak.

- Places datafiles in directories that follow standards for the environment; this helps with maintenance and manageability, which results in better long-term availability and thus better performance.

- Sets passwords to non-default values for DBA-related users; this ensures the database is more secure, which in the long run can also affect performance (e.g., if a malcontent hacks into the database and deletes data, then performance will suffer).

- Establishes three groups of online redo logs, with two members each, sized appropriately for the transaction load; the size of the redo log directly affects the rate at which they switch. When redo logs switch too often, this can degrade performance. Keep in mind that when you create a new database that you may not know the appropriate size and will have to adjust this later.

You should take the time to ensure that each database you build adheres to commonly accepted standards that help ensure you start on a firm performance foundation.

If you've inherited a database and want to verify the default permanent tablespace setting, use a query such as this:

```
SELECT *
FROM database_properties
WHERE property_name = 'DEFAULT_PERMANENT_TABLESPACE';
```

If you need to modify the default permanent tablespace, do so as follows:

```
SQL> alter database default tablespace users;
```

To verify the setting of the default temporary tablespace, use this query:

```
SELECT *
FROM database_properties
WHERE property_name = 'DEFAULT_TEMP_TABLESPACE';
```

To change the setting of the temporary tablespace, you can do so as follows:

```
SQL> alter database default temporary tablespace temp;
```

You can verify the UNDO tablespace settings via this query:

```
SELECT name, value
FROM v$parameter
WHERE name IN ('undo_management','undo_tablespace');
```

If you need to change the undo tablespace, first create a new undo tablespace and then use the ALTER SYSTEM SET UNDO_TABLESPACE statement.

1-2. Creating Tablespaces to Maximize Performance
Problem

You realize that tablespaces are the logical containers for database objects such as tables and indexes. Furthermore, you're aware that if you don't specify storage attributes when creating objects, then the tables and indexes automatically inherit the storage characteristics of the tablespaces (that the tables and indexes are created within). Therefore you want to create tablespaces in a manner that maximizes table performance and maintainability.

Solution

We recommend that you create your tablespaces with the locally managed and automatic segment space management features (ASSM) enabled. This is the default behavior starting with Oracle Database 12c:

```
create tablespace tools
datafile '/u01/dbfile/012C/tools01.dbf' size 100m;
```

You can verify that the tablespace was created locally managed and is using ASSM via this query:

```
select tablespace_name, extent_management, segment_space_management
from dba_tablespaces
where tablespace_name='TOOLS';
```

Here is some sample output:

```
TABLESPACE_NAME  EXTENT_MANAGEMENT        SEGMENT_SPACE_MANAGEMENT
---------------  -----------------------  -------------------------
TOOLS            LOCAL                    AUTO
```

How It Works

To be clear, this recipe discusses two separate desirable tablespace features:

- Locally managed tablespaces

- Automatic Segment Space Management (ASSM)

Starting with Oracle Database 12c, all tablespaces are created as locally managed. In prior versions of Oracle you had the choice of either locally managed or dictionary managed. Going forward you should always use locally managed tablespaces.

The tablespace segment space management feature can be set to either AUTO (the default) or MANUAL. Oracle strongly recommends that you use AUTO (referred to as ASSM). This allows Oracle to automatically manage many physical space characteristics that the DBA had to previously manually adjust. In most scenarios, an ASSM managed tablespace will process transactions more efficiently than a MANUAL segment space management enabled tablespace. There are a few corner cases where this may not be true. We recommend that you use ASSM unless you have a proven test case where MANUAL is better.

■ **Note** You cannot create the SYSTEM tablespace with the ASSM feature. Also, the ASSM feature is valid only for permanent, locally managed tablespaces.

When creating a tablespace, if you don't specify a uniform extent size, then Oracle will automatically allocate extents is sizes of 64 KB, 1 MB, 8 MB, and 64 MB. Use the auto-allocation behavior if the objects in the tablespace typically are of varying size. You can explicitly tell Oracle to automatically determine the extent size via the EXTENT MANAGEMENT LOCAL AUTOALLOCATE clause.

You can choose to have the extent size be consistently the same for every extent within the tablespace via the UNIFORM SIZE clause. This example uses a uniform extent size of 128k:

```
create tablespace tools
  datafile '/u01/dbfile/O12C/tools01.dbf' size 100m
  extent management local uniform size 128k;
```

If you have a good reason to set the extent size to a uniform size, then by all means do that. However, if you don't have justification, take the default of AUTOALLOCATE.

You can also specify that a datafile automatically grow when it becomes full. This is set through the AUTOEXTEND ON clause. If you use this feature, we recommend that you set an overall maximum size for the datafile. This will prevent runaway or erroneous SQL from accidentally consuming all available disk space (think about what could happen with a cloud service that automatically adds disk space as required for a database). Here's an example:

```
create tablespace tools
  datafile '/u01/dbfile/O12C/tools01.dbf' size 100m
  autoextend on maxsize 10G;
```

1-3. Matching Table Types to Business Requirements
Problem

You're new to Oracle and have read about the various table types available. For example, you can choose between heap-organized tables, index-organized tables, and so forth. You want to build a database application and need to decide which table type to use.

Solution

Oracle provides a wide variety of table types. The default table type is heap-organized. For most applications, a heap-organized table is an effective structure for storing and retrieving data. However, there are other table types that you should be aware of, and you should know the situations under which each table type should be implemented. Table 1-1 describes each table type and its appropriate use.

Table 1-1. *Oracle Table Types and Typical Uses*

Table Type/Feature	Description	Benefit/Use
Heap-organized	The default Oracle table type and the most commonly used.	Use this table type unless you have a specific reason to use a different type.
Temporary	Session private data, stored for the duration of a session or transaction; space is allocated in temporary segments.	Program needs a temporary table structure to store and modify data. Table data isn't required after the session terminates.
Index-organized (IOT)	Data stored in a B-tree index structure sorted by primary key.	Table is queried mainly on primary key columns; good for range scans, provides fast random access.
Partitioned	A logical table that consists of separate physical segments.	Type used with large tables with tens of millions of rows; dramatically affects performance scalability of large tables and indexes.
External	Tables that use data stored in operating system files outside of the database.	This type lets you efficiently access data in a file outside of the database (like a CSV or text file). External tables also provide an efficient mechanism for transporting data between databases.
Materialized view (MV)	A table that stores the output of a SQL query; periodically refreshed when you want the MV table updated with a current snapshot of the SQL result set.	Aggregating data for faster reporting or replicating data to offload performance to a reporting database.
Clustered	A group of tables that share the same data blocks.	Type used to reduce I/O for tables that are often joined on the same columns. Rarely used.
Nested	A table with a column with a data type that is another table.	Seldom used.
Object	A table with a column with a data type that is an object type.	Seldom used.

How It Works

In most scenarios, a heap-organized table is sufficient to meet your requirements. This Oracle table type is a proven structure used in a wide variety of database environments. If you properly design your database (normalized structure) and combine that with the appropriate indexes and constraints, the result should be a well-performing and maintainable system.

Normally most of your tables will be heap-organized. However, if you need to take advantage of a non-heap feature (and are certain of its benefits), then certainly do so. For example, Oracle partitioning is a scalable way to build very large tables and indexes. Materialized views are a solid feature for aggregating and replicating data. Index-organized tables are efficient structures when most of the columns are part of the primary key (like an intersection table in a many-to-many relationship). And so forth.

■ **Caution** You shouldn't choose a table type simply because you think it's a cool feature that you recently heard about. Sometimes folks read about a feature and decide to implement it without first knowing what the performance benefits or maintenance costs will be. You should first be able to test and prove that a feature has solid performance benefits.

1-4. Choosing Table Features for Performance

Problem

When creating tables, you want to implement the appropriate table features that maximize performance, scalability, and maintainability.

Solution

There are several performance and sustainability issues that you should consider when creating tables. Table 1-2 describes features specific to table performance.

Table 1-2. *Table Features That Impact Performance*

Recommendation	Reasoning
Consider setting the physical attribute PCTFREE to a value higher than the default of 10% if the table initially has rows inserted with null values that are later updated with large values. If there are never any updates, considering setting PCTFREE to a lower value.	As Oracle inserts records into a block, PCTFREE specifies what percentage of the block should be reserved (kept free) for future updates. Appropriately set, can help prevent row migration/chaining, which can impact I/O performance if a large percent of rows in a table are migrated/chained.
All tables should be created with a primary key (with possibly the exception of tables that store information like logs).	Enforces a business rule and allows you to uniquely identify each row; ensures that an index is created on primary key column(s), which allows for efficient access to primary key values.
Consider creating a numeric surrogate key to be the primary key for a table when the real-life primary key is a large character column or multiple columns.	Makes joins easier (only one column to join) and one single numeric key results in faster joins than large character-based columns or composites.
Consider using auto-incrementing columns (12c) to populate PK columns.	Saves having to manually write code and/or maintain triggers and sequences to populate PK and FK columns. However, one possible downside is potential contention with concurrent inserts.

(continued)

Table 1-2. (*continued*)

Recommendation	Reasoning
Create a unique key for the logical business key—a recognizable combination of columns that makes a row unique.	Enforces a business rule and keeps the data cleaner; allows for efficient retrieval of the logical key columns that may be frequently used in WHERE clauses. If the PK is a surrogate key, there will usually be at least one unique key that identifies the logical business key.
Define foreign keys where appropriate.	Enforces a business rule and keeps the data cleaner; helps optimizer choose efficient paths to data.
Consider creating indexes on foreign key columns.	Can speed up queries that often join on FK and PK columns and also helps prevent certain locking issues.
Consider special features such as virtual columns, invisible columns (12c), read-only, parallel, compression, no logging, and so on.	Features such as parallel DML, compression, or no logging can have a performance impact on reading and writing of data.

How It Works

The "Solution" section describes aspects of tables that relate to performance. When creating a table, you should also consider features that enhance scalability and availability. Often DBAs and developers don't think of these features as methods for improving performance. However, building a stable and supportable database goes hand in hand with good performance. Table 1-3 describes best practices features that promote ease of table management.

Table 1-3. *Table Features That Impact Scalability and Maintainability*

Recommendation	Reasoning
Use standards when naming tables, columns, views, constraints, triggers, indexes, and so on.	Helps document the application and simplifies maintenance.
Specify a separate tablespace for different schemas.	Provides some flexibility for different backup and availability requirements.
Let tables and indexes inherit storage attributes from the tablespaces (especially if you use ASSM created tablespaces).	Simplifies administration and maintenance.
Create primary-key constraints out of line (as a table constraint).	Allows you more flexibility when creating the primary key, especially if you have a situation where the primary key consists of multiple columns.
Use check constraints where appropriate.	Enforces a business rule and keeps the data cleaner; use this to enforce fairly small and static lists of values.
If a column should always have a value, then enforce it with a NOT NULL constraint.	Enforces a business rule and keeps the data cleaner.
Create comments for the tables and columns.	Helps document the application and eases maintenance.
If you use LOBs in Oracle Database 11g or higher, use the new SecureFiles architecture.	SecureFiles is the recommended LOB architecture; provides access to features such as compression, encryption, and deduplication.

1-5. Selecting Data Types Appropriately

Problem

When creating tables, you want to implement appropriate data types so as to maximize performance, scalability, and maintainability.

Solution

There are several performance and sustainability issues that you should consider when determining which data types to use in tables. Table 1-4 describes features specific to performance.

Table 1-4. *Data Type Features That Impact Performance*

Recommendation	Reasoning
If a column always contains numeric data and can be used in numeric computations, then make it a number data type. Keep in mind you may not want to make some columns that only contain digits as numbers (such as U.S. zip code or SSN).	Enforces a business rule and allows for the greatest flexibility, performance, and consistent results when using Oracle SQL math functions (which may behave differently for a "01" character vs. a 1 number); correct data types prevent unnecessary conversion of data types.
If you have a business rule that defines the length and precision of a number field, then enforce it—for example, NUMBER(7,2). If you don't have a business rule, make it NUMBER.	Enforces a business rule and keeps the data cleaner; numbers with a precision defined won't unnecessarily store digits beyond the required precision. This can affect the row length, which in turn can have an impact on I/O performance.
For most character data (even fixed length) use VARCHAR2 (and not CHAR).	The VARCHAR2 data type is more flexible and space efficient than CHAR. Having said that, you may want to use a fixed length CHAR for some data, such as a country iso-code.
If you have a business rule that specifies the maximum length of a column, then use that length, as opposed to making all columns VARCHAR2(4000).	Enforces a business rule and keeps the data cleaner.
Appropriately use date/time-related data types such as DATE, TIMESTAMP, and INTERVAL.	Enforces a business rule, ensures that the data is of the appropriate format, and allows for the greatest flexibility and performance when using SQL date functions and date arithmetic.
Avoid large object (LOB) data types if possible.	Prevents maintenance issues associated with LOB columns, like unexpected growth, performance issues when copying, and so on.

■ **Note** Prior to Oracle Database 12c the maximum length for a VARCHAR2 and NVARCHAR2 was 4,000, and the maximum length of a RAW column was 2,000. Starting with Oracle Database 12c, these data types have been extended to accommodate a length of 32,767.

How It Works

When creating a table, you must specify the columns names and corresponding data types. As a developer or a DBA, you should understand the appropriate use of each data type. We've seen many application issues (performance and accuracy of data) caused by the wrong choice of data type. For instance, if a character string is used when a date data type should have been used, this causes needless conversions and headaches when attempting to do date math and reporting. Compounding the problem, after an incorrect data type is implemented in a production environment, it can be very difficult to modify data types, as this introduces a change that might possibly break existing code. Once you go wrong, it's extremely tough to recant and backtrack and choose the right course. It's more likely you will end up with hack upon hack as you attempt to find ways to force the ill-chosen data type to do the job it was never intended to do.

Having said that, Oracle supports the following groups of data types:

- Character
- Numeric
- Date/Time
- RAW
- ROWID
- LOB

■ **Tip**   The LONG and LONG RAW data types are deprecated and should not be used.

The data types in the prior bulleted list are briefly discussed in the following subsections.

Character

There are four character data types available in Oracle: VARCHAR2, CHAR, NVARCHAR2, and NCHAR. The VARCHAR2 data type is what you should use in most scenarios to hold character/string data. A VARCHAR2 only allocates space based on the number of characters in the string. If you insert a one-character string into a column defined to be VARCHAR2(30), Oracle will only consume space for the one character.

When you define a VARCHAR2 column, you must specify a length. There are two ways to do this: BYTE and CHAR. BYTE specifies the maximum length of the string in bytes, whereas CHAR specifies the maximum number of characters. For example, to specify a string that contains at the most 30 bytes, you define it as follows:

```
varchar2(30 byte)
```

To specify a character string that can contain at most 30 characters, you define it as follows:

```
varchar2(30 char)
```

In almost all situations you're safer specifying the length using CHAR. When working with multibyte character sets, if you specified the length to be VARCHAR2(30 byte), you may not get predictable results, because some characters require more than 1 byte of storage. In contrast, if you specify VARCHAR2(30 char), you can always store 30 characters in the string, regardless of whether some characters require more than 1 byte.

The NVARCHAR2 and NCHAR data types are useful if you have a database that was originally created with a single-byte, fixed-width character set, but sometime later you need to store multibyte character set data in the same database.

■ **Tip** Oracle does have another data type named VARCHAR. Oracle currently defines VARCHAR as synonymous with VARCHAR2. Oracle strongly recommends that you use VARCHAR2 (and not VARCHAR), as Oracle's documentation states that VARCHAR might serve a different purpose in the future.

Numeric

Use a numeric data type to store data that you'll potentially need to use with mathematic functions, such as SUM, AVG, MAX, and MIN. Never store numeric information in a character data type. When you use a VARCHAR2 to store data that are inherently numeric, you're introducing future failures into your system. Eventually, you'll want to report or run calculations on numeric data, and if they're not a numeric data type, you'll get unpredictable and often wrong results.

Oracle supports three numeric data types:

- NUMBER
- BINARY_DOUBLE
- BINARY_FLOAT

For most situations, you'll use the NUMBER data type for any type of number data. Its syntax is

```
NUMBER(scale, precision)
```

where scale is the total number of digits, and precision is the number of digits to the right of the decimal point. So, with a number defined as NUMBER(5, 2) you can store values +/-999.99. That's a total of five digits, with two used for precision to the right of the decimal point.

■ **Tip** Oracle allows a maximum of 38 digits for a NUMBER data type. This is almost always sufficient for any type of numeric application.

What sometimes confuses developers and DBAs is that you can create a table with columns defined as INT, INTEGER, REAL, DECIMAL, and so on. These data types are all implemented by Oracle with a NUMBER data type. For example, a column specified as INTEGER is implemented as a NUMBER(38).

The BINARY_DOUBLE and BINARY_FLOAT data types are used for scientific calculations. These map to the DOUBLE and FLOAT Java data types. Unless your application is performing rocket science calculations, then use the NUMBER data type for all your numeric requirements.

■ **Note** The BINARY data types can lead to rounding errors that you won't have with NUMBER and also the behavior may vary depending on the operating system and hardware.

Date/Time

When capturing and reporting on date-related information, you should always use a DATE or TIMESTAMP data type (and not VARCHAR2 or NUMBER). Using the correct date-related data type allows you to perform accurate Oracle date calculations and aggregations and dependable sorting for reporting. If you use a VARCHAR2 for a field that contains date information, you are guaranteeing future reporting inconsistencies and needless conversion functions (such as TO_DATE and TO_CHAR).

The DATE data type contains a date component as well as a time component that is granular to the second. If you don't specify a time component when inserting data, then the time value defaults to midnight (0 hour at the 0 second). If you need to track time at a more granular level than the second, then use TIMESTAMP; otherwise, feel free to use DATE.

The TIMESTAMP data type contains a date component and a time component that is granular to fractions of a second. When you define a TIMESTAMP, you can specify the fractional second precision component. For instance, if you wanted five digits of fractional precision to the right of the decimal point, you would specify that as:

```
TIMESTAMP(5)
```

The maximum fractional precision is 9; the default is 6. If you specify 0 fractional precision, then you have the equivalent of the DATE data type.

RAW

The RAW data type allows you to store binary data in a column. This type of data is sometimes used for storing globally unique identifiers or small amounts of encrypted data. If you need to store large amounts (over 2000 bytes) of binary data then use a BLOB instead.

If you select data from a RAW column, SQL*Plus implicitly applies the built-in RAWTOHEX function to the data retrieved. The data are displayed in hexadecimal format, using characters 0-9 and A-F. When inserting data into a RAW column, the built-in HEXTORAW is implicitly applied.

This is important because if you create an index on a RAW column, the optimizer may ignore the index, as SQL*Plus is implicitly applying functions where the RAW column is referenced in the SQL. A normal index may be of no use, whereas a function-based index using RAWTOHEX may result in a substantial performance improvement.

ROWID

Sometimes when developers/DBAs hear the word ROWID (row identifier), they often think of a pseudocolumn provided with every table row that contains the physical location of the row on disk; that is correct. However, many people do not realize that Oracle supports an actual ROWID data type, meaning that you can create a table with a column defined as the type ROWID.

There are a few practical uses for the ROWID data type. One valid application would be if you're having problems when trying to enable a referential integrity constraint and want to capture the ROWID of rows that violate a constraint. In this scenario, you could create a table with a column of the type ROWID and store in it the ROWIDs of offending records within the table. This affords you an efficient way to capture and resolve issues with the offending data.

Never be tempted to use a ROWID data type and the associated ROWID of a row within the table for the primary key value. This is because the ROWID of a row in a table can change. For example, an ALTER TABLE...MOVE command will potentially change every ROWID within a table. Normally, the primary key values of rows within a table should never change. For this reason, instead of using ROWID for a primary key value, use a sequence-generated non-meaningful number (or in 12c, use an auto-incrementing column to populate a primary key column).

LOB

Oracle supports storing large amounts of data in a column via a LOB data type. Oracle supports the following types of LOBs:

- CLOB
- NCLOB
- BLOB
- BFILE

If you have textual data that don't fit within the confines of a VARCHAR2, then you should use a CLOB to store these data. A CLOB is useful for storing large amounts of character data, such as text from articles (blog entries) and log files. An NCLOB is similar to a CLOB but allows for information encoded in the national character set of the database.

BLOBs store large amounts of binary data that usually aren't meant to be human readable. Typical BLOB data include images, audio, word processing documents, pdf, spread sheets, and video files.

CLOBs, NCLOBs, and BLOBs are known as internal LOBs. This is because they are stored inside the Oracle database. These data types reside within data files associated with the database.

BFILEs are known as external LOBs. BFILE columns store a pointer to a file on the OS that is outside the database. When it's not feasible to store a large binary file within the database, then use a BFILE. BFILEs don't participate in database transactions and aren't covered by Oracle security or backup and recovery. If you need those features, then use a BLOB and not a BFILE.

1-6. Avoiding Extent Allocation Delays When Creating Tables

Problem

You're installing an application that has thousands of tables and indexes. Each table and index are configured to initially allocate an initial extent of 10 MB. When deploying the installation DDL to your production environment, you want install the database objects as fast as possible. You realize it will take some time to deploy the DDL if each object allocates 10 MB of disk space as it is created. You wonder if you can somehow instruct Oracle to defer the initial extent allocation for each object until data is actually inserted into a table.

Solution

The only way to defer the initial segment generation is to use the Enterprise Edition of Oracle Database 11g R2 or higher. With the Enterprise Edition of Oracle, by default the physical allocation of the extent for a table (and associated indexes) is deferred until a record is first inserted into the table. A small example will help illustrate this concept. First a table is created:

```
create table emp(
 emp_id number
,first_name varchar2(30)
,last_name varchar2(30));
```

Now query USER_SEGMENTS and USER_EXTENTS to verify that no physical space has been allocated:

```
SQL> select count(*) from user_segments where segment_name='EMP';
  COUNT(*)
----------
        0
```

```
SQL> select count(*) from user_extents where segment_name='EMP';
  COUNT(*)
----------
         0
```

Next a record is inserted, and the prior queries are run again:

```
SQL> insert into emp values(1,'John','Smith');

1 row created.

SQL> select count(*) from user_segments where segment_name='EMP';
  COUNT(*)
----------
         1

SQL> select count(*) from user_extents where segment_name='EMP';
  COUNT(*)
----------
         1
```

The prior behavior is quite different from previous versions of Oracle. In prior versions, as soon as you create an object, the segment and associated extent are allocated.

■ **Note**   Deferred segment creation also applies to partitioned tables and indexes. An extent will not be allocated until the initial record is inserted into a given segment.

How It Works

Starting with the Enterprise Edition of Oracle Database 11g R2 (and not any other editions, like the Standard Edition), with non-partitioned heap-organized tables created in locally managed tablespaces, the initial segment creation is deferred until a record is inserted into the table. You need to be aware of Oracle's deferred segment creation feature for several reasons:

- Allows for a faster installation of applications that have a large number of tables and indexes; this improves installation speed, especially when you have thousands of objects.

- As a DBA, your space usage reports may initially confuse you when you notice that there is no space allocated for objects.

- The creation of the first row will take a slightly longer time than in previous versions (because now Oracle allocates the first extent based on the creation of the first row). For most applications, this performance degradation is not noticeable.

- There may be unforeseen side effects from using this feature (more on this in a few paragraphs).

We realize that to take advantage of this feature the only "solution" is to upgrade to Oracle Database 11g R2 (Enterprise Edition), which is often not an option. However, we felt it was important to discuss this feature because you'll eventually encounter the aforementioned characteristics.

You can disable the deferred segment creation feature by setting the database initialization parameter DEFERRED_SEGMENT_CREATION to FALSE. The default for this parameter is TRUE.

You can also control the deferred segment creation behavior when you create the table. The CREATE TABLE statement has two clauses: SEGMENT CREATION IMMEDIATE and SEGMENT CREATION DEFERRED—for example:

```
create table emp(
 emp_id number
,first_name varchar2(30)
,last_name varchar2(30))
segment creation immediate;
```

It should be noted that there are some potential unforeseen side effects of the deferred segment creation. For example, MOS note 1050193.1 describes the potential for sequences that have been defined to start with the number 1, to actually start with the number 2.

Also, since the deferred segment creation feature is supported only in the Enterprise Edition of Oracle, if you attempt to export objects (that have no segments created yet) and attempt to import into a Standard Edition of Oracle, you may receive an error: ORA-00439: feature not enabled. Potential workarounds include setting ALTER SYSTEM SET DEFERRED_SEGMENT_CREATION=FALSE or creating the table with SEGMENT CREATION IMMEDIATE. See MOS note 1087325.1 for further details with this issue.

■ **Note** The COMPATIBLE initialization parameter needs to be 11.2.0.0.0 or greater before using the SEGMENT CREATION DEFERRED clause.

1-7. Maximizing Data-Loading Speeds
Problem

You're loading a large amount of data into a table and want to insert new records as quickly as possible.

Solution

First, set the table's logging attribute to NOLOGGING; this minimizes the generation redo for direct path operations (this feature has no effect on regular DML operations). Then use a direct path loading feature, such as the following:

- INSERT /*+ APPEND */ on queries that use a subquery for determining which records are inserted
- INSERT /*+ APPEND_VALUES */ on queries that use a VALUES clause
- CREATE TABLE...AS SELECT

Here's an example to illustrate NOLOGGING and direct path loading. First, run the following query to verify the logging status of a table:

```
select table_name, logging
from user_tables
where table_name = 'EMP';
```

Here is some sample output:

```
TABLE_NAME LOG
---------- ---
EMP        YES
```

The prior output verifies that the table was created with LOGGING enabled (the default). To enable NOLOGGING, use the ALTER TABLE statement as follows:

```
SQL> alter table emp nologging;
```

Now that NOLOGGING has been enabled, there should be a minimal amount of redo generated for direct path operations. The following example uses a direct path INSERT statement to load data into the table:

```
SQL> insert /*+APPEND */ into emp (first_name) select username from all_users;
```

The prior statement is an efficient method for loading data because direct path operations such as INSERT /*+APPEND */ combined with NOLOGGING generate a minimal amount of redo.

Also, make sure you commit the data loaded via direct path, otherwise you won't be able to view it as Oracle will throw an ORA-12838 error indicating that direct path loaded data must be committed before it is selected.

■ **Note** When you direct path insert into a table, Oracle will insert the new rows above the high-water mark. Even if there is ample space freed up via a DELETE statement, when direct path inserting, Oracle will always load data above the high-water mark. This can result in a table consuming a large amount of disk space but not necessarily containing that much data.

How It Works

Direct path inserts have two performance advantages over regular insert statements:

- If NOLOGGING is specified, then a minimal amount of redo is generated.
- The buffer cache is bypassed and data is loaded directly into the datafiles. This can significantly improve the loading performance.

The NOLOGGING feature minimizes the generation of redo for direct path operations only. For direct path inserts, the NOLOGGING option can significantly increase the loading speed. One perception is that NOLOGGING eliminates redo generation for the table for all DML operations. That isn't correct. The NOLOGGING feature never affects redo generation for regular INSERT, UPDATE, MERGE, and DELETE statements.

One downside to reducing redo generation is that you can't recover the data created via NOLOGGING in the event a failure occurs after the data is loaded (and before you back up the table). If you can tolerate some risk of data loss, then use NOLOGGING but back up the table soon after the data is loaded. If your data is critical, then don't use NOLOGGING with direct path operations. If your data can be easily recreated, then NOLOGGING is desirable when you're trying to improve performance of large data loads.

What happens if you have a media failure after you've populated a table in NOLOGGING mode (and before you've made a backup of the table)? After a restore and recovery operation, it will appear that the table has been restored:

```
SQL> desc emp;
```

However, when executing a query that scans every block in the table, an error is thrown.

```
SQL> select * from emp;
```

This indicates that there is logical corruption in the datafile:

```
ORA-01578: ORACLE data block corrupted (file # 4, block # 147)
ORA-01110: data file 4: '/u01/dbfile/O12C/users01.dbf'
ORA-26040: Data block was loaded using the NOLOGGING option
```

As the prior output indicates, the data in the table is unrecoverable. Use NOLOGGING only in situations where the data isn't critical or in scenarios where you can back up the data soon after it was created.

■ **Tip**   If you're using RMAN to back up your database, you can report on unrecoverable datafiles via the REPORT UNRECOVERABLE command.

There are some quirks of NOLOGGING that need some explanation. You can specify logging characteristics at the database, tablespace, and object levels. If your database has been enabled to force logging, then this overrides any NOLOGGING specified for a table. If you specify a logging clause at the tablespace level, it sets the default logging for any CREATE TABLE statements that don't explicitly use a logging clause.

You can verify the logging mode of the database as follows:

```
SQL> select name, log_mode, force_logging from v$database;
```

The next statement verifies the logging mode of a tablespace:

```
SQL> select tablespace_name, logging from dba_tablespaces;
```

And this example verifies the logging mode of a table:

```
SQL> select owner, table_name, logging from dba_tables where logging = 'NO';
```

How do you tell whether Oracle logged redo for an operation? One way is to measure the amount of redo generated for an operation with logging enabled vs. operating in NOLOGGING mode. If you have a development environment for testing, you can monitor how often the redo logs switch while the transactions are taking place. Another simple test is to measure how long the operation takes with and without logging. The operation performed in NOLOGGING mode should occur faster because a minimal amount of redo is generated during the load.

1-8. Efficiently Removing Table Data
Problem

You're experiencing performance issues when deleting data from a table. You want to remove data as efficiently as possible.

Solution

You can use either the TRUNCATE statement or the DELETE statement to remove records from a table. TRUNCATE is usually more efficient but has some side effects that you must be aware of. For example, TRUNCATE is a DDL statement. This means Oracle automatically commits the statement (and the current transaction) after it runs, so there is no way to roll back a TRUNCATE statement. Because a TRUNCATE statement is DDL, you can't truncate two separate tables as one transaction.

This example uses a TRUNCATE statement to remove all data from a table:

```
SQL> truncate table emp;
```

When truncating a table, by default all space is de-allocated for the table except the space defined by the MINEXTENTS table-storage parameter. If you don't want the TRUNCATE statement to de-allocate the currently allocated extents, then use the REUSE STORAGE clause:

```
SQL> truncate table emp reuse storage;
```

You can query the DBA/ALL/USER_EXTENTS views to verify if the extents have been de-allocated (or not)—for example:

```
SQL> select count(*) from user_extents where segment_name = 'EMP';
```

It's also worth mentioning here that the TRUNCATE statement is often used when working with partitioned tables. Especially when archiving obsolete data and therefore no longer need information in a particular partition. For example, the following efficiently removes data from a particular partition without impacting other partitions within the table:

```
SQL> alter table f_sales truncate partition p_2012;
```

How It Works

If you need the option of choosing to roll back (instead of committing) when removing data, then you should use the DELETE statement. However, the DELETE statement has the disadvantage that it generates a great deal of undo and redo information. Thus for large tables, a TRUNCATE statement is usually the most efficient way to remove data.

Another characteristic of the TRUNCATE statement is that it sets the high-water mark of a table back to zero. Oracle defines the *high-water mark* of a table as the boundary between used and unused space in a segment. When you create a table, Oracle allocates a number of extents to the table, defined by the MINEXTENTS table-storage parameter. Each extent contains a number of blocks. Before data are inserted into the table, none of the blocks have been used, and the high-water mark is zero. As data are inserted into a table, and extents are allocated, the high-water mark boundary is raised.

When you use a DELETE statement to remove data from a table, the high-water mark doesn't change. One advantage of using a TRUNCATE statement and resetting the high-water mark is that full table scan queries search only for rows in blocks below the high-water mark. This can have significant performance implications for queries that perform full table scans.

Another side effect of the TRUNCATE statement is that you can't truncate a parent table that has a primary key defined that is referenced by an enabled foreign-key constraint in a child table—even if the child table contains zero rows. In this scenario, Oracle will throw this error when attempting to truncate the parent table:

```
ORA-02266: unique/primary keys in table referenced by enabled foreign keys
```

Oracle prevents you from truncating the parent table because in a multiuser system, there is a possibility that another session can populate the child table with rows in between the time you truncate the child table and the time you subsequently truncate the parent table. In this situation, you must temporarily disable the child table–referenced foreign-key constraints, issue the TRUNCATE statement, and then re-enable the constraints.

Compare the TRUNCATE behavior to that of the DELETE statement. Oracle does allow you to use the DELETE statement to remove rows from a parent table while the constraints are enabled that reference a child table (assuming there are zero rows in the child table). This is because DELETE generates undo, is read-consistent, and can be rolled back. Table 1-5 summarizes the differences between DELETE and TRUNCATE.

Table 1-5. *Comparison of DELETE and TRUNCATE*

	DELETE	TRUNCATE
Option of committing or rolling back changes	YES	NO (DDL always commits transaction after it runs.)
Generates undo	YES	NO
Resets the table high-water mark to zero	NO	YES
Affected by referenced and enabled foreign-key constraints	NO	YES
Performs well with large amounts of data	NO	YES

If you need to use a DELETE statement, you must issue either a COMMIT or a ROLLBACK to complete the transaction. Committing a DELETE statement makes the data changes permanent:

```
SQL> delete from emp;
SQL> commit;
```

___

■ **Note**   Other (sometimes not so obvious) ways of committing a transaction include issuing a subsequent DDL statement (which implicitly commits an active transaction for a session) or normally exiting out of the client tool (such as SQL*Plus).

___

If you issue a ROLLBACK statement instead of COMMIT, the table contains data as it was before the DELETE was issued.

When working with DML statements, you can confirm the details of a transaction by querying from the V$TRANSACTION view. For example, say that you have just inserted data into a table; before you issue a COMMIT or ROLLBACK, you can view active transaction information for the currently connected session as follows:

```
SQL> insert into emp values(1, 'John', 'Smith');
SQL> select xidusn, xidsqn from v$transaction;
    XIDUSN     XIDSQN
---------- ----------
         9        369
SQL> commit;
SQL> select xidusn, xidsqn from v$transaction;
no rows selected
```

___

■ **Note**   Another way to remove data from a table is to drop and re-create the table. However, this means you also have to re-create any indexes, constraints, grants, and triggers that belong to the table. Additionally, when you drop a table, it's temporarily unavailable until you re-create it and re-issue any required grants. Usually, dropping and re-creating a table is acceptable only in a development or test environment.

___

1-9. Displaying Automated Segment Advisor Advice

Problem

You have a poorly performing query accessing a table. Upon further investigation, you discover the table has only a few rows in it. You wonder why the query is taking so long when there are so few rows. You want to examine the output of Oracle's Segment Advisor to see if there are any space-related recommendations that might help with performance in this situation.

Solution

Use the Segment Advisor to display information regarding tables that may have space allocated to them (that was once used) but now the space is empty (due to a large number of deleted rows). Tables with large amounts of unused space can cause full table scan queries to perform poorly. This is because Oracle is scanning every block beneath the high-water mark, regardless of whether the blocks contain data.

This solution focuses on accessing the Segment Advisor's advice via the DBMS_SPACE PL/SQL package. This package retrieves information generated by the Segment Advisor regarding segments that may be candidates for shrinking, moving, or compressing. One simple and effective way to use the DBMS_SPACE package (to obtain Segment Advisor advice) is via a SQL query—for example:

```
SELECT
  'Segment Advice -------------------------'|| chr(10) ||
  'TABLESPACE_NAME  : ' || tablespace_name  || chr(10) ||
  'SEGMENT_OWNER    : ' || segment_owner    || chr(10) ||
  'SEGMENT_NAME     : ' || segment_name     || chr(10) ||
  'ALLOCATED_SPACE  : ' || allocated_space  || chr(10) ||
  'RECLAIMABLE_SPACE: ' || reclaimable_space || chr(10) ||
  'RECOMMENDATIONS  : ' || recommendations  || chr(10) ||
  'SOLUTION 1       : ' || c1               || chr(10) ||
  'SOLUTION 2       : ' || c2               || chr(10) ||
  'SOLUTION 3       : ' || c3 Advice
FROM
TABLE(dbms_space.asa_recommendations('FALSE', 'FALSE', 'FALSE'));
```

Here is some sample output:

```
ADVICE
--------------------------------------------------------------------------------
Segment Advice -------------------------
TABLESPACE_NAME  : USERS
SEGMENT_OWNER    : MV_MAINT
SEGMENT_NAME     : EMP
ALLOCATED_SPACE  : 50331648
RECLAIMABLE_SPACE: 40801189
RECOMMENDATIONS  : Enable row movement of the table MV_MAINT.EMP and perform
 shrink, estimated savings is 40801189 bytes.
SOLUTION 1       : alter table "MV_MAINT"."EMP" shrink space
SOLUTION 2       : alter table "MV_MAINT"."EMP" shrink space COMPACT
SOLUTION 3       : alter table "MV_MAINT"."EMP" enable row movement
```

In the prior output, the EMP table is a candidate for freeing up space through an operation such as shrinking it or reorganizing the table.

How It Works

In Oracle Database 10g R2 and later, Oracle automatically schedules and runs a Segment Advisor job. This job analyzes segments in the database and stores its findings in internal tables. The output of the Segment Advisor contains findings (issues that may need to be resolved) and recommendations (actions to resolve the findings). Findings from the Segment Advisor are of the following types:

- Segments that are good candidates for shrink operations

- Segments that have significant row migration/chaining

- Segments that might benefit from advanced compression

When viewing the Segment Advisor's findings and recommendations, it's important to understand several aspects of this tool. First, the Segment Advisor regularly calculates advice via an automatically scheduled DBMS_SCHEDULER job. You can verify the last time the automatic job ran by querying the DBA_AUTO_SEGADV_SUMMARY view:

```
select segments_processed, end_time
from dba_auto_segadv_summary
order by end_time;
```

You can compare the END_TIME date to the current date to determine if the Segment Advisor is running on a regular basis.

■ **Note**   In addition to automatically generated segment advice, you have the option of manually executing the Segment Advisor to generate advice on specific tablespaces, tables, and indexes (see Recipe 1-10 for details).

When the Segment Advisor executes, it uses the Automatic Workload Repository (AWR) for the source of information for its analysis. For example, the Segment Advisor examines usage and growth statistics in the AWR to generate segment advice. When the Segment Advisor runs, it generates advice and stores the output in internal database tables. The advice and recommendations can be viewed via data dictionary views such as the following:

- DBA_ADVISOR_EXECUTIONS

- DBA_ADVISOR_FINDINGS

- DBA_ADVISOR_OBJECTS

■ **Note**   The DBA_ADVSIOR_* views are part of the Diagnostics Pack which requires the Enterprise Edition of Oracle and an additional license.

There are three different tools for retrieving the Segment Advisor's output:

- Executing DBMS_SPACE.ASA_RECOMMENDATIONS

- Manually querying DBA_ADVISOR_* views

- Viewing Enterprise Manager's graphical screens

In the "Solution" section, we described how to use the DBMS_SPACE.ASA_RECOMMENDATIONS procedure to retrieve the Segment Advisor advice. The ASA_RECOMMENDATIONS output can be modified via three input parameters, which are described in Table 1-6. For example, you can instruct the procedure to show information generated when you have manually executed the Segment Advisor.

Table 1-6. *Description of ASA_RECOMMENDATIONS Input Parameters*

Parameter	Meaning
all_runs	TRUE instructs the procedure to return findings from all runs, whereas FALSE instructs the procedure to return only the latest run.
show_manual	TRUE instructs the procedure to return results from manual executions of the Segment Advisor. FALSE instructs the procedure to return results from the automatic running of the Segment Advisor.
show_findings	Shows only the findings and not the recommendations

You can also directly query the data dictionary views to view the advice of the Segment Advisor. Here's a query that displays Segment Advisor advice generated within the last day:

```
select
 'Task Name       : ' || f.task_name  || chr(10) ||
 'Start Run Time  : ' || TO_CHAR(execution_start, 'dd-mon-yy hh24:mi') || chr (10) ||
 'Segment Name    : ' || o.attr2    || chr(10) ||
 'Segment Type    : ' || o.type     || chr(10) ||
 'Partition Name  : ' || o.attr3    || chr(10) ||
 'Message         : ' || f.message    || chr(10) ||
 'More Info       : ' || f.more_info  || chr(10) ||
 '---------------------------------------------------' Advice
FROM dba_advisor_findings    f
    ,dba_advisor_objects      o
    ,dba_advisor_executions  e
WHERE o.task_id    = f.task_id
AND   o.object_id = f.object_id
AND   f.task_id    = e.task_id
AND   e. execution_start > sysdate - 1
AND   e.advisor_name = 'Segment Advisor'
ORDER BY f.task_name;
```

▨ **Note** You can display Segment Advisor advice from Enterprise Manager. To view the segment advice, from the Performance tab, navigate to the Advisors Home page, then navigate to the Segment Advisor page. From this page you can generate Segment Advisor reports.

1-10. Manually Generating Segment Advisor Advice

Problem

You have a table that experiences a large amount of updates. Users have reported that queries against this table are performing slower and slower. As part of your analysis you want to manually run the Segment Advisor for this table and see if there are any space related issues such as row migration/chaining, or unused space below the high-water mark.

Solution

You can manually run the Segment Advisor and tell it to specifically analyze all segments in a tablespace or look at a specific object (such as a single table or index). Here are the steps for manually executing the Segment Advisor:

1. Create a task.

2. Assign an object to the task.

3. Set the task parameters.

4. Execute the task.

■ **Note**   The database user executing DBMS_ADVISOR needs the ADVISOR system privilege. This privilege is administered via the GRANT statement.

The following example encapsulates the four prior steps in a block of PL/SQL. The table being examined is the EMP table and the owner of the table is MV_MAINT:

```
DECLARE
  my_task_id    number;
  obj_id        number;
  my_task_name varchar2(100);
  my_task_desc varchar2(500);
BEGIN
  my_task_name := 'EMP Advice';
  my_task_desc := 'Manual Segment Advisor Run';
---------
-- Step 1
---------
  dbms_advisor.create_task (
  advisor_name => 'Segment Advisor',
  task_id      => my_task_id,
  task_name    => my_task_name,
  task_desc    => my_task_desc);
---------
-- Step 2
---------
  dbms_advisor.create_object (
  task_name   => my_task_name,
  object_type => 'TABLE',
  attr1       => 'MV_MAINT',
```

```
attr2        => 'EMP',
attr3        => NULL,
attr4        => NULL,
attr5        => NULL,
object_id    => obj_id);
---------
-- Step 3
---------
dbms_advisor.set_task_parameter(
task_name => my_task_name,
parameter => 'recommend_all',
value     => 'TRUE');
---------
-- Step 4
---------
dbms_advisor.execute_task(my_task_name);
END;
/
```

Now you can view Segment Advisor advice regarding this table by executing the DBMS_SPACE package and instructing it to pull information from a manual execution of the Segment Advisor (via the input parameters—see Table 1-7 for details)—for example:

```
SELECT
 'Segment Advice --------------------------'|| chr(10) ||
 'TABLESPACE_NAME   : ' || tablespace_name  || chr(10) ||
 'SEGMENT_OWNER     : ' || segment_owner    || chr(10) ||
 'SEGMENT_NAME      : ' || segment_name     || chr(10) ||
 'ALLOCATED_SPACE   : ' || allocated_space  || chr(10) ||
 'RECLAIMABLE_SPACE: ' || reclaimable_space || chr(10) ||
 'RECOMMENDATIONS   : ' || recommendations  || chr(10) ||
 'SOLUTION 1        : ' || c1               || chr(10) ||
 'SOLUTION 2        : ' || c2               || chr(10) ||
 'SOLUTION 3        : ' || c3 Advice
FROM
TABLE(dbms_space.asa_recommendations('TRUE', 'TRUE', 'FALSE'));
```

Table 1-7. *DBMS_ADVISOR Procedures Applicable for the Segment Advisor*

Procedure Name	Description
CREATE_TASK	Creates the Segment Advisor task; specify "Segment Advisor" for the ADVISOR_NAME parameter of CREATE_TASK. Query DBA_ADVISOR_DEFINITIONS for a list of all valid advisors.
CREATE_OBJECT	Identifies the target object for the segment advice; Table 1-8 lists valid object types and parameters.
SET_TASK_PARAMETER	Specifies the type of advice you want to receive; Table 1-9 lists valid parameters and values.
EXECUTE_TASK	Executes the Segment Advisor task
DELETE_TASK	Deletes a task
CANCEL_TASK	Cancels a currently running task

You can also retrieve Segment Advisor advice by querying data dictionary views—for example:

```
SELECT
 'Task Name       : ' || f.task_name   || chr(10) ||
 'Segment Name    : ' || o.attr2       || chr(10) ||
 'Segment Type    : ' || o.type        || chr(10) ||
 'Partition Name  : ' || o.attr3       || chr(10) ||
 'Message         : ' || f.message     || chr(10) ||
 'More Info       : ' || f.more_info TASK_ADVICE
FROM dba_advisor_findings f
    ,dba_advisor_objects  o
WHERE o.task_id = f.task_id
AND o.object_id = f.object_id
AND f.task_name like '&task_name'
ORDER BY f.task_name;
```

If the table has any space related issues, then the advice output will indicate it as follows:

```
TASK_ADVICE
--------------------------------------------------------------------------------
Task Name       : EMP Advice
Segment Name    : EMP
Segment Type    : TABLE
Partition Name  :
Message         : The object has chained rows that can be removed by re-org.
More Info       : 22 percent chained rows can be removed by re-org.
```

How It Works

The DBMS_ADVISOR package is used to manually instruct the Segment Advisor to generate advice for specific tables. This package contains several procedures that perform operations such as creating and executing a task. Table 1-7 lists the procedures relevant to the Segment Advisor.

The Segment Advisor can be invoked with various degrees of granularity. For example, you can generate advice for all objects in a tablespace or advice for a specific table, index, or partition. Table 1-8 lists the object types for which Segment Advisor advice can be obtained via the DBMS_ADVISOR.CREATE_TASK procedure.

Table 1-8. *Valid Object Types for the DBMS_ADVISOR.CREATE_TASK Procedure*

Object Type	ATTR1	ATTR2	ATTR3	ATTR4
TABLESPACE	tablespace name	NULL	NULL	NULL
TABLE	user name	table name	NULL	NULL
INDEX	user name	index name	NULL	NULL
TABLE PARTITION	user name	table name	partition name	NULL
INDEX PARTITION	user name	index name	partition name	NULL
TABLE SUBPARTITION	user name	table name	subpartition name	NULL
INDEX SUBPARTITION	user name	index name	subpartition name	NULL
LOB	user name	segment name	NULL	NULL
LOB PARTITION	user name	segment name	partition name	NULL
LOB SUBPARTITION	user name	segment name	subpartition name	NULL

You can also specify a maximum amount of time that you want the Segment Advisor to run. This is controlled via the SET_TASK_PARAMETER procedure. This procedure also controls the type of advice that is generated. Table 1-9 describes valid inputs for this procedure.

Table 1-9. *Input Parameters for the DBMS_ADVISOR.SET_TASK_PARAMETER Procedure*

Parameter	Description	Valid Values
TIME_LIMIT	Limit on time (in seconds) for advisor run	N number of seconds or UNLIMITED (default)
RECOMMEND_ALL	Generates advice for all types of advice or just space-related advice	TRUE (default) for all types of advice, or FALSE to generate only space-related advice

1-11. Automatically E-mailing Segment Advisor Output
Problem
You realize that the Segment Advisor automatically generates advice and want to automatically e-mail yourself Segment Advisor output.

Solution
First encapsulate the SQL that displays the Segment Advisor output in a shell script—for example:

```
#!/bin/bash
if [ $# -ne 1 ]; then
  echo "Usage: $0 SID"
  exit 1
fi
# source oracle OS variables
. /etc/oraset $1
#
```

```
BOX=`uname -a | awk '{print$2}'`
#
sqlplus -s <<EOF
mv_maint/foo
spo $HOME/bin/log/seg.txt
set lines 80
set pages 100
SELECT
  'Segment Advice -------------------------'|| chr(10) ||
  'TABLESPACE_NAME   : ' || tablespace_name   || chr(10) ||
  'SEGMENT_OWNER     : ' || segment_owner     || chr(10) ||
  'SEGMENT_NAME      : ' || segment_name      || chr(10) ||
  'ALLOCATED_SPACE   : ' || allocated_space   || chr(10) ||
  'RECLAIMABLE_SPACE: ' || reclaimable_space  || chr(10) ||
  'RECOMMENDATIONS   : ' || recommendations   || chr(10) ||
  'SOLUTION 1        : ' || c1                 || chr(10) ||
  'SOLUTION 2        : ' || c2                 || chr(10) ||
  'SOLUTION 3        : ' || c3 Advice
FROM
TABLE(dbms_space.asa_recommendations('FALSE', 'FALSE', 'FALSE'));
EOF
cat $HOME/bin/log/seg.txt | mailx -s "Seg. rpt. on DB: $1 $BOX" dkuhn@oracle.com
exit 0
```

The prior shell script can be regularly executed from a Linux/Unix utility such as cron. Here is a sample cron entry:

```
# Segment Advisor report
16 11 * * * /orahome/oracle/bin/seg.bsh DWREP
```

In this way, you automatically receive segment advice and proactively resolve issues before they become performance problems.

How It Works

The Segment Advisor automatically generates advice on a regular basis. Sometimes it's handy to proactively send yourself the recommendations. This allows you to periodically review the output and implement suggestions that make sense.

The shell script in the "Solution" section contains a line near the top where the OS variables are established through running an oraset script. This is a custom script that is the equivalent of the oraenv script provided by Oracle. You can use a script to set the OS variables or hard-code the required lines into the script. Calling a script to set the variables is more flexible and maintainable, as it allows you to use as input any database name that appears in the oratab file.

1-12. Rebuilding Rows Spanning Multiple Blocks

Problem

You ran a Segment Advisor report as follows:

```
SELECT
 'Task Name       : ' || f.task_name   || chr(10) ||
 'Segment Name    : ' || o.attr2       || chr(10) ||
 'Segment Type    : ' || o.type        || chr(10) ||
 'Partition Name  : ' || o.attr3       || chr(10) ||
 'Message         : ' || f.message     || chr(10) ||
 'More Info       : ' || f.more_info TASK_ADVICE
FROM dba_advisor_findings f
    ,dba_advisor_objects  o
WHERE o.task_id   = f.task_id
AND   o.object_id = f.object_id
AND   f.task_name like '&task_name'
ORDER BY f.task_name;
```

And notice that the output indicates a table with chained rows:

```
TASK_ADVICE
--------------------------------------------------------------------------------
Task Name       : EMP Advice
Segment Name    : EMP
Segment Type    : TABLE
Partition Name  :
Message         : The object has chained rows that can be removed by re-org.
More Info       : 22%chained rows can be removed by re-org.
```

You realize that migrated/chained rows leads to higher rates of I/O, and can result in poor performance; therefore you want to eliminate row migration/chaining for this table.

Solution

Row migration/chaining results when there is not enough space within one block to store a row, and therefore Oracle uses more than one block to store the row (more details on this in the "How it Works" section of this recipe). In excess, row migration/chaining can be an issue in that it results in undue I/O when reading a row. There are three basic techniques for resolving row migration/chaining:

- Move the table
- Move individual migrated/chained rows within the table
- Rebuild the table using Data Pump (export/import)

The first two bullets of the prior list are the focus of the "Solution" of this recipe. The Data Pump technique involves exporting the tables, then dropping or renaming the existing tables, and then re-importing the tables from the export file. For details on how to use Data Pump, see the Pro Oracle Database 12c Administration (available from Apress) or Oracle's Utility Guide available on Oracle's Technology Network website.

Moving the Table

One method for resolving the row migration/chaining within a table is to use the MOVE statement and rebuild the table and its rows with a lower value of PCTFREE. The idea being that with a lower value of PCTFREE, it will leave more room in the block for the migrated or chained row to fit within (as it's moved from a block with a high setting of PCTFREE to a block with more room due to the lower setting of PCTFREE).

For example, assume the table was initially built with a PCTFREE value of 40%. This next move operation rebuilds the table with a PCTFREE value of 5%:

```
SQL> alter table emp move pctfree 5;
```

However, keep in in mind if you do this, you could make the problem worse, as there will be less room in the block for future updates (which will result in more migrated/chained rows).

■ **Note**   When you move a table, Oracle requires an exclusive lock on the table; therefore you should perform this operation when there are no active transactions associated with the table being moved.

Also, as part of a MOVE operation, all of the rows are assigned a new ROWID. This will invalidate any indexes that are associated with the table. Therefore, as part of the move operation, you should rebuild all indexes associated with the table being moved. You can verify the status of the indexes by interrogating the DBA/ALL/USER_INDEXES view:

```
select owner, index_name, status
from dba_indexes
where table_name='EMP';
```

Rebuilding any indexes will make them usable again:

```
SQL> alter index emp_pk rebuild;
```

You can verify that row migration and chaining has been resolved (or not) by manually running the Segment Advisor (see Recipe 1-10) or via the ANALYZE TABLE ... COMPUTE STATISTICS command (see the "How it Works" section of this recipe for more details).

Moving Individual Migrated/Chained Rows

You can generate specific ROWIDs for rows that are either migrated or changed via the ANALYZE TABLE ... LIST INTO command. First you must create a table to hold output of the ANALYZE TABLE statement. Oracle provides a script to create a table for you:

```
SQL> @?/rdbms/admin/utlchn1.sql
```

The prior script creates a table named CHAINED_ROWS. Now you can run the ANALYZE statement to populate the CHAINED_ROWS table with rows that are migrated and/or chained:

```
SQL> analyze table emp list chained rows;
```

Now query the number of rows from the CHAINED_ROWS table:

```
SQL> select count(*) from chained_rows where table_name='EMP';
```

The advantage of identifying migrated/chained rows in this manner is that you can potentially fix the migrated/chained rows without impacting the rest of the records in the table by doing the following:

1. Create a temporary holding table to store the chained rows.

2. Delete the migrated/chained rows from the original table.

3. Insert the rows from the temporary table into the original table.

Since this technique has multiple steps, we recommend that you test this first in a non-production environment before you attempt this in a production database. Here's a short example to demonstrate the prior steps. First create a temporary table that contains the rows in the EMP table that have corresponding records in the CHAINED_ROWS table:

```
create table temp_emp
as select *
from emp
where rowid in
(select head_rowid from chained_rows where table_name = 'EMP');
```

Now delete the records from EMP that have corresponding records in CHAINED_ROWS:

```
delete from emp
where rowid in
(select head_rowid from chained_rows where table_name = 'EMP');
```

Now insert records in the temporary table into the EMP table:

```
insert into emp select * from temp_emp;
```

The prior process of moving the migrated/chained rows should clear up any row migration. Now you can delete or truncate the rows from the CHAINED_ROWS table and drop the temporary table.

How do you know if the migrated or chained rows have been fixed? Repeat the process of ANALYZE TABLE ... LIST CHAINED ROWS. If new rows are created in the CHAINED_ROWS table then this means you most likely have chained rows (and not migrated rows) and these can only be resolved by moving the table and adjusting PCTFREE to a lower value or moving the table to a tablespace that has a larger block size (see the "How It Works" section for more details).

UNDERSTANDING THE ORACLE ROWID

Every row in every table has a physical address. The address of a row is determined from a combination of the following:

- Datafile number

- Block number

- Location of the row within the block

- Object number

You can display the address of a row in a table by querying the ROWID pseudo-column—for example:

```
SQL> select rowid, emp_id from emp;
```

Here's some sample output:

```
ROWID                EMP_ID
------------------ ----------
AAAEtQAAEAAAACDAAA      100
AAAEtQAAEAAAACDAAB      101
```

The ROWID pseudo-column value isn't physically stored in the database. Oracle calculates its value when you query it. The ROWID contents are displayed as base-64 values that can contain the characters A–Z, a–z, 0–9, +, and /. You can translate the ROWID value into meaningful information via the DBMS_ROWID package. For example, to display the file number, block number, and row number in which a row is stored, issue this statement:

```
select emp_id
,dbms_rowid.rowid_to_absolute_fno(rowid,schema_name=>'MV_MAINT',object_name=>'EMP') file_num
,dbms_rowid.rowid_block_number(rowid) block_num
,dbms_rowid.rowid_row_number(rowid)    row_num
from emp;
```

Here's some sample output:

```
    EMP_ID   FILE_NUM  BLOCK_NUM    ROW_NUM
---------- ---------- ---------- ----------
       100          4        131          0
       101          4        131          1
```

You can use the ROWID value in the SELECT and WHERE clauses of a SQL statement. In most cases, the ROWID uniquely identifies a row. However, it's possible to have rows in different tables that are stored in the same cluster and so contain rows with the same ROWID (like with a clustered table).

How It Works

Oracle defines *row chaining* as a row that is too large to fit within the free space within a block and therefore two or more blocks are required to store the row. Row chaining can occur when:

- A row was initially inserted values that column values that cause the length of the row to be too long to fit within any available block. For an empty block this would roughly be the size of the block minus the space reserved by PCTFREE.

- A row that was initially inserted with column values small enough to fit within one block, but is later updated with values that cause the length of the row to be too long to fit within the free space within the block (the setting of PCTFREE determines what percentage of the block space is reserved for updates).

- A table that has more than 255 columns requires two or more blocks to store it.

Oracle will maintain pointers between the blocks that contain the chained row. This means that anytime the row is read there will be multiple I/O operations. Also updates and deletes may require writing to multiple blocks. If there is a large amount of row chaining this can impact performance. Having said that, if a row is too large to fit within any available block, the only way to fix this is to either reduce the size of the row or increase the size of the block.

For tables with 255 columns or less, you can potentially resolve row chaining by moving the table and at the same time lowering the value of PCTFREE. If that doesn't resolve the issue, then you could create a tablespace with a larger block size and move the table to that tablespace. Other than those solutions, you won't be able to avoid row chaining for large rows.

Oracle defines *row migration* as a row that was initially inserted into a block with values small enough that the row fits within a given free space within a block. The row contains columns that are later updated with larger values (like a column initially is inserted as null and is later updated with a non-null value) which causes the row not to be able to fit within its current block. However, the row is still small enough to fit within the free space of another available block. In this situation, Oracle will move (migrate) this row to another block that has enough space.

With row migration, Oracle maintains a pointer in the original block that points to the block to which the row was migrated. Row migration can impact performance because Oracle has to read/write to multiple blocks any time the row is accessed. Row migration can almost always be resolved by moving the tables as shown in the "Solution" section of this recipe.

1-13. Detecting Row Chaining and Row Migration
Problem
You're experiencing performance problems selecting from a table. You want to determine if row migration or chaining is a potential issue.

Solution
Here are the options for detecting row migration/chaining:

- Output of the Segment Advisor
- ANALYZE TABLE ... INTO CHAINED_ROWS
- ANALYZE TABLE ... COMPUTE STATISTICS
- Querying V$SYSSTAT

The first two bullets of the prior list have already been discussed in Recipe 1-12. The last two bullets are discussed in the following subsections.

Computing Statistics
A good technique for verifying row migration/chaining is to use the ANALYZE TABLE...COMPUTE STATISTICS statement. Running this for a table results in the CHAINED_CNT column of DBA_TABLES to be populated. For example:

```
SQL> analyze table emp compute statistics;
```

Now run this query to give you an idea of what percentage of rows are chained within the table:

```
select owner, chain_cnt
,round(chain_cnt/num_rows*100,2) chain_pct
,avg_row_len, pct_free
from dba_tables
where table_name = 'EMP';
```

The CHAIN_CNT contains the sum of both migrated and chained rows that have occurred within the table. If the percentage migrated/chained rows is greater than 15%, then you potentially have an issue.

Querying V$SYSSTAT

Another method for determining if you have an issue with row migration is through querying V$SYSSTAT. After you start your database instance, any time a migrated/chained row is read, the statistic with a value of "table fetch continued row" is incremented. You can view this statistic as follows:

```
SQL> select name, value from v$sysstat where name = 'table fetch continued row';
```

Viewed in a vacuum, this statistic is meaningless. If it returned a value of 10,000, you don't know if that means one migrated row was read 10,000 times or if there are 10,000 tables each with one migrated row that was read once. Furthermore, you don't know if 10,000 is a bad or good number because you have not compared it to the overall reads from the database since the instance was started.

To get a rough idea if you have an issue with row migration/chaining compare the number reads for migrated/chained rows to the overall number of rows read for your database:

```
with a as (select sum(value) total_rows_read
           from v$sysstat
           where name like '%table%'
           and name != 'table fetch continued row'),
     b as (select value total_mig_chain_rows
           from v$sysstat where name = 'table fetch continued row')
select a.total_rows_read, b.total_mig_chain_rows,
       b.total_mig_chain_rows/a.total_rows_read pct_rows_mig_or_chained
from a, b;
```

How It Works

One of the best methods for detecting row chaining or migration is by viewing the output of the Segment Advisor. If you don't have a license for this tool, then there are other methods such as using the ANALYZE TABLE statement or querying V$SYSSTAT.

If you wanted to analyze all tables in a given schema, you can use SQL to generate SQL:

```
SQL> select 'analyze table ' || table_name || ' compute statistics;'  from user_tables;
```

The prior script generates the SQL statements required to all tables for the currently connected user. If you have large tables, then keep in mind a may take some time to analyze all of them.

The second approach described in the "Solution" section involves querying V$SYSSTAT. This gives you a more dynamic look at your database. For example, when you check the number of chained rows overall, you don't necessarily know if they belong to the actively queried part of a large table. Querying V$SYSSTAT helps in this regard because it's measuring what's currently transacting in your database.

1-14. Differentiating Between Row Migration and Row Chaining
Problem

You want to determine if you have either row migration or row chaining. This will affect your strategy for resolving the problem. For example, if the issue is row chaining, which is caused by very long records that can't fit within the given free space in a block, there isn't much you can do about this. However, row migration might potentially be fixed by moving the table.

Solution

There are three basic techniques for differentiating between row chaining and row migration:

- Re-organizing the table (like moving it) will always fix row migration. It may or may not fix row chaining. So to differentiate between row migration and row chaining, re-organize the table and then compute statistics after the move and anything still showing up in the CHAIN_CNT column is a chained row that couldn't be resolved by moving the table. Consider modifying the value of PCTFREE to a lower value when you execute the move operation.

- Analyzing the table and recording the ROWIDs in a CHAINED_ROWS table, and then move the individual rows based on the ROWIDs of the migrated/chained rows. Repeat the process, and any new rows populating the CHAINED_ROWS table are chained.

- Calculate the length of each row. If the length of the row is greater than the free space available in an empty block, then most likely the issue is row chaining. If the length of the row is less than the amount of free space within a block size, then the issue is most likely row migration.

The first two bullets have already been discussed in Recipe 1-12. For the last bullet, you can manually calculate the length of a row by summing the lengths of all columns, for example:

```
SELECT NVL(vsize(emp_id),0) + NVL(vsize(first_name),0) + NVL(vsize(last_name),0)
FROM emp;
```

Rows that have a greater length than the available free space within an empty block are most likely chained and not migrated.

How It Works

Manually calculating the row length is by far the most accurate method to determine whether you have an issue with row chaining or row migration. If a row's size approaches the amount of free space within a block, then there may be no way to prevent the row from becoming chained. If the row size is much smaller than the amount of free space within a block, then it is most likely migrated and this issue can be resolved by moving the table (see Recipe 1-12).

■ **Tip** Consider using Oracle's compression options to maximize the number of rows per block (see Recipes 1-20 and 1-21 for details).

1-15. Proactively Preventing Row Migration/Chaining
Problem

You've noticed that a table has often experienced row migration and/or chaining. You want to proactively prevent this issue.

Solution

The amount of free space reserved in a block is determined by the table's storage parameter of PCTFREE. The default value of PCTFREE is 10, meaning 10% of the block is reserved space to be used for updates that result in more space usage within the row's current block. If you have a table that has columns that are initially inserted with small and/or null values and later updated to contain large values, then consider setting PCTFREE to a higher value, such as 40%. This will help prevent the row migration. However, keep in mind that a higher value of PCTFREE can result in increased row chaining.

It may help to calculate the average row length after an insert and then do a typical update to the row and again calculate its length. This will give an idea of how much a row will grow (see Recipe 1-14 for details on computing the row length.

If you have a table that is never updated after rows are inserted, then consider setting PCTFREE to 0. This will result in the maximum number of rows per block, which can lead to fewer disk reads (and thus better performance) when retrieving data.

How It Works

You can view the setting for PCTFREE by querying the DBA/ALL/USER_TABLES view—for example:

```
SQL> select table_name, pct_free from user_tables;
```

Moving a table almost always fixes migrated rows. The move operation removes each record from the block and re-inserts the record into a new block. For migrated rows, the old chained rows are deleted and rebuilt as one physical row within the block.

Chained rows can only be fixed if the length of the chained row is less than what is free within an empty block. If you have a chained row greater than the amount of free space, then consider setting PCTFREE to a lower value and moving the table or consider creating a tablespace with a larger block size.

1-16. Detecting Unused Space in a Table
Problem

You're querying a table that has no rows in it, and yet it takes several minutes for the row count to come back as zero. You know from experience that this could be an issue with vacant space within the table. The idea being that a table that initially had many rows in it was subsequently deleted from and this leaves unused space beneath the so called the high-water mark. Subsequent operations such as full table scans can take a long time because Oracle is searching the blocks that initially had data but now do not. Therefore, you want to determine if you have unused space in the table.

Solution

You can detect tables with high-water mark issues by selecting from DBA/ALL/USER_EXTENTS views. If a table has a large number of extents allocated to it but has zero rows, that's an indication that an extensive amount of data have been deleted from the table; for example:

```
SQL> select count(*) from user_extents where segment_name='EMP';

  COUNT(*)
----------
        44
```

Now, inspect the number of rows in the table:

```
SQL> select count(*) from emp;

  COUNT(*)
----------
         0
```

The prior table most likely has had data inserted into it, which resulted in extents being allocated. And, subsequently, data were deleted, and the extents remained.

Similarly you can count the number of rows and compare it to the number of blocks allocated to the table. For example:

```
SQL> select blocks from user_segments where segment_name='EMP';

    BLOCKS
----------
      1024
```

If the number of blocks is high, but the row count is low, then you most likely have free space beneath the high-water mark.

How It Works

Oracle defines the high-water mark of a table as the boundary between used and unused space in a segment. Also, when you create a table, Oracle allocates a number of extents to the table, defined by the MINEXTENTS table-storage parameter. Each extent contains a number of blocks. Before data are inserted into the table, none of the blocks have been used, and the high-water mark is 0. As data are inserted into a table, and extents are allocated, the high-water mark boundary is raised. A DELETE statement doesn't reset the high-water mark, thus leaving unused space within the table.

You need to be aware of a couple of performance-related issues regarding the high-water mark:

- SQL query full-table scans
- Direct-path load-space usage

Oracle sometimes needs to scan every block of a table (under the high-water mark) when performing a query. This is known as a full-table scan. If a significant amount of data have been deleted from a table, a full-table scan can take a long time to complete, even for a table with zero rows.

Also, when doing direct-path loads, Oracle inserts data above the high-water mark line. Potentially, you can end up with a large amount of unused space in a table that is regularly deleted from and that is also loaded via a direct-path mechanism.

Besides the technique in the solution section, there are several other ways to detect unused free space below the high-water mark:

- Autotrace tool
- DBMS_SPACE package
- Segment Advisor

See Recipe 1-17 for details on using tracing and Recipe 1-18 for details on using the DBMS_SPACE package. See Recipe 1-10 for details on how to manually run the Segment Advisor.

1-17. Tracing to Detect Space Below the High-Water Mark

Problem

You ran through the steps of Recipe 1-16 and believe you have an issue with unused space beneath the high-water mark for a table. You want to further verify the results by inspecting the output of the Autotrace tool.

Solution

You can run this simple test to detect whether you have an issue with unused space below the high-water mark:

1. SQL> set autotrace trace statistics

2. Run the query that performs the full-table scan.

3. Compare the number of rows processed with the number of blocks read from memory.

If the number of rows processed is low but the number of blocks read from memory is high, you may have an issue with the number of free blocks below the high-water mark. Here is a simple example to illustrate this technique:

```
SQL> set autotrace trace statistics
```

The next query generates a full-table scan on the INV table:

```
SQL> select * from inv;
```

Here is a snippet of the output from AUTOTRACE:

```
no rows selected

Statistics
-----------------------------------------------------------
          4  recursive calls
          0  db block gets
       7371  consistent gets
```

The number of rows returned is zero, yet there are 7,371 consistent gets (number of blocks read from buffer cache), indicating free space beneath the high-water mark.

Next, truncate the table, and run the query again:

```
SQL> truncate table inv;
SQL> select * from inv;
```

Here is a partial listing from the output of AUTOTRACE:

```
no rows selected

Statistics
-----------------------------------------------------------
          6  recursive calls
          0  db block gets
         12  consistent gets
```

Note that the number of memory accesses are now quite small.

How It Works

Any user granted the PLUSTRACE role can use the Autotrace utility. This tool is available through SQL*Plus and provides details regarding the execution plan and statistics of a successful SELECT, INSERT, UPDATE, DELETE statement. The statistics are recorded internally by Oracle and provide details on the system resources a SQL statement consumes. The consistent gets statistic gives you an indication of how many blocks are read from memory for the given SQL statement. If you have a high consistent gets number and a low row count, then you most likely have an issue with free space under the high-water mark.

1-18. Using DBMS_SPACE to Detect Space Below the High-Water Mark

Problem

You've detected evidence of unused space below the high-water mark via tracing (Recipe 1-17). You want to confirm your results via the DBMS_SPACE package.

Solution

Here is an anonymous block of PL/SQL that you can call from SQL*Plus that uses the DBMS_SPACE package to detect free space beneath the high-water mark:

```
set serverout on size 1000000
declare
    p_fs1_bytes number;
    p_fs2_bytes number;
    p_fs3_bytes number;
    p_fs4_bytes number;
    p_fs1_blocks number;
    p_fs2_blocks number;
    p_fs3_blocks number;
    p_fs4_blocks number;
    p_full_bytes number;
    p_full_blocks number;
    p_unformatted_bytes number;
    p_unformatted_blocks number;
begin
    dbms_space.space_usage(
        segment_owner      => user,
        segment_name       => 'EMP',
        segment_type       => 'TABLE',
        fs1_bytes          => p_fs1_bytes,
        fs1_blocks         => p_fs1_blocks,
        fs2_bytes          => p_fs2_bytes,
        fs2_blocks         => p_fs2_blocks,
        fs3_bytes          => p_fs3_bytes,
        fs3_blocks         => p_fs3_blocks,
        fs4_bytes          => p_fs4_bytes,
        fs4_blocks         => p_fs4_blocks,
        full_bytes         => p_full_bytes,
        full_blocks        => p_full_blocks,
```

```
      unformatted_blocks => p_unformatted_blocks,
      unformatted_bytes  => p_unformatted_bytes
   );
   dbms_output.put_line('FS1: blocks = '||p_fs1_blocks);
   dbms_output.put_line('FS2: blocks = '||p_fs2_blocks);
   dbms_output.put_line('FS3: blocks = '||p_fs3_blocks);
   dbms_output.put_line('FS4: blocks = '||p_fs4_blocks);
   dbms_output.put_line('Full blocks = '||p_full_blocks);
end;
/
```

In this scenario, you want to check the EMP table for free space below the high-water mark. Here is the output of the previous PL/SQL:

```
FS1: blocks = 0
FS2: blocks = 0
FS3: blocks = 0
FS4: blocks = 3646
Full blocks = 0
```

In the prior output the FS1 parameter shows that 0 blocks have 0% to 25% free space. The FS2 parameter shows that 0 blocks have 25% to 50% free space. The FS3 parameter shows that 0 blocks have 50% to 75% free space. The FS4 parameter shows there are 3,646 blocks with 75% to 100% free space. Finally, there are 0 full blocks. Because there are no full blocks, and a large number of blocks are mostly empty, you can deduce that free space exists below the high-water mark.

How It Works

The SPACE_USAGE procedure of the DBMS_SPACE package provides you with an alternative method for confirming that you have free space below the high-water mark. This procedure can only be used on tables created within tablespaces create using Automatic Space Segment Management (see Recipe 1-2 for details). See the Oracle PL/SQL Packages and Types Reference guide for more details on how to use this procedure.

1-19. Freeing Unused Table Space
Problem

You've analyzed the output of the Segment Advisor and have identified a table that has a large amount of free space below the high-water mark. You want to free up the unused space to improve the performance queries that perform full table scans of the table.

Solution

Do the following to shrink space and re-adjust the high-water mark for a table:

1. Enable row movement for the table.

2. Use the ALTER TABLE...SHRINK SPACE statement to free up unused space.

■ **Note**   The shrink table feature requires that the table's tablespace use automatic space segment management. See Recipe 1-2 for details on how to create an ASSM-enabled tablespace.

When you shrink a table, this requires that rows (if any) be moved which requires that row movement be enabled:

```
SQL> alter table emp enable row movement;
```

Next the table shrink operation is executed via an ALTER TABLE statement:

```
SQL> alter table emp shrink space;
```

You can also shrink the space associated with any index segments via the CASCADE clause:

```
SQL> alter table emp shrink space cascade;
```

How It Works

When you shrink a table, Oracle re-organizes the blocks in a manner that consumes the least amount of space. Oracle also re-adjusts the table's high-water mark. This has performance implications for queries that result in full table scans. During a full table scan, Oracle will inspect every block below the high-water mark to check it for data that might satisfy the result of a query. If you notice that it takes a long time for a query to return results when there aren't many rows in the table, this may be an indication that there are many unused blocks (because data was deleted) below the high-water mark.

You can also instruct Oracle to not re-adjust the high-water mark when shrinking a table. This is done via the COMPACT clause—for example:

```
SQL> alter table emp shrink space compact;
```

When you use COMPACT, Oracle defragments the table but doesn't alter the high-water mark. You will need to use the ALTER TABLE...SHRINK SPACE statement to reset the high-water mark. You might want to do this because you're concerned about the time it takes to defragment and adjust the high-water mark. This allows you to shrink a table in two shorter steps instead of one longer operation.

When you enable row movement for a table, this allows Oracle modify the ROWIDs for any records that need to be moved. This means that Oracle must also maintain indexes that reference those ROWIDs. So just keep in mind that the performance of a table shrink will correspond to the number of rows that need to be moved and indexes that must be updated.

Besides the technique shown in the Solution section, there are two other techniques you can use to free up space beneath the high water mark:

- Truncate the table.
- Move the table.
- Use Data Pump to export the table, drop the table, and then import the table.

Of course, only use TRUNCATE if you want to permanently remove all data from a table. Truncating a table may be acceptable if the table already has zero rows in it.

You can also lower the high water-mark by moving a table. For example:

```
SQL> alter table emp move;
```

If you move a table, ensure that you also rebuild any associated indexes, as the move operation will change the ROWIDs of the table rows and invalidate any indexes.

The Data Pump technique involves exporting the tables and then dropping or renaming the existing tables, and then re-importing the tables from the export file. For details on how to use Data Pump, see the Pro Oracle Database 12c Administration (available from Apress) or Oracle's Utility Guide available on Oracle's Technology Network website.

1-20. Compressing Data for Direct Path Loading

Problem

You're using the Enterprise Edition of Oracle and are working with a decision support system (DSS)-type database and you want to improve the performance of an associated reporting application. This environment contains large tables that are loaded once and then frequently subjected to full table scans. You want to compress data as it is loaded because this will compact the data into fewer database blocks and thus will require less I/O for subsequent reads from the table. Because fewer blocks need to be read for compressed data, this will improve data retrieval performance.

Solution

Use Oracle's basic compression feature to compress direct path–loaded data into a heap-organized table. Basic compression is enabled as follows:

1. Use the ROW STORE COMPRESS clause to enable compression either when creating, altering, or moving an existing table.

2. Load data via a direct path mechanism such as CREATE TABLE...AS SELECT or INSERT /*+ APPEND */.

■ **Note** Prior to Oracle Database 11g R2, basic compression was referred to as DSS compression and enabled via the COMPRESS FOR DIRECT_LOAD OPERATION clause. In 11g R2, this changed to COMPRESS BASIC. In 12c this has now changed to ROW STORE COMPRESS.

Here's an example that uses the CREATE TABLE...AS SELECT statement to create a basic compression-enabled table and direct path-load the data:

```
create table regs_dss
compress
as select reg_id, reg_name
from regs;
```

The prior statement creates a table with compressed data in it. Any subsequent direct path load operations will also load the data in a compressed format.

■ **Tip** The following clauses are synonymous: COMPRESS, COMPRESS BASIC, ROW STORE COMPRESS, or ROW STORE COMPRESS BASIC.

You can verify that compression has been enabled for a table by querying the appropriate DBA/ALL/USER_TABLES view. This example assumes that you're connected to the database as the owner of the table:

```
select table_name, compression, compress_for
from user_tables
where table_name='REGS_DSS';
```

Here is some sample output:

```
TABLE_NAME                     COMPRESS COMPRESS_FOR
------------------------------ -------- ------------
REGS_DSS                       ENABLED  BASIC
```

The prior output shows that compression has been enabled in the basic mode for this table. If you're working with a table has that already been created, then you can alter its basic compression characteristics with the ALTER TABLE statement—for example:

```
SQL> alter table regs_dss compress;
```

When you alter a table to enable basic compression, this does not affect any data currently existing in the table; rather, it only compresses subsequent direct path data load operations.

If you want to enable basic compression for data in an existing table, use the MOVE COMPRESS clause:

```
SQL> alter table regs_dss move compress;
```

Keep in mind that when you move a table, all of the associated indexes are invalidated. You'll have to rebuild any indexes associated with the moved table.

If you have enabled basic compression for a table, you can disable it via the NOCOMPRESS clause—for example:

```
SQL> alter table regs_dss nocompress;
```

When you alter a table to disable basic compression, this does not uncompress existing data within the table. Rather this operation instructs Oracle to not compress data for subsequent direct path operations. If you need to uncompress existing compressed data, then use the MOVE NOCOMPRESS clause:

```
SQL> alter table regs_dss move nocompress;
```

How It Works

The basic compression feature is available at no extra cost with the Oracle Enterprise Edition. Any heap-organized table that has been created or altered to use basic compression will be a candidate for data loaded in a compressed format for subsequent direct path load operations. There is some additional CPU overhead associated with compressing the data, but you may find in many circumstances that this overhead is offset by performance gains due to less I/O.

From a performance perspective, the main advantage to using basic compression is that once the data is loaded as compressed, any subsequent I/O operations will use fewer resources because there are fewer blocks required to read and write data. You will need to test the performance benefits for your environment. In general, tables that hold large amounts of character data are candidates for basic compression—especially in scenarios where data is direct path loaded once, and thereafter selected from many times.

Keep in mind that Oracle's basic compression feature has no effect on regular DML statements such as INSERT, UPDATE, MERGE, and DELETE. If you require compression to occur on all DML statements, then consider using advanced compression (see Recipe 1-16 for details).

You can also specify basic compression at the partition and tablespace level. Any table created within a tablespace created with the COMPRESS clause will have basic compression enabled by default. Here's an example of creating a tablespace with the COMPRESS clause:

```
CREATE TABLESPACE comp_data
  DATAFILE '/u01/dbfile/O12C/comp_data01.dbf'
  SIZE 500M
  EXTENT MANAGEMENT LOCAL
  UNIFORM SIZE 512K
  SEGMENT SPACE MANAGEMENT AUTO
  DEFAULT COMPRESS;
```

You can also alter an existing tablespace to set the default degree of compression:

```
SQL> alter tablespace comp_data default compress;
```

Run this query to verify that basic compression for a tablespace is enabled:

```
select tablespace_name, def_tab_compression, compress_for
from dba_tablespaces
where tablespace_name = 'COMP_DATA';
```

■ **Tip**   You cannot drop a column from a table created with basic compression enabled. However, you can mark a column as unused.

1-21. Compressing Data for All DML
Problem

You're in an OLTP environment and have noticed that there is a great deal of disk I/O occurring when reading data from a table. You wonder if you can increase I/O performance by compressing the data within the table. The idea is that compressed table data will consume less physical storage and thus require less I/O to read from disk.

■ **Note**   Advanced compression requires the Oracle Enterprise Edition and the Advanced Compression Option (extra cost license).

Solution

Use the ROW STORE COMPRESS ADVANCED clause when creating a table to enable data compression when using regular DML statements to manipulate data. This example creates advanced compression–enabled table:

```
create table regs
(reg_id    number
,reg_name varchar2(2000)
) row store compress advanced;
```

■ **Note**   Prior to Oracle Database 11g R2, advanced table compression was enabled using the COMPRESS FOR ALL OPERATIONS clause. In Oracle Database 11g R2, advanced table compression was enabled with COMPRESS FOR OLTP. In Oracle Database 12c, this changed to ROW STORE COMPRESS ADVANCED.

You can verify that compression has been enabled for a table by querying the appropriate DBA/ALL/USER_TABLES view. This example assumes that you're connected to the database as the owner of the table:

```
select table_name, compression, compress_for
from user_tables
where table_name='REGS';
```

If you've already created the table, you can use the ALTER TABLE statement to enable compression on an existing table—for example:

```
SQL> alter table regs row store compress advanced;
```

When you alter a table's compression mode, it doesn't impact any of the data currently within the table. Subsequent DML statements will result in data stored in a compressed fashion.

If you want to enable advanced compression for data in an existing table, use the MOVE ROW STORE COMPRESS ADVANCED clause:

```
SQL> alter table regs move row store compress advanced;
```

Keep in mind that when you move a table, all of the associated indexes are invalidated. You'll have to rebuild any indexes associated with the moved table.

If you have enabled advanced compression for a table, you can disable it via the NOCOMPRESS clause—for example:

```
SQL> alter table regs nocompress;
```

When you alter a table to disable advanced compression, this does not uncompress existing data within the table. Rather, this operation instructs Oracle to not compress data for subsequent DML operations.

How It Works

The ROW STORE COMPRESS ADVANCED clause enables compression for all DML operations. The advanced compression doesn't immediately compress data as it is inserted or updated in a table. Rather the compression occurs in a batch mode when the degree of change within the block reaches a certain threshold. When the threshold is reached, all of the uncompressed rows are compressed at the same time. The threshold at which compression occurs is determined by an internal algorithm (over which you have no control).

You can also specify advanced compression at the tablespace level. Any table created in an advanced compression-enabled tablespace will by default inherit this compression setting. Here's an example of tablespace creation script specifying advanced compression:

```
CREATE TABLESPACE comp_data
  DATAFILE '/u01/dbfile/O12C/comp_data01.dbf'
  SIZE 500M
  EXTENT MANAGEMENT LOCAL
```

```
UNIFORM SIZE 1M
SEGMENT SPACE MANAGEMENT AUTO
DEFAULT ROW STORE COMPRESS ADVANCED;
```

You can also alter an existing tablespace to set the default degree of compression:

```
SQL> alter tablespace comp_data default row store compress advanced;
```

You can verify the default compression characteristics with this query:

```
select tablespace_name, def_tab_compression, compress_for
from dba_tablespaces
where tablespace_name = 'COMP_DATA';
```

1-22. Compressing Data at the Column Level

Problem

You're using the Oracle Exadata product and you want to efficiently compress data. You have determined that compressed data will result in much more efficient I/O operations, especially when reading data from disk. The idea is that compressed data will result in much fewer blocks read for SELECT statements.

Solution

To enable column compression (Oracle refers to this feature as hybrid columnar compression), when creating a table, use either the COLUMN STORE COMPRESS FOR QUERY or the COLUMN STORE COMPRESS FOR ARCHIVE clause—for example:

```
create table emp(
 emp_id number
,first_name varchar2(30)
,last_name varchar2(30))
column store compress for query;
```

You can also specify a level of compression of either LOW or HIGH:

```
create table emp(
 emp_id number
,first_name varchar2(30)
,last_name varchar2(30))
column store compress for query high;
```

The default level of compression for QUERY is HIGH, and the default level of compression for ARCHIVE is LOW. You can validate the level of compression enabled via this query:

```
select table_name, compression, compress_for
from user_tables
where table_name='EMP';
```

If you attempt to use hybrid columnar compression in an environment other than Exadata, you'll receive the following error:

```
ORA-64307:  Exadata Hybrid Columnar Compression is not supported for
tablespaces on this storage type
```

How It Works

Exadata is Oracle's high-performance database machine. It is designed to deliver high performance for both data warehouse and OLTP databases. Exadata storage supports hybrid columnar compression and is available starting with Oracle Database 11g R2.

■ **Note**   In Oracle Database 11g R2, column compression was enabled with the COMPRESS FOR QUERY clause. Starting with Oracle Database 12c, this changed to COLUMN STORE COMPRESS FOR QUERY.

Hybrid columnar compression compresses the data on a column-by-column basis. Column-level compression results in higher compression ratios than Oracle basic compression (see Recipe 1-15) or advanced compression (see Recipe 1-16). There are four levels of hybrid columnar compression. These levels are listed here from the lowest level of compression to the highest level:

- COLUMN STORE COMPRESS FOR QUERY LOW
- COLUMN STORE COMPRESS FOR QUERY HIGH
- COLUMN STORE COMPRESS FOR ARCHIVE LOW
- COLUMN STORE COMPRESS FOR ARCHIVE HIGH

COLUMN STORE COMPRESS FOR QUERY is appropriate for bulk load operations on heap-organized tables that are infrequently updated. This type of compression is optimized for query performance and is therefore more appropriate for DSS and data warehouse databases, whereas COLUMN STORE COMPRESS FOR ARCHIVE maximizes the degree of compression and is more appropriate for data that is stored for long periods of time and will not be updated.

■ **Note**   Refer to the Oracle Exadata Storage Server Software documentation for more information on hybrid columnar compression.

CHAPTER 2

■ ■ ■

Choosing and Optimizing Indexes

An index is a database object used primarily to improve the performance of SQL queries. The function of a database index is similar to an index in the back of a book. A book index associates a topic with a page number. When you're locating information in a book, it's usually much faster to inspect the index first, find the topic of interest, and identify associated page numbers. With this information, you can navigate directly to specific page numbers in the book. In this situation, the number of pages you need to inspect is minimal.

If there were no index, you would have to inspect every page of the book to find information. This results in a great deal of page turning, especially with large books. This is similar to an Oracle query that does not use an index and therefore has to scan every used block within a table. For large tables, this results in a great deal of I/O.

The book index's usefulness is directly correlated with the rarity of occurrence of a topic within the book. For example, take this book; it would do no good to create an index on the topic of "performance" because every page in this book deals with performance. However, creating an index on the topic of "bitmap indexes" would be effective because there are only a few pages within the book that are applicable to this feature.

Keep in mind that the index isn't free. It consumes space in the back of the book, and if the material in the book is ever updated (like a second edition), every modification (insert, update, delete) potentially requires a corresponding change to the index. It's important to keep in mind that indexes consume space and require resources when updates occur.

Also, the person who creates the index for the book must consider which topics will be frequently looked up. Topics that are selective and frequently accessed should be included in the book index. If an index in the back of the book is never looked up by a reader, then it unnecessarily wastes space.

Much like the process of creating an index in the back of the book, there are many factors that must be considered when creating an Oracle index. Oracle provides a wide assortment of indexing features and options. These objects are manually created by the DBA or a developer. Therefore, you need to be aware of the various features and how to utilize them. If you choose the wrong type of index or use a feature incorrectly, there may be detrimental performance implications. Listed next are aspects to consider before you create an index:

- Type of index

- Table column(s) to include

- Whether to use a single column or a combination of columns

- Special features such as parallelism, turning off logging, compression, invisible indexes, and so on

- Uniqueness

- Naming conventions

- Tablespace placement

- Initial sizing requirements and growth

- Impact on performance of SELECT statements (improvement)

- Impact on performance of INSERT, UPDATE, and DELETE statements

- Global or local index, if the underlying table is partitioned

When you create an index, you should give some thought to every aspect mentioned in the previous list. One of the first decisions you need to make is the type of index and the columns to include. Oracle provides a robust variety of index types. For most scenarios, you can use the default B-tree (balanced tree) index. Other commonly used types are concatenated, bitmap, and function-based indexes. Table 2-1 describes the types of indexes available with Oracle.

Table 2-1. *Oracle Index Type Descriptions*

Index Type	Usage
B-tree	Default, balanced tree index, good for high-cardinality (high degree of distinct values) columns
IOT	This index is efficient when most of the column values are included in the primary key. You access the index as if it were a table. The data are stored in a B-tree-like structure.
Unique	A form of B-tree index; used to enforce uniqueness in column values; often used with primary key and unique key constraints but can be created independently of constraints.
Reverse-key	A form of B-tree index; useful for balancing I/O in an index that has many sequential inserts.
Key-compressed	Good for concatenated indexes in which the leading column is often repeated; compresses leaf block entries; applies to B-tree and IOT indexes.
Descending	A form of B-tree index; used with indexes in which corresponding column values are sorted in a descending order (the default order is ascending). You can't specify descending for a reverse-key index, and Oracle ignores descending if the index type is bitmap.
Bitmap	Excellent in data warehouse environments with low cardinality (i.e., low degree of distinct values) columns and SQL statements using many AND or OR operators in the WHERE clause. Bitmap indexes aren't appropriate for OLTP databases in which rows are frequently updated. You can't create a unique bitmap index.
Bitmap join	Useful in data warehouse environments for queries that use star schema structures that join fact and dimension tables.
Function-based	Good for columns that have SQL functions applied to them; can be used with either a B-tree or bitmap index.
Indexed virtual column	Good for columns that have SQL functions applied to them; viable alternative to using a function-based index.
Virtual	Allows you to create an index with no physical segment or extents via the NOSEGMENT clause of CREATE INDEX; useful in tuning SQL without consuming resources required to build the physical index. Any index type can be created as virtual.
Invisible	The index is not visible to the query optimizer. However, the structure of the index is maintained as table data are modified. Useful for testing an index before making it visible to the application. Any index type can be created as invisible.
Global partitioned	Global index across all partitions in a partitioned or regular table; can be a B-tree index type and can't be a bitmap index type.

(*continued*)

Table 2-1. (*contiuned*)

Index Type	Usage
Local partitioned	Local index based on individual partitions in a partitioned table; can be either a B-tree or bitmap index type.
B-tree cluster	Used with clustered tables.
Hash cluster	Used with hash clusters.
Domain	Specific for an application or cartridge.

■ **Note**   Several of the index types listed in Table 2-1 are actually just variations on the B-tree index. A reverse-key index, for example, is merely a B-tree index optimized for reducing contention when the index value is sequentially generated and inserted with similar values.

This chapter focuses on the most commonly used indexes and features. Hash cluster indexes, partitioned indexes, and domain indexes are not covered in this book. If you need more information regarding index types or features not covered in this chapter or book, see Oracle's SQL Reference Guide at http://otn.oracle.com.

The first recipe in this chapter deals with the mechanics of B-tree indexes. It's critical that you understand how this database object works. Even if you've been around Oracle for a while, we feel it's useful to work through the various scenarios outlined in this first recipe to ensure that you know how the optimizer uses this type of index. This will lay the foundation for solving many different types of performance problems (especially SQL tuning).

2-1. Understanding B-tree Indexes
Problem

You want to create an index. You understand that the default type of index in Oracle is the B-tree, but you don't quite understand how an index is physically implemented. You want to fully comprehend the B-tree index internals so as to make intelligent performance decisions when building database applications.

Solution

An example with a good diagram will help illustrate the mechanics of a B-tree index. Even if you've been working with B-tree indexes for quite some time, a good example may illuminate technical aspects of using an index. To get started, suppose you have a table created as follows:

```
create table cust(
 cust_id number
,last_name varchar2(30)
,first_name varchar2(30));
```

You determine that several SQL queries will frequently use LAST_NAME in the WHERE clause. This prompts you to create an index:

```
SQL> create index cust_idx1 on cust(last_name);
```

■ **Note** There isn't an explicit CREATE INDEX privilege (although there is a CREATE ANY INDEX privilege). If you can create a table (which requires CREATE TABLE) then you can create indexes on it. You also need space quotas for consuming space in the tablespace the table/index is placed within. Keep in mind that with the deferred segment feature (available only with Enterprise Edition of database), that it's possible to create a table and index in a tablespace, but not realize the space quotas are required until a record is inserted into the table (and attempts to consume space).

Next several thousand rows are now inserted into the table (not all of the rows are shown here):

```
insert into cust values(7, 'ACER','SCOTT');
insert into cust values(5, 'STARK','JIM');
insert into cust values(3, 'GREY','BOB');
insert into cust values(11,'KHAN','BRAD');
.....
insert into cust values(274, 'ACER','SID');
```

After the rows are inserted, we ensure that the table statistics are up to date so as to provide the query optimizer sufficient information to make good choices on how to retrieve the data:

```
SQL> exec dbms_stats.gather_table_stats(ownname=>user,tabname=>'CUST',cascade=>true);
```

■ **Note** Oracle strongly recommends that you do not use the ANALYZE statement (with the COMPUTE and ESTIMATE clauses) to collect statistics. Oracle does support using the ANALYZE statement for non-statistics gathering uses such as validating objects and listing chained/migrated rows.

As rows are inserted into the table, Oracle will allocate extents that consist of physical database blocks. Oracle will also allocate blocks for the index. For each record inserted into the table, Oracle will also create an entry in the index that consists of the ROWID and column value (the value in LAST_NAME in this example). The ROWID for each index entry points to the datafile and block that the table column value is stored in. Figure 2-1 shows a graphical representation of how data is stored in the table and the corresponding B-tree index. For this example, datafiles 10 and 15 contain table data stored in associated blocks and datafile 22 stores the index blocks.

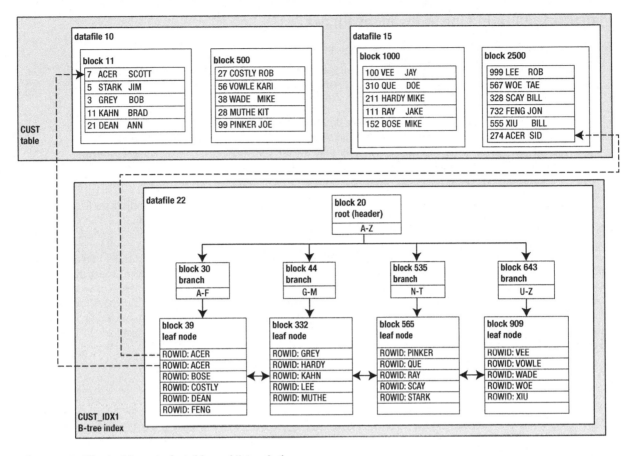

Figure 2-1. *Physical layout of a table and B-tree index*

There are two dotted lines in Figure 2-1. These lines depict how the ROWID (in the index structure) points to the physical location in the table for the column values of ACER. These particular values will be used in the scenarios in this solution. When selecting data from a table and its corresponding index, there are three basic scenarios:

- All table data required by the SQL query is contained in the index structure. Therefore only the index blocks need to be accessed. The blocks from the table are never read.

- All of the information required by the query is not contained in the index blocks. Therefore the query optimizer chooses to access both the index blocks and the table blocks to retrieve the data needed to satisfy the results of the query.

- The query optimizer chooses not to access the index. Therefore only the table blocks are accessed.

The prior situations are covered in the next three subsections.

Scenario 1: All Data Lies in the Index Blocks

There are two scenarios that will be shown in this section:

- *Index range scan*: This occurs when the optimizer determines it is efficient to use the index structure to retrieve multiple rows required by the query. Index range scans are used extensively in a wide variety of situations.

- *Index fast full scan*: This occurs when the optimizer determines that most of the rows in the table will need to be retrieved. However, all of the information required is stored in the index. Since the index structure is usually smaller than the table structure, the optimizer determines that a full scan of the index is more efficient (than a full scan of the table). This scenario is common for queries that count values.

First the index range scan is demonstrated. For this example, suppose this query is issued that selects from the table:

```
SQL> select last_name from cust where last_name='ACER';
```

Before reading on, look at Figure 2-1 and try to answer this question: "What is the minimal number of blocks Oracle will need to read to return the data for this query?" In other words, what is the most efficient way to access the physical blocks in order to satisfy the results of this query? The optimizer could choose to read through every block in the table structure. However, that would result in a great deal of I/O, and thus it is not the most optimal way to retrieve the data.

For this example, the most efficient way to retrieve the data is to use the index structure. To return the rows that contain the value of ACER in the LAST_NAME column, Oracle will need to read at least three blocks: block 20, block 30, and block 39. We can verify that this is occurring by using Oracle's Autotrace utility:

```
SQL> set autotrace on;
SQL> select last_name from cust where last_name='ACER';
```

Here is a partial snippet of the output:

```
---------------------------------------------------------------------
| Id  | Operation          | Name     | Rows  | Bytes | Cost (%CPU)| Time     |
---------------------------------------------------------------------
|   0 | SELECT STATEMENT   |          |    15 |   165 |     3   (0)| 00:00:01 |
|*  1 |   INDEX RANGE SCAN| CUST_IDX1 |    15 |   165 |     3   (0)| 00:00:01 |
---------------------------------------------------------------------
```

The prior output shows that Oracle needed to use only the CUST_IDX1 index to retrieve the data to satisfy the result set of the query. *The table data blocks were not accessed*; only the index blocks were required. This is a particularly efficient indexing strategy for the given query. Listed next are the statistics displayed by Autotrace for this example:

```
Statistics
-----------------------------------------------------------
          1  recursive calls
          0  db block gets
          3  consistent gets
          0  physical reads
```

The consistent gets value indicates that three blocks were read from memory (db block gets plus consistent gets equals the total blocks read from memory). Since the index blocks were already in memory, no physical reads were required to return the result set of this query.

Next an example that results in an index fast full scan is demonstrated. Consider this query:

```
SQL> select count(last_name) from cust;
```

Using SET AUTOTRACE ON, an execution plan is generated. Here is the corresponding output:

```
-------------------------------------------------------------------------------
| Id  | Operation            | Name      | Rows  | Bytes | Cost (%CPU)| Time     |
-------------------------------------------------------------------------------
|   0 | SELECT STATEMENT     |           |     1 |    17 |   170   (0)| 00:00:01 |
|   1 |  SORT AGGREGATE      |           |     1 |    17 |            |          |
|   2 |   INDEX FAST FULL SCAN| CUST_IDX1 |  126K | 2093K |   170   (0)| 00:00:01 |
-------------------------------------------------------------------------------
```

The prior output shows that only the index structure was used to determine the count within the table. In this situation, the optimizer determined that a full scan of the index was more efficient than a full scan of the table.

Scenario 2: All Information Is Not Contained in the Index

Now consider this situation: suppose we need more information from the CUST table. Let's begin with the previous section's query and additionally return the FIRST_NAME column in the query results. Now we need to access the table itself, for that one data element. Here's the new query:

```
SQL> select last_name, first_name from cust where last_name = 'ACER';
```

Using SET AUTOTRACE ON and executing the prior query results in the following execution plan:

```
------------------------------------------------------------------------------------------
| Id  | Operation                          | Name      | Rows | Bytes | Cost (%CPU)| Time     |
------------------------------------------------------------------------------------------
|   0 | SELECT STATEMENT                   |           |    2 |    68 |    1   (0)| 00:00:01 |
|   1 |  TABLE ACCESS BY INDEX ROWID BATCHED|CUST      |    2 |    68 |    1   (0)| 00:00:01 |
|*  2 |   INDEX RANGE SCAN                 |CUST_IDX1  |    2 |       |    1   (0)| 00:00:01 |
------------------------------------------------------------------------------------------
```

The prior output indicates that the CUST_IDX1 index was accessed via an INDEX RANGE SCAN. The INDEX RANGE SCAN identifies the index blocks required to satisfy the results of this query. Additionally the table is read by TABLE ACCESS BY INDEX ROWID BATCHED. The access to the table by the index's ROWID means that Oracle uses the ROWID (stored in the index) to locate the corresponding rows contained within the table blocks. In Figure 2-1, this is indicated by the dotted lines that map the ROWID to the appropriate table blocks that contain the value of ACER in the LAST_NAME column.

Again, looking at Figure 2-1, how many table and index blocks need to be read in this scenario? The index requires that blocks 20, 30, and 39 must be read. Since FIRST_NAME is not included in the index, Oracle must read the table blocks to retrieve these values. Oracle must read block 39 twice because there are two corresponding rows in the table. Oracle knows the ROWID of the table blocks and directly reads blocks 11 and 2500 to retrieve that data.

That makes a total of 6 blocks. With that number in mind, take a look at the statistics generated by Autotrace:

```
Statistics
----------------------------------------------------------
          1  recursive calls
          0  db block gets
          5  consistent gets
```

Notice that the prior statistics indicate that only 5 blocks were read (`consistent gets`), yet we predicted 6 blocks. This is because some block reads are not accounted for in the Autotrace generated statistics. Oracle will pin some blocks and re-read them. In our scenario, block 39 is read once, pinned, and then re-read for a second time (because there are two ROWIDs associated with the value of ACER). The count of re-reads of blocks is collected in the `buffer is pinned count` statistic (which is not displayed in the Autotrace statistics).

Regardless, the point here is that when the index is accessed there is a back-and-forth read process between index blocks and data blocks. The number of blocks read when an index is used to provide ROWIDs for table will be at least double the number of rows returned (because the index block with the ROWID is read and then the corresponding table block is read). And in many scenarios, the `consistent gets` statistic doesn't accurately reflect the actual number of buffer reads.

Scenario 3: Only the Table Blocks Are Accessed

In some situations, even if there is an index, Oracle will determine that it's more efficient to use only the table blocks. When Oracle inspects every row within a table, this is known a full table scan. For example, take this query:

```
SQL> select * from cust;
```

Here are the corresponding execution plan and statistics:

```
-----------------------------------------------------------------------------
| Id  | Operation         | Name | Rows  | Bytes | Cost (%CPU)| Time     |
-----------------------------------------------------------------------------
|   0 | SELECT STATEMENT  |      | 150K  | 4101K |   206   (1)| 00:00:01 |
|   1 |  TABLE ACCESS FULL| CUST | 150K  | 4101K |   206   (1)| 00:00:01 |
-----------------------------------------------------------------------------
```

```
Statistics
-----------------------------------------------------------
          0  recursive calls
          0  db block gets
       2586  consistent gets
          0  physical reads
```

The prior output shows that several thousand blocks were inspected. Oracle searched every row in the table to bring back the results required to satisfy the query. In this situation, all blocks of the table must be read, and there is no way for Oracle to use the index to speed up the retrieval of the data.

■ **Note** For the examples in this section, your results may vary slightly, depending on how many rows you initially insert into the table. We inserted a little over 100,000 rows to seed the table.

ARBORISTIC VIEWS

Oracle provides two types of views containing details about the structure of B-tree indexes:

- INDEX_STATS

- DBA/ALL/USER_INDEXES

The INDEX_STATS view contains information regarding the HEIGHT (number of blocks from root to leaf blocks), LF_ROWS (number of index entries), and so on. The INDEX_STATS view is only populated after you analyze the structure of the index; for example,

```
SQL> analyze index cust_idx1 validate structure;
```

The DBA/ALL/USER_INDEXES views contain statistics, such as BLEVEL (number of blocks from root to branch blocks; this equals HEIGHT – 1); LEAF_BLOCKS (number of leaf blocks); and so on. The DBA/ALL/USER_INDEXES views are populated automatically when the index is created and refreshed via the DBMS_STATS package.

How It Works

The B-tree index is the default index type in Oracle. For most OLTP-type applications, this index type is sufficient. This index type is known as B-tree because the ROWID and associated column values are stored within blocks in a balanced tree-like structure (see Figure 2-1). The B stands for balanced.

B-tree indexes are efficient because, when properly used, they result in a query retrieving data far faster than it would without the index. If the index structure itself contains the required column values to satisfy the result of the query, then the table data blocks need not be accessed. Understanding these mechanics will guide your indexing decision-making process. For example, this will help you decide which columns to index and whether a concatenated index might be more efficient for certain queries and less optimal for others. These topics are covered in detail in subsequent recipes in this chapter.

ESTIMATING THE SPACE AN INDEX WILL REQUIRE

Before you create an index, you can estimate how much space it will take via the DBMS_SPACE.CREATE_INDEX_COST procedure—for example:

```
SQL> set serveroutput on
SQL> exec dbms_stats.gather_table_stats(user,'CUST');
SQL> variable used_bytes number
SQL> variable alloc_bytes number
SQL> exec dbms_space.create_index_cost( 'create index cust_idx2 on cust(first_name)', -
                :used_bytes, :alloc_bytes );
SQL> print :used_bytes
```

Here is some sample output for this example:

```
USED_BYTES
----------
    363690

SQL> print :alloc_bytes
```

Here is some sample output for this example:

```
ALLOC_BYTES
-----------
    2097152
```

The `used_bytes` variable gives you an estimate of how much room is required for the index data. The `alloc_bytes` variable provides an estimate of how much space will be allocated within the tablespace.

2-2. Deciding Which Columns to Index

Problem

A database you manage contains hundreds of tables. Each table typically contains a dozen or more columns. You wonder which columns should be indexed.

Solution

Listed next are general guidelines for deciding which columns to index.

- Define a primary key constraint for each table that results in an index automatically being created on the columns specified in the primary key (see Recipe 2-3).

- Create unique key constraints on non-null column values that are required to be unique (different from the primary key columns). This results in an index automatically being created on the columns specified in unique key constraints (see Recipe 2-4).

- Explicitly create indexes on foreign key columns (see Recipe 2-5).

- Create indexes on columns used often as predicates in the WHERE clause of frequently executed SQL queries (if they are selective).

After you have decided to create indexes, we recommend that you adhere to index creation standards that facilitate the ease of maintenance. Specifically, follow these guidelines when creating an index:

- Use the default B-tree index unless you have a solid reason to use a different index type.

- Create ASSM managed tablespaces (see Recipe 1-2 for details). Let the index inherit its storage properties from the tablespace. This allows you to specify the storage properties when you create the tablespace and not have to manage storage properties for individual indexes.

- If you have a variety of storage requirements for indexes, then consider creating separate tablespaces for each type of index—for example, INDEX_LARGE, INDEX_MEDIUM, and INDEX_SMALL tablespaces, each defined with storage characteristics appropriate for the size of the index.

Listed next is a sample script that encapsulates the foregoing recommendations from the prior two bulleted lists:

```
CREATE TABLE cust(
 cust_id    NUMBER
,last_name  VARCHAR2(30)
,first_name VARCHAR2(30))
TABLESPACE hr_data;
--
```

```
ALTER TABLE cust ADD CONSTRAINT cust_pk PRIMARY KEY (cust_id)
USING INDEX TABLESPACE hr_data;
--
ALTER TABLE cust ADD CONSTRAINT cust_uk1 UNIQUE (last_name, first_name)
USING INDEX TABLESPACE hr_data;
--
CREATE TABLE address(
 address_id NUMBER,
 cust_id    NUMBER
,street     VARCHAR2(30)
,city       VARCHAR2(30)
,state      VARCHAR2(30))
TABLESPACE hr_data;
--
ALTER TABLE address ADD CONSTRAINT addr_fk1
FOREIGN KEY (cust_id) REFERENCES cust(cust_id);
--
CREATE INDEX addr_fk1 ON address(cust_id)
TABLESPACE hr_data;
```

In the prior script, two tables are created. The parent table is CUST and its primary key is CUST_ID. The child table is ADDRESS and its primary key is ADDRESS_ID. The CUST_ID column exists in ADDRESS as a foreign key mapping back to the CUST_ID column in the CUST table.

CREATING MULTIPLE INDEXES ON THE SAME SET OF COLUMNS

Prior to Oracle Database 12c, you could not have multiple indexes defined on the exact same combination of columns in one table. This has changed in 12c. You can now have multiple indexes on the same set of columns. However, you can only do this if there is something physically different about the indexes; for example, one index is created as a B-tree index, and the second, as a bitmap index.

Also, there can be only one visible index for the same combination of columns. Any other indexes created on that same set of columns must be declared invisible; for example,

```
SQL> create index cust_idx2 on cust(first_name, last_name);
SQL> create bitmap index cust_bmx1 on cust(first_name, last_name) invisible;
```

Prior to Oracle Database 12c, if you attempted the previous operation, the second creation statement would throw an error such as ORA-01408: such column list already indexed.

Why would you want two indexes defined on the same set of columns? You might want to do this if you originally implemented B-tree indexes and now wanted to change them to bitmap—the idea being, you create the new indexes as invisible, then drop the original indexes and make the new indexes visible. In a large database environment this would enable you to make the change quickly.

How It Works

You should add an index only when you're certain it will improve performance. Misusing indexes can have serious negative performance effects. Indexes created of the wrong type or on the wrong columns do nothing but consume space and processing resources. As a DBA, you must have a strategy to ensure that indexes enhance performance and don't negatively impact applications.

Table 2-2 encapsulates many of the index management concepts covered in this chapter. These recommendations aren't written in stone: Adapt and modify them as needed for your environment.

Table 2-2. *Index Creation and Maintenance Guidelines*

Guideline	Reasoning
Add indexes judiciously. Test first to determine quantifiable performance gains.	Indexes consume disk space and processing resources. Don't add indexes unnecessarily.
Use the correct type of index.	Correct index usage maximizes performance. See Table 2-1 for more details.
Use consistent naming standards.	This makes maintenance and troubleshooting easier.
Monitor your indexes, and drop indexes that aren't used. See Recipe 2-15 for details on monitoring indexes.	Doing this frees up physical space and improves the performance of Data Manipulation Language (DML) statements.
Don't rebuild indexes unless you have a solid reason to do so. See Recipe 2-17 for details on rebuilding an index.	Rebuilding an index is generally unnecessary unless the index is corrupt or you want to change a physical characteristic (such as the tables pace) without dropping the index.
Before dropping an index, consider marking it as unusable or invisible.	This allows you to better determine if there are any performance issues before you drop the index. These options let you rebuild or re-enable the index without requiring the Data Definition Language (DDL) index creation statement.
Consider creating concatenated indexes that result in only the index structure being required to return the result set.	Avoids having to scan any table blocks; when queries are able to use the index only, this results in very efficient execution plans.
Consider creating indexes on columns used in the ORDER BY, GROUP BY, UNION, or DISTINCT clauses.	This may result in more efficient queries that frequently use these SQL constructs.

Refer to these guidelines as you create and manage indexes in your databases. These recommendations are intended to help you correctly use index technology.

INDEXES WITH NO SEGMENTS

You can instruct Oracle to create an index that will never be used and won't have any extents allocated to it via the NOSEGMENT clause:

```
SQL> create index cust_idx1 on cust(first_name) nosegment;
```

Even though this index will never be used, you can instruct Oracle to determine if the index might be used by the optimizer via the _USE_NOSEGMENT_INDEXES initialization parameter—for example:

```
SQL> alter session set "_use_nosegment_indexes"=true;
SQL> set autotrace trace explain;
SQL> select first_name from cust where first_name = 'JIM';
```

Here's a sample execution plan showing the optimizer would use the index (assuming that you dropped and re-created it normally without the NOSEGMENT clause):

```
--------------------------------------------------------------------------
 Id | Operation          | Name      | Rows  | Bytes | Cost (%CPU)| Time     |
--------------------------------------------------------------------------
  0 | SELECT STATEMENT   |           |    1  |   17  |    1   (0)| 00:00:01 |
* 1 |  INDEX RANGE SCAN| CUST_IDX1 |    1  |   17  |    1   (0)| 00:00:01 |
--------------------------------------------------------------------------
```

That begs the question, why would you ever create an index with NOSEGMENT? If you have a very large index that you want to create without allocating space, to determine if the index would be used by the optimizer, creating an index with NOSEGMENT allows you to test that scenario. If you determine that the index would be useful, you can drop the index and re-create it without the NOSEGMENT clause.

2-3. Creating a Primary Key Constraint and Index
Problem

You want to enforce that the primary key columns are unique within a table. Furthermore many of the columns in the primary key are frequently used within the WHERE clause of several queries. You want to ensure that indexes are created on primary key columns.

Solution

When you define a primary key constraint for a table, Oracle will automatically create an associated index for you. There are several methods available for creating a primary key constraint. Our preferred approach is to use the ALTER TABLE...ADD CONSTRAINT statement. Defining a constraint in this way will create the index and the constraint at the same time. This example creates a primary key constraint named CUST_PK and also instructs Oracle to create the corresponding index (also named CUST_PK) in the USERS tablespace:

```
alter table cust add constraint cust_pk primary key (cust_id)
using index tablespace users;
```

The following queries and output provide details about the constraint and index that Oracle created. The first query displays the constraint information:

```
select constraint_name, constraint_type
from user_constraints
where table_name = 'CUST';
```

```
CONSTRAINT_NAME                 C
------------------------------- -
CUST_PK                         P
```

This query displays the index information:

```
select index_name, tablespace_name, index_type, uniqueness
from user_indexes
where table_name = 'CUST';
```

```
INDEX_NAME      TABLESPACE_NAME INDEX_TYPE       UNIQUENESS
--------------- --------------- ---------------- ---------------
CUST_PK         USERS           NORMAL           UNIQUE
```

How It Works

The solution for this recipe shows the method that we prefer to create primary key constraints and the corresponding index. In most situations, this approach is acceptable. However, you should be aware that there are several other methods for creating the primary key constraint and index. These methods are listed here:

- Create an index first, and then use ALTER TABLE...ADD CONSTRAINT.
- Specify the constraint inline (with the column) in the CREATE TABLE statement.
- Specify the constraint out of line (from the column) within the CREATE TABLE statement.

These techniques are described in the next several subsections.

Create Index and Constraint Separately

You have the option of first creating an index and then altering the table to apply the primary key constraint. Here's an example:

```
SQL> create index cust_pk on cust(cust_id);
SQL> alter table cust add constraint cust_pk primary key(cust_id);
```

The advantage to this approach is that you can drop or disable the primary key constraint independently of the index. If you work with large data volumes, you may require this sort of flexibility. This approach allows you to disable/re-enable a constraint without having to later rebuild the index.

Create Constraint Inline

You can directly create an index inline (with the column) in the CREATE TABLE statement. This approach is simple but doesn't allow for multiple column primary keys and doesn't name the constraint:

```
SQL> create table cust(cust_id number primary key);
```

If you don't explicitly name the constraint (as in the prior statement), Oracle automatically generates a name like SYS_C123456. If you want to explicitly provide a name, you can do so as follows:

```
create table cust(cust_id number constraint cust_pk primary key
using index tablespace users);
```

The advantage of this approach is that it's very simple. If you're experimenting in a development or test environment, this approach is quick and effective.

Create Constraint Out of Line

You can also define the primary key constraint out of line (from the column) within the CREATE TABLE statement:

```
create table cust(
 cust_id number
,constraint cust_pk primary key (cust_id) using index tablespace users);
```

The out-of-line approach has one advantage over the inline approach in that you can specify multiple columns for the primary key.

All of the prior techniques for creating a primary key constraint and corresponding index are valid. It's often a matter of DBA or developer preference as to which technique is used.

2-4. Ensuring Unique Column Values
Problem

You want to define a column or set of columns can be used to identify a row and must be unique. These columns are not part of the primary key.

■ **Note**　One difference between a primary key and a unique key is that you can have only one primary key definition per table, whereas you can have multiple unique keys. Also, unique key constraints allow for null values, whereas primary key constraints do not.

Solution

This solution focuses on using the ALTER TABLE...ADD CONSTRAINT statement. When you create a unique key constraint, Oracle will automatically create an index for you. This is our recommended approach for creating unique key constraints and indexes. This example creates a unique constraint named CUST_UX1 on the combination of the
LAST_NAME and FIRST_NAME columns of the CUST table:

```
alter table cust add constraint cust_ux1 unique (last_name, first_name)
using index tablespace users;
```

The prior statement creates the unique constraint, and additionally Oracle automatically creates an associated index. The following query displays the constraint that was created successfully:

```
select constraint_name, constraint_type
from user_constraints
where table_name = 'CUST';
```

Here is a snippet of the output:

```
CONSTRAINT_NAME                  C
-----------------------------    -
CUST_UX1                         U
```

This query shows the index that was automatically created along with the constraint:

```
select index_name, tablespace_name, index_type, uniqueness
from user_indexes
where table_name = 'CUST';
```

Here is some sample output:

```
INDEX_NAME           TABLESPACE INDEX_TYPE UNIQUENESS
-------------------- ---------- ---------- ---------
CUST_UX1             USERS      NORMAL     UNIQUE
```

How It Works

Defining a unique constraint ensures that when you insert or update column values, then any combination of non-null values are unique. Besides the approach we displayed in the "Solution" section, there are several additional techniques for creating unique constraints:

- Create a regular index, and then use ALTER TABLE to add a constraint.

- Use the CREATE TABLE statement.

- Create a unique index and don't add the constraint.

These techniques are described in the next few subsections.

Create Index First, Then Add Constraint

You have the option of first creating an index and then adding the constraint as a separate statement—for example:

```
SQL> create unique index cust_uidx1 on cust(last_name, first_name) tablespace users;
SQL> alter table cust add constraint cust_uidx1 unique (last_name, first_name);
```

The advantage of creating the index separate from the constraint is that you can drop or disable the constraint without dropping the underlying index. When working with large indexes, you may want to consider this approach. If you need to disable the constraint for any reason and then re-enable it later, you can do so without dropping the index (which may take a long time for large indexes).

Use CREATE TABLE

Listed next is an example of using the CREATE TABLE statement to include a unique constraint.

```
create table cust(
 cust_id number
,last_name varchar2(30)
,first_name varchar2(30)
,constraint cust_ux1 unique(last_name, first_name)
 using index tablespace users);
```

The advantage of this approach is that it's simple and encapsulates the constraint and index creation within one statement.

Creating Only a Unique Index

You can also create just a unique index without adding the unique constraint—for example:

```
SQL> create unique index cust_uidx1 on cust(last_name, first_name) tablespace users;
```

When you create only a unique index explicitly (as in the prior statement), Oracle creates a unique index but doesn't add an entry for a constraint in DBA/ALL/USER_CONSTRAINTS. Why does this matter? Consider this scenario:

```
SQL> insert into cust values (1, 'STARK', 'JIM');
SQL> insert into cust values (1, 'STARK', 'JIM');
```

Here's the corresponding error message that is thrown:

```
ORA-00001: unique constraint (MV_MAINT.CUST_UIDX1) violated
```

If you're asked to troubleshoot this issue, the first place you look is in DBA_CONSTRAINTS for a constraint named CUST_UIDX1. However, there is no information:

```
select constraint_name
from dba_constraints
where constraint_name='CUST_UIDX1';
no rows selected
```

The "no rows selected" message can be confusing: the error message thrown when you insert into the table indicates that a unique constraint has been violated, yet there is no information in the constraint-related data-dictionary views. In this situation, you have to look at DBA_INDEXES to view the details of the unique index that has been created—for example:

```
select index_name, uniqueness
from dba_indexes where index_name='CUST_UIDX1';
```

```
INDEX_NAME                        UNIQUENESS
------------------------------    ----------
CUST_UIDX1                        UNIQUE
```

When should you explicitly create a unique index versus creating a constraint and having Oracle automatically create the index? If a unique column (or set of columns) will ever have a corresponding foreign key relationship to another table, then you must explicitly create the unique constraint (and not just a unique index). Also, if you prefer to view constraint related information in DBA/ALL/USER_CONSTRAINTS, then create a constraint.

If the columns that the unique key are defined on will never be used as parent columns to foreign key constraints, then it's fine to just create a unique index (without the constraint). If you take this approach, just be aware that you may not find any information in the constraint-related data dictionary views.

■ **Tip**   If you need to enforce uniqueness on a column value with a function applied to it, such as UPPER(NAME), you can't do that with a constraint (although you could create a virtual column based on UPPER(NAME) and put a constraint on that). However, you can directly create a unique function based index on UPPER(NAME).

2-5. Indexing Foreign Key Columns
Problem

A large number of the queries in your application use foreign key columns as predicates in the WHERE clause. Therefore, for performance reasons, you want to ensure that you have foreign key columns indexed.

Solution

Unlike primary key constraints, Oracle does not automatically create indexes on foreign key columns. For example, say you have a requirement that every record in the ADDRESS table be assigned a corresponding CUST_ID column that exists in the CUST table. To enforce this relationship, you create a foreign key constraint on the ADDRESS table as follows:

```
alter table address add constraint addr_fk1
foreign key (cust_id) references cust(cust_id);
```

■ **Note**   A foreign key column must reference a column in the parent table that has a primary key or unique key constraint defined on it. Otherwise you'll receive the error "ORA-02270: no matching unique or primary key for this column-list."

You realize the foreign key column is used extensively when joining the CUST and ADDRESS tables and that an index on the foreign key column will dramatically increase performance. You have to manually create an index in this situation. For example, a regular B-tree index is created on the foreign key column of CUST_ID in the ADDRESS table:

```
SQL> create index addr_fk1 on address(cust_id);
```

You don't have to name the index the same as the foreign key name (as we did in the prior lines of code). It's a personal preference as to whether you do that. We feel it's easier to maintain environments when the constraint and corresponding index have the same name.

How It Works

Foreign keys exist to ensure that when inserting into a child table, a corresponding parent table record exists. This is the mechanism to guarantee that data conforms to parent/child business relationship rules. There are three good reasons to index foreign keys:

- Parent/child tables are typically joined on foreign key columns; therefore the query optimizer may choose to use the index on the foreign key column to identify the child records that are required to satisfy the results of the query. If no index exists, Oracle has to perform a full table scan on the child table.

- Mitigate the possibility of TM enqueue contention on the child table when rows are updated or deleted in the parent table.

- Prevent situations where Oracle will unnecessarily lock entire tables when an index on a foreign key does not exist. Thus leading to situations where the DBA or developers can't figure out why they're having strange locking issues.

If you're creating an application from scratch, it's fairly easy to create the code and ensure that each foreign key constraint has a corresponding index. However, if you've inherited a database, it's prudent to check if the foreign key columns are indexed.

You can use data dictionary views to verify if all columns of a foreign key constraint have a corresponding index. The task isn't as simple as it might first seem. For example, here is a query that gets you started in the right direction:

```
SELECT DISTINCT
  a.owner                              owner
 ,a.constraint_name                   cons_name
 ,a.table_name                        tab_name
 ,b.column_name                       cons_column
 ,NVL(c.column_name,'***Check index****') ind_column
FROM dba_constraints  a
    ,dba_cons_columns b
    ,dba_ind_columns  c
WHERE constraint_type = 'R'
AND a.owner            = UPPER('&user_name')
AND a.owner            = b.owner
AND a.constraint_name  = b.constraint_name
AND b.column_name      = c.column_name(+)
AND b.table_name       = c.table_name(+)
AND b.position         = c.column_position(+)
ORDER BY tab_name, ind_column;
```

This query, while simple and easy to understand, doesn't correctly report on unindexed foreign keys for all situations. For example, in the case of multicolumn foreign keys, it doesn't matter if the constraint is defined in an order different from that of the index columns, as long as the columns defined in the constraint are in the leading edge of the index. In other words, if the constraint is defined as COL1 and then COL2, then it's okay to have a B-tree index defined on leading-edge COL2 and then COL1.

Also if you have a multi-column index that contains more columns than just the foreign key columns, as long as the foreign key columns are in the leading edge of the index, then you're protected from locking issues.

Additionally, if you have a many-to-many intersection table, which usually has one primary key (and index) defined on all columns, the primary key index will protect the foreign key column that happens to be in the leading edge of the index, but the primary key index does not protect (from locking issues) the other foreign key columns.

Another issue is that a B-tree index protects you from locking issues, but a bitmap index does not. In this situation, the query should also check the index type.

In these scenarios (outlined in the prior paragraphs), you'll need a more sophisticated query to detect indexing issues related to foreign key columns. The following example is a more complex query that uses the LISTAGG analytical function to compare columns (returned as a string in one row) in a foreign key constraint with corresponding indexed columns:

```
SELECT
 CASE WHEN ind.index_name IS NOT NULL THEN
   CASE WHEN ind.index_type IN ('BITMAP') THEN
     '** Bitmp idx **'
   ELSE
     'indexed'
   END
 ELSE
   '** Check idx **'
 END checker
,ind.index_type
,cons.owner, cons.table_name, ind.index_name, cons.constraint_name, cons.cols
FROM (SELECT
        c.owner, c.table_name, c.constraint_name
        ,LISTAGG(cc.column_name, ',' ) WITHIN GROUP (ORDER BY cc.column_name) cols
      FROM dba_constraints  c
          ,dba_cons_columns cc
      WHERE c.owner            = cc.owner
      AND    c.owner = UPPER('&&schema')
      AND    c.constraint_name = cc.constraint_name
      AND    c.constraint_type = 'R'
      GROUP BY c.owner, c.table_name, c.constraint_name) cons
LEFT OUTER JOIN
(SELECT
  table_owner, table_name, index_name, index_type, cbr
 ,LISTAGG(column_name, ',' ) WITHIN GROUP (ORDER BY column_name) cols
 FROM (SELECT
         ic.table_owner, ic.table_name, ic.index_name
         ,ic.column_name, ic.column_position, i.index_type
         ,CONNECT_BY_ROOT(ic.column_name) cbr
       FROM dba_ind_columns ic
           ,dba_indexes     i
       WHERE ic.table_owner = UPPER('&schema')
       AND    ic.table_owner = i.table_owner
       AND    ic.table_name  = i.table_name
       AND    ic.index_name  = i.index_name
       CONNECT BY PRIOR ic.column_position-1 = ic.column_position
       AND PRIOR ic.index_name = ic.index_name)
  GROUP BY table_owner, table_name, index_name, index_type, cbr) ind
ON  cons.cols       = ind.cols
AND cons.table_name = ind.table_name
AND cons.owner      = ind.table_owner
ORDER BY checker, cons.owner, cons.table_name;
```

This query will prompt you for a schema name and then will display foreign key constraints that don't have corresponding indexes. This query also checks for the index type; as previously stated, bitmap indexes may exist on foreign key columns but don't prevent locking issues.

TABLE LOCKS AND FOREIGN KEYS

Here is a simple example that demonstrates the locking issue when foreign key columns are not indexed. First, create two tables (DEPT and EMP), and associate them with a foreign key constraint:

```
create table emp(emp_id number primary key, dept_id number);
create table dept(dept_id number primary key);
alter table emp add constraint emp_fk1 foreign key (dept_id) references dept(dept_id);
```

Next, insert some data:

```
insert into dept values(10);
insert into dept values(20);
insert into dept values(30);
insert into emp values(1,10);
insert into emp values(2,20);
insert into emp values(3,10);
commit;
```

Open two terminal sessions. From one, delete one record from the child table (don't commit):

```
delete from emp where dept_id = 10;
```

Then, attempt to delete from the parent table some data not affected by the child table delete:

```
delete from dept where dept_id = 30;
```

The delete from the parent table hangs until the child table transaction is committed. Without a regular B-tree index on the foreign key column in the child table, any time you attempt to insert or delete in the child table, a table-wide lock is placed on the parent table; this prevents deletes or updates in the parent table until the child table transaction completes.

Now, run the prior experiment, except this time, additionally create an index on the foreign key column of the child table:

```
create index emp_fk1 on emp(dept_id);
```

You should be able to run the prior two delete statements independently. When you have a B-tree index on the foreign key columns, if deleting from the child table, Oracle will not excessively lock all rows in the parent table.

2-6. Deciding When to Use a Concatenated Index

Problem

You have a combination of columns (from the same table) that are often used in the WHERE clause of several SQL queries. For example, you use LAST_NAME in combination with FIRST_NAME to identify a customer:

```
select last_name, first_name
from cust
where last_name = 'SMITH'
and first_name = 'STEVE';
```

You wonder if it would be more efficient to create a single concatenated index on the combination of LAST_NAME and FIRST_NAME columns or if performance would be better if two indexes were created separately on LAST_NAME and FIRST_NAME.

Solution

When frequently accessing two or more columns in conjunction in the WHERE clause, a concatenated index is often more selective than two single indexes. For this example, here's the table creation script:

```
create table cust(
 cust_id number primary key
,last_name varchar2(30)
,first_name varchar2(30));
```

Here's an example of a concatenated index created on LAST_NAME and FIRST_NAME:

```
SQL> create index cust_idx1 on cust(last_name, first_name);
```

To determine whether the concatenated index is used, several rows are inserted (only a subset of the rows is shown here):

```
SQL> insert into cust values(1,'SMITH','JOHN');
SQL> insert into cust values(2,'JONES','DAVE');
..........
SQL> insert into cust values(3,'FORD','SUE');
```

Next, statistics are generated for the table and index:

```
SQL> exec dbms_stats.gather_table_stats(ownname=>user,-
          tabname=>'CUST',cascade=>true);
```

Now Autotrace is turned on so that the execution plan is displayed when a query is run:

```
SQL> set autotrace on;
```

Here's the query to execute:

```
select last_name, first_name
from cust
where last_name = 'SMITH'
and first_name = 'JOHN';
```

Listed next is an explain plan that shows the optimizer is using the index:

```
---------------------------------------------------------------------
| Id  | Operation          | Name      | Rows | Bytes | Cost (%CPU)| Time     |
---------------------------------------------------------------------
|   0 | SELECT STATEMENT   |           |   13 |   143 |     1   (0)| 00:00:01 |
|*  1 |   INDEX RANGE SCAN | CUST_IDX1 |   13 |   143 |     1   (0)| 00:00:01 |
---------------------------------------------------------------------
```

The prior output indicates that an INDEX RANGE SCAN was used to access the CUST_IDX1 index. Notice that all of the information required to satisfy the results of this query was contained within the index. The table data was not required. Oracle accessed only the index.

One other item to consider: suppose you have this query that additionally selects the CUST_ID column:

```
select cust_id, last_name, first_name
from cust
where last_name = 'SMITH'
and first_name = 'JOHN';
```

If you frequently access CUST_ID in combination with LAST_NAME and FIRST_NAME, consider adding CUST_ID to the concatenated index. This will provide all of the information that the query needs in the index. Oracle will be able to retrieve the required data from the index blocks and thus not have to access the table blocks.

How It Works

Oracle allows you to create an index that contains more than one column. Multicolumn indexes are known as concatenated indexes. These indexes are especially effective when you often use multiple columns in the WHERE clause when accessing a table. Here are some factors to consider when using concatenated indexes:

- If columns are often used together in the WHERE clause, consider creating a concatenated index.

- If a column is also used (in other queries) by itself in the WHERE clause, place that column at the leading edge of the index (first column defined).

- Keep in mind that Oracle can still use a lagging edge index (not the first column defined) if the lagging column appears by itself in the WHERE clause (but not as efficiently as it would if it was an index on a column in the leading edge of the index).

In older versions of Oracle (circa v8), the optimizer would use a concatenated index only if the leading edge column(s) appeared in the WHERE clause. In modern versions, the optimizer considers using a concatenated index even if the leading edge column(s) aren't present in the WHERE clause. This ability to use an index without reference to leading edge columns is known as the skip-scan feature. For example, say you have this query that uses the FIRST_ NAME column (which is a lagging column in the concatenated index created in the "Solution" section of this recipe):

```
SQL> select last_name from cust where first_name='DAVE';
```

Here is the corresponding explain plan showing that the skip-scan feature is in play:

```
---------------------------------------------------------------------------
| Id  | Operation       | Name      | Rows  | Bytes | Cost (%CPU)| Time     |
---------------------------------------------------------------------------
|   0 | SELECT STATEMENT |          |    38 |   418 |     1   (0)| 00:00:01 |
|*  1 |   INDEX SKIP SCAN | CUST_IDX1 |    38 |   418 |     1   (0)| 00:00:01 |
---------------------------------------------------------------------------
```

A concatenated index used for skip-scanning in some scenarios can be more efficient than a full table scan. However, if you're consistently using only a lagging edge column of a concatenated index, then consider creating a single-column index on the lagging column.

■ **Note**   Keep in mind that adding an extra column to a concatenated index may help the performance of one SQL statement but may decrease the performance of other SQL statements that use the index (due to an increased number of leaf blocks in the index when the extra column is added).

2-7. Reducing Index Size Through Compression
Problem

You want to create an index that efficiently handles cases in which many rows have the same values in one or more indexed columns. For example, suppose you have a table defined as follows:

```
create table cust(
 cust_id number
,last_name varchar2(30)
,first_name varchar2(30)
,middle_name varchar2(30));
```

Furthermore, you inspect the data inserted into the prior table with this query:

```
SQL> select last_name, first_name, middle_name from cust;
```

You notice that there is a great deal of duplication in the LAST_NAME and FIRST_NAME columns:

```
LEE            JOHN           Q
LEE            JOHN           B
LEE            JOHN           A
LEE            JOE            D
SMITH          BOB            A
SMITH          BOB            C
SMITH          BOB            D
SMITH          JOHN           J
SMITH          JOHN           A
SMITH          MIKE           K
SMITH          MIKE           R
SMITH          MIKE           S
```

You want to create an index that compresses the values so as to compact entries into the blocks. When the index is accessed, the compression will result in fewer block reads and thus improve performance. Specifically you want to create a key-compressed index on the LAST_NAME and FIRST_NAME columns of this table.

Solution

Use the COMPRESS N clause to create a compressed index:

```
SQL> create index cust_cidx1 on cust(last_name, first_name) compress 2;
```

The prior line of code instructs Oracle to create a compressed index on two columns (LAST_NAME and FIRST_NAME). For this example, if we determined that there was a high degree of duplication only in the first column, we could instruct the COMPRESS N clause to compress only the first column (LAST_NAME) by specifying an integer of 1:

```
SQL> create index cust_cidx1 on cust(last_name, first_name) compress 1;
```

How It Works

Index compression is useful for indexes that contain multiple columns where the leading index column value is often repeated. Compressed indexes have the following advantages:

- Reduced storage
- More rows stored in leaf blocks, which can result in less I/O when accessing a compressed index

The degree of compression will vary by the amount of duplication in the index columns specified for compression. You can verify the degree of compression and the number of leaf blocks used by running the following two queries before and after creating an index with compression enabled:

```
SQL> select sum(bytes) from user_extents where segment_name='&ind_name';
SQL> select index_name, leaf_blocks from user_indexes where index_name='&ind_name';
```

You can verify the index compression is in use and the corresponding prefix length as follows:

```
select  index_name, compression, prefix_length
from user_indexes
where index_name = 'CUST_CIDX1';
```

Here's some sample output indicating that compression is enabled for the index with a prefix length of 2:

```
INDEX_NAME                      COMPRESS PREFIX_LENGTH
------------------------------- -------- -------------
CUST_CIDX1                      ENABLED              2
```

You can modify the prefix length by rebuilding the index. The following code changes the prefix length to 1:

```
SQL> alter index cust_cidx1 rebuild compress 1;
```

You can enable or disable compression for an existing index by rebuilding it. This example rebuilds the index with no compression:

```
SQL> alter index cust_cidx1 rebuild nocompress;
```

■ **Note**   You cannot create a key-compressed index on a bitmap index.

2-8. Implementing a Function-Based Index
Problem

A query is running slow. You examine the WHERE clause and notice that a SQL UPPER function has been applied to a column. The UPPER function blocks the use of the existing index on that column. You want to create a function-based index to support the query. Here's an example of such a query:

```
SELECT first_name
FROM cust
WHERE UPPER(first_name) = 'DAVE';
```

You inspect USER_INDEXES and discover that an index exists on the FIRST_NAME column:

```
select  index_name, column_name
from user_ind_columns
where table_name = 'CUST';

INDEX_NAME              COLUMN_NAME
-------------------     --------------------
CUST_IDX1               FIRST_NAME
```

You generate an explain plan via SET AUTOTRACE TRACE EXPLAIN and notice that with the UPPER function applied to the column, the index is not used:

```
--------------------------------------------------------------------------
| Id  | Operation         | Name | Rows  | Bytes | Cost (%CPU)| Time     |
--------------------------------------------------------------------------
|   0 | SELECT STATEMENT  |      |     1 |    17 |     2   (0)| 00:00:01 |
|*  1 |  TABLE ACCESS FULL| CUST |     1 |    17 |     2   (0)| 00:00:01 |
--------------------------------------------------------------------------
```

You need to create an index that Oracle will use in this situation.

Solution

There are two ways to resolve this issue:

- Create a function-based index.
- If using Oracle Database 11g or higher, create an indexed virtual column (see Recipe 2-9 for details).

This solution focuses on using a function-based index. You create a function-based index by referencing the SQL function and column in the index creation statement. For this example, a function-based index is created on UPPER(name):

```
SQL> create index cust_fidx1 on cust(UPPER(first_name));
```

To verify if the index is used, the Autotrace facility is turned on:

```
SQL> set autotrace trace explain;
```

Now the query is executed:

```
SELECT first_name
FROM cust
WHERE UPPER(first_name) = 'DAVE';
```

Here is the resulting execution plan showing that the function-based index is used:

```
-------------------------------------------------------------------------------------
| Id  | Operation                     | Name       | Rows | Bytes | Cost (%CPU)| Time     |
-------------------------------------------------------------------------------------
|   0 | SELECT STATEMENT              |            |    1 |    34 |    1   (0)| 00:00:01 |
|   1 |  TABLE ACCESS BY INDEX ROWID| CUST       |    1 |    34 |    1   (0)| 00:00:01 |
|*  2 |   INDEX RANGE SCAN            | CUST_FIDX1 |    1 |       |    1   (0)| 00:00:01 |
-------------------------------------------------------------------------------------
```

■ **Note** You can't modify a column that has a function-based index applied to it. You'll have to drop the index, modify the column, and then re-create the index.

How It Works

Function-based indexes are created with functions or expressions in their definitions. Function-based indexes allow index look-ups on columns referenced by SQL functions in the WHERE clause of a query. The index can be as simple as the example in the "Solution" section of this recipe, or it can be based on complex logic stored in a PL/SQL function.

■ **Note** Any user-created SQL functions must be declared deterministic before they can be used in a function-based index. Deterministic means that for a given set of inputs, the function always returns the same results. You must use the keyword DETERMINISTIC when creating a user-defined function that you want to use in a function-based index.

If you want to see the definition of a function-based index, select from the DBA/ALL/USER_IND_EXPRESSIONS view to display the SQL associated with the index. If you're using SQL*Plus, be sure to issue a SET LONG command first—for example:

```
SQL> SET LONG 5000
SQL> select index_name, column_expression from user_ind_expressions;
```

The SET LONG command in this example tells SQL*Plus to display up to 5000 characters from the COLUMN_EXPRESSION column, which is of type LONG.

2-9. Indexing a Virtual Column

Problem

You're currently using a function-based index but need better performance. You want to replace the function-based index with a virtual column and place an index on the virtual column.

■ **Note** The virtual column feature requires Oracle Database 11g or higher.

Solution

Using a virtual column in combination with an index provides you with an alternative method for achieving performance gains when using SQL functions on columns in the WHERE clause. For example, suppose you have this query:

```
SELECT first_name
FROM cust
WHERE UPPER(first_name) = 'DAVE';
```

Normally, the optimizer will ignore any indexes on the column FIRST_NAME because of the SQL function applied to the column. There are two ways to improve performance in this situation:

- Create a function-based index (see Recipe 2-8 for details).

- Use a virtual column in combination with an index.

This solution focuses on the latter bullet. First a virtual column is added to the table that encapsulates the SQL function:

```
SQL> alter table cust add(up_name generated always as (UPPER(first_name)) virtual);
```

Next an index is created on the virtual column:

```
SQL> create index cust_vidx1 on cust(up_name);
```

This creates a very efficient mechanism to retrieve data when referencing a column with a SQL function.

How It Works

You might be asking this question: "Which performs better, a function-based index or an indexed virtual column?" In our testing, we were able to create several scenarios where the virtual column performed better than the function-based index. Results may vary depending on your data.

The purpose of this recipe is not to convince you to immediately start replacing all function-based indexes in your system with virtual columns; rather, we want you to be aware of an alternative method for solving a common performance issue.

A virtual column is not free. If you have an existing table, you have to create and maintain the DDL required to create the virtual column, whereas a function-based index can be added, modified, and dropped independently from the table.

Several caveats are associated with virtual columns:

- You can define a virtual column only on a regular heap-organized table. You can't define a virtual column on an index-organized table, an external table, a temporary table, object tables, or cluster tables.

- Virtual columns can't reference other virtual columns.

- Virtual columns can reference columns only from the table in which the virtual column is defined.

- The output of a virtual column must be a scalar value (a single value, not a set of values).

To view the definition of a virtual column, use the DBMS_METADATA package to view the DDL associated with the table. If you're selecting from SQL*Plus, you need to set the LONG variable to a value large enough to show all data returned:

```
SQL> set long 5000;
SQL> select dbms_metadata.get_ddl('TABLE','CUST') from dual;
```

Here's a partial snippet of the output showing the virtual column details:

```
"UP_NAME" VARCHAR2(30) GENERATED ALWAYS AS (UPPER("FIRST_NAME")) VIRTUAL
```

You can also view the definition of the virtual column by querying the DBA/ALL/USER_IND_EXPRESSIONS view. If you're using SQL*Plus, be sure to issue a SET LONG command first—for example:

```
SQL> SET LONG 5000
SQL> select index_name, column_expression from user_ind_expressions;
```

The SET LONG command in this example tells SQL*Plus to display up to 5000 characters from the COLUMN_EXPRESSION column, which is of type LONG.

2-10. Limiting Index Contention when Several Processes Insert in Parallel

Problem

You use a sequence to populate the primary key of a table and realize that this can cause contention on the leading edge of the index because the index values are nearly similar. This leads to multiple inserts into the same block, which causes contention. You want to spread out the inserts into the index so that the inserts more evenly distribute values across the index structure. You want to use a reverse-key index to accomplish this.

Solution

Use the REVERSE clause to create a reverse-key index:

```
SQL> create index cust_idx1 on cust(cust_id) reverse;
```

You can verify that an index is reverse-key by running the following query:

```
SQL> select index_name, index_type from user_indexes;
```

Here's some sample output showing that the INV_IDX1 index is reverse-key:

```
INDEX_NAME                      INDEX_TYPE
------------------------------  ---------------------------
CUST_IDX1                       NORMAL/REV
USERS_IDX1                      NORMAL
```

■ **Note**   You can't specify REVERSE for a bitmap index or an index-organized table.

How It Works

Reverse-key indexes are similar to B-tree indexes except that the bytes of the index key are reversed when an index entry is created. For example, if the index values are 102, 103, and 104, the reverse-key index values are 201, 301, and 401:

```
Index value            Reverse key value
------------           --------------------
102                    201
103                    301
104                    401
```

Reverse-key indexes can perform better in scenarios where you need a way to spread index data that would otherwise have similar values clustered together. Thus, when using a reverse-key index, you avoid having I/O concentrated in one physical disk location within the index during large inserts of sequential values. The downside to this type of index is that it can't be used for index range scans, which may not be an issue for sequence numbers that don't correspond to any natural order that wouldn't normally be used in any type of range scan.

You can rebuild an existing index to be reverse-key by using the REBUILD REVERSE clause—for example:

```
SQL> alter index cust_idx1 rebuild reverse;
```

Similarly, if you want to make an index that is reverse-key into a normally ordered index, then use the REBUILD NOREVERSE clause:

```
SQL> alter index cust_idx1 rebuild noreverse;
```

2-11. Toggling the Visibility of an Index to the Optimizer
Problem

You want to add an index to a production environment and want a mechanism for toggling whether the optimizer will consider using the index for SELECT statements. The idea being you can observe the performance of SELECT while the index is available to the optimizer and compare that to performance with the index not being available.

Solution

Create the index as invisible and then selectively make the index visible to the optimizer for specific sessions. This will allow you to observe in a somewhat controlled setting as to whether the index will be beneficial. Here's an example of creating an invisible index:

```
SQL> create index emp_idx1 on emp(first_name) invisible;
```

Next, set the OPTIMIZER_USE_INVISIBLE_INDEXES initialization parameter to TRUE (the default is FALSE). For the currently connected session, the following instructs the optimizer to consider invisible indexes:

```
SQL> alter session set optimizer_use_invisible_indexes=true;
```

___

■ **Note** If you want all sessions to consider using invisible indexes, then alter the OPTIMIZER_USE_INVISIBLE_INDEXES parameter via the ALTER SYSTEM statement. So in a sense, when you do this the invisible indexes are no longer invisible.

___

You can verify that the index is being used by setting AUTOTRACE TRACE EXPLAIN and running the SELECT statement:

```
SQL> set autotrace trace explain;
```

Here's some sample output indicating that the optimizer chose to use the invisible index:

```
-------------------------------------------------------------------------
| Id  | Operation         | Name     | Rows  | Bytes | Cost (%CPU)| Time     |
-------------------------------------------------------------------------
|   0 | SELECT STATEMENT  |          |     1 |    17 |     1   (0)| 00:00:01 |
|*  1 |   INDEX RANGE SCAN| EMP_IDX1 |     1 |    17 |     1   (0)| 00:00:01 |
-------------------------------------------------------------------------
```

How It Works

In Oracle Database 11g and higher, you have the option of making an index invisible to the optimizer. The index is invisible in the sense that the optimizer won't directly use the index when the optimizer is creating an execution plan. As shown in the Solution section, you make the index visible to the optimizer by setting the OPTIMIZER_USE_ INVISIBLE_INDEXES parameter.

Although the index may be invisible to the optimizer, it can still impact performance in the following ways:

- Invisible indexes consume space and resources the underlying table has records inserted, updated, or deleted. This could impact performance (slow down DML statements).

- The optimizer may consider an invisible index for cardinality calculations (which could alter the choice of subsequent execution plans).

- Oracle can still use an invisible index to prevent certain locking situations when an index is placed on a foreign key column.

- If you create a unique invisible index, the uniqueness of the columns will be enforced regardless of the visibility setting.

Therefore, even if you create an index as invisible, it could have far reaching performance implications. It would be erroneous to assume that an invisible index has no impact on the applications using the tables on which invisible indexes exist. Invisible indexes are only invisible in the sense that the optimizer won't directly use them for SELECT statements unless instructed to do so.

If you want to make an invisible index visible, you can do so as follows:

```
SQL> alter index emp_idx1 visible;
```

You can verify the visibility of an index via this query:

```
SQL> select index_name, status, visibility from user_indexes;
```

Here's some sample output:

```
INDEX_NAME                      STATUS    VISIBILITY
------------------------------- --------- ----------
EMP_IDX1                        VALID     VISIBLE
```

2-12. Creating a Bitmap Index in Support of a Star Schema
Problem

You have a data warehouse that contains a star schema. The star schema consists of a large fact table and several dimension (lookup) tables. The primary key columns of the dimension tables map to foreign key columns in the fact table. You would like to create bitmap indexes on all of the foreign key columns in the fact table.

Solution

You use the BITMAP keyword to create a bitmap index. The next line of code creates a bitmap index on the CUST_ID column of the F_SALES table:

```
SQL> create bitmap index f_sales_cust_fk1 on f_sales(cust_id);
```

The type of index is verified with the following query:

```
SQL> select index_name, index_type from user_indexes where index_name='F_SALES_CUST_FK1';
```

```
INDEX_NAME                      INDEX_TYPE
------------------------------- --------------------------
F_SALES_CUST_FK1                BITMAP
```

■ **Note**   Bitmap indexes and bitmap join indexes are available only with the Oracle Enterprise Edition of the database. Also, you can't create a unique bitmap index.

How It Works

You shouldn't use bitmap indexes on OLTP databases with high INSERT/UPDATE/DELETE activities, due to locking issues. Locking issues arise because the structure of the bitmap index results in potentially many rows being locked during DML operations, which results in locking problems for high-transaction OLTP systems.

A bitmap index stores the ROWID of a row and a corresponding bitmap. You can think of the bitmap as a combination of ones and zeros. A one indicates the presence of a value, and a zero indicates that the value doesn't exist. Bitmap indexes are ideal for low-cardinality columns (few distinct values) and where the application is not frequently updating the table.

Bitmap indexes are commonly used in data warehouse environments where you have star schema design. A typical star schema structure consists of a large fact table and many small dimension (lookup) tables. In these scenarios, it's common to create bitmap indexes on fact table–foreign key columns. The fact tables are typically loaded on a daily basis and (usually) aren't subsequently updated or deleted.

Bitmap indexes are especially effective at retrieving rows when multiple AND and OR conditions appear in the WHERE clause. This is because Oracle can filter the rows by simply applying Boolean algebra operations on the bitmap values to quickly identify which rows match the specified criteria.

An example will drive home this point. In a data warehouse at the center of a star schema design sits a fact table that stores information such as sales amounts. The fact table is linked via foreign keys to several dimension tables. The dimensions store look-up values such as dates, regions, customers, and so on. The following bit of code simulates creating several dimension tables and a fact table:

```
create table d1(d1 number);
create table d2(d2 number);
create table d3(d3 number);
create table d4(d4 number);
create table d5(d5 number);
create table f_fact(d1 number, d2 number, d3 number, d4 number, d5 number, counter number);
```

Next many values are inserted into the dimension tables and the fact table:

```
insert into d1 select level from dual connect by level <= 2;
insert into d2 select level from dual connect by level <= 3;
insert into d3 select level from dual connect by level <= 5;
insert into d4 select level from dual connect by level <= 100;
insert into d5 select level from dual connect by level <= 1000;
--
insert into f_fact (d1,d2,d3,d4,d5,counter)
select d1,d2,d3,d4,d5,dbms_random.value*100
from d1,d2,d3,d4,d5;
```

Next bitmap indexes are created on the dimension columns that exist in the fact table:

```
create bitmap index f_fact_b1 on f_fact(d1);
create bitmap index f_fact_b2 on f_fact(d2);
create bitmap index f_fact_b3 on f_fact(d3);
create bitmap index f_fact_b4 on f_fact(d4);
create bitmap index f_fact_b5 on f_fact(d5);
```

Now statistics are generated:

```
exec dbms_stats.gather_schema_stats(ownname=>user);
```

Now consider what types of queries are typically issued against a fact table. They usually consist of counts or sums, and/or many varying ways of filtering the data via the dimension values. Notice what the execution plan looks like when autotracing is enabled and the fact table is queried:

```
set autotrace trace explain;
select count(*) from f_fact where d1 = 2 and (d2 = 3 or d3 = 4) and d4 IN (10,11,12);
```

Here are the execution plan details:

```
-----------------------------------------------------------------------------------------
| Id  | Operation                       | Name      | Rows  | Bytes | Cost (%CPU)| Time     |
-----------------------------------------------------------------------------------------
|   0 | SELECT STATEMENT                |           |     1 |    12 |    70   (0)| 00:00:01 |
|   1 |  SORT AGGREGATE                 |           |     1 |    12 |            |          |
|   2 |   BITMAP CONVERSION COUNT       |           | 21000 |  246K |    70   (0)| 00:00:01 |
|   3 |    BITMAP AND                   |           |       |       |            |          |
|   4 |     BITMAP OR                   |           |       |       |            |          |
|*  5 |      BITMAP INDEX SINGLE VALUE| F_FACT_B4 |       |       |            |          |
|*  6 |      BITMAP INDEX SINGLE VALUE| F_FACT_B4 |       |       |            |          |
|*  7 |      BITMAP INDEX SINGLE VALUE| F_FACT_B4 |       |       |            |          |
|*  8 |     BITMAP INDEX SINGLE VALUE | F_FACT_B1 |       |       |            |          |
|   9 |     BITMAP OR                   |           |       |       |            |          |
|* 10 |      BITMAP INDEX SINGLE VALUE| F_FACT_B2 |       |       |            |          |
|* 11 |      BITMAP INDEX SINGLE VALUE| F_FACT_B3 |       |       |            |          |
-----------------------------------------------------------------------------------------
```

The optimizer is able to make efficient use of the bitmap indexes to satisfy the results of the query. Consider what happens if you dropped the bitmap indexes and replaced them with B-tree indexes:

```
drop index f_fact_b1;
drop index f_fact_b2;
drop index f_fact_b3;
drop index f_fact_b4;
drop index f_fact_b5;
--
create index f_fact_b1 on f_fact(d1);
create index f_fact_b2 on f_fact(d2);
create index f_fact_b3 on f_fact(d3);
create index f_fact_b4 on f_fact(d4);
create index f_fact_b5 on f_fact(d5);
--
exec dbms_stats.gather_schema_stats(ownname=>user);
```

Now run the same select statement and view the execution plan:

```
set autotrace trace explain;
select count(*) from f_fact where d1 = 2 and (d2 = 3 or d3 = 4) and d4 IN (10,11,12);
```

Here's a snippet of the output (part of the output was removed so it would fit within the width of the page):

```
---------------------------------------------------------------------------
| Id  | Operation                          | Name      | Rows  | Bytes | Cost (%CPU)|
---------------------------------------------------------------------------
|   0 | SELECT STATEMENT                   |           |     1 |    12 |   961   (1)|
|   1 |  SORT AGGREGATE                    |           |     1 |    12 |            |
|   2 |   INLIST ITERATOR                  |           |       |       |            |
|*  3 |    TABLE ACCESS BY INDEX ROWID BATCHED| F_FACT  | 21000 |  246K |   961   (1)|
|*  4 |     INDEX RANGE SCAN               | F_FACT_B4 | 93314 |       |   185   (1)|
---------------------------------------------------------------------------
```

Notice that the cost is much higher for the query when it is using regular B-tree indexes. For queries against a Star schema design, which typically include many different and unpredictable combinations of AND/OR of the dimensions in the WHERE clause, bitmap indexes usually are a better choice.

■ **Tip**   One common belief is that bitmap indexes should only be used for low cardinality columns. This isn't necessarily true; a bitmap index can efficiently be used for columns that have high cardinality. When deciding whether to use a bitmap versus a B-tree index, consider how the data is updated and how the tables will be queried.

2-13. Creating a Bitmap Join Index
Problem
You're working in a data warehouse environment. You have a fairly large dimension table that is often joined to an extremely large fact table. You wonder if there's a way to create a bitmap index in such a way that it can eliminate the need for the optimizer to access the dimension table blocks to satisfy the results of a query.

Solution
Here's the basic syntax for creating a bitmap join index:

```
create bitmap index <index_name>
on <fact_table> (<dimension_table.dimension_column>)
from <fact_table>, <dimension_table>
where <fact_table>.<foreign_key_column> = <dimension_table>.<primary_key_column>;
```

Bitmap join indexes are appropriate in situations where you're joining two tables using the foreign key column(s) in one table that relate to primary key column(s) in another table. For example, suppose you typically retrieve the CUST_NAME from the D_CUSTOMERS table while joining to a large F_SHIPMENTS fact table. This example creates a bitmap join index between the F_SHIPMENTS and D_CUSTOMERS tables:

```
create bitmap index f_shipments_bm_idx1
on f_shipments(d_customers.cust_name)
from f_shipments, d_customers
where f_shipments.d_cust_id = d_customers.d_cust_id;
```

Now, consider a query such as this:

```
select d.cust_name
from f_shipments f, d_customers d
where f.d_cust_id = d.d_cust_id
and d.cust_name = 'Oracle';
```

The optimizer can choose to use the bitmap join index and thus avoid the expense of having to join the tables.

How It Works

Bitmap join indexes store the results of a join between two tables in an index. Bitmap indexes are beneficial because they avoid joining tables to retrieve results. The syntax for a bitmap join index differs from a regular bitmap index in that it contains FROM and WHERE clauses.

Bitmap join indexes are usually suitable only for data warehouse environments where you have tables that get loaded and then are not updated. When updating tables that have bitmap join indexes declared, this potentially results in several rows being locked. Therefore this type of an index is not suitable for an OLTP database.

2-14. Creating an Index-Organized Table
Problem

You want to create a table that is the intersection of a many-to-many relationship between two tables. The intersection table will consist of two columns. Each column is a foreign key that maps back to a corresponding primary key in a parent table. The combination of columns is the primary key of the intersection table.

Solution

Index-organized tables (IOTs) are efficient objects when the table data is typically accessed through querying on the primary key. Use the ORGANIZATION INDEX clause to create an IOT:

```
create table cust_assoc
(cust_id number
,user_group_id number
,create_dtt timestamp(5)
,update_dtt timestamp(5)
,constraint cust_assoc_pk primary key(cust_id, user_group_id)
)
organization index
including create_dtt
pctthreshold 30
tablespace nsestar_index
overflow
tablespace dim_index;
```

Notice that DBA/ALL/USER_TABLES includes an entry for the table name used when creating an IOT. The following two queries show how Oracle records the information regarding the IOT in the data dictionary:

```
select table_name, iot_name
from user_tables
where iot_name = 'CUST_ASSOC';
```

Here is some sample output:

```
TABLE_NAME                   IOT_NAME
---------------------------  ------------------------------
SYS_IOT_OVER_184185          CUST_ASSOC
```

Listed next is another slightly different query with its output:

```
select table_name, iot_name
from user_tables
where table_name = 'CUST_ASSOC';
```

Here is some sample output:

```
TABLE_NAME                   IOT_NAME
---------------------------  ------------------------------
CUST_ASSOC
```

Additionally, DBA/ALL/USER_INDEXES contains a record with the name of the primary key constraint specified. The INDEX_TYPE column contains a value of IOT - TOP for IOTs:

```
select index_name, index_type
from user_indexes
where table_name = 'CUST_ASSOC';
```

Here is some sample output:

```
INDEX_NAME                   INDEX_TYPE
---------------------------  ---------------------------
CUST_ASSOC_PK                IOT - TOP
```

How It Works

An IOT stores the entire contents of the table's row in a B-tree index structure. IOTs provide fast access for queries that have exact matches and/or range searches on the primary key.

All columns specified up to and including the column specified in the INCLUDING clause are stored in the same block as the CUST_ASSOC_PK primary key column. In other words, the INCLUDING clause specifies the last column to keep in the table segment. Columns listed after the column specified in the INCLUDING clause are stored in the overflow data segment. In the previous example, the UPDATE_DTT column is stored in the overflow segment.

PCTTHRESHOLD specifies the percentage of space reserved in the index block for the IOT row. This value can be from 1 to 50, and defaults to 50 if no value is specified. There must be enough space in the index block to store the primary key. The OVERFLOW clause details which tablespace should be used to store overflow data segments.

2-15. Monitoring Index Usage

Problem

You maintain a large database that contains thousands of indexes. As part of your proactive maintenance, you want to determine if any indexes are not used in SELECT statements. You realize that unused indexes have a detrimental impact on performance, because every time a row is inserted, updated, and deleted, the corresponding index has to be maintained. This consumes CPU resources and disk space.

Solution

Use the ALTER INDEX...MONITORING USAGE statement to enable basic index monitoring. The following example enables index monitoring on an index named EMP_IDX1:

```
SQL> alter index emp_idx1 monitoring usage;
```

The first time the index is used in a SELECT statement, Oracle records this; you can view whether an index has been accessed via the DBA_OBJECT_USAGE view. To report which indexes are being monitored and have ever been used, run this query:

```
SQL> select index_name, table_name, monitoring, used from dba_object_usage;
```

■ **Tip**   Prior to Oracle Database 12c, Oracle recorded monitored index usage in the V$OBJECT_USAGE view.

If the index has ever been used in a SELECT statement, then the USED column will contain the YES value. Here is some sample output from the prior query:

```
INDEX_NAME           TABLE_NAME           MON USE
-------------------- -------------------- --- ---
EMP_IDX1             EMP                  YES NO
```

Most likely, you won't monitor only one index. Rather, you'll want to monitor all indexes for a user. In this situation, use SQL to generate SQL to create a script you can run to turn on monitoring for all indexes. Here's such a script:

```
set pagesize 0 head off linesize 132
spool enable_mon.sql
select
  'alter index ' || index_name || ' monitoring usage;'
from user_indexes;
spool off;
```

To disable monitoring on an index, use the NOMONITORING USAGE clause—for example:

```
SQL> alter index emp_idx1 nomonitoring usage;
```

How It Works

Enabling the monitoring of indexes will allow you to determine which indexes are being used by Oracle for retrieving the result set of a query. If an index is never used then you should consider dropping the index. However, keep in mind that there are other scenarios in which Oracle will use an index, but its usage is not recorded in DBA_OBJECT_USAGE. Before dropping an index (that isn't used by a SELECT statement), consider these other uses:

- The optimizer may use an index for cardinality calculations (and therefore potentially impact the optimizer's choice of execution plan).

- When an index is placed on a column that has a foreign key constraint defined on it, Oracle can use an index to prevent certain locking situations.

- For unique indexes, Oracle will still use the index for enforcing uniqueness, regardless whether the index is used in a SELECT statement.

- Be certain that the index isn't crucial to end of month/quarter/year query that didn't run during the monitoring period.

If you've considered the prior reasons and an index that has been monitored for a reasonable amount of time is displayed as not used, then you can consider dropping the index. There's no hard and fast rule for how long is the right amount of time to monitor an index. Minimally you would want to monitor an index for a couple of weeks so as to give application code sufficient time such that an adequate sample of queries has been executed against the database.

Tip You can view index monitoring information for the currently connected session via the USER_OBJECT_USAGE view.

2-16. Maximizing Index Creation Speed
Problem

You're creating an index based on a table that contains millions of rows. You want to create the index as fast as possible.

Solution

This solution describes two techniques for increasing the speed of index creation:

- Turning off redo generation
- Increasing the degree of parallelism

You can use the prior two features independently of each other, or they can be used in conjunction.

Turning Off Redo Generation

You can optionally create an index with the NOLOGGING clause. Doing so has these implications:

- The redo isn't generated that would be required to recover the index in the event of a media failure.

- Subsequent direct-path operations also won't generate the redo required to recover the index information in the event of a media failure.

Here's an example of creating an index with the NOLOGGING clause:

```
create index inv_idx1 on inv(inv_id, inv_id2)
nologging
tablespace inv_mgmt_index;
```

You can run this query to determine whether an index has been created with NOLOGGING:

```
SQL> select index_name, logging from user_indexes;
```

Increasing the Degree of Parallelism

In large database environments where you're attempting to create an index on a table that is populated with many rows, you may be able to reduce the time it takes to create the index by using the PARALLEL clause. For example, this sets the degree of parallelism to 2 when creating the index:

```
create index inv_idx1 on inv(inv_id)
parallel 2
tablespace inv_mgmt_data;
```

■ **Note** If you don't specify a degree of parallelism, Oracle selects a degree based on the number of CPUs on the box times the value of PARALLEL_THREADS_PER_CPU.

You can verify the degree of parallelism on an index via this query:

```
SQL> select index_name, degree from user_indexes;
```

How It Works

The main advantage of NOLOGGING is that when you create the index, a minimal amount of redo information is generated, which can have significant performance implications when creating a large index. The disadvantage is that if you experience a media failure soon after the index is created (or have records inserted via a direct-path operation), and subsequently have a failure that causes you to restore from a backup (taken prior to the index creation), then you may see this error when the index is accessed:

```
ORA-01578: ORACLE data block corrupted (file # 4, block # 11407)
ORA-01110: data file 4: '/ora01/dbfile/O12C/inv_mgmt_index01.dbf'
ORA-26040: Data block was loaded using the NOLOGGING option
```

This error indicates that the index is logically corrupt. In this scenario, you must re-create or rebuild the index before it's usable. In most scenarios, it's acceptable to use the NOLOGGING clause when creating an index, because the index can be re-created or rebuilt without affecting the table on which the index is based.

In addition to NOLOGGING, you can use the PARALLEL clause to increase the speed of an index creation. For large indexes, this can significantly decrease the time required to create an index.

Keep in mind that you can use NOLOGGING in combination with PARALLEL. This next example rebuilds an index in parallel while generating a minimal amount of redo:

```
SQL> alter index inv_idx1 rebuild parallel nologging;
```

2-17. Reclaiming Unused Index Space
Problem

You have an index consuming space in a segment, but without actually using that space. For example, you're running the following query to display the Segment Advisor's advice (see Recipe 1-9 for further details on running the Segment Advisor):

```
SELECT
 'Task Name      : ' || f.task_name   || CHR(10) ||
 'Start Run Time : ' || TO_CHAR(execution_start, 'dd-mon-yy hh24:mi') || chr (10) ||
 'Segment Name   : ' || o.attr2       || CHR(10) ||
 'Segment Type   : ' || o.type        || CHR(10) ||
 'Partition Name : ' || o.attr3       || CHR(10) ||
 'Message        : ' || f.message     || CHR(10) ||
 'More Info      : ' || f.more_info   || CHR(10) ||
 '-------------------------------------------------' Advice
FROM dba_advisor_findings    f
    ,dba_advisor_objects     o
    ,dba_advisor_executions e
WHERE o.task_id   = f.task_id
AND   o.object_id = f.object_id
AND   f.task_id   = e.task_id
AND   e. execution_start > sysdate - 1
AND   e.advisor_name = 'Segment Advisor'
ORDER BY f.task_name;
```

The following output is displayed:

```
ADVICE
--------------------------------------------------------------------------------
Task Name      : F_REGS Advice
Start Run Time : 19-feb-11 09:32
Segment Name   : F_REGS_IDX1
Segment Type   : INDEX
Partition Name :
Message        : Perform shrink, estimated savings is 84392870 bytes.
More Info      : Allocated Space:166723584: Used Space:82330714: Reclaimable...
pace :84392870:
-------------------------------------------------------
```

You want to shrink the index to free up the unused space.

Solution

There are a couple of effective methods for freeing up unused space associated with an index:

- Rebuilding the index
- Shrinking the index

Before you perform either of these operations, first check USER_SEGMENTS to verify that the amount of space used corresponds with the Segment Advisor's advice. In this example, the segment name is F_REGS_IDX1:

```
SQL> select bytes from user_segments where segment_name = 'F_REGS_IDX1';

BYTES
----------
 166723584
```

This example uses the ALTER INDEX...REBUILD statement to re-organize and compact the space used by an index:

```
SQL> alter index f_regs_idx1 rebuild;
```

Alternatively, use the ALTER INDEX...SHRINK SPACE statement to free up unused space in an index—for example:

```
SQL> alter index f_regs_idx1 shrink space;

Index altered.
```

Now query USER_SEGMENTS again to verify that the space has been de-allocated. Here is the output for this example:

```
BYTES
----------
 524288
```

The space consumed by the index has considerably decreased.

How It Works

Usually rebuilding an index is the fastest and most effective way to reclaim unused space consumed by an index. Therefore this is the approach we recommend for reclaiming unused index space. Freeing up space is desirable because it ensures that you use only the amount of space required by an object. It also has the performance benefit that Oracle has fewer blocks to manage and sort through when performing read operations.

Besides freeing up space, you may want to consider rebuilding an index for these additional reasons:

- The index has become corrupt.
- You want to modify storage characteristics (such as changing the tablespace).
- An index that was previously marked as unusable now needs to be rebuilt to make it usable again.

Keep in mind that Oracle attempts to acquire a lock on the table and rebuild the index online. If there are any active transactions that haven't committed, then Oracle won't be able to obtain a lock, and the following error will be thrown:

```
ORA-00054: resource busy and acquire with NOWAIT specified or timeout expired
```

In this scenario, you can either wait until the there is little activity in the database or try setting the DDL_LOCK_TIMEOUT parameter:

```
SQL> alter session set ddl_lock_timeout=15;
```

The DDL_LOCK_TIMEOUT initialization parameter is available in Oracle Database 11g or higher. It instructs Oracle to repeatedly attempt to obtain a lock for the specified amount of time.

If no tablespace is specified, Oracle rebuilds the index in the tablespace in which the index currently exists. Specify a tablespace if you want the index rebuilt in a different tablespace:

```
SQL> alter index inv_idx1 rebuild tablespace inv_index;
```

■ **Tip** If you're working with a large index, you may want to consider using features such as NOLOGGING and/or PARALLEL (see Recipe 2-16 for details).

If you use the ALTER INDEX...SHRINK SPACE operation to free up unused index space, keep in mind that this feature requires that the target object must be created within a tablespace with automatic segment space management enabled. If you attempt to shrink a table or index that has been created in a tablespace using manual segment space management, you'll receive this error:

```
ORA-10635: Invalid segment or tablespace type
```

The ALTER INDEX...SHRINK SPACE statement has a few nuances to be aware of. For example, you can instruct Oracle to attempt only to merge the contents of index blocks (and not free up space) via the COMPACT clause:

```
SQL> alter index f_regs_idx1 shrink space compact;
```

The prior operation is equivalent to the ALTER INDEX...COALESCE statement. Here's an example of using COALESCE:

```
SQL> alter index f_regs_idx1 coalesce;
```

If you want to maximize the space compacted, either rebuild the index or use the SHRINK SPACE clause as shown in the "Solution" section of this recipe. It's somewhat counterintuitive that the COMPACT space doesn't actually initiate a greater degree of realized free space. The COMPACT clause instructs Oracle to only merge index blocks where possible and not to maximize the amount of space being freed up.

CHAPTER 3

■ ■ ■

Optimizing Instance Memory

Optimizing the memory you allocate to an Oracle database is one of the most critical tasks you need to perform as a DBA. Over the years, Oracle DBAs were used to spending vast amounts of their time analyzing memory usage by the database and trying to come up with the best possible allocation of memory. Since the Oracle Database 11g release, you can let Oracle manage memory allocation to your database by taking advantage of Oracle's automatic memory management feature, so you can leave the database to optimize memory usage while you focus on more important matters.

This chapter starts by explaining how to set up automatic memory management for a database. The chapter also shows you how to set minimum values for certain components of memory even under automatic memory management. It includes recipes that explain how to create multiple buffer pools, how to monitor Oracle's usage of memory, and how to use the Oracle Enterprise Manager's Database Control (or Grid Control) tool to get advice from Oracle regarding the optimal sizing of memory allocation. You'll also learn how to optimize the use of the program global area (PGA), a key Oracle memory component, especially in data warehouse environments.

The result caching feature Oracle has introduced in Oracle Database 11g enables it to cache SQL and PL/SQL results in the shared pool for easy retrieval. We discuss that server result cache in this chapter. In addition, you'll also find a recipe that explains how to take advantage of Oracle's client-side result caching feature. Finally, we'll show how to use the exciting new Oracle feature called the Oracle Database Smart Flash Cache.

3-1. Automating Memory Management
Problem

You want to automate memory management in your Oracle database. You have both OLTP and batch jobs running in this database. You want to take advantage of the automatic memory management feature built into Oracle Database 12c.

Solution

Here are the steps to implement automatic memory management in your database if you've already set either the SGA_TARGET or PGA_AGGREGATE_TARGET parameter (or both). We assume you are going to allocate 2,000 MB to the MEMORY_MAX_TARGET parameter and 1,000 MB to the MEMORY_TARGET parameter.

1. Connect to the database with the SYSDBA privilege.

2. Assuming you're using the SPFILE, first set a value for the MEMORY_MAX_TARGET parameter:

    ```
    SQL> alter system set memory_max_target=2000M scope=spfile;
    System altered.
    ```

You must specify the SCOPE parameter in the alter system command, because MEMORY_MAX_TARGET isn't a dynamic parameter, which means you can't change it on the fly while the instance is running.

3. Note that if you've started the instance with a traditional init.ora parameter file instead of the SPFILE, you must add the following to your init.ora file:

```
memory_max_target = 2000M
memory_target = 1000M
```

4. Bounce the database.

5. Turn off the SGA_TARGET and PGA_AGGREGATE_TARGET parameters by issuing the following ALTER SYSTEM commands:

```
SQL> alter system set sga_target = 0;
SQL> alter system set pga_aggregate_target = 0;
```

6. Turn on automatic memory management by setting the MEMORY_TARGET parameter:

```
SQL> alter system set memory_target = 1000M;
```

From this point on, the database runs under the automatic memory management mode, with it shrinking and growing the individual allocations to the various components of Oracle memory according to the requirements of the ongoing workload. You can change the value of the MEMORY_TARGET parameter dynamically any time, as long as you don't exceed the value you set for the MEMORY_MAX_TARGET parameter.

■ **Tip**   The term *target* in parameters such as memory_target and pga_memory_target means just that—Oracle will try to stay under the target level, but there's no guarantee it'll never go beyond that. It may exceed the target allocation on occasion, if necessary.

You don't have to set the SGA_TARGET and PGA_AGGREGATE_TARGET parameters to 0 in order to use automatic memory management. In Recipe 3-3, we show how to set minimum values for these parameters even when you choose to implement automatic memory management. Recipe 3-3 assumes you're implementing automatic memory management but that for some reason you need to specify your own minimum values for components such as the SGA and the PGA.

How It Works

In earlier releases of the Oracle Database, DBAs set values for the various SGA components or specified values for the SGA and the PGA. Since the Oracle Database 11g release, Oracle enables you to completely automate the entire instance memory allocation by just setting a single initialization parameter, MEMORY_TARGET, under what's known as *automatic memory management*. In this recipe, we show you how to set up the automatic memory management feature in your database.

If you're creating a new Oracle database with the help of the Database Configuration Assistant (DBCA), you're given a choice between automatic memory management, shared memory management, and manual memory management. Select the automatic memory management option, and specify the values for two automatic memory-related parameters: MEMORY_TARGET and MEMORY_MAX_TARGET. The first parameter sets the current value of the memory allocation to the database, and the second parameter sets the limit to which you can raise the first parameter if necessary. Do remember that past a given size, there's no point allocating more memory to an Oracle instance.

Oracle's memory structures consist of two distinct kinds of memory areas. The system global area (SGA) contains the data and control information and is shared by all server and background processes. The SGA holds the data blocks retrieved from disk by Oracle. The program global area (PGA) contains data and control information for a server process. Managing Oracle's memory allocation involves careful calibration of the needs of the database. For example, a data warehouse will need more PGA memory in order to perform the sorts that are common in such an environment and also to deal with the typically larger block sizes used in data warehousing systems. Also, during the course of a day, the memory needs of the instance might vary; during business hours, for example, the instance might be processing more online transaction processing (OLTP) work, whereas after business hours, it might be running huge batch jobs that involve data warehouse processing, which are jobs that typically need higher PGA allocations per each process.

In prior versions of the Oracle database, DBAs had to carefully decide the optimal allocation of memory to the individual components of the memory allocated to the database. Technically, you can still manually set the values of the individual components of the SGA, as well as set a value for the PGA, or partially automate the process by setting parameters such as SGA_TARGET and PGA_AGGREGATE_TARGET. Although Oracle still allows you to manually configure the various components of memory, automatic memory management is the recommended approach. Once you specify a certain amount of memory by setting the MEMORY_TARGET and MEMORY_MAX_TARGET parameters, Oracle automatically tunes the actual memory allocation by redistributing memory between the SGA and the PGA.

■ **Tip** When you create a database with the Database Configuration Assistant, automatic memory management is the default.

Since Oracle Database 11g, Oracle has allowed DBAs to automate all the memory allocations for an instance if you choose to implement automatic memory management by setting the MEMORY_TARGET and MEMORY_MAX_TARGET parameters. Under an automatic memory management regime, Oracle automatically tunes the total SGA size, the SGA component sizes, the PGA size, and the individual PGA size. This dynamic memory tuning by the Oracle instance optimizes database performance because memory allocations are changed automatically by Oracle to match changing database workloads. Automatic memory management means that once you set the MEMORY_TARGET parameter, you can simply ignore the following parameters by not setting them at all:

- SGA_TARGET
- PGA_AGGREGATE_TARGET
- DB_CACHE_SIZE
- SHARED_POOL_SIZE
- LARGE_POOL_SIZE
- JAVA_POOL_SIZE

If you're moving from a system where you were using the SGA_TARGET and PGA_AGGREGATE_TARGET parameters, you can follow the procedures shown in the "Solution" section of this recipe to move to the newer automatic memory management mode of managing Oracle's memory allocation. Note that while setting the MEMORY_TARGET parameter is mandatory for implementing automatic memory management, the MEMORY_MAX_TARGET parameter isn't—if you don't set this parameter, Oracle sets its value internally to that of the MEMORY_TARGET parameter. Also, the MEMORY_MAX_TARGET parameter acts as the upper bound for the MEMORY_TARGET parameter. Oracle has different minimum permissible settings for the MEMORY_TARGET parameter, depending on the operating system. If you try to set this parameter below its minimum allowable value, the database will issue an error. Some of the memory components can't shrink quickly, and some components must have a minimum size for the database to function properly. Therefore, Oracle won't let you set too low a value for the MEMORY_TARGET parameter. The following example shows this:

```
SQL> alter system set memory_target=360m scope=both;
alter system set memory_target=360m scope=both
*
ERROR at line 1:
ORA-02097: parameter cannot be modified because specified value is invalid
ORA-00838: Specified value of MEMORY_TARGET is too small, needs to be at least
544M

SQL> alter system set memory_target=544m scope=both;

alter system set memory_target=544m scope=both
*
ERROR at line 1:
ORA-02097: parameter cannot be modified because specified value is invalid
ORA-00838: Specified value of MEMORY_TARGET is too small, needs to be at least
624M

SQL>  alter system set memory_target=624m scope=both;

System altered.

SQL>
```

You'll notice that Oracle issued an error when we tried to set a very low value for the MEMORY_TARGET parameter. Note that Oracle took iterations to decide to let you know the minimum allowable level for the MEMORY_TARGET parameter.

■ **Note**   You can't use automatic memory management on some operating systems when implementing very large memory (VLM). To enable VLM on such operating systems, the memory_target parameter must be set to zero.

How do you go about setting the exact value of the MEMORY_MAX_TARGET parameter? The key is to adopt a trial-and-error approach to pick a value that's high enough to accommodate not only the current workloads but also the future needs of the database. Since the MEMORY_TARGET parameter is dynamic, you can alter it on the fly and, if necessary, reallocate memory among multiple instances running on a server. Always make sure to check with your system administrator so you don't allocate too high an amount of memory for your Oracle instance, which could result in problems such as paging and swapping at the operating system level.

3-2. Managing Multiple Buffer Pools
Problem

You're using automatic memory management but have decided to allocate a minimum value for the buffer pool component. You'd like to configure the buffer pool so it retains frequently accessed segments, which may run the risk of being aged out of the buffer pool.

Solution

You can use multiple buffer pools instead of Oracle's single default buffer pool to ensure that frequently used data and index blocks stay cached in the buffer pool without being recycled out of the buffer pool. The alternate buffer pool (named the *keep buffer pool*) allows you to assign frequently accessed segments to it in order to keep them from aging out because of space pressure from other segments. In this context, a segment refers to a table or an index or to a partition of a table or index.

To implement multiple buffer pools in your database, you need to create two separate buffer pools: the KEEP buffer pool and the RECYCLE buffer pool. Once you do this, you must specify the BUFFER_POOL keyword in the STORAGE clause when you create a data or index segment. For example, if you want a segment to be cached (or pinned) in the buffer pool, you must specify the KEEP buffer pool.

■ **Note**   Neither the KEEP pool nor the RECYCLE pool is part of the default buffer cache. Both of these pools are outside the default buffer cache.

Here's how you create the two types of buffer pools.

In the SPFILE or the init.ora file, specify the two parameters and the sizes you want to assign to each of the pools:

```
db_keep_cache_size=1000m
db_recycle_cache_size=100m
```

Here's how you specify the default buffer pool for a segment:

```
SQL> alter table employees
     storage (buffer_pool=keep);

Table altered.
SQL>
```

How It Works

Configuring a KEEP buffer pool is an ideal solution in situations where your database contains tables that are referenced frequently. You can store such frequently accessed segments in the KEEP buffer cache. By doing this, you not only isolate those segments to a specific part of the buffer pool but also ensure that your physical I/O is minimized. How large the KEEP buffer pool ought to be depends on the total size of the objects you want to assign to the pool. You can get a rough idea by summing up the size of all candidate objects for this pool, or you can check the value of the DBA_TABLES view (BLOCKS column) to figure this out.

While we're on this topic, we'd like to point out the counterpart to the KEEP buffer pool—the RECYCLE buffer pool. Normally, the Oracle database uses a least recently used algorithm to decide which objects it should jettison from the buffer cache when it needs more free space. If your database accesses very large objects once or so every day, you can keep these objects from occupying a big chunk of your buffer cache and instead make those objects age right out of the buffer cache after they've been accessed. You can configure such behavior by allowing candidate objects to use the RECYCLED buffer pool either when you create those objects or even later, by setting the appropriate storage parameters, as shown in the following examples (note that you must first set the DB_RECYCLE_CACHE_SIZE initialization parameter, as shown in the "Solution" section of this recipe).

You can execute the following query to figure out how many blocks for each segment are currently in the buffer cache:

```
SQL> select o.object_name, count(*) number_of_blocks
    from dba_objects o, v$bh v
    where o.data_object_id = v.objd
    and o.owner !='SYS'
    group by o.object_name
    order by count(*);
```

When your database accesses large segments and retrieves data to process a query, it may sometimes age out other segments from the buffer pool prematurely. If you need these prematurely aged-out segments later, it requires additional I/O. What exactly constitutes a large table or index segment is subject to your interpretation. It's probably safe to think of the size of the object you're concerned with by considering its size relative to the total memory you have allocated to the buffer cache. If you have other segments that the database accesses, let's say every other second, the cached blocks of these segments won't age out of the buffer pool since they are constantly in use. However, there may be other cached blocks that will be adversely affected by the few large segments the database has (infrequently) read into its buffer cache. It's in such situations that your database can benefit most by devoting the RECYCLE pool for the large segments. Of course, if you want to absolutely, positively ensure that key segments never age out at all, then you can create the KEEP buffer cache and assign these objects to this pool.

We'd like to add one final piece of advice: although Oracle allows you to create three different types of buffer pools, in most cases a well-tuned single main buffer pool is all you'll need. In most cases, the additional management work involved in tending to three separate buffer pools really doesn't warrant the extra work when compared to the potential benefits.

3-3. Setting Minimum Values for Memory
Problem

You're using automatic memory management but you think that the database sometimes doesn't allocate enough memory for the PGA_AGGREGATE_TARGET component.

Solution

Although automatic memory management is supposed to do what it says—automate memory allocation—there are times when you may want to manage certain memory allocations yourself, say because the database isn't allocating sufficient memory to the PGA memory. The next recipe, Recipe 3-4, shows how you can monitor Oracle's memory resizing operations. You can set a minimum value for any of the main Oracle memory components, including the buffer cache, shared pool, large pool, Java pool, and the PGA memory. For example, even after specifying automatic memory management, you can specify a target for the instance PGA with the following command, without having to restart the database:

```
SQL> alter system set pga_aggregate_target=1000m;
```

Oracle will, from this point forward, never decrease the PGA memory allocation to less than the value you've set; this value implicitly sets a minimum value for the memory parameter. The instance will continue to automatically allocate memory to the various components of the SGA, but first it subtracts the memory you've allocated explicitly to the PGA—in this case, 1,000 MB—from the MEMORY_TARGET parameter's value. What remains is what the database will allocate to the instance's SGA.

How It Works

Ever since Oracle introduced the SGA_TARGET (to automate shared memory management) in Oracle Database 10g and the MEMORY_TARGET parameter (to automate shared memory and PGA memory management) in Oracle Database 11g, some DBAs have complained that these parameters sometimes aren't appropriately sizing some of the components of Oracle memory, such as the buffer cache.

There's some evidence that under automatic memory management, the database could lag behind an event that requires a sudden increase in the allocation either to one of the individual components of the SGA or to the PGA. For example, you may have a spurt of activity in the database that requires a quick adjustment to the shared pool component of memory; the database may get to the optimal shared pool size allocation level only after it notices the events that require the higher memory. As a result, the instance may undergo a temporary performance hit. Several DBAs have, as a result, found that automatic memory management will work fine, as long as you set a minimum value for, say, the buffer cache or the PGA, or both, by specifying explicit values for the SGA_TARGET and PGA_AGGREGATE_TARGET initialization parameters instead of leaving them at their default value of zero. The instance will still use automatic memory management but will now use the specific values you set for any of the memory components as minimum values. Having said this, in our experience, automatic memory management works as advertised most of the time; however, your mileage may vary, depending on any special time-based workload changes in a specific database. At times like this, it's perfectly all right to set minimum values that represent your own understanding of your processing requirements instead of blindly depending on Oracle's automatic memory algorithms.

3-4. Monitoring Memory Resizing Operations
Problem

You've implemented automatic memory management in your database and want to monitor how the database is currently allocating the various dynamically tuned memory components.

Solution

When you're implementing automatic memory management, you can view the current allocations of memory in an instance by querying the V$MEMORY_DYNAMIC_COMPONENTS view. Querying this view provides vital information that helps you tune the size of the MEMORY_TARGET parameter. Here's how you execute a query against this view:

```
SQL> select * from v$memory_target_advice order by memory_size;

MEMORY_SIZE MEMORY_SIZE_FACTOR ESTD_DB_TIME ESTD_DB_TIME_FACTOR    VERSION
----------- ------------------ ------------ ------------------- ----------
        468                .75        43598              1.0061          0
        624                  1        43334                   1          0
        780               1.25        43334                   1          0
        936                1.5        43330               .9999          0
       1092               1.75        43330               .9999          0
       1248                  2        43330               .9999          0

6 rows selected.

SQL>
```

Your current memory allocation is shown by the row with the MEMORY_SIZE_FACTOR value of 1 (624 MB in our case). The MEMORY_SIZE_FACTOR column shows alternate sizes of the MEMORY_TARGET parameter as a multiple of the current MEMORY_TARGET parameter value. The ESTD_DB_TIME column shows the time Oracle estimates it will need to complete the current workload with a specific MEMORY_TARGET value. Thus, the query results show you how much faster the database can process its work by varying the value of the MEMORY_TARGET parameter.

How It Works

Use the V$MEMORY_TARGET_ADVICE view to get a quick idea about how optimal your MEMORY_TARGET allocation is. You need to run a query based on this view after a representative workload has been processed by the database to get useful results. If the view reports that there are no gains to be had by increasing the MEMORY_TARGET setting, you don't have to throw away precious system memory by allocating more memory to the database instance. Oftentimes, the query may report that potential performance, as indicated by the ESTD_DB_TIME column of the V$MEMORY_TARGET_ADVICE view, doesn't decrease at a MEMORY_SIZE_FACTOR value that's less than 1. You can safely reduce the setting of the MEMORY_TARGET parameter in such cases.

You can also use the V$MEMORY_RESIZE_OPS view to view how the instance resized various memory components over a past interval of 800 completed memory resizing operations. You'll see that the database automatically increases or shrinks the values of the SGA_TARGET and PGA_AGGREGATE_TARGET parameters based on the workload it encounters. The following query shows how to use the V$MEMORY_RESIZE_OPS view to understand Oracle's dynamic allocation of instance memory:

```
SQL> select component,oper_type, parameter, final_size,target_size
     from v$memory_resize_ops

COMPONENT             OPER_TYPE        PARAMETER         FINAL_SIZE  TARGET_SIZE
--------------------  ---------------  ---------         ----------  -----------
DEFAULT 2K buffer cache STATIC         db_2k_cache_size           0            0
DEFAULT buffer cache  STATIC           db_cache_size      150994944    150994944
DEFAULT buffer cache  INITIALIZING     db_cache_size      150994944    150994944
DEFAULT buffer cache  SHRINK IMMEDIATE db_cache_size      146800640    146800640
shared pool           GROW IMMEDIATE   shared_pool_size    96468992     96468992
DEFAULT buffer cache  GROW DEFERRED    db_cache_size      167772160    167772160
large pool            SHRINK DEFERRED  large_pool_size      8388608      8388608
...

27 rows selected.

SQL>
```

The OPER_TYPE column can take two values, GROW or SHRINK, depending on whether the database grows or shrinks individual memory components as the database workload fluctuates over time. It's this ability to respond to these changes by automatically provisioning the necessary memory to the various memory components that makes this "automatic" memory management. DBAs will do well by monitoring this view over time to ensure that automatic memory management works well for their databases.

3-5. Optimizing Memory Usage

Problem

You've set up automatic memory management in your databases and want to optimize memory usage with the help of Oracle's memory advisors.

Solution

Regardless of whether you set up automatic memory management (AMM), automatic shared memory management (ASMM), or even a manual memory management scheme, you can use Oracle's Memory Advisors to guide your memory-tuning efforts. In this example, we show how to use Oracle EM Express (Oracle Enterprise Manager Database Control 12c) to easily tune memory usage. Here are the steps:

1. Go to the Database Home page in EM Express. Click Memory after clicking the Configuration tab at the top of the page.

2. On the Memory Management page that appears, as shown in Figure 3-1, the graph titled Memory Advisor shows the improvement in database time plotted against the total memory that you've currently set for the MEMORY_TARGET parameter, as well as for various hypothetical settings for this parameter. The higher the value of improvement in database time, the better off the estimated performance will be. The graph in essence shows how performance (improvement in database time) will vary as you change the MEMORY_TARGET parameter value.

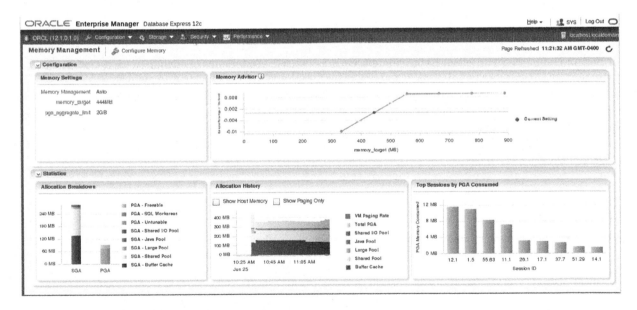

Figure 3-1. *The Memory Advisor graph in EM Express*

How It Works

When you implement automatic memory management, Oracle automatically adjusts memory between the various components of total memory—the SGA and the PGA—during the course of the instance, depending on the workload characteristics of the instance. Instead of running queries using various views to figure out whether your current memory allocation is optimal, you can follow a couple of easy steps to figure things out quickly. You can review the Automatic Database Diagnostic Monitor (ADDM) reports (provided you have the necessary licensing in place to use ADDM) to see whether they contain any comments or recommendations about inadequate memory. ADDM recommends that you add more memory to the MEMORY_TARGET parameter if it considers that the current memory allocation is insufficient for optimal performance.

If the ADDM reports recommend that you increase the size of the MEMORY_TARGET parameter, the next question is by how much you should increase the memory allocation. Oracle's built-in Memory Advisors come in handy for just this purpose. Even in the absence of a recommendation by the ADDM, you can play with the Memory Advisors to get an idea of how an increase or decrease in the MEMORY_TARGET parameter will impact performance.

You can also choose to optimize your PGA memory allocation from the same Memory Advisors page by clicking PGA at the top of the page. In the case of the PGA, in the PGA Target Advice page, the graphs plots the PGA cache hit percentage against the PGA target size. Ideally, you'd want the PGA cache ratio somewhere upward of around 75 percent. The PGA Target Advice page will help you determine approximately what value you should assign to the PGA_AGGREGATE_TARGET parameter to achieve your performance goals.

3-6. Tuning PGA Memory Allocation
Problem

You've decided to set a specific minimum memory size for the PGA_AGGREGATE_TARGET parameter, although you're using Oracle's automatic memory management to allocate memory. You want to know the best way to figure out the optimal PGA memory allocation.

Solution

There are no hard-and-fast rules for allocating the size of the PGA_AGGREGATE_TARGET parameter. Having said that, if you're operating a data warehouse, you'll more likely need much larger amounts of memory set apart for the PGA component of Oracle's memory allocation. You can follow these basic steps to allocate PGA memory levels:

1. Use a starting allocation more or less by guessing how much memory you might need for the PGA.

2. Let the database run for an entire cycle or two of representative workload. You can then access various Oracle views to figure out whether your first stab at the PGA estimation was on target.

How It Works

Although automatic memory management is designed to optimally allocate memory between the two major components of Oracle memory—the SGA and the PGA—it's certainly not uncommon for many DBAs to decide to set their own values for both the SGA and the PGA, either as part of the alternative mode of memory management, automatic shared memory management, wherein you set the SGA_TARGET and the PGA_AGGREGATE_TARGET parameters explicitly to manage memory, or under the newer automatic memory management system. Unlike the SGA_TARGET parameter, where cache hit ratios could mislead you as to the efficacy of the instance, you'll find that an analysis of the hit ratios for the PGA_AGGREGATE_TARGET parameter are not only valid but also highly useful in configuring the appropriate sizes for this parameter.

The Oracle database uses PGA memory primarily to perform operations such as sorting and hashing. The memory you allocate to the PGA component is allocated to various SQL work areas that are performing these sorting and hashing operations (along with other users of the PGA memory such as PL/SQL and Java programs). Ideally, you'd want all work areas to have an optimal PGA memory allocation. When memory allocation is ideal, a work area performs the entire operation in memory. For example, if a SQL operation involves sorting operations, under optimal PGA allocation, most, if not all, of the sorting is done within the PGA memory allocated to that process. Often, huge memory consumptions issues are because of poor execution plans caused by poorly written queries (apply a function to the wrong column, and you may get a hash join of death where the nested loop would have been faster). If the PGA memory allocation isn't optimal, the work areas make one or more passes over the data—this means they have to perform the operations on disk, involving time-consuming I/O. The more passes the database is forced to make, the more I/O and the longer it takes to process the work.

Oracle computes the PGA cache hit percentage with the following formula:

```
Bytes Processed * 100 /(Bytes processed + Extra Bytes Processed)
```

Bytes Processed is the total number of bytes processed by all the PGA memory using SQL operations since the instance started. You should seek to get this ratio as close to 100 as possible; if your PGA cache hit percentage is something like 33.37 percent, it's definitely time to increase PGA memory allocation by raising the value you've set for the PGA_AGGREGATE_TARGET parameter. Fortunately, the PGA_AGGREGATE_TARGET parameter is dynamic, so you can adjust this on the fly without a database restart to address a sudden slowdown in database performance because of heavy sorting and hashing activity.

You can issue the following simple query to find out the PGA cache hit percentage as well as a number of PGA performance-related values:

```
SQL>select  * from v$pgastat;

NAME                                  VALUE            UNIT
------------------------------------  ----------       -----
aggregate PGA target parameter        2.5770E+10       bytes
aggregate PGA auto target             9533721600       bytes
global memory bound                   1073741824       bytes
total PGA inuse                       1.5259E+10       bytes
total PGA allocated                   2.1987E+10       bytes
maximum PGA allocated                 2.9013E+10       bytes
total freeable PGA memory             5233442816       bytes
process count                               6299
max processes count                         7727
PGA memory freed back to OS           2.1836E+13       bytes
total PGA used for auto workareas       79910912       bytes
maximum PGA used for auto workareas   5302619136       bytes
total PGA used for manual workareas            0       bytes
maximum PGA used for manual workareas    1085440       bytes
over allocation count                          0
bytes processed                       2.5606E+13       bytes
extra bytes read/written              1.4300E+12       bytes
cache hit percentage                       94.71       percent
recompute count (total)                   437432

19 rows selected.

SQL>
```

Since we're using our test database here, the cache hit percentage is a full 100 percent, but don't expect that in a real-life database, especially if it is processing a lot of data warehouse–type operations!

You can also use the V$SQL_WORKAREA_HISTOGRAM view to find out how much of its work the database is performing in an optimal fashion. If a work area performs its work optimally, that is, entirely within PGA memory, it's counted as part of the OPTIMAL_COUNT column. If it makes one or more passes, it will go under the ONEPASS_COUNT or MULTIPASS_COUNT column. Here's a query that shows how to do this:

```
SQL> select optimal_count, round(optimal_count*100/total, 2) optimal_perc,
  2  onepass_count, round(onepass_count*100/total, 2) onepass_perc,
  3  multipass_count, round(multipass_count*100/total, 2) multipass_perc
  4  from
  5  (select decode(sum(total_executions), 0, 1, sum(total_executions)) total,
  6  sum(OPTIMAL_EXECUTIONS) optimal_count,
  7  sum(ONEPASS_EXECUTIONS) onepass_count,
  8  sum(MULTIPASSES_EXECUTIONS) multipass_count
  9  from  v$sql_workarea_histogram
10* )
SQL> /
OPTIMAL_COUNT OPTIMAL_PERC  ONEPA_COUNT  ONEPA_PERC MULTIPA_COUNT MULTIPA_PERC
------------- ------------  -----------  ---------- ------------- ------------
65010727             99.99        9677          .01             0            0
```

One pass is slower than none at all, but a multipass operation is usually a sign of trouble in your database, especially if it involves large work areas. We must add here that in some cases, especially when dealing with very large data sets, you may not be able to avoid these multipass operations. In most cases, you'll most likely find that your database has slowed to a crawl and is unable to scale efficiently when the database is forced to make even a moderate amount of multipass executions that involve large work areas, such as those that are sized 256 MB to 2 GB. To make sure you don't have any huge work areas running in the multipass mode, issue the following query:

```
SQL> select low_optimal_size/1024 low,
     (high_optimal_size+1)/1024 high,
     optimal_executions, onepass_executions, multipasses_executions
     from v$sql_workarea_histogram
     where total_executions !=0;
   LOW    HIGH OPTIMAL_EXECUTIONS ONEPASS_EXECUTIONS MULTIPASSES_EXECUTIONS
------- ------ ------------------ ------------------ ----------------------
      2      4           37960123                  0                      0
      4      8                  0                 37                      0
     64    128             402758                  0                      0
    128    256             744496                  0                      0
    256    512            4968100                  0                      0
    512   1024           18732748                  0                      0
   1024   2048            2082904                  0                      0
   2048   4096              60834               1245                      0
   4096   8192              31676               1519                      0
   8192  16384              12514                315                      0
  16384  32768              12585               1495                      0
  32768  65536               9559               1142                      0
  65536 131072               9883               1696                      0
 131072 262144                885               1216                      0
 262144 524288               2395                464                      0
```

524288 1048576	6	314	0
1048576 2097152	6	136	0
2097152 4194304	0	92	0
4194304 8388608	12	8	0

19 rows selected.

SQL>

You can also execute simple queries involving views such as V$SYSSTAT and V$SESSTAT as shown here, to find out exactly how many work areas the database has executed with an optimal memory size (in the PGA), one-pass memory size, and multipass memory sizes.

```
SQL>select name profile, cnt, decode(total, 0, 0, round(cnt*100/total)) percentage
    from (SELECT name, value cnt, (sum(value) over ()) total
    from V$SYSSTAT
    where name like 'workarea exec%');
```

Remember that this query shows the total number of work areas executed under each of the three different execution modes (optimal, one-pass, and multipass) since the database was started. To get the same information for a specific period of time, you can use queries involving automatic session history (ASH) or even good old Statspack.

You can also view the contents of the Automatic Workload Repository (AWR) for information regarding how the database used its PGA memory for any interval you choose. Note that here, as well as anywhere else in this book, when we mention ASH, AWR, and ADDM, we're assuming that your organization has licensed the Oracle DIAGNOSTIC and TUNING packs. If you regularly create these reports and save them, you can have a historical record of how well the PGA allocation has been over a period of time. You can also view the ADDM report for a specific time period to evaluate what proportion of work the database is executing in each of the three modes of execution we discussed earlier. In a data warehouse environment, where the database processes huge sorts and hashes, the optimal allocation of the PGA memory is one of the most critical tasks a DBA can perform.

3-7. Configuring the Server Query Cache
Problem

You want to set up the server query cache that's part of Oracle's memory allocation.

■ **Note**   Recipes 3-7 through 3-11 show how to use the result cache, which is available only in the Oracle Enterprise Edition.

Solution

You can control the behavior of the server query cache by setting three initialization parameters: RESULT_CACHE_MAX_SIZE, RESULT_CACHE_MAX_RESULT, and RESULT_CACHE_REMOTE_EXPIRATION. For example, you can use the following set of values for the three server result cache–related initialization parameters:

```
RESULT_CACHE_MAX_SIZE=500M              /* Megabytes
RESULT_CACHE_MAX_RESULT=20              /* Percentage
RESULT_CACHE_REMOTE_EXPIRATION=3600     /* Minutes
```

You can disable the server result cache by setting the RESULT_CACHE_MAX_SIZE parameter to 0 (any nonzero value for this parameter enables the cache).

If you set the RESULT_CACHE_MODE initialization parameter to FORCE, the database caches all query results unless you specify the /*+ NO_RESULT_CACHE */ hint to exclude a query's results from the cache. The default (and the recommended) value of this parameter is MANUAL, meaning that the database caches query results only if you use the appropriate query hint or table annotation (explained later). You can set this parameter at the system level or at the session level, as shown here:

```
SQL> alter session set result_cache_mode=force;
```

You can remove cached results from the server result cache by using the FLUSH procedure from the DBMS_RESULT_CACHE package, as shown here:

```
SQL> execute dbms_result_cache.flush
```

How It Works

The server result cache offers a great way to store results of frequently executed SQL queries and PL/SQL functions when data doesn't change between calls to the database. This feature is easy to configure with the help of the three initialization parameters we described in the "Solution" section. However, remember that Oracle doesn't guarantee that a specific query or PL/SQL function result will be cached no matter what.

In some ways, you can compare the Oracle result cache feature to other Oracle result-storing mechanisms such as a shared PL/SQL collection, as well as a materialized view. Note, however, that whereas Oracle stores a PL/SQL collection in private PGA areas, it stores the result cache in the shared pool as one of the shared pool components. As you know, the shared pool is part of the SGA. Materialized views are stored on disk, whereas a result cache is in the much faster random access memory. Thus, you can expect far superior performance when you utilize the result cache for storing result sets, as opposed to storing precomputed results in a materialized view. Best of all, the result cache offers the Oracle DBA a completely hands-off mode of storing frequently accessed result sets—you don't need to create any objects, as in the case of materialized views, or index or refresh them. Oracle takes care of everything for you.

The server query cache is part of the shared pool component of the SGA. You can use this cache to store both SQL query results as well as PL/SQL function results. Oracle can cache SQL results in the SQL result cache and PL/SQL function results in the PL/SQL function result cache. You usually use the server query cache to make the database cache queries that are frequently executed but need to access a large number of rows per execution. You configure the server query cache by setting the following initialization parameters in your database:

- RESULT_CACHE_MAX_SIZE: This sets the memory allocated to the server result cache.

- RESULT_CACHE_MAX_RESULT: This is the maximum amount of memory a single result in the cache can use, in percentage terms. The default is 5 percent of the server result cache.

- RESULT_CACHE_REMOTE_EXPIRATION: By default, any result that involves remote objects is not cached. Thus, the default setting of the RESULT_CACHE_REMOTE_EXPIRATION parameter is 0. You can, however, enable the caching of results involving remote objects by setting an explicit value for the RESULT_CACHE_REMOTE_EXPIRATION parameter.

Setting the three initialization parameters for the server result cache merely enables the cache. To actually use the cache for your SQL query results or for PL/SQL function results, you have to either enable the cache database-wide or, for specific queries, enable it as the following recipes explain.

Once the database stores a result in the server result cache, it retains it there either until you remove it manually with the DBMS_RESULT_CACHE.FLUSH procedure or until the cache reaches its maximum size set by the RESULT_CACHE_MAX_SIZE parameter. The database will remove the oldest results from the cache when it needs to make room for newer results after it exhausts the capacity of the server result cache.

3-8. Managing the Server Result Cache

Problem

You've enabled the server result cache, but you aren't sure if queries are taking advantage of it. You also want to find out how efficiently the server result cache is functioning.

Solution

You can check the status of the server result cache by using the DBMS_RESULT_CACHE package. For example, use the following query to check whether the cache is enabled:

```
SQL> select dbms_result_cache.status() from dual;

DBMS_RESULT_CACHE.STATUS()
--------------------------
ENABLED

SQL>
```

You can view a query's explain plan to check whether a query is indeed using the SQL query cache, after you enable that query for caching, as shown in the following example. The explain plan for the query shows that the query is indeed making use of the SQL query cache component of the result cache.

```
SQL> select  /*+ RESULT_CACHE */ department_id, AVG(salary)
     from hr.employees
     group by department_id;
.
.
.
---------------------------------------------------------------
| Id | Operation              | Name                       |Rows
---------------------------------------------------------------
| 0  | SELECT STATEMENT       |                            | 11
| 1  |   RESULT CACHE         | 8fpzao4gtwsfr6n595au15yj4y |
| 2  |    HASH GROUP BY       |                            | 11
| 3  |     TABLE ACCESS FULL| EMPLOYEES                    | 107
---------------------------------------------------------------
```

You can use the MEMORY_REPORT procedure of the DBMS_RESULT_CACHE package to view how Oracle is allocating memory to the result cache, as shown here:

```
SQL> set serveroutput on
SQL> execute dbms_result_cache.memory_report
R e s u l t    C a c h e    M e m o r y    R e p o r t
[Parameters]
Block Size         = 1K bytes
Maximum Cache Size = 1152K bytes (1152 blocks)
Maximum Result Size = 57K bytes (57 blocks)
[Memory]
Total Memory = 169408 bytes [0.119% of the Shared Pool]
```

```
... Fixed Memory = 5432 bytes [0.004% of the Shared Pool]
... Dynamic Memory = 163976 bytes [0.115% of the Shared Pool]
....... Overhead = 131208 bytes
....... Cache Memory = 32K bytes (32 blocks)
.......... Unused Memory = 29 blocks
.......... Used Memory = 3 blocks
.............. Dependencies = 1 blocks (1 count)
.............. Results = 2 blocks
................. SQL     = 2 blocks (2 count)
```

PL/SQL procedure successfully completed.

SQL>

You can monitor the server result cache statistics by executing the following query:

SQL> select name, value from V$RESULT_CACHE_STATISTICS;

NAME	VALUE
Block Size (Bytes)	1024
Block Count Maximum	1152
Block Count Current	32
Result Size Maximum (Blocks)	57
Create Count Success	2
Create Count Failure	0
Find Count	0
Invalidation Count	0
Delete Count Invalid	0
Delete Count Valid	0
Hash Chain Length	1
Find Copy Count	0
Latch (Share)	0

13 rows selected.

SQL>

SQL>

The Create Count Success column shows the number of queries that the database has cached in the server result cache, and the Invalidation Count column shows the number of times the database has invalidated a cached result. When DML activity changes data in any of the dependent tables, Oracle invalidates the result cache entries and won't use them until they're refreshed by a reexecution of the SQL statement(s).

How It Works

You can monitor and manage the server result cache with the DBMS_RESULT_CACHE package provided by Oracle. This package lets you manage both components of the server result cache, namely, the SQL result cache and the PL/SQL function result cache. You can use the DBMS_RESULT_CACHE package to manage the server result cache memory allocation, as well as to bypass and reenable the cache (when recompiling PL/SQL packages, for example), flush the cache, and view statistics relating to the server query cache memory usage.

The server result cache is part of Oracle's shared pool component of the SGA. Depending on the memory management system in use, Oracle allocates a certain proportion of memory to the server result cache upon starting the database. Here are the rules that Oracle uses for deciding what percentage of the shared pool it allocates to the server result cache:

- If you're using automatic memory management by setting the MEMORY_TARGET parameter, Oracle allocates 0.25 percent of the MEMORY_TARGET parameter's value to the server result cache.

- If you're using automatic shared memory management with the SGA_TARGET parameter, the allocation is 0.5 percent of the SGA_TARGET parameter.

- If you're using manual memory management by setting the SHARED_POOL_SIZE parameter, the allocation is 1 percent of the SHARED_POOL_SIZE parameter.

In an Oracle RAC environment, you can size the server cache differently on each instance, just as you do with MEMORY_TARGET and other instance-related parameters. Similarly, when you disable the server result cache by setting RESULT_CACHE_MAX_SIZE to 0, you must do so on all the instances of the cluster.

The server result cache can potentially reduce your CPU overhead by avoiding recomputation of results, where data may have to be fetched repeatedly from the buffer cache, which results in a higher number of logical I/Os. When you opt to cache the results in the cache instead of precomputing them and storing them in materialized views, you can also potentially reduce the database disk I/O. Just remember that the primary purpose of the result cache isn't to store just any results in memory—it's mainly designed to help with the performance of queries that involve static or mostly static data. Thus, a data warehouse or decision support system is likely to derive the greatest benefit from this new performance feature.

3-9. Caching SQL Query Results

Problem

You've configured the server result cache in your database. You now want to configure a set of queries whose result you would like to be cached in the server result cache.

Solution

Set the RESULT_CACHE_MODE initialization parameter to the appropriate value for making queries eligible for caching in the server result cache. You can set RESULT_CACHE_MODE to the value FORCE to force all SQL results to be cached by the database. Oracle recommends you set the RESULT_CACHE_MODE parameter value to MANUAL, which happens to be the default setting. The RESULT_CACHE_MODE parameter is dynamic, so you can set this parameter with the ALTER SYSTEM (or ALTER SESSION) command.

When you set the RESULT_CACHE_MODE parameter to the value MANUAL, the database caches the results of only specific queries—queries that you enable for caching by using either a query hint or a table annotation. The following example shows how to use the query hint method to specify a query's results to be cached in the server result cache:

```
SQL> select /*+ RESULT_CACHE */ prod_id, sum(amount_sold)
     from  sales
     group by prod_id
     order by prod_id;
```

The query hint /*+RESULT_CACHE */ tells the database to cache the results of the previous query. You can turn off the result caching for this query by using the /+ NO_RESULT_CACHE */ hint, as shown in the following example:

```
SQL> select /*+ NO_RESULT_CACHE */ prod_id, SUM(amount_sold)
     from  sales
     group by prod_id
     order by prod_id;
```

When you run this query, the server won't cache the results of this query any longer. The hint prevents the SQL statement results from being added to the result cache if you've set the RESULT_CACHE_MODE parameter to FORCE or if the RESULTS_CACHE property annotation for the table (or tables) involved in the query was set to FORCE.

The alternative way to specify the caching of a query's results is to use the table annotation method. Under this method, you specify the RESULT_CACHE attribute when you create a table or alter it. You can annotate a CREATE TABLE or ALTER TABLE statement with the RESULT_CACHE attribute in two different modes, DEFAULT or FORCE, as shown in the following examples:

```
SQL> create table stores (...) RESULT_CACHE (MODE DEFAULT);
SQL> alter table stores RESULT_CACHE (MODE FORCE);
```

We explain the implications of setting the RESULT_CACHE_MODE initialization parameter to FORCE in the "How It Works" section.

How It Works

If you set the value of the RESULT_CACHE parameter to FORCE, Oracle executes all subsequent queries only once. Upon subsequent executions of those queries, the database retrieves the results from the cache. Obviously, you don't want to store the results of each and every SQL statement because the server result cache may run out of room. Thus, Oracle recommends you specify the MANUAL setting for the RESULT_CACHE_MODE parameter.

If you can set the result caching behavior with the use of SQL hints, why use table annotations? Table annotations are an easy way to specify caching without having to modify the application queries directly by adding the SQL hints. It's easier to simply issue an ALTER TABLE statement for a set of tables to enable the caching of several queries that use that set of tables. Note that when you annotate a table, those annotations apply to the entire query but not for fragments of that query.

If you annotate a table *and* specify a SQL hint for query caching, which method will Oracle choose to determine whether to cache a query's results? Query hints are given precedence by the database over table annotations. However, the relationship between SQL hints and table annotations is complex, and whether the database caches a query's results also depends on the specific value of the table annotation, as summarized in the following discussion.

Table Annotations and Query Hints

As mentioned earlier, you can use both SQL hints and table annotations to specify which query results you want the result cache to store, with hints overriding annotations. Use either the ALTER TABLE or CREATE TABLE statement to annotate tables with the result cache mode. Here's the syntax for a CREATE or ALTER TABLE statement when annotating a table or a set of tables:

```
CREATE|ALTER TABLE [<schema>.]<table> ... [RESULT_CACHE (MODE {FORCE|DEFAULT})]
```

Note the following important points about table annotations:

- The mode value DEFAULT is, of course, the default value and doesn't permit caching of results that involve this table, unless you specify that the query results be cached by setting the RESULTS_CACHE_MODE parameter appropriately or by specifying the RESULTS_CACHE hint.

- If you set at least one table in a query to the DEFAULT mode, any query involving that table won't be allowed to store its results in the cache.

- If you set all the tables in a query to the FORCE mode, Oracle will always consider that query for caching—unless you turn off the caching with the NO_RESULT_CACHE hint within the query.

- If you set at least one table in a query to DEFAULT by annotating a CREATE TABLE statement, as shown here, Oracle caches results of this query only if you've either set the RESULT_CACHE_MODE parameter to FORCE or specified the RESULT_CACHE hint.

  ```
  SQL> CREATE TABLE sales (id number) RESULT_CACHE (MODE DEFAULT);
  ```

Note that the previous statement is equivalent to the following statement because the default value of the attribute RESULT_CACHE is DEFAULT:

```
SQL> CREATE TABLE sales (id number);
```

You can check that the database created the table SALES with the RESULT_CACHE attribute set to the value DEFAULT:

```
SQL> select table_name, result_cache from user_tables where table_name ='SALES';

TABLE_NAME                RESULT_
----------                -------
SALES                     DEFAULT

SQL>
```

If you specify the table creation statement with the RESULT_CACHE (MODE FORCE) option, this will prevail over the MANUAL setting of the RESULT_CACHE_MODE initialization parameter that you've set at the session level. The following example illustrates how this works:

1. Alter the table STORES to specify the RESULT_CACHE attribute with the MODE FORCE option:

    ```
    SQL> alter table stores result_cache (mode force);
    ```

2. Ensure that you've set the RESULT_CACHE_MODE initialization parameter to the value MANUAL.

3. Execute the following query:

    ```
    SQL> select prod_id, sum(amount_sold)
         from stores
         group by prod_id
         having prod_id=999;
    ```

On subsequent executions, the database will retrieve the results for the preceding query from the server result cache. The reason this is so is that when you specify the RESULT_CACHE (MODE FORCE) annotation, it overrides the MANUAL setting for the RESULT_CACHE_MODE parameter. Remember that when you set this parameter to the MANUAL mode, Oracle will cache query results only if you specify a query hint or annotation. The query shown here doesn't involve the use of a hint, but its results are cached because the RESULT_CACHE (MODE FORCE) annotation makes the database behave the same way as it does when the RESULT_CACHE_MODE parameter is set to FORCE—it caches the query results of all eligible queries.

Query hints, however, ultimately trump the RESULT_CACHE (MODE FORCE) annotation, as shown in the following example.

1. Alter the table STORES to specify the RESULT_CACHE attribute with the MODE FORCE option:

    ```
    SQL> alter table stores result_cache (mode force);
    ```

2. Ensure that you've set the RESULT_CACHE_MODE initialization parameter to the value MANUAL.

3. Execute the following query:

    ```
    SQL>select /*+ no_result_cache */ *
        from stores
        order by time_id desc;
    ```

In this example, even though you've annotated the STORES table to allow caching with the MODE FORCE option, the /*+ no_result_cache */ hint overrides the annotation and prevents the caching of the results of any query that involves the STORES table.

Requirements for Using the Result Cache

There are a few read consistency requirements that a query must satisfy in order for the database to use the result cache.

- In cases involving a snapshot, if a read-consistent snapshot builds a result, it must retrieve the latest committed state of the data, or the query must use a flashback query to point to a specific point in time.

- Whenever a session transaction is actively referencing the tables or views in a query, the database won't cache the results from this query for read consistency purposes.

In addition to the read consistency requirements for result caching, the following objects or functions, when present in a query, make that query ineligible for caching:

- CURRVAL and NEXTVAL pseudocolumns
- CURRENT_DATE, CURRENT_TIMESTAMP, USERENV_CONTEXT, SYS_CONTEXT (with nonconstant variables), SYSDATE, and SYS_TIMESTAMP
- Temporary tables
- Tables owned by SYS and SYSTEM

To realize the maximum gains from using the result cache, you must use it to cut down on repetitive work that needs to be done by the database. However, in reality, only a few select queries will qualify for the result cache because it's common for the base tables to be updated frequently.

3-10. Caching Client Result Sets

Problem

You use a lot of OCI applications that involve repetitive queries. You want to explore how you can cache the result sets on the client.

Solution

You can enable client-side query caching of SQL query results by enabling the client result cache. OCI drivers, such as OCCI, the JDBC OCI driver, and ODP.NET, support client result caching. The client result cache works similarly to the server result cache in many ways but is separate from the server cache. You set the client result cache by setting the following initialization parameters:

- CLIENT_RESULT_CACHE_SIZE: To enable the client result cache, set this parameter to 32 KB or higher (the range is 0 to an OS-dependent maximum). By default, this parameter is set to zero, meaning the client query cache is disabled. Unlike in the case of the server result cache, the CLIENT_RESULT_CACHE_SIZE parameter value sets the maximum size of result set cache per process, not for the entire instance. Since this parameter isn't a dynamic one, a reset requires that you bounce the instance. You have to determine the size of this parameter based on the potential number of results that'll be cached, as well as the average size of the result set, which depends both on the size of the rows and on the number of rows in the result set.

■ **Tip** Oracle cautions you not to set CLIENT_RESULT_CACHE_SIZE during database creation because of potential errors.

- CLIENT_RESULT_CACHE_LAG: This parameter lets you specify the maximum amount of time the client result cache can fall behind a change that affects the result set values. By default, the value of this parameter is set to 3,000 milliseconds, so you can omit this parameter if this time interval is adequate for you. Changes in this parameter also need a restart of the database because it's a static parameter.

In addition, you must specify the value of the initialization parameter COMPATIBLE at 11.0.0 or higher to enable the client result cache. If you want to cache views on the client side, the value of the COMPATIBLE parameter must be 11.2.0.0 or higher.

In addition to the initialization parameters you must set on the database server, Oracle lets you also include an optional client-side configuration file to specify values that override the values of the client query cache–related parameters in the initialization file. If you specify any of these parameters, the value of that parameter will override the value of the corresponding parameter in the server initialization file. You can specify one or more of the following parameters in the optional client configuration file, which you can include in the sqlnet.ora file on the client:

- OCI_RESULT_CACHE_MAX_SIZE: Maximum size (in bytes) for the query cache for each individual process

- OCI_RESULT_CACHE_MAX_RSET_SIZE: Maximum size of a result set in bytes in any process

- OCI_RESULT_CACHE_MAX_RSET_ROWS: Maximum size of the result set in terms of rows, in any process

You can't set any query cache lag–related parameters in the client-side file. Once you set the appropriate initialization parameters and the optional client-side configuration file, you must enable and disable queries for caching with either the /*+ result_cache +/ (and the /*+ no_result_cache +/) hint or table annotations. Once you do this, the database will attempt to cache all eligible queries in the client query cache.

How It Works

You can deploy client-side query result caching to speed up the responses of queries that your database frequently executes in an OCI application. The database keeps the result set data consistent with any database changes, including session changes. You can potentially see a huge performance improvement for repetitive queries because the database retrieves the results from the local OCI client process rather than having to reaccess the server via the network and reexecute the same query there and fetch those results. When an OCI application issues an OCIStmtExecute() or OCIStmtFetch() call, Oracle processes those calls locally on the client, if the query results are already cached in the client query cache.

The big advantage of using a client-side query cache is that it conserves your server memory usage and helps you scale up your applications to serve more processes. The client query cache is organized on a per-process basis rather than a per-session basis. Multiple client sessions can share the same cached result sets, all of which can concurrently access the same result sets through multiple threads and multiple statements. The cache automatically invalidates the cached result sets if an OCI process finds significant database changes on the database server. Once a result set is invalidated, the query will be executed again, and a fresh result set is stored in the cache.

■ **Tip** Oracle recommends you use client-side caching only for read-only or mostly read-only queries.

You can optionally set the RESULT_CACHE_MODE parameter (see Recipe 3-7) to control caching behavior, but by default, this parameter is set to the value MANUAL, so you can leave it alone. You really don't want to set this parameter to its alternative value FORCE, which compels the database to cache the results of every eligible SQL query—obviously, the cache will run out of room before too long! You can then specify either the appropriate query hint at the SQL level or table annotations at the table level to control the client-side result caching. What if you've already set up server-side result caching through the server query cache? No matter. You can still enable client result caching. Just remember that by default client-side caching is disabled and server-side result caching is enabled.

When implementing client query caching, it's important that an OCIStmtExecute() call is made so a statement handle can match a cached result. The very first OCIStmtExecute() call for an OCI statement handle goes to the server regardless of the existence of a cached result set. Subsequent OCIStmtExecute() calls will use the cached results if there's a match. Similarly, only the first OCIStmtFetch() call fetches rows until it gets the "Data Not Found" error; subsequent fetch calls don't need to fetch the data until they get this error, if the call matches the cached result set. Oracle recommends that your OCI applications either cache OCI statements or use statement caching for OCI statement handles so they can return OCI statements that have already been executed. The cached set allows multiple accesses from OCI statement handles from single or multiple sessions.

As with the server-side cache, you can set the RESULT_CACHE_MODE parameter to FORCE to specify query caching for all queries. Oracle recommends you set this parameter to the alternative value of MANUAL and use SQL hints (/*+ result_cache */) in the SQL code the application passes to the OCIStmtPrepare() and OCIStmtPrepare2() calls. You can also use table annotations, as explained in Recipe 3-7, to specify caching when you create or alter a table. All queries that include that table will follow the caching specifications subsequently.

You can query the V$CLIENT_RESULT_CACHE_STATS$ view for details such as the number of cached result sets, the number of cached result sets invalidated, and the number of cache misses. The statistic Create Count Success, for example, shows the number of cached result sets the database didn't validate before caching all rows of the result set. The statistic Create Count Failure shows the number of the cached result sets that didn't fetch all rows in the result set.

3-11. Caching PL/SQL Function Results
Problem

You've set up a server query cache in your database and want to implement the caching of certain PL/SQL function results.

Solution

Oracle's server query cache (Recipe 3-7) helps you cache both normal SQL query results as well as PL/SQL function results. By using the server result cache, you can instruct the database to cache the results of PL/SQL functions in the SGA. Other sessions can use these cached results, just as they can use cached query results with the query result cache. Once you've configured the server query cache by setting the appropriate initialization parameters (please see Recipe 3-7), you are ready to make use of this feature.

You must specify the RESULT_CACHE clause inside a function to make the database cache the function's results in the PL/SQL function result cache. When a session invokes a function after you enable caching, it first checks to see whether the cache holds results for the function with identical parameter values. If so, it fetches the cached results and doesn't have to execute the function body. Note that if you declare a function first, you must also specify the RESULT_CACHE clause in the function declaration, in addition to specifying the clause within the function itself.

Listing 3-1 shows how to cache a PL/SQL function's results.

Listing 3-1. Creating a PL/SQL Function with the /*+result_cache*/ Hint

```
SQL> create or replace package store_pkg is
     type store_sales_record is record (
     store_name stores.store_name%TYPE,
     mgr_name   employees.last_name%type,
     store_size  PLS_INTEGER
     );
     function get_store_info (store_id PLS_INTEGER)
     RETURN store_info_record
      RESULT_CACHE;
     END store_pkg;
     /
create or replace package body store_pkg is
     FUNCTION get_store_sales (store_id PLS_INTEGER)
     RETURN store_sales_record
     RESULT_CACHE RELIES_ON (stores, employees)
   IS
     rec  store_sales_record;
```

```
  BEGIN
    SELECT store_name INTO rec.store_name
    FROM stores
    WHERE store_id = store_id;
    SELECT e.last_name INTO rec.mgr_name
    FROM stores d, employees e
    WHERE d.store_id = store_id
    AND d.manager_id = e.employee_id;
     SELECT COUNT(*) INTO rec.store_size
    FROM EMPLOYEES
    WHERE store_id = store_id;
     RETURN rec;
  END get_store_sales;
END store_pkg;
/
```

Let's say you invoke the function with the following values:

```
SQL> execute store_pkg.get_store_sales(999)
```

The first execution will cache the PL/SQL function's results in the server result cache. Any future executions of this function with the same parameters (999) won't require the database to reexecute this function; the database merely fetches the results from the server result cache.

Note that in addition to specifying the RESULT_CACHE clause in the function declaration, you can optionally specify the RESULT_CACHE RELIES ON clause in the function body, as we did in this example. In this case, specifying the RESULT_CACHE_RELIES_ON clause means that the result cache relies on the tables STORES and EMPLOYEES. What this means is that whenever these tables change, the database invalidates all the cached results for the get_store_info function.

How It Works

The PL/SQL function result cache uses the same server-side result cache as the query result cache, and you set the size of the cache using the RESULT_CACHE_MAX_SIZE and RESULT_CACHE_MAX_RESULT initialization parameters, with the first parameter fixing the maximum SGA memory that the cache can use, and the latter fixing the maximum percentage of the cache a single result can use. Unlike the query result cache, the PL/SQL function cache may quickly gather numerous results for caching because the cache will store multiple values for the same function, based on the parameter values. If there's space pressure within the cache, older cached function results are removed to make room for new results.

Oracle recommends that you employ the PL/SQL function result cache to cache the results of functions that execute frequently but rely on static or mostly static data. The reason for specifying the static data requirement is simple: Oracle automatically invalidates cache results of any function whose underlying views or tables undergo committed changes. When this happens, the invocation of the function will result in a fresh execution.

Whenever you introduce a modified version of a package on which a result cache function depends (such as in Listing 3-1), the database is supposed to automatically flush that function's cached results from the PL/SQL function cache. In our example, when you hot-patch (recompile) the package store_pkg, Oracle technically must flush the cached results associated with the get_store_info function. However, Oracle doesn't automatically flush the cached results associated with the result cache function, so you must manually flush them. To ensure that the cached results of the function are removed, follow these steps whenever you recompile a PL/SQL unit such as a package that includes a cache-enabled function:

1. Place the result cache in the bypass mode:

   ```
   SQL> execute DBMS_RESULT_CACHE.bypass(true);
   ```

2. Clear the cache with the flush procedure:

   ```
   SQL> execute DBMS_RESULT_CACHE.flush;
   ```

3. Recompile the package that contains the cache-enabled function:

   ```
   SQL> alter package store_pkg compile;
   ```

4. Reenable the result cache with the bypass procedure:

   ```
   SQL> execute DBMS_RESULT_CACHE.bypass(false);
   ```

■ **Tip** If you're using both the SQL query cache and PL/SQL function result cache simultaneously, remember that both caches are actually part of the same server query cache. In cases such as this, ensure that you've sized the RESULT_CACHE_SIZE parameter high enough to hold cached results from both SQL queries and PL/SQL functions.

If you're operating in an Oracle RAC environment, you must run the cache-enabling and disabling steps on each RAC instance.

Note that the DBMS_RESULT_CACHE.FLUSH procedure flushes both the cached results for all SQL queries as well as those for all PL/SQL functions.

Of course, when you bypass the cache temporarily in this manner, during the time that the cache is bypassed, the database will execute the function instead of seeking to retrieve its results from the cache. The database will also bypass the result cache on its own for a function if a session is in the middle of a transaction involving a table or view that the function depends on. This automatic bypassing of the result cache by the database ensures that users won't see uncommitted changes of another session in their own session, thus ensuring read consistency.

You can use the V$RESULT_CACHE_STATISTICS, V$RESULT_CACHE_MEMORY, V$RESULT_CACHE_OBJECTS, and V$RESULT_CACHE_DEPENDENCY views to monitor the usage of the server result cache, which includes both the SQL result cache and the PL/SQL function result cache.

Important Considerations

While a PL/SQL function cache gets you results much faster than repetitive execution of a function, PL/SQL collections (arrays)–based processing could be even faster because the PL/SQL runtime engine gets the results from the collection cache based in the PGA rather than the SGA. However, since this requires additional PGA memory for each session, you'll have problems with the collections approach as the number of sessions grows large. The PL/SQL function is easily shareable by all concurrent sessions, whereas you can set up collections for sharing only through additional coding.

You must be alert to the possibility that if your database undergoes frequent DML changes, the PL/SQL function cache may not be ideal for you—it's mostly meant for data that never changes or does so only infrequently. DML changes will force the database to invalidate the cached PL/SQL function cache result sets.

Oracle will invalidate result cache output when it becomes out of date, so when a DML statement modifies the rows of a table that is part of a PL/SQL function that you've enabled for the function cache, the database invalidates the cached results of that function. This could happen if the specific rows that were modified aren't part of the PL/SQL function result set. Again, remember that this limitation could be "bypassed" by using the PL/SQL function cache in databases that are predominantly read-only.

Restrictions on the PL/SQL Function Cache

For its results to be cached, a function must satisfy the following requirements:

- The function doesn't use an OUT or IN OUT parameter.

- No IN parameter of a function has one of these types: BLOB, CLOB, NCLOB, REF CURSOR, Collection Object, and Record.

- The function isn't a pipelined table function.

- The function isn't part of an anonymous block.

- The function isn't part of any module that uses invoker's rights as opposed to definer's rights.

- The function's return type doesn't include the following types: BLOB, CLOB, NCLOB, REF CURSOR, Object, Record, or a PL/SQL collection that contains one of the preceding unsupported return types.

3-12. Configuring the Oracle Database Smart Flash Cache
Problem

Your Automatic Workload Repository (AWR) report indicates that you need a much larger buffer cache. You also notice that the shared pool is sized correctly, so you can't set a higher minimum level for the buffer cache by reducing the shared pool memory allocation. In addition, you're limited in the amount of additional memory you can allocate to Oracle.

Solution

Depending on your operating system, you can use the new Oracle Database Smart Flash Cache feature in cases where the database indicates that it needs a much larger amount of memory for the buffer cache. Right now, the Flash Cache feature is limited to Solaris and Oracle Linux operating systems.

Set the following parameters to turn on the Smart Flash Cache feature:

- DB_FLASH_CACHE_FILE: This parameter sets the pathname and the file name for the flash cache. The file name you specify will hold the flash cache. You must use a flash device (SSD) for the flash cache file, and it could be located in the operating system file system, a raw disk, or an Oracle ASM disk group. Here's an example:

```
DB_FLASH_CACHE_FILE= "/dev/sdc"
DB_FLASH_CACHE_FILE = "/export/home/oracle/file_raw"      /* raw file
DB_FLASH_CACHE_FILE = "+dg1/file_asm"                     /* using ASM storage
```

- DB_FLASH_CACHE_SIZE: This parameter sets the size of the flash cache storage. Here's an example:

DB_FLASH_CACHE_SIZE = 8GB

You can toggle between a system with a flash cache and one without by using the alter system command, as shown here:

```
SQL> alter system set db_flash_cache_size = 0;      /* disables the flash cache
SQL> alter system set db_flash_cache_size = 8G;     /* reenables the flash cache
```

Note that although you can successfully enable and disable the flash cache dynamically as shown here, Oracle doesn't support this method.

■ **Note** If you're using Oracle RAC, in order to utilize the Flash Cache feature, you must enable it on all the nodes of the cluster.

How It Works

Oracle Database Smart Flash Cache, a feature of the Oracle Database 11.2 release, is included as part of the Enterprise Edition of the database server. Flash Cache takes advantage of the I/O speed of flash-based devices, which perform much better than disk-based storage. For example, small disk-based reads offer a 4-millisecond response, whereas a flash-based device takes only 0.4 milliseconds to perform the same read.

Note that the Smart Flash Cache is really a read-only cache—when clean (unmodified) data blocks are evicted from the buffer cache because of space pressure, those blocks are then moved to the flash cache. If they're required later, the database will move transferred data blocks back to the SGA from the flash cache. It's not always realistic to assume that you and the Oracle database will have access to unlimited memory. What if you can allocate only a maximum of 12 GB for your Oracle SGA but it turns out that if you have 50 GB of memory, the database will run a whole lot faster? Oracle Database Smart Flash Cache is designed for those types of situations.

Oracle recommends that you size the flash cache to a value that's a multiple of your buffer cache size. There's no hard-and-fast rule here; use a trial-and-error method by setting it to anywhere between one and ten times the size of the buffer cache size and calibrate the results. Oracle also suggests that if you encounter the database file sequential read wait event (table full scans) as a top wait event and if you have sufficient CPU capacity, you should consider using the flash cache.

Once you enable the Smart Falsh Cache, Oracle moves data blocks from the buffer cache to the flash cache (the file you've created) and saves metadata about the blocks in the database buffer cache. Depending on the number of blocks moved into the flash cache, you may want to bump up the size of the MEMORY_TARGET parameter so the accumulated metadata doesn't impact the amount of memory left for the other components.

Oracle markets two devices for Smart Falsh Cache storage: Sun Storage F5100 Flash Array and the Sun Flash Accelerator F20 PCIe Card. Since you can specify only a single flash device, you will need a volume manager. It turns out that Oracle ASM is the best volume manager for these devices, based on Oracle's tests.

If you're using the Smart Falsh Cache in an Oracle RAC environment, you must create a separate flash cache file path for each of the instances, and you will also need to create a separate ASM disk group for each instance's flash cache.

Oracle testing of the Database Smart Flash Cache feature shows that it's ideally suited for workloads that are I/O bound. If you have a heavy amount of concurrent read-only transactions, the disk system could be saturated after some point. Oracle Database Smart Flash Cache increases such a system's throughput by processing more I/O per second (IOPS). Oracle's testing results of this feature also show that response times increased by five times when Smart Flash Cache was introduced to deal with workloads facing significant performance deterioration because of maxing out of disk I/O throughput. As of the writing of this book, Oracle makes these claims only for workloads that arc exclusively or mostly read-only operations. While Oracle is still in the process of testing the flash cache for write-intensive workloads, note that even for read-only operations, the reduced load on your disk system because of using the flash cache will mean that you'll have more I/O bandwidth to handle your writes.

3-13. Tuning the Redo Log Buffer

Problem

You want to know how to tune the redo log buffer because you've reviewed several AWR reports that pointed out that the redo log buffer setting for your production database is too small. Occasionally you may want to reduce the size of the current log buffer setting.

Solution

You configure the size of the redo log buffer by setting the value of the initialization parameter LOG_BUFFER. This parameter is static, so any changes to it require a restart of the database. You set the parameter in your init.ora file as follows:

```
log_buffer=4096000
```

You can also change the size of the log buffer with the following ALTER SYSTEM statement:

```
SQL> alter system set log_buffer=4096000 scope=spfile;

System altered
SQL>
```

How It Works

Oracle sets the default value for the log_buffer parameter somewhere between 5 MB and 32 MB, depending on your SGA and PGA sizes as well as on whether you're using a 32-bit or 64-bit operating system. You can set the value of the parameter as low as 2 MB and as high as 64 MB (32 bit) or 266 MB (64 bit).

When the Oracle server processes change data blocks in the buffer cache, those changes are written to the redo logs in the form of redo log entries, before they are written to disk. The redo log entries enable the database to redo or reconstruct the database changes by using various operations such as INSERT, UPDATE, and DELETE, as well as DDL operations. The Oracle redo logs are thus critical for any database recovery because it's these redo log entries that enable the database to apply all the changes made to the database from a point in time in the past. The changed data doesn't directly go to the redo logs, however; Oracle first writes the changes to a memory area called the *redo log buffer*. It's the value of this memory buffer that you can configure with the LOG_BUFFER parameter. The Oracle log writer (LGWR) process writes the redo log buffer entries to the active redo log file (or group of files). LGWR flushes the contents of the buffer to disk whenever the buffer is one-third full or if the database writer requests the LGWR to write to the redo log file. Also, upon each COMMIT or ROLLBACK by a server process, the LGWR process writes the contents of the buffer to the redo log file on disk.

The redo log buffer is a reusable cache, so as entries are written out to the redo log file, user processes copy new entries into the redo log buffer. While the LGWR usually works fast enough so there's space in the buffer, a larger buffer will have more room for new entries. Be aware that a larger buffer might increase the time for commits because there are more bytes to write to disk following each commit in the database. If your database is processing large updates, the LGWR has to frequently flush the redo log buffer to the redo log files even in the absence of a COMMIT statement, so as to keep the buffer no more than a third full. Raising the size of the redo log buffer is an acceptable solution in this situation and allows the LGWR to catch up with the heavy amount of entries into the redo log buffer. This also offsets a slow I/O system in some ways if you think the performance of the LGWR process is not fast enough. There are a couple of ways in which you keep the pressure on the redo log buffer down: you can batch COMMIT operations for all batch jobs and also specify the NOLOGGING option where possible, say during regular data loads. When you specify the NOLOGGING option during a data load, Oracle doesn't need to use the redo log files, and hence it also bypasses the redo log buffer.

It's fairly easy to tune the size of the LOG_BUFFER parameter. Just execute the following statement to get the current "redo log space request ratio":

```
SQL> select round(t.value/s.value,5) "Redo Log Space Request Ratio"
     from v$sysstat s, v$sysstat t
     where s.name = 'redo log space requests'
     and t.name = 'redo entries'
```

The redo log space request ratio is simply the ratio of total redo log space requests to redo entries. You can also query the V$SYSSTAT view to find the value of the statistic redo buffer allocation retries. This statistic shows the number of times processes waited for space in the redo log buffer:

```
SQL> select name,value from V$SYSSTAT
          where name= 'redo buffer allocation retries';
```

Execute this SQL query multiple times over a period of time. If the value of the "redo buffer allocation retries" statistic is rising steadily over this period, it indicates that the redo log buffer is under space pressure, and as a result, processes are waiting to write their redo log entries to the redo log buffer. You must increase the size of the redo log buffer if you continue to see this.

3-14. Limiting PGA Memory Allocation
Problem

You've set the PGA_AGGREGATE_TARGET parameter but find that often the database is allocating more memory for the PGA than you specified as the target.

Solution

To specify a hard limit on PGA memory usage, you must set the new PGA_AGGREGATE_LIMIT initialization parameter. Here's an example:

```
 SQL> alter system set pga_aggregate_limit=2000m;

System altered.

SQL>
```

You can set the PGA_AGGREGATE_LIMIT parameter (a dynamic initialization parameter) to the level you desire, in terms of kilobyte, megabytes, or gigabytes. The values you specify for the PGA_AGGREGATE_LIMIT parameter must be between 1070MB and 100000GB. You can disable the hard limit on PGA memory by setting the value of the PGA_AGGREGATE_LIMIT parameter to zero.

How It Works

The instance attempts to stick to the PGA_AGGREGATE_TARGET value you set by allocating appropriate amounts of PGA memory to the various work areas. However, the PGA_AGGREGATE_TARGET parameter doesn't set a hard limit but rather a soft one. Furthermore, the PGA_AGGREGATE_TARGET parameter controls only the allocation of tunable memory. If you find that your system is swapping because of excessive allocation of PGA memory beyond what you've allocated by the PGA_AGGREGATE_TARGET parameter, you can set the PGA_AGGREGATE_TARGET parameter to put a hard limit on the usage of PGA memory.

If the instance memory usage for PGA exceeds the limit you set with the PGA_AGGREGATE_TARGET parameter, the instance will first abort any new calls from sessions that are consumers of the most untunable PGA memory. If necessary, it'll terminate sessions and processes that are the consumers of the most untunable PGA memory.

The default value for the PGA_AGGREGATE_TARGET parameter is the greater of the following:

- 2 GB

- 200 percent of the PGA_AGGREGATE_TARGET parameter

- 3 MB times the value assigned to the PROCESSES parameter

The following query shows that the PGA_AGGREGATE_LIMIT parameter is set to 2 GB in the example database:

```
SQL> show parameter pga

NAME                     TYPE            VALUE
--------------------     -----------     -----
pga_aggregat             big integer     2G
pga_aggregate_target     big integer     0
SQL>
```

Note that if you set the PGA_AGGREGATE_LIMIT parameter to 0, there's no limit to the amount of PGA memory the instance can consume.

You may recall that the *c* in Oracle Database 12c stands for *cloud*; limiting PGA memory allocation as shown in this recipe can be important in cloud systems where resources are dynamically allocated (like Amazon Web Services [AWS]) and where you may get an invoice far higher than what you were expecting because a program went berserk.

CHAPTER 4

■ ■ ■

Monitoring System Performance

Monitoring system and database performance is a complex task, and there can be many aspects to managing performance, including memory, disk, CPU, database objects, and database user sessions—just for starters. This chapter zeroes in on using Oracle's Automatic Workload Repository (AWR) to gather data about the activities occurring within your database, and help convert that raw data into useful information to help gauge performance within your database for a specific period of time. Usually, when there are performance issues occurring within a database, it's easy to know when the performance problems are occurring because database activity is "slow" during that given time frame. Knowing this time frame is the starting point to perform the analysis using the AWR information.

The AWR is created automatically when you create your Oracle database and automatically gathers statistics on the activities occurring within your database. Some of this data is real-time or very near real-time, and some of the data represents historical statistics on these activities. The most current data on active sessions is stored in the Active Session History (ASH) component of the performance statistics repository. The more historical snapshots of data are generally known as the AWR snapshots.

The AWR process captures hourly snapshots by default from Oracle's dynamic performance views, and stores them within the AWR. This gives the DBA the ability to view database activity over any period of time, whether it is a single-hour time frame, up to all activity that is stored within the AWR. For instance, if you have a period of time where your database is performing poorly, you can generate an AWR report that will give statistics on the database activity for only that specific period of time.

The ASH component of the AWR is really meant to give the DBA a more real-time look at session information that is not captured within the AWR snapshots. The session information stored within the ASH repository is data that is sampled every second from the dynamic performance views.

Oracle has had similar information within the database for many years with its predecessors UTLBSTAT/UTLESTAT and Statspack, but the report data hasn't been generated or saved automatically until AWR came along with Oracle 10g. This information can help monitor your database performance much more easily, whether it be analyzing real-time data on activities currently going on within your database or historical information that could be days, weeks, or even months old, depending on the configuration of the AWR within your database. To use AWR, you need to be licensed for the Diagnostics Pack, which requires an extra cost. If you don't have a license for Diagnostics pack, you can still use Statspack, which can still be of great benefit when troubleshooting performance issues.

4-1. Implementing Automatic Workload Repository (AWR)
Problem

You want to store historical database performance statistics on your database for tuning purposes.

Solution

By implementing and using the Automatic Workload Repository (AWR) within your database, Oracle will store interval-based historical statistics in your database for future reference. This information can be used to see what was going on within your database within a given period of time. By default, the AWR should be enabled within your database. The key initialization parameter to validate is the STATISTICS_LEVEL parameter:

```
SQL> show parameter statistics_level

NAME                                 TYPE     VALUE
------------------------------------ -------- ----------
statistics_level                     string   TYPICAL
```

This parameter can be set to BASIC, TYPICAL (which is the default), and ALL. As long as the parameter is set to TYPICAL or ALL, statistics will be gathered for the AWR. If the parameter is set to BASIC, you simply need to modify the parameter in order to start gathering AWR statistics for your database:

```
alter system set statistics_level=TYPICAL scope=both;
```

How It Works

The predecessor of AWR, which is Statspack, requires manual setup and configuration to enable the statistics gathering. As stated, there generally is no setup required, unless the STATISTICS_LEVEL parameter has been changed to the BASIC setting. By default, an AWR snapshot is taken every hour on your database and is stored, by default, for 8 days. These are configurable settings that can be modified, if desired. See Recipe 4-2 for information on modifying the default settings of the AWR snapshots.

In addition to simply seeing the value of the STATISTICS_LEVEL parameter, you can also view the V$STATISTICS_LEVEL view to see this information, which has information on the STATISTICS_LEVEL setting, as well as all other relevant statistical components within your database:

```
SELECT statistics_name, activation_level, system_status
FROM v$statistics_level
order by statistics_name;

STATISTICS_NAME                       ACTIVAT SYSTEM_S
------------------------------------ ------- --------
Active Session History                TYPICAL ENABLED
Adaptive Thresholds Enabled           TYPICAL ENABLED
Automated Maintenance Tasks           TYPICAL ENABLED
Automatic DBOP Monitoring             TYPICAL ENABLED
Bind Data Capture                     TYPICAL ENABLED
Buffer Cache Advice                   TYPICAL ENABLED
Global Cache CPU Statistics           ALL     DISABLED
Global Cache Statistics               TYPICAL ENABLED
Longops Statistics                    TYPICAL ENABLED
MTTR Advice                           TYPICAL ENABLED
Modification Monitoring               TYPICAL ENABLED
OLAP row load time precision          TYPICAL ENABLED
PGA Advice                            TYPICAL ENABLED
Plan Execution Sampling               TYPICAL ENABLED
Plan Execution Statistics             ALL     DISABLED
```

```
SQL Monitoring                           TYPICAL ENABLED
Segment Level Statistics                 TYPICAL ENABLED
Shared Pool Advice                       TYPICAL ENABLED
Streams Pool Advice                      TYPICAL ENABLED
Threshold-based Alerts                   TYPICAL ENABLED
Time Model Events                        TYPICAL ENABLED
Timed OS Statistics                      ALL     DISABLED
Timed Statistics                         TYPICAL ENABLED
Ultrafast Latch Statistics               TYPICAL ENABLED
Undo Advisor, Alerts and Fast Ramp up    TYPICAL ENABLED
V$IOSTAT_* statistics                    TYPICAL ENABLED
```

26 rows selected.

The type of information that is stored in the AWR includes the following:

- Statistics regarding object access and usage

- Time model statistics

- System statistics

- Session statistics

- SQL statements

- Active Session History (ASH) information

The information gathered is then grouped and formatted by category. Some of the categories found on the report include the following:

- Load profile

- Instance efficiency

- Top 10 foreground events

- Memory, CPU, and I/O statistics

- Wait information

- SQL statement information

- Miscellaneous operating system and database statistics

- Database file and tablespace usage information

■ **Note**   To use AWR functionality, the following must apply. First, you must be licensed for the Oracle Diagnostics Pack, otherwise you need to use Statspack. Second, the CONTROL_MANAGEMENT_PACK_ACCESS parameter must be set to DIAGNOSTIC+TUNING or DIAGNOSTIC.

4-2. Modifying the Statistics Interval and Retention Periods

Problem

You need to set an interval or retention period for your AWR snapshots to values other than the default.

Solution

By using the DBMS_WORKLOAD_REPOSITORY PL/SQL package, you can modify the default snapshot settings for your database. In order to first validate your current retention and interval settings for your AWR snapshots, run the following query:

```
SQL> column awr_snapshot_retention_period format a40
SQL> SELECT EXTRACT(day from retention) || ':' ||
        EXTRACT(hour from retention) || ':' ||
        EXTRACT (minute from retention)  awr_snapshot_retention_period,
        EXTRACT (day from snap_interval) *24*60+
        EXTRACT (hour from snap_interval) *60+
        EXTRACT (minute from snap_interval) awr_snapshot_interval
FROM dba_hist_wr_control;

AWR_SNAPSHOT_RETENTION_PERIOD  AWR_SNAPSHOT_INTERVAL
-----------------------------  ---------------------
8:13:45                                           60
```

The retention period output just shown is in day:hour:minute format. So, our current retention period is 8 days, 13 hours, and 45 minutes. The interval, or how often the AWR snapshots will be gathered, is 60 minutes in the foregoing example. To then modify the retention period and interval settings, you can use the MODIFY_SNAPSHOT_SETTINGS procedure of the DBMS_WORKLOAD_REPOSITORY package. To change these settings for your database, issue a command such as the following example, which modifies the retention period to 30 days (specified by number of minutes), and the snapshot interval at which snapshots are taken to 30 minutes. Of course, you can choose to simply set one parameter or the other and do not have to change both settings. The following example shows both parameters simply for demonstration purposes:

```
SQL> exec DBMS_WORKLOAD_REPOSITORY.MODIFY_SNAPSHOT_SETTINGS(retention=>43200, interval=>30);

PL/SQL procedure successfully completed.
```

You can then simply rerun the query from the DBA_HIST_WR_CONTROL data dictionary view in order to validate that your change is now in effect:

```
SQL> /

AWR_SNAPSHOT_RETENTION_PERIOD             AWR_SNAPSHOT_INTERVAL
----------------------------------------  ---------------------
30:0:0                                                       30
```

How It Works

It is generally a good idea to modify the default settings for your database, as 8 days of retention is often not enough when diagnosing possible database issues or performing database tuning activities on your database. If you have been notified of a problem for a monthly process, for example, the last time frame that denoted an ordinary and successful execution of the process would no longer be available, unless snapshots were stored for the given interval. Because of this, it is a good idea to store a minimum of 45 days of snapshots, if at all possible, or even longer if storage is not an issue on your database. If you want your snapshots to be stored for an unlimited amount of time, you can specify a zero value, which tells Oracle to keep the snapshot information indefinitely (actually, for 40,150 days, or 110 years). See the following example:

```
SQL> exec DBMS_WORKLOAD_REPOSITORY.MODIFY_SNAPSHOT_SETTINGS(retention=>0);

PL/SQL procedure successfully completed.

SQL> /

AWR_SNAPSHOT_RETENTION_PERIOD              AWR_SNAPSHOT_INTERVAL
------------------------------------------ ----------------------
40150:0:0                                                      30
```

The default snapshot interval of 1 hour is usually granular enough for most databases, as when there are more frequent or closer to real-time needs, you can use the Active Session History (ASH) information. By increasing the default snapshot interval to greater than 1 hour, it can actually make it more difficult to diagnose performance issues, as statistics for the increased window may make it harder to distinguish and identify performance issues for a given time period.

4-3. Generating an AWR Report Manually

Problem

You want to generate an AWR report, and know the time frame on which to gather information.

Solution

In order to generate an AWR report, run the awrrpt.sql script found under the $ORACLE_HOME/rdbms/admin directory. In this example, we needed to enter information for the following:

- Report type (text or html)

- Number of days you want displayed from which to choose snapshots

- The starting snapshot number for the period on which you want to generate a report

- The ending snapshot number for the period on which you want to generate a report

- The name of the report (enter a name if you do not want the default report name and location)

The lines in bold type here denote points where user input is required:

```
$ sqlplus / as sysdba @awrrpt

Current Instance
~~~~~~~~~~~~~~~~~
  DB Id      DB Name      Inst Num Instance
----------- ------------ -------- ------------
 2334201269 ORCL                1 ORCL

Specify the Report Type
~~~~~~~~~~~~~~~~~~~~~~~~~
Would you like an HTML report, or a plain text report?
Enter 'html' for an HTML report, or 'text' for plain text
Defaults to 'html'
```
Enter value for report_type: text

```
Type Specified:  text

Instances in this Workload Repository schema
~~~~~~~~~~~~~~~~~~~~~~~~~~~~~~~~~~~~~~~~~~~~~~~~~~~

  DB Id      Inst Num DB Name      Instance     Host
----------- -------- ------------ ------------ ------------
* 2334201269        1 ORCL         ORCL         ora

Using 2334201269 for database Id
Using           1 for instance number

Specify the number of days of snapshots to choose from
~~~~~~~~~~~~~~~~~~~~~~~~~~~~~~~~~~~~~~~~~~~~~~~~~~~~~~~~~~~
```
Enter value for num_days: 7
```
Listing the last 7 days of Completed Snapshots

                                               Snap
Instance      DB Name       Snap Id   Snap Started     Level
------------ ------------ --------- ----------------- -----
ORCL          ORCL             257 28 May 2011 00:00      2

                                 258 28 May 2011 13:39      2
                                 259 28 May 2011 15:00      2
                                 260 28 May 2011 16:00      2
                                 261 28 May 2011 17:00      2
                                 262 28 May 2011 18:00      2
                                 263 28 May 2011 19:00      2
                                 264 28 May 2011 20:00      2
                                 265 28 May 2011 21:00      2
                                 266 28 May 2011 22:00      2
                                 267 28 May 2011 23:00      2
                                 268 29 May 2011 00:00      2
```

```
                        269  29 May 2011 11:52        2
                        270  29 May 2011 13:00        2
                        271  29 May 2011 14:00        2
                        272  29 May 2011 15:00        2
                        273  29 May 2011 16:00        2
                        274  29 May 2011 17:00        2

                        275  30 May 2011 17:00        2
                        276  30 May 2011 18:00        2
                        277  30 May 2011 19:00        2
                        278  30 May 2011 20:00        2
```

```
Specify the Begin and End Snapshot Ids
~~~~~~~~~~~~~~~~~~~~~~~~~~~~~~~~~~~~~~~~~
```
Enter value for begin_snap: 258
```
Begin Snapshot Id specified: 258
```

Enter value for end_snap: 268
```
End   Snapshot Id specified: 268
```

```
Specify the Report Name
~~~~~~~~~~~~~~~~~~~~~~~~~~
The default report file name is awrrpt_1_258_268.txt.  To use this name,
press <return> to continue, otherwise enter an alternative.
```

Enter value for report_name: /tmp/awrrpt_1_258_268.txt

```
Using the report name /tmp/awrrpt_1_258_268.txt

< Output of report is shown across the screen >

End of Report
Report written to /tmp/awrrpt_1_258_268.txt
```

■ **Tip** If you have an Active Data Guard environment, see My Oracle Support note 454848.1 for information on installing and using statspack on a read-only database.

How It Works

In the foregoing example, note that between some of the snapshots listed there is a blank line. Since we are getting information based on the dynamic performance views of the data dictionary, you cannot specify a snapshot period that spans bounces of the database instance, as all statistics in the dynamic performance views are lost when a database instance is shut down. Therefore, choose a snapshot period only for the life of an instance; otherwise you can experience the following error:

```
Enter value for begin_snap: 274
Begin Snapshot Id specified: 274
```

```
Enter value for end_snap: 275
End    Snapshot Id specified: 275

declare
*
ERROR at line 1:
ORA-20200: The instance was shutdown between snapshots 274 and 275
ORA-06512: at line 42
```

Although it is recommended to use the `awrrpt.sql` script to generate the desired AWR report, you can manually use the `AWR_REPORT_TEXT` or `AWR_REPORT_HTML` functions within the `DBMS_WORKLOAD_REPOSITORY` package to generate an AWR report, if needed. You need to also have your database's DBID and instance number handy as well when running either of these functions. See the following for an example:

```
SELECT  dbms_workload_repository.awr_report_text
        (l_dbid=>2334201269,l_inst_num=>1,l_bid=>258,l_eid=>268)
FROM dual;
```

Another option to get more specific and customized information normally displayed on the AWR report is to query the DBA_HIST views within the data dictionary. A listing of many of these views can be seen in Table 4-1. Refer to Chapter 6 of the Oracle 12c Performance Tuning Guide for a complete description of these views.

Table 4-1. *The DBA_HIST views*

View Name	Description
DBA_HIST_ACTIVE SESS_HISTORY	Contains Active Session History (ASH) history
DBA_HIST_BASELINE	Contains baseline information
DBA_HIST_BASELINE_DETAILS	Contains baseline details
DBA_HIST_BASELINE_TEMPLATE	Contains details for baseline templates
DBA_HIST_DATABASE_INSTANCE	Contains DB information
DBA_HIST_DB_CACHE_ADVICE	Contains historical predictions of physical reads
DBA_HIST_IOSTAT_DETAIL	Contains historical I/O statistics
DBA_HIST_SNAPSHOT	Contains historical information of all AWR snapsnots
DBA_HIST_SQL_PLAN	Contains historical explain plan information.
DBA_HIST_WR_CONTROL	Contains settings for controlling AWR

■ **Note**   For Real Application Cluster (RAC) environments, run the `awrgrpt.sql` script, which will generate an AWR report that includes all instances for a RAC database. If using the `DBMS_WORKLOAD_REPOSITORY` package, use the `AWR_GLOBAL_REPORT_TEXT` function to generate an AWR report for any or all instances in a RAC environment.

4-4. Generating an AWR Report via Enterprise Manager

Problem

You want to generate an AWR report from within Enterprise Manager.

Solution

Within Enterprise Manager, depending on your version, the manner in which to generate an AWR report may differ. There is also generally more than one way to generate an AWR report. In Figure 4-1, this particular screen shows that you enter the beginning and ending snapshot ranges, and after you click the Generate Report button, an AWR HTML report will immediately be displayed within your browser window. A sample screen of the resulting AWR report is shown in Figure 4-2.

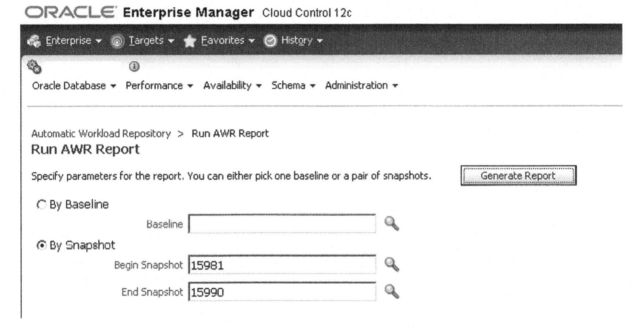

Figure 4-1. *Generating an AWR report within Enterprise Manager*

WORKLOAD REPOSITORY report for

DB Name	DB Id	Instance	Inst num	Startup Time	Release	RAC
	1175007953		1	30-Jun-13 11:06	11.2.0.2.0	NO

Host Name	Platform	CPUs	Cores	Sockets	Memory (GB)
	Linux x86 64-bit	8	8	2	47.04

	Snap Id	Snap Time	Sessions	Cursors/Session
Begin Snap:	15981	21-Jul-13 00:00:11	34	1.2
End Snap:	15990	21-Jul-13 09:00:31	34	1.4
Elapsed:		540.33 (mins)		
DB Time:		2.15 (mins)		

Report Summary

Cache Sizes

	Begin	End		
Buffer Cache:	1,328M	1,280M	Std Block Size:	8K
Shared Pool Size:	1,248M	1,296M	Log Buffer:	11,848K

Figure 4-2. *HTML AWR report*

How It Works

The AWR report via Enterprise Manager can be generated if you have Database Control configured or if you are using Grid Control. You need to be licensed for the Oracle Diagnostics Pack in order to be able to use this feature.

If you are unsure how each snapshot ID corresponds to time, you can run a query to find the snapshots you want based on a specific time period. For instance, if you wanted to see the snapshots generated within the last 4 hours, you could run the following query:

```
column begin_interval_time format a30
column end_interval_time format a30

SELECT snap_id, begin_interval_time, end_interval_time
FROM DBA_HIST_SNAPSHOT
WHERE begin_interval_time > sysdate-1/6
ORDER BY 2;

   SNAP_ID BEGIN_INTERVAL_TIME             END_INTERVAL_TIME
---------- ------------------------------- -------------------------------
     44041 12-OCT-13 11.00.53.841 AM       12-OCT-13 12.00.55.431 PM
     44042 12-OCT-13 12.00.55.431 PM       12-OCT-13 01.00.57.065 PM
     44043 12-OCT-13 01.00.57.065 PM       12-OCT-13 02.00.58.760 PM
```

4-5. Generating an AWR Report for a Single SQL Statement

Problem

You want to see statistics for a single SQL statement and do not want all other associated statistics generated from an AWR report.

Solution

You can run the `awrsqrpt.sql` script, which is very similar to `awrrpt.sql`. You will be prompted for all of the same information, except you will have an additional prompt for a specific SQL ID value—for example:

```
Specify the SQL Id
~~~~~~~~~~~~~~~~~~~
Enter value for sql_id: 5z1b3z8rhutn6
SQL ID specified:  5z1b3z8rhutn6
```

The resulting report zeroes in on information specifically for your SQL statement, including CPU Time, Disk Reads, and Buffer Gets. It also gives a detailed execution plan for review. See the following snippet from the report:

```
Stat Name                            Statement   Per Execution % Snap
-----------------------------------  ----------  -------------- -------
Elapsed Time (ms)                       210,421      105,210.3     9.4
CPU Time (ms)                            22,285       11,142.3     1.6
Executions                                    2            N/A     N/A
Buffer Gets                           1,942,525      971,262.5    12.5
Disk Reads                            1,940,578      970,289.0    14.0
Parse Calls                                   9            4.5     0.0
Rows                                          0            0.0     N/A
User I/O Wait Time (ms)                 195,394            N/A     N/A
Cluster Wait Time (ms)                        0            N/A     N/A
Application Wait Time (ms)                     0            N/A     N/A
Concurrency Wait Time (ms)                     0            N/A     N/A
Invalidations                                 0            N/A     N/A
Version Count                                 2            N/A     N/A
Sharable Mem(KB)                             22            N/A     N/A

Execution Plan
-------------------------------------------------------------------------------
|Id |Operation              |Name    |Rows |Bytes|Cost (%CPU)|Time    |PQ Dis
-------------------------------------------------------------------------------
|  0|SELECT STATEMENT       |        |     |     |73425 (100)|        |
|  1| PX COORDINATOR        |        |     |     |           |        |
|  2|  PX SEND QC (RANDOM)  |:TQ10000|    1|   39|73425   (1)|00:14:42| P->S
|  3|   PX BLOCK ITERATOR   |        |    1|   39|73425   (1)|00:14:42| PCWC
|  4|    TABLE ACCESS FULL  |EMPPART |    1|   39|73425   (1)|00:14:42| PCWP
-------------------------------------------------------------------------------

Full SQL Text

SQL ID       SQL Text
------------ ---------------------------------------------------------------
5z1b3z8rhutn /* SQL Analyze(98, 0) */ select * from emppart where empno > 12345
```

How It Works

Utilizing this feature is a handy way to get historical statistics for a given SQL statement. For current statements, you can continue to use other mechanisms such as AUTOTRACE, but after a SQL statement has been run, using the awrsqrpt.sql script provides an easy mechanism to help analyze past run statements and help retroactively tune poorly performing SQL statements.

If you are unsure how to get the SQL_ID value for your SQL statement, you can retrieve it from the data dictionary. For example, say you have the following SQL statement:

```
SELECT ename, dname
FROM emp NATURAL JOIN dept
USING deptno;
```

You could retrieve the SQL_ID from the data dictionary using the SQL statement shown in the following example:

```
SELECT sql_id, sql_text
FROM v$sqltext
WHERE sql_text LIKE '%from emp natural join dept%';

SQL_ID        SQL_TEXT
------------- ----------------------------------------------------------------
50u87jv5p37uu select ename, dname from emp natural join dept
```

■ **Tip** You can also use the Oracle SQLT utility to do detailed analysis of a given SQL statement. See My Oracle Support Note 215187.1, or the Apress publication 'Oracle SQL Tuning with Oracle SQLTXPLAIN'.

4-6. Creating a Statistical Baseline for Your Database
Problem

You want to establish baseline statistics that represent a normal view of database operations.

Solution

You can create AWR baselines in order to establish a saved workload view for your database, which can be used later for comparison to other AWR snapshots. The purpose of a baseline is to establish a normal workload view of your database for a predefined time period. Performance statistics for an AWR baseline are saved in your database and are not purged automatically. There are two types of baselines—fixed and moving.

Fixed Baselines

The most common type of baseline is called a fixed baseline. This is a single, static view that is meant to represent a normal system workload. To manually create an AWR baseline, you can use the CREATE_BASELINE procedure of the DBMS_WORKLOAD_REPOSITORY PL/SQL package. The following example illustrates how to create a baseline based on a known begin and end date and time for which the baseline will be created:

```
SQL> exec dbms_workload_repository.create_baseline -
    (to_date('2013-07-21:00:00:00','yyyy-mm-dd:hh24:mi:ss'), -
    to_date('2013-07-21:06:00:00','yyyy-mm-dd:hh24:mi:ss'),'Batch Baseline #1');

PL/SQL procedure successfully completed.
```

For the foregoing baseline, we want to establish a normal workload for a data warehouse batch window, which is between midnight and 6 a.m. This baseline will be held indefinitely unless explicitly dropped (see Recipe 4-7 for managing AWR baselines). Any fixed baseline you create stays in effect until a new baseline is created. If you want to have a set expiration for a baseline, you can simply specify the retention period for a baseline when creating it by using the EXPIRATION parameter, which is specified in days:

```
exec dbms_workload_repository.create_baseline( -
start_time=>to_date('2013-07-21:00:00:00','yyyy-mm-dd:hh24:mi:ss'), -
end_time=>to_date('2013-07-21:06:00:00','yyyy-mm-dd:hh24:mi:ss'), -
baseline_name=>'Batch Baseline #1', -
expiration=>30);
```

You can also create a baseline based on already created AWR snapshot IDs. In order to do this, you could run the CREATE_BASELINE procedure as follows:

```
exec dbms_workload_repository.create_baseline( -
start_snap_id=>258,end_snap_id=>268,baseline_name=>'Batch Baseline #1', -
expiration=>30);
```

Moving Baselines

Like the fixed baseline, the moving baseline is used to capture metrics over a period of time. The big difference is the metrics for moving baselines are captured based on the entire AWR retention period. For instance, the default AWR retention is 8 days (see Recipe 4-2 on changing the AWR retention period). These metrics, also called adaptive thresholds, are captured based on the entire 8-day window. Furthermore, the baseline changes with each passing day, as the AWR window for a given database moves day by day. Because of this, the metrics over a given period of time can change as a database evolves and performance loads change over time. A default moving baseline is automatically created—the SYSTEM_MOVING_BASELINE. It is recommended to increase the default AWR retention period, as this may give a more complete set of metrics on which to accurately analyze performance. The maximum size of the moving window is the AWR retention period. To modify the moving window baseline, use the MODIFY_BASELINE_WINDOW_SIZE procedure of the DBMS_WORKLOAD_REPOSITORY package, as in the following example:

```
SQL>  exec dbms_workload_repository.modify_baseline_window_size(30);

PL/SQL procedure successfully completed.
```

How It Works

Setting the AWR retention period is probably the most important thing to configure when utilizing the moving baseline, as all adaptive threshold metrics are based on information from the entire retention period. When setting the retention period for the moving baseline, remember again that it cannot exceed the AWR retention period, else you may get the following error:

```
SQL> exec dbms_workload_repository.modify_baseline_window_size(45);
BEGIN dbms_workload_repository.modify_baseline_window_size(45); END;
*
ERROR at line 1:
ORA-13541: system moving window baseline size (3888000) greater than retention
(2592000)
ORA-06512: at "SYS.DBMS_WORKLOAD_REPOSITORY", line 686
ORA-06512: at line 1
```

If you set your AWR retention to an unlimited value, there still is an upper bound to the moving baseline retention period, and you could receive the following error if you set your moving baseline retention period too high, and your AWR retention period is set to unlimited:

```
exec dbms_workload_repository.modify_baseline_window_size(92);
BEGIN dbms_workload_repository.modify_baseline_window_size(92); END;
*
ERROR at line 1:
ORA-13539: invalid input for modify baseline window size (window_size, 92)
ORA-06512: at "SYS.DBMS_WORKLOAD_REPOSITORY", line 708
ORA-06512: at line 1
```

For fixed baselines, the AWR retention isn't a factor and is a consideration only based on how far back in time you want to compare a snapshot to your baseline. After you have set up any baselines, you can get information on baselines from the data dictionary. To get information on the baselines in your database, you can use a query such as the following one, which would show you any fixed baselines you have configured, as well as the automatically configured moving baseline:

```
column baseline_name format a20
column baseline_id format 99 heading B_ID
column start_id heading STA
column end_id heading END
column expiration heading EXP
set lines 150
SELECT baseline_id, baseline_name, start_snap_id start_id,
       TO_CHAR(start_snap_time, 'yyyy-mm-dd:hh24:mi') start_time,
       end_snap_id end_id,
       TO_CHAR(end_snap_time, 'yyyy-mm-dd:hh24:mi') end_time,
       expiration
  FROM dba_hist_baseline
  ORDER BY baseline_id;

B_ID BASELINE_NAME         STA START_TIME       END END_TIME         EXP
---- -------------------   --- ---------------- --- ---------------- ---
   0 SYSTEM_MOVING_WINDOW    1 2013-07-21:18:00 141 2013-07-27:13:30
   4 Batch Baseline #1     127 2013-07-27:00:00 133 2013-07-27:06:00  30
```

From the foregoing results, the moving baseline includes the entire range of snapshots based on the AWR retention period; therefore the expiration is shown as NULL. You can get similar information by using the SELECT_BASELINE_DETAILS function of the DBMS_WORKLOAD_REPOSITORY package. You do need the baseline_id number to pass into the function to get the desired results:

```
column start_snap_id heading STA
column end_snap_id heading END
SELECT start_snap_id, start_snap_time, end_snap_id,
end_snap_time, pct_total_time pct
FROM (SELECT * FROM
      TABLE(DBMS_WORKLOAD_REPOSITORY.select_baseline_details(4)));


STA START_SNAP_TIME            END END_SNAP_TIME             PCT
--- ------------------------   --- ------------------------  ---
127 27-JUL-13 12.00.46.575 AM  133 27-JUL-13 06.00.33.497 AM 100
```

To get more specific information on the moving baseline in the database, you are drilling down into the statistics for the adaptive metrics. For instance, to see an average and maximum for each metric related to *reads* based on the moving window, you could use the following query:

```
column metric_name format a50
column average format 99999999.99
column maximum format 99999999.99
SELECT metric_name, average, maximum FROM
(SELECT * FROM TABLE
(DBMS_WORKLOAD_REPOSITORY.select_baseline_metric('SYSTEM_MOVING_WINDOW')))
where lower(metric_name) like '%read%'
order by metric_name;


METRIC_NAME                                     AVERAGE      MAXIMUM
----------------------------------------------- --------  ------------
Average Synchronous Single Block Read Latency       .66       821.41
Consistent Read Changes Per Sec                     .54       428.57
Consistent Read Changes Per Txn                    2.07       738.67
Consistent Read Gets Per Sec                       44.46     61030.19
Consistent Read Gets Per Txn                      621.41   1833347.00
Logical Reads Per Sec                              52.00     61030.48
Logical Reads Per Txn                             659.59   1833355.50
Logical Reads Per User Call                       297.06    916677.75
Physical Read Bytes Per Sec                      2159.48   6692928.07
Physical Read IO Requests Per Sec                   .12       511.58
Physical Read Total Bytes Per Sec               39168.45   6721045.90
Physical Read Total IO Requests Per Sec            2.35       514.30
Physical Reads Direct Lobs Per Sec                  .08       598.00
Physical Reads Direct Lobs Per Txn                  .02        55.67
Physical Reads Direct Per Sec                       .08       605.68
Physical Reads Direct Per Txn                       .02        55.67
Physical Reads Per Sec                              .26       817.01
Physical Reads Per Txn                              .59      1231.50

18 rows selected.
```

4-7. Managing AWR Baselines via Enterprise Manager

Problem

You want to create and manage AWR baselines using Enterprise Manager.

Solution

Using Enterprise Manager, you can easily configure or modify baselines. In Figure 4-3, you can see the window where you can establish or modify your existing baselines, including any fixed baselines, as well as the system moving baseline. To create a new fixed baseline, you would click the Create button, which would navigate you to the screen shown in Figure 4-4, where you can configure your new fixed baseline. Within this screen, you name your baseline, and choose between a snapshot-based or time-based baseline.

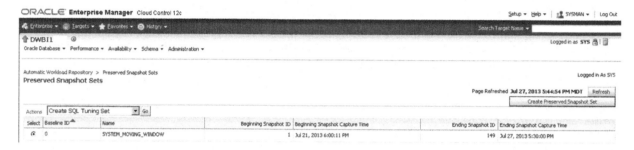

Figure 4-3. *Managing baselines within Enterprise Manager*

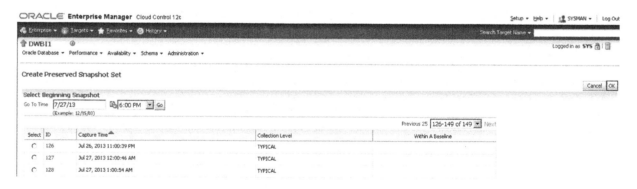

Figure 4-4. *Creating new fixed baseline within Enterprise Manager*

When deciding to work with your existing baselines, click on Actions for available options. Options include creating an SQL tuning set, viewing the AWR report associated with the baseline, and deleting a fixed baseline. The option list is shown in Figure 4-5.

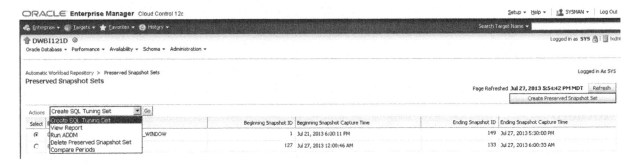

Figure 4-5. *Working with baselines in Enterprise Manager*

How It Works

For any fixed baseline created or the system moving baseline, you can also simply generate an AWR report based on a particular baseline. Figure 4-1 shows how to generate a snapshot-based AWR report by clicking the By Snapshot button. Using this same screen, you can also generate an AWR report for a baseline simply by clicking the By Baseline button.

   If you want to delete a baseline from within Enterprise Manager, simply click the radio button of the baseline you wish to delete, and then click the Delete button, as depicted in Figure 4-6. Figure 4-7 shows how to actually delete the baseline. You can choose to keep or purge the baseline data by clicking the appropriate radio button.

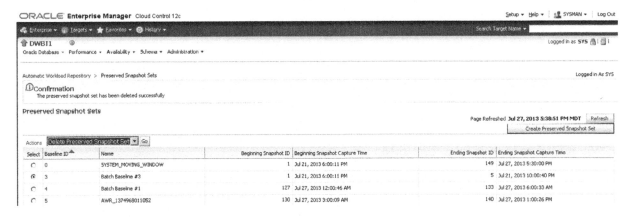

Figure 4-6. *Choosing a baseline to delete*

Figure 4-7. *Deleting a baseline*

■ **Note** You cannot delete the system moving baseline.

4-8. Managing AWR Statistics Repository

Problem

You have AWR snapshots and baselines in place for your database and need to perform regular maintenance activities for your AWR information.

Solution

By using the DBMS_WORKLOAD_REPOSITORY package, you can perform most maintenance on your baselines, including the following:

- Renaming a baseline

- Dropping a baseline

- Dropping a snapshot range

To rename a baseline, use the RENAME_BASELINE procedure of the DBMS_WORKLOAD_REPOSITORY package:

```
SQL>  exec dbms_workload_repository.rename_baseline -
     ('Batch Baseline #9','Batch Baseline #10');

PL/SQL procedure successfully completed.
```

To drop a baseline, simply use the DROP_BASELINE procedure:

```
SQL> exec dbms_workload_repository.drop_baseline('Batch Baseline #1');

PL/SQL procedure successfully completed.
```

If you have decided you have AWR snapshots you no longer need, you can reduce the number of AWR snapshots held within your database by dropping a range of snapshots using the DROP_BASELINE procedure:

```
SQL>  exec dbms_workload_repository.drop_snapshot_range(255,256);

PL/SQL procedure successfully completed.
```

How It Works

In addition to the DBMS_WORKLOAD_REPOSITORY package, there are other things you can do to analyze your AWR information in order to help manage all of the AWR information in your database, including the following:

- Viewing AWR information from the data dictionary

- Moving AWR information to a repository in another database location

If you wanted to store AWR information for an entire grid of databases in a single database, Oracle provides scripts that can be run in order to extract AWR information from a given database, based on a snapshot range, and, in turn, load that information into a different database.

To extract a given snapshot range of AWR information from your database, you need to run the awrextr.sql script. This script is an interactive script and asks for the same kind of information as when you generate an AWR report using the awrrpt.sql script. You need to answer the following questions when running this script:

1. DBID (defaults to DBID of current database)

2. Number of days of snapshots to display for extraction

3. The beginning snapshot number to extract

4. The ending snapshot number to extract

5. Oracle directory in which to place the resulting output file holding all the AWR information for the specified snapshot range; the directory must be entered in upper case.

6. Output file name (defaults to awrdat plus snapshot range numbers)

Keep in mind that the output file generated by this process does take up space, which can vary based on the number of sessions active at snapshot time. Each individual snapshot needed for extraction can take up 1 MB or more of storage, so carefully gauge the amount of snapshots needed. If necessary, you can break the extraction process into pieces if there is inadequate space on a given target directory.

In addition, for each output file generated, a small output log file is also generated, with information about the extraction process, which can be useful in determining if the information extracted matches what you think has been extracted. This is a valuable audit to ensure you have extracted the AWR information you need.

Once you have the extract output file(s), you need to transport them (if necessary) to the target server location for loading into the target database location. The load process is done using the awrload.sql script. What is needed for input into the load script includes the following:

1. Oracle directory in which to place the resulting output file holding all the AWR information for the specified snapshot range; the directory must be entered in upper case.

2. File name (would be the same name as entered in number 6 of the extraction process (for the awrextr.sql script); when entering the file name, exclude the .dmp suffix, as it will be appended automatically.

3. Target schema (default schema name is AWR_STAGE)

4. Target tablespace for object that will be created (provides list of choices)

5. Target temporary tablespace for object that will be created (provides list of choices)

After the load of the data is complete, the AWR data is moved to the SYS schema in the data dictionary tables within the target database. The temporary target schema (for example, AWR_STAGE) is then dropped.

In order to generate an AWR report generated from one database that is then loaded into a different database, use the AWR_REPORT_TEXT function of the DBMS_WORKLOAD_REPOSITORY package. For example, let's say we loaded and stored snapshots 300 through 366 into our separate AWR database. If we wanted to generate an AWR report for the information generated between snapshots 365 and 366 for a given database, we would run the following command, with the DBID of the originating, source database, as well as the beginning and ending snapshot numbers as follows:

```
SELECT  dbms_workload_repository.awr_report_text
        (l_dbid=>2334201269,l_inst_num=>1,l_bid=>365,l_eid=>366)
FROM dual;
```

4-9. Creating AWR Baselines Automatically

Problem

You want to periodically create baselines in your database automatically.

Solution

You can create an AWR repeating template, which gives you the ability to have baselines created automatically based on a predefined interval and time frame. By using the CREATE_BASELINE_TEMPLATE procedure within the DBMS_WORKLOAD_REPOSITORY package, you can have a fixed baseline automatically created for this repeating interval and time frame. See the following example to set up an AWR template:

```
SQL> alter session set nls_date_format = 'yyyy-mm-dd:hh24:mi:ss';

SQL> exec DBMS_WORKLOAD_REPOSITORY.create_baseline_template( -
>      day_of_week           => 'WEDNESDAY', -
>      hour_in_day           => 0, -
>      duration              => 6, -
>      start_time            => '2013-07-23:00:00:00', -
>      end_time              => '2013-07-23:06:00:00', -
>      baseline_name_prefix  => 'Batch Baseline ', -
>      template_name         => 'Batch Template', -
>      expiration            => 365);

PL/SQL procedure successfully completed.
```

For the foregoing template, a fixed baseline will be created based on the midnight to 6 a.m. window every Wednesday. In this case, this template creates baselines for a normal batch window time frame.

If you are using Enterprise Manager, you can create a template using the same parameters. *See* Figure 4-8 for an example.

Figure 4-8. *Creating an AWR template*

How It Works

One of the primary reasons to create baselines automatically is to maintain a current view of a statistical baseline. Over time, the load on a given database can change, and creating a single, fixed baseline at a point in time, while guaranteeing a specific view of database activity over a given period, can simply become stale over time. By creating baselines automatically at given intervals, the statistical baseline will always represent a recent view of database activity.

If you need to drop a template you created, you simply use the DROP_BASELINE_TEMPLATE procedure from the DBMS_WORKLOAD_REPOSITORY package. See the following example:

```
SQL> exec dbms_workload_repository.drop_baseline_template('Batch Template');

PL/SQL procedure successfully completed.
```

If you wish to view information on any templates you have created, you can query the DBA_HIST_BASELINE_TEMPLATE view. See the following sample query:

```
column template_name format a14
column prefix format a14
column hr format 99
column dur format 999
column exp format 999
column day format a3

SELECT template_name, baseline_name_prefix prefix,
to_char(start_time,'mm/dd/yy:hh24') start_time,
to_char(end_time,'mm/dd/yy:hh24') end_time,
substr(day_of_week,1,3) day, hour_in_day hr, duration dur, expiration exp,
to_char(last_generated,'mm/dd/yy:hh24') last
FROM dba_hist_baseline_template;
```

```
TEMPLATE_NAME   PREFIX           START_TIME    END_TIME     DAY  HR  DUR  EXP LAST
--------------- ---------------- ------------- ------------ ---  --- ---- ---- -----------
Batch Template  Batch Baseline   07/23/13:00   07/23/13:06  WED   0    6  365 07/23/13:00
```

4-10. Quickly Analyzing AWR Output

Problem

You have generated an AWR report and want to quickly interpret key portions of the report to determine if there are performance issues for your database.

Solution

The AWR report, like its predecessors Statspack and UTLBSTAT/UTLESTAT for earlier versions of Oracle, has a multitude of statistics to help you determine how your database is functioning and performing. There are many sections of the report. The first three places on the report to gauge how your database is performing are as follows:

1. DB Time

2. Instance Efficiency

3. Top 10 Foreground Events by Wait Time

The first section displayed on the report shows a summary of the snapshot window for your report, as well as a brief look at the elapsed time, which represents the snapshot window, and the DB time, which represents activity on your database. If the DB time exceeds the elapsed time, it denotes a busy database. If it is a lot higher than the elapsed time, it may mean that some sessions are waiting for resources. While not specific, it can give you a quick view to see if your overall database is busy and possibly overtaxed. We can see from the following example of this section that this is a very busy database by comparing the elapsed time to the DB time. In this case it is a data warehouse database that has both long-running data loading cycles, as well as some long-running user queries.

```
             Snap Id     Snap Time       Sessions Curs/Sess
            ---------  -------------------  --------  ---------
Begin Snap:   43210   27-Jul-13 00:00:13      75       5.3
  End Snap:   43216   27-Jul-13 06:00:53     275       5.4
  Elapsed:              360.67 (mins)
  DB Time:            12,276.01 (mins)
```

The instance efficiency section gives you a very quick view to determine if things are running adequately on your database. As indicated from the section, the ideal target for these metrics is 100%. If any of the metrics within the section fall below a general threshold of 90%, it may be an area to investigate. The Parse CPU to Parse Elapsd metric often shows a low percentage on many databases, as indicated in the below example. While the target is 100% for this metric, it is not necessary a cause for great alarm. It does, however, indicate waits occurs during parsing and may require analysis to determine why the waits are occurring during the parsing of SQL statements.

```
Instance Efficiency Percentages (Target 100%)
~~~~~~~~~~~~~~~~~~~~~~~~~~~~~~~~~~~~~~~~~~~~~~~~
              Buffer Nowait %:   99.64        Redo NoWait %:   99.99
              Buffer  Hit   %:   91.88    In-memory Sort %:   99.87
              Library Hit   %:   98.92        Soft Parse %:   94.30
           Execute to Parse %:   93.70        Latch Hit %:   99.89
   Parse CPU to Parse Elapsd %:    2.10      % Non-Parse CPU:   99.75
```

The third place to get a quick glance at your database performance is the Top 10 Foreground Events section. This section gives you a quick look at exactly where the highest amount of resources are being consumed within your database for the snapshot period. Based on these results, it may show you that there is an inordinate amount of time spent performing full-table scans or getting data across a network database link. The following example shows that the highest amount of resources is being used performing index searches (noted by "db file sequential read"). We can see there is significant time on "local write wait", "enq: CF – contention", and "free buffer waits", which gives us a quick view of what possible contention and wait events are for our database and gives us immediate direction for investigation and analysis.

```
Top 10 Foreground Events by Total Wait Time
~~~~~~~~~~~~~~~~~~~~~~~~~~~~~~~~~~~~~~~~~~~~~~~
```

Event	Waits	Total Time (sec)	Wait Avg(ms)	Wait time	% DB Wait Class
db file sequential read	3,653,606	96,468	26	20.8	User I/O
local write wait	94,358	67,996	721	14.7	User I/O
enq: CF - contention	18,621	46,944	2521	10.1	Other
free buffer waits	3,627,548	38,249	11	8.3	Configurat
db file scattered read	2,677,267	32,400	12	7.0	User I/O
SQL*Net message to client	347,401	.1	0	1.0	Network
db file sequential read	13	0	3	.3	User I/O
log file sync	20	0	0	.1	Commit
Disk file operations I/O	27	0	0	.0	User I/O
SQL*Net break/reset to client	4	0	0	.0	Applicatio

How It Works

After looking at the DB Time, Instance Efficiency, and Top 10 Foreground Events sections, if you want to look in more detail at the sections of a given AWR report, refer to Recipe 7-17 in Chapter 7 for more information. Because the sheer volume of information in the AWR report is so daunting, it is strongly recommended to create baselines that represent a normal processing window. Then, AWR snapshots can be compared to the baselines, and metrics that may just look like a number on a given AWR report will stand out when a particular metric is significantly above or below a normal range.

4-11. Manually Getting Active Session Information

Problem

You need to do performance analysis on sessions that run too frequently or are too short to be available on AWR snapshots. The AWR snapshots are not taken often enough to capture the information that you need.

Solution

You can use the Oracle Active Session History (ASH) information in order to get real-time or near real-time session information. While the AWR information is very useful, it is bound by the reporting periods, which are by default run every hour on your database. The ASH information has active session information and is sampled every second from V$SESSION, and it can show more real-time or near real-time session information to assist in doing performance analysis on your database. There are a few ways to get active session information from the database:

- Running the canned ASH report
- Running an ASH report from within Enterprise Manager (*see* Recipe 4-12)
- Getting ASH information from the data dictionary (*see* Recipe 4-13)

The easiest method to get information on active sessions is to run the ashrpt.sql script, which is similar in nature to the awrrpt.sql script that is run when generating an AWR report. When you run the ashrpt.sql script, it asks you for the following:

- Report type (text or HTML)
- Begin time for report (defaults to current time minus 15 minutes)
- End time for report (defaults to current time)
- Report name

There are many sections to the ASH report. *See* Table 4-2 for a brief description of most of the sections found on the report. See the following snippet from many of the sections of the ASH report. Some sections have been shortened for brevity.

```
Top User Events   DB/Inst: ORCL/ORCL  (Jun 18 12:00 to 12:45)
```

Event	Event Class	% Activity	Avg Active Sessions
CPU + Wait for CPU	CPU	35.36	1.66
db file scattered read	User I/O	33.07	1.55
db file sequential read	User I/O	21.33	1.00
read by other session	User I/O	6.20	0.29
direct path read temp	User I/O	2.59	0.12

Top Background Events DB/Inst: ORCL/ORCL (Jun 18 12:00 to 12:45)

Event	Event Class	% Activity	Avg Active Sessions
Log archive I/O	System I/O	12.77	0.68
CPU + Wait for CPU	CPU	6.38	0.34
log file parallel write	System I/O	5.66	0.30
log file sequential read	System I/O	4.91	0.26
log file sync	Commit	1.06	0.06

Top Event P1/P2/P3 Values DB/Inst: ORCL/ORCL (Jun 18 12:00 to 12:45)

Event	% Event	P1 Value, P2 Value, P3 Value	% Activity
Parameter 1	Parameter 2	Parameter 3	
db file scattered read	17.30	"775","246084","16"	0.14
file#	block#	blocks	
Datapump dump file I/O	6.32	"1","32","2147483647"	6.32
count	intr	timeout	
RMAN backup & recovery I/O	5.83	"1","32","2147483647"	5.80
count	intr	timeout	

Top Service/Module   DB/Inst: ORCL/ORCL (Jun 18 12:00 to 12:45)

Service	Module	% Activity	Action	% Action
SYS$BACKGROUND	UNNAMED	31.00	UNNAMED	31.00
	DBMS_SCHEDULER	18.87	GATHER_STATS_JOB	18.87
	Data Pump Worker	18.87	APP_IMPORT	18.87
SYS$BACKGROUND	MMON_SLAVE	1.95	Auto-Flush Slave A	1.42

Top SQL Command Types DB/Inst: ORCL/ORCL (Jun 18 12:00 to 12:45)

SQL Command Type	Distinct SQLIDs	% Activity	Avg Active Sessions
INSERT	2	18.88	1.00
SELECT	27	2.36	0.12

Top SQL Statements DB/Inst: ORCL/ORCL (Jun 18 12:00 to 12:45)

```
        SQL ID    Planhash % Activity Event                              % Event
------------- ----------- ---------- ------------------------------ ----------
av2f2stsjfr5k  3774074286     1.16 CPU + Wait for CPU                      0.80
  select a.tablespace_name, round(sum_free/sum_bytes,2)*100 pct_free from
(select tablespace_name, sum(bytes) sum_bytes from sys.dba_data_files group by
tablespace_name) a, (select tablespace_name, sum(bytes) sum_free , max(bytes)
 bigchunk from sys.dba_free_space group by tablespace_name) b where a.table
```

Top Sessions   DB/Inst: ORCL/ORCL (Jun 18 12:00 to 12:45)

Sid, Serial#	% Activity	Event	% Event		
User		Program	# Samples Active		XIDs
365, 3613	18.87	CPU + Wait for CPU		12.29	
D_USER		oracle@oraprod (DW01)	1,755/2,700 [65%]		8
		Datapump dump file I/O		6.32	
			903/2,700 [33%]		8
515, 8721	18.87	db file scattered read		17.26	
SYS		oracle@oraprod (J000)	2,465/2,700 [91%]		1

Top Blocking Sessions DB/Inst: ORCL/ORCL (Jun 18 12:00 to 12:45)

Blocking Sid	% Activity	Event Caused	% Event		
User		Program	# Samples Active		XIDs
549, 1	2.09	enq: CF - contention		2.03	
SYS		oracle@oraprod (CKPT)	248/2,700 [9%]		0

Top DB Objects   DB/Inst: ORCL/ORCL (Jun 18 12:00 to 12:45)

Object ID	% Activity	Event	% Event
Object Name (Type)			Tablespace
1837336	3.25	db file scattered read	3.25
STG.EMPPART.EMPPART10_11P (TAB EMP_S			
1837324	3.05	db file scattered read	3.05
STG.EMPPART.EMPPART10_10P (TAB EMP_S			

Top DB Files   DB/Inst: ORCL/ORCL   (Jun 18 12:00 to 12:45)

```
        File ID % Activity Event                          % Event
--------------- ---------- ------------------------------ ----------
File Name                                     Tablespace
------------------------------------------------------- -----------------
        200        6.31 Datapump dump file I/O                6.31
/opt/vol01/ORCL/app_s_016.dbf                 APP_S
```

Activity Over Time   DB/Inst: ORCL/ORCL   (Jun 18 12:00 to 12:45)

```
                        Slot                              Event
Slot Time (Duration)    Count Event                       Count % Event
-------------------- -------- ------------------------------ -------- -------
12:00:00   (5.0 min)    2,672 CPU + Wait for CPU            1,789   12.52
                              db file scattered read          290    2.03
                              enq: CF - contention            290    2.03
12:05:00   (5.0 min)    2,586 CPU + Wait for CPU            1,396    9.77
                              RMAN backup & recovery I/O      305    2.14
                              db file scattered read          287    2.01
12:10:00   (5.0 min)    2,392 CPU + Wait for CPU            1,068    7.48
                              Log archive I/O                 423    2.96
                              RMAN backup & recovery I/O      356    2.49
...
```

Table 4-2. *ASH Report Section Information for the Specified Report Period*

Section Name	Description
General Report Information	Contains database name, reporting period, CPU and memory information
Top User Events	Displays the top run user events for the reporting period
Top Background Events	Shows the top wait events in the database
Top P1/P2/P3 Events	Lists top wait event parameter values based on highest percentages, ordered in descending order
Top Service Module	Displays the top services or module names
Top Client IDs	Shows the top users
Top SQL Command Types	Shows all the SQL commands run
Phases of Execution	Lists phases of execution, such as SQL, PL/SQL, and Java compilation, execution
Top SQL with Top Events	Lists the SQL statements with the highest percentages of sampled session activity and associated top wait events
Top SQL with Top Row Sources	Shows SQL statements that accounted for the highest percentages of sampled session activity and associated execution plan information

(*continued*)

Table 4-2. (*continued*)

Section Name	Description
Top SQL Statements	Displays the top consuming SQL statement text
Top SQL Using Literals	Shows SQL statements using literals; this can assist in determining offending SQL for shared pool contention.
Parsing Module/Action	Displays module/action that accounted for highest percentages of sampled session activity while parsing
Top PL/SQL Procedures	Displays the PL/SQL programs run
Java Workload	Shows top Java program information
Call Types	Displays information on top program call types that have occurred during the sampled session timeframe
Top Sessions	Displays the top sessions within the database
Top Blocking Sessions	Sessions that are blocking other sessions
Top Sessions Running PQs	Sessions running parallel query processes
Top DB Objects	Objects referenced
Top DB Files	Files referenced
Top Latches	Latch information for the reporting period
Activity Over Time	Shows top three consuming events for each 5-minute reporting period shown on report

How It Works

Retrieving ASH information is necessary if you need to get session information more current than you can retrieve from the AWR report. Again, AWR information is generated only hourly by default. ASH information is gathered every second from V$SESSION and stores the most useful session information to help gauge database performance at any given moment.

The ASH information is stored within a circular buffer in the SGA. Oracle documentation states that the buffer size is calculated as follows:

```
Max [Min [ #CPUs * 2 MB, 5% of Shared Pool Size, 30MB ], 1MB ]
```

The amount of time that the information is stored within the data dictionary depends on the activity within your database. You may need to view the DBA_HIST_ACTIVE_SESS_HISTORY historical view in order to get the ASH information you need if your database is very active. For an example of querying the DBA_HIST_ACTIVE_SESS_HISTORY view, *see* Recipe 4-13. To quickly see how much data is held in your historical view, you could simply get the earliest SAMPLE_TIME from the DBA_HIST_ACTIVE_SESS_HISTORY view:

```
SELECT min(sample_time) FROM dba_hist_active_sess_history;

MIN(SAMPLE_TIME)
-------------------------------------------------------------------------
21-JUL-13 04.52.52.881 PM
```

The MMON background process, which manages the AWR hourly snapshots, also flushes ASH information to the historical view at the same time. If there is heavy activity on the database, and the buffer fills between the hourly AWR snapshots, the MMNL background process will wake up and flush the ASH data to the historical view.

The V$ACTIVE_SESSION_HISTORY and DBA_HIST_ACTIVE_SESS_HISTORY views contain much more detailed information than just the samples shown within this recipe, and you can drill down and get much more information at the session level, if desired, including information regarding actual SQL statements, the SQL operations, blocking session information, and file I/O information.

4-12. Getting ASH Information from Enterprise Manager

Problem

You want to get to ASH information from within Enterprise Manager because you use Enterprise Manager for performance tuning activities.

Solution

The ASH report generated from within Enterprise Manager has the same sections as specified in Table 4-1 (*see* Recipe 4-11). To generate an ASH report from within Enterprise Manager, you generally need to be in the Performance tab, depending on your particular version of Enterprise Manager. As with running the ashrpt.sql script, you need to specify the beginning and ending time frames for the report period desired. *See* Figure 4-9 for an example of the screen used to generate an ASH report and Figure 4-10 for a sample of the ASH report output:

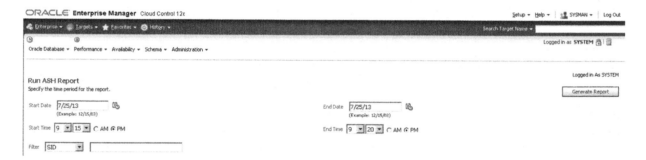

Figure 4-9. *Generating ASH report from Enterprise Manager*

Figure 4-10. *Sample ASH report from Enterprise Manager*

How It Works

When generating an ASH report, you have the option to filter on specific criteria. In Figure 4-11, see the Filter drop-down menu. If you have a very active database, and already want to zero in on a specific SQL_ID, for example, you can choose the SQL_ID option from the Filter drop-down menu, and enter the SQL_ID value. The resulting report will show information based only on the filtered criteria.

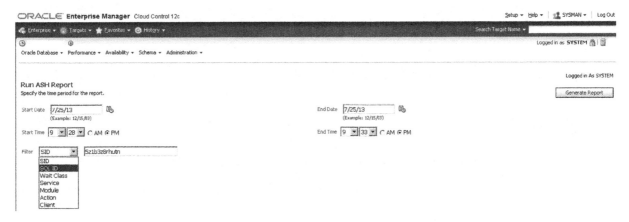

Figure 4-11. *Customizing ASH report by filter*

The choices to filter on include the following:

- SID

- SQL_ID

- Wait Class

- Service

- Module

- Action

- Client

Many of the foregoing filters can be found in the V$SESSION view. For a list of the possible wait classes, you can query the DBA_HIST_EVENT_NAME view as shown in the following example:

```
SELECT DISTINCT wait_class FROM dba_hist_event_name order by 1;

WAIT_CLASS
-------------------------
Administrative
Application
Cluster
Commit
Concurrency
Configuration
Idle
```

```
Network
Other
Queueing
Scheduler
System I/O
User I/O
```

4-13. Getting ASH Information from the Data Dictionary

Problem

You want to see what ASH information is kept in Oracle's data dictionary.

Solution

There are a couple of data dictionary views you can use to get ASH information. The first, V$ACTIVE_SESSION_HISTORY, can be used to get information on current or recent sessions within your database. The second, DBA_HIST_ACTIVE_SESS_HISTORY, is used to store older, historical ASH information.

If you wanted to see the datafiles associated with waits, which could help pinpoint access hot spots in your database, and you could perform some file management and reorganization activities to alleviate such contention, you could issue the following query:

```
SELECT
  d.file_id file#, d.file_name, count(*) wait_count,  sum(s.time_waited) time_waited
FROM
  v$active_session_history s,
  dba_data_files d
WHERE
  d.file_id = s.current_file#
GROUP BY d.file_id, d.file_name
ORDER BY 3 desc;
```

```
    FILE# FILE_NAME                                 WAIT_COUNT TIME_WAITED
---------- ------------------------------------- ---------- -----------
        1 /datafile/o1_mf_system_8yrs259o_.dbf         306   153058479
        3 /datafile/o1_mf_sysaux_8yrs0g3f_.dbf         178     3236502
        6 /datafile/o1_mf_users_8yrs3whc_.dbf           14     8381142
        4 /datafile/o1_mf_undotbs1_8yrs3xlq_.dbf         4           0
```

If you wanted to see the top five events and their total wait time for activity within the past 15 minutes in your database, you could issue the following query:

```
select * from (
SELECT NVL(event, 'ON CPU') event, COUNT(*) total_wait_tm
FROM   v$active_session_history
WHERE  sample_time > SYSDATE - 15/(24*60)
GROUP BY event
ORDER BY 2 desc
)
where rownum <= 5;
```

```
EVENT                        TOTAL_WAIT_TM
---------------------------- -------------
db file scattered read                2546
read by other session                 1152
db file sequential read                800
Datapump dump file I/O                 383
direct path read                       141
```

If you wanted to get session-specific information, and wanted to see the top five sessions that were using the most CPU resources within the last 15 minutes, you could issue the following query:

```
column username format a12
column module format a30

SELECT * FROM
(
SELECT s.username, s.module, s.sid, s.serial#, count(*)
FROM v$active_session_history h, v$session s
WHERE h.session_id = s.sid
AND    h.session_serial# = s.serial#
AND    session_state= 'ON CPU' AND
       sample_time > sysdate - interval '15' minute
GROUP BY s.username, s.module, s.sid, s.serial#
ORDER BY count(*) desc
)
where rownum <= 5;
```

```
USERNAME    MODULE                          SID    SERIAL#   COUNT(*)
----------  ------------------------------  -----  --------  --------
SYS         DBMS_SCHEDULER                   536         9        43
APPLOAD     etl1@app1 (TNS V1-V3)           1074      3588        16
APPLOAD     ctl1@app1 (TNS V1-V3)           1001      4004        12
APPLOAD     etl1@app1 (TNS V1-V3)            968       108         5
DBSNMP      emagent@ora1 (TNS V1-V3)         524         3         2
```

The SESSION_STATE column has two valid values, ON CPU and WAITING, which denote whether a session is active or is waiting for resources. If you wanted to see the sessions that are waiting for resources, you could issue the same query as previously, with a SESSION_STATE of WAITING.

How It Works

The DBA_HIST_ACTIVE_SESS_HISTORY view can give you historical information on sessions that have aged out of the V$ACTIVE_SESSION_HISTORY view. Let's say you had a day when performance was particularly bad on your database. You could zero in on historical session information for a given time frame, provided it is still held within the DBA_HIST_ACTIVE_SESS_HISTORY view. For instance, if you wanted to get the users that were consuming the most resources for a given day when performance was poor, you could issue the following query:

```
SELECT * FROM
(
SELECT u.username, h.module, h.session_id sid,
       h.session_serial# serial#, count(*)
FROM dba_hist_active_sess_history h, dba_users u
WHERE h.user_id = u.user_id
AND    session_state= 'ON CPU'
AND   (sample_time between to_date('2013-07-25:00:00:00','yyyy-mm-dd:hh24:mi:ss')
AND    to_date('2013-07-25:23:59:59','yyyy-mm-dd:hh24:mi:ss'))
AND u.username != 'SYS'
GROUP BY u.username, h.module, h.session_id, h.session_serial#
ORDER BY count(*) desc
)
where rownum <= 5;
```

```
USERNAME   MODULE                      SID    SERIAL#    COUNT(*)
---------  --------------------  ----------  ----------  ----------
RPTUSER    wireportserver.exe          637      15451        1483
LEVANS     Golden32.exe                947      22617        1082
DTOWNS     SQL*Plus                   3146      35789         251
APPLOAD1   etl1@app1 (TNS V1-V3)      2204      22055         131
RPTUSER    wireportserver.exe          323       7381          92
```

To then zero in on the database objects, you could issue the following query for the same time frame:

```
SELECT * FROM
(
select * from (
SELECT o.object_name, o.object_type, s.event, s.time_waited
FROM dba_hist_active_sess_history s, dba_objects o
WHERE s.sample_time
between to_date('2013-07-27:00:00:00','yyyy-mm-dd:hh24:mi:ss')
AND    to_date('2013-07-27:23:59:59','yyyy-mm-dd:hh24:mi:ss')
AND s.current_obj# = o.object_id
ORDER BY 4 desc
)
WHERE rownum <= 5;
```

```
OBJECT_NAME         OBJECT_TYPE         EVENT                       TIME_WAITED
------------------  ------------------  --------------------------  -----------
REVENUE_FACT        TABLE SUBPARTITION  PX Deq: Table Q Get Keys        2561946
REVENUE_FACT        TABLE SUBPARTITION  PX Deq: Table Q Get Keys        2560914
ACCTING_DIM         TABLE               DFS lock handle                 1959179
ACCTING_DIM         TABLE               enq: SS - contention            1955552
AUD$                TABLE               DFS lock handle                 1851428
```

CHAPTER 5

■ ■ ■

Minimizing System Contention

It's not uncommon for Oracle DBAs to field calls about a user being locked or "blockcd" in the database. Oracle's locking behavior is extremely sophisticated and supports simultaneous use of the database by multiple users. However, on occasion, it's possible for a user to block another user's work, mostly because of flaws in application design. This chapter explains how Oracle handles locks and how to identify a session that's blocking others.

An Oracle database can experience two main types of contention for resources. The first is contention for transaction locks on a table's rows. The second type of contention is that caused by simultaneous requests for areas of the shared memory (SGA), resulting in latch contention. In addition to showing you how to troubleshoot typical locking issues, we will show how to handle various types of latch contention in your database.

Oracle Wait Interface is Oracle's internal mechanism for classifying and measuring the different types of waits for resources in an Oracle instance. Understanding Oracle wait events is *the* key to instance tuning because high waits slow down response time. We will explain the Oracle Wait Interface in this chapter and show you how to reduce the most common Oracle wait events that beguile Oracle DBAs. We will show you how to use various SQL scripts to unravel the mysteries of the Oracle Wait Interface, and we will also show how to use Oracle Enterprise Manager to quickly track down the SQL statements and sessions that are responsible for contention in the database.

5-1. Understanding Response Time
Problem

You want to understand what database response time is and its relationship with wait time.

Solution

The most crucial performance indicator in a database is response time. Response time is the time it takes to get a response from the database for a query that a client sends to the database. Response time is simply the sum of two components:

```
response time = processing time + wait time
```

The foregoing relationship is also frequently represented as $R = S + W$, where R is the response time, S is the service time, and W stands for the wait time. The processing time component is the actual time spent by the database processing the request. Wait time, on the other hand, is time actually wasted by the database—it's the time the database spends waiting for resources such as a lock on a table's rows, library cache latch, or any of the numerous resources that a query needs to complete its processing. Oracle has hundreds of official wait events, a dozen or so of which are crucial to troubleshooting slow-running queries.

Do You Have a Wait Problem?

It's easy to find out the percentage of time the instance has spent waiting for resources instead of actually executing. Issue the following query to find out the relative percentages of wait times and actual CPU processing in the database:

```
SQL> select metric_name, value
  2 from v$sysmetric
  3 where metric_name in ('Database CPU Time Ratio',
  4 'Database Wait Time Ratio') and
  5 intsize_csec =
  6 (select max(INTSIZE_CSEC) from V$SYSMETRIC);

METRIC_NAME                          VALUE
-------------------------------      -----------
Database Wait Time Ratio             11.371689
Database CPU Time Ratio              87.831890
SQL>
```

In general, if the results of this query show a very high value for the Database Wait Time Ratio or if the Database Wait Time Ratio is much greater than the Database CPU Time Ratio, the database is spending more time waiting than processing and you must dig deeper into the Oracle wait events to identify the specific wait events causing this.

Find Detailed Information

You can use the following Oracle views to find out detailed information of what a wait event indicates that a database instance is actually waiting for and how long it has waited for each resource.

- **V$SESSION**: This view shows the specific resource currently being waited for, as well as the event last waited for in each session.

- **V$SESSION_WAIT**: This view lists either the event currently being waited for or the event last waited on for each session. It also shows the wait state and the wait time.

- **V$SESSION_WAIT_HISTORY**: This view shows the last ten wait events for each current session.

- **V$SESSION_EVENT**: This view shows the cumulative history of events waited on for each session. The data in this view is available only so long as a session is active.

- **V$SYSTEM_EVENT**: This view shows each wait event and the time the entire instance has waited on that event since you started the instance.

- **V$SYSTEM_WAIT_CLASS**: This view shows wait event statistics by wait classes.

How It Works

Your goal in tuning performance is to minimize the total response time. If the Database Wait Time Ratio (in the query shown in the "Solution" section) is high, your response time will also be high because of waits or bottlenecks in your system. On the other hand, high values for the Database CPU Time Ratio indicate a well-running database, with few waits or bottlenecks. The Database CPU Time Ratio is calculated by dividing the total CPU used by the database by the Oracle time model statistic DB Time. You must be cautious, however, and make sure that a high Database CPU Time Ratio isn't because of a session simply burning CPU cycles through wasteful work such as spinning on a latch, because of excessive parsing (even soft parsing), or because of performing needless, consistent gets because of inefficient execution plans.

Oracle uses *time model statistics* to measure the time spent in the database by the type of operation. Database time, or DB Time, is the most important time model statistic; it represents the total time spent in database calls and serves as a measure of total instance workload. Database time is total time spent by user processes either actively working or actively waiting in a database call. The DB Time we're referring to here (and the one referred to by AWR and ADDM reports) is the sum of DB Time over all sessions. DB Time is computed by adding the CPU time and wait time of all sessions (excluding the waits for idle events). An AWR report shows the total DB Time for the instance (in the section "Time Model System Stats") during the period covered by the AWR snapshots. If the time model statistic DB CPU consumes most of the database time for the instance, it shows the database was actively processing most of the time. Database time tuning, or understanding how the database is spending its time, is fundamental to understanding performance.

The total time spent by foreground sessions making database calls consists of I/O time, CPU time, and time spent waiting because of nonidle events. Your database time will increase as the system load increases; that is, as more users log on and larger queries are executed, the greater the system load. However, even in the absence of an increase in system load, database time can increase because of deterioration either in I/O or in application performance. As application performance degrades, wait time will increase, and consequently database time will increase.

Database time is captured by internal instrumentation, ASH, AWR, and ADDM, and you can find detailed performance information by querying various views or through Enterprise Manager.

■ **Note** If the host system is CPU-bound, you'll see an increase in database time. You must first tune CPU usage before focusing on wait events in that particular case.

The V$SESSION_WAIT view shows more detailed information than the V$SESSION_EVENT and V$SYSTEM_EVENT views. While both the V$SESSION_EVENT and V$SESSION_WAIT views show that there are waits such as the event db file scattered read, for example, only the V$SESSION_WAIT view shows information such as the amount of time waited for the current wait (SECONDS_IN_WAIT) and the wait state. The STATE column in V$SESSION_WAIT captures the wait state, which could be one of the following:

- WAITING: Session is currently waiting

- WAITED UNKNOWN TIME: Duration of the last wait is unknown (value when you set the parameter TIMED_STATISTICS to false)

- WAITED SHORT TIME: Last wait was less than 100th of a second

- WAITED KNOWN TIME: Duration of the last wait is specified in the WAIT_TIME column

---

■ **Note** The Automatic Workload Repository (AWR) queries the V$SYSTEM_EVENT view for its wait event–related analysis.

You can first query the V$SYSTEM_EVENT view to rank the top wait events by total and average time waited for that event. You can then drill down to the wait event level by focusing on the events at the top of the event list. In addition to providing information about blocking and blocked users and the current wait events, the V$SESSION view also shows the objects that are causing the problem by providing the file number and block number for the object.

5-2. Identifying SQL Statements with the Most Waits
Problem

You want to identify the SQL statements responsible for the most waits in your database.

Solution

Execute the following query to identify the SQL statements that are experiencing the most waits in your database:

```
SQL> select ash.user_id,
  2  u.username,
  3  s.sql_text,
  4  sum(ash.wait_time +
  5  ash.time_waited) ttl_wait_time
  6  from v$active_session_history ash,
  7  v$sqlarea s,
  8  dba_users u
  9  where ash.sample_time between sysdate - 60/2880 and sysdate
 10  and ash.sql_id = s.sql_id
 11  and ash.user_id = u.user_id
 12  group by ash.user_id,s.sql_text, u.username
 13* order by ttl_wait_time
SQL>
```

The preceding query ranks queries that ran during the past 30 minutes, according to the total time waited by each query.

How It Works

When you're experiencing a performance problem, it's a good idea to see which SQL statements are waiting the most. These are the statements that are using most of the database's resources. To find the queries that are waiting the most, you must sum the values in the wait_time and time_waited columns of V$ACTIVE_SESSION_HISTORY for a specific SQL statement. To do this, you must join the V$SQLAREA view with the V$ACTIVE_SESSION_HISTORY view, using SQL_ID as the join column.

■ **Note**　To query the V$ACTIVE_SESSION_HISTORY view, you must first license the Oracle Database Diagnostic Pack and the Tuning Pack. If you can't license the packs, all is not lost; you can still examine wait times through views such as V$SQLAREA.

Besides the SQL_ID of the SQL statements, the V$ACTIVE_SESSION_HISTORY view contains information about the execution plans used by the SQL statements. You can use this information to identify why a SQL statement is experiencing a high number of waits. You can also run an active session history (ASH) report, using a SQL script or through Oracle Enterprise Manager, to get details about the top SQL statements in the sampled session activity. The Top SQL section of an ASH report helps you identify the high-load SQL statements that are responsible for performance problems. Examining the Top SQL report may show you, for example, that one bad query is responsible for most of the database activity.

5-3. Analyzing Wait Events
Problem

You want to analyze Oracle wait events while troubleshooting database performance.

Solution

Several recipes in this chapter show you how to analyze the most important Oracle wait events. It's not uncommon to find that a significant portion of the total wait time in most cases is because of I/O–related waits, such as those caused by either full table scans or indexed reads. While indexed reads may seem to be completely normal on the face of it, too many indexed reads can also slow down performance. Therefore, you must investigate why the database is performing a large number of indexed reads. For example, if you see the db file sequential read event (indicates indexed reads) at the top of the wait event list, you must look a bit further to see how the database is accumulating these read events. If you find that the database is performing hundreds of thousands of query executions, with each query doing only a few indexed reads, that's fine. However, if you find that just a couple of queries in an OLTP environment are contributing to a high number of logical reads, then, most likely, those queries are reading more data than necessary. You must tune those queries to reduce the db file sequential read events.

How It Works

Wait events are statistics that a server process or thread increments when it waits for an operation to complete in order to continue its processing. For example, a SQL statement may be modifying data, but the server process may have to wait for a data block to be read from disk because it's not available in the SGA. Although there's a large number of wait events, some the most common wait events are the following:

- *Buffer busy waits*: These occur when multiple processes attempt to concurrently access the same buffers in the buffer cache.

- *Free buffer waits*: These waits occur when a server process posts the database writer process to write out dirty buffers in order to make free buffers available.

- *Db file scattered read*: These are waits incurred by an user process for a physical I/O to return when reading buffers into the SGA buffer cache. The scattered reads are multiblock reads and can occur because of a full table scan or a fast full scan of an index.

- *Db file sequential read*: These are waits incurred by an user process for a physical I/O to return when reading buffers into the SGA buffer cache. The reads are single block reads and are usually because of indexed reads.

- *Enqueue waits*: These are waits on Oracle locking mechanisms that control access to internal database resources and that occur when a session waits on a lock held by another session. You actually won't see a wait event named enqueue (or enq) because the enqueue wait event types are always held for a specific purpose, such as *enq: TX - contention, enq:TX - index contention*, and *enq:TX - row lock contention*.

- *Log buffer space*: These are waits caused by server processes waiting for free space in the log buffer.

- *Log file sync*: These are waits by server processes that are performing a commit (or rollback) for the LGWR to complete its write to the redo log file.

Analyzing Oracle wait events is the starting point when troubleshooting a slow-running query. When a query is running slow, it usually means that there are excessive waits of one type or another. Some of the waits may be because of excessive I/O due to missing indexes. Other waits may be caused by a latch or a locking event. Several recipes in this chapter show you how to identify and fix various types of Oracle wait-related performance problems. In general, wait events that account for the most wait time warrant further investigation.

> ■ **Tip** It's important to understand that wait events show only the symptoms of underlying problems. Thus, you should view a wait event as a window into a particular problem, and not the problem itself.

When Oracle encounters a problem such as buffer contention or latch contention, it simply increments a specific type of wait event relating to that latch or buffer. By doing this, the database is showing where it had to wait for a specific resource and was thus unable to continue processing. The buffer or latch contention can often be traced to faulty application logic, but some wait events could also emanate from system issues such as a misconfigured RAID system. Missing indexes, inappropriate initialization parameters, inadequate values for initialization parameters that relate to memory, and inadequate sizing of redo log files are just some of the things that can lead to excessive waits in a database. The great benefit of analyzing Oracle wait events is that it takes the guesswork out of performance tuning—you can see exactly what is causing a performance slowdown so you can immediately focus on fixing the problem. The bottom line is that you won't be spending inordinate amounts of time on marginal improvements because you can clearly see the contribution of each type of wait.

In most cases, you probably will notice that events such as "rdbms ipc message," "pmon timer," and "SQL*Net message from client" might be the most common wait events in your database. However, all of these are considered "idle waits," and you can safely ignore them. For example, if the client program is busy computing something after having retrieved data, the DBMS is "idle" until the program sends another statement. Similarly, when performing backups with RMAN, you may notice a high number of "RMAN backup and recovery I/O" wait events. As you can tell, these are wait events associated with the RMAN backups and don't usually signify anything important.

5-4. Understanding Wait Class Events
Problem

You want to understand how Oracle classifies wait events into various classes.

Solution

Every Oracle wait event belongs to a specific wait event class. Oracle groups wait events into classes, such as Administrative, Application, Cluster, Commit, Concurrency, Configuration, Scheduler, System I/O, and User I/O, to facilitate the analysis of wait events. Here are the characteristics of typical waits in some of these wait classes:

- Application: Waits resulting from application code issues such as lock waits because of row-level locking

- Commit: Waits for confirmation of a redo log write after committing a transaction

- Network: Waits caused by delays in sending data over the network

- User I/O: Waits for reading blocks from disk

Two key wait classes are the Application and User I/O wait classes. The Application wait class contains waits because of row and table locks caused by an application. The User I/O class includes the db file scattered read, db file sequential read, direct path read, and direct path write events. The System I/O class includes redo log-related wait events among other waits. The Commit class contains just the log file sync wait information. There's also an "idle" class of wait events such as SQL*Net message from client, for example, that merely indicate an inactive session. You can ignore the idle waits.

How It Works

Classes of wait events help you quickly find out what type of activity is affecting database performance. For example, the Administrative wait class may show a high number of waits because you're rebuilding an index. Concurrency waits point to waits for internal database resources such as latches. If the Cluster wait class shows the most wait events, then your RAC instances may be experiencing contention for global cache resources (gc cr block busy event). Note that the System I/O wait class includes waits for background process I/O such as the database writer (DBWR) wait event db file parallel write.

The Application wait class contains waits that result from user application code—most of your enqueue waits fall in this wait class. The only wait event in the Commit class is the log file sync event, which we examine in detail later in this chapter. The Configuration class waits include waits such as those caused by log files that are sized too small.

5-5. Examining Session Waits

Problem

You want to find out the wait events in a session.

Solution

You can use the V$SESSION_WAIT view to get a quick idea about what a particular session is waiting for, as shown here:

```
SQL> select event, count(*) from v$session_wait
     group by event;
```

```
EVENT                                               COUNT(*)
-----------------------------------------------     --------
SQL*Net message from client                               11
Streams AQ: waiting for messages in the queue              1
enq: TX - row lock contention                              1
...
15 rows selected.
```

```
SQL>
```

The output of the query indicates that one session is waiting for an enqueue lock, possibly because of a blocking lock held by another session. If you see a large number of sessions experiencing row lock contention, you must investigate further and identify the blocking session.

Here's one more way you can query the V$SESSION_WAIT view to find out what's slowing down a particular session:

```
SQL> select event, state, seconds_in_wait siw
     from   v$session_wait
     where  sid = 81;
```

```
EVENT                           STATE         SIW
-----------------------------   -----------   ------
enq: TX - row lock contention   WAITING       976
```

The preceding query shows that the session with SID 81 has been waiting for an enqueue event because the row (or rows) it wants to update is locked by another transaction.

■ **Note** Since Oracle Database 11g, the database counts each resource wait as just one wait, even if the session experiences many internal time-outs caused by the wait. For example, a wait for an enqueue for 15 seconds may include 5 different 3-second wait calls—the database considers these as just a single enqueue wait.

How It Works

The first query shown in the "Solution" section offers an easy way to find out which wait events, if any, are slowing down user sessions. When you issue the query without specifying a SID, it displays the current and last waits for all sessions in the database. If you encounter a locking situation in the database, for example, you can issue the query periodically to see whether the total number of enqueue waits is coming down. If the number of enqueue waits across the instance is growing, that means more sessions are encountering slowdowns because of blocked locks.

The V$SESSION_WAIT view shows the current or last wait for each session. The STATE column in this view tells you whether a session is currently waiting. Here are the possible values for the STATE column:

- WAITING: The session is currently waiting for a resource.

- WAITED UNKNOWN TIME: The duration of the last wait is unknown. (This value is shown only if you set the TIMED_STATISTICS parameter to false, so in effect this depends on the value set for the STATISTICS_LEVEL parameter. If you set STATISTICS_LEVEL to TYPICAL or ALL, the TIMED_STATISTICS parameter will be TRUE by default. If the STATISTICS_LEVEL parameter is set to BASIC, TIMED_STATISTICS will be FALSE by default.)

- WAITED SHORT TIME: The most recent wait was less than a 100th of a second long.

- WAITED KNOWN TIME: The WAIT_TIME column shows the duration of the last wait.

Note that the query utilizes the seconds_in_wait column to find out how long this session has been waiting. Oracle has deprecated this column in favor of the wait_time_micro and TIME_SINCE_LAST_WAIT_MICRO columns. The WAIT_TIME_MICRO column shows the amount of time waited in microseconds. If the session is currently waiting, the value is the time spent in the current wait. If the session is currently not in a wait, then the value is the amount of time waited during the last wait. The TIME_SINCE_LAST_WAIT_MIRCO column shows time elapsed since the end of the last wait (in microseconds). All three columns show the amount of time waited for the current wait if the session is currently waiting. If the session is not currently waiting, the wait_time_micro column shows the amount of time waited during the last wait. We chose to use the deprecated column SECONDS_IN_WAIT simply because we wanted to show the wait in seconds.

■ **Note** We want to mention here that since Oracle Database 10g Release 1, several of the wait columns from the V$SESSION_WAIT view are made available in the V$SESSION view as well.

5-6. Examining Wait Events by Class
Problem

Your database is exhibiting poor performance and you want to quickly find out which Oracle wait event class could be responsible for the performance deterioration.

Solution

The following query shows the different types of wait classes and the wait events associated with each wait class:

```
SQL> select  wait_class, name
  2  from v$event_name
  3  where name LIKE 'enq%'
  4  and wait_class <> 'Other'
  5* order by wait_class
SQL> /

WAIT_CLASS                            NAME
--------------                        --------------------------
Administrative                        enq: TW - contention
Concurrency                           enq: TX - index contention
...
SQL>
```

To view the current waits grouped into various wait classes, issue the following query:

```
SQL>
SQL> select wait_class, sum(time_waited), sum(time_waited)/sum(total_waits)
  2  sum_waits
  3  from v$system_wait_class
  4  group by wait_class
  5* order by 3 desc;

WAIT_CLASS          SUM(TIME_WAITED)           SUM_WAITS
-----------         ----------------           ----------
Idle                     249659211             347.489249
Commit                     1318006             236.795904
Concurrency                  16126               4.818046
User I/O                    135279               2.228869
Application                    912                .0928055
Network                        139                .0011209
...
SQL>
```

Do not worry if you see a very high sum of waits for the Idle wait class. You should actually expect to see a high number of Idle waits in any healthy database. In a typical production environment, however, you'll certainly see more waits under the User I/O and Application wait classes. If you notice that the database has accumulated a very large wait time for the Application wait class or the User I/O wait class, for example, it's time to investigate those two wait classes further. In the following example, we drill down into a couple of wait classes to find out which specific waits are causing the high sum of total wait time under the Application and Concurrency classes. To do this, we use the V$SYSTEM_EVENT and $EVENT_NAME views in addition to the V$SYSTEM_WAIT_CLASS view. Focus not just on the total time waited but also on the average wait to gauge the effect of the wait event.

```
SQL>  select sea.event, sea.total_waits, sea.time_waited, sea.average_wait
  2    from v$system_event sea, v$event_name enb, v$system_wait_class swc
  3    where sea.event_id=enb.event_id
```

```
  4    and enb.wait_class#=swc.wait_class#
  5    and swc.wait_class in ('Application','Concurrency')
  6*   order by average_wait desc
SQL> /
```

EVENT	TOTAL_WAITS	TIME_WAITED	AVERAGE_WAIT
enq: TX - index contention	2	36	17.8
library cache load lock	76	800	10.53
buffer busy waits	9	89	9.87
row cache lock	26	100	3.84
cursor: pin S wait on X	484	1211	2.5
SQL*Net break/reset to client	2	2	1.16
library cache: mutex X	12	13	1.10
latch: row cache objects	183	158	.86
latch: cache buffers chains	5	3	.69
enq: RO - fast object reuse	147	70	.47
library cache lock	4	1	.27
cursor: pin S	20	5	.27
latch: shared pool	297	74	.25

```
13 rows selected.

SQL>
```

■ **Tip**   Two of the most common Oracle wait events are the db file scattered read and db file sequential read events. The db file scattered read wait event is because of full table scans of large tables. If you experience this wait event, investigate the possibility of adding indexes to the table or tables. Sometimes, an index may already exist, but the instance is unable to use it because of the existence of a function. Make sure that this isn't the case. The db file sequential read wait event is because of indexed reads. While an indexed read may seem like it's a good thing, a high amount of indexed reads could potentially indicate an inefficient query that you must tune. If high values for the db file sequential read wait event are because of a large number of small indexed reads, it's not really a problem in most cases—this is natural in a database. You should be concerned if a handful of queries are responsible for most of the waits.

You can see that the enqueue waits caused by the row lock contention are what's causing the most waits under these two classes. Now you know exactly what's slowing down the queries in your database! To get at the session whose performance is being affected by the contention for the row lock, drill down to the session level using the following query:

```
SQL> select se.sid, se.event, se.total_waits, se.time_waited, se.average_wait
     from v$session_event se, v$session ss
     where time_waited > 0
     and se.sid=ss.sid
     and ss.username is not NULL
     and se.event='enq: TX - row lock contention';
```

```
SID   EVENT                        TOTAL_WAITS  time_waited   average_wait
----  ---------------------------  -----------  ------------  -----------
68    enq: TX - row lock content            24          8018          298
SQL>
```

The output shows that the session with SID 68 had waited (or still might be waiting) for a row lock that's held by another transaction.

How It Works

Understanding the various Oracle wait event classes enhances your ability to quickly diagnose Oracle wait-related problems. Analyzing wait events by classes lets you know whether contention, user I/O, or a configuration issue is responsible for high waits. The examples in the "Solution" section show you how to start analyzing the waits based on the wait event classes. This helps identify the source of the waits, such as concurrency issues, for example. Once you identify the wait event class responsible for most of the waits, you can drill down into that wait event class to find out the specific wait events that are contributing to high total waits for that wait event class. You can then identify the user sessions waiting for those wait events using the final query shown in the "Solution" section.

5-7. Resolving Buffer Busy Waits
Problem

Your database is experiencing a high number of buffer busy waits, based on the output from the AWR report. You want to resolve those waits.

Solution

Oracle has several types of buffer classes, such as data block, segment header, undo header, and undo block. How you fix a buffer busy wait situation will depend on the types of buffer classes that are causing the problem. You can find out the type of buffer causing the buffer waits by issuing the following two queries. Note that you first get the value of row_wait_obj# from the first query and use it as the value for object_id in the second query.

```
SQL> select row_wait_obj#
     from v$session
     where event = 'buffer busy waits';

SQL> select owner, object_name, subobject_name, object_type
     from dba_objects
     where object_id = &row_wait_obj;
```

The preceding queries will reveal the specific type of buffer causing the high buffer waits. How you resolve the problem depends on which buffer class causes the buffer waits, as summarized in the following subsections.

Segment Header

If your queries show that the buffer waits are being caused by contention on the segment header, there's free list contention in the database because of several processes attempting to insert into the same data block; each of these processes needs to obtain a free list before it can insert data into that block. If you aren't already using it, an automatic segment space management (ASSM) is recommended—under ASSM, the database doesn't use free lists. In cases where you can't implement ASSM, you must increase the free lists for the segment in question. You can also try increasing the free list groups. Partitioning the segment can also help in some cases.

Data Block

Data block buffer contention could be related to a table or an index. This type of contention is often caused by right-hand indexes, that is, indexes that result in several processes inserting into the same point, such as when you use sequence number generators to produce the key values. Again, if you're using manual segment management, move to ASSM or increase free lists for the segment. A good solution would be to implement a reverse key index if possible.

Undo Header and Undo Block

If you're using automatic undo management, few or none of the buffer waits will be because of contention for an undo segment header or an undo segment block. If you do see one of these buffer classes as the culprit, however, you may increase the size of your undo tablespace to resolve the buffer busy waits.

How It Works

A buffer busy wait occurs when a session tries to access a block in the buffer cache but can't do so because the buffer is busy. Another session is modifying the required data block, and the contents of the block are going through a change. To provide the requester with a consistent image of the data block (with all of the changes or none of the changes), the session that's changing the data block will mark the block header with a flag to indicate the block is being modified and that the other session needs to wait until all the changes are applied to the block. During the time the block is being modified, the block is marked unreadable by other sessions.

Buffer busy waits occur in two important types of cases:

- Another session is reading the block into the buffer
- Another session is holding the buffer in a mode that's incompatible to our request

High concurrent inserts into a hot block where multiple users are inserting into the same block at the same time leads to high buffer busy waits. You also see these waits when several users are running full table scans simultaneously on the same table. As the first user reads the data blocks off the disk storage, the rest of the sessions will wait on the Buffer Busy Wait for the physical I/O to finish.

If your investigation of buffer busy waits reveals that the same block or set of blocks is involved most of the time, a good strategy would be to delete some of these rows and insert them back into the table, thus forcing them onto different data blocks.

Check your current memory allocation to the buffer cache, and, if necessary, increase it. A larger buffer cache can reduce the waiting by sessions to read data from disk, since more of the data will already be in the buffer cache. You can also place the offending table in memory by using the keep pool in the buffer cache (please see Recipe 3-7). By making the hot block always available in memory, you'll avoid the high buffer busy waits.

Indexes that have a very low number of unique values are called *low cardinality indexes*. Low cardinality indexes generally result in too many block reads. Thus, if several DML operations are occurring concurrently, some of the index blocks could become "hot" and lead to high buffer busy waits. As a long-term solution, you can try to reduce the number of the low cardinality indexes in your database.

Each Oracle data segment such as a table or an index contains a header block that records information such as free blocks available. When multiple sessions are trying to insert or delete rows from the same segment, you could end up with contention for the data segment's header block.

Buffer busy waits are also caused by a contention for free lists. A session that's inserting data into a segment needs to first examine the free list information for the segment to find blocks with free space into which the session can insert data.

You can identify the query that's involved by executing the following two queries:

```
SQL> select sql_id from v$session
     where sid in (SELECT sid FROM v$session_wait WHERE event = 'buffer
                   busy waits');
SQL> SELECT sql_text FROM v$sqlarea WHERE sql_id = <sql_id>;
```

If you use ASSM in your database, you shouldn't see any waits due to contention for a free list.

5-8. Resolving Log File Sync Waits

Problem

You're seeing a high amount of log file sync wait events, which are at the top of all wait events in your database. You want to reduce these wait events.

Solution

The following are two strategies for dealing with high log file sync waits in your database:

- If you notice a large number of waits with a short average wait time per wait, that's an indication that too many commit statements are being issued by the database. You must change the commit behavior by batching the commits. Instead of committing after each row, for example, you can specify that the commits occur after a large number of inserts or updates.

- If you notice that the large amount of wait time accumulated because of the redo log file sync event was caused by long waits for writing to the redo log file (high average time waited for this event), it's more a matter of how fast your I/O subsystem is. You can alternate the redo log files on various disks to reduce contention. You can also see whether you can dedicate disks entirely for the redo logs instead of allowing other files on those disks—this will reduce I/O contention when the LGWR is writing the buffers to disk. Finally, as a long-term solution, you can look into placing redo logs on faster devices, say, by moving them from a RAID 5 device to a RAID 1 device or even by moving to solid-state (SSD) disks.

How It Works

■ **Note**   Oracle (actually the LGWR background process) flushes a session's redo information to the redo log file whenever a session issues a COMMIT statement. The database writes commit records to disk before it returns control to the client. The server process thus waits for the completion of the write to the redo log. This is the default behavior.

The session will tell the LGWR process to write the session's redo information from the redo log buffer to the redo log file on disk. The LGWR process posts the user session after it finishes writing the buffer's contents to disk. The log file sync wait event includes the wait during the writing of the log buffer to disk by LGWR and the posting of that information to the session. The server process will have to wait until it gets confirmation that the LGWR process has completed writing the log buffer contents out to the redo log file.

The log file sync events are caused by contention during the writing of the log buffer contents to the redo log files. Check the V$SESSION_WAIT view to ascertain whether Oracle is incrementing the SEQ# column. If Oracle is incrementing this column, it means that the LGWR process is the culprit, and it may be stuck.

As the log file sync wait event is caused by contention caused by the LGWR process, see if you can use the NOLOGGING option to get rid of these waits. Of course, in a production system, you can't use the NOLOGGING option when the database is processing user requests, so this option is of limited use in most cases.

The log file sync wait event can also be caused by too large a setting for the LOG_BUFFER initialization parameter. Too large a value for the LOG_BUFFER parameter will lead the LGWR process to write data less frequently to the redo log files. For example, if you set the LOG BUFFER to something like 64 MB, it sets an internal parameter, _log_io_size, to a high value. The _log_io_size parameter acts as a threshold for when the LGWR writes to the redo log files. In the absence of a commit request or a checkpoint, LGWR waits until the _log_io_size threshold is met. Thus, when the database issues a COMMIT statement, the LGWR process would be forced to write a large amount of data to the redo log files at once, resulting in sessions waiting on the log file sync wait event. This happens because each of the waiting sessions is waiting for LGWR to flush the contents of the redo log buffer to the redo log files before these sessions can write to the log buffer. Although the database automatically calculates the value of the _log_io_size parameter, you can specify a value for it by issuing a command such as the following:

```
SQL> alter system set "_log_io_size"=1024000 scope=spfile;

System altered.

SQL>
```

It's important here to remember that regardless of the value of the _log_io_size parameter, by default the instance writes the contents of the redo log buffer to the log every three seconds. Finally, be sure to check the CPU usage on your server because a CPU starvation condition could result in excessive time spent on the log file sync wait event.

5-9. Minimizing Read by Other Session Wait Events
Problem

Your AWR report shows that the read by other session wait event is responsible for the highest number of waits. You'd like to reduce the high read by other session waits.

Solution

The main reason you'll see the read by other session wait event is that multiple sessions are seeking to read the same data blocks, whether they are table or index blocks, and are forced to wait behind the session that's currently reading those blocks. You can find the data blocks a session is waiting for by executing the following command:

```
SQL> select p1 "file#", p2 "block#", p3 "class#"
     from v$session_wait
     where event = 'read by other session';
```

You can then take the block# and use it in the following query to identify the exact segments (table or index) that are causing the read by other session waits:

```sql
SQL> select relative_fno, owner, segment_name, segment_type
    from dba_extents
    where file_id = &file
    and &block between block_id
    and block_id + blocks - 1;
```

Once you identify the hot blocks and the segments they belong to, you need to identify the queries that use these data blocks and segments and tune those queries if possible. You can also try deleting and re-inserting the rows inside the hot blocks.

The query shown here using the DBA_EXTENTS view may run quite slow in large databases. You can alternatively query the ROW_WAIT_OBJ# column from the V$SESSION view to quickly retrieve the associated OBJECT_ID and then use the OBJECT_ID to look up the OWNER, OBJECT_NAME, and OJBECT_TYPE column values from the DBA_OBJECTS view. Use this first query that follows to determine the possible causes when a session is waiting for buffered busy waits. This will get you the ROW_WAIT_OBJ# that you can use in the second query.

```sql
SQL> select row_wait_obj# from v$session     where event = 'buffer_busy_waits';
```

You can also query the DBA_OBJECTS view using the value for ROW_WAIT_OBJ# from the previous query. In that way you can identify the object and object type that sessions are contending for. Here's an example:

```sql
SQL> select owner, object_name, subobject_name, object_type
    from dba_objects
    where data_object_id = &row_wait_obj;
```

To reduce the amount of data in each of the hot blocks and thus reduce these types of waits, you can also try to create a new tablespace with a smaller block size and move the segment to that tablespace. It's also a good idea to check whether any low cardinality indexes are being used because this type of an index will make the database read a large number of data blocks into the buffer cache, potentially leading to the read by other session wait event. If possible, rewrite queries so that they use an index on a column with a high rather than low cardinality.

How It Works

The read by other session wait event indicates that one or more sessions are waiting for another session to read the same data blocks from disk into the SGA. Your first goal should be to identify the actual data blocks and the objects the blocks belong to. For example, these waits can be caused by multiple sessions trying to read the same index blocks into memory. Multiple sessions can also be trying to execute a full table scan simultaneously on the same table.

We've suggested diagnostic and remedial strategies to handle the read by other session wait event. However, as with just about any wait that is related to SQL performance, one of the first things you probably ought to do is to examine the execution plan for the SQL query.

5-10. Reducing Direct Path Read Wait Events
Problem

You notice a high amount of the direct path read wait events and also of the direct path read temp wait events and you want to reduce the occurrence of those events.

Solution

The `direct path read` and `direct path read temp` events are related wait events that occur when sessions are reading data directly into the PGA instead of reading it into the SGA. Reading data into the PGA isn't the problem here—that's normal behavior for certain operations, such as sorting, for example. The `direct path read temp` event usually indicates that the sorts being performed are large and that the PGA is unable to accommodate those sorts.

■ **Note**   The `direct path read temp` wait event may also appear when the instance is performing hash joins.

Issue the following command to get the file ID for the blocks that are being waited for:

```
SQL> select p1 "file#", p2 "block#", p3 "class#"
     from v$session_wait
     where event = 'direct path read temp';
```

The column P1 shows the file ID for the read call. Column P2 shows the start BLOCK_ID, and column P3 shows the number of blocks. You can then execute the following statement to check whether this file ID is for a temporary tablespace tempfile:

```
SQL> select relative_fno, owner, segment_name, segment_type
     from dba_extents
     where file_id = &file
     and &block between block_id and block_id + &blocks - 1;
```

The direct read type waits can be caused by excessive sorts to disk or full table scans. To find out what the reads are actually for, check the P1 column (file ID for the read call) of the V$SESSION_WAIT view. By doing this, you can find out whether the reads are being caused by reading data from the TEMP tablespace because of disk sorting or whether they're occurring because of full table scans by parallel slaves.

■ **Note**   It must be understood that `direct path read` waits are more common in Oracle Database 11.1 and higher releases and are likely to happen during full table scans even when a parallel query isn't used, that is, unless you disable serial direct path reads by setting event 10949 to a value of 1.

If you determine that sorts to disk are the main culprit in causing high `direct read` wait events, increase the value of the PGA_AGGREGATE_TARGET parameter (or specify a minimum size for it, if you're using automatic memory management). Increasing PGA size is also a good strategy when the queries are doing large hash joins, which could result in excessive I/O on disk if the PGA is inadequate for handling the large hash joins. When you set a high degree of parallelism for a table, Oracle tends to go for full table scans, using parallel slaves. If your I/O system can't handle all the parallel slaves, you'll notice a high amount of direct path reads. The solution for this is to reduce the degree of parallelism for the table or tables in question. Also investigate whether you can avoid the full table scan by specifying appropriate indexes.

As far as efficient query writing is concerned, a DISTINCT at the top level of a query that returns a lot of data is a wrong idea, especially if it's there to mask duplicates returned by badly written joins. Some unwanted hash joins are sometimes simply because a poor use of functions in queries prevents Oracle from running the nested loops or correlated subquery that would be appropriate.

How It Works

Normally, during both a sequential database read or a scattered database read operation, the database reads data from disk into the SGA. A direct path read is one where a single or multiblock read is made from disk directly to the PGA, bypassing the SGA. Ideally, the database should perform the entire sorting of the data in the PGA. When a huge sort doesn't fit into the available PGA, Oracle writes part of the sort data directly to disk. A direct read occurs when the server process reads this data from disk (instead of the PGA).

You're most likely to encounter significant direct path read waits when the I/O subsystem is overloaded, most likely because of full table scans caused by setting a high degree of parallelism for tables, causing the database to return buffers slower than what the processing speed of the server process requires. Direct path read waits will occur even when the I/O system isn't overloaded, but the duration of these waits is likely to increase significantly when you face an overloaded I/O system. A good disk striping strategy would help out here. Oracle's Automatic Storage Management (ASM) automatically stripes data for you. If you aren't already using ASM, consider implementing it in your database.

The direct path write and direct path write temp wait events are analogous to the direct path read and direct path read temp waits. Normally, it's the DBWR that writes data from the buffer cache. Oracle uses a direct path write when a process writes data buffers directly from the PGA. If your database is performing heavy sorts that spill onto disk or parallel DML operations, you can on occasion expect to encounter the direct path write events. You may also see this wait event when you execute direct path load events such as a parallel CTAS (create table as select) or a direct path INSERT operation. As with the direct path read events, the solution for direct path write events depends on what's causing the waits. If the waits are being mainly caused by large sorts, then you may think about increasing the value of the PGA_AGGREGATE_TARGET parameter. If operations such as parallel DML are causing the waits, you must look into the proper spreading of I/O across all disks and also ensure that your I/O subsystem can handle the high degree of parallelism during DML operations.

5-11. Minimizing Recovery Writer Waits
Problem

You've turned on the Oracle Flashback Database feature in your database. You're now seeing a large number of wait events because of a slow recovery writer (RVWR) process. You want to reduce the recovery writer waits.

Solution

Oracle writes all changed blocks from memory to the flashback logs on disk. You may encounter the flashback buf free by RVWR wait event as a top wait event when the database is writing to the flashback logs. To reduce these recovery writer waits, you must tune the flash recovery area file system and storage. Specifically, you must do the following:

- Since flashback logs tend to be quite large, operating system caching may not only be ineffectual, but the instance is likely to incur some CPU overhead when writing to these files. One of the things you may consider is moving the flash recovery area to a faster file system. Also, Oracle recommends that you use file systems based on ASM because they won't be subject to operating system file caching, which tends to slow down I/O.

- Increase the disk throughput for the file system where you store the flash recovery area by configuring multiple disk spindles for that file system. This will speed up the writing of the flashback logs.

- Stripe the storage volumes, ideally with small stripe sizes (for example, 128 KB).

- Set the LOG_BUFFER initialization parameter to a minimum value of 8 MB—the memory allocated for writing to the flashback database logs depends on the setting of the LOG_BUFFER parameter.

How It Works

Unlike in the case of the redo log buffer, Oracle writes flashback buffers to the flashback logs at infrequent intervals to keep overhead low for the Oracle Flashback Database. The flashback buf free by RVWR wait event occurs when sessions are waiting on the RVWR process. The RVWR process writes the contents of the flashback buffers to the flashback logs on disk. When the RVWR falls behind during this process, the flashback buffer is full and free buffers aren't available to sessions that are making changes to data through DML operations. The sessions will continue to wait until RVWR frees up buffers by writing their contents to the flashback logs. High RVWR waits indicate that your I/O system is unable to support the rate at which the RVWR needs to flush flashback buffers to the flashback logs on disk.

5-12. Finding Out Who's Holding a Blocking Lock
Problem

Your users are complaining that some of their sessions are very slow. You suspect that those sessions may be locked by Oracle for some reason and want to find the best way to go about figuring out who is holding up these sessions.

Solution

As we've explained in the introduction to this chapter, Oracle uses several types of locks to control transactions being executed by multiple sessions to prevent destructive behavior in the database. A blocking lock could "slow" down a session; in fact, the session is merely waiting on another session that is holding a lock on an object (such as a row or a set of rows or even an entire table). Or, in a development scenario, a developer might have started multiple sessions, some of which are blocking each other.

When analyzing Oracle locks, some of the key database views you must examine are the V$LOCK and V$SESSION views. The V$LOCKED_OBJECT and DBA_OBJECTS views are also useful in identifying the locked objects. To find out whether a session is being blocked by the locks being applied by another session, you can execute the following query:

```
SQL> select s1.username || '@' || s1.machine
  2  || ' ( SID=' || s1.sid || ' ) is blocking '
  3  || s2.username || '@' || s2.machine || ' ( SID=' || s2.sid || ' ) ' AS blocking_status
  4  from v$lock l1, v$session s1, v$lock l2, v$session s2
  5  where s1.sid=l1.sid and s2.sid=l2.sid
  6  and l1.BLOCK=1 and l2.request > 0
  7  and l1.id1 = l2.id1
  8  and l2.id2 = l2.id2 ;


BLOCKING_STATUS
-----------------------------------------------------------------

HR@MIRO\MIROPC61 ( SID=68 )  is blocking SH@MIRO\MIROPC61 ( SID=81 )

SQL>
```

Note that the BLOCK column can have the value 2 in an Oracle RAC environment. The output of the query shows the blocking session as well as all the blocked sessions.

A quick way to find out whether you have any blocking locks in your instance at all, for any user, is to simply run the following query:

```
SQL> select * from V$lock where block > 0;
```

If you don't get any rows back from this query, good—you don't have any blocking locks in the instance right now! We'll explain this view in more detail in the explanation section.

You can also issue a SELECT statement on the V$SESSION view with the clause where blocking_session is not null to identify blocking locks in the instance. Here's an example:

```
SQL> select process,sid, blocking_session
       from v$session
       where blocking_session is not null;
```

```
PROCESS             SID              BLOCKING_SESSION
-------             ====             ---------------
6789                123                          456
SQL>
```

You can use the SID to find the SERIAL# value for the blocking session and kill the blocking session.

How It Works

Oracle uses two types of locks to prevent destructive behavior: exclusive and shared locks. Only one transaction can obtain an exclusive lock on a row or a table, while multiple shared locks can be obtained on the same object. Oracle uses locks at two levels: the row and table levels. Row locks, indicated by the symbol TX, lock just a single row of a table for each row that'll be modified by a DML statement such as INSERT, UPDATE, and DELETE. This is true also for a MERGE or a SELECT ... FOR UPDATE statement. The transaction that includes one of these statements grabs an exclusive row lock as well as a row share table lock. Note that each time a transaction intends to modify a row or rows of a table, it holds a table lock (TM) as well on that table to prevent the database from allowing any DDL operations (such as DROP TABLE) on that table while the transaction is trying to modify some of its rows. The transaction (and the session) will hold these locks until it commits or rolls back the statement. Until it does one of these two things, all other sessions that intend to modify that particular row are blocked.

In an Oracle database, locking works this way:

- A reader won't block another reader.
- A reader won't block a writer.
- A writer won't block a reader of the same data.
- A writer will block another writer that wants to modify the same data.

It's the last case in the list, where two sessions intend to modify the same data in a table, that Oracle's automatic locking kicks in to prevent destructive behavior. The first transaction that contains the statement that updates an existing row will get an exclusive lock on that row. While the first session that locks a row continues to hold that lock (until it issues a COMMIT or ROLLBACK statement), other sessions can modify any other rows in that table other than the locked row. The concomitant table lock held by the first session is merely intended to prevent any other session from issuing a DDL statement to alter the table's structure. Oracle uses a sophisticated locking mechanism whereby a row-level lock isn't automatically escalated to the table or even the block level.

5-13. Identifying Blocked and Blocking Sessions

Problem

You notice enqueue locks in your database and suspect that a blocking lock may be holding up other sessions. You'd like to identify the blocking and blocked sessions.

Solution

When you see an enqueue wait event in an Oracle database, chances are that it's a locking phenomenon that's holding up some sessions from executing their SQL statements. When a session waits on an "enqueue" wait event, that session is waiting for a lock that's held by a different session. The blocking session is holding the lock in a mode that's incompatible with the lock mode that's being requested by the blocked session. You can issue the following command to view information about the blocked and blocking sessions:

```
SQL> select decode(request,0,'Holder: ','Waiter: ')||sid sess,
     id1, id2, lmode, request, type
     from v$lock
     where (id1, id2, type) in
     (select id1, id2, type from v$lock where request>0)
     order by id1, request;
```

The V$LOCK view shows whether there are any blocking locks in the instance. If there are blocking locks, it also shows the blocking session(s) and the blocked session(s). Note that a blocking session can block multiple sessions simultaneously, if all of them need the same object that's being blocked. Here's an example that shows there are locks present:

```
SQL> select sid,type,lmode,request,ctime,block from v$lock;
```

SID	TY	LMODE	REQUEST	CTIME	BLOCK
127	MR	4	0	102870	0
81	TX	0	6	778	0
191	AE	4	0	758	0
205	AE	4	0	579	0
140	AE	4	0	11655	0
68	TM	3	0	826	0
68	TX	6	0	826	1

```
...
SQL>
```

The key column to watch is the BLOCK column—the blocking session will have the value 1 for this column. In our example, session 68 is the blocking session because it shows the value 1 under the BLOCK column. Thus, the V$LOCK view confirms our initial finding in the "Solution" section of this recipe. The blocking session, with a SID of 68, also shows a lock mode 6 under the LMODE column, indicating that it's holding this lock in the exclusive mode; this is the reason session 81 is "hanging," unable to perform its update operation. The blocked session, of course, is the victim, so it shows a value of 0 in the BLOCK column. It also shows a value of 6 under the REQUEST column because it's requesting a lock in the exclusive mode to perform its update of the column. The blocking session, in turn, will show a value of 0 for the REQUEST column because it isn't requesting any locks; it's already holding it.

If you want to find out the wait class and for how long a blocking session has been blocking others, you can do so by querying the V$SESSION view, as shown here:

```
SQL> select  blocking_session, sid,  wait_class,
    seconds_in_wait
    from      v$session
    where blocking_session is not NULL
    order by blocking_session;
```

```
BLOCKING_SESSION        SID     WAIT_CLASS        SECONDS_IN_WAIT
----------------        -----   ------------      ----------------
          68            81      Application                  7069
```

SQL>

The query shows that the session with SID=68 is blocking the session with SID=81 and that it started blocking the session 7,069 seconds ago. You can replace the WAIT_CLASS clause from the V$SESSION view with the EVENT column if you want to find the exact wait event instead of the wait class. The EVENT column shows the resource or event for which the session is waiting, while the WAIT_CLASS column shows the name of the class for the wait event.

How It Works

The following are the most common types of enqueue locks you'll see in an Oracle database:

- TX: These are because of a transaction lock and usually caused by faulty application logic.

- TM: These are table-level DML locks, and the most common cause is that you haven't indexed foreign key constraints in a child table and you're modifying the parent table.

In addition, you are also likely to notice ST enqueue locks on occasion. These indicate sessions that are waiting while Oracle is performing space management operations, such as the allocation of temporary segments for performing a sort.

5-14. Dealing with a Blocking Lock
Problem

You've identified blocking locks in your database. You want to know how to deal with those locks.

Solution

There are two basic strategies when dealing with a blocking lock: a short-term strategy and a long-term strategy. The short-term solution is to quickly get rid of the blocking locks so they don't hurt the performance of your database. You get rid of them by simply killing the blocking session. If you see a long queue of blocked sessions waiting behind a blocking session, kill the blocking session so that the other sessions can get going.

The first thing you need to do is get rid of the blocking lock so the sessions don't keep queuing up—it's not at all uncommon for a single blocking lock to result in dozens and even hundreds of sessions, all waiting for the blocked object. Since you already know the SID of the blocking session (session 68 in our example), just kill the session in this way after first querying the V$SESSION view for the corresponding serial# for the session:

```
SQL> select serial# from v$session where sid=68;
SQL> alter system kill session '68, 1234';
```

■ **Tip** If you want and if things aren't in a panic mode, you can query the V$SESSION view's active column before proceeding to kill the session.

For the long run, though, you must investigate why the blocking session is behaving the way it is. Usually, you'll find a flaw in the application logic. You may, though, need to dig deep into the SQL code that the blocking session is executing.

How It Works

In this example, obviously the blocking lock is a DML lock. However, even if you didn't know this ahead of time, you can figure out the type of lock by examining the TYPE (TY) column of the V$LOCK view. Oracle uses several types of internal "system" latches to maintain the library cache and other instance-related components, but those locks are normal, and you won't find anything related to those locks in the V$LOCK view.

■ **Note** In more recent versions of the database, most of the library cache–related caches are termed *mutexes*. Mutexes, which is short for mutual exclusion algorithms, are a much lighter and finer-grained concurrency management mechanism than latches. Mutexes are typically used in concurrent programming to control access to common resources. Mutexes protect single structures whereas latches typically protect access to multiple structures. In Oracle Database 10g Oracle introduced the use of mutexes for certain library cache operation and in Oracle Database 11g replaced all library cache latches with mutexes. A typical concurrency wait involving mutexes is the library cache: mutex X concurrency wait event.

For DML operations, Oracle uses two basic types of locks: transaction locks (TX) and DML locks (TM). There is also a third type of lock, a user lock (UL), but it doesn't play a role in troubleshooting general locking issues. Transaction locks are the most frequent type of locks you'll encounter when troubleshooting Oracle locking issues. Each time a transaction modifies data, it invokes a TX lock, which is a row transaction lock. The DML lock, TM, on the other hand, is acquired once for each object that's being changed by a DML statement.

The LMODE column shows the lock mode, with a value of 6 indicating an exclusive lock. The REQUEST column shows the requested lock mode. The session that first modifies a row will hold an exclusive lock with LMODE=6. This session's REQUEST column will show a value of 0, since it's not requesting a lock—it already has one! The blocked session needs but can't obtain an exclusive lock on the same rows, so it requests a TX in the exclusive mode (MODE=6) as well. So, the blocked session's REQUEST column will show a value of 6 and its LMODE column a value of 0 (a blocked session has no lock at all in any mode).

The preceding discussion applies to row locks, which are always taken in the exclusive mode. A session may attempt to acquire a TX-type lock in a mode other than the exclusive mode (mode 6), as is the case when a session enqueues because of a potential primary key violation, where the session will attempt to acquire a TX lock in share mode (mode 4). A TM lock is normally acquired in mode 3, which is a Shared Row Exclusive mode, whereas a DDL statement will need a TM exclusive lock.

5-15. Identifying a Locked Object
Problem

You are aware of a locking situation, and you want to find out the object that's being locked.

Solution

You can find the locked object's identity by looking at the value of the ID1 (LockIdentifier) column in the V$LOCK view (see Recipe 5-13). The value of the ID1 column where the TYPE column is TM (DML enqueue) identifies the locked object. Let's say you've ascertained that the value of the ID1 column is 99999. You can then issue the following query to identify the locked table:

```
SQL> select object_name from dba_objects where object_id=99999;

OBJECT_NAME
------------
TEST
SQL>
```

An even easier way is to use the V$LOCKED_OBJECT view to find out the locked object, the object type, and the owner of the object.

```
SQL> select lpad(' ',decode(l.xidusn,0,3,0)) || l.oracle_username "User",
        o.owner, o.object_name, o.objcct_type
        from v$locked_object l, dba_objects o
        where l.object_id = o.object_id
        order by o.object_id, 1 desc;
```

User	OWNER	OBJECT_NAME	OBJECT_TYPE
HR	HR	TEST	TABLE
SH	HR	TEST	TABLE

```
SQL>
```

Note that the query shows both the blocking and blocked users.

How It Works

As the "Solution" section shows, it's rather easy to identify a locked object. You can certainly use Oracle Enterprise Manager (Cloud Control 12c or the new Enterprise Manager Database Express) to quickly identify a locked object, the ROWID of the object involved in the lock, and the SQL statement that's responsible for the locks. However, it's always important to understand the underlying Oracle views that contain the locking information, and that's what this recipe demonstrates. Using the queries shown in this recipe, you can easily identify a locked object without recourse to a monitoring tool such as Oracle Enterprise Manager, for example.

In the example shown in the solution, the locked object was a table, but it could be any other type of object, including a PL/SQL package. Often, it turns out that the reason a query is just hanging is that one of the objects the query needs is locked. You may have to kill the session holding the lock on the object before other users can access the object.

5-16. Resolving enq: TM Lock Contention

Problem

Several sessions in your database are taking a long time to process some insert statements. As a result, the "active" sessions count is very high, and the database is unable to accept new session connections. Upon checking, you find that the database is experiencing a lot of enq: TM - contention wait events.

Solution

The enq: TM - contention event is usually because of indexes on foreign key columns on a table that's part of an Oracle DML operation. Once you fix the problem by indexing the foreign key constraint, the enq: TM - contention event will go away.

The waits on the enq: TM - contention event for the sessions that are waiting to perform insert operations are almost always because of an unindexed foreign key constraint. This happens when a dependent or child table's foreign key constraint that references a parent table is missing an index on the associated key. Oracle acquires a table lock on a child table if it's performing modifications on the primary key column in the parent table that's referenced by the foreign key of the child table. Note that these are full table locks (TM) and not row-level locks (TX); thus, these locks aren't restricted to a row but to the entire table. Naturally, once this table lock is acquired, Oracle will block all other sessions that seek to modify the child table's data. Once you create an index in the child table performing on the column that references the parent table, the waits due to the TM contention will go away.

How It Works

Oracle takes out an exclusive lock on a child table if you don't index the foreign key constraints in that table, when a SQL statement modifies a table that is referenced by another table. To illustrate how an unindexed foreign key will result in contention because of locking, we use the following example. Create two tables, STORES and PRODUCTS, as shown here:

```
SQL> create table stores
     (store_id       number(10)      not null,
      supplier_name     varchar2(40)      not null,
      constraint stores_pk PRIMARY KEY (store_id));
SQL>create table products
     (product_id      number(10)      not null,
      product_name     varchar2(30)      not null,
      supplier_id      number(10)      not null,
      store_id      number(10)      not null,
      constraint fk_stores
      foreign key (store_id)
      references stores(store_id)
      on delete cascade);
```

If you now delete any rows in the STORES table, you'll notice waits because of locking. You can get rid of these waits by simply creating an index on the column you've specified as the foreign key in the PRODUCTS table:

```
create index fk_stores on products(store_id);
```

You can find all unindexed foreign key constraints in a specific schema by issuing the following query. (Recipe 2-5 shows a query to get all such constraints in the entire database.)

```
SQL> select * from (
    select ct.table_name, co.column_name, co.position column_position
    from   user_constraints ct, user_cons_columns co
    where  ct.constraint_name = co.constraint_name
    and    ct.constraint_type = 'R'
    minus
    select ui.table_name, uic.column_name, uic.column_position
    from   user_indexes ui, user_ind_columns uic
    where  ui.index_name = uic.index_name
    )
    order by table_name, column_position;
```

If you don't index a foreign key column, you'll notice the child table is often locked, thus leading to contention-related waits. Oracle recommends that you always index your foreign keys.

■ **Tip** If the matching unique or primary key for a child table's foreign key never gets updated or deleted, you don't have to index the foreign key column in the child table.

As mentioned earlier, Oracle tends to acquire a table lock on the child table if you don't index the foreign key column. If you insert a row into the parent table, the parent table doesn't acquire a lock on the child table; however, if you update or delete a row in the parent table, the database will acquire a full table lock on the child table. That is, any modifications to the primary key in the parent table will result in a full table lock (TM) on the child table. In our example, the STORES table is a parent of the PRODUCTS table, which contains the foreign key STORE_ID. The table PRODUCTS being a dependent table, the values of the STORE_ID column in that table must match the values of the unique or primary key of the parent table, STORES. In this case, the STORE_ID column in the STORES table is the primary key of that table.

Whenever you modify the parent table's (STORES) primary key, the database acquires a full table lock on the PRODUCTS table. Other sessions can't change any values in the PRODUCTS table, including the columns other than the foreign key column. The sessions can query but not modify the PRODUCTS table. During this time, any sessions attempting to modify any column in the PRODUCTS table will have to wait (TM: enq contention wait). Oracle will release this lock on the child table PRODUCTS only after the transaction has finished the modifying the primary key in the parent table, STORES. If you have a bunch of sessions waiting to modify data in the PRODUCTS table, they'll all have to wait, and the active session count naturally will go up very fast if you have an online transaction processing–type database that has many users who perform short DML operations. Note that any DML operations you perform on the child table don't require a table lock on the parent table.

5-17. Identifying Recently Locked Sessions
Problem

A session is experiencing severe waits in the database, most likely because of a blocking lock placed by another session. You've tried to use V$LOCK and other views to drill deeper into the locking issue but are unable to "capture" the lock while it's in place. You want to use a different view to "see" the older locking data that you might have missed while the locking was going on.

Solution

You can execute the following statement based on ASH (needs licensing) to find out information about all locks held in the database during the previous ten minutes. Of course, you can vary the time interval to a smaller or larger period, so long as there's ASH data covering that time period.

```
SQL> select to_char(h.sample_time, 'HH24:MI:SS') TIME,ash.session_id,
     decode(ash.session_state, 'WAITING' ,ash.event, ash.session_state) STATE,
     ash.sql_id,
     ash.blocking_session BLOCKER
     from v$active_session_history ash, dba_users du
     where du.user_id = ash.user_id
     and ash.sample_time > SYSTIMESTAMP-(10/1440);

TIME       SID    STATE                           SQL_ID          BLOCKER
---------  -----  ------------------------------  --------------  -------
17:00:52   197    116 enq: TX - row lock conten   094w6n53tnywr      191
17:00:51   197    116 enq: TX - row lock conten   094w6n53tnywr      191
17:00:50   197    116 enq: TX - row lock conten   094w6n53tnywr      191

...

SQL>
```

You can see that ASH has recorded all the blocks placed by session 1, the blocking session (SID=191) that led to a "hanging" situation for session 2, the blocked session (SID=197). Be aware that the data in the V$ACTIVE_SESSION_HISTORY view doesn't show all enqueues. It shows only those enqueues that the sessions were waiting on at the instant that the ASH sample was collected. And ASH samples are collected every second.

How It Works

Often, when your database users complain about a performance problem, you may query the V$SESSION or V$LOCK view, but you may not find anything useful there because the wait issue may have been already resolved by then. In these circumstances, you can query the V$ACTIVE_SESSION_HISTORY view to find out what transpired in the database during the previous 60 minutes. This view offers a window into the active session history (ASH), which is a memory buffer that collects information about all active sessions, every second. V$ACTIVE_SESSION_HISTORY contains one row for each active session, and newer information continuously overwrites older data, since ASH is a rolling buffer.

We can best demonstrate the solution by creating the scenario that we're discussing and then working through that scenario. Begin by creating a test table with a couple of columns:

```
SQL> create table test (name varchar(20), id number (4));
Table created.
SQL>
```

Insert some data into the test table:

```
SQL> insert into test values ('alapati',9999);
1 row created.
SQL> insert into test values ('sam', 1111);
1 row created.
SQL> commit;
Commit complete.
SQL>
```

In session 1 (the current session), execute a SELECT * FOR UPDATE statement on the table TEST—this will place a lock on that table.

```
SQL> select * from test for update;

SQL>
```

In a different session, session 2, execute the following UPDATE statement:

```
SQL> update test set name='Jackson' where id = 9999;
```

Session 2 will hang now because it's being blocked by the SELECT FOR UPDATE statement issued by session 1. Go ahead now and issue either a ROLLBACK or a COMMIT from session 1.

```
SQL> rollback;
Rollback complete.
SQL>
```

When you issue the ROLLBACK statement, session 1 releases all locks it's currently holding on table TEST. You'll notice that session 2, which has been blocked thus far, immediately processes the UPDATE statement, which was previously "hanging," waiting for the lock held by session 2.

Therefore, we know for sure that there was a blocking lock in your database for a brief period, with session 1 the blocking session and session 2 the blocked session. You can't find any evidence of this in the V$LOCK view, though, because that and all other lock-related views show you details only about currently held locks. Here's where the ASH views shine—they can provide you with information about locks that have been held recently but are gone already before you can view them with a query on the V$LOCK or V$SESSION view.

■ **Caution** Be careful when executing the ASH query shown in the "Solution" section of this recipe. As the first column (SAMPLE_TIME) shows, ASH will record session information every second. If you execute this query over a long time frame, you may get a large amount of output just repeating the same locking information. To deal with that output, you may specify the SET PAUSE ON option in SQL*Plus. That will pause the output every page, enabling you to scroll through a few rows of the output to identify the problem.

Use the following query to find out the wait events that occurred in this session during the past hour.

```
SQL> select sample_time, event, wait_time
     from v$active_session_history
     where session_id = 81
     and session_serial# = 422;
```

The column SAMPLE_TIME lets you know precisely when this session suffered a performance hit because of a specific wait event. You can identify the actual SQL statement that was being executed by this session during that period by using the V$SQL view along with the V$ACTIVE_SESSION_HISTORY view, as shown here:

```
SQL> select sql_text, application_wait_time
     from v$sql
     where sql_id in ( select sql_id from v$active_session_history
     where sample_time =   '08-MAR-14 05.00.52.00 PM'
     and session_id = 68 and session_serial# = 422);
```

Alternatively, if you have the SQL_ID already from the V$ACTIVE_SESSION_HISTORY view, you can get the value for the SQL_TEXT column from the V$SQLAREA view, as shown here:

```
SQL> select sql_text FROM v$sqlarea WHERE sql_id = '7zfmhtu327zm0';
```

Once you have the SQL_ID, it's also easy to extract the SQL plan for this SQL statement, by executing the following query based on the DBMS_XPLAN package:

```
SQL> select * FROM table(dbms_xplan.display_cursor('7zfmhtu327zm0'));
```

■ **Tip**   Since a SQL statement can have multiple execution plans, you may want to add the SQL_PLAN_HASH_VALUE column's value from the V$ACTIVE_SESSION_HISTORY view when you execute the DBMS_XPLAN.DISPLAY_CURSOR procedure.

The background process MMON flushes ASH data to disk every hour, when the AWR snapshot is created. What happens when MMON flushes ASH data to disk? Well, you won't be able to query older data any longer with the V$ACTIVE_SESSION_HISTORY view. No worry, because you can still use the DBA_HIST_ACTIVE_SESS_HISTORY view to query the older data. The structure of this view is similar to that of the V$ACTIVE_SESSION_HISTORY view. The DBA_HIST_ACTIVE_SESS_HISTORY view shows the history of the contents of the in-memory active session history of recent system activity. You can also query the V$SESSION_WAIT_HISTORY view to examine the last ten wait events for a session while it's still active. This view offers more reliable information for very recent wait events than the V$SESSION and V$SESSION_WAIT views, both of which show wait information for only the most recent wait. Here's a typical query using the V$SESSION_WAIT_HISTORY view:

```
SQL> select sid from v$session_wait_history
     where wait_time = (select max(wait_time) from v$session_wait_history);
```

Any nonzero values under the WAIT_TIME column represent the time waited by this session for the last wait event. A zero value for this column means that the session is currently waiting for a resource.

5-18. Analyzing Recent Wait Events in a Database

Problem

You want to find out the most important waits in your database in the recent past, as well as the users, SQL statements, and objects that are responsible for most of those waits.

Solution

Query the V$ACTIVE_SESSION_HISTORY view to get information about the most common wait events and the SQL statements, database objects, and users responsible for those waits. The following are some useful queries you can use.

To find the most important wait events in the last 15 minutes, issue the following query:

```
SQL> select event,
    sum(wait_time +
    time_waited) total_wait_time
    from v$active_session_history
    where sample_time between
    sysdate -15/1440 and sysdate
    group by event
    order by total_wait_time desc
```

To find out which of your users experienced the most waits in the past 15 minutes, issue the following query:

```
SQL> select s.sid, s.username,
    sum(a.wait_time +
    a.time_waited) total_wait_time
    from v$active_session_history a,
    v$session s
    where a.sample_time between sysdate - 15/1440 and sysdate
    and a.session_id=s.sid
    group by s.sid, s.username
    order by total_wait_time desc;
```

You can identify the SQL statements that have been waiting the most during the last 15 minutes with this query:

```
SQL> select a.user_id,u.username,s.sql_text,
    sum(a.wait_time + a.time_waited) total_wait_time
    from v$active_session_history a,
    v$sqlarea s,
    dba_users u
    where a.sample_time between sysdate - 15/1440 and sysdate
    and a.sql_id = s.sql_id
    and a.user_id = u.user_id
    group by a.user_id,s.sql_text, u.username
    order by 4;
```

How It Works

The "Solution" section shows how to join the V$ACTIVE_SESSION_HISTORY view with other views, such as the V$SESSION, V$SQLAREA, DBA_USERS, and DBA_OBJECTS views, to find out exactly what's causing the highest number of wait events or who's waiting the most, in the past few minutes. This information is valuable when troubleshooting "live" database performance issues.

5-19. Identifying Time Spent Waiting Because of Locking
Problem

You want to identify the total time spent waiting by sessions because of locking issues.

Solution

You can use the following query to identify (and quantify) waits caused by the locking of a table's rows. Since the query orders the wait events by time waited, you can quickly see which type of wait events accounts for most of the waits in your instance.

```
SQL> select wait_class, event, time_waited / 100 time_secs
  2  from v$system_event e
  3  where e.wait_class <> 'Idle' AND time_waited > 0
  4  union
  5  select 'Time Model', stat_name NAME,
  6  round ((value / 1000000), 2) time_secs
  7  from v$sys_time_model
  8  where stat_name NOT IN ('background elapsed time', 'background cpu time')
  9* order by 3 desc;

WAIT_CLASS              EVENT                            TIME_SECS
-----------            -----------------------------    ----------
System I/O             log file parallel write           45066.32
System I/O             control file sequential read      23254.41
Time Model             DB time                           11083.91
Time Model             sql execute elapsed time           7660.04
Concurrency            latch: shared pool                 5928.73
Application            enq: TX - row lock contention      3182.06
...
SQL>
```

In this example, the wait event enq: TX - row lock contention reveals the total time because of row lock enqueue wait events. Note that the shared pool latch events are classified under the Concurrency wait class, while the enqueue TX - row lock contention event is classified as an Application class wait event.

How It Works

The query in the "Solution" section joins the V$SYSTEM_EVENT and V$SYS_TIME_MODEL views to show you the total time waited because of various wait events. In our case, we're interested in the total time waited because of enqueue locking. If you're interested in the total time waited by a specific session, you can use a couple of different V$ views to find out how long sessions have been in a wait state, but we recommend using the V$SESSION view because it shows you various useful attributes of the blocking and blocked sessions. Here's an example showing how to find out how long a session has been blocked by another session:

```
SQL>select sid, username, event, blocking_session,
    seconds_in_wait, wait_time
    from v$session where state in ('WAITING');
```

The query reveals the following about the session with SID 81, which is in a WAITING state:

```
SID  : 81 (this is the blocked session)
username: SH (user who's being blocked right now)
event: TX - row lock contention (shows the exact type of lock contention)
blocking session: 68 (this is the "blocker")
seconds_in_wait: 3692 (how long the blocked session is in this state)
```

The query reveals that the user SH, with a SID of 81, has been blocked for more than an hour (3,692 seconds). User SH is shown as waiting for a lock on a table that is currently locked by session 68. While the V$SESSION view is highly useful for identifying the blocking and blocked sessions, it can't tell you the SQL statement that's involved in the blocking of the table. Often, identifying the SQL statement that's involved in a blocking situation helps in finding out exactly why the statement is leading to the locking behavior. To find out the actual SQL statement that's involved, you must join the V$SESSION and V$SQL views, as shown here:

```
SQL> select sid, sql_text
     from v$session s, v$sql q
     where sid in (68,81)
     and (
     q.sql_id = s.sql_id or  q.sql_id = s.prev_sql_id)
SQL> /

    SID                     SQL_TEXT
    ----    --------------------------------------------------------
    68      select * from test for update
    81      update hr.test set name='nalapati' where user_id=1111

SQL>
```

■ **Note** Developers can also use Oracle's built-in DBMS_APPLICATION_INFO package to Oracle Trace and the SQL trace facility to record the names of executing modules or transactions in the database. They can later use this information for tracking the performance of the modules and for debugging.

The output of the query shows that session 81 is being blocked because it's trying to update a row in a table that has been locked by session 68, using the SELECT ... FOR UPDATE statement. In cases such as this, if you find a long queue of user sessions being blocked by another session, you must kill the blocking session so the other sessions can process their work. You'll also see a high active user count in the database during these situations—killing the blocking session offers you an immediate solution to resolving contention caused by enqueue locks. Later, you can investigate why the blocks are occurring so as to prevent these situations.

For any session, you can identify the total time waited by a session for each wait class by issuing the following query:

```
SQL> select wait_class_id, wait_class,
    total_waits, time_waited
    from v$session_wait_class
    where sid = <SID>;
```

If you find, for example, that this session endured a high number of waits in the application wait class (the wait class ID for this class is 4217450380), you can issue the following query using the V$SYSTEM_EVENT view to find out exactly which waits are responsible:

```
SQL> select event, total_waits, time_waited
    from v$system_event e, v$event_name n
    where n.event_id = e.event_id
    and e.wait_class_id = 4217450380;
```

EVENT	TOTAL_WAITS	TIME_WAITED
enq: TM - contention	82	475

```
...
SQL>
```

In our example, the waits in the Application class (ID 4217450380) are because of locking contention as revealed by the wait event enq:TM - contention. You can further use the V$EVENT_HISTOGRAM view to find out how many times and for how long sessions have waited for a specific wait event since you started the instance. Here's the query you need to execute to find out the wait time pattern for enqueue lock waits:

```
SQL> select wait_time_milli bucket, wait_count
    from v$event_histogram
    where event = 'enq: TX - row lock contention';
```

A high number of enqueue waits because of locking behavior is usually because of faulty application design. You'll sometimes encounter this when an application executes many updates against the same row or a set of rows. Since this type of high waits due to locking is because of inappropriately designed applications, there's not much you can do by yourself to reduce these waits. Let your application team know why these waits are occurring, and ask them to consider modifying the application logic to avoid the waits.

Any of the following four DML statements can cause locking contention: INSERT, UPDATE, DELETE, and SELECT FOR UPDATE. INSERT statements wait for a lock because another session is attempting to insert a row with an identical value. This usually happens when you have a table that has a primary key or unique constraint, with the application generating the keys. Use an Oracle sequence instead to generate the key values to avoid these types of locking situations. You can specify the NOWAIT option with a SELECT FOR UPDATE statement to eliminate session blocking because of locks. You can also use the SELECT FOR UPDATE NOWAIT statement to avoid waiting by sessions for locks when they issue an UPDATE or DELETE statement. The SELECT FOR UPDATE NOWAIT statement locks the row without waiting. You can specify SELECT FOR UPDATE SKIP UNLOCKED to skip all rows in the candidate result set that have already been locked and return the rest of the rows.

5-20. Minimizing Latch Contention
Problem

You're seeing a high number of latch waits, and you want to reduce the latch contention.

Solution

Severe latch contention can slow your database down noticeably. When you're dealing with a latch contention issue, start by executing the following query to find out the specific types of latches and the total wait time caused by each wait:

```
SQL> select event, sum(P3), sum(seconds_in_wait) seconds_in_wait
    from v$session_wait
    where event like 'latch%'
    group by event;
```

The previous query shows the latches that are currently being waited for by this session. To find out the amount of time the entire instance has waited for various latches, execute the following SQL statement:

```
SQL> select wait_class, event, time_waited / 100 time_secs
    from v$system_event e
    where e.wait_class <> 'Idle' AND time_waited > 0
    union
    select 'Time Model', stat_name NAME,
    round ((value / 1000000), 2) time_secs
    from v$sys_time_model
    where stat_name not in ('background elapsed time', 'background cpu time')
    order by 3 desc;
```

WAIT_CLASS	EVENT	TIME_SECS
Concurrency	library cache pin	622.24
Concurrency	latch: library cache	428.23
Concurrency	latch: library cache lock	93.24
Concurrency	library cache lock	24.20
Concurrency	latch: library cache pin	60.28

. . .

The partial output from the query shows the latch-related wait events, which are part of the Concurrency wait class.

You can also view the Top 5 Timed Events in the AWR report to see whether latch contention is an issue, as shown here:

Event	Waits	Time (s)	(ms)	Time	Wait Class
db file sequential read	42,005,780	232,838	6	73.8	User I/O
CPU time		124,672		39.5	Other
latch free	11,592,952	76,746	7	24.3	Other
wait list latch free	107,553	2,088	19	0.7	Other
latch: library cache	1,135,976	1,862	2	0.6	Concurrency

Here are the most common Oracle latch wait types and how you can reduce them:

- `Shared pool` and `library latches`: These are caused mostly by the database repeatedly executing the same SQL statement that varies slightly each time. For example, a database may execute a SQL statement 10,000 times, each time with a different value for a variable. The solution in all such cases is to use bind variables. Too small a shared pool may also contribute to the latch problem, so check your SGA size.

- `Cache buffers LRU chain`: These latch events are usually because of excessive buffer cache usage and may be caused both by excessive physical reads and by logical reads. Either the database is performing large full table scans or it's performing large index range scans. The usual cause for these types of latch waits is either the lack of an index or the presence of an unselective index. Also check to see whether you need to increase the size of the buffer cache.

- `Cache buffer chains`: These waits are because of one or more hot blocks that are being repeatedly accessed. Application code that updates a table's rows to generate sequence numbers, rather than using an Oracle sequence, can result in such hot blocks. You might also see the cache buffer chains wait event when too many processes are scanning an unselective index with similar predicates.

Also, if you're using Oracle sequences, re-create them with a larger cache size setting and try to avoid using the ORDER clause. The CACHE clause for a sequence determines the number of sequence values the database must cache in the SGA. If your database is processing a large number of inserts and updates, consider increasing the cache size to avoid contention for sequence values. By default, the cache is set to 20 values. Contention can result if values are being requested fast enough to frequently deplete the cache. If you're dealing with a RAC environment, using the NOORDER clause will prevent enqueue contention because of the forced ordering of queued sequence values.

How It Works

Oracle uses internal locks called *latches* to protect various memory structures. When a server process attempts to get a latch but fails to do so, that attempt is counted as a latch-free wait event. Oracle doesn't group all latch waits into a single latch-free wait event. Oracle does use a generic latch-free wait event, but this is only for the minor latch-related wait events. For the latches that are most common, Oracle uses various subgroups of latch wait events, with the name of the wait event type. You can identify the exact type of latch by looking at the latch event name. For example, the latch event `latch: library cache` indicates contention for library cache latches. Similarly, the `latch: cache buffer chains` event indicates contention for the buffer cache.

Oracle uses various types of latches to prevent multiple sessions from updating the same area of the SGA. Various database operations require sessions to read or update the SGA. For example, when a session reads a data block into the SGA from disk, it must modify the buffer cache least recently used chain. Similarly, when the database parses a SQL statement, that statement has to be added to the library cache component of the SGA. Oracle uses latches to prevent database operations from stepping on each other and corrupting the SGA.

A database operation needs to acquire and hold a latch for very brief periods, typically lasting a few nanoseconds. If a session fails to acquire a latch at first because the latch is already in use, the session will try a few times before going to "sleep." The session will re-awaken and try a few more times, before going into the sleep mode again if it still can't acquire the latch it needs. Each time the session goes into the sleep mode, it stays longer there, thus increasing the time interval between subsequent attempts to acquire a latch. Thus, if there's a severe contention for latches in your database, it results in a severe degradation of response times and throughput.

Don't be surprised to see latch contention even in a well-designed database running on very fast hardware. Some amount of latch contention, especially the cache buffers chain latch events, is pretty much unavoidable. You should be concerned only if the latch waits are extremely high and are slowing down database performance.

Contention because of the library cache latches as well as shared pool latches is usually because of applications not using bind variables. If your application can't be recoded to incorporate bind variables, all is not lost. You can set the CURSOR_SHARING parameter to force Oracle to use bind variables, even if your application hasn't specified them in the code. You must set the CURSOR_SHARING parameter to FORCE to force the substituting of bind variables for hard-coded values of variables.

The default setting for the CURSOR_SHARING parameter is EXACT, which means the database won't substitute bind variables for literal values. Rather, Oracle only allows statements with identical text to share cursors. When you set the CURSOR_SHARING parameter to FORCE, Oracle converts all literals to bind variables. The setting of the parameter to FORCE allows the creation a new cursor if an existing cursor is being shared or if the cursor's execution plan isn't optimal.

Although there are some concerns about the safety of setting the CURSOR_SHARING parameter to FORCE, we haven't seen any real issues with using this setting. The library cache contention usually disappears once you set the CURSOR_SHARING parameter to FORCE.

While the CURSOR_SHARING parameter does seem to help in a number of instances when dealing with library cache latch contention, be sure to review the bug reports in My Oracle Support to make sure your applications don't fall prey to various reported issues with setting the CURSOR_SHARING parameter to FORCE. These issues include wrong results being returned at times, instance crashes, excessively long parse times, problems with function-based indexes, and so forth. Also, when the distribution of values is everything but uniform, systematically binding constants may result in much worse performance.

The cache buffer chains latch contention is usually because of a session repeatedly reading the same data blocks. First identify the SQL statement that's responsible for the highest number of the cache buffers chain latches and see whether you can tune it. If this doesn't reduce the latch contention, you must identify the actual hot blocks that are being repeatedly read.

If a hot block belongs to an index segment, you may consider partitioning the table and using local indexes. For example, a hash partitioning scheme lets you spread the load among multiple partitioned indexes. You can also consider converting the table to a hash cluster based on the indexed columns. This way, you can avoid the index altogether. If the hot blocks belong to a table segment instead, you can still consider partitioning the table to spread the load across the partitions. You may also want to reconsider the application design to see why the same blocks are being repeatedly accessed, thus rendering them "hot."

CHAPTER 6

■ ■ ■

Analyzing Operating System Performance

Solving database performance issues sometimes requires the use of operating system (OS) utilities. These tools often provide information that can help isolate database performance problems. Consider the following situations:

- You're running multiple databases and multiple applications on one server and want to use OS utilities to identify which process is consuming the most OS resources. This approach is invaluable when a process (that may or may not be related to a database) is consuming resources to the point of causing one or more of the databases on the box to perform poorly.

- You need to verify if the database server is adequately sized for current application workload in terms of CPU, memory, storage I/O, and network bandwidth.

- An analysis is needed to determine at what point the server will not be able to handle larger (future) workloads.

- You're leasing resources within a cloud and want to verify that you're consuming the resources you're paying for.

- You've used database tools to identify system bottlenecks and want to double-check the analysis via OS tools.

In these scenarios, to effectively analyze, tune, and troubleshoot, you'll need to employ OS tools to identify resource-intensive processes. Furthermore, if you have multiple databases and applications running on one server, when troubleshooting performance issues, it's often more efficient to first determine which database and process is consuming the most resources. Operating system utilities help pinpoint whether the bottleneck is CPU, memory, storage I/O, or a network issue. Once you've identified the OS identifier, you can then query the database to show any corresponding database processes and SQL statements.

Take a look at Figure 6-1. This flowchart details the decision-making process and the relevant OS tools that a DBA steps through when diagnosing sluggish server performance. For example, when you're dealing with performance problems, one common first task is to log on to the box and quickly check for disk space issues using OS utilities like df and du. A full mount point is a common cause of database unresponsiveness.

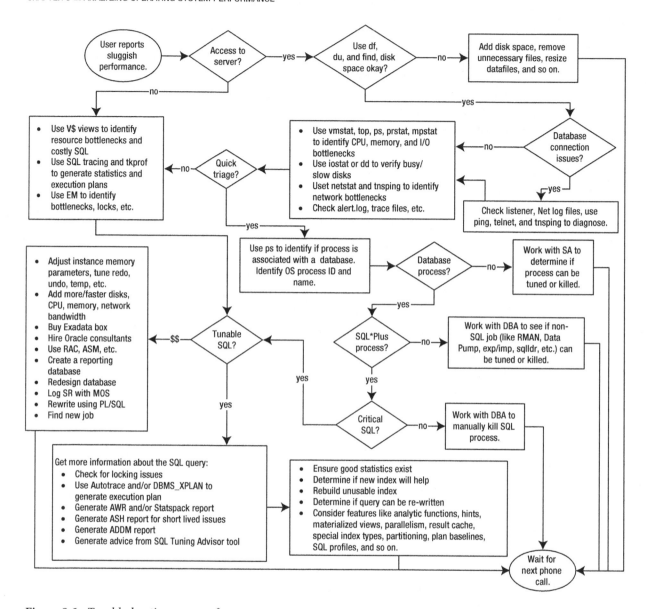

Figure 6-1. *Troubleshooting poor performance*

After inspecting disk space issues, the next task is to use an OS utility such as vmstat, top, or ps to determine what type of bottleneck you have (CPU, memory, I/O, or network). After determining the type of bottleneck, the next step is to determine if a database process is causing the problem.

The ps command is useful for displaying the process name and ID of the resource-consuming session. When you have multiple databases running on one box, you can determine which database is associated with the process from the process name. Once you have the process ID and associated database, you can then log on to the database and run SQL queries to determine if the process is associated with a SQL query. If the problem is SQL-related, then you can identify further details regarding the SQL query and where it might be tuned.

Figure 6-1 encapsulates the difficulty of troubleshooting performance problems. Correctly pinpointing the cause of performance issues and recommending an efficient solution is often easier said than done. When trying to resolve issues, some paths result in relatively efficient and inexpensive solutions, such as terminating a runaway OS process, creating an index, or generating fresh statistics. Other decisions may lead you to conclude that you need to add expensive hardware or redesign the system. Your performance tuning conclusions can have long-lasting financial impact on your company and thus influence your ability to retain a job. Obviously you want to focus on the cause of a performance problem and not just address the symptom. If you can consistently identify the root cause of the performance issue and recommend an effective and inexpensive solution, this will greatly increase your value to your employer.

The focus of this chapter is to provide detailed examples that show how to use Linux/Unix OS utilities to identify server performance issues. These utilities are invaluable for providing extra information used to diagnose performance issues outside of tools available within the database. Operating system utilities act as an extra set of eyes to help zero in on the cause of poor database performance.

■ **Tip** If you work in a Windows environment, consider downloading the Cygwin (www.cygwin.com). This provides you a collection of Linux/Unix tools in your Windows environment.

6-1. Detecting Disk Space Issues
Problem

Users are reporting that they can't connect to a database. You log on to the database server, attempt to connect to SQL*Plus, and receive this error:

```
ORA-09817: Write to audit file failed.
Linux Error: 28: No space left on device
Additional information: 12
```

You want to quickly determine if a mount point is full and where the largest files are within this mount point.

Solution

In a Linux/Unix environment, use the df command to identify disk space issues. This example uses the h (human readable) parameter to format the output so that space is reported in megabytes or gigabytes:

```
$ df -h
```

Here is some sample output:

```
Filesystem            Size  Used Avail Use% Mounted on
/dev/mapper/VolGroup00-LogVol00
                      222G  210G     0 100% /
/dev/sda1              99M   23M   71M  25% /boot
```

The prior output indicates that the root (/) file system is full on this server. In this situation, once a full mount point is identified, then use the find command to locate the largest files contained in a directory structure. This example navigates to the ORACLE_HOME directory and then combines the find, ls, sort, and head commands to identify the largest files beneath that directory:

```
$ cd $ORACLE_HOME
$ find . -ls | sort -nrk7 | head -10
```

If you have a full mount point, also consider looking for the following types of files that can be moved or removed:

- Deleting database trace files (these files often have the extension of .trm or .trc)

- Removing large Oracle Net log files

- Moving, compressing, or deleting old archive redo log files

- Removing old installation files or binaries

- If you have datafiles with ample free space, consider resizing them to smaller sizes

---

■ **Tip** You can view the names and values of directories where Oracle writes trace files with this query: select value from v$diag_info where name='Diag Trace';

Another way to identify where the disk space is being used is to find the largest space-consuming directories beneath a given directory. This Linux example combines the du, sort, and head commands to show the 10 largest directories beneath the current working directory:

```
$ du -S . | sort -nr | head -10
```

The prior command is particularly useful for identifying a directory that might not necessarily have large files in it but lots of small files consuming space (like trace files).

■ **Note** On Solaris Unix systems, the prior command will need to use du with the –o option.

How It Works

When you have a database that is hung because there is little or no free disk space, you should quickly find files that can be safely removed without compromising database availability. On Linux/Unix servers, the df, find, and du commands are particularly useful.

When working with production database servers, it's highly desirable to proactively monitor disk space so that you're warned about a mount point becoming full. Listed next is a simple shell script that monitors disk space for a given set of mount points:

```
#!/bin/bash
mntlist="/orahome /oraredo1 /oraarch1 /ora01 /oradump01 /"
for ml in $mntlist
do
echo $ml
usedSpc=$(df -h $ml | awk '{print $5}' | grep -v capacity | cut -d "%" -f1 -)
```

```
BOX=$(uname -a | awk '{print $2}')
#
case $usedSpc in
[0-9])
arcStat="relax, lots of disk space: $usedSpc"
;;
[1-7][0-9])
arcStat="disk space okay: $usedSpc"
;;
[8][0-9])
arcStat="space getting low: $usedSpc"
;;
[9][0-9])
arcStat="warning, running out of space: $usedSpc"
echo $arcStat $ml | mailx -s "space on: $BOX" dkuhn@gmail.com
;;
[1][0][0])
arcStat="update resume, no space left: $usedSpc"
echo $arcStat $ml | mailx -s "space on: $BOX" dkuhn@gmail.com
;;
*)
arcStat="huh?: $usedSpc"
esac
#
BOX=$(uname -a | awk '{print $2}')
echo $arcStat
#
done
#
exit 0
```

You'll have to modify the script to match your environment. For example, the second line of the script specifies the mount points on the box being monitored:

```
mntlist="/orahome /oraredo1 /oraarch1 /ora01 /oradump01 /"
```

These mount points should match the mount points listed in the output of the df -h command. For a Solaris box that this script runs on, here's the output of df:

```
Filesystem         size    used   avail capacity  Mounted on
/                   35G    5.9G    30G    17%      /
/ora01             230G    185G    45G    81%      /ora01
/oraarch1          100G     12G    88G    13%      /oraarch1
/oradump01         300G     56G   244G    19%      /oradump01
/orahome            20G     15G   5.4G    73%      /orahome
/oraredo1           30G    4.9G    25G    17%      /oraredo1
```

Also, depending on what version of Linux/Unix you're using, you'll have to modify this line as well:

```
usedSpc=$(df -h $ml | awk '{print $5}' | grep -v capacity | cut -d "%" -f1 -)
```

The prior code runs several Linux/Unix commands and places the output in the usedSpc variable. The code depends on the output of the df command, which can vary somewhat depending on the OS vendor and version. For example, on some Linux systems, the output of df reports on Use% instead of capacity, so in this scenario, the usedSpc variable is populated as shown:

```
usedSpc=$(df -h $ml | grep % | grep -v Use | awk '{print $4}' | cut -d "%" -f1 -)
```

The command first runs df -h, which is piped to the grep command to find any string with the "%" character in it, and then uses -v to eliminate any strings that contain "Use" from the output. Then the awk command takes the output and prints out the fourth column. This is finally piped to the cut command, which removes the "%" character from the output.

On a Linux/Unix system, a shell script such as the prior one can easily be run from a scheduling utility such as cron. For example, if the shell script is named filesp.bsh, here is a sample cron entry:

```
#----------------------------------------------------------------
# Filesystem check
7 * * * * /orahome/oracle/bin/filesp.bsh 1>/orahome/oracle/bin/log/filesp.log 2>&1
#----------------------------------------------------------------
```

The prior entry instructs the system to run the filesp.bsh shell script at 7 minutes after the hour for every hour of the day.

6-2. Identifying System Bottlenecks

Problem

You want to determine if a server performance issue is specifically related to CPU, memory, I/O, or network.

Solution

Use vmstat to determine where the system is resource-constrained. For example, the following command reports on system resource usage every 5 seconds on a Linux system:

```
$ vmstat 5
```

Here is some sample output:

```
procs -----------memory---------- ---swap-- -----io---- --system-- -----cpu------
 r  b   swpd   free   buff  cache   si   so    bi    bo   in    cs us sy id wa st
 2  0 228816 2036164  78604 3163452    0    0     1    16     0     0 29  0 70  0  0
 2  0 228816 2035792  78612 3163456    0    0     0    59   398   528 50  1 49  0  0
 2  0 228816 2035172  78620 3163448    0    0     0    39   437   561 50  1 49  0  0
```

To exit out of vmstat in this mode, press Ctrl+C. You can also have vmstat report for a specific number of runs. For example, this instructs vmstat to run every 6 seconds for a total of 10 reports:

```
$ vmstat 6 10
```

- Here are some general heuristics you can use when interpreting the output of vmstat. If b (processes sleeping) is consistently greater than 0, then you may be using more CPU than available. See Recipe 6-5 for details on identifying Oracle processes and SQL statements consuming CPU resources.

- If so (memory swapped out to disk) and si (memory swapped in from disk) are consistently greater than 0, you may have a memory bottleneck. Paging and swapping occur when there isn't enough physical memory to accommodate the memory needs of the processes on the server. When paging and swapping take place, performance usually suffers because the process of copying memory contents to and from disk is an inherently slow activity. See Recipe 6-5 for details on identifying Oracle processes and SQL statements consuming the most memory.

- If the wa (time waiting for I/O) column is high, this is usually an indication that the storage subsystem is overloaded. See Recipe 6-6 for identifying the sources of I/O contention.

■ **Note** The vmstat tool is available on most Linux/Unix platforms. This tool does vary somewhat by platform; use the man vmstat command to list descriptions of the output and options available for your environment.

How It Works

The vmstat (virtual memory statistics) tool helps quickly identify bottlenecks on your server. This provides a system wide view of the server health. Use the output of vmstat to help determine if the performance bottleneck is related to CPU, memory, or disk I/O.

Most OS monitoring tools focus on one aspect of system performance. The vmstat tool differs from other monitoring tools in that it displays statistics for all of the major components of the OS—namely:

- Processing jobs
- Memory
- Swap
- I/O
- System
- CPU

The processing jobs (procs) section has two columns: r and b. The r column displays the number of processes waiting for access to a processor. The b column displays the number of processes in a sleep state. These values are usually zero.

The memory area displays information about memory usage. This output is approximately the same as obtained by running the free command with the -m parameter:

```
$ free -m
```

The swpd column indicates how much virtual memory has been swapped out to a file or disk. The free column indicates the amount of unused memory.

The swap section displays the amount of memory swapped to and from disk. The si column displays the amount of memory per second swapped in from disk and so column displays the amount of memory per second swapped out to disk.

The IO section displays the number of blocks read and written per second. The bo column is blocks received from the block device and the bi column is the numbers sent to the block device.

The system area shows the number of system operations per second. The in column is the number system interrupts and the cs column is the number context switches.

The CPU section shows the percentage of system usage of the CPUs. These columns should sum to approximately 100 and reflect the percentage of available CPU time. The us column signifies the amount of time spent on non-kernel processes, whereas the si column shows the amount of time spent on kernel operations. The id column shows the amount of idle time. The wa column shows the amount of time waiting for IO operations to complete.

■ **Tip** Use the watch -d vmstat command to highlight differences in the report output as it refreshes.

OS WATCHER

Oracle provides a collection of OS scripts that gather and store metrics for CPU, memory, disk I/O, and network usage. The OS Watcher tool suite automates the gathering of statistics using tools such as vmstat, top, iostat, mpstat, netstat, and so on.

You can obtain OS Watcher from the My Oracle Support web site (support.oracle.com). The OS Watcher User Guide can be found under document ID **301137.1**. This tool is supported on most Linux/Unix systems, and there is also a version for the Windows platform.

6-3. Determining Top System-Resource-Consuming Processes
Problem

You have a server that hosts multiple databases. Users are reporting sluggishness with an application that uses one of the databases. You want to identify which processes are consuming the most resources on the server and then determine if the top consuming process is associated with a database.

Solution

The top command shows a real-time display of the highest CPU and memory resource-consuming processes on a server. Here's the simplest way to run top:

```
$ top
```

Listed next is a fragment of the output:

```
top - 10:57:47 up 65 days,  1:32,  2 users,  load average: 0.22, 0.08, 0.05
Tasks: 165 total,   2 running, 163 sleeping,   0 stopped,   0 zombie
Cpu(s): 46.4%us,  2.3%sy,  0.0%ni, 47.9%id,  3.3%wa,  0.0%hi,  0.0%si,  0.0%st
Mem:   2049404k total,  2033308k used,    16096k free,    95108k buffers
Swap:  4095992k total,    55744k used,  4040248k free,  1362984k cached
```

```
  PID USER      PR  NI  VIRT  RES   SHR S %CPU %MEM      TIME+  COMMAND
29603 oracle    20   0  966m 219m   69m R 34.4 11.0    0:10.16  oracle_29603_o1
   54 root      20   0     0    0     0 S  1.3  0.0    6:37.51  kswapd0
23255 oracle    -2   0  805m  15m   15m S  1.0  0.8   23:53.83  ora_vktm_o12c
 2516 root      20   0     0    0     0 S  0.3  0.0   14:26.21  kondemand/0
23293 oracle    20   0  805m  26m   24m S  0.3  1.3    1:17.38  ora_ckpt_o12c
23317 oracle    20   0  817m 126m  119m S  0.3  6.3    3:14.04  ora_mmon_o12c
```

Type q or press Ctrl+C to exit top. In the prior output, the first section of the output displays general system information such as how long the server has been running, number of users, CPU information, and so on.

■ **Tip** The w command will display the same information contained in the first line of the output of the top command. Additionally, w will display who is logged onto the box.

The second section shows which processes are consuming the most CPU resources (listed top to bottom). In the prior output, the process ID of 29603 is consuming a large amount of CPU and memory. To determine which database this process is associated with, use the ps command:

```
$ ps 29603
```

Here is the associated output:

```
  PID TTY      STAT   TIME COMMAND
29603 ?        Rs     1:08 oracleO12C (DESCRIPTION=(LOCAL=YES)(ADDRESS=(PROTOCOL=beq)))
```

In the prior output, the command column displays the value of oracleO12C. This indicates that this is an Oracle process associated with the O12C database. If the process continues to consume resources, you can next determine if there is a SQL statement associated with the process (see Recipe 6-8) or terminate the process (see Recipe 6-9).

■ **Note** If you're on a Windows box, you can press the ctrl+alt+delete keys at the same time to start the Task Manager utility. This utility allows you to view which applications and processes are consuming the most CPU and memory.

How It Works

The top utility is often the first investigative tool employed by DBAs and system administrators to identify resource-intensive processes on a server. If a process is continuously consuming excessive system resources, then you should further determine if the process is associated with a database and a specific SQL statement.

By default, top will repetitively refresh (every few seconds) information regarding the most CPU-intensive processes. While top is running, you can interactively change its output. For example, if you type >, this will move the column that top is sorting one position to the right. Table 6-1 lists the most useful hot key features to alter the top display to the desired format.

Table 6-1. *Commands to Interactively Change the top Output*

Command	Function
Spacebar	Immediately refreshes the output
< or >	Moves the sort column one to the left or to the right; by default, top sorts on the CPU column
d	Changes the refresh time
R	Reverses the sort order
z	Toggles the color output
h	Displays help menu
F or O	Chooses a sort column

Table 6-2 describes several of the columns displayed by top. Use these descriptions to help interpret the output.

Table 6-2. *Column Descriptions of the top Output*

Column	Description
PID	Unique process identifier
USER	OS username running the process
PR	Priority of the process
NI	Nice value of process; negative value means high priority; positive value means low priority
VIRT	Total virtual memory used by process
RES	Non-swapped physical memory used
SHR	Shared memory used by process
S	Process status
%CPU	Processes percent of CPU consumption since last screen refresh
%MEM	Percent of physical memory the process is consuming
TIME+	Total CPU time, showing hundredths of seconds
COMMAND	Command line used to start a process

6-4. Detecting CPU Bottlenecks

Problem

You want to determine if there is an excessive load on the CPUs on your server.

■ **Note** There are two main utilities for identifying system wide CPU bottlenecks: vmstat and mpstat. The vmstat utility was described in Recipe 6-2. This recipe focuses on using mpstat.

Solution

The mpstat utility reports on system wide CPU statistics. You can specify an interval and count when running this utility. The following instructs mpstat to run 10 times while refreshing the output every 2 seconds:

```
$ mpstat 2 10
```

Here is a snippet of the output:

```
10:17:44 AM  CPU  %user  %nice  %sys %iowait  %irq  %soft  %steal  %idle   intr/s
10:17:46 AM  all   0.50   0.00   0.50    0.75  0.00   0.00    0.00  98.25  1135.18
10:17:48 AM  all   0.25   0.00   0.74    0.00  0.00   0.00    0.00  99.01  1085.00
```

Here are some general guidelines for interpreting the output of the previous report:

- If %idle is high, then your CPUs are most likely not overburdened
- If the %iowat output is a non-zero number, then you may have some disk I/O contention
- If you identify that the CPUs are overloaded, see Recipe 6-5 for techniques to pinpoint sessions consuming the most CPU resources

---

■ **Tip** On Solaris systems, see MOS document ID 1278725.1 for details on using dtrace to interpret mpstat output.

How It Works

The default output of mpstat will only show one line of aggregated statistics for all CPUs on the server. You can also view CPU snapshots that report statistics accumulated between intervals. The following example uses the -P option to report only on processor 0; it displays output every 2 seconds for a total of 20 different reports:

```
$ mpstat -P 0 2 20
```

Here is a snippet of the output:

```
12:20:35 PM  CPU  %user  %nice  %sys %iowait  %irq  %soft  %steal  %idle   intr/s
12:20:37 PM    0   0.00   0.00   0.50    0.00  0.00   0.00    0.00  99.50    2.51
12:20:39 PM    0   0.00   0.00   1.00    0.00  0.00   0.00    0.00  99.00    2.00
```

You can also use the -P ALL option to print on separate lines each CPU's statistics:

```
$ mpstat -P ALL
```

Here is the corresponding output:

```
12:22:45 PM  CPU  %user  %nice  %sys %iowait  %irq  %soft  %steal  %idle   intr/s
12:22:45 PM  all   1.62   0.01   1.05    2.51  0.00   0.00    0.00  94.81  807.99
12:22:45 PM    0   1.22   0.01   1.03    0.64  0.00   0.00    0.00  97.11    1.56
12:22:45 PM    1   2.02   0.01   1.06    4.34  0.01   0.01    0.00  92.56   12.06
```

■ **Tip** To view the configuration of CPUs on a Linux server view the /proc/cpuinfo file. Similarly you can view the /proc/meminfo file to view memory configuration. On Solaris systems, run the prtdiag utility to view configured memory (and CPUs).

6-5. Identifying Processes Consuming CPU and Memory
Problem

You want to view which processes are consuming the most CPU and memory resources on your system.

■ **Note** There are two main utilities for identifying specific processes consuming the most CPU and memory resources: top and ps. The top utility was described in Recipe 6-3. This recipe focuses on using ps.

Solution

The ps (process status) command is handy for quickly identifying top resource-consuming processes. For example, this command displays the top 10 CPU-consuming resources on the box:

```
$ ps -e -o pcpu,pid,user,tty,args | sort -n -k 1 -r | head
```

Here is a partial listing of the output:

```
65.5  5017 oracle   ?        oracleO12C (DESCRIPTION=(LOCAL=YES)(ADDRESS=(PROTOCOL=beq)))
 0.8  5014 oracle   pts/1    sqlplus
 0.8 23255 oracle   ?        ora_vktm_O12C
```

In the prior output, the process named oracleO12C is consuming an inordinate amount of CPU resources on the server. The process name identifies this as an Oracle process associated with the O12C database.

Similarly, you can also display the top memory-consuming processes:

```
$ ps -e -o pmem,pid,user,tty,args | sort -n -k 1 -r | head
```

Here is a snippet of the output:

```
11.2  5017 oracle   ?        oracleO12C (DESCRIPTION=(LOCAL=YES)(ADDRESS=(PROTOCOL=beq)))
 7.1 23317 oracle   ?        ora_mmon_O12C
 6.3 23285 oracle   ?        ora_dbw0_O12C
```

How It Works

The Linux/Unix ps command displays information about currently active processes on the server. The pcpu switch instructs the process status to report the CPU usage of each process. Similarly the pmem switch instructs ps to report on process memory usage. This gives you a quick and easy way to determine which processes are consuming the most CPU or memory resources.

When using multiple commands on one line (such as ps, sort, and head), it's often desirable to associate the combination of commands with a shortcut (alias). Here's an example of creating aliases:

```
$ alias topc='ps -e -o pcpu,pid,user,tty,args | sort -n -k 1 -r | head'
$ alias topm='ps -e -o pmem,pid,user,tty,args | sort -n -k 1 -r | head'
```

Now instead of typing in the long line of commands, you can use the alias—for example:

```
$ topc
```

Also consider establishing the aliases in a startup file (like .bashrc or .profile) so that the commands are automatically defined when you log on to the database server.

On Solaris systems, the prstat utility can also be used to identify which processes are consuming the most CPU and memory resources. For example, you can instruct the prstat to report system statistics every 5 seconds:

```
$ prstat 5
```

Here is some sample output:

```
  PID USERNAME  SIZE   RSS STATE   PRI NICE      TIME  CPU PROCESS/NLWP
24448 oracle    12G 8216M sleep     59    0   0:22:40 0.4% oracle/51
24439 oracle    12G 8214M sleep     59    0   0:08:48 0.3% oracle/14
24387 oracle    12G 4025M sleep     59    0   0:09:45 0.1% oracle/258
```

Type q or press Ctrl+C to exit prstat. After identifying a top resource-consuming process, you can determine which database the process is associated with by using the ps command. This example reports on process information associated with the PID of 24448:

```
$ ps -ef | grep 24448
  oracle 24448    1    1 16:33:42 ?          22:48 ora_pr00_DWREP
```

In this example, the name of the process is ora_pr00_DWREP and the associated database is DWREP.

■ **Tip** Use the ipcs or the sysresv commands to view memory segments allocated by Oracle (and associated semaphores).

6-6. Determining I/O Bottlenecks

Problem

You are experiencing performance problems and want to determine if the issues are related to slow disk I/O.

Solution

Use the iostat command with the -x (extended) option combined with the -d (device) option to generate I/O statistics. This next example displays extended device statistics every 10 seconds:

```
$ iostat -xd 10
```

You need a fairly wide screen to view this output; here's a partial listing:

```
Device: rrqm/s   wrqm/s   r/s   w/s   rsec/s   wsec/s avgrq-sz avgqu-sz   await  svctm  %util
sda       0.00     2.00  0.00  0.80     0.00    22.40    28.00     0.01   15.88  15.87   1.27
```

This periodic extended output allows you to view in real time which devices are experiencing spikes in read and write activity. To exit from the previous iostat command, press Ctrl+C. The options and output may vary depending on your OS. For example, on some Linux/Unix distributions, the iostat output may report the disk utilization as %b (percent busy).

When trying to determine whether device I/O is the bottleneck, here are some general guidelines when examining the iostat output:

- Watch for devices with high reads (r/s) or writes (w/s) per second. To determine if I/O is abnormally high, you'll have to compare the rates with maximum I/O rate of your storage subsystem.

- If any device is near 100% utilization, that's a sign that I/O is a bottleneck.

DETERMINING I/O RATES

To get an estimate of the I/O rate of your storage system, use the dd command in combination with the time command. For example:

```
$ time dd if=/u01/dbfile/O12C/system01.dbf of=test.out
```

Here is some sample output:

```
1024016+0 records in
1024016+0 records out
524296192 bytes (524 MB) copied, 27.3087 seconds, 19.2 MB/s

real    0m27.349s
user    0m0.385s
sys     0m9.846s
```

You can divide the data file size by the total time the command too to run, this will give you the disk I/O rate (which is also displayed in the output). This is a useful metric in determining the speed at which the OS is able to read and write a file.

If you want an estimate of just the read rate, then send then use /dev/null for the output file (nothing gets written):

```
$ time dd if=/u01/dbfile/O12C/system01.dbf of=/dev/null
```

In this way you can estimate the I/O writes of your storage subsystem.

How It Works

The iostat command can help you determine whether disk I/O is potentially a source of performance problems. Table 6-3 describes the columns displayed in the iostat output.

Table 6-3. *Column Descriptions of iostat Disk I/O Output*

Column	Description
Device	Device or partition name
tps	I/O transfers per second to the device
Blk_read/s	Blocks per second read from the device
Blk_wrtn/s	Blocks written per second to the device
Blk_read	Number of blocks read
Blk_wrtn	Number of blocks written
rrqm/s	Number of read requests merged per second that were queued to device
wrqm/s	Number of write requests merged per second that were queued to device
r/s	Read requests per second
w/s	Write requests per second
rsec/s	Sectors read per second
wsec/s	Sectors written per second
rkB/s	Kilobytes read per second
wkB/s	Kilobytes written per second
avgrq-sz	Average size of requests in sectors
avgqu-sz	Average queue length of requests
await	Average time in milliseconds for I/O requests sent to the device to be served
svctm	Average service time in milliseconds
%util	Percentage of CPU time during which I/O requests were issued to the device. Near 100% indicates device saturation

You can also instruct iostat to display reports at a specified interval. The first report displayed will report averages since the last server reboot; each subsequent report shows statistics since the previously generated snapshot. The following example displays a device statistic report every 3 seconds:

```
$ iostat -d 3
```

You can also specify a finite number of reports that you want generated. This is useful for gathering metrics to be analyzed over a period of time. This example instructs iostat to report every 2 seconds for a total of 15 reports:

```
$ iostat 2 15
```

Also consider running `iostat` in combination with the `watch` command. The watch command is particularly useful when you want to highlight differences in the output with each screen refresh. For example:

```
$ watch -d iostat
```

When working with locally attached disks, the output of the `iostat` command will clearly show where the I/O is occurring. However, it is not that clear-cut in environments that use external arrays for storage. What you are presented with at the file system layer is some sort of a virtual disk that might also have been configured by a volume manager. In virtualized storage environments, you'll have to work with your system administrator or storage administrator to determine exactly which disks are experiencing high I/O activity.

Once you have determined that you have a disk I/O contention issue, then you can use utilities such as AWR (if licensed), Statspack (no license required), or the V$ views to determine if your database is I/O stressed. For example, the AWR report contains an I/O statistics section with the following subsections:

- IOStat by Function summary

- IOStat by Filetype summary

- IOStat by Function/Filetype summary

- Tablespace IO Stats

- File IO Stats

If you want to display current database sessions that are waiting for I/O resources, you can query the data dictionary as follows:

```
SELECT a.username, a.sql_id, b.object_name, b.object_type, a.event
FROM v$session a
    ,dba_objects b
    ,v$event_name c
WHERE b.object_id = a.row_wait_obj#
AND    a.event = c.name
AND    c.wait_class = 'User I/O';
```

6-7. Detecting Network-Intensive Processes
Problem

You're investigating performance issues on a database server. As part of your investigation, you want to determine if there are network bottlenecks on the system.

Solution

Use the `netstat` (network statistics) command to display network traffic. Perhaps the most useful way to view `netstat` output is with the `-ptc` options. These options display the process ID and TCP connections, and they continuously update the output:

```
$ netstat -ptc
```

Press Ctrl+C to exit the previous command. Here's a partial listing of the output:

```
Active Internet connections (w/o servers)
Proto Recv-Q Send-Q Local Address Foreign Address            State
PID/Program name
tcp       0      0 speed3:ssh    dhcp-brk-bl8-214-2w-e:59032 ESTABLISHED -
tcp       0      0 speed3:6204   speed3.us.oracle.c:ncube-lm ESTABLISHED -
tcp       0      0 speed3:ssh    dhcp-brk-bl8-214-2w-e:63682 ESTABLISHED -
```

If the Send-Q (bytes not acknowledged by remote host) column has an unusually high value for a process, this may indicate an overloaded network. The useful aspect about the previous output is that you can determine the OS process ID (PID) associated with a network connection. If you suspect the connection in question is an oracle session, you can use the techniques described in the "Solution" section of Recipe 6-8 to map an OS PID to an Oracle process or SQL statement.

How It Works

When experiencing performance issues, usually the network bandwidth is not the cause. Most likely you'll determine that bad performance is related to a poorly constructed SQL statement, inadequate disk I/O, badly designed processes, or not enough CPU or memory resources. However, as a DBA, you need to be aware of all sources of performance bottlenecks and how to diagnose them. In today's highly interconnected world, you must possess network troubleshooting and monitoring skills. The netstat utility is a good starting place for monitoring server network connections.

TROUBLESHOOTING DATABASE NETWORK CONNECTIVITY

Use these steps as guidelines when diagnosing Oracle database network connectivity issues:

Step 1. Use the OS ping utility to determine whether the remote box is accessible—for example:

```
$ ping dwdb
dwdb is alive
```

If ping doesn't work, work with your system or network administrator to ensure you have server-to-server connectivity in place.

Step 2. Use telnet to see if you can connect to the remote server and port (that the listener is listening on)—for example:

```
$ telnet dwdb 1521
Trying 127.0.0.1...
Connected to dwdb.
Escape character is '^]'.
```

The prior output indicates that connectivity to a server and port is okay. If the prior command hangs, then contact your SA or network administrator for further assistance.

Step 3. Use `tnsping` to determine whether Oracle Net is working. This utility will verify that an Oracle Net connection can be made to a database via the network—for example:

```
$ tnsping dwrep
..........
Used TNSNAMES adapter to resolve the alias
Attempting to contact (DESCRIPTION = (ADDRESS = (PROTOCOL = TCP)
(HOST = dwdb.us.farm.com)(PORT = 1521))
(CONNECT_DATA = (SERVER = DEDICATED) (SERVICE_NAME = DWREP)))
OK (500 msec)
```

If `tnsping` can't contact the remote database, verify that the remote listener and database are both up and running. On the remote box, use the `lsnrctl status` command to verify that the listener is up. Verify that the remote database is available by establishing a local connection as a non-SYS account (SYS can often connect to a troubled database when other schemas will not work).

Step 4. Verify that the TNS information is correct. If the remote listener and database are working, then ensure that the mechanism for determining TNS information (like the `tnsnames.ora` file) contains the correct information.

Sometimes the client machine will have multiple TNS_ADMIN locations and `tnsnames.ora` files. One way to verify whether a particular `tnsnames.ora` file is being used is to rename it and see whether you get a different error when attempting to connect to the remote database.

Step 5. If you're still having issues, examine the client `sqlnet.log` file and the remote server `listener.log` file. Sometimes these log files will show additional information that will pinpoint the issue.

6-8. Mapping a Resource-Intensive Process to a Database Process
Problem

The system is performing poorly and you want to identify which OS intensive process on the box is consuming the most resources. Furthermore, you want to map an OS process back to a database process. If the database process is a SQL process, you want to display the details of the SQL statement (such as the user, explain plan, and so on).

Solution

In Linux/Unix environments, if you can identify the resource intensive OS process, then you can easily check to see if that process is associated with a database process. This procedure consists of the following:

1. Run an OS command to identify resource-intensive processes and associated IDs.

2. Identify the database associated with the process.

3. Extract details about the process from the database data dictionary views.

4. If it's a SQL statement, get those details.

5. Generate an execution plan for the SQL statement.

For example, suppose you identify the top CPU-consuming queries with the ps command:

```
$ ps -e -o pcpu,pid,user,tty,args|grep -i oracle|sort -n -k 1 -r|head
```

Here is some sample output:

```
45.7 23651 oracle    ?          oracle012C (DESCRIPTION=(LOCAL=YES)(ADDRESS=(PROTOCOL=beq)))
 0.8 23255 oracle    ?          ora_vktm_012C
 0.2 23317 oracle    ?          ora_mmon_012C
```

The prior output identifies one OS process consuming an excessive amount of CPU. The process ID is 23651 and name is oracle012C. From the process name, it's an Oracle process associated with the 012C database.

You can determine what type of Oracle process this is by querying the data dictionary:

```
SELECT
  'USERNAME    : ' || s.username      || CHR(10) ||
  'SCHEMA      : ' || s.schemaname    || CHR(10) ||
  'OSUSER      : ' || s.osuser        || CHR(10) ||
  'MODUEL      : ' || s.program       || CHR(10) ||
  'ACTION      : ' || s.schemaname    || CHR(10) ||
  'CLIENT_INFO : ' || s.osuser        || CHR(10) ||
  'PROGRAM     : ' || s.program       || CHR(10) ||
  'SPID        : ' || p.spid          || CHR(10) ||
  'SID         : ' || s.sid           || CHR(10) ||
  'SERIAL#     : ' || s.serial#       || CHR(10) ||
  'KILL STRING : ' || '''' || s.sid || ',' || s.serial# || '''' || CHR(10) ||
  'MACHINE     : ' || s.machine       || CHR(10) ||
  'TYPE        : ' || s.type          || CHR(10) ||
  'TERMINAL    : ' || s.terminal      || CHR(10) ||
  'SQL ID      : ' || q.sql_id        || CHR(10) ||
  'CHILD_NUM   : ' || q.child_number  || CHR(10) ||
  'SQL TEXT    : ' || q.sql_text
FROM v$session s
    ,v$process p
    ,v$sql     q
WHERE s.paddr  = p.addr
AND    p.spid   = '&PID_FROM_OS'
AND    s.sql_id = q.sql_id(+)
AND    s.status = 'ACTIVE';
```

The prior script prompts you for the OS process ID. Here is the output for this example:

```
USERNAME    : MV_MAINT
SCHEMA      : MV_MAINT
OSUSER      : oracle
MODUEL      : sqlplus@speed2 (TNS V1-V3)
ACTION      : MV_MAINT
CLIENT_INFO : oracle
PROGRAM     : sqlplus@speed2 (TNS V1-V3)
SPID        : 28191
SID         : 10
SERIAL#     : 2039
```

```
KILL STRING : '10,2039'
MACHINE     : speed2
TYPE        : USER
TERMINAL    : pts/1
SQL ID      : 3k8vqz6yycr3g
CHILD_NUM   : 0
SQL TEXT    : select a.table_name from dba_tables a, dba_indexes b, dba_objects
```

The output indicates that this is a SQL*Plus process with a database SID of 10 and SERIAL# of 2039. You'll need this information if you decide to terminate the process with the ALTER SYSTEM KILL SESSION statement (see Recipe 6-9 for details).

In this example, since the process is running a SQL statement, further details about the query can be extracted by generating an execution plan:

```
SQL> SELECT * FROM table(DBMS_XPLAN.DISPLAY_CURSOR('&sql_id',&child_num));
```

You'll be prompted for the sql_id and child_num when you run the prior statement. Here is a partial listing of the output:

```
SQL_ID  3k8vqz6yycr3g, child number 0
-------------------------------------
select a.table_name from dba_tables a, dba_indexes b, dba_objects c
...
```

This output will help you determine the efficiency of the SQL statement and provide insight on how to tune it. Refer to Chapter 9 for details on how to manually tune a query and Chapter 11 for automated SQL tuning.

Keep in mind that when selecting from V$SESSION, the records displayed within that view show the current SQL statement that the session is executing. It's entirely possible that a given session can run several resource consuming queries in succession. Therefore it's conceivable you might identify a query for a session (Step 3) that wasn't the SQL executing when you first identified the OS process (Step 1). That said, the prior solution works well for long running queries consuming large amounts of system resources.

How It Works

The process described in the "Solution" section of this recipe allows you to quickly identify resource-intensive processes, then map the OS process to a database process, and subsequently map the database process to a SQL statement. Once you know which SQL statement is consuming resources, then you can generate an execution plan to further attempt to determine any possible inefficiencies.

When generating the execution plan for a SQL statement, you need to provide DBMS_XPLAN both the SQL_ID and CHILD_NUMBER to correctly identify an execution plan. The SQL_ID uniquely identifies the SQL statement. If the SQL statement has executed more than once, it is possible for the optimizer to generate and use one or more execution plans. If a given SQL statement has more than one execution plan associated with it, then the combination of SQL_ID and CHILD_NUMBER uniquely identifies an execution plan for a given SQL statement.

Sometimes the resource-consuming process will not be associated with a database. In these scenarios, you'll have to work with your SA to determine what the process is and if it can be tuned or terminated. Also, you may encounter resource-intensive processes that are database-specific but not associated with a SQL statement. For example, you might have a long-running RMAN backup process, Data Pump, or PL/SQL jobs running. In these cases, work with your DBA to identify whether these types of processes can be tuned, scheduled to run at another time of day, or killed.

ORADEBUG

You can use Oracle's oradebugutility to display top consuming SQL statements if you know the OS ID. For example, suppose that you have used a utility such as top or ps to identify a high CPU-consuming OS process, and from the name of the process you determine it's a database process. Now log in to SQL*Plus and use oradebug to display any SQL associated with the process. In this example, the OS process ID is 23651:

```
SQL> oradebug setospid 23651;
Oracle pid: 32, Unix process pid: 23651, image: oracle@speed2 (TNS V1-V3)
```

Now show the SQL associated with this process (if any):

```
SQL> oradebug current_sql;
```

If there is a SQL statement associated with the process, it will be displayed—for example:

```
select a.table_name from dba_tables a, dba_indexes b, dba_objects c
...
```

The oradebug utility can be used in a variety of methods to help troubleshoot performance issues. Use oradebug help to display all options available.

6-9. Terminating a Resource-Intensive Process

Problem

You have identified a database process that is consuming inordinate amounts of system resources (see Recipe 6-8) and determined that it's a runaway SQL statement that needs to be killed.

Solution

There are three basic ways to terminate a SQL process:

- If you have access to the terminal where the SQL statement is running, you can press Ctrl+C and attempt to halt the process.

- Determine the session ID and serial number, and then use the SQL ALTER SYSTEM KILL SESSION statement.

- Determine the OS process ID, and use the kill utility to stop the process.

If you happen to have access to the terminal from which the resource-consuming SQL statement is running, you can attempt to press Ctrl+C to terminate the process. Often you don't have access to the terminal and will have to use a SQL statement or an OS command to terminate the process.

Using SQL to Kill a Session

If it's an Oracle process and you have identified the SID and SERIAL# (see Recipe 6-8), you can terminate a process from within SQL*Plus. Here is the general syntax:

```
alter system kill session 'integer1, integer2 [,integer3]' [immediate];
```

In the prior syntax statement, integer1 is the value of the SID column and integer2 is the value from the SERIAL# column (of V$SESSION). In a RAC environment, you can optionally specify the value of the instance ID for integer3. The instance ID can be retrieved from the GV$SESSION view.

Here's an example that terminates a process with a SID of 1177 and a SERIAL# of 38583:

```
SQL> alter system kill session '1177,38583';
```

If successful, you should see this output:

```
System altered.
```

When you kill a session, this will mark the session as terminated, roll back active transactions (within the session), and release any locks (held by the session). The session will stay in a terminated state until any dependent transactions are rolled back. If it takes a minute or more to roll back the transaction, Oracle reports the session as "marked to be terminated" and returns control to the SQL prompt. If you specify IMMEDIATE (optional), Oracle will roll back any active transactions and immediately return control back to you.

■ **Caution**   Killing a session that is executing a select statement is fairly harmless. However, if you terminate a session that is performing a large insert/update/delete then you may see a great deal of database activity (including I/O in the online redo logs) associated with Oracle rolling back the terminated transaction.

Using the OS Kill Command

If you have access to the database server and access to an OS account that has privileges to terminate an Oracle process (such as the oracle OS account), you can also terminate a process directly with the kill command.

■ **Caution**   Ensure that you don't kill the wrong Oracle process. If you accidentally kill a required Oracle background process, this will cause your instance to abort.

For example, suppose you run the ps command and have done the associated work to determine that you have a SQL statement that has been running for hours and needs to be terminated. The kill command directly terminates the OS process. In this example, the process ID of 6254 is terminated:

```
$ kill -9 6254
```

■ **Caution** In some rare situations killing an Oracle process associated with a SQL transaction can have an adverse impact on the stability of the instance. For example, killing a process participating in a distributed transaction may cause the instance to crash. To determine if this is an issue for the version of the database you're using see MOS bug IDs 8686128 and 12961905. In older versions of Oracle various other bugs associated with killing a process have been identified and fixed and are documented in MOS bug IDs 5929055 and 6865378.

How It Works

Sometimes you'll find yourself in a situation where you need to kill hung SQL processes, database jobs, or SQL statements that are consuming inordinate amounts of resources. For example, you may have a test server where a job has been running for several hours, is consuming much of the server resources, and needs to be stopped so that other jobs can continue to process in a timely manner.

Manually killing a SQL statement will cause the transaction to be rolled back. Therefore take care when doing this. Ensure that you are killing the correct process. If you erroneously terminate a critical process, this obviously will have an adverse impact on the application and associated data.

CHAPTER 7

■ ■ ■

Troubleshooting the Database

This chapter contains several recipes that show how to use the database's built-in diagnostic infrastructure to resolve database performance issues. You'll learn how to use ADRCI, the Automatic Diagnostic Repository Command Interpreter, to perform various tasks such as checking the database alert log, creating a diagnostic package for sending to Oracle Support engineers, and running a proactive health check of the database.

Many common Oracle database performance-related issues occur when you have space issues with the temporary tablespace or when you're creating a large index or a large table with the create table as select (CTAS) technique. Undo tablespace space issues are another common source of trouble for many DBAs. This chapter has several recipes that help you proactively monitor, diagnose, and resolve temporary tablespace and undo tablespace-related issues. When a production database seems to hang, there are ways to collect critical diagnostic data for analyzing the causes, and this chapter shows you how to log in to an unresponsive database to collect diagnostic data.

7-1. Determining the Optimal Undo Retention Period
Problem

You need to determine the optimal length of time for undo retention in your database.

Solution

You can specify the length of time Oracle will retain undo data after a transaction commits, by specifying the UNDO_RETENTION parameter. To determine the optimal value for the UNDO_RETENTION parameter, you must first calculate the actual amount of undo that the database is generating. Once you know approximately how much undo the database is generating, you can calculate a more precise value for the UNDO_RETENTION parameter. Use the following formula to calculate the optimal value of the UNDO_RETENTION parameter:

```
OPTIMAL UNDO_RETENTION = UNDO SIZE/(DB_BLOCK_SIZE*UNDO_BLOCK_PER_SEC)
```

You can calculate the space allocated for undo in your database by issuing the following query:

```
SQL> select sum(d.bytes) "undo"
  2  from v$datafile d,
  3  v$tablespace t,
  4  dba_tablespaces s
  5  where s.contents = 'UNDO'
  6  and s.status = 'ONLINE'
  7  and t.name = s.tablespace_name
  8  and d.ts# = t.ts#;
```

```
UNDO
----------
104857600
SQL>
```

You can calculate the value of UNDO_BLOCKS_PER_SEC with the following query:

```
SQL> select max(undoblks/((end_time-begin_time)*3600*24))
  2  "UNDO_BLOCK_PER_SEC"
  3  FROM v$undostat;

UNDO_BLOCK_PER_SEC
------------------
             7.625
SQL>
```

You most likely remember the block size for your database—if not, you can look it up in the SPFILE or find it by issuing the command show parameter db_block_size. Let's say the db_block_size is 8 KB (8,192 bytes) for your database. You can then calculate the optimal value for the UNDO_RETENTION parameter using the formula shown earlier in this recipe—for example, giving a result in seconds: 1,678.69 = 104,857,600/(7.625 * 8,192). In this case, assigning a value of 1,800 seconds for the undo_retention parameter is appropriate, because it's a bit more than what is indicated by our formula for computing the value of this parameter.

The previous example is predicated on the assumption that you have a limited amount of disk space available. If disk space isn't an issue for you, you can instead choose the ideal value for the UNDO_RETENTION parameter for your instance. In this case, you choose a value for the UNDO_RETENTION parameter first and use that to calculate the size of your undo tablespace. The formula now becomes:

```
size of undo = undo_retention * db_block_size :undo_block_per_sec
```

You can use the following query to do all the calculations for you:

```
select d.undo_size/(1024*1024) "Current UNDO SIZE",
       SUBSTR(e.value,1,25) "UNDO RETENTION",
       (to_number(e.value) * to_number(f.value) *
       g.undo_block_per_sec) / (1024*1024)
      "Necessary UNDO SIZE"
    from (
      select sum(a.bytes) undo_size
        from v$datafile a,
             v$tablespace b,
             dba_tablespaces c
     where c.contents = 'UNDO'
       and c.status = 'ONLINE'
       and b.name = c.tablespace_name
       and a.ts# = b.ts#
    ) d,
    v$parameter e,
    v$parameter f,
    (
    Select max(undoblks/((end_time-begin_time)*3600*24))
      undo_block_per_sec
      from v$undostat
    ) g
```

```
    where e.name = 'undo_retention'
    and f.name = 'db_block_size';
```

```
Current UNDO SIZE
-----------------
500
UNDO RETENTION
--------------
10800
Necessary UNDO SIZE
-------------------
674.611200
```

The query shows that you should set the size of the undo tablespace in this database to around 675 MB. The final result is 674.611200. That rounds to 675 MB.

Here is how to set the undo retention to 30 minutes for an instance by updating the value of the UNDO_RETENTION parameter in the SPFILE:

```
SQl> alter system set undo_retention=1800 scope=both;

System altered.

SQL>
```

How It Works

Oracle retains the undo data for both read consistency purposes as well as to support Oracle Flashback operations, for the duration you specify with the UNDO_RETENTION parameter. Automatic undo management is the default mode for undo management starting with release 11g. If you create a database with the Database Configuration Assistant (DBCA), Oracle automatically creates an auto-extending undo tablespace named UNDOTBS1. If you're manually creating a database, you specify the undo tablespace in the database creation statement, or you can add the undo tablespace at any point. If a database doesn't have an explicit undo tablespace, Oracle will store the undo records in the SYSTEM tablespace.

Once you set the UNDO_TABLESPACE initialization parameter, Oracle automatically manages undo retention for you. Optionally, you can set the UNDO_RETENTION parameter to specify how long Oracle retains older undo data before overwriting it with newer undo data.

The first formula in the Solution section shows how to set the length of the UNDO_RETENTION parameter for a specific undo tablespace size. The second query calculates the size of the undo tablespace for a specifc value for the UNDO_RETENTION parameter that's based on your instance's undo needs, which in turn depend on current database activity. Note that we rely on the dynamic view V$UNDOSTAT to calculate the value for the undo retention period. Therefore, it's essential that you execute your queries after the database has been running for some time, thus ensuring that it has had the chance to process a typical workload.

If you configure the UNDO_RETENTION parameter, the undo tablespace must be large enough to hold the undo generated by the database within the time you specify with the UNDO_RETENTION parameter. When a transaction commits, the database may overwrite its undo data with newer undo data. The undo retention period is the minimum time for which the database will attempt to retain older undo data. After it saves the undo data for the period you specified for the UNDO_RETENTION parameter, the database marks that undo data as *expired* and makes the space occupied by that data available to write undo data for new transactions.

By default, the database uses the following criteria to determine how long it needs to retain undo data:

- Length of the longest-running query

- Length of the longest-running transaction

- Longest flashback duration

It's somewhat difficult to understand how the Oracle database handles the retention of undo data. Here's a brief summary of how things work:

- If you don't configure the undo tablespace with the AUTOEXTEND option, the database simply ignores the value you set for the UNDO_RETENTION parameter. The database will automatically tune the undo retention period based on database workload and the size of the undo tablespace. So, make sure you set the undo tablespace to a large value if you're receiving errors indicating (*snapshot too old*) that the database is not retaining undo for a long enough time. Typically, the undo retention in this case is for a duration significantly longer than the longest-running active query in the database.

- If you want the database to try to honor the settings you specify for the UNDO_RETENTION parameter, make sure that you enable the AUTOEXTEND option for the undo tablespace. This way, Oracle will automatically extend the size of the undo tablespace to make room for undo from new transactions, instead of overwriting the older undo data. However, if you're receiving ORA-0155 (snapshot too old) errors—say, due to Oracle Flashback operations—it means that the database isn't able to dynamically tune the undo retention period effectively. In a case such as this, try increasing the value of the UNDO_RETENTION parameter to match the length of the longest Oracle Flashback operation. Alternatively, you can try going to a larger fixed-size undo tablespace (without the AUTOEXTEND option).

The key to figuring out the right size for the undo tablespace or the correct setting for the UNDO_RETENTION parameter is to understand the nature of the current database workload. In order to understand the workload characteristics, it's important to examine the V$UNDOSTAT view, because it contains statistics showing how the database is utilizing the undo space, as well as information such as the length of the longest-running queries. You can use this information to calculate the size of the undo space for the current workload your database is processing. Note that each row in the V$UNDOSTAT view shows undo statistics for a 10-minute time interval. The table contains a maximum of 576 rows, each for a 10-minute interval. Thus, you can review undo usage for up to 4 days in the past.

Here are the key columns you should monitor in the V$UNDOSTAT view for the time period you're interested in—ideally, the time period should include the time when your longest-running queries are executing. You can use these statistics to size both the UNDO_TABLESPACE as well as the UNDO_RETENTION initialization parameters.

begin_time: Beginning of the time interval.

end_time: End of the time interval.

undoblks: Number of undo blocks the database consumed in a 10-minute interval; this is what we used in our formula for the estimation of the size of the undo tablespace.

txncount: Number of transactions executed in a 10-minute interval.

maxquerylen: This shows the length of the longest query (in seconds) executed in this instance during a 10-minute interval. You can estimate the size of the UNDO_RETENTION parameter based on the maximum value of the MAXQUERYLEN column.

maxqueryid: Identifier for the longest-running SQL statement in this interval.

nospaceerrcnt: The number of times the database didn't have enough free space available in the undo tablespace for new undo data, because the entire undo tablespace was being used by active transactions; of course, this means that you need to add space to the undo tablespace.

tuned_undoretention: The time, in seconds, for which the database will retain the undo data after the database commits the transaction to which the undo belongs.

The following query based on the V$UNDOSTAT view shows how Oracle automatically tunes undo retention (check the TUNED_UNDORETENTION column) based on the length of the longest-running query (MAXQUERYLEN column) in the current instance workload.

```
SQL> select to_char(begin_time,'hh24:mi:ss') BEGIN_TIME,
  2  to_char(end_time,'hh24:mi:ss') END_TIME,
  3  maxquerylen,nospaceerrcnt,tuned_undoretention
  4  from v$undostat;
```

BEGIN_TI	END_TIME	MAXQUERYLEN	NOSPACEERRCNT	TUNED_UNDORETENTION
12:15:35	12:25:35	592	0	1492
12:05:35	12:15:35	1194	0	2094
11:55:35	12:05:35	592	0	1493
11:45:35	11:55:35	1195	0	2095
11:35:35	11:45:35	593	0	1494
11:25:35	11:35:35	1196	0	2097
11:15:35	11:25:35	594	0	1495
11:05:35	11:15:35	1195	0	2096
10:55:35	11:05:35	593	0	1495
10:45:35	10:55:35	1198	0	2098

```
...
SQL>
```

Note that the value of the TUNED_UNDORETENTION column fluctuates continuously, based on the value of the maximum query length (MAXQUERYLEN) during any interval. You can see that the two columns are directly related to each other, with Oracle raising or lowering the tuned undo retention based on the maximum query length during a given interval (of 10 minutes). The following query shows the usage of undo blocks and the transaction count during each 10-minute interval.

```
SQL> select to_char(begin_time,'hh24:mi:ss'),to_char(end_time,'hh24:mi:ss'),
  2  maxquerylen,ssolderrcnt,nospaceerrcnt,undoblks,txncount from v$undostat
  3  order by undoblks
  4  /
```

TO_CHAR(	TO_CHAR(	MAXQUERYLEN	SSOLDERRCNT	NOSPACEERRCNT	UNDOBLKS	TXNCOUNT
17:33:51	17:36:49	550	0	0	1	18
17:23:51	17:33:51	249	0	0	33	166
17:13:51	17:23:51	856	0	0	39	520
17:03:51	17:13:51	250	0	0	63	171
16:53:51	17:03:51	850	0	0	191	702
16:43:51	16:53:51	245	0	0	429	561

```
6 rows selected.

SQL>
```

Oracle provides an easy way to help set the size of the undo tablespace as well as the undo retention period, through the OEM Undo Advisor interface. You can specify the length of time for the advisor's analysis, for a period going back to a week—the advisor uses the AWR hourly snapshots to perform its analysis. You can specify the undo retention period to support a flashback transaction query. Alternatively, you can let the database determine the desired undo retention based on the longest query in the analysis period.

7-2. Finding What's Consuming the Most Undo
Problem

Often, one or two user sessions seem to be hogging the undo tablespaces. You'd like to identify the user and the SQL statement that are using up all that undo space.

Solution

Use the following query to find out which SQL statement has run for the longest time in your database.

```
SQL> select s.sql_text from v$sql s, v$undostat u
    where u.maxqueryid=s.sql_id;
```

You can join the V$TRANSACTION and the V$SESSION views to find out the most undo used by a session for a currently executing transaction, as shown here:

```
SQL> select s.sid, s.username, t.used_urec, t.used_ublk
    from v$session s, v$transaction t
    where s.saddr = t.ses_addr
    order by t.used_ublk desc;
```

You can also issue the following query to find out which session is currently using the most undo in an instance:

```
SQL>select s.sid, t.name, s.value
    from v$sesstat s, v$statname t
    where s.statistic# = t.statistic#
    and t.name = 'undo change vector size'
    order by s.value desc;
```

The query's output relies on the statistic undo change vector size in the V$STATNAME view, to show the SID for the sessions consuming the most undo right now. The V$TRANSACTION view shows details about active transactions. Here's a query that joins the V$TRANSACTION, V$SQL and V$SESSION views and shows you the user and the SQL statement together with the amount of undo space that's consumed by the SQL statement:

```
SQL> select sql.sql_text sql_text, t.USED_UREC Records,
    t.USED_UBLK Blocks,
    (t.USED_UBLK*8192/1024) KBytes from v$transaction t,
    v$session s,
    v$sql sql
    where t.addr = s.taddr
    and s.sql_id = sql.sql_id
    and s.username ='&USERNAME';
```

The column USED_UREC shows the number of undo records used, and the USED_UBLK column shows the undo blocks used by a transaction.

How It Works

You can issue the queries described in the "Solution" section to identify the sessions that are responsible for the most undo usage in your database, as well as the users that are responsible for those sessions. You can query the V$UNDOSTAT with the appropriate begin_time and end_time values to get the SQL identifier of the longest-running SQL statement during a time interval. The MAXQUERYID column captures the SQL identifier. You can use this ID to query the V$SQL view in order to find out the actual SQL statement. Similarly, the V$TRANSACTION and the V$SESSION views together help identify the users that are consuming the most undo space. If excessive undo usage is affecting performance, you might want to look at the application to see why the queries are using so much undo.

If you are experiencing excessive undo, then the following query can help. Executing the query helps you find the users and the instance responsible for undo usage in an Oracle RAC Database.

```
SQL> select a.inst_id, a.sid, c.username, c.osuser, c.program, b.name,
     a.value, d.used_urec, d.used_ublk
     from gv$sesstat a, v$statname b, gv$session c, gv$transaction d
     where a.statistic# = b.statistic#
     and a.inst_id = c.inst_id
     and a.sid = c.sid
     and c.inst_id = d.inst_id
     and c.saddr = d.ses_addr
     and b.name = 'undo change vector size'
     and a.value > 0
     order by a.value;
```

Once you know the users and the instances responsible, you can take a closer look at just what those users and instances are doing that is causing such a high rate of undo usage.

7-3. Resolving an ORA-01555 Error
Problem

You're receiving the ORA-01555 (snapshot too old) errors during nightly runs of key production batch jobs. You want to eliminate these errors.

Solution

While setting a high value for the UNDO_RETENTION parameter can potentially minimize the possibility of receiving "snapshot too old" errors, it doesn't guarantee that the database won't overwrite older undo data that may be needed by a running transaction. You can move long-running batch jobs to a separate time interval when other programs aren't running in the database, to avoid these errors. Remember that you don't always need several concurrent programs to generate "snapshot too old". You can do generate that error by running one poorly written query on a big table in a cursor, and update the same table in the loop.

Regardless, while you can minimize the occurrence of "snapshot too old" errors with these approaches, you can't completely eliminate such errors without specifying the *guaranteed undo retention* feature. When you configure guaranteed undo retention in a database, no SELECT statement can fail because of the "snapshot too old" error. Oracle will keep new DML statements from executing when you set up guaranteed undo retention. Implementing the guaranteed undo feature is simple. Suppose you want to ensure that the database retains undo for at least an hour (3,600 seconds). First set the undo retention threshold with the alter system command shown here, and then set up guaranteed undo retention by specifying the retention guarantee clause to alter the undo tablespace.

```
SQL> alter system set undo_retention=3600;
System altered.
SQL> alter tablespace undotbs1 retention guarantee;
Tablespace altered.
SQL>
```

You can switch off guaranteed undo retention by executing the alter tablespace command with the retention noguarantee clause.

■ **Tip**   You can enable guaranteed undo retention by using the alter system command as shown in this recipe, as well as with the create database and create undo tablespace statements.

How It Works

Oracle uses the undo records stored in the undo tablespace to help roll back transactions, provide read consistency, and to help recover the database. In addition, the database also uses undo records to read data from a past point in time using Oracle Flashback Query. Undo data serves as the underpinning for several Oracle Flashback features that help you recover from logical errors.

Occurrence of the Error

The ORA-01555 error (snapshot too old) may occur in various situations. The following is a case where the error occurs during an export.

```
EXP-00008: ORACLE error 1555 encountered
ORA-01555: snapshot too old: rollback segment number 10 with name "_SYSSMU10$" too small
EXP-00000: Export terminated unsuccessfully
```

And you can receive the same error when performing a flashback transaction:

```
ERROR at line 1:
ORA-01555: snapshot too old: rollback segment number  with name "" too small
ORA-06512: at "SYS.DBMS_FLASHBACK", line 37
ORA-06512: at "SYS.DBMS_FLASHBACK", line 70
ORA-06512: at li
```

The "snapshot too old" error occurs when Oracle overwrites undo data that's needed by another query. The error is a direct result of how Oracle's read consistency mechanism works. The error occurs during the execution of a long-running query when Oracle tries to read the "before image" of any changed rows from the undo segments.

For example, if a long-running query starts at 1 A.M. and runs until 6 A.M. it's possible for the database to change the data that's part of this query during the period in which the query executes. When Oracle tries to read the data as it appeared at 1 A.M., the query may fail if that data is no longer present in the undo segments.

If your database is experiencing a lot of updates, Oracle may not be able to fetch the changed rows, because the before changes recorded in the undo segments may have been overwritten. The transactions that changed the rows will have already committed, and the undo segments don't have a record of the before change row values because the database overwrote the relevant undo data. Since Oracle fails to return consistent data for the current query, it issues the ORA-01555 error. The query that's currently running requires the before image to construct read-consistent data, but the before image isn't available.

The ORA-01555 error may be the result of one or both of the following: a heavy amount of queries during a time of intense changes in the database or too small an undo tablespace. You can increase the size of the undo tablespace, but that doesn't ensure that the error won't occur again.

Influence of Extents

The database stores undo data in undo extents, and there are three distinct types of undo extents:

Active: Transactions are currently using these extents.

Unexpired: These are extents that contain undo that's required to satisfy the undo retention time specified by the UNDO_RETENTION initialization parameter.

Expired: These are extents with undo that's been retained longer than the duration specified by the UNDO_RETENTION parameter.

If the database doesn't find enough expired extents in the undo tablespace or it can't get new undo extents, it'll re-use the unexpired (but never an active undo extent) extents, and this leaves the door open for an ORA-01555, "snapshot too old" error. By default, the database will essentially stop honoring the undo retention period you specify if it encounters space pressure to accommodate the undo from new transactions. Since the unexpired undo extents contain undo records needed to satisfy the undo retention period, overwriting those extents in reality means that the database is lowering the undo retention period you've set. Enabling the undo retention guarantee helps assure the success of long-running queries as well as Oracle Flashback operations. The "guarantee" part of the undo retention guarantee is *real*—Oracle will certainly retain undo at least for the time you specify and will never overwrite any of the unexpired undo extents that contain the undo required to satisfy the undo retention period. However, there's a stiff price attached to this guarantee—Oracle will guarantee retention even if it means that DML transactions fail because the database can't find space to record the undo for those transactions. Therefore, you must exercise great caution when enabling the guaranteed undo retention capability.

7-4. Monitoring Temporary Tablespace Usage
Problem

You want to monitor the usage of the temporary tablespace.

Solution

Execute the following query to find out the used and free space in a temporary tablespace.

```
SQL> select * from (select a.tablespace_name,
     sum(a.bytes/1024/1024) allocated_mb
     from dba_temp_files a
```

```
where a.tablespace_name = upper('&&temp_tsname') group by a.tablespace_name) x,
(select sum(b.bytes_used/1024/1024) used_mb,
sum(b.bytes_free/1024/1024) free_mb
from v$temp_space_header b
where b.tablespace_name=upper('&&temp_tsname') group by b.tablespace_name);
```

```
Enter value for temp_tsname: TEMP
...
TABLESPACE_NAME              ALLOCATED_MB   USED_MB   FREE_MB
---------------             ------------   -------   -------
TEMP                                  60        12        48
SQL>
```

How It Works

Oracle uses temporary tablespaces for storing intermediate results from sort operations as well as any temporary tables, temporary LOBs, and temporary B-trees. You can create multiple temporary tablespaces, but only one of them can be the default temporary tablespace. If you don't explicitly assign a temporary tablespace to a user, that user is assigned the default temporary tablespace.

You won't find information about temporary tablespaces in the DBA_FREE_SPACE view. Use the V$TEMP_SPACE_HEADER as shown in this example to find how much free and used space there is in any temporary tablespace.

7-5. Identifying Who Is Using the Temporary Tablespace
Problem

You notice that the temporary tablespace is filling up fast, and you want to identify the user and the SQL statements responsible for the high temporary tablespace usage.

Solution

Issue the following query to find out which SQL statement is using up space in a sort segment.

```
SQL> select se.sid, se.username,
    su.blocks * ts.block_size / 1024 / 1024 mb_used, su.tablespace,
    su.sqladdr address, sq.hash_value, sq.sql_text
    from v$sort_usage su, v$session se, v$sqlarea sq, dba_tablespaces ts
    where su.session_addr = se.saddr
    and su.sqladdr = sq.address (+)
    and su.tablespace = ts.tablespace_name;
```

The preceding query shows information about the session that issued the SQL statements well as the name of the temporary tablespace and the amount of space the SQL statement is using in that tablespace.

You can use the following query to find out which sessions are using space in the temporary tablespace. Note that the information is in the summary form, meaning it doesn't separate the various sort operations being run by a session—it simply gives the total temporary tablespace usage by each session.

```
SQL> select se.sid,
    se.username, se.osuser, pr.spid,
    se.module,se.program,
    sum (su.blocks) * ts.block_size / 1024 / 1024 mb_used, su.tablespace,
    count(*) sorts
    from v$sort_usage su, v$session se, dba_tablespaces ts, v$process pr
    where su.session_addr = se.saddr
    and se.paddr = pr.addr
    and su.tablespace = ts.tablespace_name
    group by se.sid, se.serial#, se.username, se.osuser, pr.spid, se.module,
    se.program, ts.block_size, su.tablespace;
```

The output of this query will show you the space that each session is using in the temporary tablespace, as well as the number of sort operations that session is performing right now.

How It Works

Oracle tries to perform sort and hash operations in memory (PGA), but if a sort operation is too large to fit into memory, it uses the temporary tablespace to do the work. It's important to understand that even a single large sort operation has the potential to use up an entire temporary tablespace. Since all database sessions share the temporary tablespace, the session that runs the large sort operation could potentially result in other sessions receiving errors due to lack of room in that tablespace, or fail itself. Once the temporary tablespace fills up, all SQL statements that seek to use the temporary tablespace will fail with the ORA-1652: unable to extend temp segment error. New sessions may not be able to connect, and queries can sometimes hang and users may not be able to issue new queries. You try to find any blocking locks, but none exists. If the temporary tablespace fills up, transactions won't complete. If you look in the alert log, you'll find that the temporary tablespace ran out of space.

Operations that use an ORDER BY or GROUP BY clause frequently use the temporary tablespace to do their work. Large hash joins also need the temp space while they're execting. You must also remember that creating an index or rebuilding one also makes use of the temporary tablespace for sorting the index.

Oracle uses the PGA memory for performing the sort and hash operations. Thus, one of the first things you must do is to review the current value set for the PGA_AGGREGATE_TARGET initialization parameter and see if bumping it up will help if you happen to see a lot of I/O occurring in the temporary tablespace. Nevertheless, even a larger setting for the PGA_AGGREGATE_TARGET parameter doesn't guarantee that Oracle will perform a huge sort entirely in memory. Oracle allocates each session a certain amount of PGA memory, with the amount it allocates internally determined, based on the value of the PGA_AGGREGATE_TARGET parameter. Once a large operation uses its share of the PGA memory, Oracle will write intermediary results to disk in the temporary tablespace. These types of operations are called *one-pass* or *multi-pass* operations, and since they are performed on disk, they are much slower than an operation performed entirely in the PGA.

If your database is running out of space in the temporary tablespace, you must increase its size by adding a tempfile. Enabling *autoextend* for a temporary tablespace will also help prevent "out of space" errors. Since Oracle allocates space in a temporary tablespace that you have assigned for the user performing the sort operation, you can assign users that need to perform heavy sorting a temporary tablespace that's different from that used by the rest of the users, thus minimizing the effect of the heavy sorting activity on overall database performance.

Note that unlike table or index segments, of which there are several for each object, a temporary tablespace has just one segment called the sort segment. All sessions share this sort segment. A single SQL statement can use multiple sort and hash operations. In addition, the same session can have multiple SQL statements executing simultaneously, with each statement using multiple sort and hash operations. Once a sort operation completes, the database immediately marks the blocks used by the operations as free and allocates them to another sort operation. The database adds extents to the sort segment as the sort operation gets larger, but if there's no more free space in the temporary tablespace to allocate additional extents, it issues the ORA-1652:unable to extend temp segment error. The SQL statement that's using the sort operation will fail as a result.

■ **Note** Although you'll receive an ORA-1652 error when a SQL statement performing a huge sort fails due to lack of space in the temporary tablespace, that's not the only reason you'll get this error. You'll also receive this error when performing a table move operation (alter table ... move), if the tablespace to which you're moving the table doesn't have room to hold the table. Same is the case sometimes when you're creating a large index. Please *see* Recipe 7-6 for an explanation of this error.

7-6. Resolving the "Unable to Extend Temp Segment" Error

Problem

While creating a large index, you receive an Oracle error indicating that the database is unable to extend a TEMP segment. However, you have plenty of free space in the temporary tablespace.

Solution

When you get an error such as the following, your first inclination may be to think that there's no free space in the temporary tablespace.

```
ORA-01652: unable to extend temp segment by 1024 in tablespace INDX_01
```

You cannot fix this problem by adding space to the temporary tablespace. The error message clearly indicates the tablespace that ran out of space. In this case, the offending tablespace is INDX_01, and not the TEMP tablespace. Obviously, an index creation process failed because there was insufficient space in the INDX_01 tablespace. You can fix the problem by adding a datafile to the INDX_01 tablespace, as shown here:

```
SQL>alter tablespace INDX_01 add datafile '/u01/app/oracle/data/indx_01_02.dbf'
  2 size 1000m;
```

How It Works

When you receive the ORA-01652 error, your normal tendency is to check the temporary tablespace. You check the DBA_TEMP_FREE_SPACE view, and there's plenty of free space in the default temporary tablespace, TEMP. Well, if you look at the error message carefully, it tells you that the database is unable to extend the temp segment in the INDX_01 tablespace. When you create an index, as in this case, you provide the name of the permanent tablespace in which the database must create the new index. Oracle starts the creation of the new index by putting the new index structure into a temporary segment in the tablespace you specify (INDX_01 in our example) for the index. The reason is that if your index creation process fails, Oracle (to be more specific, the SMON process) will remove the temporary segment from the tablespace you specified for creating the new index. Once the index is successfully created (or rebuilt), Oracle converts the temporary segment into a permanent segment within the INDX_01 tablespace. However, as long as Oracle is still creating the index, the database deems it a temporary segment and thus when an index creation fails, the database issues the ORA-01652 error, which is also the error code for an "out of space" error for a temporary tablespace. The TEMP segment the error refers to is the segment that was holding the new index while it was being built. Once you increase the size of the INDX_01 tablespace, the error will go away.

■ **Tip** The temporary segment in an ORA-1652 error message may not be referring to a temporary segment in a temporary tablespace.

The key to resolving the ORA-01652 error is to understand that Oracle uses temporary segments in places other than a temporary tablespace. While a temporary segment in the temporary tablespace is for activities such as sorting, a permanent tablespace can also use temporary segments when performing temporary actions necessary during the creation of a table (CTAS) or an index.

■ **Tip** When you create an index, the creation process uses two different temporary segments. One temporary segment in the TEMP tablespace is used to sort the index data. Another temporary segment in the permanent tablespace holds the index while it is being created. After creating the index, Oracle changes the temporary segment in the index's tablespace into a permanent segment. The same is the case when you create a table with the CREATE TABLE...AS SELECT (CTAS) option.

As the "Solution" section explains, the ORA-01652 error refers to the tablespace where you're rebuilding an index. If you are creating a new index, Oracle uses the temporary tablespace for sorting the index data. When creating a large index, it may be a smart idea to create a large temporary tablespace and assign it to the user who's creating the index. Once the index is created, you can re-assign the user the original temporary tablespace and remove the large temporary tablespace. This strategy helps avoid enlarging the default temporary tablespace to a very large size to accommodate the creation of a large index.

If you specify autoextend for a temporary tablespace, the temp files may get very large, based on one or two large sorts in the database. When you try to reclaim space for the TEMP tablespace, you may get the following error.

```
SQL> alter database tempfile '/u01/app/oracle/oradata/prod1/temp01.dbf'
    resize 500M;
alter database tempfile '/u01/app/oracle/oradata/prod1/temp01.dbf'
    resize 500M
*ERROR at line 1:
ORA-03297: file contains used data beyond requested RESIZE value
```

One solution is to create a new temporary tablespace, make that the default temporary tablespace, and then drop the larger temporary tablespace (provided no other sessions are using it, of course). You can simplify matters by using the following alter tablespace command to shrink the temporary tablespace:

```
SQL> alter tablespace temp shrink space;

Tablespace altered.

SQL>
```

In this example, we shrank the entire temporary tablespace, but you can shrink a specific tempfile by issuing the command alter tablespace temp shrink tempfile <file_name>. The command will shrink the tempfile to the smallest size possible.

7-7. Resolving Open Cursor Errors

Problem

You are frequently getting the Maximum Open Cursors exceeded error, and you want to resolve the error.

Solution

One of the first things you need to do when you receive the ORA-01000: "maximum open cursors exceeded" error is to check the value of the initialization parameter open_cursors. You can view the current limit for open cursors by issuing the following command:

```
SQL> sho parameter open_cursors
```

NAME	TYPE	VALUE
open_cursors	integer	300
SQL>		

The parameter OPEN_CURSORS sets the maximum number of cursors a session can have open at once. You specify this parameter to control the number of open cursors. Keeping the parameter's value too low will result in a session receiving the ORA-01000 error. There's no harm in specifying a large value for the OPEN_CURSORS parameter (unless you expect all sessions to simultaneously max out their cursors, which is unlikely), so you can usually resolve cursor-related errors simply by raising the parameter value to a large number. However, you may sometimes find that raising the value of the open_cursors parameter doesn't "fix" the problem. In such cases, investigate which processes are using the open cursors by issuing the following query:

```
SQL> select a.value, s.username,s.sid,s.serial#,s.program,s.inst_id
     from gv$sesstat a,gv$statname b,gv$session s
     where a.statistic# = b.statistic# and s.sid=a.sid
     and b.name='opened cursors current'
```

The GV$OPEN_CURSOR (or the V$OPEN_CURSOR) view shows all the cursors that each user session has currently opened and parsed, or cached. You can issue the following query to identify the sessions with a high number of opened and parsed or cached cursors.

```
SQL> select saddr, sid, user_name, address,hash_value,sql_id, sql_text
     from gv$open_cursor
     where sid in
     (select sid from v$open_cursor
     group by sid having count(*)  > &threshold);
```

The query lists all sessions with an open cursor count greater than the threshold you specify. This way, you can limit the query's output and focus just on the sessions that have opened, parsed, or cached a large number of cursors.

You can get the actual SQL code and the open cursor count for a specific session by issuing the following query:

```
SQl> select sql_id,substr(sql_text,1,50) sql_text, count(*)
     from gv$open_cursor where sid=81
     group by sql_id,substr(sql_text,1,50)
     order by sql_id;
```

The output shows the SQL code for all open cursors in the session with the SID 81. You can examine all SQL statements with a high open cursor count to see why the session was keeping a large number of cursors open.

How It Works

If your application is not closing open cursors, then setting the OPEN_CURSORS parameter to a higher value won't really help you. You may momentarily resolve the issue, but you're likely to run into the same issue a little later. If the application layer never closes the ref cursors created by the PL/SQL code, the database will simply hang on to the server resources for the used cursors. You must fix the application logic so it closes the cursors—the problem isn't really in the database.

If you're using a Java application deployed on an application server such as the Oracle WebLogic Server, the WebLogic Server's JDBC connection pools provide open database connections for applications. Any prepared statements in each of these connections will use a cursor. Multiple application server instances and multiple JDBC connection pools will mean that the database needs to support all the cursors. If multiple requests share the same session ID, the open cursor problem may be due to implicit cursors. The only solution then is to close the connection after each request, unless developers are using the close() method of the PreparedStatement and ResultSet objects.

A *cursor leak* is when the database opens cursors but doesn't close them.

You can use the SESSION_CACHED_CURSORS initialization parameter to set the maximum number of cached closed cursors for each session. The default setting is 50. You can use this parameter to prevent a session from opening an excessive number of cursors, thereby filling the library cache or forcing excessive hard parses. Repeated parse calls for a SQL statement leads Oracle to move the session cursor for that statement into the session cursor cache. The database satisfies subsequent parse calls by using the cached cursor instead of re-opening the cursor.

When you re-execute a SQL statement, Oracle will first try to find a parsed version of that statement in the shared pool—if it finds the parsed version in the shared pool, a soft parse occurs. Oracle is forced to perform the much more expensive hard parse if it doesn't find the parsed version of the statement in the shared pool. While a soft parse is much less expensive than a hard parse, a large number of soft parses can affect performance, because they do require CPU usage and library cache latches. To reduce the number of soft parses, Oracle caches the recent closed cursors of each session in a local session cache for that session—Oracle stores any cursor for which a minimum of three parse calls were made, thus avoiding having to cache every single session cursor, which will fill up the cursor cache.

The default value of 50 for the SESSION_CACHED_CURSORS initialization parameter may be too low for many databases. You can check if the database is bumping against the maximum limit for session-cached cursors by issuing the following statement:

```
SQL> select max(value) from v$sesstat
  2  where statistic# in (select statistic# from v$statname
  3* where name = 'session cursor cache count');


MAX(VALUE)
----------
        49

SQL>
```

The query shows the maximum number of session cursors that have been cached in the past. Since this number (49) is virtually the same as the default value (or the value you've set) for the SESSION_CACHED_CURSORS parameter, you must set the parameter's value to a larger number. Session cursor caches use the shared pool. If you're using automatic memory management, there's nothing for you to do after you reset the SESSION_CACHED_CURSORS parameter—the database will bump up the shared pool size if necessary. You can find out how many cursors each session has in its session cursor cache by issuing the following query:

```
SQL> select a.value,s.username,s.sid,s.serial#
  2  from v$sesstat a, v$statname b,v$session s
  3  where a.statistic#=b.statistic# and s.sid=a.sid
  4* and b.name='session cursor cache count';
```

7-8. Resolving a Hung Database

Problem

Your database is hung. Users aren't able to log in, and existing users can't complete their transactions. The DBAs with SYSDBA privileges may also be unable to log in to the database. You need to find out what is causing the database to hang, and fix the problem.

Solution

Follow these general steps when facing a database that appears to be hung:

1. Check your alert log to see if the database has reported any errors, which may indicate why the database is hanging.

2. See if you can get an AWR or ASH report or query some of the ASH views, as explained in Chapter 5. You may notice events such as hard parses at the top of the Load Profile section of the AWR report, indicating that this is what is slowing down the database.

3. A single ad hoc query certainly has the potential to bring an entire database to its knees. See if you can identify one or more very poorly performing SQL statements that may be leading to the hung (or a very poorly performing) database.

4. Check the database for blocking locks as well as latch contention.

5. Check the server's memory usage as well as CPU usage. Make sure the sessions aren't stalling because you've sized the PGA too low, as explained in Chapter 3.

6. Don't overlook the fact that a scary-looking database hang may be caused by something as simple as the filling up of all archive log destinations. If the archive destination is full, the database will hang, and new user connections will fail. You can, however, still connect as the SYS user, and once you make room in the archive destination by moving some of the archived redo log files, the database becomes accessible to the users.

7. Check the Flash Recovery Area (FRA). A database also hangs when it's unable to write Flashback Database logs to the recovery area. When the FRA fills up, the database won't process new work and it won't spawn new database connections. You can fix this problem by making the recovery area larger with the alter system set db_recovery_file_dest_size command.

If you're still unable to resolve the reasons for the hung database, you most likely have a truly hung database. While you're investigating such a database, you may sometimes find yourself unable to connect and log in. In that case, use the "prelim" option to log in to the database. The prelim option doesn't require a real database connection. Here's an example that shows how to use the prelim option to log into a database:

```
$ sqlplus /nolog

SQL> set _prelim on
SQL> connect / as sysdba
Prelim connection established
SQL>
```

■ **Note**   You can't set prelim while connected to a database. Alternatively, you can use the command `sqlplus -prelim` `"/ as sysdba"` to log in with the `-prelim` option. Note that you use the `nolog` option to open a SQL*Plus session. You can't execute the `set _prelim on` command if you're already connected to the database. Once you establish a `prelim` connection as shown here, you can execute the `oradebug hanganalyze` command to analyze a hung database—for example:

```
SQL> oradebug hanganalyze 3

Statement processed.

SQL>
```

The integer 3 in the oradebug comamnd specifes the level at which you want to run the command. We explain this in more detail in the How it Works section of this recipe.

In an Oracle RAC environment, specify the oradebug hanganalyze command with additional options, as shown here:

```
SQL> oradebug setinst all
SQL> oradebug -g def hanganalyze 3
```

You can repeat the oradebug hanganalyze command a couple of times to generate dump files for varying process states.

In addition to the dump files generated by the hanganalyze command, Oracle Support may often also request a process state dump, also called a systemstate dump, to analyze hung database conditions. The systemstate dump will report on what the processes are doing and the resources they're currently holding. You can get a systemstate dump from a non-RAC system by executing the following set of commands.

```
SQL> oradebug setmypid
Statement processed.
SQL> oradebug dump systemstate 266
Statement processed.
SQL>
```

Issue the following commands to get a `systemstate` dump in a RAC environment:

```
SQL> oradebug setmypid
SQL> oradebug unlimit
SQL> oradebug -g all dump systemstate 266
```

Note that unlike the `oradebug hanganalyze` command, you must connect to a process. The `setmypid` option specifies the process, in this case your own process. You can also specify a process ID other than yours, in which case you issue the command `oradebug setmypid <pid>` before issuing the `dump systemstate` command. If you try to issue the `dump systemstate` command without setting the PID, you'll receive an error:

```
SQL> oradebug dump systemstate 10
ORA-00074: no process has been specified
SQL>
```

You must take the `systemstate` dumps a few times, with an interval of about a minute or so in between the dumps. Oracle Support usually requests several systemstate dumps along with the trace files generated by the hanganalyze command.

How It Works

The key thing you must ascertain when dealing with a "hung" database is whether the database is really hung, or just slow. If one or two users complain about a slow-running query, you need to analyze their sessions, using the techniques described in Chapter 5, to see if the slowness is due to a blocking session or to an Oracle wait event. If several users report that their work is going slowly, it could be due to various reasons, including CPU, memory (SGA or PGA), or other system resource issues.

Check the server's CPU usage as one of your first steps in troubleshooting a hung database. If your server is showing 100% CPU utilization, or if it's swapping or paging, the problem may not lie in the database at all. As for memory, if the server doesn't have enough free memory, new sessions can't connect to the database.

■ **Tip** The "prelim" option shown in the "Solution" section lets you connect to the SGA without opening a session. You can thus "log" in to the hung database even when normal SQL*Plus logins don't work. The `oradebug` session you start once you connect to the SGA actually analyzes what's in the SGA and dumps it into a trace file.

A true database hang can be due to a variety of reasons, including a system that has exhausted resources such as the CPU or memory, or because several sessions are stuck waiting for a resource such as a lock. In fact, a true database hang is more likely due to to an Oracle bug than to any other reason. Oracle is sometimes unable to automatically detect and resolve internal deadlocks—and this leads to what Oracle Support calls a "true database hang." A true database hang is thus an internal deadlock or a cyclical dependency among multiple processes. Oracle Support will usually ask you to provide them the hanganalyze trace files and multiple systemstate dumps to enable them to diagnose the root cause of your hang. At times like this, you may not even be able to log into the database. Your first instinct when you realize that you can't even log in to a database is to try shutting down and restarting, often referred to as bouncing the database. Unfortunately, while shutting down and restarting the database may "resolve" the issue, it'll also disconnect all users—and you're no wiser as to what exactly caused the problem. If you do decide to bounce your database, quickly generate a few hanganalyze and systemstate dumps first.

■ **Tip** As unpleasant as it may be at times, if you find that you simply can't connect to a hung database, then collect any trace dumps you may need, and quickly bounce the database so that users can access their applications. Especially when you're dealing with a database that's hanging because of memory issues, bouncing the instance may get things going again quickly.

If you find that the database is completely unresponsive, and you can't even log in to the database with the SYSDBA privilege, you can use the prelim option to log into the database. The prelim option stands for preliminary connection, and it starts an Oracle process and attaches that process to the SGA shared memory. However, this is not a full or complete connection, but a limited connection where the structures for query execution are not set up—so, you cannot even query the V$ views. However, the prelim option lets you run oradebug commands to get error dump stacks for diagnostic purposes. The output of the hanganalyze command can tell Oracle Support engineers if your database is really hanging, because of sessions waiting for some resource. The command makes internal kernel calls to find out all sessions that are waiting for a resource and shows the relationship between the blocking and waiting sessions. The hanganalyze option that you can specify with either the oradebug command or an alter session statement produces details about hung sessions. Once you get the dump file, Oracle Support personnel can analyze it and let you know the reasons for the database hang.

You can invoke the hanganalyze command at various levels ranging from 1 to 10. Level 3 dumps processes that are in a hanging (IN_HANG) state. You normally don't need to specify a level higher than 3, because higher levels will produce voluminous reports with too many details about the processes.

■ **Note** The dump files you create with the hanganalyze and the systemstate commands are created in ADR's trace directory.

Note that we issued the oradebug command to get a systemstate dump with a level of 266. Level 266 (combination of Level 256, which produces short stack information, and Level 10) is for Oracle releases 9.2.0.6 and onward (earlier releases used systemstate level 10). Level 266 allows you to dump the short stacks for each process, which are Oracle function calls that help Oracle development teams determine which Oracle function is causing the problem. The short stack information also helps in matching known bugs in the code. On Solaris and Linux systems, you can safely specify level 266, but on other systems, it may take a long time to dump the short stacks. Therefore, you may want to stick with level 10 for the other operating systems.

If you can find out the blocking session, you can also take a dump just for that session, by using the command oradebug setospid nnnn, where nnnn is the blocking session's PID, and then invoking the oradebug command, as shown here:

```
SQL> oradebug setospid  9999
SQL> oradebug unlimit
SQL> oradebug dump errorstack  3
```

Note that you can generate the hanganalyze and systemstate dumps in a normal session (as well as in a prelim session), without using the oradebug command. You can invoke the hanganalyze command with an alter session command, as shown here.

```
SQL>alter session set  events 'immediate trace name hanganalyze level 3';
```

Similarly, you can get a systemstate dump with the following command:

```
SQL> alter session set events 'immediate trace name SYSTEMSTATE level 10';
Session altered.
SQL>
```

The oradebug and systemstate dumps are just two of the many dumps you can collect. Use the oradebug dumplist command to view the various error dumps you can collect.

```
SQL> oradebug dumplist
TRACE_BUFFER_ON
TRACE_BUFFER_OFF
LATCHES
PROCESSSTATE
SYSTEMSTATE
INSTANTIATIONSTATE
REFRESH_OS_STATS
CROSSIC
CONTEXTAREA
HANGDIAG_HEADER
HEAPDUMP
...
```

Note that while you can read some of the dump files in an editor, these files are mainly for helping Oracle Support professionals troubleshoot a database hang situation. There's not much you can do with the dump files, especially when a database hang situation is due to an Oracle bug or a kernel-level lock, except to send them along to Oracle Support for analysis.

7-9. Invoking the Automatic Diagnostic Repository Command Interpreter

Problem

You'd like to invoke the Automatic Diagnostic Repository Command Interpreter (ADRCI) and work with various components of the Automatic Diagnostic Repository (ADR).

Solution

ADRCI is a tool to help you manage Oracle diagnostic data. You can use ADRCI commands in both an interactive as well as a batch mode.

To start ADRCI in the interactive mode, type **adrci** at the command line, as shown here:

```
$ adrci

ADR base = "c:\app\ora"
adrci>
```

You can issue the adrci command from any directory, so long as the PATH environment variable includes ORACLE_HOME/bin/. You can enter each command at the adrci prompt, and when you're done using the utility, you can type **EXIT** or **QUIT** to exit. You can view all the ADRCI commands available to you by typing **HELP** at the ADRCI command line, as shown here:

```
adrci> HELP

HELP [topic]
  Available Topics:
        CREATE REPORT
        ECHO
        EXIT
        HELP
        HOST
        IPS
...
        SHOW HOMES | HOME | HOMEPATH
        SHOW INCDIR
        SHOW INCIDENT
        SHOW PROBLEM
        SHOW REPORT
        SHOW TRACEFILE
        SPOOL

There are other commands intended to be used directly by Oracle, type
"HELP EXTENDED" to see the list

adrci>
```

You can get detailed information for an individual ADRCI command by adding the name of the command as an attribute to the HELP command. For example, here is how to get the syntax for the show tracefile command:

```
adrci> help show tracefile

  Usage: SHOW TRACEFILE [file1 file2 ...] [-rt | -t]
                        [-i inc1 inc2 ...] [-path path1 path2 ...]

  Purpose: List the qualified trace filenames.
...
  Options:
  Examples:
...
adrci>
```

You can also execute ADRCI commands in the batch mode by incorporating the commands in a script or batch file. For example, if you want to run the ADRCI commands SET HOMEPATH and SHOW ALERT from within an operating system script, include the following line inside a shell script:

```
SET HOMEPATH diag/rdbms/orcl/orcl; SHOW ALERT -term
```

Let's say your script name is myscript.txt. You can then execute this script by issuing the following command inside an operating system shell script or batch file:

```
$ adrci script=myscript.txt
```

Note that the parameter SCRIPT tells ADRCI that it must execute the commands within the text file myscript.txt. If the text file is not within the same directory from where the shell script or batch file is running, you must provide the path for the directory where you saved the text file.

To execute an ADRCI command directly at the command line instead of invoking ADRCI first and working interactively with the ADR interface, specify the parameter EXEC with the ADRCI command, as shown here:

```
$ adrci EXEC="SHOW HOMES; SHOW INCIDENT"
```

This example shows how to include two ADRCI commands—SHOW HOMES and SHOW INCIDENT—by executing the ADRCI command at the command line.

How It Works

The Automatic Diagnostic Repository is a directory structure that you can access even when the database is down, because it's stored outside the database. The root directory for the ADR is called the *ADR base* and is set by the DIAGNOSTIC_DEST initialization parameter. Each Oracle product or component has its own *ADR home* under the ADR base. The location of each of the ADR homes follows the path diag/product_type/product_id/instance_id. Thus, the ADR home for a database named orcl1 with the instance name orcl1 and the ADR base set to /app/oracle will be /app/oracle/diag/rdbms/orcl1/orcl1. Under each of the ADR homes are the diagnostic data, such as the trace and dump files and the alert log, as well as other diagnostic files, for that instance of an Oracle product.

The ADRCI utility helps you manage the diagnostic data in the ADR. ADRCI lets you perform the following types of diagnostic tasks:

- *View diagnostic data in the ADR (Automatic Diagnostic Repository)*: The ADR stores diagnostic data such as alert logs, dump files, trace files, health check reports, etc.

- *View health check reports*: The diagnosability infrastructure automatically runs health checks to capture details about the error and adds them to other diagnostic data it collects for that error. You can also manually invoke a health check.

- *Package incidents and problem information for transmission to Oracle Support*: A *problem* is a critical database error, and an *incident* is a single occurrence of a specific problem. An incident package is a collection of diagnostic data that you send to Oracle Support for troubleshooting purposes. ADRCI has special commands that enable you to create packages and generate zipped diagnostic packages to send to Oracle Support.

You can view all ADR locations for the current database instance by querying the V$DIAG_INFO view, as shown here.

```
SQL> select * from v$diag_info;

INST_ID      NAME          VALUE                                              CON_ID
-------      -------------  -------------------------------------------------  ------
      1      Diag Enabled  TRUE                                                    0
      1      ADR Base      /u01/app/oracle                                         0
      1      ADR Home      /u01/app/oracle/diag/rdbms/orcl/orcl                    0
      1      Diag Trace    /u01/app/oracle/diag/rdbms/orcl/orcl/trace             0
      1      Diag Alert    /u01/app/oracle/diag/rdbms/orcl/orcl/alert             0
      1      Diag Incident /u01/app/oracle/diag/rdbms/orcl/orcl/incident 0
```

1	Diag Cdump	/u01/app/oracle/diag/rdbms/orcl/orcl/cdump	0
1	Health Monitor	/u01/app/oracle/diag/rdbms/orcl/orcl/hm	0
1	Default Trace File	/u01/app/oracle/diag/rdbms/orcl/orcl/	
2		trace/orcl_ora_3263.trc	0
1	Active Problem Count	0	0
1	Active Incident Count	0	0

```
11 rows selected.

SQL>
```

The ADR home is the root directory for a database's diagnostic data. All diagnostic files such as the alert log and the various trace files are located under the ADR home. The ADR home is located directly underneath the ADR base, which you specify with the DIAGNOSTIC_DEST initialization parameter. Here's how to find out the location of the ADR base directory:

```
adrci> show base
ADR base is "/u01/app/oracle"
adrci>
```

You can view all the ADR homes under the ADR base by issuing the following command:

```
adrci> show homes
ADR Homes:
diag/rdbms/orcl/orcl
diag/tnslsnr/localhost/listener
adrci>
```

You can have multiple ADR homes under the ADR base, and multiple ADR homes can be current at any given time. Your ADRCI commands will work only with diagnostic data in the current ADR home. How do you know which ADR home is current at any point in time? The ADRCI homepath helps determine the ADR homes that are current, by pointing to the ADR home directory under the ADR base hierarchy of directories.

■ **Note** Some ADRCI commands require only one ADR home to be current—these commands will issue an error if multiple ADR homes are current.

You can use either the show homes or the show homepath command to view all ADR homes that are current:

```
adrci> show homepath
ADR Homes:
diag/rdbms/orcl/orcl
diag/tnslsnr/localhost/listener
adrci>
```

If you want to work with diagnostic data from multiple database instances or components, you must ensure that all the relevant ADR homes are current. Most of the time, however, you'll be dealing with a single database instance or a single Oracle product or component such as the listener, for example. An ADR homepath is always relative to the ADR. If you specify /u01/app/oracle/ as the value for the ADR base directory, for example, all ADR homes will be under the ADR_Base/diag directory. Issue the set homepath command to set an ADR home directory to a single home, as shown here:

```
adrci> set homepath diag\rdbms\orcl1\orcl1

adrci> show homepath

ADR Homes:
diag\rdbms\orcl1\orcl1
adrci>
```

■ **Note**   Diagnostic data includes descriptions of incidents and problems, health monitoring reports, and traditional diagnostic files such as trace files, dump files, and alert logs.

Note that before you set the homepath with the set homepath command, the show homepath command shows all ADR homepaths. However, once you set the homepath to a specific home, the show homepath command shows just a single homepath. It's important to set the homepath before you execute several ADRCI commands, as they are applicable to only a single ADR home. For example, if you don't set the homepath before issuing the following command, you'll receive an error:

```
adrci> ips create package
DIA-48448: This command does not support multiple ADR homes
adrci>
```

The error occurs because the ips create package command is not valid with multiple ADR homes. The command will work fine after you issue the set homepath command to set the homepath to a single ADR home. Commands such as the one shown here work only with a single current ADR home, but others work with multiple current ADR homes—there are also commands that don't need a current ADR home. The bottom line is that all ADRCI commands will work with a single current ADR home.

7-10. Viewing an Alert Log from ADRCI
Problem

You want to view an alert log by using ADRCI commands.

Solution

To view an alert log with ADRCI, follow these steps:
    Invoke ADRCI.

```
$ adrci
```

8. Set the ADR home with the `set homepath` command.

   ```
   adrci> set homepath diag/rdbms/orcl/orcl
   ```

9. Enter the following command to view the alert log:

   ```
   adrci> show alert

   ADR Home = /u01/app/oracle/diag/rdbms/orcl/orcl:
   *************************************************************************
   Output the results to file: /tmp/alert_3573_13986_orcl_1.ado
   adrci>
   show alert
   ```

The alert log will pop up in your default editor. The ADRCI prompt will return once you close the text file in the editor.

You can also query the V$DIAG_INFO view to find the path that corresponds to the Diag Trace entry. You can change the directory to that path and open the alert_<db_name>.log file with a text editor.

How It Works

The alert log holds runtime information for an Oracle instance and provides information such as the initialization parameters the instance is using, as well as a record of key changes such as redo log file switches and, most importantly, messages that show Oracle errors and their details. The alert log is critical for troubleshooting purposes, and is usually the first place you'll look when a problem occurs. Oracle provides the alert log as both a text file as well as an XML-formatted file.

The show alert command brings up the XML-formatted alert log without displaying the XML tags. You can set the default editor with the SET EDITOR command, as shown here:

```
adrci> set editor notepad.exe
```

The previous command changes the default editor to Notepad. The show alert -term command shows the alert log contents in the terminal window. If you want to examine just the latest events in the alert log, issue the following command:

```
adrci>show alert -tail 50
```

The tail option shows you a set of the most recent lines from the alert log in the command window. In this example, it shows the last 50 lines from the alert log. If you don't specify a value for the tail parameter, by default, it shows the last 10 lines from the alert log.

The following command shows a "live" alert log, in the sense that it will show changes to the alert log as the entries are added to the log.

```
adrci> show alert -tail -f
```

The previous command shows the last 10 lines of the alert log and prints all new messages to the screen, thus offering a "live" display of ongoing additions to the alert log. The CTRL+C sequence will take you back to the ADRCI prompt.

When troubleshooting, it is very useful to see if the database issued any ORA-600 errors. You can issue the following command to trap the ORA-600 errors.

```
adrci> show alert -p "MESSAGE_TEXT LIKE '%ORA-600%'"
```

Although you can view the alert log directly by going to the file system location where it's stored, you can also do so through the ADRCI tool. ADRCI is especially useful for working with the trace files of an instance. The SHOW TRACEFILE command shows all the trace files in the trace directory of the instance. You can issue the SHOW TRACEFILE command with various filters—the following example looks for trace files that reference the background process mmon:

```
$ adrci> show tracefile %mmon%
    diag\rdbms\orcl1\orcl1\trace\orcl1_mmon_1792.trc
    diag\rdbms\orcl1\orcl1\trace\orcl1_mmon_2340.trc
adrci>
```

This command lists all trace files with the string mmon in their file names. You can apply filters to restrict the output to just the trace files associated with a specific incident number (the next recipe, Recipe 7-11, explains how to get the incident number), as shown here:

```
adrci> show tracefile -I 43417
        diag\rdbms\orcl1\orcl1\incident\incdir_43417\orcl1_ora_4276_i43417.trc
adrci>
```

The previous command lists the trace files related to the incident number 43417.

7-11. Viewing Incidents with ADRCI
Problem

You want to use ADRCI to view incidents.

Solution

You can view all incidents in the ADR with the show incident command (be sure to set the homepath first):

```
$ adrci
$ set homepath diag\rdbms\orcl1\orcl1

adrci> show incident

ADR Home = c:\app\ora\diag\rdbms\orcl1\orcl1:
*************************************************************************
INCIDENT_ID          PROBLEM_KEY
 CREATE_TIME
-------------------- ---------------------------------------------------
 43417               ORA 600 [kkqctinvvm(2): Inconsistent state space!]
 2013-08-17 09:26:15.091000 -05:00
43369                ORA 600 [kkqctinvvm(2): Inconsistent state space!]
 2013-08-17 11:08:40.589000 -05:00
79451                ORA 445
 2013-03-04 03:00:39.246000 -05:00
84243                ORA 445
 2013-03-14 19:12:27.434000 -04:00
84244                ORA 445
 2013-03-20 16:55:54.501000 -04:00
5 rows fetched
```

You can specify the detail mode to view details about a specific incident, as shown here:

```
adrci> show incident -mode detail -p "incident_id=43369"

ADR Home = c:\app\ora\diag\rdbms\orcl1\orcl1:
*************************************************************************

INCIDENT INFO RECORD 1
*************************************************************************
    INCIDENT_ID                 43369
    STATUS                      ready
    CREATE_TIME                 2013-08-17 11:08:40.589000 -05:00
    PROBLEM_ID                  1
    CLOSE_TIME                  <NULL>
    FLOOD_CONTROLLED            none
    ERROR_FACILITY              ORA
    ERROR_NUMBER                600
    ERROR_ARG1                  kkqctinvvm(2): Inconsistent state space!
    SIGNALLING_COMPONENT        SQL_Transform
    PROBLEM_KEY                 ORA 600 [kkqctin: Inconsistent state space!]
    FIRST_INCIDENT              43417
    FIRSTINC_TIME               2013-08-17 09:26:15.091000 -05:00
    LAST_INCIDENT               43369
    LASTINC_TIME                2013-08-17 11:08:40.589000 -05:00
    KEY_VALUE                   ORACLE.EXE.3760_3548
    KEY_NAME                    PQ
    KEY_NAME                    SID
    KEY_VALUE                   71.304
    OWNER_ID                    1
    INCIDENT_FILE               c:\app\ora\diag\rdbms\orcl1\orcl1\trace\orcl1_ora_3548.trc

adrci>
```

How It Works

The show incident command reports on all open incidents in the database. For each incident, the output for this command shows the problem key, incident ID, and the time when the incident occurred. In this example, we first set the ADRCI homepath, so the command shows incidents from just this ADR home. If you don't set the homepath, you'll see incidents from all the current ADR homes.

As mentioned earlier, an incident is a single occurrence of a problem. A problem is a critical error such as an ORA-600 (internal error) or an ORA-07445 error relating to operating system exceptions. The problem key is a text string that shows the problem details. For example, the problem key ORA 600 [kkqctinvvm(2): Inconsistent state space!] shows that the problem is due to an internal error.

When a problem occurs several times, the database creates an incident for each occurrence of the problem, each with a unique incident ID. The database logs the incident in the alert log and sends an alert to the Oracle Enterprise Manager, where they show up in the Home page. The database automatically gathers diagnostic data for the incident, called incident dumps, and stores them in the ADR trace directory.

Since a critical error can potentially generate numerous identical incidents, the fault diagnosability infrastructure applies a "flood control" mechanism to limit the generation of incidents. For a given problem key, the database allows only 5 incidents within 1 hour and a maximum of 25 incidents in 1 day. Once a problem triggers incidents beyond these thresholds, the database merely logs the incidents in the alert log and the Oracle Enterprise Manager but stops generating new incident dumps for them. You can't alter the default threshold settings for the incident flood control mechanism.

7-12. Packaging Incidents for Oracle Support
Problem

You want to send the diagnostic files related to a specific problem to Oracle Support.

Solution

You can package the diagnostic information for one more incidents through either Database Control or through commands that you can execute from the ADRCI interface. In this solution, we show you how to package incidents through ADRCI. You can use various IPS commands to package all diagnostic files related to a specific problem in a zipped format and send the file to Oracle Support. Here are the steps to create an incident package.

Create an empty logical package as shown here:

```
adrci> ips create package
Created package 1 without any contents, correlation level typical
adrci>
```

In this example, we created an empty package, but you can also create a package based on an incident number, a problem number, a problem key or a time interval. In all these cases, the package won't be empty—it'll include the diagnostic information for the incident or problem that you specify. Since we created an empty package, we need to add diagnostic information to that package in the next step.

10. Add diagnostic information to the logical package with the `ips add incident` command:

```
adrci> ips add incident 43369 package 1
Added incident 43369 to package 1
adrci>
```

At this point, the incident 43369 is associated with package 1, but there's no diagnostic data in it yet.

11. Generate the physical package.

```
adrci> ips generate package 1 in \app\ora\diagnostics
Generated package 1 in file \app\ora\diagnostics\IPSPKG_20110419131046_COM_1.zip, mode complete
adrci>
```

When you issue the generate package command, ADRCI gathers all relevant diagnostic files and adds them to a zip file in the directory you designate.

12. Send the resulting zip file to Oracle Support.

If you decide to add supplemental diagnostic data to an existing physical package (zipped file), you can do so by specifying the incremental option with the generate package command:

```
adrci> ips generate package 1 in \app\ora\diagnostics incremental
```

The incremental zip file created by this command will have the term INC in the file name, indicating that it is an incremental zip file.

How It Works

A physical package is the zip file that you can send to Oracle Support for diagnosing a problem in your database. Since an incident is a single occurrence of a problem, adding the incident number to the logical package and generating the physical package rolls up all the diagnostic data for that problem (incident) into a single zipped file. In this example, we showed you how to first create an empty logical package and then associate it with an incident number. However, the ipc create package command has several options: you can specify the incident number or a problem number directly when you create the logical package, and skip the add incident command. You can also create a package that contains all incidents between two points in time, as shown here:

```
adrci> ips create package time '2013-09-12 10:00:00.00 -06:00' to '2013-09-12 23
:00:00.00 -06:00'
Created package 2 based on time range 2011-04-12 12:00:00.000000 -06:00 to 2011-
04-12 23:00:00.000000 -06:00, correlation level typical
adrci>
```

The package generated by the previous command contains all incidents that occurred between 10 A.M. and 11 P.M. on April 12, 2011.

Note that you can also manually add a specific diagnostic file to an existing package. To add a file, you specify the file name in the ips add file command—you are limited to adding only those diagnostic files that are within the ADR base directory. Here is an example:

```
adrci> ips add file <ADR_BASE>/diag/rdbms/orcl1/orcl1/trace/orcl_ora12345.trc package 1
```

By default, the ips generate package command generates a zip file that includes all files for a package. The incremental option will limit the files to those that the database has generated since you originally generated the zipped file for that package. The ips show files command shows all the files in a package and the ips show incidents command shows all the incidents in a package. You can issue the ips remove file command to remove a diagnostic file from a package.

7-13. Running a Database Health Check
Problem

You'd like to run a comprehensive diagnostic health check on your database. You'd like to find out if there's any data dictionary or file corruption, as well as any other potential problems in the database.

Solution

You can use the database health monitoring infrastructure to run a health check of your database. You can run various integrity checks, such as transaction integrity checks and dictionary integrity checks. You can get a list of all the health checks you can run by querying the V$HM_CHECK view:

```
SQL> select name from v$hm_check where internal_check='N';
```

Once you decide on the type of check, specify the name of the check in the DBMS_HM package's RUN_CHECK procedure, as shown here:

```
SQL> begin
  2    dbms_hm.run_check('Dictionary Integrity Check','testrun1');
  3    end;
  4  /

PL/SQL procedure successfully completed.

SQL>
```

You can also run a health check from the Enterprise Manager. Go to Advisor Central ➤ Checkers, and select the specific checker from the Checkers subpage to run a health check.

How It Works

Oracle automatically runs a health check when it encounters a critical error. You can run a manual check using the procedure shown in the "Solution" section. The database stores all health check findings in the ADR.

You can run most of the health checks while the database is open. You can run the Redo Integrity Check and the DB Structure Integrity Check only when the database is closed—you must place the database in the NOMOUNT state to run these two checks.

You can view a health check's findings using either the DBMS_HM package or through the Enterprise Manager. Here is how to get a health check using the DBMS_HM package:

```
SQL> set long 100000
SQL> set longchunksize 1000
SQL> set pagesize 1000
SQL> set linesize 512

SQL> select dbms_hm.get_run_report('testrun1') from dual;

DBMS_HM.GET_RUN_REPORT('TESTRUN1')
--------------------------------------------------------------------------------
--------------------------------------------------------------------------------
--------------------------------------------------------------------------------
--------------------------------------------------------------------------------
--------------------------------------------------------------------------------
----------------------------------
Basic Run Information
Run Name                     : testrun1
 Run Id                      : 141
 Check Name                  : Dictionary Integrity Check
```

```
Mode                      : MANUAL
Status                    : COMPLETED
Start Time                : 2013-09-09 15:11:22.779917 -04:00
End Time                  : 2013-07-09 15:11:40.046797 -04:00
Error Encountered         : 0

Source Incident Id        : 0
Number of Incidents Created : 0
Input Paramters for the Run
TABLE_NAME=ALL_CORE_TABLES
CHECK_MASK=ALL


Run Findings And Recommendations
 Finding
 Finding Name  : Dictionary Inconsistency
Finding ID     : 142
 Type          : FAILURE
 Status        : OPEN

Priority       : CRITICAL
 Message       : SQL dictionary health check: seg$.type# 31 on object SEG$
                 Failed
Message        : Damaged rowid is AIAABAAAUUjAAf - description: Ts# 1
                 File# 3 Block# 83328 is referenced
...

SQL>
```

You can also go to Advisor Central ➤ Checkers and run a report from the Run Detail page for any health check you have run. Use the show hm run, create report, and show report commands to view health check reports with the ADRCI utility. You can use the views V$HM_FINDING and V$HM_RECOMMENDATION to investigate the findings as well as the recommendations pursuant to a health check.

7-14. Creating a SQL Test Case

Problem

You need to create a SQL test case in order to reproduce a SQL failure on a different machine, either to support your own diagnostic efforts, or to enable Oracle Support to reproduce the failure.

Solution

In order to create a SQL test case, first you must export the SQL statement along with several bits of useful information about the statement. The following example shows how to capture the SQL statement that is throwing an error. In this example, the user SH is doing the export (you can't do the export as the user SYS).

First, connect to the database as SYSDBA and create a directory to hold the test case:

```
SQL> conn / as sysdba
Connected.
SQL> create or replace directory TEST_DIR1 as 'c:\myora\diagnsotics\incidents\';
```

```
Directory created.
SQL> grant read,write on directory TEST_DIR1 to sh;

Grant succeeded.
SQL>
```

Then grant the DBA role to the user through which you will create the test case, and connect as that user:

```
SQL> grant dba to sh;

Grant succeeded.

SQL> conn sh/sh
Connected.
```

Issue the SQL command that's throwing the error:

```
SQL> select * from  my_mv  where max_amount_sold >100000 order by 1;
```

Now you're ready to export the SQL statement and relevant information, which you can import to a different system later on. Use the EXPORT_SQL_TESTCASE procedure to export the data, as shown here:

```
SQL> set serveroutput on

SQL> declare mycase clob;
  2   begin
  3   dbms_sqldiag.export_sql_testcase
  4   (directory      =>'TEST_DIR1',
  5   sql_text        => 'select * from my_mv where max_amount_sold >100000 order by 1',
  6   user_name       => 'SH',
  7   exportData      =>   TRUE,
  8   testcase        => mycase
  9   );
 10   end;
 11   /

PL/SQL procedure successfully completed.

SQL>
```

Once the export procedure completes, you are ready to perform the import, either on the same or on a different server. The following example creates a new user named TEST, and imports the test case into that user's schema. Here are the steps for importing the SQL statement and associated information into a different schema.

```
SQL> conn /as sysdba
Connected.
SQL> create or replace directory TEST_DIR2 as 'c:\myora\diagnsotics\incidents\'; /

Directory created.
SQL> grant read,write on directory TEST_dir2 to test;
```

Transfer all the files in the TEST_DIR1 directory to the TEST_DIR2 directory. Then grant the DBA role to user TEST, and connect as that user:

```
SQL> grant dba to test;

Grant succeeded.

SQL> conn test/test
Connected.
```

Perform the import of the SQL data as the user TEST, by invoking the IMPORT_SQL_TESTCASE procedure, as shown here:

```
SQL> begin
  2  dbms_sqldiag.import_sql_testcase
  3  (directory=>'TEST_DIR2',
  4  filename=>'oratcb1_008602000001main.xml',
  5  importData=>TRUE
  6  );
  7  end;
  8  /

PL/SQL procedure successfully completed.

SQL>
```

The user TEST will now have all the objects to execute the SQL statement that you want to investigate. You can verify this by issuing the original select statement. It should give you the same output as under the SH schema.

How It Works

Oracle offers the SQL Test Case Builder (TCB) to reproduce a SQL failure. You can create a test case through Enterprise Manager or through a PL/SQL package. The "Solution" section of this recipe shows how create a test case using the EXPORT_SQL_TESTCASE procedure of the DBMS_SQLDIAG package. There are several variants of this package, and our example shows how to use a SQL statement as the source for creating a SQL test case. Please review the DBMS_SQLDIAG.EXPORT_TESTCASE procedure in Oracle's PL/SQL Packages manual for details about other options to create test cases.

■ **Note**   You can use the Test Case Builder without a need to licnese either the Orcle Diagnostics Pack or the Oracle Tuning Pack. Often, you'll find yourself trying to provide a test case for Oracle, without which the Oracle Support personnel won't be able to investigate a particular problem they are helping you with. The SQL Test Case Builder is a tool that is part of Oracle Database 11g, and its primary purpose is to help you quickly obtain a reproducible test case. The SQL Test Case Builder helps you easily capture pertinent information relating to a failed SQL statement and package it in a format that either a developer or an Oracle support person can use to reproduce the problem in a different environment.

You access the SQL Test Case Builder through the DBMS_SQLDIAG package. To create a test case, you must first export the SQL statement, including all the objects that are part of the statement, and all other related information. The export process is very similar to an Oracle export with the EXPDP command and thus uses a directory, just as EXPDP does. Oracle creates the SQL test case as a script that contains the statements that will re-create the necessary database objects, along with associated runtime information such as statistics, which enable you to reproduce the error. The following are the various types of information captured and exported as part of the test case creation process:

- SQL text for the problem statement
- Table data—this is optional, and you can export a sample or complete data.
- The execution plan
- Optimizer statistics
- PL/SQL functions, procedure, and packages
- Bind variables
- User privileges
- SQL profiles
- Metadata for all the objects that are part of the SQL statement
- Dynamic sampling results
- Runtime information such as the degree of parallelism, for example

In the `DBMS_SQLDIAG` package, the `EXPORT_SQL_TESTCASE` procedure exports a SQL test case for a SQL statement to a directory. The `IMPORT_SQL_TESTCASE` procedure imports the test case from a directory.

In the `EXPORT_SQL_TESTCASE` procedure, here is what the attributes stand for:

`DIRECTORY`: The directory where you want to store the test case files

`SQL_TEXT`: The actual SQL statement that's throwing the error

`TESTCASE`: The name of the test case

`EXPORTDATA`: By default, Oracle doesn't export the data. You can set this parameter to `TRUE` in order to export the data. You can optionally limit the amount of data you want to export, by specifying a value for the Sampling Percent attribute. The default value is 100.

The Test Case Builder automatically exports the PL/SQL package specifications but not the package body. However, you can specify that the TCB export the package body as well. The export process creates several files in the directory you specify. Of these files, the file in the format `oratcb1_008602000001main.xml` contains the metadata for the test case.

7-15. Generating an AWR Report

Problem

You'd like to generate an AWR report to analyze performance problems in your database.

Solution

The database automatically takes an AWR (needs additional licensing) snapshot every hour and saves the statistics in the AWR for 8 days. An AWR report contains data captured between two snapshots, which need not be consecutive. Thus, an AWR report lets you examine instance performance between two points in time. You can generate an AWR report through Oracle Enterprise Manager. However, we show you how to create an AWR report using Oracle-provided scripts.

To generate an AWR report for a single instance database, execute the `awrrpt.sql` script as shown here.

```
SQL> @?/rdbms/admin/awrrpt.sql

Current Instance
~~~~~~~~~~~~~~~~~

   DB Id    DB Name      Inst Num Instance
----------- ------------ -------- --------
 1118243965 ORCL1              1 orcl1
Specify the Report Type
~~~~~~~~~~~~~~~~~~~~~~~~~
Would you like an HTML report, or a plain text report?
Enter 'html' for an HTML report or 'text' for plain text
Defaults to 'html'
Enter value for report_type: text
```

Type Specified:

Select a text- or an HTML-based report. The HTML report is the default report type, and it provides a nice-looking, well-formatted, easy-to-read report. Press Enter to select the default HTML-type report.

```
Instances in this Workload Repository schema
~~~~~~~~~~~~~~~~~~~~~~~~~~~~~~~~~~~~~~~~~~~~~~~

   DB Id     Inst Num DB Name     Instance    Host
----------- -------- -------     --------    --------
* 1118243965       1 ORCL1       orcl1       MIROPC61

Using 1118243965 for database Id
Using           1 for instance number
```

You must specify the DBID for the database at this point. In our example, however, there's only one database and therefore one DBID, so there's no need to enter the DBID.

```
Specify the number of days of snapshots to choose from
~~~~~~~~~~~~~~~~~~~~~~~~~~~~~~~~~~~~~~~~~~~~~~~~~~~~~~~~~
Entering the number of days (n) will result in the most recent
(n) days of snapshots being listed.  Pressing <return> without
specifying a number lists all completed snapshots.
Enter value for num_days: 1
```

Enter the number of days for which you want the database to list the snapshot IDs. In this example, we chose 1 because we want to generate an AWR for a time period that falls in the last day.

```
Listing the last day's Completed Snapshots
                                                      Snap
Instance     DB Name       Snap Id   Snap Started   Level
--------     -------       -------- ----------------  -----
orcl1        ORCL1            1877 09 Sep 2013 00:00      1
                             1878 09 Sep 2013 07:47      1
```

Specify a beginning and an ending snapshot for the AWR report.

```
Specify the Begin and End Snapshot Ids
~~~~~~~~~~~~~~~~~~~~~~~~~~~~~~~~~~~~~~~~
Enter value for begin_snap: 1877
Begin Snapshot Id specified: 1877

Enter value for end_snap: 1878
End Snapshot Id specified: 1878
```

You can either accept the default name for the AWR report by pressing Enter, or enter a name for the report.

```
Specify the Report Name
~~~~~~~~~~~~~~~~~~~~~~~~~
The default report file name is awrrpt_1_1877_1878.txt.  To use this name,
press <return> to continue, otherwise enter an alternative.

Enter value for report_name:
Using the report name awrrpt_1_1877_1878.html
```

The database generates an AWR report in the same directory from which you invoked the awrrpt.sql script. For example, if you choose an HTML-based report, the AWR report will be in the following format: awrrpt_1_1881_1882.html.

■ **Tip**   You can generate an AWR report to analyze the performance of a single SQL statement by executing the awrsqrpt.sql script.

How It Works

The AWR reports that you generate show performance statistics captured between two points in time, each of which is called a snapshot. You can gain significant insights into your database performance by reading the AWR reports carefully. An AWR report takes less than a minute to run in most cases, and holds a treasure trove of performance information. The report consists of multiple sections. Walking through an AWR report usually shows you the reason that your database isn't performing at peak levels.

To generate an AWR report for all instances in an Oracle RAC environment, use the awrgrpt.sql script instead. You can generate an AWR report for a specific instance in a RAC environment by using the awrrpti.sql script. You can also generate an AWR report for a single SQL statement by invoking the awrsqrpt.sql script and providing the SQL_ID of the SQL statement.

You can generate an AWR report to span any length of time, as long as the AWR has snapshots covering that period. By default, the AWR retains its snapshots for a period of eight days.

You can generate an AWR snapshot any time you want, either through the Oracle Enterprise Manager or by using the DBMS_WORKLOAD_REPOSITORY package. That ability is useful when, for example, you want to investigate a performance issue from 20 minutes and the next snapshot is 40 minutes away. In that case, you must either wait 40 minutes or create a manual snapshot. Here's an example that shows how to create an AWR snapshot manually:

```
SQL> exec dbms_workload_repository.create_snapshot();

PL/SQL procedure successfully completed.
SQL>
```

Once you create the snapshot, you can run the `awrrpt.sql` script. Then select the previous two snapshots to generate an up-to-date AWR report.

You can generate an AWR report when your user response time increases suddenly, say from 1 to 10 seconds during peak hours. An AWR report can also be helpful if a key batch job is suddenly taking much longer to complete. Of course, you must check the system CPU, I/O, and memory usage during the period as well, with the help of operating system tools such as `sar`, `vmstat`, and `iosat`.

If the system CPU usage is high, that doesn't necessarily mean that it's the CPU that's the culprit. CPU usage percentages are not always a true measure of throughput, nor is CPU usage always useful as a database workload metric. Make sure to generate the AWR report for the precise period that encompasses the time during which you noticed the performance deterioration. An AWR report that spans a 24-hour period is of little use in diagnosing a performance dip that occurred 2 hours ago for only 30 minutes. Match your report to the time period of the performance problem.

7-16. Comparing Database Performance Between Two Periods
Problem

You want to examine and compare how the database performed during two different periods.

Solution

Use the `awrddrpt.sql` script (located in the `$ORACLE_HOME/rdbms/admin` directory) to generate an AWR Compare Periods Report that compares performance between two periods. Here are the steps.

Invoke the `awrddrpt.sql` script.

```
SQL> @$ORACLE_HOME/rdbms/admin/awrddrpt.sql
```

13. Select the report type (default is text).

    ```
    Enter value for report_type: html
    Type Specified:  html
    ```

14. Specify the number of days of snapshots from which you want to select the beginning and ending snapshots for the first time period.

    ```
    Specify the number of days of snapshots to choose from
    Enter value for num_days: 4
    ```

15. Choose a pair of snapshots over which you want to analyze the first period's performance.

    ```
    Specify the First Pair of Begin and End Snapshot Ids
    ~~~~~~~~~~~~~~~~~~~~~~~~~~~~~~~~~~~~~~~~~~~~~~~~~~~~~~~
    Enter value for begin_snap: 2092
    First Begin Snapshot Id specified: 2092

    Enter value for end_snap: 2093
    First End   Snapshot Id specified: 2093
    ```

16. Select the number of days of snapshots from which you want to select the pair of snapshots for the second period. Enter the value 4 so you can select a pair of snapshots from the previous 4 days.

```
                 Specify the number of days of snapshots to choose from
                 Enter value for num_days: 4
```

17.   Specify the beginning and ending snapshots for the second period.

```
        Specify the Second Pair of Begin and End Snapshot Ids
        ~~~~~~~~~~~~~~~~~~~~~~~~~~~~~~~~~~~~~~~~~~~~~~~~~~~~~~~
        Enter value for begin_snap2: 2134
        Second Begin Snapshot Id specified: 2134

        Enter value for end_snap2: 2135
        Second End   Snapshot Id specified: 2135
```

18.   Specify a report name or accept the default name.

```
        Specify the Report Name
        ~~~~~~~~~~~~~~~~~~~~~~~~~
        The default report file name is awrdiff_1_2092_1_2134.html  To use this name,
        press <return> to continue, otherwise enter an alternative.

        Enter value for report_name:
        Using the report name awrdiff_1_2092_1_2134.html
        Report written to awrdiff_1_2092_1_2134.html
        SQL>
```

How It Works

Generating an AWR Compare Periods report is a process very similar to the one for generating a normal AWR report. The big difference is that the report does not show what happened between two snapshots, as the normal AWR report does. The AWR Compare Periods report compares performance between two different time periods, with each time period involving a different pair of snapshots. If you want to compare the performance of your database between 9 A.M. and 10 A.M. today and the same time period three days ago, you can do it with the AWR Compare Periods report. You can run an AWR Compare Periods report on one or all instances of a RAC database.

The AWR Compare Periods report is organized similarly to the normal AWR report, but it shows each performance statistic for the two periods side by side, so you can quickly see the differences (or similarities) in performance. Here's a section of the report showing how you can easily review the differences in performance statistics between the first and the second periods.

```
                                First       Second        Diff
                                -----       ------       ------
% Blocks changed per Read:      61.48        15.44       -46.04
Recursive Call %:               98.03        97.44        -0.59
Rollback per transaction %:      0.00         0.00         0.00
Rows per Sort:                   2.51         2.07        -0.44
Avg DB time per Call (sec):      1.01         0.03        -0.98
```

7-17. Analyzing an AWR Report

Problem

You've generated an AWR report that covers a period when the database was exhibiting performance problems. You want to analyze the report.

Solution

An AWR report summarizes its performance-related statistics under various sections. The following is a quick summary of the most important sections in an AWR report.

Session Information

You can find out the number of sessions from the section at the very top of the AWR report, as shown here:

```
             Snap Id    Snap Time            Sessions  Curs/Sess
             ---------  -------------------  --------  ---------
Begin Snap:  1878       12-Sep-13 07:47:33        38        1.7
  End Snap:  1879       12-Sep-13 09:00:48        34        3.7
  Elapsed:              73.25 (mins)
  DB Time:              33.87 (mins)
```

Be sure to check the Begin Snap and End Snap times, to confirm that the period encompasses the time when the performance problem occurred. If you notice a very high number of sessions, you can investigate if shadow processes are being created—for example, if the number of sessions goes up by 200 between the Begin Snap and End Snap times when you expect the number of sessions to be the same at both times, the most likely cause is an application start-up issue, which is spawning all those sessions.

Load Profile

The load profile section shows the per-second and per-transaction statistics for various indicators of database load such as hard parses and the number of transactions.

```
Load Profile              Per Second    Per Transaction
~~~~~~~~~~~~~~~~~~~        ----------    ---------------
       DB Time(s):               0.5                1.4
        DB CPU(s):               0.1                0.3
        Redo size:           6,165.3           19,028.7
    Logical reads:             876.6            2,705.6
    Block changes:              99.2              306.0
   Physical reads:              10.3               31.8
  Physical writes:               1.9                5.9
       User calls:               3.4               10.4
           Parses:              10.2               31.5
      Hard parses:               1.0                3.0
           Logons:               0.1                0.2
     Transactions:               0.3
```

The Load Profile section is one of the most important parts of an AWR report. Of particular significance are the physical I/O rates and hard parses. In an efficiently performing database, you should see mostly soft parses and very few hard parses. A high hard parse rate usually is a result of not using bind variables. If you see a high per second value for logons, it usually means that your applications aren't using persistent connections. A high number of logons or an unusually high number of transactions tells you something unusual is happening in your database. However, the only way you'll know the numbers are unusual is if you regularly check the AWR reports and know what the various statistics look like in a normally functioning database, at various times of the day!

Instance Efficiency Percentages

The instance efficiency section shows several hit ratios as well as the "execute to parse" and "latch hit" percentages.

```
Instance Efficiency Percentages (Target 100%)
~~~~~~~~~~~~~~~~~~~~~~~~~~~~~~~~~~~~~~~~~~~~~~~~~~~~~~~~~~~~~~~~~~~~~~~~~~~
            Buffer Nowait %:  100.00        Redo NoWait %:  100.00
            Buffer  Hit   %:   99.10     In-memory Sort %:  100.00
            Library Hit   %:   95.13         Soft Parse %:   90.35
         Execute to Parse %:   70.71          Latch Hit %:   99.97
  Parse CPU to Parse Elapsd %:  36.71      % Non-Parse CPU:   83.60


Shared Pool Statistics           Begin    End
                                 -----    -----
            Memory Usage %:      81.08    88.82
       % SQL with executions>1:  70.41    86.92
  % Memory for SQL w/exec>1:     69.60    91.98
```

The *execute to parse ratio* should be very high in a well-running instance. A low value for the % SQL with exec>1 statistic means that the database is not re-using shared SQL statements, usually because the SQL is not using bind variables.

Top 5 Foreground Events

The Top 5 Timed Foreground Events section shows the events that were responsible for the most waits during the time spanned by the AWR report.

```
Top 5 Timed Foreground Events
~~~~~~~~~~~~~~~~~~~~~~~~~~~~~~~~~~~
```

| | | | Avg Wait | % DB | |
Event	Waits	Time(s)	(ms)	time	Wait Class
db file sequential read	13,735	475	35	23.4	User I/O
DB CPU		429		21.1	
latch: shared pool	801	96	120	4.7	Concurren
db file scattered read	998	49	49	2.4	User I/O
control file sequential read	9,785	31	3	1.5	System I/O

The Top 5 Timed Foreground Events section is where you can usually spot the problem, by showing you why the sessions are "waiting." The Top 5 Events information shows the total waits for all sessions, but usually one or two sessions are responsible for most of the waits. Make sure to analyze the total waits and average waits (ms) separately, in order to determine if the waits are significant. Merely looking at the total number of waits or the total wait time for a wait event could give you a misleading idea about its importance. You must pay close attention to the average wait times for an event as well. In a nicely performing database, you should see CPU and I/O as the top wait events, as is the case here. If any wait events from the concurrent wait class such as latches show up at the top, investigate those waits further. For example, if you see events such as enq: TX - row lock contention, gc_buffer_busy (RAC), or latch free, it usually indicates contention in the database. If you see an average wait of more than 2 ms for the log file sync event, investigate the wait event further (Chapter 5 shows how to analyze various wait events). If you see a high amount of waits due to the db file sequential read or the db file scattered read wait events, there are heavy indexed reads (this is normal) or full table scans going on. You can find out the SQL statement and the tables involved in these read events in the AWR report.

Time Model Statistics

Time model statistics give you an idea about how the database has spent its time, including the time it spent on executing SQL statements as against parsing statements. If parsing time is very high, or if hard parsing is significant, you must investigate further.

```
Time Model Statistics                  DB/Inst: ORCL1/orcl1  Snaps: 1878-1879

Statistic Name                                Time (s) % of DB Time
-----------------------                       -------- ------------
sql execute elapsed time                       1,791.5         88.2
parse time elapsed                               700.1         34.5
hard parse elapsed time                          653.7         32.2
```

Top SQL Statements

This section of the AWR report lets you quickly identify the most expensive SQL statements.

```
SQL ordered by Elapsed Time           DB/Inst: ORCL1/orcl1  Snaps: 1878-1879
-> Captured SQL account for      13.7% of Total DB Time (s):        2,032
-> Captured PL/SQL account for   19.8% of Total DB Time (s):        2,032

Elapsed           Elapsed Time
Time (s) Executions  per Exec (s) %Total  %CPU   %IO   SQL Id
-------- ---------- ------------ ------  ----  ---- ------------
292.4       1           292.41    14.4   8.1  61.2 b6usrg82hwsas
...
```

You can generate an explain plan for the expensive SQL statements using the SQL ID from this part of the report.

PGA Histogram

The PGA Aggregate Target Histogram shows how well the database is executing the sort and hash operations—for example:

```
PGA Aggr Target Histogram             DB/Inst: ORCL1/orcl1  Snaps: 1878-1879
-> Optimal Executions are purely in-memory operations
```

Low Optimal	High Optimal	Total Execs	Optimal Execs	1-Pass Execs	M-Pass Execs
2K	4K	13,957	13,957	0	0
64K	128K	86	86	0	0
128K	256K	30	30	0	0

In this example, the database is performing all sorts and hashes optimally in the PGA. If you see a high number of one-pass executions and even a few large multi-pass executions, that's an indication that the PGA is too small and you should consider increasing it.

How It Works

Analyzing an AWR report should be your first step when troubleshooting database performance issues such as a slow-running query. An AWR report lets you quickly find out things such as the number of connections, transactions per second, cache-hit rates, wait event information, and the SQL statements that are using the most CPU and I/O. It shows you which of your SQL statements are using the most resources, and which wait events are slowing down the database. Most importantly, probably, the report tells you if the database performance is unusually different from its typical performance during a given time of the day (or night). The AWR report sections summarized in the "Solution" section are only a small part of the AWR report. Here are some other key sections of the report that you must review when troubleshooting performance issues:

- Foreground Wait Events
- SQL Ordered by Gets
- SQL Ordered by Reads
- SQL Ordered by Physical Reads
- Instance Activity Stats
- Log Switches
- Enqueue Activity
- Reads by Tablespace, Datafile, and SQL Statement
- Segments by Table Scans
- Segments by Row Lock Waits
- Undo Segment Summary

Depending on the nature of the performance issue you're investigating, several of these sections in the report may turn out to be useful. In addition to the performance and wait statistics, the AWR report also offers advisories for both the PGA and the SGA. The AWR report is truly your best friend when you are troubleshooting just about any database performance issue. In a matter of minutes, you can usually find the underlying cause of the issue and figure out a potential fix. AWR does most of the work for you—all you need to do is know what to look for!

CHAPTER 8

▪ ▪ ▪

Creating Efficient SQL

Structured Query Language is like any other programming language in that it can be coded well, coded poorly, and everywhere in between. Learning to create efficient SQL statements has been discussed in countless books. This chapter zeroes in on basic SQL coding fundamentals and addresses some techniques to improve performance of your SQL statements. In addition, some emphasis is given to ramifications of poorly written SQL, along with a few common pitfalls to avoid in your SQL statements within your application. Most database performance issues are caused by poorly written SQL statements. Therefore, this chapter focuses on SQL fundamentals, which leads to better performing SQL, which leads to a more efficient use of database resources and overall better database performance. In addition, this can be extended to fundamental SQL code design as part of an overall software development lifecycle (SDLC) process. Good, fundamental code is also easy to read and therefore easier to maintain. This improves the performance of the overall SDLC process within an organization.

Writing good SQL statements the first time is the best way to get good performance from your SQL queries. Knowing the fundamentals is the key to accomplishing the goal of good performance. This chapter focuses on the following basic aspects of the SQL language:

- SELECT statement
- WHERE clause
- Joining tables
- Subqueries
- Set operators

Then, we'll focus on basic techniques to improve performance of your queries, as well as help ensure your queries are not hindering the performance of other queries within your database. It's important to take the time to write efficient SQL statements the first time, which is easy to say but tough to accomplish when balancing client requirements, budgets, and project timelines. However, if you adhere to basic coding practices and fundamentals, you can greatly improve the performance of your SQL queries.

▪ **Note**   Several times in this chapter, we make a distinction between ISO syntax and traditional Oracle syntax. Specifically, we do that with respect to join syntax. However, that distinction is a bit mis-stated. With the exception of Oracle's use of the (+) to indicate an outer join, all of Oracle's join syntax complies with the ISO SQL standard, so it is *all* ISO syntax. However, it is common in the field to refer to the newer syntax as "ISO syntax," and we follow that pattern in this chapter.

8-1. Retrieving All Rows from a Table

Problem

You need to write a query to retrieve all rows from a given table within your database.

Solution

Within the SQL language, you use the SELECT statement to retrieve data from the database. Everything following the SELECT statement tells Oracle what data you need from the database. The first thing you need to determine is from which table(s) you need to retrieve data. Once this has been determined, you have what you need to be able to run a query to get data from the database. If we have an EMPLOYEES table within our Oracle database, we can perform a describe on that table in order to see the structure of the table. By doing this, we can see the column names for the table and can determine which columns we want to select from the database.

```
SQL> describe employees
 Name                                      Null?    Type
 ----------------------------------------- -------- ----------------------------
 EMPLOYEE_ID                               NOT NULL NUMBER(6)
 FIRST_NAME                                         VARCHAR2(20)
 LAST_NAME                                 NOT NULL VARCHAR2(25)
 EMAIL                                     NOT NULL VARCHAR2(25)
 PHONE_NUMBER                                       VARCHAR2(20)
 HIRE_DATE                                 NOT NULL DATE
 JOB_ID                                    NOT NULL VARCHAR2(10)
 SALARY                                             NUMBER(8,2)
 COMMISSION_PCT                                     NUMBER(2,2)
 MANAGER_ID                                         NUMBER(6)
 DEPARTMENT_ID                                      NUMBER(4)
```

If we want to retrieve a list of all the employees' names from our EMPLOYEES table, we now have all the information we need to assemble a simple query against the EMPLOYEES table in the database. We know we are selecting from the EMPLOYEES table, which is needed for the FROM clause. We also know we want to select the names of the employees, which is needed to satisfy the SELECT clause. At this point, we can issue the following query against the database:

```
SELECT last_name, first_name
FROM employees;
```

```
LAST_NAME                 FIRST_NAME
------------------------- --------------------
Abel                      Ellen
Baer                      Hermann
Cabrio                    Anthony
Dilly                     Jennifer
Ernst                     Bruce
```

If we want to select all columns from the EMPLOYEES table, we can list every column from the table in the SELECT clause, or we can substitute listing every column with the asterisk, which indicates that we want to retrieve all the columns:

```
SELECT *
FROM employees;
```

If our manager wants the format of the output to be a list of employee name in last-comma-first format, we can modify our query to accomplish this task:

```
SELECT last_name || ', ' || first_name AS "Employee Name"
FROM employees;

Employee Name
-----------------------------------------------
Abel, Ellen
Baer, Hermann
Cabrio, Anthony
Dilly, Jennifer
Ernst, Bruce
```

In the foregoing case, we placed the concatenation characters, which are comprised of two vertical bars, in the query to indicate that we are combining the contents of multiple columns into a single output column. At the same time, we are creating a column alias by using the AS clause and calling the combined last and first names "Employee Name".

How It Works

SELECT is the most fundamental statement needed to retrieve data from an Oracle database. While there are many clauses and features of a SELECT statement, at its most basic, there are really only two clauses needed to first retrieve data out of an Oracle database—and those clauses are the SELECT clause and the FROM clause. Normally, more is required to accurately retrieve the desired result set. You may want only a subset of the columns within a database table, and you may want only a subset of rows from a given table. Furthermore, you may want to perform manipulation on data pulled from the database. All this requires more sophisticated components of the SQL language than the simple SELECT statement. However, the SELECT and FROM clauses are the basic building blocks to assemble a query, from the most simple of queries to the most complex of queries.

■ **Note**   In order to select data from any database table, you need to either own the table or have been given the privilege to select data from the given set of tables.

8-2. Retrieve a Subset of Rows from a Table
Problem

You want to filter the data from a database SELECT query to return only a subset of rows from a database table.

Solution

The WHERE clause gives the user the ability to filter rows and return only the desired result set back from the database. There are various ways to construct a WHERE clause, a few of which will be reviewed within this recipe. The first thing that occurs within a WHERE clause is that one or more columns' values are compared to some other value. See Table 8-1 for a list of comparison operators that can be used within the WHERE clause. One of the more common comparison operators is the equal sign, which denotes an equality condition:

```
SELECT *
FROM EMP
WHERE deptno = 20;
```

Table 8-1. *Comparison Operators Used in the WHERE Clause*

Operator	Description
=	Equal to
!= , <> , ^=	Not equal to
<	Less than
>	Greater than
<=	Less than or equal to
>=	Greater than or equal to
IS NULL IS NOT NULL	Checking for existence of null values
LIKE NOT LIKE	Used to search when entire column value is not known

In the foregoing query, we are selecting all columns from the EMP table, which is denoted by using the asterisk, and we want only those rows for department 20, which is determined by the WHERE clause.

How It Works

In many SQL statements, there can be multiple conditions in a WHERE clause. Coding multiple conditions is done by using the logical operators OR, AND, and IN. If you have multiple logical operators within your SQL statement, and if no parentheses are present, then Oracle will first evaluate all AND clauses prior to any of the OR clauses. This can be confusing when constructing a complex WHERE condition. Therefore, when coding multiple conditions within a WHERE clause, delimit each clause with parentheses, or else you may not get the results you are expecting. This is good SQL coding practice and makes SQL code simpler to read and maintain—for example:

```
SELECT last_name, first_name, salary, email
FROM employees
WHERE (department_id = 20
OR department_id = 80)
AND commission_pct > 0;
```

If we have the need for multiple OR logical operators within our statement, we can replace them with the IN logical operator, which can simplify our SQL statement. By rewriting the foregoing query to use the IN logical operator, our query would look like the following:

```
SELECT last_name, first_name, salary, email
FROM employees
WHERE department_id IN (20,80)
AND commission_pct > 0;
```

If you want to find all the same information for all departments except department 20 or 80, the SQL code would look like the following:

```
SELECT last_name, first_name, salary, email
FROM employees
WHERE (department_id != 20
AND department_id <> 80)
AND commission_pct > 0;
```

Note that in the foregoing, for demonstration, we used two of the "not equal" comparison operators. It is generally good coding practice to be consistent, and use the same operators across all of your SQL code. This avoids confusion with others who need to look at or modify your SQL code. Even subtle differences like this can make someone else ponder why one piece of SQL code was done one way, and another piece of SQL code was done a different way. When writing SQL code, writing for efficiency is important, but it is equally important to write the code with an eye on maintainability. If SQL code is consistent, it simply will be easier to read and maintain.

Taking the previous SQL statement, we again will use the logical OR operator, add the NOT operand, and accomplish the same task:

```
SELECT last_name, first_name, salary, email
FROM employees
WHERE department_id NOT IN(20,80)
AND commission_pct > 0;
```

The last two queries both provided the proper results, but in this case, using the IN clause simplified our SQL statement.

8-3. Joining Tables with Corresponding Rows
Problem

Within a single query, you wish to retrieve matching rows from multiple tables. These tables have at least one common column on which to match the data between the tables.

Solution

A join condition within the SQL language is used to combine data from multiple tables within a single query. The most common join condition is called an *inner join*. What this means is that the result set is based on the common join columns between the tables and that only data that matches between the two tables will be returned.

Let's say you want to get the city where all departments in your company are based. There are two different ways to approach this before writing your SQL statement. You can use either traditional SQL syntax, or the newer, so-called ISO syntax. (In truth, both approaches represent ISO syntax). Using traditional SQL, the syntax would be as follows:

```
SELECT d.location_id, department_name, city
FROM departments d, locations l
WHERE d.location_id = l.location_id;
```

To write the same statement using ISO syntax, there are several methods that can be used:

- Natural Join

- JOIN ... USING clause

- JOIN ... ON clause

If using the NATURAL JOIN clause, you are letting Oracle determine the natural join condition and which columns will be joined on, and therefore there are no join clauses or conditions in the statement. Oracle will join the tables based on all columns in both tables that share the same names. See the following example:

```
SELECT location_id, department_name, city
FROM departments NATURAL JOIN locations;
```

If tables you are joining have common named join columns, you can also specify the JOIN ... USING clause, and you specify this common column within parentheses:

```
SELECT location_id, department_name, city
FROM departments JOIN locations
USING (location_id);
```

It is very common for the join condition between tables to have differently named columns that are needed to complete the join criteria. In these cases, the JOIN ... ON clause is appropriate:

```
SELECT d.location_id, d.department_name, l.city
FROM departments d JOIN locations l
ON (l.location_id = d.location_id);
```

How It Works

When using traditional Oracle SQL, you need to specify all join conditions in the WHERE clause. Therefore, the WHERE clause will contain all join conditions, along with any filtering criteria.

With ISO SQL, a key advantage is that the join conditions are done in the FROM clause, and the WHERE clause is used solely for filtering criteria. This makes SQL statements easier to read and decipher. No longer do you need to determine within a WHERE clause which statements are join conditions and which are filtering criteria. The advantage of this is more evident when you are joining three or more tables. The filtering criteria are solely in the WHERE clause and are easily visible:

```
SELECT last_name, first_name, department_name, city,
state_province state, postal_code zip, country_name
FROM employees
JOIN departments USING (department_id)
JOIN locations USING (location_id)
JOIN countries USING (country_id)
JOIN regions USING (region_id)
WHERE department_id = 20;
```

If you prefer to write SQL statements with traditional Oracle SQL, good practice just for readability and more maintainable SQL code is to place all join conditions first in the WHERE clause, and place all filtering criteria at the end of the WHERE clause. It also makes the code easier to read and maintain if you can simply line up the code. This is an optional practice but helps anyone else who may need to look at your SQL code:

```
SELECT last_name, first_name, department_name, city,
state_province state, postal_code zip, country_name
FROM employees e, departments d, locations l, countries c, regions r
WHERE e.department_id = d.department_id
  AND d.location_id   = l.location_id
  AND l.country_id    = c.country_id
  AND c.region_id     = r.region_id
  and d.department_id = 20;
```

Also, when using the JOIN ... ON or JOIN ... USING clause, it may be more clear to specify the optional INNER keyword, as it would immediately be known it is an inner join that is being done:

```
SELECT location_id, department_name, city
FROM departments INNER JOIN locations
USING (location_id);
```

USE NATURAL JOIN WITH CAUTION

As a general rule, it may simply be beneficial to avoid the use of NATURAL JOIN with applications, as the output can be different than what is intended. By using this syntax, you are giving Oracle control to handle the join condition between tables, and it may decide to join two tables differently than expected. See the following example of two statements that query the data dictionary. The first example uses the USING clause to join the tables.

```
select s.owner, segment_name, e.bytes
from dba_segments s join dba_extents e
using (segment_name)
where segment_name = 'EMPLOYEES';

OWNER   SEGMENT_NAME              BYTES
------  --------------------  ----------
HR      EMPLOYEES                 65536
```

The second example uses the NATURAL JOIN keyword:

```
select owner, segment_name, bytes
from dba_segments natural join dba_extents
where segment_name = 'EMPLOYEES';


no rows selected
```

Let's see if we can run a test to determine why the foregoing sample query using NATURAL JOIN returned no rows. If we look at the common columns between DBA_SEGMENTS and DBA_EXTENTS and construct a query to retrieve data for the EMPLOYEES table based on only the common columns, the results look identical:

```
select 'DBA_SEGMENTS' tab, owner, segment_name, partition_name,
segment_type, tablespace_name, bytes, blocks, relative_fno
from dba_segments
where segment_name = 'EMPLOYEES'
union all
select 'DBA_EXTENTS', owner, segment_name, partition_name,
segment_type, tablespace_name, bytes, blocks, relative_fno
from dba_extents
where segment_name = 'EMPLOYEES';

TAB             OW SEGMENT_NA P TYPE   TABLES BYTES BLK FNO
------------    -- ---------- - ------ ------ ------ --- ---
DBA_SEGMENTS HR EMPLOYEES      TABLE  USERS   65536   8   6
DBA_EXTENTS  HR EMPLOYEES      TABLE  USERS   65536   8   6
```

In the foregoing query using NATURAL JOIN, all common columns between DBA_SEGMENTS and DBA_EXTENTS should have been used to complete the join operation. Our query against the data dictionary appeared to show all common columns indeed had matching values. However, no match was found when using NATURAL JOIN, whereas a row was returned from the query having the USING clause. This doesn't mean the query with NATURAL JOIN returned incorrect results, but it does mean we made assumptions about the join conditions that were incorrect. Because of this, it's always better to be explicit when coding SQL, in which case NATURAL JOIN should generally be avoided.

8-4. Joining Tables When Corresponding Rows May Be Missing
Problem

You need data from two or more tables, but some of the data have no match in one or more of the tables. For instance, you want to get a list of all of the departments for your company, along with their base locations. For whatever reason, you've been told that there are locations listed within your company that do not map to a single department, in which case there are no department locations listed.

Solution

You need to show all locations, so an inner join will not work in this case. Instead, you can write what is termed an *outer join*. Notice the (+) syntax in the following example:

```
SELECT l.location_id, city, department_id, department_name
FROM locations l, departments d
WHERE l.location_id = d.location_id(+)
ORDER BY 1;
```

LOCATION_ID	CITY	DEPARTMENT_ID	DEPARTMENT_NAME
1100	Venice		
1400	Southlake	60	IT
1500	South San Francisco	50	Shipping
1700	Seattle	170	Manufacturing
1700	Seattle	240	Sales
1700	Seattle	270	Payroll
1700	Seattle	120	Treasury
1700	Seattle	110	Accounting
1700	Seattle	100	Finance
1700	Seattle	30	Purchasing
1800	Toronto	20	Marketing
2000	Beijing		
2400	London	40	Human Resources
2700	Munich	70	Public Relations
3200	Mexico City		

To specify an outer join using traditional Oracle SQL, simply place a plus sign within parentheses in the WHERE clause join condition next to a column from the table that you know has no matching data. We know in the foregoing case that there are locations that are not assigned to a department. From the results, we can see the locations that have no departments assigned to them.

To execute the same query using ISO SQL syntax, you use the LEFT OUTER JOIN or RIGHT OUTER JOIN clauses, which can be shortened to LEFT JOIN or RIGHT JOIN—for example:

```
SELECT location_id, city, department_id, department_name
FROM locations LEFT JOIN departments d
USING (location_id)
ORDER BY 1;
```

Now let's say you must execute a query in which either table, on either side of the join, could be missing one or more corresponding rows. One approach is to create a union of two outer join queries:

```
SELECT last_name, first_name, department_name
FROM employees e, departments d
WHERE e.department_id = d.department_id(+)
UNION
SELECT last_name, first_name, department_name
FROM employees e, departments d
WHERE e.department_id(+) = d.department_id
ORDER BY department_name, last_name, first_name;
```

```
LAST_NAME       FIRST_NAME      DEPARTMENT_NAME
------------    --------------  ----------------------
Gietz           William         Accounting
Higgins         Shelley         Accounting
Whalen          Jennifer        Administration
                                Benefits
                                Construction
Kochhar         Neena           Executive
Chen            John            Finance
Bates           Elizabeth       Sales
Zlotkey         Eleni           Sales
                                Shareholder Services
Weiss           Matthew         Shipping
                                Treasury
Grant           Kimberely
Lee             Linda
Morse           Steve
```

From the foregoing results, we can see all employees that manage departments, all employees that do not manage departments, as well as those departments with no assigned manager.

In order to do the same query using ISO SQL syntax, use the FULL OUTER JOIN clause, which can be shortened to FULL JOIN:

```
SELECT last_name, first_name, department_name
FROM employees FULL JOIN departments
USING (department_id)
ORDER BY department_name, last_name, first_name;
```

How It Works

There are really three outer joins that can be done based on your circumstances. Table 8-2 describes all the possible join conditions. SQL statements using traditional syntax or ISO SQL syntax are both perfectly acceptable. However, it is generally easier to write, read, and maintain ISO SQL than traditional Oracle SQL.

Table 8-2. *Oracle Join Conditions*

Join Type	Traditional Join Syntax	ISO Join Syntax	Description
Inner join	WHERE clause, with one clause specified for each join condition	FROM clause, along with: NATURAL JOIN JOIN ... USING JOIN ... ON	There are corresponding rows in each table matching the condition.
Left outer join	WHERE clause, the 3-character sequence of (+) placed next to column from table with missing data	FROM clause, along with: LEFT OUTER JOIN LEFT JOIN	There may not be corresponding rows in the table on the right side of the join condition.
Right outer join	WHERE clause, the 3-character sequence of (+) placed next to table with missing data	FROM clause, along with: RIGHT OUTER JOIN RIGHT JOIN	This means there may not be corresponding rows on table on the left side of the join condition.
Full outer join	Two SELECT statements with union condition specified, with one side of the outer join specified on first part of the union, and the other side of the outer join specified on second part of the union	FROM clause, along with: FULL OUTER JOIN FULL JOIN	This means there may not always be corresponding rows in both tables. It cannot be specified natively with traditional Oracle SQL syntax and must be constructed with a UNION, while ISO SQL has the syntax built in.
Cross join	WHERE clause; there are no join conditions between the joined tables.	FROM clause, along with: CROSS JOIN	This means a Cartesian join is indicated.

One of the main advantages of the ISO syntax is that for multiple table joins, all the join conditions are specified in the FROM clause, and are therefore isolated and easy to see. In Oracle SQL, the join conditions are specified in the WHERE clause, along with any other filtering criteria needed for the query. If you inherited poorly structured SQL code, it is simply harder to read longer and more complex SQL statements that have join conditions and filtering criteria interspersed within a single WHERE clause.

One other type of join not already mentioned is the cross join, which is a Cartesian join, which is all possible combinatinos of all rows from both tables. While this type of join is rarely useful, it can be occasionally beneficial. As a DBA, let's say you are gathering database size information for your enterprise of databases and are placing the results in a single spreadsheet. You need to get database and host information for each query. You can execute the following query:

```
SELECT d.name, i.host_name, round(sum(f.bytes)/1048576) megabytes
FROM v$database d
CROSS JOIN v$instance i
CROSS JOIN v$datafile f
GROUP BY d.name, i.host_name;
```

NAME	HOST_NAME	MEGABYTES
ORCL	DREGS-PC	2333

In this case, the v$instance and v$database views contain only a single row, so there is no harm in doing a Cartesian join. The foregoing join could also be written with traditional Oracle SQL:

```
SELECT d.name, i.host_name, round(sum(f.bytes)/1048576) megabytes
FROM v$database d, v$instance i, v$datafile f
GROUP BY d.name, i.host_name;
```

Starting with Oracle 12c release 1, if using LEFT OUTER Join syntax, you can now place multiple tables on the left-hand side of the join operation. For instance, see the following query and resulting error message when run in Oracle 11g:

```
SELECT d.department_name, e.manager_id, l.location_id, sum(e.salary)
FROM departments d, employees e, locations l
WHERE d.department_id = e.department_id
AND e.manager_id = d.manager_id  (+)
AND l.location_id = d.location_id (+)
GROUP BY d.department_name, e.manager_id, l.location_id
ORDER BY 2,3;

AND e.manager_id = d.manager_id  (+)
             *
ERROR at line 4:
ORA-01417: a table may be outer joined to at most one other table
```

When now running in Oracle 12c, the syntax is now valid and returns an efficient execution plan:

```
---------------------------------------------------------------------
| Id | Operation                               | Name            |
---------------------------------------------------------------------
|  0 | SELECT STATEMENT                        |                 |
|  1 |  SORT GROUP BY                          |                 |
|  2 |   HASH JOIN                             |                 |
|  3 |    TABLE ACCESS BY INDEX ROWID BATCHED| DEPARTMENTS     |
|  4 |     INDEX FULL SCAN                     | DEPT_LOCATION_IX |
|  5 |    TABLE ACCESS FULL                    | EMPLOYEES       |
```

8-5. Constructing Simple Subqueries

Problem

You are finding it easiest to think in terms of executing two queries to get your desired results. Your thought process is to execute a first query to get some intermediate results and then executing a second query to get to the results that you really are after.

Solution

It is common that data needs from a relational database are complex enough that the data cannot be retrieved within a simple SQL SELECT statement. Rather than having to run two or more queries serially, it is possible to construct several SQL SELECT statements and place them within a single query. These additional SELECT statements are called subqueries, subselects, or nested selects.

Let's say you want to get the name of the employee with the highest salary in your company so you can ask your boss for a raise. Since you don't know what the highest salary is, you first have to run a query to determine the following:

```
SELECT MAX(salary) FROM employees;

MAX(SALARY)
-----------
      24000
```

Then, knowing what the highest salary is, you could run a second query to get the employee(s) with that salary:

```
SELECT last_name, first_name
FROM employees
WHERE salary = 24000;

LAST_NAME                FIRST_NAME
------------------------ --------------------
King                     Steven
```

It's very simple to combine the foregoing two queries, and construct a single SQL statement with a subquery to accomplish the same task:

```
SELECT last_name, first_name
FROM employees
WHERE salary =
(SELECT MAX(salary) FROM employees);

LAST_NAME                FIRST_NAME
------------------------ --------------------
King                     Steven
```

How It Works

Within a SQL statement, a subquery can be placed within the SELECT, WHERE, or HAVING clauses. You can also place a query within the FROM clause, which is also called an inline view, which is addressed in a different recipe. There are several kinds of subqueries that can be constructed:

- Single-row or scalar subquery

- Multiple-row subquery

- Multiple-column subquery

- Correlated subquery (addressed in a different recipe)

In the solution example, the inner query is executed first, and then the results of the inner query are passed to the outer query, which is then executed.

Single-Row Subqueries

Single-row subqueries return a single column of a single row. The example shown in the "Solution" section is a single-row subquery. Use caution and be certain that the subquery can return only a single value; otherwise you can get an error from your subquery:

```
SELECT last_name, first_name
FROM employees
WHERE salary =
(SELECT salary FROM employees WHERE department_id = 30);

(SELECT salary FROM employees WHERE department_id = 30)
 *
ERROR at line 4:
ORA-01427: single-row subquery returns more than one row
```

In the foregoing example, there are multiple employees in department 30, so the subquery would return all of the matching rows.

If you want to see how your salary stacks up against the average salaries of employees in your company, you can issue a subquery in the SELECT clause to accomplish this:

```
SELECT last_name, first_name, salary, ROUND((SELECT AVG(salary) FROM employees)) avg_sal
FROM employees
WHERE last_name = 'King';
```

LAST_NAME	FIRST_NAME	SALARY	AVG_SAL
King	Steven	24000	6462

Let's say you want to know which departments overall had a higher salary than the average for your company. By placing the subquery in the HAVING clause, you can get the desired results:

```
column avg_sal format 99999.99

SELECT department_id, ROUND(avg(salary),2) avg_sal
FROM employees
GROUP BY department_id
HAVING avg(salary) > (SELECT AVG(salary) FROM employees)
ORDER BY 2;
```

DEPARTMENT_ID	AVG_SAL
40	6500.00
100	8600.00
80	8955.88
20	9500.00
70	10000.00
110	10150.00
90	19333.33

```
8 rows selected.
```

Multiple-Row Subqueries

If you know the desired subquery is going to return multiple rows, you can use the IN, ANY, ALL, and SOME operators. The IN operator is the same as having multiple OR conditions in a select statement. For example, in the following SQL statement, we are getting the DEPARTMENT_NAME for departments 20, 30, and 40.

```
SELECT department_id, department_name
FROM departments
WHERE department_id = 20
OR department_id = 30
OR department_id = 40;


DEPARTMENT_ID DEPARTMENT_NAME
------------- ------------------------------
           20 Marketing
           30 Purchasing
           40 Human Resources
```

Using the IN operator, we can simplify our SQL statement and achieve the same result:

```
SELECT department_id, department_name
FROM departments
WHERE department_id IN (20,30,40);
```

The ANY and SOME operators function identically. They are used to compare a value retrieved from the database to each value shown in the list of values in the query. They are used with the comparison operators =, !=, <>, <, <=, >, or >=. Use care with ANY or SOME, as it evaluates each value separately, without regard to the entire list of values. For example, using the same query to get the department name for departments 20, 30, or 40, if we modify this query to use ANY or SOME, we can see how Oracle evaluates each value in the ANY clause. Because we used the ANY clause, departments 10, 20, and 30 were included in the result, even though departments 20 and 30 were within our ANY clause. This is because each value is evaluated separately before the result set is returned.

```
SELECT department_id, department_name
FROM departments
WHERE department_id < ANY (20,30,40);

SELECT department_id, department_name
FROM departments
WHERE department_id < SOME (20,30,40);

DEPARTMENT_ID DEPARTMENT_NAME
------------- ------------------------------
           10 Administration
           20 Marketing
           30 Purchasing
```

The ALL operator essentially uses a logical AND operator to do the comparison of values shown in the query. While with the ANY operator, each value was compared individually to see if there was a match, the ALL operator needs to compare every value in the list before determining if there is a match. Using our department table as an example, see the following query. In this query, we are retrieving the department names from the table if the DEPARTMENT_ID value is less than or equal to *all* values in the list:

```
SELECT department_id, department_name
FROM departments
WHERE department_id <= ALL (20,30,40);


DEPARTMENT_ID DEPARTMENT_NAME
------------- ------------------------------
           10 Administration
           20 Marketing
```

Multiple-Column Subqueries

At times, you need to match data based on multiple columns. If placed within the WHERE clause, the column list needs to be placed within parentheses. As an example, if you want to get a list of the employees with the highest salary in their respective departments, you can write a multiple-column subquery such as the following:

```
SELECT last_name, first_name, department_id, salary
FROM employees
WHERE (department_id, salary) IN
(SELECT department_id, max(salary)
FROM employees
GROUP BY department_id)
ORDER BY department_id;
```

LAST_NAME	FIRST_NAME	DEPARTMENT_ID	SALARY
Whalen	Jennifer	10	4400
Hartstein	Michael	20	13000
Raphaely	Den	30	11000
Mavris	Susan	40	6500
Fripp	Adam	50	8200
Hunold	Alexander	60	9000
Baer	Hermann	70	10000
Russell	John	80	14000
King	Steven	90	24000
Greenberg	Nancy	100	12000
Higgins	Shelley	110	12000

```
11 rows selected.
```

8-6. Constructing Correlated Subqueries

Problem

You are writing a subquery to retrieve data from a given set of tables from your database. In order to retrieve the proper results, you really need to reference the outer query from inside the inner query.

Solution

The correlated subquery is a powerful component of the SQL language. The reason it is called "correlated" is that it allows you to reference the outer query from within the inner query. For example, we want to see the employees in our company whose salary was the minimum for their specific job title:

```
SELECT department_id, last_name, salary
FROM employees e
WHERE salary =
   (SELECT min_salary
    FROM jobs j
    WHERE e.job_id = j.job_id);

DEPARTMENT_ID LAST_NAME          SALARY
------------- --------------- ----------
          50 Olson               2000
          80 Russell            10000
```

How It Works

Because you reference the outer query from inside the inner query, the process of executing a correlated subquery is essentially the opposite compared to a simple subquery. In a correlated subquery, normally the outer query is executed first, as the inner query needs the data from the outer query in order to be able to process the query and retrieve the results. Depending on the specific query, the optimizer may actually choose to transform the query to a standard join. This can be determined by running an explain plan for a given query. The traditional steps to execute a correlated subquery are as follows. These steps repeat for each row in the outer query:

1. Retrieve row from the outer query.

2. Execute the inner query.

3. The outer query compares the value returned from the inner query.

4. If there is a value match in step 3, the row is returned to the user.

Another type of correlated subquery is to use the EXISTS clause in a subquery. When you use EXISTS, a test is done to see if the inner query returns at least one row. This is the important test that occurs when using the EXISTS operator. As you can see from the following example, the column list of the SELECT clause within the inner query is irrelevant. Something is included there simply to have proper SQL syntax only. If we want to see all the jobs each current employee has ever held in our company, we can use the EXISTS operator to help us get this information:

```
SELECT employee_id, job_id
FROM job_history h
WHERE EXISTS
(SELECT job_id FROM employees e
```

```
WHERE e.job_id = h.job_id)
ORDER BY 1;

EMPLOYEE_ID JOB_ID
----------- ----------
        101 AC_ACCOUNT
        101 AC_MGR
        102 IT_PROG
        114 ST_CLERK
        122 ST_CLERK
        176 SA_REP
        176 SA_MAN
        200 AD_ASST
        200 AC_ACCOUNT
        201 MK_REP

10 rows selected.
```

You can also use NOT EXISTS if you want to test the opposite condition within a query. For example, your CEO wants to determine the manager-to-employee ratio within your company. Using the query from the previous example, we can first use the EXISTS operator to determine the number of managers within the company:

```
SELECT count(*)
FROM employees e
WHERE EXISTS
(SELECT 'TESTING 1,2,3'
FROM employees m
WHERE e.employee_id = manager_id);

  COUNT(*)
----------
        18
```

If we convert EXISTS to NOT EXISTS, we can determine the number of non-managers within the company:

```
SELECT count(*)
FROM employees e
WHERE NOT EXISTS
(SELECT 'X'
FROM employees m
WHERE e.employee_id = manager_id);

  COUNT(*)
---------
        89
```

8-7. Comparing Two Tables to Find Missing Rows

Problem

You need to compare data for a subset of columns between two tables. You need to find rows in one table that are missing from the other.

Solution

You can use the Oracle MINUS set operator to compare two sets of data, and show data missing from one of the tables. When using any of the Oracle set operators, the SELECT clauses must be identical in terms of number of columns, and the datatypes of each column.

As an example, you work for a cable television company, and you want to find out what channels are offered free of charge. To test this, you could first simply get a list of the channels offered by your company:

```
SELECT channel_id FROM channels;

CHANNEL_ID
----------
         2
         3
         4
         5
         9
```

Then, you can run a query to find out which channels have costs associated with them by querying the COSTS table:

```
SELECT DISTINCT channel_id FROM costs
ORDER BY channel_id;

CHANNEL_ID
----------
         2
         3
         4
```

By quickly doing a visual examination of the results, the free channels are channels 5 and 9. By using a set operator, in this case, MINUS, you can get this result from a single query:

```
SELECT channel_id
FROM channels
MINUS
SELECT channel_id
FROM costs;

CHANNEL_ID
----------
         5
         9
```

How It Works

It is also very common to use set operators in queries to get more information about the missing data. For instance, you have gotten the free channel list, but you really need to get more information about those free channels, and would like to accomplish everything within a single query:

```
SELECT channel_id, channel_desc FROM channels
WHERE channel_id IN
(SELECT channel_id
FROM channels
MINUS
SELECT channel_id
FROM costs);


CHANNEL_ID CHANNEL_DESC
---------- --------------------
         5 Catalog
         9 Tele Sales
```

The MINUS operator is very simple to use. However, use MINUS with care. MINUS can easily consume a large amount of temporary tablespace if the data set being retrieved is large, and it can be slow performing as volumes increase. An alternative to using MINUS is to rewrite such a query using an OUTER JOIN. In the first example in the SOLUTION section, see the query repeated below and its associated explain plan:

```
SELECT channel_id
FROM channels
MINUS
SELECT channel_id
FROM costs;
```

```
-----------------------------------------
| Id | Operation           | Name      |
-----------------------------------------
|  0 | SELECT STATEMENT    |           |
|  1 |  MINUS              |           |
|  2 |   SORT UNIQUE       |           |
|  3 |    TABLE ACCESS FULL| CHANNELS  |
|  4 |   SORT UNIQUE       |           |
|  5 |    TABLE ACCESS FULL| COSTS     |
-----------------------------------------
```

Now, see the same query rewritten as an outer join, and it's associated explain plan:

```
select h.channel_id
from costs o right join channels h
on o.channel_id = h.channel_id
Where o.channel_id is null and o.cost is null;
```

```
------------------------------------------
| Id  | Operation              | Name      |
------------------------------------------
|   0 | SELECT STATEMENT       |           |
|   1 |  FILTER                |           |
|   2 |   HASH JOIN OUTER      |           |
|   3 |    TABLE ACCESS FULL| CHANNELS |
|   4 |    TABLE ACCESS FULL| COSTS    |
------------------------------------------
```

In the foregoing example, using a join method can be more efficient and better performing than using a MINUS set operator. The basic rule of thumb to keep in mind is volume. With very small volumes, MINUS works well. As volumes grow, consider using OUTER JOIN rather than MINUS.

8-8. Comparing Two Tables to Find Matching Rows
Problem

You need to compare data for a subset of columns between two tables. You need to see all matching rows from those tables.

Solution

You can use the SQL INTERSECT set operator to compare two sets of data and show the matching data between the two tables. Again, when using any of the SQL set operators, the SELECT clauses must be identical in terms of number of columns, and the datatypes of each column.

Using the example of the free channels, we now want to see which channels are not free, and have costs associated with them. By using the INTERSECT set operator, we will see only the matching rows between the two tables:

```
SELECT channel_id
FROM channels
INTERSECT
SELECT channel_id
FROM costs;

CHANNEL_ID
----------
         2
         3
         4
```

How It Works

When using INTERSECT, think of it as the overlapping data between two tables, based on the column list in the SELECT statement.

8-9. Combining Results from Similar SELECT Statements

Problem

You need to combine the results between two similar SELECT statements, and would like to accomplish it within a single query.

Solution

You can use the SQL set operators UNION or UNION ALL to combine results from two like queries. The difference between using UNION and UNION ALL is that UNION will automatically eliminate any duplicate rows, and each row of the result set will be unique. When using UNION ALL, it will show all matching rows, including duplicate rows. Using UNION ALL may yield better performance than UNION, because a sort to eliminate duplicates is avoided. If your application can eliminate duplicates during processing, it may be worth the performance gained from using UNION ALL.

In Oracle's sample schemas, we have the SCOTT.EMP table and the HR.EMPLOYEES table. If we want to see all the employees on both tables, we can use a UNION set operator to get the results:

```
SELECT empno, hiredate FROM scott.emp
UNION
SELECT employee_id, hire_date FROM hr.employees;

    EMPNO HIREDATE
---------- ---------
       100 17-JUN-87
       101 21-SEP-89
       102 13-JAN-93
       ...
      7902 03-DEC-81
      7934 23-JAN-82
      7997 15-AUG-11

122 rows selected.
```

How It Works

You are running two queries where you have a nearly identical column list, but let's say you have one additional column on one table. In this case, we have the COMM column on the SCOTT.EMP table, which is the commission amount an employee has earned. You don't have an equivalent column on the HR.EMPLOYEES table. By using NULL in the missing column, you can still use a set operator such as UNION as long as you account for any missing columns on either side of the operation:

```
SELECT empno, mgr, hiredate, sal, deptno, comm
FROM scott.emp
UNION
SELECT employee_id, manager_id, hire_date, salary, department_id, NULL
FROM hr.employees;
```

EMPNO	MGR	HIREDATE	SAL	DEPTNO	COMM
100		17-JUN-87	24000	90	
101	100	21-SEP-89	17000	90	
102	100	13-JAN-93	17000	90	
...					
7369	7902	17-DEC-80	800	20	
7499	7698	20-FEB-81	1600	30	300
7521	7698	22-FEB-81	1250	30	500
7566	7839	02-APR-81	2975	20	
7654	7698	28-SEP-81	1250	30	1400

After examining the HR.EMPLOYEES table, there is a column named COMMISSION_PCT. We can derive the actual commission based on this column and add it to the previous query. Also, our manager has told us that he or she wants to see a value in the commission column for all employees, even if they earn no commission:

```
SELECT empno, mgr, hiredate, sal, deptno, nvl(comm,0)
FROM scott.emp
UNION
SELECT employee_id, manager_id, hire_date, salary, department_id,
nvl(salary*commission_pct/100,0)
FROM hr.employees;
```

EMPNO	MGR	HIREDATE	SAL	DEPTNO	NVL(COMM,0)
100		17-JUN-87	24000	90	0
101	100	21-SEP-89	17000	90	0
102	100	13-JAN-93	17000	90	0
...					
147	100	10-MAR-97	12000	80	36
148	100	15-OCT-99	11000	80	33
149	100	29-JAN-00	10500	80	21
...					
7499	7698	20-FEB-81	1600	30	300
7521	7698	22-FEB-81	1250	30	500
7566	7839	02-APR-81	2975	20	0

One point to stress again is that the datatypes for each column also must be the same. For example, we are doing a union between the SCOTT.EMP table and the HR.DEPARTMENTS table and want to see a combined list of the department numbers, along with their locations. However, based on the datatype list, we cannot use an Oracle set operator such as UNION for this, as the location column for each table is different:

```
SQL> desc scott.dept
```

Name	Null?	Type
DEPTNO	NOT NULL	NUMBER(2)
DNAME		VARCHAR2(14)
LOC		**VARCHAR2(13)**

```
SQL> desc hr.departments
```

Name	Null?	Type
DEPARTMENT_ID	NOT NULL	NUMBER(4)
DEPARTMENT_NAME	NOT NULL	VARCHAR2(30)
MANAGER_ID		NUMBER(6)
LOCATION_ID		**NUMBER(4)**

```
SQL> l
  1  SELECT deptno, loc FROM scott.dept
  2  UNION
  3* select department_id, location_id from hr.departments
SQL> /
SELECT deptno, loc FROM scott.dept
              *
ERROR at line 1:
ORA-01790: expression must have same datatype as corresponding expression
```

8-10. Searching for a Range of Values

Problem

You need to retrieve data from your database based on a range of values for a given column.

Solution

The BETWEEN clause is commonly used to retrieve a range of values from a database. It is most commonly used with dates, timestamps, and numbers but can also be used with alphanumeric data. It is an efficient way of retrieving data from the database when an exact set of values is not known for a column within the WHERE clause. For instance, if we wanted to see all employees that were hired between the year 2000 and through the year 2010, the query could be written as follows:

```
SELECT last_name, first_name, hire_date
FROM employees
WHERE hire_date BETWEEN to_date('2000-01-01','yyyy-mm-dd')
AND to_date('2010-12-31','yyyy-mm-dd')
ORDER BY hire_date;
```

When using the BETWEEN clause, it is an efficient way to find a range of values for a column and works for a multitude of datatypes. If you want to get a range of values for a NUMBER datatype as in the SALARY column, a range can be given:

```
SELECT last_name, first_name, salary
FROM employees
WHERE salary BETWEEN 20000 and 30000
ORDER BY salary;
```

If you want to add to the foregoing query and get only those employees whose last names are in the first half of the alphabet, you can supply a range to satisfy this request. In order to guarantee all values, we filled out the possible values to the 25-character length of the last_name column:

```
SELECT last_name, first_name, salary
FROM employees
WHERE salary BETWEEN 20000 and 30000
AND last_name BETWEEN 'Aaaaaaaaaaaaaaaaaaaaaaaaa'
AND 'Mzzzzzzzzzzzzzzzzzzzzzzzz'
ORDER BY salary;
```

For the above specific example, since the first half of the alphabet is inclusive between "A" and "M", you could simply the above query by using both BETWEEN in the first clause and a comparison operator in the second clause:

```
SELECT last_name, first_name, salary
FROM employees
WHERE salary BETWEEN 20000 and 30000
AND last_name < 'N'
ORDER BY salary;
```

The foregoing two examples demonstrate that the data needed may drive the methods that can and cannot be used when writing a query.

How It Works

One common pitfall when using the BETWEEN clause is with the use of date-based columns, whether it be the DATE datatype, the TIMESTAMP datatype, or any other date-based datatype. If not constructed carefully, desired rows can be missed from the result set.

One way this occurs is that often queries on dates are done using a combination of year, month, and day. It is important to remember that even though the format of the date-based fields on an Oracle database usually defaults to a year, month, and day type of format, the element of time must always be accounted for, else rows can be missed from a query. In this first example, we have an employee, Sarah Bell, who was hired February 4, 1996:

```
SELECT to_char(hire_date,'yyyy-mm-dd:hh24:mi:ss') hire_date
FROM employees
WHERE email = 'SBELL';


HIRE_DATE
-------------------
1996-02-04:12:30:46
```

If we query the database and don't consider the time element for any date column, we can omit critical rows from our result set. Therefore it is important to know whether the time portion of the column is included in the makeup of the data. In this case, there is indeed a time element present in the hire_date column:

```
SELECT last_name, first_name, hire_date
FROM employees
WHERE hire_date = to_date('1996-02-04','yyyy-mm-dd');

no rows selected
```

When coding SQL, it is important to always assume there is a time element present for any and all date-based columns. Based on that assumption, we can modify the foregoing query to consider the time element in the hire_ date column. Two examples are shown. The first uses BETWEEN to delimit the date range, while the second uses comparison operators to delimit the date range. Both return the same result:

```
SELECT last_name, first_name, to_char(hire_date,'yyyy-mm-dd:hh24:mi:ss') hire_date
FROM employees
WHERE hire_date
BETWEEN TO_DATE('1996-02-04:00:00:00','yyyy-mm-dd:hh24:mi:ss')
AND TO_DATE('1996-02-04:23:59:59','yyyy-mm-dd:hh24:mi:ss');

SELECT last_name, first_name, to_char(hire_date,'yyyy-mm-dd:hh24:mi:ss') hire_date
FROM employees
WHERE hire_date >= TO_DATE('1996-02-04:00:00:00','yyyy-mm-dd:hh24:mi:ss')
    AND hire_date <= TO_DATE('1996-02-04:23:59:59','yyyy-mm-dd:hh24:mi:ss');
```

```
LAST_NAME                FIRST_NAME            HIRE_DATE
------------------------ -------------------- --------------------
Bell                     Sarah                1996-02-04:12:30:46
```

Using the foregoing example, we can also use the TRUNC function to eliminate this issue, and although using functions on the left side of the comparison operator generally may hurt performance, the optimizer in this case will still use an index. Below is the explain plan of the query without using TRUNC:

```
-----------------------------------------------------------
| Id  | Operation                           | Name          |
-----------------------------------------------------------
|   0 | SELECT STATEMENT                    |               |
|   1 |  TABLE ACCESS BY INDEX ROWID BATCHED| EMPLOYEES     |
|   2 |   INDEX RANGE SCAN                  | EMP_HIRE_DT_IX |
-----------------------------------------------------------
```

In turn, below is the query and resulting plan using the TRUNC function:

```
SELECT last_name, first_name, hire_date
FROM employees
WHERE trunc(hire_date) = '1996-02-04';
```

```
LAST_NAME    FIRST_NAME     HIRE_DATE
------------ -------------- ----------
Bell         Sarah          1996-02-04
```

```
-----------------------------------------------------
| Id  | Operation             | Name            |
-----------------------------------------------------
|   0 | SELECT STATEMENT      |                 |
|   1 |  VIEW                 | index$_join$_001 |
|   2 |   HASH JOIN           |                 |
|   3 |    INDEX FAST FULL SCAN| EMP_NAME_IX    |
|   4 |    INDEX FAST FULL SCAN| EMP_HIRE_DT_IX |
-----------------------------------------------------
```

Here is a similar case, where we are performing a SELECT to retrieve all data for a given month specified in the query. In this case, we are retrieving all employees who were hired in the month of September 1997. If we omit the time element from the BETWEEN clause, we can actually omit data that meets the criteria for our query:

```
SELECT last_name, first_name, to_char(hire_date,'yyyy-mm-dd:hh24:mi:ss') hire_date
FROM employees
WHERE hire_date

BETWEEN TO_DATE('1997-09-01','yyyy-mm-dd')
AND TO_DATE('1997-09-30','yyyy-mm-dd');
```

```
LAST_NAME                    FIRST_NAME              HIRE_DATE
------------------------     --------------------    ----------
Chen                         John                    1997-09-28
```

```
SELECT last_name, first_name, to_char(hire_date,'yyyy-mm-dd:hh24:mi:ss') hire_date
FROM employees
WHERE hire_date
BETWEEN TO_DATE('1997-09-01:00:00:00','yyyy-mm-dd:hh24:mi:ss')
AND TO_DATE('1997-09-30:23:59:59','yyyy-mm-dd:hh24:mi:ss');
```

```
LAST_NAME     FIRST_NAME      HIRE_DATE
------------  --------------  --------------------
Chen          John            1997-09-28:00:00:00
Sciarra       Ismael          1997-09-30:08:00:00
```

If you are using a BETWEEN clause or in some way delimit the value range in your query, and there is an index on the column specified in the WHERE clause, the Oracle optimizer can use the index to retrieve the data. By using BETWEEN or some other means to delimit a value range, it is more likely that an index can often be used if one is present. As shown with the following example, you would need to perform an explain plan to validate the use of an index:

```
SELECT last_name, first_name, salary
FROM employees
WHERE last_name between 'Ba' and 'Bz'
ORDER BY salary;
```

```
-----------------------------------------------------
| Id  | Operation                     | Name        |
-----------------------------------------------------
|   0 | SELECT STATEMENT              |             |
|   1 |  SORT ORDER BY                |             |
|   2 |   TABLE ACCESS BY INDEX ROWID | EMPLOYEES   |
|   3 |    INDEX RANGE SCAN           | EMP_NAME_IX |
-----------------------------------------------------
```

8-11. Handling Null Values

Problem

You have null values in some of your database data and need to understand the ramifications of dealing with null values in data. You also need to write queries to correctly deal with such nulls.

Solution

Null values have to be dealt with in a certain manner, depending on whether you are searching for null values in your data in the SELECT clause, or you are attempting to make a determination of what to do when a null value is found in the WHERE clause.

Handling Nulls in the SELECT Clause

Within the SELECT clause, if you are dealing with data within a column that contains null values, there are Oracle-provided functions you can use within SQL to transform a null value into a more usable form. Two of these functions are NVL and NVL2.

■ **Note**   Actually, there are more than just the two functions NVL and NVL2. However, those are widely used and are a good place to begin.

With NVL, you simply pass in the column name, along with the value you want to give the output based on whether that value is null in the database. For instance, in our employees table, not all employees get a commission based on their jobs, and the value in that column for these employees is null:

```
SELECT ename , sal , comm
FROM emp
ORDER BY ename;
```

```
ENAME           SAL       COMM
----------  ----------  ----------
ADAMS         1100
ALLEN         1600        300
BLAKE         2850
KING          5000
MARTIN        1250        1400
```

If we simply want to see a zero in the commission column for employees not eligible for a commission, we can use the NVL function to accomplish this:

```
SELECT ename , sal , NVL(comm,0) comm
FROM emp
ORDER BY ename;
```

ENAME	SAL	COMM
ADAMS	1100	0
ALLEN	1600	300
BLAKE	2850	0
KING	5000	0
MARTIN	1250	1400

If we decide to perform arithmetic on a null value, the result will always be null; therefore if we want to compute "Total Compensation" as salary plus commission, we must apply the NVL function to properly compute this with consideration of the null values. In the following example, we compute the sum of these columns, both with and without the NVL function. Without using NVL, we get an incorrect result, which can be seen in the TOTAL_COMP_NO_NVL output field:

```
SELECT ename , sal , nvl(comm,0) comm, sal+comm total_comp_no_nvl,
       sal+NVL(comm,0) total_comp_nvl
FROM emp
ORDER BY ename;
```

ENAME	SAL	COMM	TOTAL_COMP_NO_NVL	TOTAL_COMP_NVL
ADAMS	1100	0		1100
ALLEN	1600	300	1900	1900
BLAKE	2850	0		2850
KING	5000	0		5000
MARTIN	1250	1400	2650	2650

The NVL2 is similar to NVL, except that NVL2 takes in three arguments—the value or column, the value to return if the column is not null, and finally the value to return if the column is null. For instance, if we use the same foregoing example when determining if an employee gets a commission, we simply want to assign a value to each employee stating whether he or she is a "commissioned" or "non-commissioned" employee. We can accomplish this with the NVL2 function:

```
SELECT ename , sal ,
NVL2(comm,'Commissioned','Non-Commissioned') comm_status
FROM emp
ORDER BY ename;
```

ENAME	SAL	COMM_STATUS
ADAMS	1100	Non-Commissioned
ALLEN	1600	Commissioned
BLAKE	2850	Non-Commissioned
KING	5000	Non-Commissioned
MARTIN	1250	Commissioned

Handling Nulls in the WHERE Clause

Within the WHERE clause, if you simply want to check a column to see if it contains a null value, use IS NULL or IS NOT NULL as the comparison operator—for example:

```
SELECT ename , sal
FROM emp
```

```
WHERE comm IS NULL
ORDER BY ename;

ENAME           SAL
---------- ----------
ADAMS           1100
BLAKE           2850
KING            5000


SELECT ename , sal
FROM emp
WHERE comm IS NOT NULL
ORDER BY ename;

ENAME           SAL
---------- ----------
ALLEN           1600
MARTIN          1250
```

You can also use the NVL or NVL2 function in the WHERE clause just as it was used in the SELECT statement:

```
SELECT ename , sal
FROM emp
WHERE NVL(comm,0) = 0
ORDER BY ename;

ENAME           SAL
---------- ----------
ADAMS           1100
BLAKE           2850
KING            5000
```

How It Works

It is best to always explicitly handle the possibility of null values, so if a column of a table is nullable, assume nulls exist, else output results can be undesired or unpredictable. One quick check that can be made to determine if a column has null values is to compare a count of rows in the table (COUNT *) to a count of rows for that column (COUNT <column_name>). A count on a nullable column will count only those rows that do not have null values. Here's an example:

```
SELECT count(*) FROM emp;

  COUNT(*)
----------
        14

SELECT count(comm) FROM emp;

COUNT(COMM)
-----------
          4
```

This technique of comparing row count to a count of values in a column is a handy way to check if nulls exist in a column.

Another very useful function that can be used in the handling of null values is the COALESCE function. With COALESCE, you can pass in a series of values, and the function will return the first non-NULL value. If all values within COALESCE are NULL, a NULL value is returned. Here is a simple example:

```
SELECT coalesce(NULL,'ABC','DEF') FROM dual;

COA
---
ABC
```

Let's say you wanted to get the shipping address for your customers, and if none were present, you would then get the billing address. If the billing address was not present, you would state that the address is unknown. Using COALESCE, you could achieve this as shown in the following example:

```
SELECT COALESCE(shipping_address, billing_address,'Address Unknown')
FROM customers
WHERE cust_id = 9342;
```

All arguments used in a statement with COALESCE must be with the same datatype, else you will receive an error, as shown here:

```
SELECT coalesce(NULL,123,'DEF') FROM dual;
                            *
ERROR at line 1:
ORA-00932: inconsistent datatypes: expected NUMBER got CHAR
```

When deciding on whether to use NVL or COALESCE in handling NULL values, evaluate the complexity of the conditions within your statement. NVL is more suited to simple evaluations, while the COALESCE function is better suited to more complex conditions.

8-12. Searching for Partial Column Values

Problem

You need to search for a string from a column in the database, but do not know the exact value of the column data.

Solution

When you are unsure of the data values in the columns you are filtering on in your WHERE clause, you can utilize the LIKE operator. Unlike the normal comparison operators such as the equal sign, the BETWEEN clause, or the IN clause, the LIKE operator allows you to search for matches based on a partial string of the column data. When you use the LIKE clause, you need to also use the "%" symbol or the "_" symbol within the data itself in order to search for the data you need. The percent sign is used to replace one to many characters. For example, if you want to see the list of employees that were hired in 1995, regardless of the exact date, the LIKE clause can be used to search for any matches within hire_date that contain the string 1995. When using LIKE with a date or timestamp datatype, you need to ensure that the date format you are using is compatible with your search criteria in your LIKE statement. For instance, if the default date format for your database is DD-MON-YY, then the string 1995 is not compatible with that format and a match would never be found. In order to search in this manner, set your date format within your session before issuing your query:

```
alter session set nls_date_format = 'yyyy-mm-dd';

Session altered.

SELECT employee_id, last_name, first_name, hire_date
FROM employees
WHERE hire_date LIKE '%1995%';
```

EMPLOYEE_ID	LAST_NAME	FIRST_NAME	HIRE_DATE
122	Kaufling	Payam	1995-05-01
115	Khoo	Alexander	1995-05-18
137	Ladwig	Renske	1995-07-14
141	Rajs	Trenna	1995-10-17

An easy way to remedy having to worry about the date format of your session is to simply use the TO_CHAR function within the query. The advantage of this method is it is very easy to code, without having to worry about your session's date format. See the following equivalent example:

```
SELECT employee_id, last_name, first_name, hire_date
FROM employees
WHERE to_char(hire_date,'yyyy') = '1995';
```

Yet a third way to do the same thing is to use the EXTRACT function:

```
SELECT employee_id, last_name, first_name, hire_date
FROM employccs
WHERE extract(year from hire_date) = '1995';
```

The underscore symbol ("_") is used to replace exactly one character. Let's say you were looking for an employee that had a last name of "Olsen" or "Olson," but were unsure of the spelling. In a single query, you can use the underscore in conjunction with the LIKE clause to find all employees with that name variation in your database:

```
SELECT last_name, first_name, phone_number
FROM employees
WHERE last_name like 'Ols_n';
```

LAST_NAME	FIRST_NAME	PHONE_NUMBER
Olsen	Christopher	011.44.1344.498718
Olson	TJ	650.124.8234

How It Works

The LIKE clause is extremely useful for finding data within your database when you are unsure of the exact column values stored within the data. There are performance ramifications that need to be considered when using the LIKE clause. The primary consideration is that when the LIKE clause is used, the likelihood of the optimizer using an index to aid in retrieving the data are reduced, especially if the wild card character is placed on the leading edge of the value.

Since an index is based on a complete value for a column, having to search for only a portion of the complete value of a column is problematic for the optimizer to be able to use an index.

Using our foregoing example of finding employees that started during the year 1995, here is the explain plan for that query:

```
--------------------------------------------------------------------
| Id | Operation          | Name      | Rows | Bytes | Cost (%CPU)| Time     |
--------------------------------------------------------------------
|  0 | SELECT STATEMENT   |           |    5 |   135 |     3  (0)| 00:00:01 |
|* 1 |  TABLE ACCESS FULL | EMPLOYEES |    5 |   135 |     3  (0)| 00:00:01 |
--------------------------------------------------------------------

Predicate Information (identified by operation id):
---------------------------------------------------

   1 - filter(INTERNAL_FUNCTION("HIRE_DATE") LIKE '%1995%')
```

If you need to use the LIKE clause for a given query, do not expect an index to be used. There can be exceptions, however. A couple of scenarios include if you have an ORDER BY clause on an indexed column. If we take the previous example and add an ORDER BY clause, the optimizer will use the index to assist in sorting the data:

```
SELECT employee_id, last_name, first_name, hire_date
FROM employees
WHERE hire_date LIKE '%1995%'
ORDER BY hire_date;
```

```
--------------------------------------------------------
| Id | Operation                    | Name         |
--------------------------------------------------------
|  0 | SELECT STATEMENT             |              |
|  1 |  TABLE ACCESS BY INDEX ROWID | EMPLOYEES    |
|  2 |   INDEX FULL SCAN            | EMP_HIRE_DT_IX |
--------------------------------------------------------
```

The INDEX FULL SCAN shown in the foregoing example isn't the most efficient index usage but is still more efficient than a full table scan. If your query only queried on column(s) that are part of an index, the optimizer may choose to use the index, even with the LIKE clause:

```
SELECT employee_id, hire_date
FROM employees
WHERE hire_date LIKE '%1995%';
```

```
--------------------------------------------------------
| Id | Operation                | Name           |
--------------------------------------------------------
|  0 | SELECT STATEMENT         |                |
|  1 |  VIEW                    | index$_join$_001 |
|  2 |   HASH JOIN              |                |
|  3 |    INDEX FAST FULL SCAN  | EMP_EMP_ID_PK  |
|  4 |    INDEX FAST FULL SCAN  | EMP_HIRE_DT_IX |
--------------------------------------------------------
```

Each statement is different, along with the environment, statistics, and other factors relating to your specific database. The best course of action is to always run an explain plan, as one given statement may produce different execution plans on different databases, depending on the circumstances.

Sometimes it is very possible for an underscore to be part of the data that is being searched. In these cases, it is important to preface the underscore with the escape character. If you are a DBA and are searching for a tablespace name in your database, which easily can contain the underscore character, make sure you consider that underscore is a wildcard symbol and must be considered. See the following example:

```
SELECT tablespace_name FROM dba_tablespaces
WHERE tablespace_name like '%EE_DATA';


TABLESPACE_NAME
-------------------------------
EMPLOYEE_DATA
EMPLOYEE1DATA
```

If you insert an escape character within the query, you can avoid getting undesired results. By inserting the escape character directly in front of the underscore, then the underscore will be considered as part of the data, rather than a substitution character:

```
SELECT tablespace_name FROM dba_tablespaces
WHERE tablespace_name LIKE '%EE^_DATA' ESCAPE '^';


TABLESPACE_NAME
-------------------------------
EMPLOYEE_DATA
```

The benefit of the LIKE clause is the flexibility it gives you in finding data based on a partial value of the column data. The likely trade-off is performance. Queries using the LIKE clause are often much less likely to use an index. As an alternative to LIKE, the BETWEEN clause, although not as simple to code within your SQL statement, can generally be more likely to use an index.

In the TO_CHAR example of the "Solution" section, you will note that the TO_CHAR function is placed on the left side of the comparison operator. Generally, when this occurs, it means no index on the filtering column will be used (*see* Recipe 8-14 for more discussion on this topic). However, with certain Oracle functions and the manner in which they are translated, an index still may be used. The only way to be certain is to simply run an explain plan on your query. For our foregoing query using TO_CHAR, it still used an index even though the function was placed on the left side of the comparison operator:

```
SELECT employee_id, last_name, first_name, hire_date
FROM employees
WHERE to_char(hire_date,'yyyy') = '1995'
ORDER BY hire_date;
---------------------------------------------------------
| Id  | Operation                   | Name         |
---------------------------------------------------------
|   0 | SELECT STATEMENT            |              |
|   1 |  TABLE ACCESS BY INDEX ROWID| EMPLOYEES    |
|   2 |   INDEX FULL SCAN           | EMPLOYEES_I1 |
---------------------------------------------------------
```

8-13. Re-using SQL Statements Within the Shared Pool
Problem

You are getting an excessive amount of hard parsing for your SQL statements and want to lower the number of SQL statements that go through the hard-parse process.

Solution

Implementing bind variables within an application can tremendously improve the efficiency and performance of queries. Bind variables are used to replace literals within a query. By placing bind variables within your SQL statements, the statements can be re-used in memory and do not have to go through the entire expensive SQL parsing process.

Here is an example of a normal SQL statement, with literal values shown in the WHERE clause:

```
SELECT employee_id, last_name || ', ' || first_name employee_name
FROM employees
WHERE employee_id = 115;

EMPLOYEE_ID EMPLOYEE_NAME
----------- ------------------------
        115 Khoo, Alexander
```

There are a couple of ways to define bind variables within Oracle. First, you can simply use SQL Plus. To accomplish this within SQL Plus, you first need to define a variable, along with a datatype to the variable. Then, you can use the exec command, which actually will run a PL/SQL command to populate the variable with the desired value. Notice that when referencing a bind variable in SQL Plus, it is prefaced with a colon:

```
SQL> variable g_emp_id number
SQL> exec :g_emp_id := 115;

PL/SQL procedure successfully completed.
```

After you have defined a variable and assigned a value to it, you can simply substitute the variable name within your SQL statement. Again, since it is a bind variable, you need to preface it with a colon:

```
SELECT employee_id, last_name || ', ' || first_name employee_name
FROM employees
WHERE employee_id = :g_emp_id;

EMPLOYEE_ID EMPLOYEE_NAME
----------- ------------------------
        115 Khoo, Alexander
```

You can also assign variables within PL/SQL. The nice advantage of PL/SQL is that just by using variables in PL/SQL, they are automatically bind variables. And, unlike in SQL*Plus, no colon is required when referencing a variable that was defined within the PL/SQL block:

```
SQL> set serveroutput on
  1 DECLARE
  2    v_emp_id employees.employee_id%TYPE := 200;
```

```
 3    v_last_name employees.last_name%TYPE;
 4    v_first_name employees.first_name%TYPE;
 5  BEGIN
 6    SELECT last_name, first_name
 7    INTO v_last_name, v_first_name
 8    FROM employees
 9    WHERE employee_id = v_emp_id;
10  dbms_output.put_line('Employee Name = ' || v_last_name || ', ' || v_first_name);
11* END;
SQL> /
Employee Name = Whalen, Jennifer
```

How It Works

When bind variables are used, it increases the likelihood that a SQL statement can be re-used within the shared pool. Oracle uses a hashing algorithm to assign a value to every unique SQL statement. If literals are used within a SQL statement, the hash values between two otherwise identical statements will be different. By using the bind variables, the statements will have the same hash value within the shared pool, and part of the expensive parsing process can be avoided.

Re-use Is Efficient

Re-use is efficient because Oracle does not have to go through the entire parsing process for those SQL statements. If you do not use bind variables within your SQL statements, and instead use literals, the statements need to be completely parsed.

See Table 8-3 for a review of the steps taken to process a SQL statement. A statement that is "hard parsed" must execute all of the steps. If a statement is "soft parsed," the optimizer generally does not execute the optimization and row source generation steps.

Table 8-3. *Steps to Execute a SQL Statement*

Step	Description
Syntax checking	Determines if SQL statement is syntactically correct
Semantic checking	Determines if objects referenced in SQL statement exist and user has proper privileges to those objects
Check shared pool	Oracle uses hashing algorithm to generate hash value for SQL statement and checks shared pool for existence of that statement in the shared pool.
Optimization	The Oracle optimizer chooses what it perceives as the best execution plan for the SQL statement based on gathered statistics.
Row source generation	This is an Oracle program that received the execution plan from the optimization step and generates a query plan. When you generate an explain plan for a statement, it shows the detailed query plan.
Execution	Each step of the query plan is executed, and the result set is returned to the user.

Hard Parsing Can Be Avoided

By using bind variables, a hard parse can be avoided and can help the performance of SQL queries, as well as reduce the amount of memory thrashing that can occur in the shared pool. The TKPROF utility is one way to verify whether SQL statements are being re-used in the shared pool. Later, there are examples of PL/SQL code that use bind variables, and PL/SQL code that does not use bind variables.

By using the TKPROF utility, we can see how these statements are processed. In order to see this information with the TKPROF utility, we first must turn tracing on within our session. The easiest method is with ALTER SESSION, and while supported in Oracle 12c, is now deprecated:

```
alter session set sql_trace=true;
```

Another method to enable session tracing is by using the DBMS_MONITOR PL/SQL package. To turn monitoring on for your current session, see the below example. We first must obtain session information, and then we can turn tracing on:

```
SELECT dbms_debug_jdwp.current_session_id sid,
dbms_debug_jdwp.current_session_serial serial#
from dual;

       SID    SERIAL#
---------- ----------
        64      21713


exec dbms_monitor.session_trace_enable(session_id=>64,serial_num=>21713);
```

There are many options available with the DBMS_MONITOR package. Refer to the Oracle 12c Packages and Types Reference manual for a complete list of these options, which can help customize the trace output.

Once session tracing is set, the trace file gets generated in the location specified by the diagnostic_dest or user_dump_dest parameter settings. To demonstrate, the following PL/SQL block updates the employees table and gives all employees a 3% raise. Since all PL/SQL variables are treated as bind variables, we can see with the TKPROF output that the update statement was parsed only once but executed many times:

```
BEGIN
FOR i IN 100..206
LOOP
UPDATE employees
SET salary=salary*1.03
WHERE employee_id = i;
END LOOP;
COMMIT;
END;
```

Here is an excerpt from the TKPROF-generated report, which summarizes information about the session on which tracing was enabled:

```
UPDATE EMPLOYEES_BIG SET SALARY=SALARY*1.03
WHERE
 EMPLOYEE_ID = :B1
```

call	count	cpu	elapsed	disk	query	current	rows
Parse	1	0.00	0.00	0	0	0	0
Execute	16	142.10	380.62	0	729	13979390	12583424
Fetch	0	0.00	0.00	0	0	0	0
total	17	142.11	380.62	0	729	13979390	12583424

In the following example, we do the same thing using dynamic SQL with the execute immediate command:

```
BEGIN
FOR i IN 100..206
LOOP
execute immediate 'UPDATE employees SET salary=salary*1.03 WHERE employee_id = ' || i;
END LOOP;
COMMIT;
END;
```

Since the entire statement is assembled together prior to execution, the variable is converted to a literal before execution. We can see with the TKPROF output that the statement was parsed with each execution. There is an entry in the TKPROF output for each statement executed.

```
SQL ID: 5ad0n7d74j9au Plan Hash: 751015319
UPDATE employees SET salary=salary*1.03
WHERE
 employee_id = 206
```

call	count	cpu	elapsed	disk	query	current	rows
Parse	1	0.00	0.01	0	0	0	0
Execute	1	0.04	21.12	0	27	265	256
Fetch	0	0.00	0.00	0	0	0	0
total	2	0.04	21.13	0	27	265	256

At the bottom of the TKPROF report, a summarization confirms that each statement was parsed and then executed:

```
OVERALL TOTALS FOR ALL RECURSIVE STATEMENTS
```

call	count	cpu	elapsed	disk	query	current	rows
Parse	168	0.07	0.08	0	0	120	0
Execute	168	261.00	707.14	4	911	27688705	12583424
Fetch	151	0.00	0.01	2	405	0	103
total	487	261.08	707.24	6	1316	27688825	12583527

```
   1  session in tracefile.
 109  user  SQL statements in trace file.
   0  internal SQL statements in trace file.
 109  SQL statements in trace file.
 109  unique SQL statements in trace file.
1016  lines in trace file.
   8  elapsed seconds in trace file.
```

Bind Variables Are Usable with EXECUTE IMMEDIATE

If we want to use the execute immediate command more efficiently, we can convert that execute immediate command to use a bind variable with the USING clause and specify a bind variable within the execute immediate statement. The result shows that the statement was parsed only one time:

```
BEGIN
FOR i IN 100..206
LOOP
execute immediate 'UPDATE employees SET salary=salary*1.03 WHERE employee_id = :empno' USING i;
END LOOP;
COMMIT;
END;


SQL ID : 4y09bqzjngvq4
update employees set salary=salary*1.03
where
 employee_id = :empno
```

call	count	cpu	elapsed	disk	query	current	rows
Parse	1	0.00	0.00	0	0	0	0
Execute	16	146.65	399.63	3	730	13983401	12583424
Fetch	0	0.00	0.00	0	0	0	0
total	17	146.65	399.63	3	730	13983401	12583424

■ **Tip** Hard-parsing always occurs for DDL statements.

8-14. Avoiding Accidental Full Table Scans
Problem

You have queries that should be using indexes, but instead are doing full table scans. You want to avoid performing full table scans when the optimizer could be using an index to retrieve the data.

Solution

When constructing a SQL statement, a fundamental rule to try to always observe in the WHERE clause, if possible, is to avoid doing function calls on indexed columns, which typically are on the left side of the comparison operator. In these cases, the optimizer will not use any available index, unless a function-based index exists that the query can use. A function essentially turns a column into a literal value, and therefore the Oracle optimizer does not recognize that converted value as a column any longer but as a value instead.

Here, we're trying to get a list of all the employees that started since the year 1999. Because we placed a function on the left side of the comparison operator, the optimizer will choose a full table scan, even though the HIRE_DATE column is indexed:

```
SELECT employee_id, salary, hire_date
FROM employees
WHERE TO_CHAR(hire_date,'yyyy-mm-dd') >= '2000-01-01';
```

```
----------------------------------------
| Id | Operation          | Name        |
----------------------------------------
|  0 | SELECT STATEMENT   |             |
|  1 |  TABLE ACCESS FULL | EMPLOYEES   |
----------------------------------------
```

By moving the function to the right side of the comparison operator and leaving HIRE_DATE as a pristine column in the WHERE clause, the optimizer can now use the index on HIRE_DATE:

```
SELECT employee_id, salary, hire_date
FROM employees
WHERE hire_date >= TO_DATE('2000-01-01','yyyy-mm-dd');
```

```
--------------------------------------------------------
| Id | Operation                   | Name       |
--------------------------------------------------------
|  0 | SELECT STATEMENT            |            |
|  1 |  TABLE ACCESS BY INDEX ROWID| EMPLOYEES  |
|  2 |   INDEX RANGE SCAN          | EMP_I5     |
--------------------------------------------------------
```

How It Works

Functions are wonderful tools to convert a value or return the desired value based on what you need from the database, but they can be a performance killer if used incorrectly within a SQL statement. Make sure all functions apply to constants, to unindexed columns, or at least to the least-selective indexed column when two indexed columns are involved in a comparison. Then the optimizer will be able to use any indexes on columns specified in the WHERE clause. This rule holds true for most functions. In certain cases, it is possible Oracle will still use an index even if a function is on the left side of the comparison operator, but this is usually the exception. *See* Recipe 8-12 for an example of this.

Keep in mind that the datatype for a given column in the WHERE clause may change how the SQL statement needs to be modified to move the function to the right side of the comparison operator. With the following example, we had to change the comparison operator in order to effectively move the function:

```
SELECT last_name, first_name
FROM employees
WHERE SUBSTR(phone_number,1,3) = '515';
```

```
-------------------------------------
| Id | Operation         | Name      |
-------------------------------------
|  0 | SELECT STATEMENT  |           |
|  1 |  TABLE ACCESS FULL| EMPLOYEES |
-------------------------------------
```

In order to effectively get all numbers in the 515 area code, we can use a BETWEEN clause and capture all possible values. We can also use a LIKE clause, as long as the wildcard character is on the trailing end of the condition. By using either of these methods, the optimizer changed the execution plan to use an index:

```
SELECT last_name, first_name
FROM employees
WHERE phone_number BETWEEN '515.000.0000' and '515.999.9999';
```

```
SELECT last_name, first_name
FROM employees
WHERE phone_number LIKE'515%';
```

```
---------------------------------------------------------
| Id | Operation              | Name             |
---------------------------------------------------------
|  0 | SELECT STATEMENT       |                  |
|  1 |  VIEW                  | index$_join$_001 |
|  2 |   HASH JOIN            |                  |
|  3 |    INDEX RANGE SCAN    | EMP_PH_NO        |
|  4 |    INDEX FAST FULL SCAN| EMP_NAME_IX      |
---------------------------------------------------------
```

8-15. Creating Efficient Temporary Views

Problem

You need a table or a view of data that does not exist to construct a needed query and do not have the authority to create such a table or view on your database.

Solution

At times, within a single SQL statement, you want to create a table "on the fly" that is used solely for your query and will never be used again. In the FROM clause of your query, you normally place the name of your table or view on which to retrieve the data. In cases where a needed view of the data does not exist, you can create a temporary view of that data with what is called an "inline view," where you specify the characteristics of that view right in the FROM clause of your query:

```
SELECT last_name, first_name, department_name dept, salary
FROM employees e join
      ( SELECT department_id, max(salary) high_sal
        FROM employees
        GROUP BY department_id ) m
USING (department_id) join departments
USING (department_id)
```

```
WHERE e.salary = m.high_sal
ORDER BY SALARY desc;
```

LAST_NAME	FIRST_NAME	DEPT	SALARY
King	Steven	Executive	24000
Russell	John	Sales	14000
Hartstein	Michael	Marketing	13000
Greenberg	Nancy	Finance	12000
Higgins	Shelley	Accounting	12000
Raphaely	Den	Purchasing	11000
Baer	Hermann	Public Relations	10000
Hunold	Alexander	IT	9000
Fripp	Adam	Shipping	8200
Mavris	Susan	Human Resources	6500
Whalen	Jennifer	Administration	4400

In the foregoing query, we are getting the employees with the highest salary for each department. There isn't such a view in our database. Moreover, there isn't a way to directly join the employees table to the departments table to retrieve this data within a single query. Therefore, the inline view is created as part of the SQL statement and holds only the key information we needed—it has the high salary and department information, which now can easily be joined to the employees table based on the employee with that matching salary.

How It Works

Inline views, as with many components of the SQL language, need to be used carefully. While extremely useful, if misused or overused, inline views can cause database performance issues, especially in terms of the use of the temporary tablespace. Since inline views are created and used only for the duration of a query, their results are held in the program global memory area and, if too large, the temporary tablespace. Before using an inline view, the following questions should be considered:

1. Most importantly, how often will the SQL containing the inline view be run? If only once or rarely, then it might be best to simply execute the query and not worry about any potential performance impact.

2. How many rows will be contained in the inline view?

3. What will the row length be for the inline view?

4. How much memory is allocated for the pga_aggregate_target or memory_target setting?

5. How big is the temporary tablespace that is used by your Oracle user or schema?

If you have a simple ad hoc query you are doing, this kind of analysis may not be necessary. If you are creating a SQL statement that will run in a production environment, it is important to perform this analysis, as if all the temporary tablespace is consumed by an inline view, it affects not only the completion of that query, but also the successful completion of any processing for any user that may use that specific temporary tablespace. In many database environments, there is only a single temporary tablespace. Therefore, if one user process consumes all the temporary space with a single operation, this affects the operations for every user in the database.

Consider the following query:

```
WITH service_info AS
(SELECT
product_id,
```

```
geographic_id,
sum(qty) quantity
FROM services
GROUP BY
product_id,
geographic_id),
product_info AS
(SELECT product_id, product_group, product_desc
FROM products
WHERE source_sys = 'BILLING'),
billing_info AS
(SELECT journal_date, billing_date, product_id
FROM BILLING
WHERE journal_date = TO_DATE('2013-08-15', 'YYYY-MM-DD'))
SELECT
product_group,
product_desc,
journal_date,
billing_date,
sum(service_info.quantity)
FROM service_info JOIN product_info
ON service_info.product_id = product_info.product_id JOIN billing_info
ON  service_info.product_id = billing_info.product_id
WHERE
service_info.quantity > 0
GROUP BY
product_group,
product_desc,
journal_date,
billing_date;
```

The WITH clause is also known as subquery factoring. In the foregoing query, there are three portions created either as inline views or temporary tables: the SERVICE_INFO view, the PRODUCT_INFO view, and the BILLING_INFO view. Each of these queries will be processed and the results stored in the program global area or the temporary tablespace before finally processing the true end-user query, which starts with the final SELECT statement shown in the query. While efficient in that the desired results can be done by executing a single query, the foregoing query, depending on the size of the data within the tables, can be tremendously inefficient to process, as storing potentially millions of rows in the temporary tablespace uses critical resources needed by an entire community of users that use the database. In examples such as these, it is generally more efficient at the database level to create permanent objects such as tables or materialized views that hold the data. Then, the final query can be extracted from joining the three permanent tables to generate the results. While this may be more upfront work by the development team and the DBA, it could very well pay dividends if the query is run on a regular basis. Furthermore, as complexity increases with a SQL statement, ease of maintenance decreases. So, overall, it is more efficient, and usually more maintainable, to break a complex statement into chunks.

■ **Note**   There are SQL experts who disagree with me and prefer to do everything in one query whenever possible. My feeling is that sometimes in doing so, an unmaintainable query is written that eventually leads to trouble down the road when it inevitably must be modified. For me, simplicity in the long run is sometimes the better path.

Inline views provide great benefit. However, do the proper analysis and investigation prior to implementing the use of such a view in a production environment.

■ **Caution** Large inline views can easily consume a large amount of temporary tablespace.

8-16. Avoiding the NOT Clause
Problem

You have queries that use the NOT clause that are not performing adequately and wish to modify them to improve performance.

Solution

Just as often as we query our database for equality conditions, we will query our database for non-equality conditions. It is the nature of retrieving data from a database and the nature of the SQL language to allow users to do this.

There are performance drawbacks in using the NOT clause within your SQL statements, as they trigger full table scans. Here's an example query from a previous recipe:

```
SELECT last_name, first_name, salary, email
FROM employees_big
WHERE department_id NOT IN(20,30)
AND commission_pct > 0;
```

Elapsed: **00:00:21.65**

```
-----------------------------------------------------------------
|Id |Operation          |Name         |Rows|Bytes|Cost (%CPU)|Time      |
-----------------------------------------------------------------
|  0|SELECT STATEMENT   |             |   1|   43|  535   (1)|00:00:01|
|* 1| TABLE ACCESS FULL|EMPLOYEES_BIG|   1|   43|  535   (1)|00:00:01|
-----------------------------------------------------------------
```

Even though we have an index on the department_id column, by using the NOT clause we cause Oracle to bypass the use of that index in order to properly search and ensure all rows were not those in department 20 or 30. One of the easiest ways to avoid the NOT IN clause in this example is simply to convert it to an IN clause. While it may be simpler to code the NOT IN because there are less values, using IN will more likely use an index. In the following example, the NOT IN has been converted to an IN clause showing all values except the ones shown in the NOT IN clause:

```
SELECT last_name, first_name, salary, email
FROM employees_big
WHERE department_id IN(10,40,50,60,70,80,90,100,110)
and commission_pct > 0;
```

Elapsed: **00:00:00.02**

```
-----------------------------------------------------------------
|Id|Operation                  |Name         |Rows|Bytes|Cost (%CPU)|Time    |
-----------------------------------------------------------------
| 0|SELECT STATEMENT           |             |  1 |  43 |  11   (0)|00:00:01|
| 1| INLIST ITERATOR           |             |    |     |          |        |
|*2|  TABLE ACCESS BY          |EMPLOYEES_BIG|  1 |  43 |  11   (0)|00:00:01|
           INDEX ROWID BATCHED
|*3|   INDEX RANGE SCAN        |EMP_BIG_DEPTNO|  5 |     |  10   (0)|00:00:01|
-----------------------------------------------------------------
```

Note now that after our change, the query now uses an index and is substantially faster in run time. Keep in mind that based on the make-up of the data in the table, the optimizer may still decide it is more optimal to do a full table scan, even if there is an index on the filtering column. In these cases, one option to improve performance is to use parallelism (discussed in Chapter 15).

Another way to get the optimizer to use an index is to use the NOT EXISTS clause. Using the foregoing example and modifying it to use a NOT EXISTS clause, an index is used:

```
SELECT last_name, first_name, salary, email
FROM employees
WHERE NOT EXISTS
(SELECT department_id FROM departments
WHERE department_id in(20,30))
AND commission_pct > 0;
```

```
-----------------------------------------------------------------
|Id|Operation                  |Name         |Rows|Bytes|Cost (%CPU)|Time    |
-----------------------------------------------------------------
| 0|SELECT STATEMENT           |             |  1 |  40 |  536  (1)|00:00:01|
|*1| FILTER                    |             |    |     |          |        |
|*2|  TABLE ACCESS FULL        |EMPLOYEES_BIG|  1 |  40 |  535  (1)|00:00:01|
| 3|  INLIST ITERATOR          |             |    |     |          |        |
|*4|   INDEX UNIQUE SCAN       |DEPT_ID_PK   |  2 |   8 |    1  (0)|00:00:01|
-----------------------------------------------------------------
```

How It Works

You can effectively use the NOT clause several ways:

- Comparison operators ('<>', '!=', '^=')

- NOT IN

- NOT LIKE

By using NOT, each of the following queries has the same basic effect in that it will negate the use of any possible index on the columns to which NOT applies:

```
SELECT last_name, first_name, salary, email
FROM employees
WHERE department_id != 20
AND commission_pct > 0;
```

```
SELECT last_name, first_name, salary, email
FROM employees
WHERE department_id NOT IN(20,30)
AND commission_pct > 0;

SELECT last_name, first_name, salary, email
FROM employees
WHERE hire_date NOT LIKE '2%'
AND commission_pct > 0;
```

```
----------------------------------------
| Id | Operation        | Name      |
----------------------------------------
|  0 | SELECT STATEMENT |           |
|  1 |   TABLE ACCESS FULL| EMPLOYEES |
----------------------------------------
```

At times, a full table scan is simply required. Even if an index is present, if you need to read more than a certain percentage of rows of a table, the Oracle optimizer may perform a full table scan regardless of whether an index is present. Still, if you simply try to avoid using NOT where possible, you may be able to improve performance of your queries.

8-17. Controlling Transaction Sizes
Problem

You are performing a series of DML activities and want to better manage the units of work and the recoverability of your transactions.

Solution

With the use of savepoints, you can split up transactions more easily into logical chunks and can manage them more effectively upon failure. With the use of savepoints, you can roll back a series of DML statements to an incremental savepoint you have created. Within your SQL session, simply create a savepoint at an appropriate place during your processing that allows you to more easily isolate a "logical unit of work." With larger units of work, savepoints can help overall database performance by reducing the amount of data held in undo tablespaces at any given point in time. The following is an example showing how to create a savepoint:

```
SQL> savepoint A;

Savepoint created.
```

If you have an online bookstore, for instance, and you have a customer placing an online order, when he or she submits an order, a logical unit of work for this transaction would be as follows:

- Adding a row to the orders table

- Adding one to many rows to the orderitems table

When processing this online order, you will want to commit all the information for the order and all items for an order as one transaction. This particular customer order represents multiple database DML statements but needs to be processed one at a time to preserve the integrity of the order; therefore, it can be regarded as one "logical unit of work." By using savepoints, you can more easily process multiple DML statements as logical units of work. When a savepoint is created, it is essentially creating an alias based on a system change number (SCN). After creating a savepoint, you then have the luxury to roll back a transaction to that SCN based on the savepoint you created.

How It Works

Let's say your company has established two new departments, as well as employees for those departments. You need to insert rows in the corresponding DEPT and EMP tables, but you need to do this in one logical, grouped transaction. In case of an error, you can roll back to the point the last logical transaction completed. First, we can see a current picture of the DEPT table:

```
SELECT * FROM dept;

    DEPTNO DNAME          LOC
---------- -------------- -------------
        10 ACCOUNTING     NEW YORK
        20 RESEARCH       DALLAS
        30 SALES          CHICAGO
        40 OPERATIONS     BOSTON
```

We first insert the information for the first department into the DEPT and EMP tables, and then create a savepoint:

```
INSERT INTO dept VALUES (50,'PAYROLL','LOS ANGELES');

1 row created.

INSERT INTO emp VALUES (7997,'EVANS','ACCTNT',7566,'2011-08-15',900,0,50);

1 row created.

savepoint A;

Savepoint created.
```

We then start processing information for the second department. Let's say in the middle of the transaction, an unknown error occurs between the insert into the DEPT table and the insert into the EMP table. In this case, we know this transaction of inserting the information into the recruiting department must be rolled back. At the same time, we wish to commit the transaction to the payroll department. Using the savepoint we created, we can commit a portion of the transaction, while rolling back the portion of the transaction we do not want to keep:

```
INSERT INTO dept VALUES (60,'RECRUITING','DENVER');

1 row created.

ROLLBACK to savepoint A;

Rollback complete.

COMMIT;

Commit complete.
```

Because of the savepoint, our rollback rolled back the incomplete transaction only for department 60, and the subsequent commit wrote the complete transaction for department 50 to the database in both the DEPT and EMP tables:

```
SELECT * FROM dept;

    DEPTNO DNAME          LOC
---------- -------------- -------------
        10 ACCOUNTING     NEW YORK
        20 RESEARCH       DALLAS
        30 SALES          CHICAGO
        40 OPERATIONS     BOSTON
        50 PAYROLL        LOS ANGELES

SELECT * FROM emp
WHERE empno = 7997;

    EMPNO ENAME      JOB             MGR HIREDATE    SAL   COMM DEPTNO
---------- ---------- --------- ---------- ---------- ---- ---------- -------
     7997 EVANS      ACCTNT         7566 2011-08-15  900      0     50
```

There are many similar mechanisms or coding techniques you can use in programming languages such as PL/SQL. The SAVEPOINT command in the SQL language is a simple way to manage transactions without having to code more complex programming structures.

CHAPTER 9

■ ■ ■

Manually Tuning SQL

It has been said many times in books, articles, and other publications that over 90% of all performance problems on a database are due to poorly written SQL. Often, database administrators are given the task of "fixing the database" when queries are not performing adequately. The database administrator is often guilty before proven innocent—and often has the task of proving that a performance problem is not the database itself but, rather, simply, SQL statements that are not written efficiently. The goal, of course, is to have SQL statements written efficiently the first time. This chapter's focus is to help monitor and analyze existing queries to help show why they may be underperforming, as well as show some steps to improve queries.

If you have SQL code that you are maintaining or that needs help to improve performance, some of the questions that need to be asked first include the following:

- Has the query run before successfully? If so, how often does it run?

- Was the query performance acceptable in the past?

- Are there any metrics on how long the query has run when successful?

- How much data is typically returned from the query?

- When was the last time statistics were gathered on the objects referenced in the query?

Once these questions are answered, it helps to direct the focus to where the problem may lie. You then may want to run an explain plan for the query to see if the execution plan is reasonable at first glance. The skill of reading an explain plan takes time and improves with experience. Sometimes, especially if there are views on top of the objects being queried, an explain plan can be lengthy and intimidating. Therefore, it's important to simply know what to look for first, and then dig as you go.

At times, poorly running SQL can expose database configuration issues, but normally, poorly performing SQL queries occur due to poorly written SQL statements. Again, as a database administrator or database developer, the best approach is to take time up front whenever possible to tune the SQL statements prior to ever running in a production environment. Often, a query's elapsed time is a benchmark for efficiency, which is an easy trap in which to fall. Over time, database characteristics change, more historical data may be stored for an application, and a query that performed well on initial install simply doesn't scale as an application matures. Therefore, it's important to take the time to do it right the first time, which is easy to say but tough to accomplish when balancing client requirements, budgets, and project timelines.

There are many tools on the market to help in tuning SQL that can be used as well. While this chapter focuses on manual methods of tuning SQL, there are other methods to aid in tuning your SQL. One Oracle-provided tool that does in-depth analysis, but is outside the scope of this text, is the SQLTXPLAIN utility, for which you can reference the Apress publication "Oracle SQL Tuning with Oracle SQLTXPLAIN," which covers this tool in detail.

9-1. Displaying an Execution Plan for a Query
Problem

You want to quickly retrieve an execution plan from within SQL Plus for a query.

Solution

From within SQL Plus, you can use the AUTOTRACE feature to quickly retrieve the execution plan for a query. This SQL Plus utility is very handy at getting the execution plan, along with getting statistics for the query's execution plan. In the most basic form, to enable AUTOTRACE within your session, execute the following command within SQL Plus:

```
SQL> set autotrace on
```

Then, you can run a query using AUTOTRACE, which will show the execution plan and query execution statistics for your query:

```
SELECT last_name, first_name
FROM employees NATURAL JOIN departments
WHERE employee_id = 101;
```

```
LAST_NAME                 FIRST_NAME
------------------------  --------------------
Kochhar                   Neena
```

Id	Operation	Name	Rows	Bytes	Cost (%CPU)	Time
0	SELECT STATEMENT		1	33	2 (0)	00:00:01
1	NESTED LOOPS		1	33	2 (0)	00:00:01
2	TABLE ACCESS BY INDEX ROWID	EMPLOYEES	1	26	1 (0)	00:00:01
* 3	INDEX UNIQUE SCAN	EMP_EMP_ID_PK	1		0 (0)	00:00:01
* 4	TABLE ACCESS BY INDEX ROWID	DEPARTMENTS	11	77	1 (0)	00:00:01
* 5	INDEX UNIQUE SCAN	DEPT_ID_PK	1		0 (0)	00:00:01

```
Statistics
----------------------------------------------------------
          0  recursive calls
          0  db block gets
          4  consistent gets
          0  physical reads
          0  redo size
        490  bytes sent via SQL*Net to client
        416  bytes received via SQL*Net from client
          2  SQL*Net roundtrips to/from client
          0  sorts (memory)
          0  sorts (disk)
          1  rows processed
```

How It Works

There are several options to choose from when using AUTOTRACE, and the basic factors are as follows:

1. Do you want to execute the query?

2. Do you want to see the execution plan for the query?

3. Do you want to see the execution statistics for the query?

As you can see from Table 9-1, you can abbreviate each command, if so desired. The portions of the words in brackets are optional.

Table 9-1. *Options of AUTOTRACE Within SQL Plus*

AUTOTRACE Option	**Execution Plan Shown**	**Statistics Shown**	**Query Executed**
AUTOT[RACE] OFF	No	No	Yes
AUTOT[RACE] ON	Yes	Yes	Yes
AUTOT[RACE] ON EXP[LAIN]	Yes	No	Yes
AUTOT[RACE] ON STAT[ISTICS]	No	Yes	Yes
AUTOT[RACE] TRACE[ONLY]	Yes	Yes	Yes, but query output is suppressed.
AUTOT[RACE] TRACE[ONLY] EXP[LAIN]	Yes	No	No

A common use for AUTOTRACE is to get the execution plan for the query without running the query. By doing this, you can quickly see whether you have a reasonable execution plan and can do this without having to execute the query:

```
SQL> set autot trace exp

SELECT l.location_id, city, department_id, department_name
  FROM locations l, departments d
  WHERE l.location_id = d.location_id(+)
  ORDER BY 1;
```

```
----------------------------------------------------------------------
|Id|Operation                  |Name            |Rows|Bytes|Cost(%CPU)|Time     |
----------------------------------------------------------------------
| 0|SELECT STATEMENT           |                | 43| 1333|   5  (0)|00:00:01|
| 1| SORT ORDER BY             |                | 43| 1333|   5  (0)|00:00:01|
|*2|  HASH JOIN OUTER          |                | 43| 1333|   5  (0)|00:00:01|
| 3|   VIEW                    |index$_join$_001| 23|  276|   2  (0)|00:00:01|
|*4|    HASH JOIN              |                |   |     |         |        |
| 5|     INDEX FAST FULL SCAN|LOC_CITY_IX     | 23|  276|   1  (0)|00:00:01|
| 6|     INDEX FAST FULL SCAN|LOC_ID_PK       | 23|  276|   1  (0)|00:00:01|
| 7|   TABLE ACCESS FULL       |DEPARTMENTS     | 27|  513|   3  (0)|00:00:01|
----------------------------------------------------------------------
```

For the foregoing query, if you wanted to see only the execution statistics for the query and did not want to see all the query output, you would do the following:

```
SQL> set autot trace stat
SQL> set timi on
SQL> /

43 rows selected.

Statistics
-----------------------------------------------------------
          0  recursive calls
          0  db block gets
         14  consistent gets
          0  physical reads
          0  redo size
       1862  bytes sent via SQL*Net to client
        438  bytes received via SQL*Net from client
          4  SQL*Net roundtrips to/from client
          1  sorts (memory)
          0  sorts (disk)
         43  rows processed
```

By setting timing on in the foregoing example, it can be helpful simply by giving you the elapsed time of your query, which can be one of the most basic benchmarks of a query's performance.

Once you are done using AUTOTRACE for a given session and want to turn it off and run other queries without using AUTOTRACE, run the following command from within your SQL Plus session:

```
SQL> set autot off
```

The default for each SQL Plus session is AUTOTRACE OFF, but if you want to check to see what your current AUTOTRACE setting is for a given session, you can do that by executing the following command:

```
SQL> show autot
autotrace OFF
```

9-2. Customizing Execution Plan Output
Problem

You want to configure the explain plan output for your query based on your specific needs.

Solution

The Oracle-provided PL/SQL package DBMS_XPLAN has extensive functionality to get explain plan information for a given query. There are many functions within the DBMS_XPLAN package. The DISPLAY function can be used to quickly get the execution plan for a query and also to customize the information that is presented to meet your specific needs. The following is an example that invokes the basic display functionality:

```
explain plan for
SELECT last_name, first_name
FROM employees JOIN departments USING(department_id)
WHERE employee_id = 101;

Explained.

SELECT * FROM table(dbms_xplan.display);

PLAN_TABLE_OUTPUT
-----------------------------------------------------------------------
Plan hash value: 1833546154


-----------------------------------------------------------------------
|Id|Operation             |Name        |Rows|Bytes |Cost(%CPU)|Time    |
-----------------------------------------------------------------------
| 0|SELECT STATEMENT      |            |  1|  22 |   1   (0)|00:00:01|
|*1| TABLE ACCESS         |EMPLOYEES   |  1|  22 |   1   (0)|00:00:01|
          BY INDEX ROWID
|*2|  INDEX UNIQUE SCAN   |EMP_EMP_ID_PK|  1|      |   0   (0)|00:00:01|
-----------------------------------------------------------------------


Predicate Information (identified by operation id):
---------------------------------------------------

   1 - filter("EMPLOYEES"."DEPARTMENT_ID" IS NOT NULL)
   2 - access("EMPLOYEES"."EMPLOYEE_ID"=101)
```

The DBMS_XPLAN.DISPLAY procedure is very flexible in configuring how you would like to see output. If you wanted to see only the most basic execution plan output, using the foregoing query, you could configure the DBMS_XPLAN.DISPLAY function to get that output:

```
SELECT * FROM table(dbms_xplan.display(null,null,'BASIC'));

------------------------------------------------------
| Id  | Operation                   | Name          |
------------------------------------------------------
|   0 | SELECT STATEMENT            |               |
|   1 |  TABLE ACCESS BY INDEX ROWID| EMPLOYEES     |
|   2 |   INDEX UNIQUE SCAN         | EMP_EMP_ID_PK |
------------------------------------------------------
```

How It Works

The DBMS_XPLAN.DISPLAY function has a lot of built-in functionality to provide customized output based on your needs. The function provides four basic levels of output detail:

- BASIC
- TYPICAL (default)
- SERIAL
- ALL

Table 9-2 shows the format options that are included within each level of detail option.

Table 9-2. DBMS_XPLAN.DISPLAY Options

Format Option	BASIC	TYPICAL	SERIAL	ALL	Description
Basic (ID, Operation, Object Name	X	X	X	X	
ALIAS (Section)				X	Information on object aliases and query block information
BYTES (Column)		X	X	X	Estimated bytes
COST (Column)		X	X	X	Displays optimizer cost
NOTE (Section)		X	X	X	Shows NOTE section of the explain plan
PARALLEL (Detail within plan)		X		X	Show parallelism information related to the explain plan
PARTITION (Columns)		X	X	X	Displays partition pruning information
PREDICATE (Section)		X	X	X	Shows PREDICATE section of the explain plan
PROJECTION (Section)				X	Shows PROJECTION section of the explain plan
REMOTE (Detail within plan)				X	Shows information for distributed queries
ROWS (Column)		X	X	X	Shows estimated number of rows

If you simply want the default output format, there is no need to pass in any special format options:

```
SELECT * FROM table(dbms_xplan.display);
```

If you want to get all available output for a query, use the ALL level of detail format output option:

```
SELECT * FROM table(dbms_xplan.display(null,null,'ALL'));
```

```
-------------------------------------------------------------------------------
|Id|Operation                     |Name        |Rows|Bytes|Cost(%CPU)|Time     |
-------------------------------------------------------------------------------
| 0|SELECT STATEMENT              |            |   1|   22|    1  (0)|00:00:01|
|*1| TABLE ACCESS BY INDEX ROWID|EMPLOYEES   |   1|   22|    1  (0)|00:00:01|
|*2|  INDEX UNIQUE SCAN           |EMP_EMP_ID_PK|   1|     |    0  (0)|00:00:01|
-------------------------------------------------------------------------------
```

Query Block Name / Object Alias (identified by operation id):

```
   1 - SEL$38D4D5F3 / EMPLOYEES@SEL$1
   2 - SEL$38D4D5F3 / EMPLOYEES@SEL$1
```

Predicate Information (identified by operation id):

```
   1 - filter("EMPLOYEES"."DEPARTMENT_ID" IS NOT NULL)
   2 - access("EMPLOYEES"."EMPLOYEE_ID"=101)
```

Column Projection Information (identified by operation id):

```
   1 - "EMPLOYEES"."FIRST_NAME"[VARCHAR2,20], "EMPLOYEES"."LAST_NAME"[VARCHAR2,25]
   2 - "EMPLOYEES".ROWID[ROWID,10]
```

One of the very nice features of the DBMS_XPLAN.DISPLAY function is after deciding the base level of detail you need, you can add individual options to be displayed in addition to the base output for that level of detail. For instance, if you want just the most basic output information, but also want to know cost information, you can format the DBMS_XPLAN.DISPLAY as follows:

```
SELECT * FROM table(dbms_xplan.display(null,null,'BASIC +COST'));
```

```
-------------------------------------------------------------------
| Id  | Operation                    | Name          | Cost (%CPU)|
-------------------------------------------------------------------
|   0 | SELECT STATEMENT             |               |     1   (0)|
|   1 |  TABLE ACCESS BY INDEX ROWID | EMPLOYEES     |     1   (0)|
|   2 |   INDEX UNIQUE SCAN          | EMP_EMP_ID_PK |     0   (0)|
-------------------------------------------------------------------
```

You can also do the reverse—that is, subtract information you do not want to see. If you wanted to see the output using the TYPICAL level of output but did not want to see the ROWS or BYTES information, you could issue the following query to display that level of output:

```
SELECT * FROM table(dbms_xplan.display(null,null,'TYPICAL -BYTES -ROWS'));
```

```
--------------------------------------------------------------------------
| Id  | Operation                    | Name          | Cost (%CPU)| Time     |
--------------------------------------------------------------------------
|   0 | SELECT STATEMENT             |               |     1   (0)| 00:00:01 |
|*  1 |  TABLE ACCESS BY INDEX ROWID | EMPLOYEES     |     1   (0)| 00:00:01 |
|*  2 |   INDEX UNIQUE SCAN          | EMP_EMP_ID_PK |     0   (0)| 00:00:01 |
--------------------------------------------------------------------------
```

9-3. Graphically Displaying an Execution Plan

Problem

You want to quickly view an execution plan without having to run SQL statements to retrieve the execution plan. You would like to use a GUI to view the plan, so that you can just click your way to it.

Solution

From within Enterprise Manager, you can quickly find the execution plan for a query. In order to use this functionality, you will have to have Enterprise Manager configured within your environment. This can be either Database Control, which manages a single database, or Grid Control, which manages an enterprise of databases. In order to see the execution plan for a given query, you will need to navigate to the Top Sessions screen of Enterprise Manager. (Refer to the Oracle Enterprise Manager documentation for your specific release.) Once on the Top Sessions screen, you can drill down into session specific information. First, find your session. Then, click the SQL ID shown under Current SQL. From there, you can click Plan, and the execution plan will appear, such as the one shown in Figure 9-1.

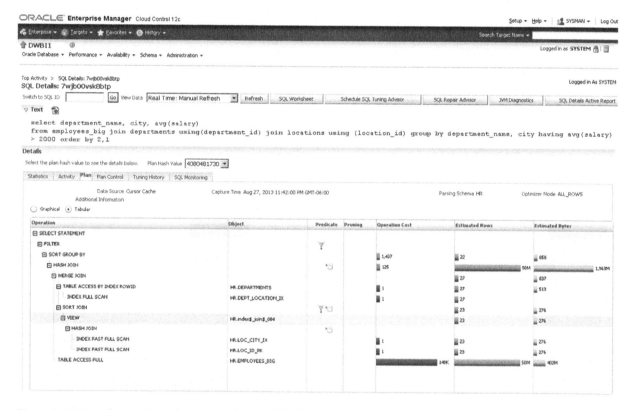

Figure 9-1. *Sample execution plan output from within Enterprise Manager*

How It Works

Using Enterprise Manager makes it very easy to find the execution plan for currently running SQL operations within your database. If a particular SQL statement isn't performing as expected, this method is one of the fastest ways to determine the execution plan for a running query or other SQL operation. In order to use this feature, you must be licensed for the Tuning Pack of Enterprise Manager.

9-4. Reading an Execution Plan
Problem

You have run an explain plan for a given SQL statement, and want to understand how to read the plan.

Solution

The execution plan for a SQL operation tells you step-by-step exactly how the Oracle optimizer will execute your SQL operation. Using AUTOTRACE, let's get an explain plan for the following query:

```
set autotrace trace explain

SELECT ename, dname
FROM emp JOIN dept USING (deptno);
```

```
-------------------------------------------------------------
|Id|Operation            |Name   |Rows|Bytes|Cost (%CPU)|Time     |
-------------------------------------------------------------
| 0|SELECT STATEMENT     |       | 14| 308|   6  (17)|00:00:01 |
| 1| MERGE JOIN          |       | 14| 308|   6  (17)|00:00:01 |
| 2|  TABLE ACCESS BY    |DEPT   |  4|  52|   2   (0)|00:00:01 |
|  |    INDEX ROWID      |       |   |    |          |         |
| 3|   INDEX FULL SCAN   |PK_DEPT|  4|    |   1   (0)|00:00:01 |
|*4|  SORT JOIN          |       | 14| 126|   4  (25)|00:00:01 |
| 5|   TABLE ACCESS FULL |EMP    | 14| 126|   3   (0)|00:00:01 |
-------------------------------------------------------------

Predicate Information (identified by operation id):
---------------------------------------------------

   4 - access("EMP"."DEPTNO"="DEPT"."DEPTNO")
       filter("EMP"."DEPTNO"="DEPT"."DEPTNO")

Note
-----
   - automatic DOP: Computed Degree of Parallelism is 1
     because of parallel threshold
```

Once you have an explain plan to interpret, you can tell which steps are executed first because the innermost or most indented steps are executed first and are executed from the inside out, in top-down order. In the foregoing query, we are joining the EMP and DEPT tables. Here are the steps of how the query is processed based on the execution plan:

1. The PK_DEPT index is scanned (ID 3).

2. Rows are retrieved from the DEPT table based on the matching entries in the PK_DEPT index (ID 2).

3. All EMP table rows are scanned (ID 5).

4. Resulting data from the EMP table is sorted (ID 4).

5. Data from the EMP and DEPT tables are then joined via a MERGE JOIN (ID 1).

6. The resulting data from the query is returned to the user (ID 0).

How It Works

When first looking at an explain plan and wanting to quickly get an idea of the steps in which the query will be executed, do the following:

1. Look for the most indented rows in the plan (the right-most rows). These will be executed first.

2. If multiple rows are at the same level of indentation, they will be executed in top-down fashion in the plan, with the highest rows in the plan first moving downward in the plan.

3. Look at the next most indented row or rows and continue working your way outward.

4. The top of the explain plan corresponds with the least indented or left-most part of the plan, and usually is where the results are returned to the user.

Remember that the indentation top-down rule cannot be taken literally when examining each and every explain plan. In the above example, the highest, most indented line is the full scan of the PK_DEPT index. Once this step is complete, it means by default step 2 is complete—since there is only one child step in the group. The same logic applies to the sort operation in step 4. Each explain plan needs to be interpreted separately in order to determine the absolute order, but looking at each plan from the inside out and top down will always be the right place to start when reading explain plan output.

Once you have an explain plan for a query, and can understand the sequence of how the query should be processed, you then can move on and perform some analysis to determine if the explain plan you are looking at is efficient. When looking at your explain plan, answer these questions and consider these factors when determining if you have an efficient plan:

- What is the access path for the query (is the query performing a full table scan or is the query using an index)?

- What is the join method for the query (if a join condition is present)?

- Look at the columns within the filtering criteria found within the WHERE clause of the query. What is the cardinality of these columns? Are the columns indexed?

- Get the volume or number of rows for each table in the query. Are the tables small, medium-sized, or large? This may help you determine the most appropriate join method. See Table 9-3 for a synopsis of the types of join methods.

Table 9-3. *Join Methods*

Method	Description
Hash	Most appropriate if at least one table involved in the query returns a large result set
Nested loop	Appropriate for smaller tables
Sort merge	Appropriate for pre-sorted data
Cartesian	Signifies either no join condition or a missing join condition; usually signifies an unwanted condition and query needs to be scrutinized to ensure there is a join condition for each and every table in the query

- When were statistics last gathered for the objects involved in the query?

- Look at the COST column of the explain plan to get a starting cost.

By looking at our original explain plan, we determined that the EMP table is larger in size and also that there is no index present on the DEPTNO column, which is used within a join condition between the DEPT and EMP tables. By placing an index on the DEPTNO column on the EMP table and gathering statistics on the EMP table, the plan now uses an index:

```
-----------------------------------------------------------------
|Id|Operation           |Name   |Rows|Bytes|Cost(%CPU)|Time     |
-----------------------------------------------------------------
| 0|SELECT STATEMENT    |       |  14| 280|   6  (17)|00:00:01|
| 1| MERGE JOIN         |       |  14| 280|   6  (17)|00:00:01|
| 2|  TABLE ACCESS BY   |EMP    |  14|  98|   2   (0)|00:00:01|
|  |       INDEX ROWID  |       |    |    |          |        |
| 3|   INDEX FULL SCAN  |EMP_I2 |  14|    |   1   (0)|00:00:01|
|*4|  SORT JOIN         |       |   4|  52|   4  (25)|00:00:01|
| 5|   TABLE ACCESS FULL|DEPT   |   4|  52|   3   (0)|00:00:01|
-----------------------------------------------------------------
```

For information on parallel execution plans, *see* Chapter 15.

■ **Tip**   One of the most common reasons for a suboptimal explain plan is the lack of current statistics on one or more objects involved in a query.

9-5. Monitoring Long-Running SQL Statements
Problem

You have a SQL statement that runs a long time, and you want to be able to monitor the progress of the statement and find out when it will finish.

Solution

By viewing information for a long-running query in the V$SESSION_LONGOPS data dictionary view, you can gauge about when each operation within a query will finish. Let's say you are running the following query, with join conditions, against a large table:

```
SELECT last_name, first_name FROM employees_big
WHERE last_name = 'EVANS';
```

With a query against the V$SESSION_LONGOPS view, you can quickly get an idea of how long a given query component will execute, and when it will finish:

```
SELECT username, target, sofar blocks_read, totalwork total_blocks,
round(time_remaining/60) minutes
FROM v$session_longops
WHERE sofar <> totalwork
and username = 'HR';
```

USERNAME	TARGET	BLOCKS_READ	TOTAL_BLOCKS	MINUTES
HR	HR.EMPLOYEES_BIG	81101	2353488	10

As the query progresses, you can see the BLOCKS_READ column increase, as well as the MINUTES column decrease. It is usually necessary to place the WHERE clause to eliminate rows that have been completed, which is why in the foregoing query it asked for rows where the SOFAR column did not equal TOTALWORK. Keep in mind that for complex queries with many steps within the explain plan, you will see each associated step in the V$SESSION_LONGOPS view, which can at times make it more challenging to really know when the overall query may finish.

How It Works

In order to be able to monitor a query within the V$SESSION_LONGOPS view, the following requirements apply:

- The query must run for six seconds or greater.
- The table being accessed must be greater than 10,000 database blocks.
- TIMED_STATISTICS must be set or SQL_TRACE must be turned on.
- The objects within the query must have been analyzed via DBMS_STATS or ANALYZE.

This view can contain information on SELECT statements, DML statements such as UPDATE, as well as DDL statements such as CREATE INDEX. Some common operations that find themselves in the V$SESSION_LONGOPS view include table scans, index scans, join operations, parallel operations, RMAN backup operations, sort operations, and Data Pump operations.

9-6. Identifying Resource-Consuming SQL Statements That Are Currently Executing

Problem

You have contention issues within your database and want to identify the SQL statement consuming the most system resources.

■ **Note** Recipe 9-9 shows how to examine the historical record to find resource-consuming SQL statements that have executed in the past but that are not currently executing.

Solution

Look at the V$SQLSTATS view, which gives information about currently or recently run SQL statements. If you wanted to get the five recent SQL statements that performed the most disk I/O, you could issue the following query:

```
SELECT sql_text, disk_reads FROM
  (SELECT sql_text, buffer_gets, disk_reads, sorts,
   cpu_time/1000000 cpu, rows_processed, elapsed_time
   FROM v$sqlstats
   ORDER BY disk_reads DESC)
WHERE rownum <= 5;
```

If you wanted to see the top five SQL statements by CPU time, sorts, loads, invalidations, or any other column, simply replace the disk_reads column in the foregoing query with your desired column. For instance, if you were more interested in the queries that ran the longest, you could issue the following query:

```
SELECT sql_text, elapsed_time FROM
  (SELECT sql_text, buffer_gets, disk_reads, sorts,
   cpu_time/1000000 cpu, rows_processed, elapsed_time
   FROM v$sqlstats
   ORDER BY elapsed_time DESC)
WHERE rownum <= 5;
```

The SQL_TEXT column can make the results look messy, so another alternative is to substitute the SQL_TEXT column with SQL_ID, and then, based on the statistics shown, you can run a query to simply get the SQL_TEXT based on a given SQL_ID.

How It Works

The V$SQLSTATS view is meant to help more quickly find information on resource-consuming SQL statements. V$SQLSTATS has the same information as the V$SQL and V$SQLAREA views, but V$SQLSTATS has only a subset of columns of the other views. However, data is held within the V$SQLSTATS longer than either V$SQL or V$SQLAREA.

Sometimes, there are SQL statements that are related to the database background processing of keeping the database running, and you may not want to see those statements, but only the ones related to your application. If you join V$SQLSTATS to V$SQL, you can see information for particular users. See the following example:

```
SELECT schema, sql_text, disk_reads, round(cpu,2) FROM
  (SELECT s.parsing_schema_name schema, t.sql_id, t.sql_text, t.disk_reads,
   t.sorts, t.cpu_time/1000000 cpu, t.rows_processed, t.elapsed_time
   FROM v$sqlstats t join v$sql s on(t.sql_id = s.sql_id)
  WHERE parsing_schema_name = 'SCOTT'
  ORDER BY disk_reads DESC)
WHERE rownum <= 5;
```

Keep in mind that V$SQL represents SQL held in the shared pool, and is aged out faster than the data in V$SQLSTATS, so this query will not return data for SQL that has been already aged out of the shared pool.

9-7. Seeing Execution Statistics for Currently Running SQL

Problem

You want to view execution statistics for SQL statements that are currently running.

Solution

You can use the V$SQL_MONITOR view to see real-time statistics of currently running SQL and see the resource consumption used for a given query based on such statistics as CPU usage, buffer gets, disk reads, and elapsed time of the query. Let's first find a current executing query within our database:

```
SELECT sid, sql_text FROM v$sql_monitor
WHERE status = 'EXECUTING';

       SID SQL_TEXT
---------- ----------------------------------------------------------
       100 select department_name, city, avg(salary)
           from employees_big join departments using(department_id)
           join locations using (location_id)
           group by department_name, city
           having avg(salary) > 2000
           order by 2,1
```

For the foregoing executing query found in V$SQL_MONITOR, we can see the resource utilization for that statement as it executes:

```
SELECT sid, buffer_gets, disk_reads, round(cpu_time/1000000,1) cpu_seconds
FROM v$sql_monitor
WHERE SID=100
AND status = 'EXECUTING';

       SID BUFFER_GETS DISK_READS CPU_SECONDS
---------- ----------- ---------- -----------
       100      149372       4732        39.1
```

The V$SQL_MONITOR view contains currently running SQL statements, as well as recently run SQL statements. If you wanted to see the sessions that are running the top five CPU-consuming queries in your database, you could issue the following query:

```
SELECT * FROM (
  SELECT sid, buffer_gets, disk_reads, round(cpu_time/1000000,1) cpu_seconds
  FROM v$sql_monitor
  ORDER BY cpu_time desc)
WHERE rownum <= 5;

       SID BUFFER_GETS DISK_READS CPU_SECONDS
---------- ----------- ---------- -----------
        20     1332665      30580       350.5
       105      795330      13651       269.7
        20      259324       5449        71.6
        20      259330       5485        71.3
       100      259236       8188        67.9
```

How It Works

SQL statements are monitored in V$SQL_MONITOR under the following conditions:

- Automatically for any parallelized statements

- Automatically for any DML or DDL statements

- Automatically if a particular SQL statement has consumed at least 5 seconds of CPU or I/O time

- Monitored for any SQL statement that has monitoring set at the statement level

To turn monitoring on at the statement level, a hint can be used. See the following example:

```
SELECT /*+ monitor */ ename, dname
FROM emppart JOIN dept USING (deptno);
```

If, for some reason, you do not want certain statements monitored, you can use the NOMONITOR hint in the statement to prevent monitoring from occurring for a given statement.

Statistics in V$SQL_MONITOR are updated near real-time,—that is, every second. Any currently executing SQL statement that is being monitored can be found in V$SQL_MONITOR. Completed queries can be found there for at least 1 minute after execution ends and can exist there longer, depending on the space requirements needed for newly executed queries. One advantage of the V$SQL_MONITOR view is it has detailed statistics for each and every execution of a given query, unlike V$SQL, where results are cumulative for several executions of a SQL statement. In order to drill down, then, to a given execution of a SQL statement, you need three columns from V$SQL_MONITOR:

1. SQL_ID

2. SQL_EXEC_START

3. SQL_EXEC_ID

If we wanted to see all executions for a given query (based on the SQL_ID column), we can get that information by querying on the three necessary columns to drill to a given execution of a SQL query:

```
SELECT * FROM (
  SELECT sql_id, to_char(sql_exec_start,'yyyy-mm-dd:hh24:mi:ss') sql_exec_start,
         sql_exec_id, sum(buffer_gets) buffer_gets,
         sum(disk_reads) disk_reads, round(sum(cpu_time/1000000),1) cpu_secs
  FROM v$sql_monitor
  WHERE sql_id = '21z86kt10h3rp'
  GROUP BY sql_id, sql_exec_start, sql_exec_id
  ORDER BY 6 desc)
WHERE rownum <= 5;
```

SQL_ID	SQL_EXEC_START	SQL_EXEC_ID	BUFFER_GETS	DISK_READS	CPU_SECS
21z86kt10h3rp	2013-08-26:14:06:02	16777218	591636	6	28.3
21z86kt10h3rp	2013-08-26:14:06:36	16777219	507484	0	27.8
21z86kt10h3rp	2013-08-26:14:07:17	16777220	507484	0	27.6

Keep in mind that if a statement is running in parallel, one row will appear for each parallel thread for the query, including one for the query coordinator. However, they will share the same SQL_ID, SQL_EXEC_START, and SQL_EXEC_ID values. In this case, you could perform an aggregation on a particular statistic, if desired. See the following example for a parallelized query, along with parallel slave information denoted by the PX_SERVER# column:

```
SELECT sql_id, sql_exec_start, sql_exec_id, px_server# px#, disk_reads,
       cpu_time/1000000 cpu_secs, buffer_gets
FROM v$sql_monitor
WHERE status = 'EXECUTING'
ORDER BY px_server#;
```

SQL_ID	SQL_EXEC_S	SQL_EXEC_ID	PX#	DISK_READS	CPU_SECS	BUFFER_GETS
55x73dhhx277n	2013-08-26	16777216	1	98	.673897	11869
55x73dhhx277n	2013-08-26	16777216	2	100	.664898	12176
55x73dhhx277n	2013-08-26	16777216	3	72	.481927	8715
55x73dhhx277n	2013-08-26	16777216	4	143	.752885	17283
55x73dhhx277n	2013-08-26	16777216		0	.007999	27

```
33 rows selected.
```

Then, to perform a simple aggregation for a given query, in this case, our parallelized query, the aggregation is done on the three key columns that make up a single execution of a given SQL statement:

```
SELECT sql_id,sql_exec_start, sql_exec_id, sum(buffer_gets) buffer_gets,
       sum(disk_reads) disk_reads, round(sum(cpu_time/1000000),1) cpu_seconds
FROM v$sql_monitor
WHERE sql_id = '21z86kt10h3rp'
GROUP BY sql_id, sql_exec_start, sql_exec_id;
```

SQL_ID	SQL_EXEC_S	SQL_EXEC_ID	BUFFER_GETS	DISK_READS	CPU_SECONDS
21z86kt10h3rp	2013-08-26	16777218	591636	6	28.3

If you wanted to perform an aggregation for one SQL statement, regardless of the number of times is has been executed, simply run the aggregate query only on the SQL_ID column, as shown here:

```
SELECT sql_id, sum(buffer_gets) buffer_gets,
       sum(disk_reads) disk_reads, round(sum(cpu_time/1000000),1) cpu_seconds
FROM v$sql_monitor
WHERE sql_id = '21z86kt10h3rp '
GROUP BY sql_id;
```

■ **Note** Initialization parameter STATISTICS_LEVEL must be set to TYPICAL or ALL, and CONTROL_MANAGEMENT_PACK_ACCESS must be set to DIAGNOSTIC+TUNING for SQL monitoring to occur. Diagnostic and Tuning Pack Licenses are required to use V$SQL_MONITOR.

9-8. Monitoring Progress of a SQL Execution Plan

Problem

You want to see the progress a query is making from within the execution plan used.

Solution

There are a couple of ways to get information to see where a query is executing in terms of the execution plan. First, by querying the V$SQL_PLAN_MONITOR view, you can get information for all queries that are in progress, as well as recent queries that are complete. For instance, we will use a query from a previous recipe that performs a three table join:

```
SELECT department_name, city, avg(salary)
FROM employees_big join departments using(department_id)
JOIN locations using (location_id)
GROUP BY department_name, city
HAVING avg(salary) > 2000
ORDER BY 2,1;
```

```
-------------------------------------------------------------
| Id  | Operation                    | Name           |
-------------------------------------------------------------
|   0 | SELECT STATEMENT             |                |
|   1 |  FILTER                      |                |
|   2 |   SORT GROUP BY              |                |
|   3 |    HASH JOIN                 |                |
|   4 |     MERGE JOIN               |                |
|   5 |      TABLE ACCESS BY INDEX ROWID| DEPARTMENTS |
|   6 |       INDEX FULL SCAN        | DEPT_LOCATION_IX |
|   7 |      SORT JOIN               |                |
|   8 |       VIEW                   | index$_join$_004 |
|   9 |        HASH JOIN             |                |
|  10 |         INDEX FAST FULL SCAN | LOC_CITY_IX    |
|  11 |         INDEX FAST FULL SCAN | LOC_ID_PK      |
|  12 |     TABLE ACCESS FULL        | EMPLOYEES_BIG  |
-------------------------------------------------------------
```

To see information for the foregoing query while it is currently running, you can issue a query like the one shown here (some rows have been removed for conciseness):

```
column operation format a25
column plan_line_id format 9999 heading 'LINE'
column plan_options format a10 heading 'OPTIONS'
column status format a10
column output_rows heading 'ROWS'
break on sid on sql_id on status

SELECT sid, sql_id, status, plan_line_id,
plan_operation || ' ' || plan_options operation, output_rows
FROM v$sql_plan_monitor
WHERE status not like '%DONE%'
ORDER BY 1,4;
```

SID	SQL_ID	STATUS	LINE	OPERATION	ROWS
423	7wjb00vsk8btp	EXECUTING	0	SELECT STATEMENT	0
			1	FILTER	0
			2	SORT GROUP BY	0
			3	HASH JOIN	9785901
			4	MERGE JOIN	27
			5	TABLE ACCESS BY INDEX ROWID	27
			6	INDEX FULL SCAN	27
			7	SORT JOIN	27
			8	VIEW	23
			9	HASH JOIN	23
			10	INDEX FAST FULL SCAN	23
			11	INDEX FAST FULL SCAN	23
			12	TABLE ACCESS FULL	9785901

In this particular example, there is a full table scan against the EMPLOYEES_BIG table, and indexes are being used for the DEPARTMENTS and LOCATIONS tables. The MERGE JOIN indicates that the optimizer is joining the data between the DEPARTMENTS and LOCATIONS tables . The HASH JOIN is joining data between the EMPLOYEES_BIG table, and the result set from the join between the DEPARTMENTS and LOCATIONS tables. The resulting data is being passed back to the SORT GROUP BY operation. Finally, the FILTER represents paring the data down based on the HAVING clause. If we simply run subsequent queries against the V$SQL_PLAN_MONITOR view, we can see the progress of the query as it is executing. In the foregoing example, we simply see the output row values increasing as the query progresses.

Another method of seeing the progress of a query via the execution plan is by using the DBMS_SQLTUNE.REPORT_SQL_MONITOR function. If we use the same foregoing query used in the previous example, we can run the REPORT_SQL_MONITOR function to get a graphical look at the progress. See the following example of how to generate the file that would produce the HTML file that could be, in turn, used to view our progress. Figure 9-2 shows portions of the resulting report.

```
set pages 9999
set long 1000000
SELECT DBMS_SQLTUNE.REPORT_SQL_MONITOR
   (sql_id=> '7wjb00vsk8btp ',type=>'HTML')
FROM dual;
```

SQL Text

select department_name, city, avg(salary) from employees_big join departments using(department_id) join locations using (location_id) group by department_name, city having avg(salary) > 2000 order by 2,1

Global Information: DONE

Instance ID	: 1
Session	: HR (423:25891)
SQL ID	: 7wjb00vsk8btp
SQL Execution ID	: 16777219
Execution Started	: 08/26/2013 16:20:52
First Refresh Time	: 08/26/2013 16:20:58
Last Refresh Time	: 08/26/2013 16:21:12
Duration	: 20s
Module/Action	: SQL*Plus/-
Service	: SYS$USERS
Program	: sqlplus@lxdnt24b (TNS V1-V3)
Fetch Calls	: 1

Buffer Gets	Database Time	Wait Activity
372K	20s	

SQL Plan Monitoring Details (Plan Hash Value=4080481730)

Id	Operation	Name	Estimated Rows	Cost	Active Period (20s)	Execs	Rows	Memory (Max)	Temp (Max)	IO Requests	CPU Activity	Wait Activity
0	SELECT STATEMENT					1						
1	FILTER					1						
2	SORT GROUP BY		1	752		1	0					
3	HASH JOIN		6M	594		1	36M	1.4MB				
4	MERGE JOIN		27	4		1	27					
5	TABLE ACCESS BY INDEX ROWID	DEPARTMENTS	27	2		1	27					
6	INDEX FULL SCAN	DEPT_LOCATION_IX	27	1		1	27					
7	SORT JOIN		23	2		27	27					
8	VIEW	index$_join$_004	23	2		1	23					
9	HASH JOIN					1	23	1.5MB				
10	INDEX FAST FULL SCAN	LOC_CITY_IX	23	1		1	23					
11	INDEX FAST FULL SCAN	LOC_ID_PK	23	1		1	23					
12	TABLE ACCESS FULL	EMPLOYEES_BIG	6M	574		1	36M					

Figure 9-2. *Sample HTML report from DBMS_SQLTUNE.REPORT_SQL_MONITOR*

How It Works

The V$SQL_PLAN_MONITOR is populated from the V$SQL_MONITOR view (*see* Recipe 9-7). Both of these views are updated every second that a statement executes. The V$SQL_MONITOR view is populated each time a SQL statement is monitored.

The DBMS_SQLTUNE.REPORT_SQL_MONITOR function can be invoked in several ways. The level of detail, as well as the type of detail you wish to see in the report, can be changed based on the parameters passed into the function. The output can be viewed in several formats, including plain text, HTML, and XML. The default output format is plain text. As an example, let's say we wanted to see the output for our join against the EMPLOYEES_BIG, DEPARTMENTS, and LOCATIONS tables. In this instance, we want the output in text format. We want the detail aggregated, and we want to see just the most basic level of detail. Our query would then be run as follows:

```
SELECT DBMS_SQLTUNE.REPORT_SQL_MONITOR
(sql_id=>'7wjb00vsk8btp ',event_detail=>'NO',report_level=>'BASIC') FROM dual;


SQL Monitoring Report

SQL Text
--------------------------------
select department_name, city, avg(salary)
from employees_big join departments using(department_id)
join locations using (location_id)
group by department_name,city
having avg(salary) > 2000 order by 2,1
```

```
Global Information
------------------------------
 Status              :  DONE
 Instance ID         :  1
 Session             :  HR (423:25891)
 SQL ID              :  7wjb00vsk8btp
 SQL Execution ID    :  16777219
 Execution Started   :  08/26/2013 16:20:52
 First Refresh Time  :  08/26/2013 16:20:58
 Last Refresh Time   :  08/26/2013 16:21:12
 Duration            :  20s
 Module/Action       :  SQL*Plus/-
 Service             :  SYS$USERS
 Program             :  sqlplus@lxdnt24b (TNS V1-V3)
 Fetch Calls         :  1

Global Stats
=================================================
| Elapsed |   Cpu   |  Other   | Fetch | Buffer |
| Time(s) | Time(s) | Waits(s) | Calls |  Gets  |
=================================================
|      20 |      20 |     0.03 |     1 |   372K |
=================================================
```

Refer to the Oracle PL/SQL Packages and Types Reference for a complete list of all the parameters that can be used to execute the REPORT_SQL_MONITOR function. It is a very robust function, and there are a myriad of permutations to report on, based on your specific need.

■ **Note** A license for Tuning Pack is required to use DBMS_SQLTUNE package.

9-9. Identifying Resource-Consuming SQL Statements That Have Executed in the Past

Problem

You want to view information on previously run SQL statements to aid in identifying resource-intensive operations.

■ **Note** Recipe 9-6 shows how to identify *currently executing* statements that are resource-intensive.

Solution

The DBA_HIST_SQLSTAT and DBA_HIST_SQLTEXT views are two of the views that can be used to get historical information on SQL statements and their resource consumption statistics. For example, to get historical information on what SQL statements are incurring the most disk reads, you can issue the following query against DBA_HIST_SQLSTAT:

```
SELECT * FROM (
  SELECT sql_id, sum(disk_reads_delta) disk_reads_delta,
                 sum(disk_reads_total) disk_reads_total,
                 sum(executions_delta) execs_delta,
                 sum(executions_total) execs_total
  FROM dba_hist_sqlstat
  GROUP BY sql_id
  ORDER BY 2 desc)
WHERE rownum <= 5;
```

SQL_ID	DISK_READS_DELTA	DISK_READS_TOTAL	EXECS_DELTA	EXECS_TOTAL
36bdwxutr5n75	6306401	10933153	13	24
0bx1z9rbm10a1	1590538	1590538	2	2
0gzf8010xdasr	970292	1848743	1	3
1gtkxf53fk7bp	969785	969785	7	7
4h81qj5nspx6s	869588	869588	2	2

Since the actual text of the SQL isn't stored in DBA_HIST_SQLSTAT, you can then look at the associated DBA_HIST_SQLTEXT view to get the SQL text for the query with the highest number of disk reads:

```
SELECT sql_text FROM dba_hist_sqltext
WHERE sql_id = '7wjb00vsk8btp ';
```

```
SQL_TEXT
------------------------------------------------------------
select department_name, city, avg(salary)
from employees_big join departments using(department_id)
join locations using (location_id)
group by department_name, city
having avg(salary) > 2000
order by 2,1
```

How It Works

There are many useful statistics to get from the DBA_HIST_SQLSTAT view regarding historical SQL statements, including the following:

- CPU utilization

- Elapsed time of execution

- Number of executions

- Total disk reads and writes

- Buffer get information

- Parallel server information

- Rows processed

- Parse calls

- Invalidations

Furthermore, this information is separated by two views of the data. There is a set of "Total" information in one set of columns, and there is a "Delta" set of information in another set of columns. The "Total" set of columns is calculated based on instance startup. The "Delta" columns are based on the values seen in the BEGIN_INTERVAL_TIME and END_INTERVAL_TIME columns of the DBA_HIST_SNAPSHOT view.

If you want to see explain plan information for historical SQL statements, there is an associated view available to retrieve that information for a given query. You can access the DBA_HIST_SQL_PLAN view to get the explain plan information for historical SQL statements. See the following example:

```
SELECT id, operation || ' ' || options operation, object_name, cost, bytes
FROM dba_hist_sql_plan
WHERE sql_id = '7wjb00vsk8btp '
ORDER BY 1;
```

ID	OPERATION	OBJECT_NAME	COST	BYTES
0	SELECT STATEMENT		549	
1	FILTER			
2	SORT GROUP BY		549	858
3	HASH JOIN		546	7668102
4	MERGE JOIN		4	837
5	TABLE ACCESS BY INDEX ROWID	DEPARTMENTS	2	513
6	INDEX FULL SCAN	DEPT_LOCATION_IX	1	
7	SORT JOIN		2	276
8	VIEW	index$_join$_004	2	276
9	HASH JOIN			
10	INDEX FAST FULL SCAN	LOC_CITY_IX	1	276
11	INDEX FAST FULL SCAN	LOC_ID_PK	1	276
12	TABLE ACCESS FULL	EMPLOYEES_BIG	541	15729449

Comparing SQL Performance After a System Change
Problem

You are making a system change and want to see the impact that change will have on performance of a SQL statement.

Solution

By using the Oracle SQL Performance Analyzer, and specifically the DBMS_SQLPA package, you can quantify the performance impact a system change will have on one or more SQL statements. A system change can be an initialization parameter change, a database upgrade, or any other change to your environment that could affect SQL statement performance.

Let's say you are going to be performing a database upgrade and want to see the impact the upgrade is going to have on a series of SQL statements run within your database. Using the DBMS_SQLPA package, the basic steps to get the information needed to perform the analysis generally are as follows:

1. Create an analysis task based on a single or series of SQL statements.

2. Run an analysis for those statements based on your current configuration.

3. Perform the given change to your environment (like a database upgrade).

4. Run an analysis for those statements based on the new configuration.

5. Run a "before and after" comparison to determine what impact the change has on the performance of your SQL statement(s).

6. Generate a report to view the output of the comparison results.

■ **Note**   You must be licensed for Real Application Testing in order to use the SQL Performance Analyzer.

Using the foregoing steps, see the following example for a single query. First, we need to create an analysis task. For the database upgrade example, this would be done on an appropriate test database that is Oracle 12c. In this case, within SQL Plus, we will do the analysis for one specific SQL statement:

```
variable g_task varchar2(100);

EXEC :g_task := DBMS_SQLPA.CREATE_ANALYSIS_TASK(sql_text => 'select last_name
|| ',' || first_name, department_name from employees join departments using(department_id)');
```

In order to properly simulate this scenario on our Oracle 12c database, we then set the optimizer_features_enable parameter back to Oracle 11g. We then run an analysis for our query using the "before" conditions—in this case, with a previous version of the optimizer:

```
alter session set optimizer_features_enable='11.2.0.3';

EXEC DBMS_SQLPA.EXECUTE_ANALYSIS_TASK(task_name=>:g_task,execution_type=>'test execute',
execution_name=>'before_change');
```

After completing the before analysis, we set the optimizer to the current version of our database, which, for this example, represents the version to which we are upgrading our database:

```
alter session set optimizer_features_enable='12.1.0.1.1';

EXEC DBMS_SQLPA.EXECUTE_ANALYSIS_TASK(task_name=>:g_task,execution_type=>'test execute',
execution_name=>'after_change');
```

Now that we have created our analysis task based on a given SQL statement, and have run "before" and "after" analysis tasks for that statement based on the changed conditions, we can now run an analysis task to compare the results of the two executions of our query. There are several metrics that can be compared. In this case, we are comparing "buffer gets":

```
EXEC DBMS_SQLPA.EXECUTE_ANALYSIS_TASK(task_name=>:g_task,execution_type=>'COMPARE
PERFORMANCE',execution_name=>'compare change',execution_params =>
dbms_advisor.arglist('comparison_metric','buffer_gets'));
```

Finally, we can now use the REPORT_ANALYSIS_TASK function of the DBMS_SQLPA package in order to view the results. In the following example, we want to see output only if the execution plan has changed. The output can be in several formats, the most popular being HTML and plain text. For our example, we produced text output:

```
set long 100000 longchunksize 100000 linesize 200 head off feedback off echo off
spool compare_report.txt

SELECT DBMS_SQLPA.REPORT_ANALYSIS_TASK(:g_task, 'TEXT', 'CHANGED_PLANS', 'ALL')
FROM DUAL;

General Information
---------------------------------------------

Task Information:
---------------------------------------------
  Task Name    : TASK_1603
  Task Owner   : HR
  Description  :

Execution Information:
-----------------------------------------------------------------------
Execution Name:compare change       Started          :08/26/2013 17:47:21
Execution Type:COMPARE PERFORMANCE Last Updated      :08/26/2013 17:47:21
Description   :                     Global Time Limit :UNLIMITED
Scope         :COMPREHENSIVE        Per-SQL Time Limit:UNUSED
Status        :COMPLETED            Number of Errors  :0

Analysis Information:
-----------------------------------------------------------------------
Before Change Execution:             After Change Execution:
-------------------------------      -------------------------------
Execution Name    :before_change     Execution Name    :after_change
Execution Type    :TEST EXECUTE      Execution Type    :TEST EXECUTE
Scope             :COMPREHENSIVE     Scope             :COMPREHENSIVE
Status            :COMPLETED         Status            :COMPLETED
Started           :08/26/2013 17:46:17 Started         :08/26/2013 17:47:09
Last Updated      :08/26/2013 17:46:17 Last Updated    :08/26/2013 17:47:10
Global Time Limit :UNLIMITED         Global Time Limit :UNLIMITED
Per-SQL Time Limit:UNUSED            Per-SQL Time Limit:UNUSED
Number of Errors  :0                 Number of Errors  :0


-------------------------------
 Comparison Metric: BUFFER_GETS
-------------------------------
 Workload Impact Threshold: 1%
-------------------------
 SQL Impact Threshold: 1%
-------------------------
```

Report Details

SQL Details:

```
 Object ID             : 4
 Schema Name           : HR
 Container Name        : Unknown (con_dbid: 253609779)
 SQL ID                : 6jrgypw4rcq70
 Execution Frequency   : 1
 SQL Text              : select last_name , first_name, department_name from
                         employees join departments using(department_id)
```

Execution Statistics:

| | Impact on | Value | Value | Impact |
Stat Name	Workload	Before	After	on SQL
elapsed_time	-10.05%	.000378	.000416	-10.05%
parse_time	24.49%	.001127	.000851	24.49%
cpu_time	-100%	.000222	.000444	-100%
user_io_time	0%	0	0	0%
buffer_gets	0%	8	8	0%
cost	33.33%	6	4	33.33%
reads	0%	0	0	0%
writes	0%	0	0	0%
io_interconnect_bytes	0%	0	0	0%
rows		107	107	

Note: time statistics are displayed in seconds

Notes:

Before Change:
 1. The statement was first executed to warm the buffer cache.
 2. Statistics shown were averaged over next 9 executions.

After Change:
 1. The statement was first executed to warm the buffer cache.
 2. Statistics shown were averaged over next 9 executions.

Execution Plan Before Change:

```
 Plan Id           : 954
 Plan Hash Value   : 1473400139
```

```
-------------------------------------------------------------------
|Id|Operation                    |Name             |Rows|Bytes|Cost|Time     |
-------------------------------------------------------------------
| 0|SELECT STATEMENT             |                 | 106| 3604|   6|00:00:01|
| 1|  MERGE JOIN                 |                 | 106| 3604|   6|00:00:01|
| 2|   TABLE ACCESS BY           |DEPARTMENTS      |  27|  432|   2|00:00:01|
  |      INDEX ROWID
| 3|    INDEX FULL SCAN          |DEPT_ID_PK       |  27|     |   1|00:00:01|
|*4|   SORT JOIN                 |                 | 107| 1926|   4|00:00:01|
| 5|    VIEW                     |index$_join$_001 | 107| 1926|   3|00:00:01|
|*6|     HASH JOIN               |                 |    |     |    |        |
| 7|      INDEX FAST FULL SCAN|EMP_DEPARTMENT_IX| 107| 1926|   1|00:00:01|
| 8|      INDEX FAST FULL SCAN|EMP_NAME_IX      | 107| 1926|   1|00:00:01|
-------------------------------------------------------------------
```

Predicate Information (identified by operation id):
----
* 4 - access("EMPLOYEES"."DEPARTMENT_ID"="DEPARTMENTS"."DEPARTMENT_ID")
* 4 - filter("EMPLOYEES"."DEPARTMENT_ID"="DEPARTMENTS"."DEPARTMENT_ID")
* 6 - access(ROWID=ROWID)

Execution Plan After Change:

```
Plan Id       : 955
Plan Hash Value : 1473400139
```

```
-------------------------------------------------------------------
|Id|Operation                    |Name             |Rows|Bytes|Cost|Time     |
-------------------------------------------------------------------
| 0|SELECT STATEMENT             |                 | 106| 3604|   4|00:00:01|
| 1|  MERGE JOIN                 |                 | 106| 3604|   4|00:00:01|
| 2|   TABLE ACCESS BY           |DEPARTMENTS      |  27|  432|   2|00:00:01|
  |      INDEX ROWID
| 3|    INDEX FULL SCAN          |DEPT_ID_PK       |  27|     |   1|00:00:01|
|*4|   SORT JOIN                 |                 | 107| 1926|   2|00:00:01|
| 5|    VIEW                     |index$_join$_001 | 107| 1926|   2|00:00:01|
|*6|     HASH JOIN               |                 |    |     |    |        |
| 7|      INDEX FAST FULL SCAN|EMP_DEPARTMENT_IX| 107| 1926|   1|00:00:01|
| 8|      INDEX FAST FULL SCAN|EMP_NAME_IX      | 107| 1926|   1|00:00:01|
-------------------------------------------------------------------
```

Predicate Information (identified by operation id):
----
* 4 - access("EMPLOYEES"."DEPARTMENT_ID"="DEPARTMENTS"."DEPARTMENT_ID")
* 4 - filter("EMPLOYEES"."DEPARTMENT_ID"="DEPARTMENTS"."DEPARTMENT_ID")
* 6 - access(ROWID=ROWID)

In the foregoing example output, we can see the before and after execution statistics, as well as the before and after execution plans. We can also see an estimated workload impact and SQL impact percentages, which are very useful in order to see, at a quick glance, if there is a large impact by making the system change being made. In this example, we can see there would be a 1% change, and by looking at the execution plans, we see no difference. So, for the foregoing query, the database upgrade will essentially have minimal or no impact on the performance of our query. If you see an impact percentage of 10% or greater, it may mean more analysis and tuning need to occur to proactively tune the query or the system prior to making the change to your production environment. In order to get an accurate comparison, it is also recommended to export production statistics and import them into your test environment prior to performing the analysis using DBMS_SQLPA.

■ **Tip** In SQL Plus, remember to SET LONG and SET LONG CHUNKSIZE in order for output to be displayed properly.

How It Works

The SQL Performance Analyzer and the DBMS_SQLPA package can be used to analyze a SQL workload, which can be defined as any of the following:

- A SQL statement
- A SQL ID stored in cache
- A SQL tuning set (*see* Chapter 11 for information on SQL tuning sets)
- A SQL ID based on a snapshot from the Automatic Workload Repository (*see* Chapter 4 for more information)

In normal circumstances, it is easiest to gather information on a series of SQL statements, rather than one single statement. Getting information via Automatic Workload Repository (AWR) snapshots or via SQL tuning sets is the easiest way to get information for a series of statements. The AWR snapshots will contain information based on a specific time period, while SQL tuning sets will contain information on a specifically targeted set of SQL statements. Some of the possible key reasons to consider doing a "before and after" performance analysis include the following:

- Initialization parameter changes
- Database upgrades
- Hardware changes
- Operating system changes
- Application schema object additions or changes
- The implementation of SQL baselines or profiles

There is an abundance of information available for comparison. When reporting on the information gathered in your analysis, it may be beneficial to show only the output for SQL statements affected adversely by the system change. For instance, you may want to narrow down the information shown from the REPORT_ANALYSIS_TASK function to show information only on SQL statements such as the following:

- Those statements that show regressed performance
- Those statements with a changed execution plan
- Those statements that show errors in the SQL statements

It may be beneficial to flush the shared_pool and/or the buffer_cache prior to gathering information on each of your tasks, which will aid in getting the best possible information for comparison. Information on analysis tasks is stored in the data dictionary. You can reference any of the data dictionary views prefaced with "DBA_ADVISOR" to get information on performance analysis tasks you have created, executions performed, as well as execution statistics, execution plans, and report information. Refer to the Oracle PL/SQL Packages and Types Reference for your version of the database for a complete explanation of the DBMS_SQLPA package.

■ **Note**   The ADVISOR system privilege is needed to perform the analysis tasks using DBMS_SQLPA.

Tracing SQL Execution

Tracing session activity is at the heart of most SQL performance tuning exercises. Oracle provides a rich set of tools to trace SQL activity. This chapter introduces the Oracle SQL trace facility and shows you how to set up SQL tracing in your environment. Oracle provides numerous "events" that help you perform various types of traces.

Although there are several tracing methods available, Oracle now recommends that you use the DBMS_MONITOR package for most types of tracing. The chapter contains several recipes that explain how to use this package to generate traces. In addition, we show how to trace sessions by setting various Oracle events, the setting of which is often requested by Oracle Support. You'll learn how to trace a single SQL statement, a session as well as an entire instance, as well as how to trace parallel queries. There are recipes that show how to trace another user's session and how to use a trigger to start a session trace. You'll also learn how to trace the Oracle optimizer's execution path.

Oracle provides the TKPROF utility as well as the freely downloadable profiler named Oracle Trace Analyzer. This chapter shows how to use both of these profilers to analyze the raw trace files you generate.

10-1. Preparing Your Environment

Problem

You want to make sure your database is set up correctly for tracing SQL sessions.

Solution

You must do three things before you can start tracing SQL statements:

1. Enable timed statistics collection.

2. Specify a destination for the trace dump file.

3. Adjust the trace dump file size.

You can enable the collection of timed statistics by setting the timed_statistics parameter to true. Check the current value of this parameter first:

```
SQL> sho parameter statistics

NAME                                 TYPE         VALUE
------------------------------------ ----------- -----------
statistics_level                     string       TYPICAL
timed_statistics                     boolean      TRUE
SQL>
```

If the value of the timed_statistics parameter is false, you set it to true with the following statement.

```
SQL> alter system set timed_statistics=true scope=both;

System altered.

SQL>
```

You can also set this parameter at the session level with the following statement:

```
SQL> alter session set timed_statistics=true
```

You can find the location of the trace directory with the following command:

```
SQL> select name,value from v$diag_info
  2* where name='Diag Trace'
SQL> /

NAME                                 VALUE
----------------------------         ----------------------------------------

Diag Trace                           c:\app\ora\diag\rdbms\orcl1\orcl1\trace


SQL>
```

Tthe default value of the max_dump_file_size parameter is unlimited, as you can verify by issuing the following command:

```
SQL> sho parameter dump

NAME                                 TYPE         VALUE
------------------------------------ -----------  ----------
...
max_dump_file_size                   string       unlimited
...
SQL>
```

An unlimited dump file size means that the file can grow as large as the operating system permits.

How It Works

Before you can trace any SQL sessions, ensure that you've set the timed_statistics initialization parameter to true. If the value for this parameter is false, SQL tracing is disabled. Setting the timed_statistics parameter to true enables the database to collect statistics such as the CPU and elapsed times and store them in various dynamic performance tables. The default value of this parameter, starting with the Oracle 11.1.0.7.0 release, depends on the value of the initialization parameter statistics_level (default value is TYPICAL). If you set the statistics_level parameter to basic, the default value of the timed_statistics parameter is false. If you set statistics_level to the value typical or all, the default value of the timed_statistics parameter is true. The timed_statistics parameter is dynamic, meaning you don't have to restart the database to turn it on—you can turn this parameter on for the entire database without a significant overhead. You can also turn the parameter on only for an individual session.

When you trace a SQL session, Oracle generates a trace file that contains diagnostic data that's very useful in troubleshooting SQL performance issues. Starting with Oracle Database 11g, the database stores all diagnostic files under a dedicated diagnostic directory that you specify through the diagnostic_dest initialization parameter. The structure of the diagnostic directory is as follows:

<diagnostic_dest>/diag/rdbms/<dbname>/<instance>

The diagnostic directory is called the ADR Home. If your database name is prod1 and the instance name is prod1 as well, then the ADR home directory will be the following:

<diagnostic_dest>/diag/rdbms/prod1/prod1

The ADR home directory contains trace files in the <ADR Home>/trace subdirectory. Trace files usually have the extension .trc. You'll notice that several trace files have a corresponding trace map file with the .trm extension. The .trm files contain structural information about trace files, which the database uses for searching and navigation. You can view the diagnostic directory setting for a database with the following command:

```
SQL> sho parameter diagnostic_dest

NAME                                 TYPE         VALUE
------------------------------------ ------------ -----------
diagnostic_dest                      string       C:\APP\ORA
SQL>
```

The V$DIAG_INFO view shows the location of the various diagnostic directories, including the trace directory, which is listed in this view under the name Diag Trace. Although the new database diagnosability infrastructure introduced in Oracle Database 11g ignores the user_dump_dest initialization parameter, the parameter still exists and points to the same directory as the $ADR_BASE\diag\rdbms\<database>\<instance>\trace directory, as the following command shows:

```
SQL> show parameter user_dump_dest

NAME                    TYPE     VALUE
----------------------- ------   -------------------------------------
user_dump_dest          string   /u01/app/oracle/diag/rdbms/orc
                                            /orcl/trace

SQL>
```

In Oracle Database 12g, you don't have to set the max_dump_file_size parameter to specify the maximum size of a trace file.

10-2. Tracing a Specific SQL Statement

Problem

You want to trace a specific SQL statement, in order to find out where the database is spending its time during the execution of the statement.

Solution

In an Oracle 11.1 or higher release, you can use the enhanced SQL tracing interface to trace one or more SQL statements. Here are the steps to tracing a set of SQL statements.

1. Issue the `alter session set events` statement, as shown here, to set up the trace.

    ```
    SQL> alter session set events 'sql_trace level 12';

    Session altered.
    SQL>
    ```

2. Execute the SQL statements.

    ```
    SQL> select count(*) from sales;
    ```

3. Set tracing off.

    ```
    SQL> alter session set events 'sql_trace off';

    Session altered.

    SQL>
    ```

The previous example showed how to trace a SQL statement as a one-off operation. You can alternatively set up a trace for a specific SQL statement each time the instance executes the SQL statement. You can choose to trace specific SQL statements by specifying the SQL ID of a statement in the `alter session set events` statement. Here are the steps:

1. Find the SQL ID of the SQL statement by issuing this statement:

    ```
    SQL> select sql_id,sql_text
         from v$sql
         where sql_text='select sum(quantity_sold) from sales';

    SQL_ID                    SQL_TEXT
    ----------------          ------------------------------------
    fb2yu0p1kgvhr             select sum(quantity_sold) from sales

    SQL>
    ```

2. Set tracing on for the specific SQL statement whose SQL ID you've retrieved.

```
SQL> alter session set events 'sql_trace [sql:fb2yuOp1kgvhr] level 12';

Session altered.

SQL>
```

3. Execute the SQL statement.

```
SQL> select sum(quantity_sold) from sales;

SUM(QUANTITY_SOLD)
------------------
            918843
```

4. Turn off tracing.

```
SQL> alter session set events 'sql_trace[sql:fb2yuOp1kgvhr] off';

Session altered.

SQL>
```

You can trace multiple SQL statements by separating the SQL IDs with the pipe (|) character, as shown here:

```
SQL> alter session set events 'sql_trace [sql: fb2yuOp1kgvhr|4v433su9vvzsw]';
```

You can trace a specific SQL statement running in a different session by issuing an alter system set events statement:

```
SQL> alter system set events 'sql_trace[sql:fb2yuOp1kgvhr] level 12';

System altered.
SQL>
```

You can get the SQL ID for the statement by querying the V$SQL view as shown earlier in this recipe, or you can get it through the Oracle Enterprise Manager. Once the user in the other session completes executing the SQL statement, turn off tracing with the following command:

```
SQL> alter system set events 'sql_trace[sql:fb2yuOp1kgvhr] off';

System altered.

SQL>
```

How It Works

In Oracle Database 11g, you can set the Oracle event SQL_TRACE to trace the execution of one or more SQL statements. You can issue either an alter session or an alter system statement for tracing a specific SQL statement. Here's the syntax of the command:

```
alter session/system set events 'sql_trace [sql:<sql_id>|<sql_id>] ... event specification';
```

Even if you execute multiple SQL statements before you turn the tracing off, the trace file will show just the information pertaining to the SQL_ID or SQL_IDs you specify.

10.3. Enabling Tracing in Your Own Session
Problem

You want to trace your own session.

Solution

Ordinary users can use the DBMS_SESSION package to trace their sessions, as shown in this example:

```
SQL>execute dbms_session.session_trace_enable(waits=>true, binds=> false);
```

To disable tracing, the user must execute the session_trace_disable procedure, as shown here:

```
SQL> execute dbms_session.session_trace_disable();
```

How It Works

The DBMS_MONITOR package, which Oracle recommends for all tracing, is by default executable only by a user with the DBA role. You as an Oracle DBA can grant the execute privilege on the DBMS_MONITOR package to a user, and that'll let the user trace their own sessions using the DBMS_MONITOR package instead of the DBMS_SESSION package. And no matter the case, users can use the dbms_session.session_trace_enable procedure to trace their own session.

10-4. Finding the Trace Files
Problem

You'd like to find a way to easily identify your trace files.

Solution

Issue the following statement to set an identifier for your trace files, before you start generating the trace:

```
SQL> alter session set tracefile_identifier='MyTune1';
```

To view the most recent trace files the database has created, in Oracle Database 11.1 and newer releases, you can query the Automatic Diagnostic Repository (ADR) by executing the following command (see Chapter 5 for details on the adrci utility):

```
adrci> show tracefile -t
05-NOV-13 11:44:54  diag/rdbms/orcl/orcl/trace/orcl_ckpt_3047.trc
   05-NOV-13 11:50:06  diag/rdbms/orcl/orcl/trace/alert_orcl.log
   05-NOV-13 11:56:03  diag/rdbms/orcl/orcl/trace/orcl_tmon_3085.trc
```

```
   05-NOV-13 12:22:23  diag/rdbms/orcl/orcl/trace/orcl_vktm_3024.trc
   05-NOV-13 12:36:26  diag/rdbms/orcl/orcl/trace/orcl_mmon_3055.trc
adrci>
```

To find out the path to your current session's trace file, issue the following command:

```
SQL> select value from v$diag_info
     where name = 'Default Trace File';

VALUE
--------------------------------------------------------------
/u01/app/oracle/diag/rdbms/orcl/orcl/trace/orcl_ora_4287.trc

SQL>
```

To find all trace files for the current instance, issue the following query:

```
SQL> select value from v$diag_info where name = 'Diag Trace'
```

How It Works

Often, it's hard to find the exact trace file you're looking for, because there may be a bunch of other trace files in the trace directory, all with similar-looking file names. A best practice during SQL tracing is to associate your trace files with a unique identifier. Setting an identifier for the trace files you're going to generate makes it easy to identify the SQL trace files from among the many trace files the database generates in the trace directory.

You can confirm the value of the trace identifier with the following command:

```
SQL> sho parameter tracefile_identifier
NAME                                 TYPE        VALUE
------------------------------------ ----------- ---------------
tracefile_identifier                 string      MyTune1
SQL>
```

The column TRACEID in the V$PROCESS view shows the current value of the tracefile_identifier parameter as well. The trace file identifier you set becomes part of the trace file name, making it easy to pick the correct file name for a trace from among a large number of trace files in the trace directory. You can modify the value of the tracefile_identifier parameter multiple times for a session. The trace file names for a process will contain information to indicate that they all belong to the same process.

Once you set the tracefile_identifier parameter, the trace files will have the following format, where sid is the Oracle SID, pid is the process ID, and traceid is the value you've set for the tracefile_identifier initialization parameter.

```
sid_ora_pid_traceid.trc
```

10-5. Examining a Raw SQL Trace File

Problem

You want to examine a raw SQL trace file.

Solution

Open the trace file in a text editor to inspect the tracing information. Here are portions of a raw SQL trace generated by executing the dbms_monitor.session_trace_enable procedure:

```
PARSING IN CURSOR #3 len=490 dep=1 uid=85 oct=3 lid=85 tim=269523043683 hv=672110367
ad='7ff18986250' sqlid='bqasjasn0z5sz'

PARSE #3:c=0,e=647,p=0,cr=0,cu=0,mis=1,r=0,dep=1,og=1,plh=0,tim=269523043680
EXEC #3:c=0,e=1749,p=0,cr=0,cu=0,mis=1,r=0,dep=1,og=1,plh=3969568374,tim=269523045613
WAIT #3: nam='Disk file operations I/O' ela= 15833 FileOperation=2 fileno=4 filetype=2 obj#=-1
tim=269523061555
FETCH #3:c=0,e=19196,p=0,cr=46,cu=0,mis=0,r=1,dep=1,og=1,plh=3969568374,tim=269523064866
STAT #3 id=3 cnt=12 pid=2 pos=1 obj=0 op='HASH GROUP BY (cr=46 pr=0 pw=0 time=11 us cost=4 size=5317
card=409)'
STAT #3 id=4 cnt=3424 pid=3 pos=1 obj=89079 op='TABLE ACCESS  FULL DEPT (cr=16 pr=0 pw=0 time=246 us
cost=3 size=4251 card=327)'
```

As you can see from this excerpt of the raw trace file, you can glean useful information, such as parse misses, waits, and the execution plan of the SQL statement.

How It Works

The usual practice after getting a session trace file is to analyze it using a tool such as TKPROF. However, you can examine a trace file by visually reading the trace output. The main benefit in doing so is having the actual sequence of all the events that have happened during the course of the execution of a query. The raw trace files capture information for each of the following three steps of SQL statement processing:

Parse: During this stage, the database converts the SQL statement into an execution plan and checks for authorization and the existence of tables and other objects.

Execute: The database executes the SQL statement during this phase. For a SELECT statement, the execute phase identifies the rows the database must retrieve. The database modifies the data for DML statements such as insert, update, and delete.

Fetch: This step applies only for a SELECT statement. During this phase, the database retrieves the selected rows.

A SQL trace file will contain detailed statistics for each of the three phases of execution, in addition to wait event information. You usually format the raw trace files with a utility such as TKPROF. However, there are times when a raw trace file can show you useful information very quickly, by a simple scroll through the file. A locking situation is a good example where you can visually inspect a raw trace file. TKPROF doesn't provide you details about latches and locks (enqueues). If you suspect that a query was waiting on a lock, digging deep into a raw trace file shows you exactly where and why a query was waiting. In the WAIT line, the elapsed time (ela) shows the amount of time waited (in microseconds). In our example, elapsed wait time for "Disk file operations I/O" is 15,833 microseconds. Since 1 second = 1,000,000 microseconds, this is not a significant wait time. The raw trace file clearly shows if an I/O wait event, as is true in this case, or another type of wait event held up the query. If the query was waiting on a lock, you'll see something similar to the following: WAIT #2: nam='enqueue ela-300....

We've purposefully kept the discussion short in this recipe, because tools such as TKPROF and the Oracle Trace Analyzer provide you sophisticated diagnostic information by profiling the raw trace files.

10-6. Analyzing Oracle Trace Files

Problem

You want to know how to analyze an Oracle trace file.

Solution

There are multiple ways to interpret a SQL trace file. Here are the different approaches:

- Read the raw SQL trace file in a text editor.

- Use the Oracle-provided TKPROF (Trace Kernel Profiler) utility.

- Use Oracle Trace Analyzer, a free product you can download from Oracle Support.

- Use third-party tools.

How It Works

Getting a SQL trace is often the easy part—analyzing it is, of course, more of a task than collecting the trace. Sometimes, if you're particularly adept at it, you can certainly directly view the source trace file itself, but in most cases, you need a tool to interpret and profile the huge amount of data that a trace file can contain..

You can easily read certain trace files such as the trace file for event 10053 (which details the choices made by the optimizer in evaluating the execution path of a query), since the file doesn't contain any SQL execution statistics (such as parsing, executing, and fetching statistics), and no wait event analysis—it mostly shows how the cost-based optimizer (CBO) selected a particular execution plan.. However, for any SQL execution trace files, such as those you generate with the dbms_monitor.session_trace_enable procedure, a visual inspection of the trace file, while technically possible, is not only time-consuming but the raw data is not in a summary form and key events are often described in obscure ways. Therefore, using a profiler such as the TKPROF utility is really your best option.

The TKPROF utility is an Oracle-supplied profiling tool that most Oracle DBAs use on a routine basis. Recipes 10-7 and 10-8 show how to use TKPROF.

Oracle's Trace Analyzer is free (you have to download it from Oracle Support), easy to install and use, and produces clear reports with plenty of useful diagnostic information. You do have to install the tool first, but it takes only a few minutes to complete the installation. Thereafter, you just pass the name of the trace file to a script to generate the formatted output. Recipe 10-9 shows how to install and use the Oracle Trace Analyzer.

There are also third-party profiling tools that offer features not found in the TKPROF utility. Some of these tools generate pretty HTML trace reports and some include charts as well to help you visually inspect the details of the execution of the SQL statement that you've traced. Note that in order to use some of these products, you'll have to upload your trace files for analysis. If your trace files contain sensitive data or security information, this may not work for you.

10-7. Formatting Trace Files with TKPROF

Problem

You've traced a session, and you want to use TKPROF to format the trace file.

Solution

You run the TKPROF utility from the command line. Here's an example of a typical tkprof command for formatting a trace file.

```
$ tkprof user_sql_001.trc user1.prf explain=hr/hr table=hr.temp_plan_table_a sys=no
  sort=exeela,prsela,fchela
```

In the example shown here, the tkprof command takes the user_sql_001.trc trace file as input and generates an output file named user1.prf. The "How it Works" section of this recipe explains key optional arguments of the TKPROF utility.

How It Works

TKPROF is a utility that lets you format any extended trace files that you generate with the dbms_monitor.session_trace_enable procedure. You can use this tool to generate reports for analyzing results of the various types of SQL tracing explained in this chapter. You can run TKPROF on a single trace file or a set of trace files that you've concatenated with the trcsess utility. TKPROF shows details of various aspects of SQL statement execution, such as:

- SQL statement text
- SQL trace statistics
- Number of library cache misses during the parse and execute phases
- Execution plans for all SQL statements
- Recursive SQL calls

You can view a list of all the arguments you can specify issuing the tkprof command without any arguments, as shown here:

```
$ tkprof
Usage: tkprof tracefile outputfile [explain= ] [table= ]
              [print= ] [insert= ] [sys= ] [sort= ]
...
```

Here's a brief explanation of the important arguments you can specify with the tkprof command:

filename1: Specifies the name of the trace file

filename2: Specifies the formatted output file

waits: Specifies whether the output file should record a summary of the wait events; default is *yes*.

sort: By default, TKPROF lists the SQL statements in the trace file in the order they were executed. You can specify various options with the sort argument to control the order in which TKPROF lists the various SQL statements.

- prscpu: CPU time spent parsing

- prsela: Elapsed time spent parsing

- execpu: CPU time spent executing

- exeela: Elapsed time spent executing

- fchela: Elapsed time spent fetching

print: By default TKPROF will list all traced SQL statements. By specifying a value for the print option, you can limit the number of SQL statements listed in the output file.

sys: By default TKPROF lists all SQL statements issued by the user SYS, as well as recursive statements. Specify the value no for the sys argument to make TKPROF omit these statements.

explain: Writes execution plans to the output file; TKPROF connects to the database and issues explain plan statements using the username and password you provide with this parameter.

table: By default, TKPROF uses a table named PLAN_TABLE in the schema of the user specified by the explain parameter, to store the execution plans. You can specify an alternate table with the table parameter.

width: This is an integer that determines the output line widths of some types of output, such as the explain plan information.

10-8. Analyzing TKPROF Output

Problem

You've formatted a trace file with TKPROF, and you now want to analyze the TKPROF output file.

Solution

Invoke the TKPROF utility with the tkprof command as shown here:

```
c:\>tkprof orcl1_ora_6448_mytrace1.trc ora6448.prf explain=hr/hr sys=no sort=prsela,exeela,fchela

TKPROF: Release 11.2.0.1.0 - Development on Sat May 14 11:36:35 2011

Copyright (c) 1982, 2009, Oracle and/or its affiliates.  All rights reserved.

c:\app\ora\diag\rdbms\orcl1\orcl1\trace>
```

In this example, orcl1_ora_6448_mytrace1.trc is the trace file you want to format. The ora6448.prf file is the TKPROF output file. The "How it Works" section that follows shows how to interpret a TKPROF output file.

How It Works

In our example, there's only a single SQL statement. Thus, the sort parameters (prsecla, exeela, fchela) don't really matter, because they come into play only when TKPROF needs to list multiple SQL statements. Here's a brief description of the key sections in a TKPROF output file.

Header

The header section shows the trace file name, the sort options, and a description of the terms used in the output file.

```
Trace file: orcl1_ora_6448_mytrace1.trc
Sort options: prsela  exeela  fchela
********************************************************************************
count    = number of times OCI procedure was executed
cpu      = cpu time in seconds executing
elapsed  = elapsed time in seconds executing
disk     = number of physical reads of buffers from disk
query    = number of buffers gotten for consistent read
current  = number of buffers gotten in current mode (usually for update)
rows     = number of rows processed by the fetch or execute call
********************************************************************************
```

Execution Statistics

TKPPROF lists execution statistics for each SQL statement in the trace file. TKPROF lists the execution statistics for the three steps that are part of SQL statement processing: parse, execute, and fetch.

call	count	cpu	elapsed	disk	query	current	rows
Parse	1	0.01	0.03	0	64	0	0
Execute	1	0.00	0.00	0	0	0	0
Fetch	5461	0.29	0.40	0	1299	0	901
total	5463	0.31	0.43	0	1363	0	81901

The following is what the SQL execution statistics in the table stand for:

count: The number of times the database parsed, executed, or fetched this statement

cpu: The CPU time used for the parse/execute/fetch phases

elapsed: Total elapsed time (in seconds) for the parse/execute/fetch phases

disk: Number of physical block reads for the parse/execute/fetch phases

query: Number of data blocks read with logical reads from the buffer cache in consistent mode for the parse/fetch/execute phases (for a select statement)

current: Number of data blocks read and retrieved with logical reads from the buffer cache in current mode (for insert, update, delete, and merge statements)

rows: Number of fetched rows for a select statement or the number of rows inserted, deleted, or updated, respectively, for an insert, delete, update, or merge statement

Row Source Operations

The next section of the report shows the number of misses in the library cache, the current optimizer mode, and the row source operations for the query. Row source operations show the number of rows that the database processes for each operation such as joins or full table scans. It's important to note that the row source operation information shows the actual execution plan used by the SQL statement. The actual execution plan may differ from that showed by explain plan statemenet because of the following reasons:

- Optimizer stats, cursor sharing, bind variable peeking, and dynamic instance parameters all impact execution plans.

- EXPLAIN PLAN doesn't do "bind peeking" to glean the values of the bind variables used in a SQL statement.

- EXPLAIN PLAN doesn't check the library cache for an aleready parsed version of the SQL statement.

That's why it's often said that an explain plan may "lie" but not the actual trace of the execution.

```
Misses in library cache during parse: 1
Optimizer mode: ALL_ROWS
Parsing user id: 85   (HR)

Rows     Row Source Operation
-------  -----------------------------------------------------------------------
  81901  HASH JOIN  (cr=1299 pr=0 pw=0 time=3682295 us cost=22 size=41029632 card=217088)
   1728    TABLE ACCESS FULL DEPT (cr=16 pr=0 pw=0 time=246 us cost=6 size=96768 card=1728)
   1291    TABLE ACCESS FULL EMP (cr=1283 pr=0 pw=0 time=51213 us cost=14 size=455392 card=3424)
```

The "Misses in library cache during parse" indicates the number of hard parses during the parse and execute database calls. In the Row Source Operation column, the output includes several statistics for each row source operation. These statistics quantify the various types of work performed during a row source operation. The following is what the different statistics stand for (you may not see all of these for every query):

cr: Blocks retrieved through a logical read in the consistent mode (consistent read mode, also known as "query mode", means the data that's read as of a fixed point in time—more specifically, data as it existed when the query began).

pr: Number of blocks read through a physical disk read

pw: Number of blocks written with a physical write to a disk

time: Total time (in microseconds) spent processing the operation

cost: Estimated cost of the operation

size: Estimated amount of data (bytes) returned by the operation

card: Estimated number of rows returned by the operation

The Execution Plan

If you specified the explain parameter when issuing the tkprof command, you'll find an execution table showing the execution plan for each SQL statement.

```
Rows     Execution Plan
-------  ----------------------------------------
      0  SELECT STATEMENT   MODE: ALL_ROWS
  81901   HASH JOIN
   1728    TABLE ACCESS (FULL) OF 'DEPT' (TABLE)
   1291    TABLE ACCESS (FULL) OF 'EMP' (TABLE)
```

In our example, the execution plan shows that there were two full table scans and a hash join following it. It's important to understand the execution plan displayed here may not be the execution plan that is actually used to execute the statement. This is just like with the execution plan generated by autotrace and Explain Plan, which also might not be the actual execution plan used to execute the statement.

Wait Events

You'll see the wait events section only if you've specified waits=>true in your trace command. The wait events table summarizes waits during the trace period:

```
Elapsed times include waiting on following events:
  Event waited on                         Times      Max. Wait   Total Waited
                                          Waited
  ---------------------------------       ---------  ----------- -----------
SQL*Net message from client                  5461       2.95         62.81
db file sequential read                         1       0.05          0.05
  *************************************************************************
```

In this example, the SQL*Net message from client waits account for most of the waits, but these are usually idle waits. The "SQL *Net message from client" message means that the server has completed its work by returning the results requested by the client and is waiting for the client to give the server more work to perform. Even though "SQL*Net message from client" is classified as an idle wait, do pay attention to the average wait time for the client (and in theory, the network) side wait. If the average duration for this wait event is high, it could mean that the network link is slow. You should usually expect to see average network wait tiems between 0.00001 and 0.002 seconds.

A long, average wait time for "SQL*Net message from client" can also be due to the fact that the client receiving the data was very busy. If you see wait events such as the "db file sequential read event" (due to indexed reads) or the db file scattered read event (due to full table scans) with a significant number of waits (and/or total wait time), you need to investigate those wait events further.

Note that the TKPROF output doesn't show you information about any bind variables.

10-9. Analyzing Trace Files with Oracle Trace Analyzer
Problem

You want to use the Oracle Trace Analyzer to analyze trace files.

Solution

The Oracle Trace Analyzer, also known as TRCANLZR or TRCA, is a SQL trace profiling tool that's an alternative to the TKPROF utility. You must download the TRCA from Oracle Support. Once you download TRCA, unzip the files and install TRCA by executing the /trca/install/trcreate.sql script.

Once you install TRCA, you must log in as a user with the SYSDBA privilege to execute the tacreate.sql script. The tacreate.sql generates the formatted output files for any traces you've generated. The script asks you for information relating to the location of the trace files, the output file, and the tablespace where you want TRCA to store its data.

Here are the steps for installing and running TRCA.

1. Installing TRCA is straightforward, so we just show you a summary of the installation here:

```
SQL> @tacreate.sql
Uninstalling TRCA, please wait ...
TADOBJ completed.
SQL>
SQL> WHENEVER SQLERROR EXIT SQL.SQLCODE;
SQL> REM If this DROP USER command fails that means a session is connected wi
this user.
SQL> DROP USER trcanlzr CASCADE;
SQL> WHENEVER SQLERROR CONTINUE;
SQL>
SQL> SET ECHO OFF;
TADUSR completed.
TADROP completed.

Creating TRCA$ INPUT/BDUMP/STAGE Server Directories
...

TACREATE completed. Installation completed successfully.
SQL>
```

2. Set up tracing.

```
SQL> alter session set events '10046 trace name context forever, level 12';

System altered.

SQL>
```

3. Execute the SQL statement you want to trace.

```
SQL> select ...
```

4. Turn off tracing.

```
SQL> alter session set events '10046 trace name context off';
System altered.

SQL>
```

5. Run the /trca/run/trcanlzr script (START trcanlzr.sql) to profile the trace you've just generated. You must pass the trace file name as input to this script:

```
c:\trace\trca\trca\run>sqlplus hr/hr
SQL> START trcanlzr.sql orcl1_ora_7460_mytrace7.trc
Parameter 1:
Trace Filename or control_file.txt (required)
Value passed to trcanlzr.sql:
~~~~~~~~~~~~~~~~~~~~~~~~~~~~~~~
```

```
TRACE_FILENAME: orcl1_ora_7460_mytrace7.trc
Analyzing orcl1_ora_7460_mytrace7.trc
... analyzing trace(s) ...
Trace Analyzer completed.
Review first trcanlzr_error.log file for possible fatal errors.
  ...
   233387  08/14/2013 15:59   trca_e21106.html
   115885  08/14/2013 15:59   trca_e21106.txt
File trca_e21106.zip has been created
TRCANLZR completed.
SQL>
c:\trace\trca\trca\run>
```

You can now view the profiled trace data in text or HTML format—TRCA provides both of these in the ZIP file that it creates when it completes profiling the trace file. TRCA places the ZIP file in the directory from which you run the /trca/run/trcanlzr.sql script.

How It Works

Oracle Support Center of Expertise (CoE) provides the TRCA diagnostic tool. Although many DBAs are aware of the TRCA, few use it on regular basis. Some of us have used it in response to a request by Oracle Support. As you learned in the "Solution" section, the TRCA tool accepts a SQL trace generated by you and outputs a diagnostic report in both text and HTML formats. The TRCA tool also provides you a TKPROF report (it executes the tkprof command as part of its diagnostic data collection). Since TRCA provides a rich set of diagnostic information, consider using it instead of TKPROF.

Apart from the data normally collected by the TKPROF utility, TRCA also identifies expensive SQL statements and gathers their explain plans. It also shows the optimizer statistics and configuration parameters that have a bearing on the performance of the SQL statements in the trace.

■ **Tip** Use TRCA instead of TKPROF for analyzing your trace files—it provides you a wealth of diagnostic information, besides giving you a TKPROF output file as part of the bargain.

In our example, we used TRCA to format a trace file on the same system where we generated the trace. However, if you can't install TRCA in a production system, not to worry. TRCA can also analyze production traces using a different system. The details are in the trca_instructions HTML document, which is part of the TRCA download ZIP file.

Here are the major sections of a TRCA report, and as you can see already, the report offers a richer set of diagnostic information than that offered by TKPROF.

Summary: Provides a breakdown of elapsed time, response time broken down into CPU and non-idle wait time, and other response time-related information

Non-Recursive Time and Totals: Provides a breakdown of response time and elapsed time during the parse, execute, and fetch steps; the report also contains a table that provides total and average waits for each idle and non-idle wait event.

Top SQL: Provides detailed information about SQL statements that account for the most response time, elapsed time, and CPU time, as shown in the following extract from the report:

```
There are 2 SQL statements with "Response Time Accounted-for" larger than
threshold of 10.0% of the "Total Response Time Accounted-for".
These combined 2 SQL statements are responsible for a total of 99.3% of the
"Total Response Time Accounted-for".

There are 3 SQL statements with "Elapsed Time" larger than threshold of 10.0%
of the "Total Elapsed Time".
These combined 3 SQL statements are responsible for a total of 75.5% of the
"Total Elapsed Time".

There is only one SQL statement with "CPU Time" larger than threshold of
10.0% of the "Total CPU Time".
```

Individual SQL: This is a highly useful section, as it lists all SQL statements and shows their elapsed time, response time, and CPU time. It provides the hash values and SQL IDs of each statement.

SQL Self - Time, Totals, Waits, Binds and Row Source Plan: Shows parse, execute, and fetch statistics for each statement, similar to the TKPROF utility; it also shows the wait event breakdown (average and total times) for each statement. There's also a very nice explain plan for each statement, which shows the time and the cost of each execution step.

Tables and Indexes: Shows the number of rows, partitioning status, the sample size, and the last time the object was analyzed; for indexes, it additionally shows the clustering factor and the number of keys.

Summary: Shows I/O related wait (such as the db file sequential read event) information including average and total waits, for tables and indexes

Hot I/O Blocks: Shows the list of blocks with the largest wait time or times waited

Non-default Initialization Parameters: Lists all non-default initialization parameters

As this brief review of TRCA shows, it's a far superior tool than TKPROF. Besides, if you happen to love TKPROF reports, it includes them as well in its ZIP file. So, what are you waiting for? Download the TRCA and benefit from its rich diagnostic profiling of problem SQL statements.

10-10. Tracing a Parallel Query

Problem

You'd like to trace a parallel query.

Solution

You can get an event 10046 trace for a parallel query in the same way as you would for any other query. The only difference is that the 10046 event will generate as many trace files as the number of parallel query servers. Here's an example:

```
SQL>alter session set tracefile_identifier='MyTrace1';

SQL> alter session set events '10046 trace name context forever, level 12';
```

```
Session altered.

SQL> select /*+ full(sales) parallel (sales 6) */ count(quantity_sold) from
     sales;

COUNT(QUANTITY_SOLD)
--------------------
              918843

SQL> alter session set events '10046 trace name context off';

Session altered.

SQL>
```

You'll now see a total of seven trace files with the trace file identifier MyTrace1 in the trace directory. Depending on what you're looking for, you can analyze each of the trace files separately or consolidate them into one big trace file with the trcsess utility before analyzing it with TKPROF or another profiler such as the Oracle Trace Analyzer. You'll also find several files with the suffix .trm in the trace directory—you can ignore these files, as they are for use by the database.

How It Works

The only real difference between getting an extended trace for a single query and one for a parallel query is that you'll have multiple trace files, one for each parallel query server. When a user executes a parallel query, Oracle creates multiple parallel query processes to process the query, with each process getting its own session. That's the reason Oracle creates multiple trace files for a parallel query.

Once you turn off the trace, go to the trace directory and execute the following command to find all the trace files for the parallel query:

```
$ find . -name '*MyTrace1*'
```

The find command lists all the trace files for your parallel query (ignore the files ending with .trm in the trace directory). You can move the trace files to another directory and use the trcsess utility to consolidate those files, as shown here:

```
$ trcsess output=MyTrace1.trc clientid='px_test1' orcl1_ora_8432_mytrace1.trc orcl1_ora_8432_
mytrace2.trc
```

You're now ready to use the TKPROF utility to profile the parallel query.

When you issue a parallel query, the parallel execution coordinator/query coordinator (QC) controls the execution of the query. The parallel execution servers/slaves (QS) do the actual work. The parallel execution server *set* is the set of all the query servers that execute an operation. The query coordinator and each of the execution servers generate their own trace files. For example, if one of the slave processes waits for a resource, the database records the resulting wait events in that slave process's trace file but not in the query coordinator's trace file.

Note that if you're using a 10.2 or an older release, the trace files for the user process will be created in the user dump directory and the background processes (slaves) will generate trace files in the background dump directory. In 11.1 and newer databases, the trace files for both background and user processes are in the same directory (trace). You can find the trace file names by issuing the show tracefile -t command after invoking ADRCI or by querying the V$DIAG_INFO view from SQL*Plus.

10-11. Tracing Specific Parallel Query Processes

Problem

You want to trace one or more specific parallel query processes.

Solution

Identify the parallel query processes you want to trace with the following command.

```
SQL> select inst_id,p.server_name,
      p.status as p_status,
      p.pid as p_pid,
      p.sid as p_sid
    from  gv$px_process p
    order by p.server_name;
```

Let's say you decide to trace the processes p002 and p003. Issue the following alter system set events command to trace just these two parallel processes.

```
SQL> alter system set events 'sql_trace  {process: pname = p002 | p003}';
```

Once you're done tracing, turn off the trace by issuing the following command:

```
SQL> alter system set events 'sql_trace  {process: pname = p002 | p003} off';
```

How It Works

Tracing parallel processes is always tricky. One of the improvements made to the tracing infrastructure in the Oracle Database 11g release is the capability to trace a specific statement or a set of statements. This capability comes in handy when there are a large number of SQL statements being executed by a session and you're sure about the identity of the SQL statement whose execution you want to trace.

10-12. Tracing Parallel Queries in a RAC System

Problem

You're tracing a parallel query in a RAC environment but aren't sure in which instance the trace files are located.

Solution

Finding the trace files for the server (or thread or slave) processes is sometimes difficult in a RAC environment, because you aren't sure on which node or node(s) the database has created the trace files. Here are the steps to follow to make it easier to find the trace files on the different nodes.

1. Set the px_trace with an alter session command, to help identify the trace files, as shown here:

   ```
   SQL> alter session set tracefile_identifier='10046';
   SQL> alter session set  "_px_trace" = low , messaging;
   SQL> alter session set events '10046 trace name context forever,level 12';
   ```

2. Execute your parallel query.

    SQL> alter table bigsales (parallel 4);
    SQL> select count(*) from bigsales;

3. Turn all tracing off.

    ```
    SQL> alter session set events '10046 trace name context off';
    SQL> alter session set "_px_trace" = none;
    ```

Specifying px_trace will cause the query coordinator's trace file to include information about the slave processes that are part of the query and the instance each slave process belongs to. You can then retrieve the trace files from the instances listed in the query coordinator's trace file.

How It Works

The _px_trace (px trace) parameter is an undocumented, internal Oracle parameter that has existed since the 9.2 release. Once you run the trace commands as shown in the "Solution" section of this recipe, the trace file for the query coordinator (QC) process will show within it the name of each of the slave processes and the instances the processes have run on—for example:

```
Acquired 4 slaves on 1 instances avg height=4 in 1 set q serial:2049
        P000 inst 1 spid 7512
        P001 inst 1 spid 4088
        P002 inst 1 spid 7340
        P003 inst 1 spid 9256
```

In this case, you know that Instance 1 is where you must look to get the trace files for the slave processes P000, P001, P002, and P003. On Instance 1, in the ADR trace subdirectory, look for file names that contain the words P000 (or P001/P002/P003), to identify the correct trace files.

10-13. Consolidating Multiple Trace Files
Problem

You have generated multiple trace files for a session in order to tune performance, and you want to consolidate those files into a single trace file.

Solution

Use the trcsess command to merge multiple trace files into a single trace file. Here's a simple example:

```
c:\trace> trcsess output=combined.trc session=196.614 orcl1_ora_8432_mytrace1.trc orcl1_ora_8432_
mytrace2.trc
C:\trace>
```

The trcsess command shown here combines two trace files generated for a session into a single trace file. The session parameter identifies the session with a session identifier, consisting of the session index and session serial number, which you can get from the V$SESSION view.

How It Works

The trcsess utility is part of the Oracle database and helps by letting you consolidate multiple trace files during performance tuning and debugging exercises. Here's the syntax of the trcsess command:

```
trcsess [output=output_file_name]
        [session=session_id]
        [client_id=cleint_id]
        [service=service_name]
        [action=action_name]
        [module=module_name]
        [trace_files]
```

You must specify one of these five options when issuing the trcess command: session, client_id, service, action, and module. For example, if you issue the command in the following manner, the command includes all the trace files in the current directory for a session and combines them into a single file:

```
$ trcsess output=main.trc session=196.614
```

In our example, we specified the name of the consolidated trace file with the output option. If you don't specify the output option, trcsess prints the output to standard out. Once you use trcsess to combine the output of multiple trace files into one consolidated file, you can use the TKPROF utility to analyze the file, just as you'd do in the case of a single trace file.

10-14. Finding the Correct Session for Tracing

Problem

You want to initiate a session trace for a user from your own session, and you would like to find out the correct session to trace.

Solution

You must have the SID and the serial number for the user whose session you want to trace. You can find these from the V$SESSION view, of course, once you know the user's name. However, you must get several other details about the user's session to identify the correct session, since the user may have multiple sessions open. Use the following query to get the user's information:

```
SQL> select a.sid, a.serial#, b.spid, b.pid,
     a.username, a.osuser, a.machine
     from
     v$session a,
     v$process b
     where a.username IS NOT NULL
     and a.paddr=b.addr;
```

The query provides several attributes such as USERNAME, OSUSER, and MACHINE, which help you unambiguously select the correct session.

How It Works

You can't always rely on the first set of SID and serial number you manage to find for the user whose session you want to trace. Together, the SID and serial number uniquely identify a session. However, you may find multiple SID and serial number combinations for the same user, because your database may be using common user logins. Therefore, querying the V$SESSION view for other information such as OSUSER and MACHINE besides the SID and serial number helps to identify the correct user session.

V$SESSION view columns such as COMMAND, SERVER, LOGON_TIME, PROGRAM, and LAST_CALL_ET help identify the correct session to trace. The LAST_CALL_ET column stands for Elasped Time of the Last Call, and following is how Oracle documentation describes this column:

- If the session STATUS is currently ACTIVE, then the value represents the elapsed time (in seconds) since the session has become active.

- If the session STATUS is currently INACTIVE, then the value represents the elapsed time (in seconds) since the session has become inactive.

If you still can't find the correct session, you may want to join the V$SESSION and V$SQLAREA views to identify the correct session.

10-15. Tracing a SQL Session

Problem

You want to turn on SQL tracing for a session to diagnose a performance problem.

Solution

There are multiple ways to trace a session, but the Oracle-recommended approach is to use the DBMS_MONITOR package to access the SQL tracing facility. To trace a session, first identify the session using the SQL statement shown in Recipe 10-14 (the previous recipe).

Once you get the SID and SERIAL# from the query shown in Recipe 10-14, invoke the session_trace_enable procedure of the DBMS_MONITOR package, as shown here:

```
SQL> execute dbms_monitor.session_trace_enable(session_id=>138,serial_num=>242,
waits=>true,binds=>false);
PL/SQL procedure successfully completed.
SQL>
```

▪ **Caution** SQL tracing does impose an overhead on the database—you need to be very selective in tracing sessions in a production environment, as a trace can fill up a disk or affect CPU usage adversely.

In this example, we chose to trace the wait information as well, but it's optional. Once you execute this command, have the user execute the SQL statements that you're testing (in a dev or test environment). In a production environment, wait for a long enough period to make sure you've captured the execution of the SQL statements, before turning the tracing off. Invoke the session_trace_disable procedure to disable the SQL tracing for the session, as shown here:

```
SQL> execute dbms_monitor.session_trace_disable(138,242);
PL/SQL procedure successfully completed.
SQL>
```

Once you complete tracing the session activity, you can get the trace file for the session from the trace directory and use the TKPROF utility (or a different profiler) to get a report. To trace the current user session, use the following pair of commands:

```
SQL> execute dbms_monitor.session_trace_enable();
SQL> execute dbms_monitor.session_trace_disable();
```

How It Works

Tracing an entire session is expensive in terms of resource usage and you must do so only when you haven't identified a poorly performing SQL statement already. A session trace gathers the following types of information.

- Physical and logical reads for each statement that's running in the session
- CPU and elapsed times
- Number of rows processed by each statement
- Misses in the library cache
- Number of commits and rollbacks
- Row operations that show the actual execution plan for each statement
- Wait events for each SQL statement

You can specify the following parameters for the session_trace_enable procedure:

session_id: Identifies the session you want to trace (SID); if you omit this, your own session will be traced.

serial_num: Serial number for the session

waits: Set it to true if you want to capture wait information (default = false).

binds: Set it to true to capture bind information (default=false).

plan_stat: Determines the frequency with which the row source statistics (execution plan and execution statistics) are dumped

All the parameters for the session_trace_enable procedure are self-evident, except the plan_stat parameter. You can set the following values for this parameter:

never: The trace file won't contain any information about row source operations.

first_execution (same as setting the plan_stat parameter to the value null): Row source information is written once, after the first execution of a statement.

all_executions: Execution plan and execution statistics are written for each execution of the cursor, instead of only when the cursor is closed.

Since an execution plan for a statement can change during the course of a program run, you may want to set the plan_stat parameter to the value all_executions if you want to capture all possible execution plans for a statement.

10-16. Tracing a Session by Process ID
Problem

You want to identify and trace a session using an operating system process ID.

Solution

Execute the alter session (or alter system) set events command to trace a session by its operating system process ID, which is shown by the SPID column in the V$PROCESS view. The general format of this command is as follows:

```
alter system set events 'sql_trace {process:pid}'
```

Here are the steps to tracing a session by its OS PID.

1. Get the OS process ID by querying the V$PROCESS view.

   ```
   SQL> select spid,pname from v$process;
   ```

2. Once you identify the SPID of the user, issue the following statement to start the trace for that session:

   ```
   SQL> alter system set events 'sql_trace {process:2714}';
   Session altered.
   SQL>
   ```

3. Turn off tracing the following way:

   ```
   SQL> alter system set events 'sql_trace {process:2714} off';
   Session altered.
   SQL>
   ```

4. You can also execute the set events command in the following manner, to trace two processes at once:

   ```
   SQL> alter system set events 'sql_trace {process:2714|2936}';
   System altered.
   SQL> alter system set events 'sql_trace {process:2714|2936} off';
   System altered.
   SQL>
   ```

When you trace tow processes simultaneously, Oracle generates two separate trace files, one for each process, as shown here:

```
orcl1_ora_2714.trc
orcl1_ora_2936.trc
```

How It Works

The `alter system set events` command allows you to trace a process by specifying the process ID (PID), process name (PNAME), or the Oracle Process ID (ORAPID). Here's the syntax of the command:

```
alter session set events 'sql_trace {process : pid = <pid>, pname = <pname>,
orapid = <orapid>} rest of event specification'
```

The V$PROCESS view contains information about all currently active processes. In the V$PROCESS view, the following columns help you identify the three process-related values:

```
PID: the Oracle process identifier
SPID: the Operating System process identifier
PNAME: name of the process
```

In this recipe, we showed how to generate a trace file using the OS process identifier (SPID column in the V$PROCESS view). You can use the general syntax shown here to generate a trace using the PID or the process name.

10-17. Tracing Multiple Sessions
Problem

You want to trace multiple SQL sessions that belong to a single user.

Solution

You can trace multiple sessions that belong to a user by using the `client_id_trace_enable` procedure from the DBMS_MONITOR package. Before you can execute the `dbms_monitor.client_id_trace_enable` procedure, you must set the `client_identifier` for the session by using the DBMS_SESSION package, as shown here:

```
SQL> execute dbms_session.set_identifier('MySQLTune1')
```

Once you set the client identifier as shown here, the `client_identifier` column in the V$SESSION view is populated. You can confirm the value of the `client_identifier` column by executing the following statement:

```
SQL> select sid, serial#,username from v$session where client_identifier='MySQLTune1';
```

Now you can execute the `dbms_monitor.client_id_trace_enable` procedure:

```
SQL> execute dbms_monitor.client_id_trace_enable(client_id=>'SH', waits=>true, binds=>false);
```

You can disable the trace with the following command:

```
SQL> execute dbms_monitor.client_id_trace_disable(client_id=>'SH');
```

How It Works

Setting the `client_identifier` column lets you enable the tracing of multiple sessions, when several users may be connecting as the same Oracle user, especially in applications that use connection pools. The `client_id_trace_enable` procedure collects statistics for all sessions with a specific client ID. Note that the `client_id` that you must specify doesn't have to belong to a currently active session. By default, the waits and binds parameters are set to false and you can set the tracing of both waits and binds by adding those parameters when you execute the client_id_trace_enable procedure:

```
SQL> exec dbms_monitor.client_id_trace_enable('SH',true,true);

PL/SQL procedure successfully completed.
```

You can query the DBA_ENABLED_TRACES view to find the status of a trace that you executed with a client identifier. In this view, the column TRACE_TYPE shows the value CLIENT_ID and the PRIMARY_ID shows the value of the client identifier.

```
SQL> select trace_type, primary_id,waits,binds from dba_enabled_traces;

TRACE_TYPE      PRIMARY_ID        WAITS     BINDS
------------    ---------------   --------  --------------
CLIENT_ID       SH                TRUE      TRUE
```

10-18. Tracing an Instance or a Database
Problem

You want to trace the execution of all SQL statements in the entire instance or database.

Solution

Use the dbms_monitor.database_trace_enable procedure to trace a specific instance or an entire database. Issue the following pair of commands to start and stop tracing for an *individual instance*.

```
SQL> execute dbms_monitor.database_trace_enable(instance_name=>'instance1');
SQL> execute dbms_monitor.database_trace_disable(instance_name=>'instance1');
```

You can optionally specify the waits and binds attributes. The following commands enable and disable SQL tracing at the *database level*:

```
SQL> execute dbms_monitor.database_trace_enable();
SQL> execute dbms_monitor.database_trace_disable();
```

You can also set the sql_trace initialization parameter to true to turn on and turn off SQL tracing, but this parameter is deprecated. Oracle recommends that you use the dbms_monitor (or the dbms_session) package for SQL tracing.

How It Works

Obviously, instance-level and database-level SQL tracing is going to impose a serious overhead and may well turn out to be another source of performance problems! It's possible for background processes to continue writing to their trace files until the trace files reach their maximum size, the directory containing the trace files exhausts all the space allocated to it, or until you bounce the database. This is so because even after you disable this type of tracing, background processes may keep writing to the trace files. You normally don't ever have to do this—use the session-level tracing instead to identify performance problems. If you must trace an entire instance, because you don't know from which session a query may be executed, turn off tracing as soon as possible to reduce the overhead.

10-19. Generating an Event 10046 Trace for a Session

Problem

You want to get an Oracle event 10046 trace for a session.

Solution

You can get an Oracle event 10046 trace, also called an extended trace, by following these steps:

1. Set your trace file identifier.

    ```
    SQL> alter session set tracefile_identifier='My_Trace';
    ```

2. Issue the following statement to start the trace.

    ```
    SQL> alter session set events '10046 trace name context forever, level 12'
    ```

3. Execute the SQL statement(s) that you want to trace.

    SQL> select sum(amount_sold) from sales;

4. Turn tracing off with the following command:

    ```
    SQL> alter session set events '10046 trace name context off';
    ```

You'll find the trace dump file in the trace directory that's specified by the diagnostic_dest parameter ($DIAG_HOME/rdbms/db/inst/trace). You can analyze this trace file with TKPROF or another utility such as the Oracle Trace Analyzer.

How It Works

Here's what the various keywords in the syntax for setting a 10046 trace mean:

set events: Sets a specific Oracle event, in this case, the event 10046

10046: Specifies when an action should be taken

trace: The database must take this action when the event (10046) occurs.

name: Indicates the type of dump or trace

context: Specifies that Oracle should generate a context-specific trace; if you replace context with errorstack, the database will not trace the SQL statement. It dumps the error stack when it hits the 10046 event.

forever: Specifying the keyword forever tells the database to invoke the action (trace) every time the event (10046) is invoked, until you disable the 10046 trace. If you omit the keyword forever, the action is invoked just once, following which the event is automatically disabled.

level 12: Specifies the trace level—in this case, it captures both bind and wait information.

While the Oracle event 10046 has existed for several years, this trace is identical to the trace you can generate with the session_trace_enable procedure of the DBMS_MONITOR package:

```
SQL> execute dbms_monitor.session_trace_enable(session_id=>99,
serial_num=>88,waits=>true,binds=>true);
```

Both the 10046 event and the dbms_monitor.session_trace_enable procedure shown here generate identical tracing information, called extended tracing because the trace includes wait and bind variable data.

If you aren't using the new diagnostic infrastructure (ADR) introduced in Oracle Database 11g, make sure you set the dump file size to the value unlimited, as the 10046 trace often produces very large trace files, and the database will truncate the dump file if there isn't enough space in the trace dump directory.

The level of tracing you specify for the 10046 trace determines which types of information is gathered by the trace. The default level is 1, which collects basic information. Level 4 allows you to capture the bind variable values, which are shown as :bi, :b2, and so on. You can see the actual values that Oracle substitutes for each of the bind variables. Level 8 provides all the information from a Level 1 trace plus details about all the wait events during the course of the execution of the SQL query. A Level 12 trace is a combination of the Level 4 and Level 8 traces, meaning it'll include both bind variable and wait information. Level 16 is new in Oracle Database 11g and provides STAT line dumps for each execution of the query. Note that this is the same as setting the value all_executions for the plan_level parameter when you trace with the dbms_monitor.session_trace_enable procedure.

■ **Tip** If the session doesn't close cleanly before you disable tracing, your trace file may not include important trace information.

While getting a 10046 trace and analyzing it does provide valuable information regarding the usage of bind variables and the wait events, you need to be careful about when to trace sessions. If the instance as a whole is poorly performing, your tracing might even make performance worse due to overhead imposed by running the trace. In addition, it takes time to complete the trace, run it through TKPROF or some other profiler, and go through the dozens of SQL statements in the report. Here is a general strategy that has worked for us in our own work:

If you're diagnosing general performance problems, a good first step would be to get an AWR report, ideally taking several snapshots spaced 1–15 minutes apart. Often, you can identify the problem from a review of the AWR report. The report will highlight things such as inefficient SQL statements, contention of various types, memory issues, latching, and full table scans that are affecting performance. You can get all this information without running a 10046 trace.

Run a 10046 trace when a user reports a problem and you can't identify a problem through the AWR reports. If you've clearly identified a process that is performing poorly, you can trace the relevant session. You can also run this trace in a development environment to help developers understand the query execution details and tune their queries.

10-20. Generating an Event 10046 Trace for an Instance

Problem

You want to trace a problem SQL query, but you can't identify the session in advance. You would like to trace all SQL statements executed by the instance.

Solution

You can turn on tracing at the instance level with the following `alter system` command, after connecting to the instance you want to trace.

```
SQL> alter system set events '10046 trace name context forever,level 12';
```

The previous command enables the tracing of all sessions that start after you issue the command—it won't trace sessions that are already connected.

You disable the trace by issuing the following command:

```
SQL> alter system set events '10046 trace name context off';
```

This command disables tracing for all sessions.

How It Works

Instance-wide tracing helps in cases where you know a problem query is running, but there's no way to identify the session ahead of time. Make sure that you enable instance-wide tracing only when you have no other alternative, and turn it off as soon as you capture the necessary diagnostic information. Any instance-wide tracing is going to not only generate very large trace files in a busy environment but also contribute significantly to the system workload.

As in the case of Recipe 10-18, it's possible for background processes to continue writing to their trace files until the trace files reach their maximum size, the directory containing the trace files exhausts all the space allocated to it, or until you bounce the database. This is so because even after you disable this type of tracing, background processes may keep writing to the trace files.

10-21. Setting a Trace in a Running Session

Problem

You want to set a trace in a session, but the session has already started.

■ **Note**   A user who phones to ask for help with a long-running query is a good example of a case in which you might want to initiate a trace in a currently executing session. Some business-intelligence queries, for example, run for dozens of minutes, even hours, so there is time to initiate a trace mid-query and diagnose a performance problem.

Solution

You can set a trace in a running session using the operating system process ID (SPID), with the help of the oradebug utility. Once you identify the PID of the session you want to trace, issue the following commands to trace the session.

```
SQL> connect / as sysdba
SQL> oradebug setospid <SPID>
SQL> oradebug unlimit
SQL> oradebug event 10046 trace name context forever,level 12
SQL> oradebug event 10046 trace name context off
```

In the example shown here, we specified Level 12, but as with the 10046 trace you set with the `alter session` command, you can specify the lower tracing levels 4 or 8.

How It Works

The oradebug utility comes in handy when you can't access the session you want to trace, or when the session has already started before you can set tracing. oradebug lets you attach to the session and start the SQL tracing. If you aren't sure about the operating system PID (or SPID) associated with an Oracle session, you can find it with the following query.

```
SQL> select p.PID,p.SPID,s.SID
  2  from v$process p,v$session s
  3  where s.paddr = p.addr
  4* and s.sid = &SESSION_ID
```

oradebug is only a facility that allows you to set tracing—it's not a tracing procedure by itself. The results of the 10046 trace you obtain with oradebug are identical to those you obtain with a normal event 10046 trace command.

In the example shown in the "Solution" section, we use the OS PID of the Oracle users. You can also specify the Oracle Process Identifier (PID) to trace a session instead of the OS PID.

```
SQL> connect / as sysdba
SQL> oradebug setorapid 9834
SQL> oradebug unlimit
SQL> oradebug event 10046 trace name context forever,level 12
```

In an Oracle RAC environment, as is the case with all other types of Oracle tracing, make sure you connect to the correct instance before starting the trace. As an alternative to using oradebug, you can use the dbms_system.set_sql_trace_in_session procedure to set a trace in a running session. Note that DBMS_SYSTEM is an older package, and the recommended way to trace sessions starting with the Oracle Database 10g release is to use the DBMS_MONITOR package.

10-22. Enabling Tracing in a Session After a Login
Problem

You want to trace a user's session, but that session starts executing queries immediately after it logs in.

Solution

If a session immediately begins executing a query after it logs in, it doesn't give you enough time to get the session information and start tracing the session. In cases like this, you can create a *logon trigger* that automatically starts tracing the session once the session starts. Here is one way to create a logon trigger to set up a trace for sessions created by a specific user:

```
SQL> create or replace trigger trace_my_user
  2    after logon on database
  3    begin
  4      if user='SH' then
  5      dbms_monitor.session_trace_enable(null,null,true,true);
  6      end if;
  8*   end;
SQL> /

Trigger created.

SQL>
```

How It Works

Often, you find it hard to trace session activity because the session already starts executing statements before you can set up the trace. This is especially so in a RAC environment, where it is harder for the DBA to identify the instance and quickly set up tracing for a running session. A logon trigger is the perfect solution for such cases. Note that in a RAC environment, the database generates the trace files in the trace directory of the instance to which a user connected.

A logon trigger for tracing sessions is useful for tracing SQL statements issued by a specific user, by setting the trace as soon as the user logs in. From that point on, the database traces all SQL statements issued by that user. Make sure you disable the tracing and drop the logon trigger once you complete tracing the SQL statements you are interested in. Remember to revoke the alter session privilege from the user as well.

10-23. Tracing the Optimizer's Execution Path
Problem

You want to trace the cost-based optimizer (CBO) to examine the execution path for a SQL statement.

Solution

You can trace the optimizer's execution path by setting the Oracle event 10053. Here are the steps.

1. Set the trace identifier for the trace file.

   ```
   SQL> alter session set tracefile_identifier='10053_trace1'
   Session altered.
   SQL>
   ```

2. Issue the alter session set events statement to start the trace.

   ```
   SQL> alter session set events '10053 trace name context forever,level 1';
   Session altered.
   SQL>
   ```

3. Execute the SQL statement whose execution path you want to trace.

    ```
    SQL> select * from users
      2  where user_id=88 and
      3  account_status='OPEN'
      4  and username='SH';
    ...
    SQL>
    ```

4. Turn the tracing off.

    ```
    SQL> alter session set events '10053 trace name context off';
    Session altered.
    SQL>
    ```

You can examine the raw trace file directly to learn how the optimizer went about its business in selecting the execution plan for the SQL statement.

How It Works

An event 10053 trace gives you insight into the way the optimizer does its job in selecting what it estimates to be the optimal execution plan for a SQL statement. For example, you may wonder why the optimizer didn't use an index in a specific case—the event 10053 trace shows you the logic used by the optimizer in skipping that index. The optimizer considers the available statistics for all objects in the query and evaluates various join orders and access paths. The event 10053 trace also reveals all the evaluations performed by the optimizer and how it arrived at the best join order and the best access path to use in executing a query.

You can set either Level 1 or Level 2 for the event 10053 trace. Level 2 captures the following types of information:

- Column statistics

- Single access paths

- Table joins considered by the optimizer

- Join costs

- Join methods considered by the optimizer

A Level 1 trace includes all the foregoing, plus a listing of all the default initialization parameters used by the optimizer. You'll also find detailed index statistics used by the optimizer in determining the best execution plan. The trace file captures the amazing array of statistics considered by the cost optimizer and explains how the CBO creates the execution plan. Here are some of the important things you'll find in the CBO trace file.

- List of all internal optimizer-related initialization parameters

- Peeked values of the binds in the SQL statement

- Final query after optimizer transformations

- System statistics (CPUSPEEDNW, IOTFRSPEED, IOSEEKTIM, MBRC)

- Access path analysis for all objects in the query

- Join order evaluation

Unlike a raw 10046 event trace file, a 10053 event trace file is quite easy (and interesting) to read. You must understand here that a 10053 trace will be generated only when a hard parse is required. Bear in mind that the trace files might at times be hard to follow when several tables with multiple indexes are analyzed during optimization. Also, the contents of a 10053 event trace file are subject to change from one Oracle Database release to the next.

Here are key excerpts from our trace file. The trace file shows the cost-based query transformations applied by the optimizer:

```
OBYE:   Considering Order-by Elimination from view SEL$1 (#0)
OBYE:      OBYE performed.
```

In this case, the optimizer eliminated the order by clause in our SQL statement. After performing all its transformations, the optimizer arrives at the "final query after transformations," which is shown here:

```
select channel_id,count(*)
from sh.sales
group by channel_id
```

Next, the output file shows the access path analysis for each of the tables in your query.

```
Access path analysis for SALES
****************************************
SINGLE TABLE ACCESS PATH
  Single Table Cardinality Estimation for SALES[SALES]
  Table: SALES  Alias: SALES
    Card: Original: 918843.000000  Rounded: 918843  Computed: 918843.00  Non Adjusted: 918843.00
  Access Path: TableScan
    Cost:  495.47  Resp: 495.47  Degree: 0
      Cost_io: 481.00  Cost_cpu: 205554857
      Resp_io: 481.00  Resp_cpu: 205554857
  Access Path: index (index (FFS))
    Index: SALES_CHANNEL_BIX
    resc_io: 42.30  resc_cpu: 312277
    ix_sel: 0.000000  ix_sel_with_filters: 1.000000
  Access Path: index (FFS)
    Cost:  42.32  Resp: 42.32  Degree: 1
      Cost_io: 42.30  Cost_cpu: 312277
      Resp_io: 42.30  Resp_cpu: 312277
  ****** trying bitmap/domain indexes ******
  Access Path: index (FullScan)
    Index: SALES_CHANNEL_BIX
    resc_io: 75.00  resc_cpu: 552508
    ix_sel: 1.000000  ix_sel_with_filters: 1.000000
    Cost: 75.04  Resp: 75.04  Degree: 0
  Access Path: index (FullScan)
    Index: SALES_CHANNEL_BIX
    resc_io: 75.00  resc_cpu: 552508
    ix_sel: 1.000000  ix_sel_with_filters: 1.000000
    Cost: 75.04  Resp: 75.04  Degree: 0
  Bitmap nodes:
    Used SALES_CHANNEL_BIX
      Cost = 75.038890, sel = 1.000000
  Access path: Bitmap index - accepted
    Cost: 75.038890 Cost_io: 75.000000 Cost_cpu: 552508.000000 Sel: 1.000000
    Believed to be index-only
```

```
****** finished trying bitmap/domain indexes ******
******** Begin index join costing ********
******** End index join costing ********
  Best:: AccessPath: IndexFFS
  Index: SALES_CHANNEL_BIX
        Cost: 42.32  Degree: 1  Resp: 42.32  Card: 918843.00  Bytes: 0
```

In this case, the optimizer evaluates various access paths and shows the optimal access path as an Index Fast Full Scan (IndexFFS).

The optimizer then considers various permutations of join orders and estimates the cost for each join order it considers:

```
Considering cardinality-based initial join order.
Join order[1]:  SALES[SALES]#0
GROUP BY sort
GROUP BY adjustment factor: 1.000000
      Total IO sort cost: 0      Total CPU sort cost: 834280255
      Best so far:  Table#: 0  cost: 101.0459  card: 918843.0000  bytes: 2756529
Number of join permutations tried: 1
GROUP BY adjustment factor: 1.000000
GROUP BY cardinality:  4.000000, TABLE cardinality:  918843.000000
      Total IO sort cost: 0      Total CPU sort cost: 834280255
  Best join order: 1
  Cost: 101.0459  Degree: 1  Card: 918843.0000  Bytes: 2756529
```

As our brief review of the 10053 trace output shows, you can get answers to puzzling questions such as why exactly the optimizer chose a certain join order or an access path, and why it ignored an index. The answers are all there!

10-24. Generating Automatic Oracle Error Traces
Problem

You want to create an automatic error dump file when a specific Oracle error occurs.

Solution

You can create error dumps to diagnose various problems in the database by specifying the error number in a hanganalyze or systemstate command. For example, diagnosing the causes for deadlocks is often tricky. You can ask the database to dump a trace file when it hits the ORA-00060: Deadlock detected error. To do this, specify the event number 60 with the hanganalyze or the systemstate command:

```
SQL> alter session set events '60 trace name hanganalyze level 4';

Session altered.

SQL> alter session set events '60 trace name systemstate level 266';

Session altered.

SQL>
```

Both of these commands will trigger the automatic dumping of diagnostic data when the database next encounters the ORA-00060 error. You can use the same technique in an Oracle RAC database. For example, you can issue the following command to generate automatic hanganalyze dumps:

```
SQL>alter session set events '60 trace name hanganalyze_global level 4';
```

This alter session statement invokes the hanganalyze command in any instance in which the database encounters the ORA-00060 error.

Although we showed how to set the error trace event at the session level, it would be better, for some hard-to-catch unfortunate conditions, to set this trace event at the system level. It isn't always easy to reproduce a problem in one's session.

How It Works

Setting event numbers for an error will ensure that when the specified error occurs the next time, Oracle automatically dumps the error information for you. This comes in very handy when you're diagnosing an error that occurs occasionally and getting a current systemstate dump or a hanganalyze dump is unhelpful. Some events such as deadlocks have a text alias, in which case you can specify the alias instead of the error number. For the ORA-00060 error, the text alias is deadlock, and so you can issue the following command for tracing the error:

```
SQL> alter session set events 'deadlock trace name systemstate level 266';

Session altered.

SQL>
```

Similarly, you can use text aliases wherever they're available for other error events.

10-25. Tracing a Background Process
Problem

You want to trace a background process.

Solution

If you aren't sure of the correct name of the background process you want to trace, you can list the exact names of all background processes by issuing the following command:

```
SQL> select name,description from v$bgprocess;
```

Suppose you want to trace the dbw0 process. Issue the following commands to start and stop the trace.

```
SQL> alter system set events 'sql_trace {process:pname=dbw0}';
System altered.
SQL> alter system set events 'sql_trace {process:pname=dbw0} off';
System altered.
SQL>
```

You can trace two background processes at the same time by specifying the pipe (|) character to separate the process names:

```
SQL> alter system set events 'sql_trace {process:pname=dbw0|dbw1}';
System altered.

SQL> alter system set events 'sql_trace {process:pname=dbw0|dbw1} off';
System altered.
SQL>
```

How It Works

Oracle lets you to issue an `alter system set events` command to trace a process (or a set of processes) or a specific SQL statement (or a set of statements).This recipe shows how to trace a background process by specifying the process name.

As in the case of Recipes 10-18 and 10-20, it's possible for background processes to continue writing to their trace files until the trace files reach their maximum size, the directory containing the trace files exhausts all the space allocated to it, or until you bounce the database. This is so because even after you disable this type of tracing, background processes may keep writing to the trace files.

10-26. Enabling Oracle Listener Tracing
Problem

You want to trace the Oracle listener, in order to diagnose and troubleshoot user connection issues.

Solution

To generate a trace for the Oracle listener, add the following two lines in the `listener.ora` file, which is by default located in the `$ORACLE_HOME/network/admin` directory.

```
trace_level_listener=support
trace_timestamp_listener=true
```

You can optionally specify a file name for the listener trace by adding the line `trace_file_listener=<file_name>`. Reload the listener with the `lsnrctl reload` command, and then check the status of the listener with the `lsnrctl status` command. You should see the trace file listed in the output:

```
C:\>lsnrctl reload

The command completed successfully

C:\>lsnrctl status
...

Listener Parameter File   C:\app\ora\product\11.2.0\dbhome_1\network\admin\liste
ner.ora
Listener Log File         c:\app\ora\diag\tnslsnr\MIROPC61\listener\alert\log.xm
```

```
1
Listener Trace File           c:\app\ora\diag\tnslsnr\MIROPC61\listener\trace\ora_86
40_9960.trc
...
  Instance "orcl1", status READY, has 1 handler(s) for this service...
Service "orcl1XDB.miro.local" has 1 instance(s).
  Instance "orcl1", status READY, has 1 handler(s) for this service...
The command completed successfully

C:\>
```

The output shows the listener trace file you've just configured.

■ **Note**   This and the next recipe don't have anything to with SQL tracing, which is the focus of this chapter. However, we thought we'd add these two recipes because they're useful, and there's no better chapter to put them in!

How It Works

You can specify various levels for listener tracing. You can specify Level 4 (user) for user trace information and Level 10 (admin) for administrative trace information. Oracle Support may request Level 16 (support) for troubleshooting Oracle listener issues.

If you can't reload or restart the listener, you can configure the tracing dynamically by issuing the following commands:

```
C:>lsnrctl

LSNRCTL> set current_listener listener
Current Listener is listener
LSNRCTL> set trc_level 16
Connecting to (DESCRIPTION=(ADDRESS=(PROTOCOL=IPC)(KEY=EXTPROC
listener parameter "trc_level" set to support
The command completed successfully
LSNRCTL>
```

You can turn off listener tracing by issuing the command set trc_level off, which is the default value for this parameter:

```
LSNRCTL> set trc_level off
Connecting to (DESCRIPTION=(ADDRESS=(PROTOCOL=IPC)(KEY=EXTPROC1521)))
LISTENER parameter "trc_level" set to off
The command completed successfully
LSNRCTL>
```

You'll notice that the lsnrctl status command doesn't show the listener trace file any longer. Note that the trace file for the listener will not be in the $ORACLE_HOME\rdbms\network\admin directory. Rather, the database stores the trace file in the diag directory of the database diagnosability infrastructure (ADR), under the tnslsnr directory, as shown here:

```
Listener Trace File        c:\app\ora\diag\tnslsnr\myhost\listener\trace\ora_86
                           40_9960.trc
```

10-27. Setting Archive Tracing for Data Guard

Problem

You want to trace the creation and transmission of the archive logs in a Data Guard environment.

Solution

You can trace the archive logs on either the primary or the standby database by setting the log_archive_trace initialization parameter:

```
log_archive_trace=trace_level(integer)
```

For example, if you want to trace the archive log destination activity, you set tracing at level 8, as shown here:

```
SQL> alter system set log_archive_trace=8
```

By default the log_archive_trace parameter is set to zero, meaning archive log tracing is disabled.

How It Works

Although archive log tracing is disabled when you leave the log_archive_trace parameter at its default level of zero, the database will still record error conditions in the trace files and the alert log. When you set the log_archive_trace parameter to a non-zero value, Oracle writes the appropriate trace output generated by the archive log process to an audit trail. The audit trail is the same trace directory as that for the SQL trace files—the *trace* directory in the ADR (this is the same as the user dump directory specified by the user_dump_dest initialization parameter).

On the primary database, the log_archive_trace parameter controls the output of the ARCn (archiver), FAL (fetch archived log), and the LGWR (log writer) background processes. On the standby databases, it traces the work of the ARCn, RFS (remote file server), and the FAL processes.

You can specify any of 17 levels of archive log tracing. Here's what the tracing levels mean:

> 0: Disables archivelog tracing (default)
>
> 1: Tracks archival of redo log file
>
> 2: Tracks archival status of each archivelog destination
>
> 4: Tracks archival operational phase
>
> 8: Tracks archivelog destination activity
>
> 16: Tracks detailed archivelog destination activity
>
> 32: Tracks archivelog destination parameter modifications

64: Tracks ARCn process state activity

128: Tracks FAL (fetch archived log) server related activities

256: Tracks RFS Logical Client

512: Tracks LGWR redo shipping network activity

1024: Tracks RFS Physical Client

2048: Tracks RFS/ARCn Ping Heartbeat

4096: Tracks Real Time Apply

8192: Tracks Redo Apply (Media Recovery or Physical Standby)

16384: Tracks redo transport buffer management

32768: Tracks LogMiner dictionary

When you specify a higher level of tracing, the trace will include information from all lower tracing levels. For example, if you specify Level 15, the trace file will include trace information from Levels 1, 2, 4, and 8.

CHAPTER 11

■ ■ ■

Automated SQL Tuning

Starting with Oracle Database 11g and higher, Oracle provides several tools that help automate the SQL tuning process. This chapter focuses on the following automated SQL tuning tools:

- Automatic SQL Tuning Advisor
- SQL tuning sets (STS)
- Tuning task feature
- SQL Tuning Advisor
- Automatic Database Diagnostic Monitor (ADDM)

The *Automatic SQL Tuning Advisor* is a preset background database job (11g and higher) that by default runs daily. This task examines high resource-consuming statements captured in the Automatic Workload Repository (AWR) and generates tuning advice (if any) for each statement analyzed. As part of automated SQL tuning, you can configure characteristics such as the automatic acceptance of some recommendations like SQL profiles (see Chapter 12 for details on SQL profiles).

Central to SQL tuning tools are *SQL tuning sets*. A SQL tuning set (STS) is a database object that contains one or more SQL statements and the associated execution statistics. You can populate a SQL tuning set from multiple sources, such as historical SQL recorded in the automatic workload repository (AWR) or SQL currently in memory. It's critical that you be familiar with SQL tuning sets. This feature is used as an input to several of Oracle's performance tuning and management tools, such as the SQL Tuning Advisor, SQL Plan Management, SQL Access Advisor, and SQL Performance Advisor. Additionally, you can use SQL tuning sets to capture a set of SQL statements in production and transport them to a test environment (where you can tune the statements without impacting production).

A *tuning task* defines that SQL statements are used for input to the SQL Tuning Advisor. A tuning task can be populated from the following sources:

- The text of a single SQL statement
- A SQL statement currently in memory
- A historical SQL statement in the AWR
- A SQL tuning set (consisting of one or more SQL statements)

The *SQL Tuning Advisor* is a tool that provides advice on how to improve the performance of SQL statements. This tool can be invoked via the DBMS_SQLTUNE package, SQL Developer, or Enterprise Manager. The SQL Tuning Advisor offers advice in the form of:

- Rewriting the SQL

- Adding indexes

- Implementing a SQL profile or plan baselines

- Generating statistics

The *Automatic Database Diagnostic Monitor* (ADDM) analyzes information in the AWR and provides recommendations on database performance issues, including high resource-consuming SQL statements. The main goal of ADDM is to help you reduce the overall time (the DB time metric) spent by the database processing user requests. This tool can be invoked from an Oracle-provided SQL script, the DBMS_ADDM package, or Enterprise Manager.

■ **Note** All of the prior listed tools require an extra license from Oracle. You may not have a license to run these tools. Even if you don't have one, we still recommend that you know how these tools function. For example, you might have a manager asking if these automated tools are worth the cost, or you might be working with a developer who is investigating the use of these tools in a test environment. As a SQL tuning guru, you need to be familiar with these tools, as you will sooner or later encounter these automated features.

With the advent of automated SQL tuning features, anybody from novice to expert can generate solutions for SQL performance problems. This opens the door for new ways to address problematic SQL. For example, imagine your boss (who has access to automated SQL tuning tools) coming to you each morning with tuning recommendations and asking what the plan is to implement enhancements. This is different from SQL tuning being mainly the purview of SQL tuning experts.

Automated SQL tuning features are not a panacea for SQL performance angst. If you are an expert SQL tuner, there's no need to fear your skills are obsolete or your job is lost. There will always be a need to verify recommendations and successfully implement solutions. A human is still required to review the automated SQL tuning output and confirm the worthiness of fixes.

Still, there's been a change in the way SQL performance problems can be identified and solutions can be recommended. Some old-school folks may disagree and argue that you can't allow just anybody to generate SQL tuning advice. Regardless, Oracle has made these automated tools accessible and usable by the general population. Therefore you need to understand the underpinnings of these features and how to use them.

Before investigating the recipes in this chapter, take a long look at Figure 11-1. This diagram demonstrates how the various automated tools interact and in what scenarios you would use a particular feature. Refer back to this diagram as you work through the recipes in this chapter. Particularly notice that you can easily use SQL statements found in the AWR or SQL currently in memory as input for various Oracle tuning tools. This allows you to systematically identify and use high-resource SQL statements as the target for various performance tuning activities.

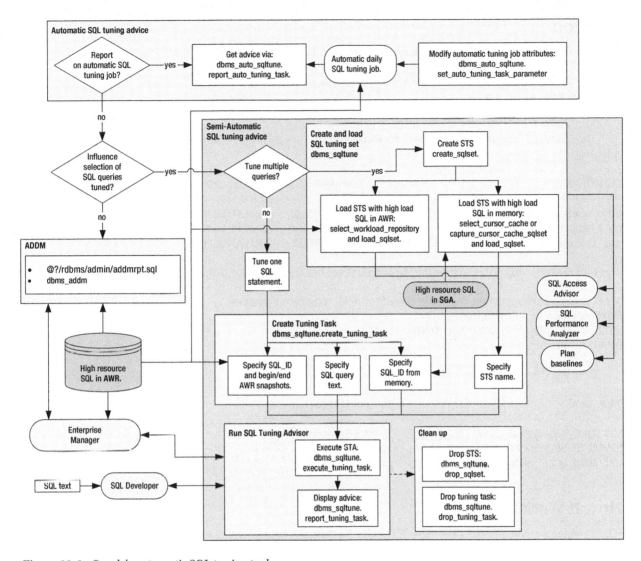

Figure 11-1. *Oracle's automatic SQL tuning tools*

The first several recipes in this chapter deal with the Automatic SQL Tuning Advisor tool. You'll be shown how to determine if and when the automated job is running and how to modify its characteristics. The middle section of this chapter focuses on how to create and manage SQL tuning sets. SQL tuning sets are used widely as input to various Oracle performance tuning tools. Lastly, the chapter shows you how to create tuning tasks, run the SQL Tuning Advisor, and execute the ADDM to generate performance recommendations for SQL statements.

11-1. Displaying Automatic SQL Tuning Job Details
Problem

You want to determine if the Automatic SQL Tuning job is enabled and regularly running. If the job is enabled, you want to display other aspects, such as when it starts and how long it executes.

377

Solution

Use the following query to determine if any Automatic SQL Tuning jobs are enabled:

```
SELECT client_name, status, consumer_group, window_group
FROM dba_autotask_client
ORDER BY client_name;
```

The following output shows that there are three enabled automatic jobs running, one of which is the SQL Tuning Advisor:

```
CLIENT_NAME                       STATUS      CONSUMER_GROUP    WINDOW_GROUP
-----------------------------     ----------  ---------------   ---------------
auto optimizer stats collection   ENABLED     ORA$AUTOTASK      ORA$AT_WGRP_OS
auto space advisor                ENABLED     ORA$AUTOTASK      ORA$AT_WGRP_SA
sql tuning advisor                ENABLED     ORA$AUTOTASK      ORA$AT_WGRP_SQ
```

Run the following query to view the last several times the Automatic SQL Tuning Advisor job has run:

```
SELECT task_name, status, TO_CHAR(execution_end,'DD-MON-YY HH24:MI')
FROM dba_advisor_executions
WHERE task_name='SYS_AUTO_SQL_TUNING_TASK'
ORDER BY execution_end;
```

Here is some sample output:

```
TASK_NAME                  STATUS        TO_CHAR(EXECUTION_END,'D
------------------------   ------------  ------------------------
SYS_AUTO_SQL_TUNING_TASK   COMPLETED     19-MAY-13 06:00
SYS_AUTO_SQL_TUNING_TASK   COMPLETED     20-MAY-13 22:00
SYS_AUTO_SQL_TUNING_TASK   COMPLETED     21-MAY-13 22:00
```

How It Works

When you create a database (11g or higher), Oracle automatically implements three automatic maintenance jobs:

- Automatic SQL Tuning Advisor
- Automatic Segment Advisor
- Automatic Optimizer Statistics Collection

These tasks are automatically configured to run in maintenance windows. A maintenance window is a specified time and duration for the task to run. You can view the maintenance window details with this query:

```
SELECT window_name,TO_CHAR(window_next_time,'DD-MON-YY HH24:MI:SS')
,sql_tune_advisor, optimizer_stats, segment_advisor
FROM dba_autotask_window_clients;
```

Here's a snippet of the output for this example:

```
WINDOW_NAME          TO_CHAR(WINDOW_NEXT_TIME,'D SQL_TUNE OPTIMIZE SEGMENT_
-------------------  -------------------------- -------- -------- --------
SUNDAY_WINDOW        26-MAY-13 06:00:00          ENABLED  ENABLED  ENABLED
THURSDAY_WINDOW      23-MAY-13 22:00:00          ENABLED  ENABLED  ENABLED
TUESDAY_WINDOW       28-MAY-13 22:00:00          ENABLED  ENABLED  ENABLED
```

There are several data dictionary views related to the automatically scheduled jobs. See Table 11-1 for descriptions of these views.

Table 11-1. *Automatic Maintenance Task View Descriptions*

View Name	Description
DBA_AUTOTASK_CLIENT	Statistical information about automatic jobs
DBA_AUTOTASK_CLIENT_HISTORY	Window history of job execution
DBA_AUTOTASK_CLIENT_JOB	Currently running automatic scheduled jobs
DBA_AUTOTASK_JOB_HISTORY	History of automatic scheduled job runs
DBA_AUTOTASK_SCHEDULE	Schedule of automated tasks for next 32 days
DBA_AUTOTASK_TASK	Information regarding current and past tasks
DBA_AUTOTASK_OPERATION	Operations for automated tasks
DBA_AUTOTASK_WINDOW_CLIENTS	Displays windows that belong to the MAINTENANCE_WINDOW_GROUP
DBA_AUTOTASK_STATUS	Displays status information for current and past automated maintenance tasks
DBA_AUTOTASK_WINDOW_HISTORY	Displays historical information for automated maintenance task windows

11-2. Displaying Automatic SQL Tuning Advisor Advice

Problem

You're aware that Oracle automatically runs a daily job that generates SQL tuning advice. You want to view the advice.

Solution

If you're using Oracle Database 11g Release 2 or higher, here's the quickest way to display automatically generated SQL tuning advice (run this from SQL*Plus):

```
SET LINESIZE 80 PAGESIZE 0 LONG 100000
SELECT DBMS_AUTO_SQLTUNE.REPORT_AUTO_TUNING_TASK FROM DUAL;
```

Depending on the activity in your database, there may be a great deal of output. Here's a small sample of the advice:

```
GENERAL INFORMATION SECTION
-------------------------------------------------------------------------
Tuning Task Name                  : SYS_AUTO_SQL_TUNING_TASK
Tuning Task Owner                 : SYS
```

```
Workload Type                          : Automatic High-Load SQL Workload
Execution Count                        : 37
Current Execution                      : EXEC_3032
Execution Type                         : TUNE SQL
Scope                                  : COMPREHENSIVE
Global Time Limit(seconds)             : 3600
Per-SQL Time Limit(seconds)            : 1200
Completion Status                      : COMPLETED
Started at                             : 05/22/2013 22:00:03
Completed at                           : 05/22/2013 22:00:53
Number of Candidate SQLs               : 2
Cumulative Elapsed Time of SQL (s)     : 3
-------------------------------------------------------------------------------
```

AUTOMATICALLY E-MAILING SQL OUTPUT

On Linux/Unix systems, it's quite easy to automate the e-mailing of output from a SQL script. First encapsulate the SQL in a shell script, and then use a utility such as cron to automatically generate and e-mail the output. Here's a sample shell script:

```
#!/bin/bash
# Source oracle OS variables
export ORACLE_SID=O12C
export ORACLE_HOME='/ora01/app/oracle/product/12.1.0.3/db_1'
#
BOX=`uname -a | awk '{print$2}'`
OUTFILE=$HOME/bin/log/sqladvice.txt
#
sqlplus -s <<EOF
mv_maint/foo
SPO $OUTFILE
SET LINESIZE 80 PAGESIZE 0 LONG 100000
SELECT DBMS_AUTO_SQLTUNE.REPORT_AUTO_TUNING_TASK FROM DUAL;
EOF
cat $OUTFILE | mailx -s "SQL Advice: $1 $BOX" dkuhn@gmail.com
exit 0
```

Here's the corresponding cron entry that runs the report on a daily basis:

```
#----------------------------------------------------------------
# SQL Advice report from SQL auto tuning
16 11 * * * /orahome/oracle/bin/sqladvice.bsh
1>/orahome/oracle/bin/log/sqladvice.log 2>&1
#----------------------------------------------------------------
```

In this manner, you can automatically receive the output of the Automatic SQL Tuning Advisor.

How It Works

The "Solution" section describes a simple method to display in-depth automatic tuning advice for high-load queries in your database. Depending on the activity and load on your database, the report may contain no suggestions or may provide a great deal of advice. The advice can be of the following types:

- New/fresh statistics
- SQL profiles
- Addition of indexes
- Modifying the SQL statement

The Automatic SQL Tuning Advisor uses the high-workload SQL statements identified in the AWR as the target SQL statements to report on. The advice report consists of one or more of the following general subsections:

- General information
- Summary
- Details
- Findings
- Explain plans
- Alternate plans
- Errors

The general information section contains high-level information regarding the start and end time, number of SQL statements considered, cumulative elapsed time of the SQL statements, and so on.

The summary section contains information regarding the SQL statements analyzed—for example:

```
-------------------------------------------------------------------------
SUMMARY SECTION
-------------------------------------------------------------------------
                         Global SQL Tuning Result Statistics
-------------------------------------------------------------------------
Number of SQLs Analyzed                       : 2
Number of SQLs in the Report                  : 1
Number of SQLs with Findings                  : 1
Number of SQLs with SQL profiles recommended : 1


-------------------------------------------------------------------------
    SQLs with Findings Ordered by Maximum (Profile/Index) Benefit, Object ID
-------------------------------------------------------------------------
object ID  SQL ID        statistics profile(benefit) index(benefit) restructure
---------- ------------- ---------- --------------- -------------- -----------
       196 0g55kd7p78gnb                    31.74%
```

The details section contains information describing specific SQL statements, such as the owner and SQL text. Here is a small sample:

```
-------------------------------------------------------------------------
DETAILS SECTION
-------------------------------------------------------------------------
 Statements with Results Ordered by Maximum (Profile/Index) Benefit, Object ID
-------------------------------------------------------------------------
```

```
Object ID  : 196
Schema Name: SYS
SQL ID     : 0g55kd7p78gnb
SQL Text   : SELECT registration_id FROM registrations ...
```

The findings section contains recommendations such as accepting a SQL profile or creating an index—for example:

```
--------------------------------------------------------------------------
FINDINGS SECTION (1 finding)
--------------------------------------------------------------------------


1- SQL Profile Finding (see explain plans section below)
--------------------------------------------------------
  A potentially better execution plan was found for this statement.
  The SQL profile was not automatically created because the verified benefit
  was too low.

  Recommendation (estimated benefit: 31.74%)
  -----------------------------------------
  - Consider accepting the recommended SQL profile.
    execute dbms_sqltune.accept_sql_profile(task_name =>
            'SYS_AUTO_SQL_TUNING_TASK', object_id => 196, replace => TRUE);
```

Where appropriate, the original execution plan for a query is displayed along with a suggested fix and new execution plan. This allows you to see the before and after plan differences. This is very useful when determining if the findings (such as adding an index) would improve performance.

Lastly, there is an error section of the report. For most scenarios, there typically will not be an error section in the report.

The "Solution" section showed how to execute the REPORT_AUTO_TUNING_TASK function from a SQL statement. This function can also be called from an anonymous block of PL/SQL. Here's an example:

```
VARIABLE tune_report CLOB;
BEGIN
  :tune_report := DBMS_AUTO_SQLTUNE.report_auto_tuning_task(
    begin_exec   => NULL
   ,end_exec     => NULL
   ,type         => DBMS_AUTO_SQLTUNE.type_text
   ,level        => DBMS_AUTO_SQLTUNE.level_typical
   ,section      => DBMS_AUTO_SQLTUNE.section_all
   ,object_id    => NULL
   ,result_limit => NULL);
END;
/
--
SET LONG 1000000
PRINT :tune_report
```

The parameters for the REPORT_AUTO_TUNING_TASK function are described in detail in Table 11-2. These parameters allow you a great deal of flexibility to customize the advice output.

Table 11-2. *Parameter Details for the REPORT_AUTO_TUNING_TASK Function*

Parameter Name	Description
BEGIN_EXEC	Name of beginning task execution; NULL means the most recent task is used.
END_EXEC	Name of ending task; NULL means the most recent task is used.
TYPE	Type of report to produce; TEXT specifies a text report.
LEVEL	Level of detail; valid values are BASIC, TYPICAL, and ALL.
SECTION	Section of the report to include; valid values are ALL, SUMMARY, FINDINGS, PLAN, INFORMATION, and ERROR.
OBJECT_ID	Used to report on a specific statement; NULL means all statements.
RESULT_LIMIT	Maximum number of SQL statements to include in report

11-3. Generating a SQL Script to Implement Automatic Tuning Advice

Problem

You've reviewed the automatic SQL tuning advice (see Recipe 11-2 for details). Now you want to generate a SQL script that can be used to implement the tuning advice.

Solution

Use the DBMS_SQLTUNE.SCRIPT_TUNING_TASK function to generate the SQL statements to implement the advice of a tuning task. You need to provide as input the name of the automatic tuning task. The default task name generated by the automatic SQL tuning advice is SYS_AUTO_SQL_TUNING_TASK (run this from SQL*Plus):

```
SET LINES 132 PAGESIZE 0 LONG 10000
SELECT DBMS_SQLTUNE.SCRIPT_TUNING_TASK('SYS_AUTO_SQL_TUNING_TASK') FROM dual;
```

Here is a small snippet of the output for this example:

```
-----------------------------------------------------------------
-- Script generated by DBMS_SQLTUNE package, advisor framework --
-- Use this script to implement some of the recommendations    --
-- made by the SQL tuning advisor.                             --
--                                                             --
-- NOTE: this script may need to be edited for your system     --
--        (index names, privileges, etc.) before it is executed. --
-----------------------------------------------------------------
execute dbms_sqltune.accept_sql_profile(task_name => 'SYS_AUTO_SQL_TUNING_TASK',
 object_id => 196, replace => TRUE);
```

You can edit the script as required and then execute it directly from SQL*Plus to implement the automatic tuning advice.

How It Works

The DBMS_SQLTUNE.SCRIPT_TUNING_TASK function generates the SQL required to implement the advice recommended by the Automatic SQL Tuning Advisor (such as new statistics, creating profiles, indexes, or re-writing the SQL statement). If the tuning task doesn't have any advice to give, then there won't be any SQL statements generated in the output. SYS_AUTO_SQL_TUNING_TASK is the default name of the Automatic SQL Tuning task. If you're unsure of the details regarding this task, then query the DBA_ADVISOR_LOG view:

```
select task_name, execution_start from dba_advisor_log
where task_name='SYS_AUTO_SQL_TUNING_TASK'
order by 2;
```

Here's some sample output for this example:

```
TASK_NAME                       EXECUTION
------------------------------  ---------
SYS_AUTO_SQL_TUNING_TASK        22-MAY-13
```

11-4. Modifying Automatic SQL Tuning Features
Problem

You've noticed that sometimes the Automatic SQL Tuning Advisor job recommends that a SQL profile be applied to a SQL statement (see Chapter 12 for details on SQL profiles). The default behavior of the automatic tuning advice job is to not automatically accept SQL profile recommendations. You want to modify this behavior and have the job place any SQL profiles that it recommends into an accepted state.

Solution

Use the DBMS_AUTO_SQLTUNE.SET_AUTO_TUNING_TASK_PARAMETER procedure to modify the default behavior of the Automatic SQL Tuning Advisor. For example, if you want SQL profiles to be automatically accepted, you can do so as follows:

```
BEGIN
  DBMS_AUTO_SQLTUNE.SET_AUTO_TUNING_TASK_PARAMETER(
    parameter => 'ACCEPT_SQL_PROFILES', value => 'TRUE');
END;
/
```

You can verify that auto SQL profile accepting is enabled via this query:

```
SELECT parameter_name, parameter_value
FROM dba_advisor_parameters
WHERE task_name = 'SYS_AUTO_SQL_TUNING_TASK'
AND  parameter_name ='ACCEPT_SQL_PROFILES';
```

Here is some sample output:

```
PARAMETER_NAME                  PARAMETER_VALUE
------------------------------  ------------------------------
ACCEPT_SQL_PROFILES             TRUE
```

To disable automatic acceptance of SQL profiles, pass a FALSE value to the procedure:

```
BEGIN
  DBMS_AUTO_SQLTUNE.SET_AUTO_TUNING_TASK_PARAMETER(
    parameter => 'ACCEPT_SQL_PROFILES', value => 'FALSE');
END;
/
```

How It Works

The DBMS_AUTO_SQLTUNE.SET_AUTO_TUNING_TASK_PARAMETER procedure allows you to modify the default behavior of the Automatic SQL Tuning Advisor job. You can view all of the current settings for the automated job via this query:

```
SELECT parameter_name,parameter_value
FROM dba_advisor_parameters
WHERE task_name = 'SYS_AUTO_SQL_TUNING_TASK'
AND   parameter_name IN ('ACCEPT_SQL_PROFILES',
                         'MAX_SQL_PROFILES_PER_EXEC',
                         'MAX_AUTO_SQL_PROFILES',
                         'EXECUTION_DAYS_TO_EXPIRE');
```

Here's some sample output:

```
PARAMETER_NAME                  PARAMETER_VALUE
------------------------------  ------------------------------
ACCEPT_SQL_PROFILES             FALSE
EXECUTION_DAYS_TO_EXPIRE        30
MAX_SQL_PROFILES_PER_EXEC       20
MAX_AUTO_SQL_PROFILES           10000
```

The prior parameters are described in Table 11-3.

Table 11-3. *Description of SET_AUTO_TUNING_TASK_PARAMETER Parameters*

Parameter Name	Description
ACCEPT_SQL_PROFILE	Determines if SQL profiles are automatically accepted
EXECUTION_DAYS_TO_EXPIRE	Number of days to save task history
MAX_SQL_PROFILES_PER_EXEC	Limit of SQL profiles accepted per execution of tuning task
MAX_AUTO_SQL_PROFILES	Maximum limit of SQL profiles automatically accepted

You can also use Enterprise Manager to modify the behavior of the Automatic SQL Tuning Advisor. Click on the "Performance" tab, then "Advisors home", then "SQL Advisors", then "Automatic SQL Tuning Advisor Results." You should be presented with a screen similar to Figure 11-2.

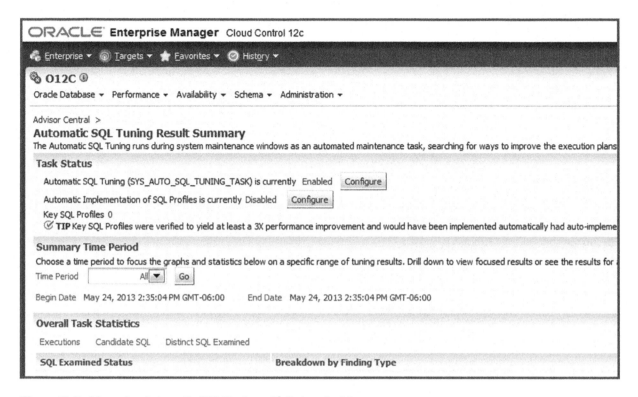

Figure 11-2. *Managing Automatic SQL Tuning with Enterprise Manager*

From this screen, you can configure, view results, disable, and enable various aspects of Automatic SQL Tuning job.

11-5. Disabling and Enabling Automatic SQL Tuning
Problem
You want to completely disable and later re-enable the Automatic SQL Tuning Advisor job.

Solution
Use the DBMS_AUTO_TASK_ADMIN.DISABLE procedure to disable the Automatic SQL Tuning Advisor job. For example:

```
BEGIN
  DBMS_AUTO_TASK_ADMIN.DISABLE(
  client_name => 'sql tuning advisor',
  operation => NULL,
  window_name => NULL);
END;
/
```

You can report on the status of the automatic tuning job via this query:

```
SELECT client_name,status,consumer_group
FROM dba_autotask_client
ORDER BY client_name;
```

Here's some sample output:

```
CLIENT_NAME                             STATUS   CONSUMER_GROUP
--------------------------------------- -------- --------------------
auto optimizer stats collection         ENABLED  ORA$AUTOTASK
auto space advisor                      ENABLED  ORA$AUTOTASK
sql tuning advisor                      DISABLED ORA$AUTOTASK
```

To re-enable the job, use the DBMS_AUTO_TASK_ADMIN.ENABLE procedure as shown:

```
BEGIN
  DBMS_AUTO_TASK_ADMIN.ENABLE(
  client_name => 'sql tuning advisor',
  operation => NULL,
  window_name => NULL);
END;
/
```

How It Works

You might want to disable the Automatic SQL Tuning Advisor job because you have a very active database and want to ensure that this job doesn't impact the overall performance of the database. The DBMS_AUTO_TASK_ADMIN.ENABLE/ DISABLE procedures allow you to turn on and off this automated job. These procedures take three parameters (see Table 11-4 for details).

Table 11-4. *Parameter Descriptions for DBMS_AUTO_TASK_ADMIN.ENABLE and DISABLE Procedures*

Parameter	Description
CLIENT_NAME	Name of client; query DBA_AUTOTASK_CLIENT for details.
OPERATION	Name of operation; query DBA_AUTOTASK_OPERATION for details.
WINDOW_NAME	Operation name of the window

The behavior of the procedures varies depending on which parameters you pass in:

- If CLIENT_NAME is provided and both OPERATION and WINDOW_NAME are NULL, then the client is disabled.

- If OPERATION is provided, then the operation is disabled.

- If WINDOW_NAME is provided, and OPERATION is NULL, then the client is disabled in the provided window name.

The prior parameters allow you to control at a granular detail the schedule of the automatic task. Given the prior rules, you would disable the Automatic SQL Tuning Advisor job during the Tuesday maintenance window as follows:

```
BEGIN
  dbms_auto_task_admin.disable(
  client_name => 'sql tuning advisor',
  operation => NULL,
  window_name => 'TUESDAY_WINDOW');
END;
/
```

You can verify that the window has been disabled via this query:

```
SELECT window_name,TO_CHAR(window_next_time,'DD-MON-YY HH24:MI:SS')
,sql_tune_advisor
FROM dba_autotask_window_clients;
```

Here is a snippet of the output:

```
WINDOW_NAME         TO_CHAR(WINDOW_NEXT_TIME,'D SQL_TUNE
------------------  -------------------------- --------
SUNDAY_WINDOW       26-MAY-13 06:00:00         ENABLED
THURSDAY_WINDOW     30-MAY-13 22:00:00         ENABLED
TUESDAY_WINDOW      28-MAY-13 22:00:00         DISABLED
```

11-6. Modifying Maintenance Window Attributes
Problem

You realize that the automatic tasks (such as the Automatic SQL Tuning Advisor job) run during regularly scheduled maintenance windows. You want to limit the time the job runs and so lessen the impact the job has on overall database performance.

Solution

Here's an example that changes the duration of the Sunday maintenance window to 2 hours:

```
BEGIN
  dbms_scheduler.set_attribute(
  name => 'SUNDAY_WINDOW',
  attribute => 'DURATION',
  value => numtodsinterval(2, 'hour'));
END;
/
```

You can confirm the changes to the maintenance window with this query:

```
SELECT window_name, next_start_date, duration
FROM dba_scheduler_windows;
```

Here is a snippet of the output:

```
WINDOW_NAME         NEXT_START_DATE                        DURATION
------------------  -------------------------------------  ----------------
SUNDAY_WINDOW       26-MAY-13 06.00.00.000000 AM MST7MDT   +000 02:00:00
SATURDAY_WINDOW     25-MAY-13 06.00.00.000000 AM MST7MDT   +000 20:00:00
```

How It Works

The key to understanding how to modify a maintenance window is that it is an attribute of the database job scheduler and therefore must be modified via the DBMS_SCHEDULER package. Starting with Oracle 11g and higher, when you create a database, by default three automatic maintenance jobs are configured:

- Automatic SQL Tuning
- Statistics gathering
- Segment advice

You can view the high-level details of these jobs via this query:

```
SELECT client_name, status, consumer_group, window_group
FROM dba_autotask_client
ORDER BY client_name;
```

Here is some sample output:

```
CLIENT_NAME                          STATUS    CONSUMER_GROUP       WINDOW_GROUP
-----------------------------------  --------  -------------------  --------------------
auto optimizer stats collection      ENABLED   ORA$AUTOTASK         ORA$AT_WGRP_OS
auto space advisor                   ENABLED   ORA$AUTOTASK         ORA$AT_WGRP_SA
sql tuning advisor                   ENABLED   ORA$AUTOTASK         ORA$AT_WGRP_SQ
```

These jobs automatically execute in preconfigured daily maintenance windows. A maintenance window consists of a day of the week and the length of time the job runs.

You can view the future 1 month's worth of scheduled jobs via this query:

```
SELECT window_name, to_char(start_time,'dd-mon-yy hh24:mi'), duration
FROM dba_autotask_schedule
ORDER BY start_time;
```

Here is a small sample of the output:

```
WINDOW_NAME         TO_CHAR(START_TIME,'DD-M DURATION
------------------  ------------------------ ----------------
FRIDAY_WINDOW       24-may-13 22:00          +000 04:00:00
SATURDAY_WINDOW     25-may-13 06:00          +000 20:00:00
SUNDAY_WINDOW       26-may-13 06:00          +000 02:00:00
```

■ **Tip** See Oracle's Database Administrator's Guide (available on the Oracle Technology Network web site) for further details on managing scheduled jobs.

11-7. Creating a SQL Tuning Set Object

Problem

You're working on improving a business process comprised of multiple SQL statements. This requires that you create a SQL tuning set object that will be used to associate a set of SQL statements (and corresponding statistics).

Solution

Use the DBMS_SQLTUNE.CREATE_SQLSET procedure to create a SQL tuning set object—for example:

```
BEGIN
  DBMS_SQLTUNE.CREATE_SQLSET(
  sqlset_name => 'HIGH_IO',
  description => 'High disk read tuning set');
END;
/
```

The prior code creates an STS named HIGH_IO. The tuning set does not yet contain any SQL statements (see Recipes 11-9, 11-11, and 11-12 for details on adding SQL statements to an STS).

How It Works

A SQL tuning set object must be created before populating a tuning set with SQL statements. You can view any defined SQL tuning sets in the database by querying the DBA_SQLSET view:

```
SQL> select owner, name, id, created, statement_count from dba_sqlset;
```

Here is some sample output:

```
OWNER       NAME                    ID CREATED   STATEMENT_COUNT
----------  --------------------  ---------- ---------  ---------------
MV_MAINT    HIGH_IO                  1 23-AUG-13                 0
```

If you need to drop a SQL tuning set object, then use the DBMS_SQLTUNE.DROP_SQLSET procedure to drop a tuning set. The following example drops the previously created SQL tuning set:

```
SQL> EXEC DBMS_SQLTUNE.DROP_SQLSET(sqlset_name => 'HIGH_IO');
```

11-8. Viewing Resource-Intensive SQL in the AWR

Problem

You want to view SQL statements in the AWR that are consuming the most resources. This will lay the foundation for understanding how you can populate a SQL tuning set with high resource-consuming SQL statements recorded in the AWR.

Solution

First determine what snapshots are available and which range you would like to report on:

```
SELECT snap_id, instance_number, end_interval_time
FROM dba_hist_snapshot
ORDER BY snap_id;
```

Next use the DBMS_SQLTUNE.SELECT_WORKLOAD_REPOSITORY function to extract SQL stored in the AWR. This particular query selects queries in the AWR between snapshots 1669 and 1671 ordered by the top 10 in the disk reads usage category:

```
SELECT sql_id
,substr(sql_text,1,20)
,disk_reads, cpu_time, elapsed_time
FROM table(DBMS_SQLTUNE.SELECT_WORKLOAD_REPOSITORY(1669,1671,
          null, null, 'disk_reads',null, null, null, 10))
ORDER BY disk_reads DESC;
```

Here is a small snippet of the output:

```
SQL_ID          SUBSTR(SQL_TEXT,1,20 DISK_READS     CPU_TIME  ELAPSED_TIME
--------------  -------------------- ----------  ------------- -------------
achffburdff9j   delete from "MVS"."     101145      814310000     991574249
5vku5ap6g6zh8   INSERT /*+ BYPASS_RE     98172       75350000      91527239
```

■ **Note**   See Recipe 11-9 for details on using DBMS_SQLTUNE.SELECT_WORKLOAD_REPOSITORY to populate a SQL tuning set with resource intensive SQL statements stored in the AWR.

How It Works

The DBMS_SQLTUNE.SELECT_WORKLOAD_REPOSITORY function is used to retrieve high resource-usage SQL from the AWR. Table 11-5 provides details regarding the SELECT_WORKLOAD_REPOSITORY function parameters.

Table 11-5. Parameter Descriptions of the SELECT_WORKLOAD_REPOSITORY Function

Parameter	Description
BEGIN_SNAP	Non-inclusive beginning snapshot ID
END_SNAP	Inclusive ending snapshot ID
BASELINE_NAME	Name of AWR baseline
BASIC_FILTER	SQL predicate to filter SQL statements from workload; if not set, then only SELECT, INSERT, UPDATE, DELETE, MERGE, and CREATE TABLE statements are captured.
OBJECT_FILTER	Not currently used
RANKING_MEASURE(n)	Order by clause on selected SQL statement(s), such as elapsed_time, cpu_time, buffer_gets, disk_reads, and so on; N can be 1, 2, or 3. The elapsed_time and cpu_time are measured in seconds.
RESULT_PERCENTAGE	Filter for choosing top N% for ranking measure
RESULT_LIMIT	Limit of the number of SQL statements returned in the result set
ATTRIBUTE_LIST	List of SQL statement attributes (TYPICAL, BASIC, ALL, and so on)
RECURSIVE_SQL	Include/exclude recursive SQL (HAS_RECURSIVE_SQL or NO_RECURSIVE_SQL)

You have a great deal of flexibility in how you use this function. A few examples will help illustrate this. Say you want to retrieve SQL from the AWR that was not parsed by the SYS user. Here is the SQL to do that:

```
SELECT sql_id, substr(sql_text,1,20)
,disk_reads, cpu_time, elapsed_time, parsing_schema_name
FROM table(
DBMS_SQLTUNE.SELECT_WORKLOAD_REPOSITORY(1669,1671,
'parsing_schema_name <> "SYS"',
NULL, NULL,NULL,NULL, 1, NULL, 'ALL'));
```

The following example retrieves the top 10 queries ranked by buffer gets for non-SYS users:

```
SELECT sql_id, substr(sql_text,1,20)
,disk_reads, cpu_time, elapsed_time, buffer_gets, parsing_schema_name
FROM table(
DBMS_SQLTUNE.SELECT_WORKLOAD_REPOSITORY(
 begin_snap => 1669
,end_snap => 1671
,basic_filter => 'parsing_schema_name <> "SYS"'
,ranking_measure1 => 'buffer_gets'
,result_limit => 10
));
```

In the prior queries, the SYS keyword is enclosed by two single quotes (in other words, those aren't double quotes around SYS).

You can also automatically calculate and pass in a pair of AWR snapshot IDs to the DBMS_SQLTUNE.SELECT_WORKLOAD_REPOSITORY function. For example, say you wanted to view the highest CPU-consuming SQL in the last 7 days for non-SYS users:

```
COL bsnap NEW_VALUE begin_snap
COL esnap NEW_VALUE end_snap
--
SELECT MAX(snap_id) bsnap
FROM dba_hist_snapshot
WHERE begin_interval_time < sysdate-7;
--
SELECT MAX(snap_id) esnap
FROM dba_hist_snapshot;
--
COL sql_text             FORMAT A40
COL sql_id               FORMAT A15
COL parsing_schema_name  FORMAT A15
COL cpu_seconds          FORMAT 999,999,999,999,999
SET LONG 10000 LINES 132 PAGES 100 TRIMSPOOL ON
--
SELECT sql_id, sql_text
,disk_reads, cpu_time cpu_seconds, elapsed_time, buffer_gets, parsing_schema_name
FROM table(
DBMS_SQLTUNE.SELECT_WORKLOAD_REPOSITORY(
 begin_snap => &begin_snap
,end_snap => &end_snap
```

```
,basic_filter => 'parsing_schema_name <> "SYS"'
,ranking_measure1 => 'cpu_time'
,result_limit => 10
));
```

The prior examples give a small sampling of the power of the DBMS_SQLTUNE.SELECT_WORKLOAD_REPOSTIORY function. This lays the foundation for using this tool to automatically populate a SQL tuning set with high-resource usage SQL in the AWR.

11-9. Populating a SQL Tuning Set from High-Resource SQL in AWR

Problem

You want to create a SQL tuning set and populate it with the top resource-consuming SQL statements found in the AWR.

Solution

Use the following steps to populate a SQL tuning set from high resource-consuming statements in the AWR:

1. Create a SQL tuning set object.

2. Determine begin and end AWR snapshot IDs.

3. Populate the SQL tuning set with high-resource SQL found in AWR using the DBMS_SQLTUNE package.

The prior steps are detailed in the following subsections.

Step 1: Create a SQL Tuning Set Object

Create a SQL tuning set. This next bit of code creates a tuning set named IO_STS:

```
BEGIN
  dbms_sqltune.create_sqlset(
    sqlset_name => 'IO_STS',
   description => 'STS from AWR');
END;
/
```

Step 2: Determine Begin and End AWR Snapshot IDs

If you're unsure of the available snapshots in your database, you can run an AWR report or select the SNAP_ID from DBA_HIST_SNAPSHOTS:

```
select snap_id, begin_interval_time
from dba_hist_snapshot order by 1;
```

Step 3: Populate the SQL Tuning Set with High-Resource SQL Found in AWR

Now the SQL tuning set is populated with the top 15 SQL statements ordered by disk reads. The begin and end AWR snapshot IDs are 1668 and 1695, respectively:

```
DECLARE
  base_cur dbms_sqltune.sqlset_cursor;
BEGIN
  OPEN base_cur FOR
    SELECT value(x)
    FROM table(dbms_sqltune.select_workload_repository(
      1668,1695, null, null,'disk_reads',
      null, null, null, 15)) x;
  --
  dbms_sqltune.load_sqlset(
    sqlset_name => 'IO_STS',
    populate_cursor => base_cur);
END;
/
```

The prior code populates the top 15 SQL statements contained in the AWR ordered by disk reads. The DBMS_SQLTUNE.SELECT_WORKLOAD_REPOSITORY function is used to populate a PL/SQL cursor with AWR information based on a ranking criterion. Then the DBMS_SQLTUNE.LOAD_SQLSET procedure is used to populate the SQL tuning set using the cursor as input.

How It Works

The DBMS_SQLTUNE.SELECT_WORKLOAD_REPOSITORY function can be used in a variety of ways to populate a SQL tuning set using queries in the AWR. You can instruct it to load SQL statements by criteria such as disk reads, elapsed time, CPU time, buffer gets, and so on. See Table 11-5 for descriptions for parameters to this function. When designating the AWR as input, you can use either of the following:

- Begin and end AWR snapshot IDs

- An AWR baseline that you've previously created (see Chapter 7 for details)

You can view the details of the SQL tuning set (created in the "Solution" section) via this query:

```
SELECT sqlset_name, elapsed_time
,cpu_time, buffer_gets, disk_reads, sql_text
FROM dba_sqlset_statements
WHERE sqlset_name = 'IO_STS';
```

11-10. Viewing Resource-Intensive SQL in Memory
Problem

You want to view resource-consuming SQL statements currently in memory. This will lay the foundation for understanding how you can populate a SQL tuning set with high resource-consuming SQL statements stored in memory.

Solution

Use the DBMS_SQLTUNE.SELECT_CURSOR_CACHE function to view current high resource-consuming SQL statements in memory. This query selects SQL statements in memory that have read more than a million blocks from disk:

```
SELECT sql_id, substr(sql_text,1,20)
,disk_reads, cpu_time, elapsed_time
FROM table(DBMS_SQLTUNE.SELECT_CURSOR_CACHE('disk_reads > 1000000'))
ORDER BY sql_id;
```

Here is some sample output:

```
SQL_ID          SUBSTR(SQL_TEXT,1,20 DISK_READS   CPU_TIME ELAPSED_TIME
------------- -------------------- ---------- ---------- ------------
0s6gq1c890p4s  delete from "MVS"."    3325320 8756130000    1.0416E+10
b63h4skwvpshj  BEGIN dbms_mview.ref   9496353 1.4864E+10    3.3006E+10
```

■ **Note**   See Recipe 11-11 for details on using DBMS_SQLTUNE.SELECT_CURSOR_CACHE to populate a SQL tuning set with resource-intensive SQL statements in the shared pool (memory).

How It Works

The DBMS_SQLTUNE.SELECT_CURSOR_CACHE function is used to display high resource-usage SQL currently in the shared pool memory area. See Table 11-6 for a description of the SELECT_CURSOR_CACHE function parameters.

Table 11-6. Parameter Descriptions of the SELECT_CURSOR_CACHE Function

Parameter	Description
BASIC_FILTER	SQL predicate to filter SQL in the cursor cache
OBJECT_FILTER	Currently not used
RANKING_MEASURE(n)	ORDER BY clause for the SQL returned
RESULT_PERCENTAGE	Filter for the top N percent queries for the ranking measure provided; invalid if more than one ranking measure provided
RESULT_LIMIT	Top number of SQL statements filter
ATTRIBUTE_LIST	List of SQL attributes to return in result set
RECURSIVE_SQL	Include recursive SQL

You have a great deal of flexibility in how you use the SELECT_CURSOR_CACHE function. For example, this next query selects the top 10 queries in memory in terms of CPU time for non-SYS users:

```
SELECT sql_id, substr(sql_text,1,20), disk_reads
,cpu_time, elapsed_time
,buffer_gets, parsing_schema_name
```

```
FROM table(
DBMS_SQLTUNE.SELECT_CURSOR_CACHE(
 basic_filter => 'parsing_schema_name <> "SYS"'
,ranking_measure1 => 'cpu_time'
,result_limit => 10
));
```

Here's another example that selects SQL in memory but excludes statements parsed by the SYS user and also returns statements with an elapsed time greater than 1 second (1,000,000 microseconds):

```
SELECT sql_id, substr(sql_text,1,20)
,disk_reads, cpu_time, elapsed_time
FROM table(DBMS_SQLTUNE.SELECT_CURSOR_CACHE('parsing_schema_name <> "SYS"
                                          AND elapsed_time > 1000000'))
ORDER BY sql_id;
```

In the prior query, the SYS keyword is enclosed by two single quotes (in other words, those aren't double quotes around SYS). The SQL_TEXT column is a LOB data type and is truncated to 20 characters so that the output can be displayed on the page more easily. Here is some sample output:

```
SQL_ID          SUBSTR(SQL_TEXT,1,20 DISK_READS   CPU_TIME ELAPSED_TIME
------------    -------------------- ---------- ---------- ------------
byzwu34haqmh4 SELECT /* DS_SVC */            0     140000      1159828
```

Once you have identified a SQL_ID for a resource-intensive SQL statement, you can view all of its execution details via this query:

```
SELECT *
FROM table(DBMS_SQLTUNE.SELECT_CURSOR_CACHE('sql_id = "byzwu34haqmh4"'));
```

Note that the SQL_ID in the prior statement is enclosed by two single quotes (not double quotes).

11-11. Populating a SQL Tuning Set from Resource-Consuming SQL in Memory

Problem

You want to populate a tuning set from high resource-consuming SQL statements that are currently in the memory.

Solution

Use the DBMS_SQLTUNE.SELECT_CURSOR_CACHE function to populate a SQL tuning set with statements currently in memory. This example creates a SQL tuning set named HIGH_DISK_READS and populates it with high-load resource-consuming statements not belonging to the SYS schema and having disk reads greater than 1,000,000:

```
-- Create the tuning set
EXEC DBMS_SQLTUNE.CREATE_SQLSET('HIGH_DISK_READS');
-- Populate the tuning set from the cursor cache
DECLARE
  cur DBMS_SQLTUNE.SQLSET_CURSOR;
```

```
BEGIN
  OPEN cur FOR
  SELECT VALUE(x)
  FROM table(
  DBMS_SQLTUNE.SELECT_CURSOR_CACHE(
  'parsing_schema_name <> "SYS" AND disk_reads > 1000000',
  NULL, NULL, NULL, NULL, NULL, 1, NULL,'ALL')) x;
--
  DBMS_SQLTUNE.LOAD_SQLSET(sqlset_name => 'HIGH_DISK_READS',
    populate_cursor => cur);
END;
/
```

In the prior code, notice that the SYS user is bookended by sets of two single quotes (not double quotes). The SELECT_CURSOR_CACHE function loads the SQL statements into a PL/SQL cursor, and the LOAD_SQLSET procedure populates the SQL tuning set with the SQL statements.

How It Works

The DBMS_SQLTUNE.SELECT_CURSOR_CACHE function (see Table 11-6 for function parameter descriptions) allows you to extract from memory SQL statements and associated statistics into a SQL tuning set. The procedure allows you to filter SQL statements by various resource-consuming criteria, such as the following:

- ELAPSED_TIME
- CPU_TIME
- BUFFER_GETS
- DISK_READS
- DIRECT_WRITES
- ROWS_PROCESSED

This allows you a great deal of flexibility on how to filter and populate the SQL tuning set.

If you want to view the SQL statements contained within the STS, then query the DBA_SQLSET_STATEMENTS view. This query shows the details of the STS created previously in the "Solution" section:

```
SELECT sqlset_name, elapsed_time
,cpu_time, buffer_gets, disk_reads, sql_text
FROM dba_sqlset_statements
WHERE sqlset_name = 'HIGH_DISK_READS';
```

11-12. Populating a SQL Tuning Set With All SQL in Memory
Problem

You're experiencing performance problems with a production database. You want to populate a SQL tuning set with all SQL statements currently in memory. The idea being that you can use the SQL Tuning Advisor to analyze the SQL statements as a set to better determine which statements should be tuned.

Solution

Use the following steps to populate a SQL tuning set from high resource-consuming statements in memory:

1. Create a SQL tuning set object.

2. Populate the SQL tuning set with high-resource SQL found in memory via the DBMS_SQLTUNE.CAPTURE_CURSOR_CACHE_SQLSET procedure.

The prior steps are detailed in the following subsections.

Step 1: Create a SQL Tuning Set Object

The following code creates a SQL tuning set named PROD_WORKLOAD:

```
BEGIN
  -- Create the tuning set
  DBMS_SQLTUNE.CREATE_SQLSET(
    sqlset_name => 'PROD_WORKLOAD'
   ,description => 'Prod workload sample');
END;
/
```

Step 2: Populate the SQL Tuning Set With High-Resource SQL Found in Memory

Use the DBMS_SQLTUNE.CAPTURE_CURSOR_CACHE_SQLSET procedure to capture all of the SQL currently stored in the cursor cache (in memory). This example creates a SQL tuning set named PROD_WORKLOAD and then populates by sampling memory for one hour (3,600 seconds) and waiting 20 seconds between each polling event:

```
BEGIN
  DBMS_SQLTUNE.CAPTURE_CURSOR_CACHE_SQLSET(
    sqlset_name      => 'PROD_WORKLOAD'
   ,time_limit       => 3600
   ,repeat_interval => 20);
END;
/
```

How It Works

The DBMS_SQLTUNE.CAPTURE_CURSOR_CACHE_SQLSET procedure allows you to poll for queries and memory and use any queries found to populate a SQL tuning set. This is a powerful technique that you can use when it's required to capture a sample set of all SQL statements currently in memory.

You have a great deal of flexibility on instructing DBMS_SQLTUNE.CAPTURE_CURSOR_CACHE_SQLSET to capture SQL statements in memory (see Table 11-7 for details on all parameters). For example, you can instruct the procedure to capture a cumulative set of statistics for each SQL statement by specifying a CAPTURE_MODE of DBMS_SQLTUNE.MODE_ACCUMULATE_STATS.

Table 11-7. CAPTURE_CURSOR_CACHE_SQLSET Parameter Descriptions

Parameter	Description	Default Value
SQLSET_NAME	SQL tuning set name	none
TIME_LIMIT	Total time in seconds to spend sampling	1800
REPEAT_INTERVAL	While sampling, amount of time to pause in seconds before polling memory again	300
CAPTURE_OPTION	Either INSERT, UPDATE, or MERGE statements when new statements are detected	MERGE
CAPTURE_MODE	When capture option is UPDATE or MERGE, either replace statistics or accumulate statistics. Possible values are MODE_REPLACE_OLD_STATS or MODE_ACCUMULATE_STATS.	MODE_REPLACE_OLD_STATS
BASIC_FILTER	Filter type of statements captured	NULL
SQLSET_OWNER	SQL tuning set owner; NULL indicates the current user.	NULL
RECURSIVE_SQL	Include (or not) recursive SQL; possible values are HAS_RECURSIVE_SQL, NO_RECURSIVE_SQL.	HAS_RECURSIVE_SQL

```
BEGIN
  DBMS_SQLTUNE.CAPTURE_CURSOR_CACHE_SQLSET(
    sqlset_name      => 'PROD_WORKLOAD'
    ,time_limit      => 60
    ,repeat_interval => 10
    ,capture_mode    => DBMS_SQLTUNE.MODE_ACCUMULATE_STATS);
END;
/
```

This is more resource-intensive than the default settings, but produces more accurate statistics for each SQL statement. For example, you may want to use values other than the default settings because you suspect there are queries being flushed out of memory quickly and the default sampling of every 300 seconds is too long of a period to capture these statements.

11-13. Displaying the Contents of a SQL Tuning Set
Problem
You have populated a SQL tuning set and want to verify its characteristics such as the SQL statements and corresponding statistics.

Solution
You can determine the name and number of SQL statements for SQL tuning sets in your database via this query:

```
SELECT name, created, statement_count
FROM dba_sqlset;
```

Here is some sample output:

```
NAME                 CREATED   STATEMENT_COUNT
-------------------- --------- ---------------
IO_STS               26-MAY-13              15
```

Use the following query to display the SQL text and associated statistical information for each query within the SQL tuning set:

```
SELECT sqlset_name, elapsed_time, cpu_time, buffer_gets, disk_reads, sql_text
FROM dba_sqlset_statements;
```

Here is a small snippet of the output. The SQL_TEXT column has been truncated in order to fit the output on the page:

```
SQLSET_NAME     ELAPSED_TIME   CPU_TIME BUFFER_GETS DISK_READS SQL_TEXT
--------------- ------------ ---------- ----------- ---------- ---------------------------
IO_STS             235285363   45310000      112777       3050 INSERT ......
IO_STS              52220149   22700000      328035      18826 delete from.....
```

How It Works

Recall that a SQL tuning set consists of one or more SQL statements and the corresponding execution statistics. This information is viewable from the DBA_SQLSET_* views. Table 11-8 describes the type of SQL tuning set information contained within each of these views.

Table 11-8. *Views Containing SQL Tuning Set Information*

View Name	Description
DBA_SQLSET	Displays information regarding SQL tuning sets
DBA_SQLSET_BINDS	Displays bind variable information associated with SQL tuning sets
DBA_SQLSET_PLANS	Shows execution plan information for queries in a SQL tuning set
DBA_SQLSET_STATEMENTS	Contains SQL text and associated statistics
DBA_SQLSET_REFERENCES	Shows whether a SQL tuning set is active

You can also use the DBMS_SQLTUNE.SELECT_SQLSET function to retrieve information about SQL tuning set. For example:

```
SELECT sql_id, elapsed_time
,cpu_time, buffer_gets
,disk_reads, sql_text
FROM TABLE(DBMS_SQLTUNE.SELECT_SQLSET('&sqlset_name'));
```

Whether you use the DBMS_SQLTUNE.SELECT_SQLSET function or directly query the data dictionary views depends entirely on your personal preference.

11-14. Selectively Deleting Statements from a SQL Tuning Set

Problem

You want to prune SQL statements from an SQL tuning set that don't meet a performance measure, such as queries that have less than 2,000,000 disk reads.

Solution

First view the existing SQL information associated with an STS:

```
select sqlset_name, disk_reads, cpu_time, elapsed_time, buffer_gets
from dba_sqlset_statements;
```

Here is some sample output:

SQLSET_NAME	DISK_READS	CPU_TIME	ELAPSED_TIME	BUFFER_GETS
IO_STS	3112941	3264960000	7805935285	2202432
IO_STS	2943527	3356460000	8930436466	1913415
IO_STS	2539642	2310610000	5869237421	1658465
IO_STS	1999373	2291230000	6143543429	1278601
IO_STS	1993973	2243180000	5461607976	1272271
IO_STS	1759096	1930320000	4855618689	1654252

Now use the DBMS_SQLTUNE.DELETE_SQLSET procedure to remove SQL statements from the STS based on the specified criterion. This example removes SQL statements that have less than 2,000,000 disk reads from the SQL tuning set named IO_STS:

```
BEGIN
  DBMS_SQLTUNE.DELETE_SQLSET(
    sqlset_name   => 'IO_STS'
    ,basic_filter => 'disk_reads < 2000000');
END;
/
```

How It Works

The key to understanding that you can modify SQL tuning set is understanding that a SQL tuning set consists of the following:

- One or more SQL statements
- Associated metrics/statistics for each SQL statement

Because the metrics/statistics are part of the SQL tuning set, you can remove SQL statements from a SQL tuning set based on characteristics of the associated metrics/statistics. You can use the DBMS_SQLTUNE.DELETE_SQLSET procedure to remove statements from the STS based on statistics such as the following:

- ELAPSED_TIME
- CPU_TIME

- BUFFER_GETS
- DISK_READS
- DIRECT_WRITES
- ROWS_PROCESSED

If you want to delete all SQL statements from a SQL tuning set, then don't specify a filter—for example:

```
SQL> exec  DBMS_SQLTUNE.DELETE_SQLSET(sqlset_name  => 'IO_STS');
```

11-15. Transporting a SQL Tuning Set

Problem

You've identified some resource-intensive SQL statements in a production environment. You want to transport these statements and associated statistics to a test environment, where you can tune the statements without impacting production.

Solution

The following steps are used to copy a SQL tuning set from one database to another:

1. Create a staging table in source database.

2. Populate the staging table with SQL tuning set data.

3. Copy the staging table to the destination database.

4. Unpack the staging table in the destination database.

The prior steps are elaborated on in the following subsections.

Step 1: Create a Staging Table in the Source Database

Use the DBMS_SQLTUNE.CREATE_STGTAB_SQLSET procedure to create a table that will be used to contain the SQL tuning set metadata. This example creates a table named STS_TABLE with the MV_MAINT schema:

```
BEGIN
  dbms_sqltune.create_stgtab_sqlset(
  table_name => 'STS_TABLE'
 ,schema_name => 'MV_MAINT');
END;
/
```

In the prior code, you must specify a non-SYS schema name (otherwise, you'll get this error: ORA-19381: cannot create staging table in SYS schema). If you omit the SCHEMA_NAME parameter, the table will be created in the currently connected schema executing the code.

Step 2: Populate Staging Table with STS Data

Now populate the staging table with SQL tuning set metadata using DBMS_SQLTUNE.PACK_STGTAB_SQLSET. In the following code, the SQL tuning set name is PROD_WORKLOAD:

```
BEGIN
  dbms_sqltune.pack_stgtab_sqlset(
  sqlset_name            => 'PROD_WORKLOAD'
 ,sqlset_owner           => 'SYS'
 ,staging_table_name     => 'STS_TABLE'
 ,staging_schema_owner   => 'MV_MAINT');
END;
/
```

If you're unsure of the name of the SQL tuning set you want to transport, run the following query to get the details:

```
SELECT name, owner, created, statement_count
FROM dba_sqlset;
```

Here is some sample output:

```
NAME                   OWNER       CREATED     STATEMENT_COUNT
---------------------  ----------  ---------   ---------------
HIGH_IO                MV_MAINT    23-AUG-13                 0
PROD_WORKLOAD          SYS         23-AUG-13               148
IO_STS                 MV_MAINT    23-AUG-13                15
```

Step 3: Copy the Staging Table to the Destination Database

You can copy the table (created in Step 1) from one database to the other via Data Pump, the old exp/imp utilities, or by using a database link. This example creates a database link in the destination database and then copies the table from the source database:

```
create database link source_db
connect to mv_maint
identified by foo
using 'source_db';
```

In the destination database, the table can be copied directly from the source with the CREATE TABLE AS SELECT statement:

```
SQL> create table STS_TABLE as select * from STS_TABLE@source_db;
```

Step 4: Unpack the Staging Table in the Destination Database

Connect to the destination database as the user that owns the SQL tuning set. Then use the
DBMS_SQLTUNE.UNPACK_STGTAB_SQLSET procedure to take the contents of the staging table and populate the data
dictionary with the SQL tuning set metadata. This example unpacks all SQL tuning sets contained within the
staging table:

```
BEGIN
DBMS_SQLTUNE.UNPACK_STGTAB_SQLSET(
  sqlset_name         => '%'
 ,replace             => TRUE
 ,staging_table_name  => 'STS_TABLE'
 ,staging_schema_owner=> 'MV_MAINT');
END;
/
```

How It Works

A SQL tuning set consists of one or more queries and corresponding execution statistics. You will occasionally have
a need to copy a SQL tuning set from one database to another. For example, you might be having performance
problems with a production database but want to capture and move the top resource-consuming statements to a test
database where you can diagnose the SQL (within the SQL tuning set) without impacting production.

Keep in mind that an STS can be used as input for any of the following tools:

- SQL Tuning Advisor

- SQL Access Advisor

- SQL Plan Management

- SQL Performance Analyzer

The prior tools are used extensively to troubleshoot and test SQL performance. Transporting a SQL tuning set
from one environment to another allows you to use these tools in a testing or development environment.

■ **Note**   SQL tuning sets can be transported to Oracle Database 10g R2 or higher versions of the database only.

11-16. Creating a Tuning Task
Problem

You realize that as part of manually running the SQL Tuning Advisor, you need to first create a tuning task.

■ **Tip**   Refer to Figure 11-1 for the details on the flow of processes required when manually running the SQL
Tuning Advisor.

Solution

Use the DBMS_SQLTUNE.CREATE_TUNING_TASK procedure to create a SQL tuning task. You can use the following as inputs when creating a SQL tuning task:

- Text for a specific SQL statement

- SQL identifier for a specific SQL statement from the cursor cache in memory

- Single SQL statement from the AWR given a range of snapshot IDs

- SQL tuning set name (see Recipes 11-7 through 11-12 for details on how to create and populate a SQL tuning set)

Examples of the prior techniques for creating a SQL tuning task are described in the following subsections.

■ **Note**   The user creating the tuning task needs the ADMINISTER SQL MANAGEMENT OBJECT system privilege.

Text for a Specific SQL Statement

This example provides the text of a SQL statement when creating the tuning task:

```
DECLARE
  tune_task VARCHAR2(30);
  tune_sql  CLOB;
BEGIN
  tune_sql := 'select count(*) from emp';
  tune_task := DBMS_SQLTUNE.CREATE_TUNING_TASK(
    sql_text     => tune_sql
   ,user_name    => 'MV_MAINT'
   ,scope        => 'COMPREHENSIVE'
   ,time_limit   => 60
   ,task_name    => 'tune_test1'
   ,description  => 'Provide SQL text'
);
END;
/
```

SQL ID for a Specific SQL Statement from the Cursor Cache

First identify the SQL_ID and PLAN_HASH_VALUE by querying V$SQL:

```
SELECT sql_id, plan_hash_value , sql_text
FROM v$sql where sql_text like '%&mytext%'
and sql_text not like '%FROM v$sql%';
```

Once you have the SQL_ID, and PLAN_HASH_VALUE, you can provide those values as input to DBMS_SQLTUNE.CREATE_TUNING_TASK:

```
DECLARE
  tune_task VARCHAR2(30);
  tune_sql  CLOB;
BEGIN
  tune_task := DBMS_SQLTUNE.CREATE_TUNING_TASK(
    sql_id           => '1ybqt7wu5hwas'
   ,plan_hash_value => '3956160932'
   ,task_name        => 'tune_test2'
   ,description       => 'Provide SQL ID'
);
END;
/
```

Single SQL Statement from the AWR Given a Range of Snapshot IDs

You may need to use the AWR repository as a source of information for a SQL statement that has been aged out of memory. Here's an example of creating a SQL tuning task by providing a SQL_ID and range of AWR snapshot IDs:

```
DECLARE
  tune_task VARCHAR2(30);
  tune_sql  CLOB;
BEGIN
  tune_task := DBMS_SQLTUNE.CREATE_TUNING_TASK(
    sql_id      => '1tbu2jp7kv0pm'
   ,begin_snap => 21690
   ,end_snap   => 21864
   ,task_name  => 'tune_test3'
);
END;
/
```

If you're not sure which SQL_ID (and associated query) to use, then run this query:

```
SQL> select sql_id, sql_text from dba_hist_sqltext;
```

If you're unaware of the available snapshot IDs, then run this query:

```
SQL> select snap_id, end_interval_time from dba_hist_snapshot order by snap_id;
```

The following query provides information about which SQL statement was recorded during which snapshot:

```
select snap_id, sql_id, plan_hash_value
from dba_hist_sqlstat
order by snap_id;
```

■ **Tip** By default, the AWR contains only high resource-consuming queries. You can modify this behavior and ensure that a specific SQL statement is included in every snapshot (regardless of its resource consumption) by adding it to the AWR via the following:

```
SQL> exec dbms_workload_repository.add_colored_sql('98u3gf0xzq03f');
```

SQL Tuning Set Name

If you have the requirement of running the SQL Tuning Advisor against multiple SQL queries, then a SQL tuning set is required. To create a tuning task using a SQL tuning set as input, do so as follows:

```
SQL> variable mytt varchar2(30);
SQL> exec :mytt := DBMS_SQLTUNE.CREATE_TUNING_TASK(sqlset_name => 'PROD_WORKLOAD', -
                                                   task_name => 'tune_test4');
SQL> print :mytt
```

How It Works

Before manually executing the SQL Tuning Advisor, you first need to define what SQL statements will be used as input. You do this by creating a SQL tuning task and associating SQL statements with the tuning task. Oracle provides a great deal of flexibility on how you add SQL statements to a tuning task. As shown in the "Solution" section, you can do the following:

- Hard-code the text for a specific SQL query

- Use a SQL query currently in memory

- Use a SQL query in the AWR

- Define a SQL tuning set when tuning multiple queries

The prior techniques provide a variety of ways to identify SQL statements to be analyzed by the SQL Tuning Advisor. Once you've created a tuning task, you can view its details via this query:

```
select owner, task_name, advisor_name, how_created, created
from dba_advisor_tasks
where advisor_name = 'SQL Tuning Advisor'
order by created;
```

Once you have created a tuning task, you can now manually execute the SQL Tuning Advisor (Recipe 11-17). If you need to drop the tuning task, you can do so as follows:

```
SQL> exec dbms_sqltune.drop_tuning_task(task_name => '&&task_name');
```

11-17. Running the SQL Tuning Advisor
Problem

You want to manually execute SQL Tuning Advisor and get tuning advice for a SQL statement.

Solution

You can run the SQL Tuning Advisor from several different tools:

- SQL*Plus

- SQL Developer

- Enterprise Manager

Examples of accessing the SQL Tuning Advisor are shown in the following subsections:

From SQL*Plus

Use the following steps to run the SQL Tuning Advisor form SQL*Plus:

1. Create a tuning task (see Recipe 11-16 for complete details); this defines which SQL statements will be tuned. This can be a single SQL statement or several SQL statements within a SQL tuning set.

2. Execute the tuning task.

3. Display the results of the tuning task.

This example runs the SQL Tuning Advisor for a single SQL statement. First a tuning task is created.

```
DECLARE
  tune_task VARCHAR2(30);
  tune_sql  CLOB;
BEGIN
  tune_sql := 'select a.emp_id, b.dept_name ' ||
              'from emp a, dept b ' ||
              'where a.dept_id = b.dept_id';
  --
  tune_task := DBMS_SQLTUNE.CREATE_TUNING_TASK(
    sql_text     => tune_sql
   ,user_name    => 'MV_MAINT'
   ,scope        => 'COMPREHENSIVE'
   ,time_limit   => 60
   ,task_name    => 'tune_test5'
   ,description  => 'Tune a SQL statement.'
);
END;
/
```

Next the tuning task is executed:

```
SQL> exec dbms_sqltune.execute_tuning_task(task_name => 'tune_test5');
```

Lastly, a report is generated that displays the tuning advice:

```
SQL> set long 10000 longchunksize 10000 linesize 132 pagesize 200
SQL> select dbms_sqltune.report_tuning_task('tune_test5') from dual;
```

Here is some sample output:

```
1- Statistics Finding
---------------------
  Table "MV_MAINT"."DEPT" was not analyzed.
  Recommendation
  --------------
  - Consider collecting optimizer statistics for this table.
....
2- Index Finding (see explain plans section below)
--------------------------------------------------
  The execution plan of this statement can be improved by creating one or more
  indices.
  Recommendation (estimated benefit: 97.98%)
  ------------------------------------------
  - Consider running the Access Advisor to improve the physical schema design
    or creating the recommended index.
    create index MV_MAINT.IDX$$_21E10001 on MV_MAINT.EMP("DEPT_ID");
```

The prior output has specific recommendations on generating statistics for a table in the query and adding an index. You'll need to test the recommendations to ensure that performance does improve before implementing them in a production environment.

From SQL Developer

If you have access to SQL Developer 3.0 or higher, then it's very easy to run the SQL Tuning Advisor for a query. Follow these simple steps:

1. Open a SQL worksheet.

2. Type in the query.

3. Click the button associated with the SQL Tuning Advisor.

You will be presented with any findings and recommendations. If you have access to SQL Developer (it's a free download available on Oracle's OTN website), this provides a simple way to run the SQL Tuning Advisor.

■ **Note** Before running SQL Tuning Advisor from SQL Developer, ensure the user that you're connected to has the ADVISOR system privilege granted to it.

From Enterprise Manager

You can also run the SQL Tuning Advisor from within Enterprise Manager. Login to Enterprise Manager and follow these steps:

1. From the main database page, click on the "Performance" tab.

2. Select the "Advisors Home" page and then select the SQL Advisors page.

3. Click the "SQL Tuning Advisor" link.

You should be presented with a page similar to the one shown in Figure 11-3.

Figure 11-3. *Scheduling SQL Tuning Advisor jobs from Enterprise Manager*

From here you can run a SQL Tuning Advisor tuning task on the top SQL statements in memory, or historical SQL in the AWR, or provide a SQL tuning set as input.

How It Works

The SQL Tuning Advisor helps automate the task of tuning poorly performing queries. The tool is fairly easy to use, and it provides suggestions on how to tune a query, such as the following:

- Rewriting the SQL

- Adding indexes

- Implementing a SQL profile or plan baselines

- Generating statistics

The SQL Tuning advisor is easily accessed through the DBMS_SQLTUNE package, Enterprise Manager, or SQL Developer. This easy access provides everybody on the team a way to identify problematic SQL queries and generate potential tuning advice.

One key to understanding how the SQL Tuning Advisor operates is that the query optimizer can operate in two different modes: normal and tuning. When a user runs a SQL statement, the optimizer operates in *normal mode* and quickly identifies a reasonable execution plan. In this mode, the optimizer spends only a fraction of a second to try to determine the best plan.

Whereas when the SQL Tuning Advisor analyzes a query, it runs the optimizer in *tuning mode*. In this mode, the optimizer can take several minutes to analyze each step of the execution plan and generate an execution plan that is potentially much more efficient than the plan generated under normal mode.

This is somewhat similar to a computer chess game. When you allow the chess software to spend only a second or less on each move, it's easy to beat the game. However, if you allow the chess game to spend a minute or more on each move, in this mode the game makes much more optimal decisions.

11-18. Generating SQL Tuning Advice from the Automatic Database Diagnostic Monitor

Problem

You're having performance issues. You realize that the Automatic Database Diagnostic Monitor (ADDM) report is a good place to get initial advice on identifying problematic SQL statements and potential recommendations. Therefore you want to run an ADDM report.

Solution

You can view an ADDM report from the following tools:

- SQL*Plus script

- DBMS_ADDM package

- Enterprise Manager

These techniques are elaborated on in the following subsections.

SQL Approach

You can run the ADDM report manually as shown:

```
SQL> @?/rdbms/admin/addmrpt.sql
```

You'll be prompted to specify a beginning and ending snapshot. Here's some sample output:

```
Instance     DB Name        Snap Id    Snap Started        Level
-----------  ------------   ---------  ------------------  -----
012C         012C              1766  29 May 2013 08:00      1
                               1767  29 May 2013 09:00      1
                               1768  29 May 2013 10:00      1

Specify the Begin and End Snapshot Ids
~~~~~~~~~~~~~~~~~~~~~~~~~~~~~~~~~~~~~~~~
Enter value for begin_snap:
```

You'll then be prompted for a report name:

```
The default report file name is addmrpt_1_26468_26486.txt. To use this name,
press <return> to continue, otherwise enter an alternative.
Enter value for report_name:
```

After the report executes, you can inspect the output. There's a Top SQL Statements section that reports on tuning recommendations for the top resource-consuming SQL statement. Here's some sample output:

```
Finding 1: Top SQL Statements
Impact is .79 active sessions, 72.17% of total activity.
-------------------------------------------------------
SQL statements consuming significant database time were found. These
statements offer a good opportunity for performance improvement.
   Recommendation 1: SQL Tuning
   Estimated benefit is .58 active sessions, 53.07% of total activity.
   ----------------------------------------------------------------
   Action
      Investigate the INSERT statement with SQL_ID "2nw0mmysuma43" for
      possible performance improvements. You can supplement the information
      given here with an ASH report for this SQL_ID.
      Related Object
         SQL statement with SQL_ID 2nw0mmysuma43.
         INSERT INTO bling
         ( registration_id,company
         ,soa_id,product_name
```

DBMS_ADDM Package

The DBMS_ADDM package is available with Oracle Database 11g R2 or higher. When using the DBMS_ADDM package, you must pass in a valid range of begin and end AWR snapshot IDs. Query the DBA_HIST_SNAPSHOT view if you're not sure of what snapshots are available. Here's an example of running DBMS_ADDM:

```
SQL> var task_name varchar2(30);
SQL> exec DBMS_ADDM.ANALYZE_DB(:task_name, 1766, 1767);
SQL> print :task_name
```

Here is some sample output displaying the task name:

```
TASK_NAME
-------------------------------
TASK_3041
```

Next the ADDM report is displayed:

```
SQL> SET LONG 1000000 PAGESIZE 0;
SQL> SELECT DBMS_ADDM.GET_REPORT('TASK_3041') FROM DUAL;
```

The output can be quite lengthy. Here is a small snippet recommending that you run the SQL Tuning Advisor for a specific SQL statement:

```
Action
    Run SQL Tuning Advisor on the DELETE statement with SQL_ID
    "0s6gq1c890p4s".
    Related Object
        SQL statement with SQL_ID 0s6gq1c890p4s.
        delete from "MVS"."MGMT_DB_FFAT_USE_ECM_LATEST"
Rationale
    The SQL spent 98% of its database time on CPU, I/O and Cluster waits.
    This part of database time may be improved by the SQL Tuning Advisor.
```

Enterprise Manager

First, login to Enterprise Manager. From the main login page, you can access the ADDM reports in Enterprise Manager as follows:

1. Click the "Performance" tab.

2. Click on the "Advisors Home" link

3. Then click on the "ADDM" link

You should be presented with a page similar to the one shown in Figure 11-4.

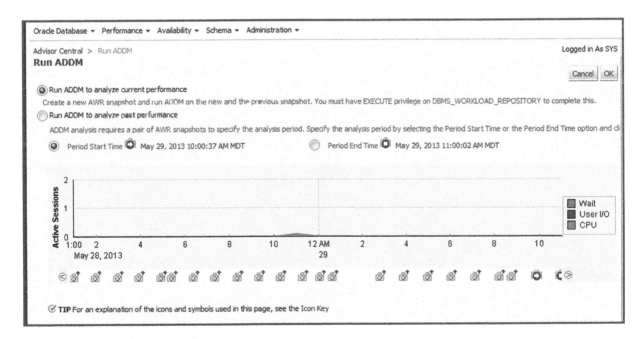

***Figure 11-4.** Running ADDM from Enterprise Manager*

From this page, you can run ADDM to analyze current performance or investigate past performance issues.

How It Works

The ADDM analyzes AWR snapshots every hour (by default) and produces performance recommendations. The suggestions are ranked by the expected benefit of implementing a recommendation. Listed next are the types of recommendations you can expect from ADDM:

- Expensive SQL statements

- Expensive PL/SQL

- RAC issues

- CPU bottlenecks

- Memory sizing recommendations

- Database configuration recommendations

- I/O bottlenecks

If you are having database performance issues, the ADDM report is an excellent place to first look for bottlenecks and problem areas of the database. The ADDM also details top resource-consuming SQL statements and makes recommendations on how to tune these queries.

CHAPTER 12

■ ■ ■

Execution Plan Optimization and Consistency

When you issue a SQL statement, the query optimizer creates an *execution plan* that describes the combination of steps Oracle takes to retrieve or modify the data. For example when you submit a query, the optimizer quickly produces several execution plans and will determine which plan is most efficient. In most scenarios, the prior behavior results in adequate-performing execution plan. However, you will encounter situations where query performance is poor and you need to understand the optimizer's choice of an execution plan. Listed next are features you can use to guide the decision path the optimizer uses when selecting an execution plan:

- Initialization parameters

- Statistics

- Hints

- SQL profiles

- SQL plan management (plan baselines)

- Adaptive SQL plan management (12c)

- Adaptive query optimization (12c)

■ **Note**   As of Oracle Database 12c, stored outlines have been deprecated in favor of plan baselines.

It's critical you understand how these features affect the optimizer's choice of an execution plan. When troubleshooting SQL performance problems, you must determine which of the prior features are enabled and how they influence query behavior. The performance of a SQL statement can vary significantly depending on which feature is implemented.

Background

Initialization parameters (that impact the optimizer) and statistics gathering are detailed in Chapter 13. Using hints is the emphasis of Chapter 14. The focus of this chapter is SQL profiles and SQL plan management (plan baselines). Also where appropriate, we will discuss Oracle Database 12c features such as adaptive SQL plan management and adaptive query optimization.

A *SQL profile* is a database object that contains optionally generated corrections and improvements to statistics for a particular SQL statement. The recommendation (and code) to implement a SQL profile is manifested through the output of the SQL Tuning Advisor. You can manually enable SQL profiles or configure them to be automatically accepted. SQL profiles help the optimizer derive better execution plans.

SQL plan management allows you to store and manage execution plans within tables in the database. *Plan baselines* consist of one or more stored execution plans that have been accepted for a SQL query. When you run a query, and if a valid execution plan exists within a plan baseline (for that query), then the optimizer will use that execution plan (instead of using an execution plan generated on-the-fly). *Plan history* is the super set of both accepted and unaccepted execution plans for a query. You can manually change the state of an unaccepted plan to accepted (this moves it to the plan baseline). This is known as *evolving* a plan baseline.

Plan baselines help ensure that the optimizer consistently chooses the same execution plan, regardless of changes in the database environment. Plan baselines provide the following benefits:

- Preserving performance when upgrading from one database version to another; in other words, helping ensure that the same execution plan is used for a query before and after the upgrade

- Keeping performance stable and consistent when data changes, or statistics are updated, or new SQL profiles become available

- Providing a mechanism for adding more efficient executions plans as they become available (like a new index is added or a SQL profile becomes available)

Starting with Oracle Database 12c, if a plan baseline exists for a query, and if a new plan is generated that has a significantly lower cost than an existing plan in the plan baseline, then Oracle will automatically add the new plan to the plan baseline. This is known as *adaptive SQL plan management*. This feature can be disabled/enabled as desired (see Recipe 12-17 for details).

Also new with Oracle database 12c is the *adaptive query optimization* feature that consists of the following features:

- Adaptive plans

- Automatic re-optimization

- SQL plan directives

- Dynamic statistics enhancements

An *adaptive plan* is an execution plan that optimizer can improve through metrics automatically gathered when a query executes. If the actual execution statistics vary significantly from the original plan statistics, then the optimizer will store the statistics.

When a query first executes, the optimizer monitors the query and if the actual execution statistics vary significantly from the original plan statistics then the optimizer will *automatically re-optimize* the query (and generate a more efficient execution plan) the next time it executes.

As a query executes, the optimizer will collect metrics and determine if additional statistics might help generate a more efficient execution plan. If so, a *SQL plan directive* is created that records the desirable statistics. Any subsequent call to DBMS_STATS (for the affected objects) will result in additional statistics being collected at the direction of the SQL plan directive. The SQL plan directives are stored in the SYSAUX tablespace and details are visible via the DBA_SQL_PLAN_DIRECTIVES view.

If a table in a query doesn't have any statistics, the optimizer will dynamically generate a minimal amount of statistics for input into formulating an execution plan. This feature has been enhanced in 12c where the optimizer will automatically decide if dynamic statistics are useful and at what level of dynamic statistics to use (see Handling Missing Statistics in Chapter 13 for details on levels).

Adaptive query optimization features are enabled by default. You can instruct the optimizer not to automatically optimize plans by setting the database parameter of OPTIMIZER_ADAPTIVE_REPORTING_ONLY to TRUE (the default setting is FALSE).

You can view adaptive reports by passing the value of ADAPTIVE to the FORMAT parameter of DBMS_XPLAN.DISPLAY_CURSOR, for example:

```
SQL> SELECT * FROM table (DBMS_XPLAN.DISPLAY_CURSOR('0rc4km05kgzb9', NULL, 'ADAPTIVE'));
```

Seeing the Big Picture

Figure 12-1 displays the flow of choices that the optimizer makes when choosing an execution plan. Please take a few minutes to analyze this diagram and ensure you grasp how the various features influence the optimizer's behavior. As you view the diagram, keep in mind the following:

- Hints are the only feature that requires a physical modification to the SQL query. All of the other techniques can be used to improve performance without changing the query.

- Initialization parameters, statistics, hints, SQL profiles, and plan baselines can all operate independently of each other. No one feature is dependent on the existence of another feature.

- The optimizer works fine with out-of-the-box settings. You don't need to use any of these features (hints, SQL profiles, and so on). However, to get the maximum performance from SQL queries, we highly recommend you know when and how to use these features to help the query optimizer make optimal decisions (and thus maximize performance).

- If you are using Oracle Database 12c, then adaptive query optimization will automatically be utilized by the optimizer to derive more efficient execution plans.

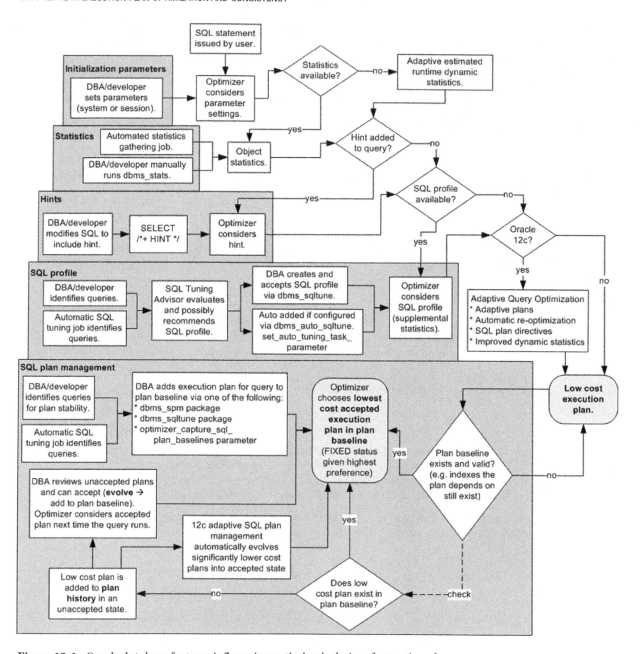

Figure 12-1. Oracle database features influencing optimizer's choice of execution plan

As you look at skep-shaped (beehive) Figure 12-1, to help understand how the optimizer chooses between the low-cost plan and a plan baseline, consider the general steps taken when formulating an execution plan:

1. The optimizer first considers initialization parameters, hints, and SQL profiles when choosing the lowest-cost plan. If using Oracle Database 12c, the optimizer will also factor in adaptive query optimization features.

2. Regardless of the plan arrived at in step 1, if a plan baseline exists for the query, the optimizer will choose the lowest-cost accepted plan from the plan baseline. Additionally, the optimizer will give preference to accepted plans that have a fixed state in the plan baseline.

3. If the accepted plans in the plan baseline are not reproducible (say an index has been dropped that all of the plan baseline plans depend on), then the optimizer chooses the lowest-cost plan generated in step 1. Lowest cost in this situation means using the least amount of database resources such as CPU, I/O, and memory.

4. If a plan baseline exists for a query, and if the low-cost plan (from step 1) has a lower cost than the plan from the plan baseline, then the low-cost plan is automatically added to the plan history for the query in an unaccepted state. You can choose to move plans from the plan history into the plan baseline so that the optimizer will consider them when choosing an execution plan. This provides you the flexibility to use better plans as they become available (evolving the plan).

5. If using a plan baseline for a query, in Oracle 12c adaptive SQL plan management is enabled by default. In this mode, if a significantly more cost-efficient plan is generated by the optimizer, then the execution plan will automatically be added to the plan baseline.

Features such as initialization parameters and hints don't require an extra license and are available with all editions of the Oracle database. Other features such as SQL profiles require an extra license and ship only with the Enterprise Edition. Table 12-1 summarizes the characteristics of each query optimizer-influencing feature.

Table 12-1. *Oracle Features Influencing the Generation of an Execution Plan*

Feature	Purpose	How to Enable	Enterprise Edition Required?	Extra License Required?	Require Change to SQL?
Initialization parameters	Influence aspects such as efficiently delivering query result sets to the client application	ALTER SYSTEM or SESSION statement	No	No	No
Statistics	Provide optimizer with characteristics of the table, data, and indexes so as to better generate execution plans	Statistics are automatically enabled and gathered, and can also be manually collected.	No	No	No
Hints	Suggestions coded into the query to influence optimizer decisions when choosing an execution plan	Add a SQL hint to the query	No	No	Yes

(continued)

Table 12-1. (*continued*)

Feature	Purpose	How to Enable	Enterprise Edition Required?	Extra License Required?	Require Change to SQL?
SQL profiles	Corrections and enhancements to statistics that enable the optimizer to craft a more efficient execution plan	1. Run SQL Tuning Advisor. 2. If SQL Tuning Advisor recommends a profile, enable via DBMS_TUNE package.	Yes	Yes	No
Plan baselines	Instructs the optimizer to consistently select a certain execution plan	1. Identify queries. 2. Enable via DBMS_SPM package.	Yes	No	No
12c Adaptive SQL plan management	Automatically added new low cost execution plan added to plan baseline	Automatically enabled. Can be disabled by DBA.	Yes	No	No
12c Adaptive query optimization	Runtime adjustments to execution plan and better use of statistics	Automatically enabled.	No	No	No
Stored Outlines	Deprecated plan stability tool; use fixed plan baselines to achieve stored outline functionality.	1. Identify queries. 2. CREATE OR REPLACE OUTLINE ... FOR <query>.	No	No	No

The first part of this chapter focuses on managing SQL profiles. The rest of the chapter deals with the implementation and use of plan baselines. We describe practical and real-world examples of the use of these tools. Where appropriate, we also have added instructions on how to use a given feature via Enterprise Manager.

12-1. Creating and Accepting a SQL Profile

Problem

You have a poorly performing query, and you want to get advice from the SQL Tuning Advisor. If the SQL Tuning Advisor recommends a SQL profile, then you want to accept the SQL profile (for the poorly performing query).

Solution

Run the SQL Tuning Advisor for the problem query. Keep in mind that the SQL Tuning Advisor may or may not recommend a SQL profile as a solution for performance issues. To run the SQL Tuning Advisor manually, perform the following steps:

1. Use DBMS_SQLTUNE to create a tuning task.

2. Execute the tuning task.

3. Generate the tuning advice report.

4. If SQL profile is part of the tuning advice output, then create and accept it.

The following example follows the prior steps. In this scenario, the SQL Tuning Advisor recommends that a SQL profile be applied to the given query.

■ **Tip** See Chapter 11 for details on creating SQL tuning tasks. Chapter 11 covers topics such as using historical SQL stored in the AWR, SQL currently in memory, or SQL tuning sets as the source of SQL for a tuning task.

Step 1: Use DBMS_SQLTUNE to Create a Tuning Task

The first step is to create a tuning task that is associated with the problem SQL statement. In the following code, the SQL text is hard-coded as input to the tune_sql variable:

```
DECLARE
  tune_sql  CLOB;
  tune_task VARCHAR2(30);
BEGIN
  tune_sql := 'select count(*) from emp';
  tune_task := DBMS_SQLTUNE.CREATE_TUNING_TASK(
    sql_text    => tune_sql
   ,user_name   => 'MV_MAINT'
   ,scope       => 'COMPREHENSIVE'
   ,time_limit  => 60
   ,task_name   => 'TUNE1'
   ,description => 'Calling SQL Tuning Advisor for one statement'
);
END;
/
```

The prior code is placed in a file named sqltune.sql and executed as follows:

```
SQL> @sqltune.sql
```

■ **Note** When working with tuning advice and SQL profiles, ensure that the database account you're using has the ADMINISTER SQL MANAGEMENT OBJECT system privilege granted to it. This privilege contains all of the privileges required to manage tuning tasks and SQL profiles.

Step 2: Execute the Tuning Task

This step runs the SQL Tuning Advisor to generate advice regarding any queries associated with the tuning task (created in step 1):

```
SQL> exec dbms_sqltune.execute_tuning_task(task_name=>'TUNE1');
```

Step 3: Run Tuning Advice Report

Now use DBMS_SQLTUNE to extract any tuning advice generated in step 2:

```
set long 10000
set longchunksize 10000
set lines 132
set pages 200
select dbms_sqltune.report_tuning_task('TUNE1') from dual;
```

For this example, the SQL Tuning Advisor recommends creating a SQL profile. Here is a snippet from the output that contains the recommendation and the code required to create the SQL profile:

```
Recommendation (estimated benefit: 86.11%)
------------------------------------------
  - Consider accepting the recommended SQL profile to use parallel execution
    for this statement.
    execute dbms_sqltune.accept_sql_profile(task_name => 'TUNE1', task_owner
          => 'SYS', replace => TRUE, profile_type =>
          DBMS_SQLTUNE.PX_PROFILE);
------------------------------------------
  Executing this query parallel with DOP 8 will improve its response time
  86.11% over the original plan. However, there is some cost in enabling
  parallel execution...
```

Step 4: Create and Accept the SQL Profile

To create the SQL profile, you need to run the code recommended by the SQL Tuning Advisor (from step 3)—for example:

```
begin
-- This is the code from the SQL Tuning Advisor
dbms_sqltune.accept_sql_profile(
    task_name => 'TUNE1',
    task_owner => 'SYS',
    replace => TRUE,
    profile_type => DBMS_SQLTUNE.PX_PROFILE);
--
end;
/
```

When the prior code is run, it creates and enables the SQL profile. Now whenever the associated SQL query is executed, the SQL profile will be considered by the optimizer when formulating an execution plan.

If you need to later drop the tuning task, you can use the DBMS_SQLTUNE.DROP_TUNING_TASK procedure. Here's an example of dropping the tuning task:

```
SQL> exec DBMS_SQLTUNE.DROP_TUNING_TASK(task_name=>'TUNE1');
```

How It Works

The only Oracle-supported method for creating a SQL profile is to run the SQL Tuning Advisor and, if recommended, create a SQL profile using the Tuning Advisor's output. In other words, the SQL Tuning Advisor determines if a SQL profile will help and, if so, generates the code required to create a SQL profile for a given query.

Keep in mind that a SQL profile is not a silver bullet for improving query performance. It may be that the SQL Tuning Advisor recommends a SQL profile for a query and it does nothing to improve performance. We recommend that you observe the performance characteristics of the query before and after the SQL profile has been created. If there is a significant performance gain, then keep the SQL profile in place, otherwise drop it (see Recipe 12-8 for details on how to drop a SQL profile).

The "Solution" section detailed how to manually run the SQL Tuning Advisor. Keep in mind that with Oracle Database 11g and higher, this tuning task job automatically runs on a regularly scheduled basis. The automatic tuning task will oftentimes recommend the application of a SQL profile for a poorly performing query. See Chapter 11 for details on automatic SQL tuning features. You can review the output of the automatic tuning job via this query:

```
SQL> SELECT DBMS_AUTO_SQLTUNE.REPORT_AUTO_TUNING_TASK FROM DUAL;
```

We recommend that you review the output of the automatic tuning job on a regular basis. If a SQL profile is recommended then consider creating it with the code provided in the output from the tuning task.

■ **Tip** See Recipe 12-3 for details on how to configure the automatic acceptance of SQL profiles.

As noted in the "Solution" section, a SQL profile is created and accepted via the DBMS_SQLTUNE.ACCEPT_SQL_PROFILE procedure. There are many options available when using this procedure (see Table 12-2 for details).

Table 12-2. *Parameters for the ACCEPT_SQL_PROFILE Procedure*

Parameter Name	Description
TASK_NAME	Mandatory name of tuning task
OBJECT_ID	The identifier of the advisor object representing the SQL statement
NAME	Name of SQL profile (case-sensitive)
DESCRIPTION	Description of SQL profile
CATEGORY	Category name that must match the session value of the SQLTUNE_CATEGORY initialization parameter
TASK_OWNER	Tuning task owner
REPLACE	Specify TRUE to replace profile if it already exists
FORCE_MATCH	Specify TRUE for SQL statement matching after normalization of literal values into bind values
PROFILE_TYPE	REGULAR_PROFILE specifies no change to parallel execution; PX_PROFILE changes regular profile to parallel execution.

The FORCE_MATCH parameter of ACCEPT_SQL_PROFILE requires further explanation. Recall that a SQL profile is associated with a SQL statement. The SQL statement is identified via a hash function (SQL signature). The hash function is generated after converting the SQL text and removing extra white space. When setting FORCE_MATCH to TRUE, this additionally normalizes literal values into bind values. This is similar to the algorithm generated via the FORCE option of the CURSOR_SHARING database initialization parameter.

For example, with FORCE_MATCH set to TRUE, the following two SQL statements will generate the same SQL signature:

```
SQL> select value from my_table where value = 'AA';
SQL> select value from my_table where value = 'bb';
```

This allows SQL statements that use literal values to share the same SQL profile. If there is a combination of literal values and bind variables in a SQL statement, then literal values are not normalized.

SQL PROFILE VS. DATABASE PROFILE

It's puzzling that Oracle would choose the name of "profile" and apply it to two diverse database features—namely, SQL profiles and database profiles. Perhaps in a future release, Oracle might consider renaming SQL profiles to something like SQL Optional More Intelligent Statistics That Make Your Queries Run Faster. Regardless, ensure you don't confuse a SQL profile with a database profile.

Briefly, a SQL profile is associated with a SQL statement and contains adjustments to statistics that help the optimizer generate a more efficient execution plan. The SQL Tuning Advisor recommends and generates the code required to create and accept a SQL profile, whereas a database profile is an object assigned to a user that constrains database resource usage and also enforces password security. A database profile is created with the CREATE PROFILE statement.

12-2. Determining if a Query is Using a SQL Profile

Problem

You've created a SQL profile for a query and wonder if the SQL profile is being used by the optimizer when the query executes.

Solution

Query the SQL_PROFILE column of V$SQL to display any SQL queries currently in memory that have used a SQL profile. For example:

```
select sql_id, child_number, sql_profile
from v$sql
where sql_profile is not null;
```

To view historical high resource-consuming SQL statements that have used a SQL profile, then query the DBA_HIST_SQLSTAT view:

```
select sql_id, sql_profile
from dba_hist_sqlstat
where sql_profile is not null;
```

How It Works

When a SQL query executes, the query optimizer will detect whether there is an associated SQL profile. If so, the optimizer can choose to use the SQL profile to adjust the execution plan for the query. If the optimizer does use a SQL profile, it will record that in the SQL_PROFILE column in the V$SQL view.

Also recall that the AWR is a historical repository that contains information on high resource-consuming SQL statements. If a high resource usage SQL statement is recorded in the AWR and if it was using a SQL profile, that information is noted in the SQL_PROFILE column of DBA_HIST_SQL_STAT.

If you are manually tuning a query and are using tools such as Autotrace or the DBMS_XPLAN package, then the use of a SQL profile is displayed in the output of these tools. For example:

```
SQL> set autotrace trace explain
SQL> <run the query in question>
```

If a SQL profile is being used, then you should see this in the output:

```
Note
-----
   - SQL profile "SYS_SQLPROF_013f199ac5990000" used for this statement
```

The same type of SQL profile information is displayed in the output of DBMS_XPLAN.DISPLAY_CURSOR and DBMS_XPLAN.DISPLAY.

RENAMING A SQL PROFILE

When you create and accept a SQL profile (see Recipe 12-1), the name is usually consists of a system-generated non-meaningful name. If you want to rename a SQL profile, use the DBMS_SQLTUNE package and the ALTER_SQL_PROFILE procedure. For example:

```
BEGIN dbms_sqltune.alter_sql_profile ( NAME => 'SYS_SQLPROF_013f199ac5990000',
attribute_name =>
'NAME', VALUE => 'ORDER_ACCEPT_QUERY_SP');
END;
/
```

This allows you to provide a descriptive name for the SQL profile. You can verify the name change by querying DBA_SQL_PROFILES.

12-3. Automatically Accepting SQL Profiles

Problem

You realize that the Automatic SQL Tuning job runs on a daily basis (in Oracle Database 11g or higher). You determine that the automatic tuning job generates reasonable SQL profiles for problematic queries and now want to enable the automatic acceptance of SQL profiles generated by the automatic tuning job.

■ **Tip** See Chapter 11 for full details on modifying the Automatic SQL Tuning job.

Solution

Use the DBMS_AUTO_SQLTUNE.SET_AUTO_TUNING_TASK_PARAMETER procedure to enable the automatic acceptance of SQL profiles recommended by the Automatic SQL Tuning task—for example:

```
BEGIN
DBMS_AUTO_SQLTUNE.SET_AUTO_TUNING_TASK_PARAMETER(
  parameter => 'ACCEPT_SQL_PROFILES', value => 'TRUE');
END;
/
```

If you want to disable the automatic acceptance of SQL profiles, then do so as follows (using the FALSE parameter):

```
BEGIN
DBMS_AUTO_SQLTUNE.SET_AUTO_TUNING_TASK_PARAMETER(
  parameter => 'ACCEPT_SQL_PROFILES', value => 'FALSE');
END;
/
```

■ **Note** The DBMS_AUTO_SQLTUNE package requires the DBA role or that EXECUTE on the package has been granted explicitly to a user. This package is available in Oracle Database 11g R2 or higher. If you are using a lower version of the database, then use the DBMS_SQLTUNE package.

How It Works

In Oracle Database 11g or higher, an automatically configured job runs the SQL Tuning Advisor on a periodic basis (determined by a configured maintenance window). This job identifies high resource-consuming SQL statements from performance metrics contained in the AWR. When the automatic tuning job runs, it will occasionally recommend that a SQL profile be implemented for a poorly performing SQL statement. If you have configured the automatic acceptance via DBMS_AUTO_SQLTUNE.SET_AUTO_TUNING_TASK_PARAMETER, and if the SQL Tuning Advisor deems the query's performance will significantly improve with the SQL Profile, then it will be automatically implemented. You can report on the details of the automatic tuning task configuration via this query:

```
SELECT
 parameter_name
,parameter_value
FROM dba_advisor_parameters
WHERE task_name = 'SYS_AUTO_SQL_TUNING_TASK'
AND   parameter_name
  IN ('ACCEPT_SQL_PROFILES',
      'MAX_SQL_PROFILES_PER_EXEC',
      'MAX_AUTO_SQL_PROFILES',
      'EXECUTION_DAYS_TO_EXPIRE');
```

Here is some sample output:

```
PARAMETER_NAME           PARAMETER_VALUE
------------------------ --------------------
EXECUTION_DAYS_TO_EXPIRE 30
ACCEPT_SQL_PROFILES      TRUE
MAX_SQL_PROFILES_PER_EXEC 20
MAX_AUTO_SQL_PROFILES    10000
```

■ **Tip** SQL profiles that have automatically been implemented display the value of AUTO in the TYPE column of the DBA_SQL_PROFILES view.

You can also use Enterprise Manager to configure the automatic acceptance of SQL profiles. From the Performance tab, click on Advisors Home, then select SQL Advisors. Next click on Automatic SQL Tuning Results. You should see a page similar to Figure 12-2.

Figure 12-2. Configuring automatic acceptance of SQL profiles

From this screen, you can configure features such as the automatic implementation of SQL profiles, maximum time for a tuning session, and so on.

12-4. Displaying SQL Profile Information

Problem

You have created and accepted several SQL profiles and now want to view information related to these database objects.

Solution

Use the DBA_SQL_PROFILES view to display information about SQL profiles. Here's an example that selects the most interesting columns:

```
SQL> select name, type, status, sql_text from dba_sql_profiles;
```

Here is a snippet of the output:

```
NAME                            TYPE     STATUS    SQL_TEXT
------------------------------- -------- --------- -------------------------------
SYS_SQLPROF_012eda58a1be0001    MANUAL   ENABLED   SELECT ecm_snapshot_id AS id...
SYS_SQLPROF_012ea20305980000    MANUAL   ENABLED   SELECT *  FROM inv_maint...
SYS_SQLPROF_012edf0316930003    MANUAL   ENABLED   SELECT /* + parallel(mgmt_db_f...
```

For this database, there are several manually enabled SQL profiles (as shown in the prior output).

■ **Note** Since a SQL profile is associated with a specific SQL statement (and not a user), there are no ALL- or USER-level views associated with SQL profiles. Having said that, keep in mind that it is possible for two SQL statements to have the same signature, yet be based on tables that exist in separate schemas.

How It Works

Recall that a SQL profile contains improvements to existing statistics. The DBA_SQL_PROFILES view is the best source for viewing the SQL profile name, attributes, and associated SQL text.

To view the internal SQL profile hint-related information, you can additionally query the DBMSHSXP_SQL_PROFILE_ATTR view—for example:

```
SELECT
 a.name
,b.comp_data
FROM dba_sql_profiles          a
    ,dbmshsxp_sql_profile_attr b
WHERE a.name = b.profile_name;
```

Here is some sample output:

```
SYS_SQLPROF_0130520c90dc0002
<outline_data><hint><![CDATA[OPT_ESTIMATE(@"SEL$2",
NLJ_INDEX_SCAN, "FS"@"SEL$2", ("MAP"@"SEL$2"), "DB_FEAT_OPT_112_SUM_MV_IDX3",
SCALE_ROWS=0.3369001041)]]></h
```

The prior output gives you an indication of the types of hints within a SQL profile. This information is used by the optimizer to better estimate the cardinality of each execution step. This data allows the optimizer to make better decisions when generating an execution plan.

You can also view this internal SQL profile information by querying the SQLOBJ$ and SQLOBJ$DATA views. The data in these views is in XML format, and therefore you must format the output with Oracle XML functions when querying—for example:

```
SELECT
  extractvalue(value(a), '.') sqlprofile_hints
FROM sqlobj$      o
    ,sqlobj$data d
    ,table(xmlsequence(extract(xmltype(d.comp_data),'/outline_data/hint'))) a
WHERE o.name      = '&profile_name'
AND   o. plan_id = d.plan_id
AND   o.signature = d.signature
AND   o.category = d.category
AND   o.obj_type = d.obj_type;
```

Here is a small sample of the output:

```
OPT_ESTIMATE(@"SEL$EF0E05FC", INDEX_SCAN, "MGMT_TARGETS"@"SEL$4",
"MIDX3", SCALE_ROWS=50.68489486)
OPT_ESTIMATE(@"SEL$EF0E05FC", NLJ_INDEX_FILTER,
"MGMT_ECM_GEN_SNAPSHOT"@"SEL$3", ("MGMT_TARGETS"@"SEL$4"),
"IDX$$_1197C0001", SCALE_ROWS=0.4308705)
```

Again, these profile statistics don't force the optimizer to use a certain execution plan. Rather, these statistics provide the optimizer with information that enables it to construct a more efficient execution plan.

12-5. Selectively Testing a SQL Profile
Problem

You have a SQL profile that the SQL Tuning Advisor has recommended you enable for a SQL query. You want to test to see if the SQL profile helps performance but want to restrict the SQL profile being used to one session before enabling the profile for all sessions in the database. The idea being that you want to first verify the performance impact before allowing the optimizer to consider the SQL profile for all sessions running the given SQL query.

Solution

When you create a SQL profile, its category is assigned a value of DEFAULT (the category can be viewed by querying DBA_SQL_PROFILES). Also, when you start a SQL*Plus session by default the initialization parameter of SQTUNE_CATEOGRY has a value of DEFAULT. When you execute a SQL statement, the optimizer will check to see if there are any SQL profiles for the query, and also it will check to see if the category of the SQL profile matches the session's (or system level) initialization parameter setting for SQLTUNE_CATEGORY. If those values match, then the optimizer will use the SQL profile as input when generating the execution plan.

Unless manually modified, the SQL profile category (value of DEFAULT) will always match the SQLTUNE_CATEGORY (value of DEFAULT). This means that if you alter a SQL profile's category to something other than DEFAULT, then the optimizer will not consider using a SQL profile for query unless the session running the query has its SQLTUNE_CATEGORY modified to match the category of the SQL profile.

For example, say you modify the SQL profile to have a category of TEST1:

```
BEGIN
  DBMS_SQLTUNE.ALTER_SQL_PROFILE(
    name => 'SYS_SQLPROF_012eda58a1be0001',
    attribute_name => 'CATEGORY',
    value => 'TEST1');
END;
/
```

■ **Note** You need the ALTER ANY SQL PROFILE privilege to alter a SQL profile.

Now the optimizer will only consider using the SQL profile for sessions executing the SQL query that have the initialization parameter of SQLTUNE_CATEGORY set to TEST1. You can set SQLTUNE_CATEGORY for a session as follows:

```
SQL> alter session set sqltune_category=TEST1;
```

You can verify the session setting of the SQLTUNE_CATEGORY via this statement:

```
SQL> show parameter sqltune_category
```

And you can verify the category of a SQL profile via this query:

```
SQL> select name, category from dba_sql_profiles;
```

How It Works

Setting a SQL profile's category to something other than DEFAULT allows you to isolate a SQL profile's use to only those sessions that have the SQLTUNE_CATEGORY set to match the category of the SQL profile. This allows you to test the impact of implementing a SQL profile and back it out quickly, simply by altering a session's SQLTUNE_CATEGORY.

■ **Tip** The SQLTUNE_CATEGORY can be set at either the session or system level. This means at the system level you could effectively disable and enable the optimizer's consideration of SQL profiles by setting the system level SQLTUNE_CATEGORY to something other than DEFAULT.

12-6. Transporting a SQL Profile to a Different Database

Problem

You have a test database and want to extract all of the SQL profiles from the test database and move them to a production database.

Solution

Listed next are the steps involved with transporting a SQL profile from one database to another:

1. Create a staging table.

2. Populate the staging table.

3. Move the table from the source database to the destination database (use Data Pump or a database link).

4. On the destination database, extract information from the staging table to populate the data dictionary with SQL profile information.

These steps are detailed in the following subsections.

Step 1: Create a Staging Table

Use the DBMS_SQLTUNE.CREATE_STGTAB_SQLPROF procedure to create the staging table. This example creates a table named PROF_STAGE owned by the MV_MAINT user:

```
BEGIN
  dbms_sqltune.create_stgtab_sqlprof(
    table_name => 'PROF_STAGE',
    schema_name => 'MV_MAINT' );
END;
/
```

Step 2: Populate the Staging Table

Use the DBMS_SQLTUNE.PACK_STGTAB_SQLPROF procedure to populate the table created in step 1 with SQL profile information. This example populates the table with information regarding a specific SQL profile:

```
BEGIN
  dbms_sqltune.pack_stgtab_sqlprof(
    profile_name => 'SYS_SQLPROF_012edf84806e0004',
    staging_table_name => 'PROF_STAGE',
    staging_schema_owner => 'MV_MAINT' );
END;
/
```

■ **Tip** The PROFILE_NAME parameter can include wildcard characters. For example, if you want to transport all SQL profiles in a database, you can use '%' for the PROFILE_NAME.

Step 3: Copy the Staging Table to the Destination Database

You can copy the table from one database to the other via Data Pump or by using a database link. This example creates a database link in the destination database and then copies the table from the source database:

```
create database link source_db
connect to mv_maint
identified by foo
using 'source_db';
```

Once the database link has been created, the table can be copied directly from the source with the CREATE TABLE...AS SELECT statement:

```
SQL> create table PROF_STAGE as select * from PROF_STAGE@source_db;
```

Step 4: Load the Contents of the Staging Table into the Destination Database

Now in the destination database, unpack the table to load profile information into the database:

```
BEGIN
  DBMS_SQLTUNE.UNPACK_STGTAB_SQLPROF(
    replace => TRUE,
    staging_table_name => 'PROF_STAGE');
END;
/
```

If no profile name is specified, the default is the % wildcard character (meaning all profiles in the table will be loaded into the destination database).

How It Works

It's fairly easy to copy SQL profiles from one database to another. You simply have to create a special table to hold the profile information, then populate the table, copy the table to the destination database, and lastly unpack the table's contents. Table 12-3 describes all of the parameters for the profile packing procedure.

Table 12-3. Parameters for the DBMS_SQLTUNE.PACK_STGTAB_SQLPROF Procedure

Parameter Name	Description	Default Value
PROFILE_NAME	Name of profile (% wildcard characters can be used)	%
PROFILE_CATEGORY	Name of category, can use % wildcards in name	DEFAULT
STAGING_TABLE_NAME	Name of the staging table to store profile information	No default value
STAGING_SCHEMA_OWNER	Owner of staging table (NULL means use current schema)	NULL

The DBMS_SQLTUNE.UNPACK_STGTAB_SQLPROF procedure takes the same parameters as the packing procedure with an additional REPLACE parameter. The REPLACE parameter specifies whether to replace profiles if they already exist (can be TRUE or FALSE).

12-7. Disabling a SQL Profile

Problem

You created a SQL profile for a query (see Recipe 12-1) and sometime later you added an index to one of the tables used by the query and subsequently noticed that the SQL_PROFILE column of V$SQL is not populated (see Recipe 12-2) when the query is executing. You therefore want to disable the SQL profile and verify that there is no performance decline.

Solution

First verify the name of the SQL profile that you want to disable:

```
SQL> select name, status from dba_sql_profiles;
```

Here's a partial snippet of the output:

```
NAME                            STATUS
------------------------------ --------
SYS_SQLPROF_013f199ac5990000 ENABLED
```

Now use the DBMS_SQLTUNE.ALTER_SQL_PROFILE procedure to modify the status of the profile to DISABLED:

```
BEGIN
  DBMS_SQLTUNE.ALTER_SQL_PROFILE(
    name => 'SYS_SQLPROF_013f199ac5990000',
    attribute_name => 'STATUS',
    value => 'DISABLED');
END;
/
```

How It Works

Disabling a SQL profile is fairly easy. You may want to do this because you have determined the SQL profile is no longer being used by the optimizer for a query. Or you may want to ascertain the impact of a SQL profile by disabling it, running the query, re-enabling it, and running the query. You can enable a disabled SQL profile as shown:

```
BEGIN
  DBMS_SQLTUNE.ALTER_SQL_PROFILE(
    name => 'SYS_SQLPROF_013f199ac5990000',
    attribute_name => 'STATUS',
    value => 'ENABLED');
END;
/
```

You can also disable a SQL profile from Enterprise Manager. From the Performance tab click on the SQL link, then click on SQL Plan Control. You should be presented with a screen similar to Figure 12-3.

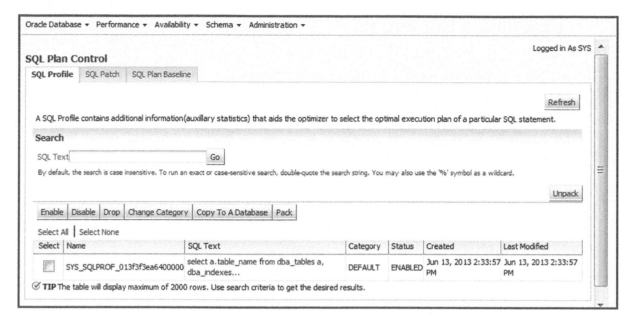

Figure 12-3. *Managing SQL profiles*

From this screen, you can manage features such as enabling, disabling, changing the category, and dropping a SQL profile.

12-8. Dropping a SQL Profile
Problem

You have determined that a SQL profile is no longer being used by a SQL query (see Recipe 12-2) and want to drop it.

Solution

Execute the DBMS_SQLTUNE.DROP_SQL_PROFILE procedure to drop a SQL profile. Pass in the name of the SQL profile you want to drop—for example:

```
SQL> exec dbms_sqltune.drop_sql_profile('SYS_SQLPROF_012eda58a1be0001');
```

■ **Note**   You need the DROP ANY SQL PROFILE privilege to drop a SQL profile.

How It Works

It's fairly easy to drop a SQL profile. You might want to do this if you're cleaning up a database or if you want to remove profiles from a testing environment. If you're unsure of the SQL profile name, you can query DBA_SQL_PROFILES for more information.

If you want to drop all profiles in a database, you can use PL/SQL to loop through all profiles and drop them:

```
declare
  cursor c1 is select name from dba_sql_profiles;
begin
  for r1 in c1 loop
    dbms_sqltune.drop_sql_profile(r1.name);
  end loop;
end;
/
```

12-9. Creating a Plan Baseline for a SQL Statement in Memory

Problem

You're planning a database upgrade. You know from past experience that sometimes after the database is upgraded SQL queries can perform more poorly. This is caused by the new version of the optimizer choosing a different execution plan that is less efficient than the plan used by the prior version of the optimizer. Therefore, to ensure that the optimizer consistently chooses the same execution plan before and after the upgrade, you want to establish a plan baseline for the query. You want to start by establishing plan baseline for a SQL query in memory.

■ **Note**   Recall that a plan baseline is one or more accepted execution plans associated with a SQL statement. If a plan baseline exists for a SQL statement, the optimizer will choose the lowest cost execution plan that exists within the plan baseline for the given SQL query.

Solution

The procedure for manually associating a plan baseline with a SQL statement is as follows:

1. Identify the SQL statement for which you want a plan baseline.

2. Provide an identifier such as the SQL_ID as input to the DBMS_SPM package to create a plan baseline for the SQL statement.

For example, suppose you have a SQL statement you've been working with such as the following:

```
SQL> select first_name from emp where emp_id = 100;
```

Now query the V$SQL view to determine the SQL_ID for the query:

```
select sql_id, plan_hash_value, sql_text
from v$sql
where sql_text like 'select first_name from emp where emp_id = 100'
and sql_text not like '%v$sql';
```

Here is a snippet of the output:

```
SQL_ID          PLAN_HASH_VALUE SQL_TEXT
------------- --------------- ----------------------------------------------------------
dv73f7y69ny8z      3956160932 select first_name from emp where emp_id = 100
```

Now that the SQL_ID has been identified, use it as input to the DBMS_SPM.LOAD_PLANS_FROM_CURSOR_CACHE function to create a plan baseline for the given query—for example:

```
DECLARE
  plan1 PLS_INTEGER;
BEGIN
  plan1 := DBMS_SPM.LOAD_PLANS_FROM_CURSOR_CACHE(sql_id => 'dv73f7y69ny8z');
END;
/
```

The query now should have an entry in the DBA_SQL_PLAN_BASELINES view showing that it has an enabled plan baseline associated with it—for example:

```
SQL> select sql_handle, plan_name, sql_text from dba_sql_plan_baselines;
```

Here's a small snippet of the output:

```
SQL_HANDLE                  PLAN_NAME                            SQL_TEXT
------------------------- ------------------------------------ ---------------
SQL_30c98e5c7bb6b95d        SQL_PLAN_31kcfbjxvdfaxd8a279cc       select first_name...
```

How It Works

Keep in mind that it's possible that a single SQL statement can have more than one execution plan associated with it in memory. This can happen when the SQL executes multiple times and something in the environment changes that causes the optimizer to choose a different plan (like updated statistics, use of bind variables, changes with database initialization parameters, adding/deleting a SQL profile, and so on).

You can uniquely identify a single plan via the combination of SQL_ID and the PLAN_HASH_VALUE column of V$SQL and use that as input to DBMS_SPM, for example:

```
DECLARE
  plan1 PLS_INTEGER;
BEGIN
  plan1 := DBMS_SPM.LOAD_PLANS_FROM_CURSOR_CACHE(sql_id => 'dv73f7y69ny8z',
          plan_hash_value => 3956160932);
END;
/
```

If you don't specify a PLAN_HASH_VALUE when loading a plan baseline from memory, then Oracle will load all plans available for a SQL query in memory. The next time the query executes, the optimizer will use the lowest cost accepted plan in the plan baseline. If multiple plans exist in the plan baseline for a query, and if you have a specific plan that you want the optimizer to always use, then consider altering the plan to a FIXED state. See Recipe 12-12 for details on altering a given execution plan within the plan baseline to a FIXED state.

The "Solution" section described how to identify a single SQL statement for which you want to create a plan baseline (based on the SQL_ID) using a query in the cursor cache. There are many methods for creating a plan baseline for a query, such as using the SQL text, schema, module, and so on. For example, next a plan baseline is loaded based on a partial SQL string:

```
DECLARE
  plan1 PLS_INTEGER;
BEGIN
  plan1 := DBMS_SPM.LOAD_PLANS_FROM_CURSOR_CACHE(
            attribute_name => 'sql_text'
            ,attribute_value => 'select emp_id from emp%');
END;
/
```

See Table 12-4 for details on input parameters available with the DBMS_SPM.LOAD_PLANS_FROM_CURSOR_CACHE function.

Table 12-4. *Parameters for the LOAD_PLANS_FROM_CURSOR_CACHE Function*

Parameter Name	Description
SQL_ID	SQL statement identifier.
PLAN_HASH_VALUE	Plan identifier; if NULL, then capture all plans for the given SQL_ID.
SQL_TEXT	Text used for identifying plan baseline into which plans are loaded.
SQL_HANDLE	SQL handle used for identifying plan baseline into which plans are loaded.
FIXED	Value of NO means plans are not loaded in a fixed state. YES means plans are loaded as fixed. Fixed plan baselines are given preference over non-fixed.
ATTRIBUTE_NAME	One of the following: SQL_TEXT, PARSING_SCHEMA_NAME, MODULE, ACTION.
ATTRIBUTE_VALUE	Value of the attribute; when using SQL_TEXT attribute, the value can contain wildcard values.
ENABLED	Plans are loaded in an enabled state (default is YES).

■ **Note**   See Recipe 12-10 for an example of how to create plan baselines for SQL statements contained in a SQL tuning set.

12-10. Creating Plan Baselines for SQL Contained in SQL Tuning Set
Problem

You have the following scenario:

- You're upgrading a database to a new version.

- You know from past experience that upgrading to newer versions of Oracle can sometimes cause SQL statements to perform poorly because the optimizer in the upgraded version of the database is choosing a less efficient (worse) execution plan than the optimizer from the prior version of the database.

- You want to ensure that a set of critical SQL statements execute with acceptable performance after the upgrade.

In essence, you are upgrading and would prefer that the optimizer choose the same execution plans (for the given set of SQL queries) both before and after the upgrade. You don't want the upgrade to result in new plans that risk degrading performance.

Solution

To deal with this problem, use the most resource-intensive SQL queries in the AWR as candidates for the creation of plan baselines. This solution uses the technique of creating an AWR baseline. An AWR baseline is a snapshot of activity in the AWR designated by begin/end snapshot IDs. Listed next are the steps for creating and populating a SQL tuning set with high resource-consuming SQL statements found in an AWR baseline and then creating plan baselines for those queries:

1. Create an AWR baseline.

2. Create a SQL tuning set object.

3. Populate the SQL tuning set with the queries found in the AWR baseline.

4. Use the tuning set as input to DBMS_SPM to create a plan baseline for each query contained in the SQL tuning set.

■ **Note** You have a great deal of flexibility on how to populate a SQL tuning set with high resource-consuming queries in the AWR or currently in memory. See Chapter 11 for complete details on working with SQL tuning sets.

Step 1: Create an AWR Baseline

The first step is to create an AWR baseline. For example, suppose you knew you had high-load queries running between two snapshots in your database. The following creates an AWR baseline using two snapshot IDs:

```
BEGIN
  DBMS_WORKLOAD_REPOSITORY.create_baseline (
    start_snap_id => 2150,
    end_snap_id   => 2155,
    baseline_name => 'peak_baseline_jun14_13');
END;
/
```

If you're unsure of the available snapshots in your database, you can run an AWR report or select the SNAP_ID from DBA_HIST_SNAPSHOTS:

```
SQL> select snap_id, begin_interval_time from dba_hist_snapshot order by 1;
```

Step 2: Create a SQL Tuning Set Object

Now create a SQL tuning set. This next bit of code creates a tuning set named test1:

```
BEGIN
  dbms_sqltune.create_sqlset(
    sqlset_name => 'test1'
    ,description => 'STS from AWR');
END;
/
```

Step 3: Populate the SQL Tuning Set with High-Resource Queries Found in AWR Baseline

Now the SQL tuning set (created in step 2) is populated with any queries found within the AWR baseline (created in step 1):

```
DECLARE
  base_cur dbms_sqltune.sqlset_cursor;
BEGIN
  OPEN base_cur FOR
    SELECT value(x)
    FROM table(dbms_sqltune.select_workload_repository(
      'peak_baseline_jun14_13', null, null,'elapsed_time',
      null, null, null, 15)) x;
  dbms_sqltune.load_sqlset(
    sqlset_name => 'test1',
    populate_cursor => base_cur);
END;
/
```

In the prior lines of a code, the AWR baseline name is passed to the DBMS_SQLTUNE package. The queries within the baseline are select by the elapsed time, and the top 15 are specified. To view the queries within the SQL tuning set, query the data dictionary as follows:

```
SELECT sqlset_name, elapsed_time
,cpu_time, buffer_gets, disk_reads, sql_text
FROM dba_sqlset_statements
WHERE sqlset_name = 'test1';
```

CHAPTER 12 ■ EXECUTION PLAN OPTIMIZATION AND CONSISTENCY

Step 4: Use the Tuning Set As Input to DBMS_SPM to Create Plan Baselines for Each Query Contained in the SQL Tuning Set

Now the tuning set (created in step 2 and populated in step 3) is provided as input to the DBMS_SPM package:

```
DECLARE
  test_plan1 PLS_INTEGER;
BEGIN
  test_plan1 := dbms_spm.load_plans_from_sqlset(
                  sqlset_name=>'test1');
END;
/
```

Each query in the SQL tuning set should now have an entry in the DBA_SQL_PLAN_BASELINES view showing that it has an enabled plan baseline associated with it—for example:

```
SQL> select sql_handle, plan_name, sql_text from dba_sql_plan_baselines;
```

How It Works

The technique shown in the "Solution" section is a very powerful method for creating plan baselines for the most resource-consuming queries running in your database. The key to this recipe is understanding that you can use as input (to the DBMS_SPM package) queries contained in a SQL tuning set. A SQL tuning set can be populated from high resource-consuming statements found in the AWR and memory. This allows you to easily create plan baselines for the most problematic queries.

Having plan baselines in place for resource-intensive queries helps ensure that the same execution plan is used after there are changes to your system, such as a database upgrades, changes in statistics, different data sets, and so on.

Keep in mind that it's possible to have more than one accepted execution plan within the plan baseline. If you have a specific plan that you want the optimizer to always use, then consider altering the plan to a FIXED state. See Recipe 12-12 for details on altering a plan baseline to a FIXED state.

12-11. Automatically Adding Plan Baselines

Problem

You want to automatically create plan baselines for every SQL query that repeatedly executes in your database.

Solution

Listed next are the steps for automatically creating plan baselines for SQL statements that execute more than once:

1. Set the OPTIMIZER_CAPTURE_SQL_PLAN_BASELINES parameter to TRUE (either at the session or system level).

2. Execute two times or more the queries for which you want plan baselines captured.

3. Set the OPTIMIZER_CAPTURE_SQL_PLAN_BASELINES to FALSE.

This next example illustrates the process for adding a plan baseline (for a query) using the prior steps. First, set the specified initialization parameter at the session level:

```
SQL> alter session set optimizer_capture_sql_plan_baselines=true;
```

Now a query is executed twice. Oracle will automatically create a plan baseline for a query that is run two or more times while the OPTIMIZER_CAPTURE_SQL_PLAN_BASELINES parameter is set to TRUE:

```
SQL> select first_name from emp where emp_id=3000;
SQL> select first_name from emp where emp_id=3000;
```

Now set the initialization parameter back to FALSE.

```
SQL> alter session set optimizer_capture_sql_plan_baselines=false;
```

The query now should have an entry in the DBA_SQL_PLAN_BASELINES view showing that it has an enabled plan baseline associated with it—for example:

```
SELECT
 sql_handle, plan_name, enabled, accepted,
 created, optimizer_cost, sql_text
FROM dba_sql_plan_baselines;
```

Here is a partial listing of the output:

```
SQL_HANDLE           PLAN_NAME                      ENA ACC...
-------------------  -----------------------------  --- ---...
SQL_790bd425fe4a0125 SQL_PLAN_7k2yn4rz4n095d8a279cc YES YES...
```

How It Works

Enabling OPTIMIZER_CAPTURE_SQL_PLAN_BASELINES allows you to automatically capture plan baselines for queries running repeatedly (more than once) in your database. The "Solution" section described how to use this feature at the session level. You can also set the parameter so that all repeating queries in the database have plan baselines generated—for example:

```
SQL> alter system set optimizer_capture_sql_plan_baselines=true;
```

From this point, any query in the database that runs more than once will automatically have a plan baseline created for it. We wouldn't recommend that you do this in a production environment unless you have first carefully tested this feature and ensured that there will be no adverse side effects (from storing a plan baseline for every query executing more than once). However, you may have a test environment where you want to purposely create a plan baseline for every SQL statement that is repeatedly run.

▄ **Note** By default, the OPTIMIZER_CAPTURE_SQL_PLAN_BASELINES parameter is FALSE.

12-12. Altering a Plan Baseline

Problem

You've been monitoring the plan baseline of a SQL query and notice there are two execution plans with an accepted and enabled status. You've examined at both of the execution plans and are confident that one plan is superior to the other based on the value of OPTIMIZER_COST in DBA_SQL_PLAN_BASELINES. You want to instruct the optimizer to always use the plan with the lowest cost.

Solution

The optimizer will give preference to plan baselines with a FIXED state. Use the DBMS_SPM package and ALTER_SQL_PLAN_BASELINE function to alter a current plan baseline execution plan to FIXED. Here's an example:

```
DECLARE
 pf PLS_INTEGER;
BEGIN
  pf := dbms_spm.alter_sql_plan_baseline(
    plan_name => 'SQL_PLAN_1wskqhvrwf8g60e23be79'
    ,attribute_name => 'fixed'
    ,attribute_value => 'YES');
END;
/
```

You can query the FIXED column of DBA_SQL_PLAN_BASELINES to verify that it is now fixed within the baseline. Listed next is such a query:

```
SQL> SELECT sql_handle, plan_name, enabled, accepted, fixed FROM dba_sql_plan_baselines;
```

Here is some sample output:

```
SQL_HANDLE           PLAN_NAME                      ENA ACC FIX
-------------------- ------------------------------ --- --- ---
SQL_457bf2f82571bd38 SQL_PLAN_4ayzkz0kr3g9s90e466fd YES YES NO
SQL_790bd425fe4a0125 SQL_PLAN_7k2yn4rz4n095d8a279cc YES YES YES
```

How It Works

You can think of fixing a plan baseline as a way of establishing a preference hierarchy for how the optimizer chooses an execution plan from within the plan baseline. The optimizer will give first priority to any fixed plans within the plan baseline. If no fixed plan is available, then accepted non-fixed plan baselines are considered. Execution plans that are added to a plan baseline that already contains a fixed plan baseline will be considered secondary (unless you add them as fixed).

Table 12-5 describes the parameters available with ALTER_SQL_PLAN_BASELINE. You can specify either the SQL_HANDLE or PLAN_NAME or both. If the SQL_HANDLE is NULL, then a PLAN_NAME must be specified and vice versa.

Table 12-5. *Parameters for the* ALTER_SQL_PLAN_BASELINE *Function*

Parameter	Description
SQL_HANDLE	SQL handle identifier for the SQL statement in the plan baseline
PLAN_NAME	Unique identifier for a plan baseline
ATTRIBUTE_NAME	Name of the attribute being modified
ATTRIBUTE_VALUE	Attribute value being modified

The ATTRIBUTE_NAME and ATTRIBUTE_VALUE parameters consist of a name/value pairing that can be used to alter various attributes of a plan baseline. See Table 12-6 for a complete description of the possible pairings.

Table 12-6. *Values for* ATTRIBUTE_NAME *and* ATTRIBUTE_VALUE

Attribute Name	Possible Attribute Values	Description
ENABLED	YES or NO	YES means the plan is available for use. The plan may or may not have been accepted.
FIXED	YES or NO	YES means the plan is fixed.
AUTOPURGE	YES or NO	YES means the plan can be purged if the plan isn't used within a time period. NO means the plan is never purged.
PLAN_NAME	String up to 30 characters	Name of plan
DESCRIPTION	String up to 500 characters	Description of plan

■ **Tip** Use the ENABLED attribute of ALTER_SQL_PLAN_BASELINE to either disable or re-enable a plan baseline for use.

12-13. Determining If Plan Baselines Exist
Problem

You recently implemented a plan baseline for a query. You want to verify the configuration of a plan baseline.

Solution

Run the following query to view details regarding any plan baselines that have been configured:

```
set pages 100 linesize 150
col sql_handle form a20
col plan_name form a30
col sql_text form a40
col created form a20
--
SELECT sql_handle, plan_name, enabled
,accepted, created, optimizer_cost, sql_text
FROM dba_sql_plan_baselines;
```

The output from the prior query is very wide and has been modified to fit within the page width:

```
SQL_HANDLE            PLAN_NAME                       ENA ACC
-------------------- ------------------------------- --- ---
SQL_b98d2ae2145eec3d SQL_PLAN_bm39aw8a5xv1xae72d2f5 YES YES
CREATED              OPTIMIZER_COST SQL_TEXT
-------------------- -------------- --------------------
21-MAR-11 10.53.29.0              2 select last_name from custs...
```

In the output, there are two key columns: the SQL_HANDLE and PLAN_NAME. Each query has an associated SQL_HANDLE that is an identifier for a query. Each execution plan has a unique PLAN_NAME. The PLAN_NAME is unique within DBA_SQL_PLAN_BASELINES, whereas one query (identified by SQL_HANDLE) can have multiple execution plans (identified by PLAN_NAME).

How It Works

The DBA_SQL_PLAN_BASELINES view provides a quick and easy way to determine if plan baselines exist and are in use. If a plan is enabled and accepted, then the query has a plan baseline in use.

■ **Note** There is no ALL or USER-level data dictionary views for plan baselines. This is because the plan baseline is associated with a specific SQL statement and not a user.

You can also view and manage plan baselines from Enterprise Manager. From the Performance tab, click on SQL, then click on SQL Plan Control. Next, click the SQL Plan Baseline tab. You should see a screen similar to Figure 12-4.

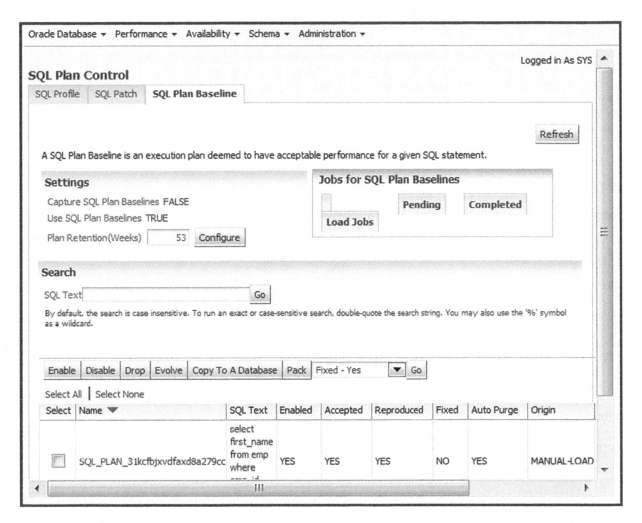

Figure 12-4. *Viewing and managing plan baselines*

From this screen, you can perform tasks such as enabling, disabling, dropping, and evolving plan baselines.

12-14. Determining if a Query is Using a Plan Baseline
Problem

You've been assigned to investigate performance issues with a database and application. As a preliminary task of understanding the environment, you want to determine if any SQL statements are using plan baselines.

Solution

You can directly determine if a SQL statement currently in memory has utilized a plan baseline via the following query:

```
select sql_id, child_number, sql_plan_baseline, sql_text
from v$sql
where sql_plan_baseline is not null
and sql_text like 'select first_name%';
```

Here is a snippet of the output:

```
SQL_ID          CHILD_NUMBER SQL_PLAN_BASELINE              SQL_TEXT
------------- ------------ ------------------------------ -------------------------
898c46878bm3f            0 SQL_PLAN_31kcfbjxvdfaxc4b18358 select first_name from ...
```

How It Works

The technique shown in the "Solution" section only shows SQL statements that are currently in memory (V$SQL). You can manually verify the optimizer's use of a plan baseline by viewing the output from tools such as Autotrace or DBMS_XPLAN. For example:

```
SQL> set autotrace trace explain;
SQL> select first_name from emp where emp_id = 3000;
```

Here is a partial listing of the output indicating that a SQL plan baseline execution plan is used for this query:

```
Note
-----
   - SQL plan baseline "SQL_PLAN_5jjxkya4jrxv5d8a279cc" used for this statement
```

Here's an example of using DBMS_XPLAN:

```
EXPLAIN PLAN
SET STATEMENT_ID = 'myplan' FOR
select first_name from emp where emp_id=3000;
--
set pagesize 100
set linesize 132
set long 1000000
col xplan format a132
--
SELECT dbms_xplan.display_plan(statement_id => 'myplan') AS XPLAN
FROM dual;
```

Here's the output indicating a plan baseline was used by the optimizer to determine the execution plan:

```
Note
-----
- SQL plan baseline "SQL_PLAN_5jjxkya4jrxv5d8a279cc" used for this statement
```

12-15. Displaying Plan Baseline Execution Plans

Problem

You want to view any execution plans for a given plan baseline.

Solution

If you're not sure which plan baseline you want to view, then first query the DBA_SQL_PLAN_BASELINES view:

```
SQL> SELECT plan_name, sql_text FROM dba_sql_plan_baselines;
```

After you determine the plan name, then use the DBMS_XPLAN.DISPLAY_SQL_PLAN_BASELINE function to display the execution plan and corresponding plan baseline details. This example reports details for a specific plan:

```
SELECT *
FROM TABLE(
DBMS_XPLAN.DISPLAY_SQL_PLAN_BASELINE(plan_name=>'SQL_PLAN_5jjxkya4jrxv5d8a279cc'));
```

Here is a partial listing of the output:

```
--------------------------------------------------------------------------------
SQL handle: SQL_58c7b2f2891bf765
SQL text:  select first_name from emp where emp_id=3000
--------------------------------------------------------------------------------
Plan name: SQL_PLAN_5jjxkya4jrxv5d8a279cc        Plan id: 3634526668
Enabled: YES      Fixed: NO      Accepted: YES      Origin: AUTO-CAPTURE
Plan rows: From dictionary
--------------------------------------------------------------------------------

PLAN_TABLE_OUTPUT
--------------------------------------------------------------------------------
Plan hash value: 3956160932

---------------------------------------------------------------------------
| Id  | Operation          | Name | Rows  | Bytes | Cost (%CPU)| Time     |
---------------------------------------------------------------------------
|   0 | SELECT STATEMENT   |      |     1 |     6 |    34   (3)| 00:00:01 |
|*  1 |  TABLE ACCESS FULL | EMP  |     1 |     6 |    34   (3)| 00:00:01 |
---------------------------------------------------------------------------
```

How It Works

The DBMS_XPLAN.DISPLAY_SQL_PLAN_BASELINE function allows you to display one or more execution plans in a plan baseline. The return type for this function is a PL/SQL table type. This function takes three parameters (described in Table 12-7).

Table 12-7. Parameters for the DISPLAY_SQL_PLAN_BASELINE Function

Parameter	Description
SQL_HANDLE	Identifier for the SQL statement; instructs function to display all plans for the SQL statement
PLAN_NAME	Instructs function to display a specific plan for a SQL statement
FORMAT	Determines the detail of information displayed; takes values of BASIC, TYPICAL, and ALL

If you want to display all plans for a SQL statement, then use as input the SQL_HANDLE parameter—for example:

```
SELECT *
FROM TABLE(
DBMS_XPLAN.DISPLAY_SQL_PLAN_BASELINE(sql_handle=>'SQL_b98d2ae2145eec3d'));
```

If there are multiple plans, then each plan will be displayed in the output.

12-16. Manually Adding a New Execution Plan to Plan Baseline (Evolving)

Problem

You have the following scenario:

- You have an existing plan baseline for the query.

- You have recently added an index that the query can use.

- The optimizer determines a new lower-cost plan is now available for the query and adds the new plan to the plan history in an unaccepted state.

- You notice the new plan either from a recommendation by the SQL Tuning Advisor or by querying the DBA_SQL_PLAN_BASELINES view.

- You have examined the new execution plan, have run the query in a test environment, and are confident that the new plan will result in better performance.

You want to evolve the low-cost plan in the history so that it's moved to an accepted plan in the baseline. You realize that once the plan is accepted in the baseline, the optimizer will use it (if it's the lowest-cost plan in the baseline).

■ **Note** Starting with Oracle Database 12c, new low-cost execution plans will automatically be entered into an existing plan baseline for a query in an accepted state. See Recipe 12-17 for details on how to modify this behavior.

Solution

First verify that there are plans in the unaccepted state for the query in question. Here's a quick example:

```
SELECT sql_handle, plan_name, enabled, accepted, optimizer_cost
FROM dba_sql_plan_baselines
WHERE sql_text like '%select first_name from emp where emp_id=3000%';
```

Here is the output indicating there are two plans, one unaccepted but with a much lower cost:

```
SQL_HANDLE                PLAN_NAME                      ENA ACC OPTIMIZER_COST
------------------------- ------------------------------ --- --- --------------
SQL_58c7b2f2891bf765      SQL_PLAN_5jjxkya4jrxv5c4b18358  YES NO               2
SQL_58c7b2f2891bf765      SQL_PLAN_5jjxkya4jrxv5d8a279cc  YES YES             34
```

Use the DBMS_SPM.EVOLVE_SQL_PLAN_BASELINE function to move a plan from the history to the baseline (evolve the plan). In this example, the SQL handle (unique SQL string associated with a SQL statement) is used to evolve a plan:

```
SET SERVEROUT ON SIZE 1000000
SET LONG 100000
DECLARE
  rpt CLOB;
BEGIN
  rpt := DBMS_SPM.EVOLVE_SQL_PLAN_BASELINE(
    sql_handle => 'SQL_58c7b2f2891bf765');
  DBMS_OUTPUT.PUT_LINE(rpt);
END;
/
```

If Oracle determines that there is an unaccepted plan with a lower cost, then you'll see output similar to this indicating that the plan has been moved to the accepted state (evolved):

```
GENERAL INFORMATION SECTION
-------------------------------------------------------------------------------------

  Task Information:

  ---------------------------------------------
  Task Name          : TASK_3772
  Task Owner         : SYS
  Execution Name     : EXEC_3979
  Execution Type
: SPM EVOLVE
  Scope              : COMPREHENSIVE
  Status             : COMPLETED
  Started            : 06/15/2013 15:41:01
  ...
FINDINGS
SECTION
-------------------------------------------------------------------------------------

Findings (2):
-----------------------------
  1. The plan was verified in 0.31000 seconds. It
passed the benefit criterion
     because its verified performance was 40.07033 times better than that of the
     baseline plan.
  2. The plan was automatically accepted.
```

You can quickly verify that the new plan baseline is now in use by setting AUTOTRACE on and running the query—for example:

```
SQL> set autotrace trace explain;
SQL> select first_name from emp where emp_id=3000;
```

Here's a small snippet of the output indicating the new plan baseline is in use:

```
Note
-----
   - SQL plan baseline "SQL_PLAN_5jjxkya4jrxv5c4b18358" used for this statement
```

How It Works

One key feature of SQL plan management is that when a new low-cost plan is generated by the query optimizer, if the new low-cost plan has a lower cost than the accepted plan(s) in the plan baseline, the new low-cost plan will automatically be added to the query's plan history in an unaccepted state.

You can choose to accept this new low-cost plan, which then moves it into the plan baseline as accepted. Moving an unaccepted execution plan from the plan history to the plan baseline (ENABLED and ACCEPTED) is known as evolving the plan baseline.

Why would a new plan ever be generated by the optimizer? There are several factors that would cause the optimizer to create a new execution plan that doesn't match an existing one in the plan baseline:

- New statistics are available.

- A new SQL profile has been assigned to the query.

- An index has been added or dropped.

This gives you a powerful technique to manage and use new plans as they become available. We should also point out again that starting with Oracle Database 12c, new low-cost execution plans that are added to the plan history will automatically be evolved (added to the plan baseline). See Recipe 12-17 for details on modifying this default behavior.

You can use the DBMS_SPM.EVOLVE_SQL_PLAN_BASELINE function in the following modes:

- Specify the name of the plan to evolve.

- Provide a list of plans to evolve.

- Run it with no value, meaning that Oracle will evolve all non-accepted plans contained within the plan baseline repository.

Table 12-8 describes the parameters used in the DBMS_SPM.EVOLVE_SQL_PLAN_BASELINE function.

Table 12-8. *Parameters for the EVOLVE_SQL_PLAN_BASELINE Function*

Parameter	Description	Default Value
SQL_HANDLE	SQL statement ID; NULL means consider all statements with unaccepted plans.	NULL
PLAN_NAME	Plan name; NULL means consider all unaccepted plans in plan baseline.	NULL
PLAN_LIST	List of plan names	DBMS_SPM.NAME_LIST
TIME_LIMIT	Valid only if VERIFY=YES. Time limit in minutes to verify plans. DBMS_SPM.AUTO_LIMIT lets Oracle choose the time limit; DBMS_SPM.NO_LIMIT means no time limit.	DBMS_SPM.AUTO_LIMIT
VERIFY	Verify that performance will be improved before accepting the plan	YES
COMMIT	Updates accepted status from NO to YES	YES

12-17. Toggling the Automatic Acceptance of New Low-Cost Execution Plans

Problem

In Oracle Database 12c, if a plan baseline exists for a query, and a new lower cost execution plan is generated by the optimizer, the new execution plan will automatically be entered into the plan baseline in an accepted state. You want to change the behavior of Oracle so as to not automatically add new execution plans to the plan baseline.

Solution

You can disable the automatic acceptance of a plan added to the plan baseline via the following code:

```
BEGIN
  DBMS_SPM.SET_EVOLVE_TASK_PARAMETER('SYS_AUTO_SPM_EVOLVE_TASK',
  'ACCEPT_PLANS', 'false');
END;
/
```

How It Works

New in Oracle Database 12c, execution plans will automatically be evolved for you when the daily SYS_AUTO_SPM_EVOLVE_TASK job runs. You can verify that plans will be automatically evaluated and potentially moved to the accepted state via this query:

```
select parameter_name, parameter_value
from dba_advisor_parameters
where task_name = 'SYS_AUTO_SPM_EVOLVE_TASK'
and parameter_name = 'ACCEPT_PLANS';
```

You can re-enable the automatic acceptance of plans with this code:

```
BEGIN
  DBMS_SPM.SET_EVOLVE_TASK_PARAMETER('SYS_AUTO_SPM_EVOLVE_TASK',
  'ACCEPT_PLANS', 'true');
END;
```

12-18. Disabling Plan Baselines

Problem

You're working with a test database that has many SQL statements with associated plan baselines. You want to determine what the performance difference would be without the plan baselines enabled and therefore want to temporarily disable the use of plan baselines.

Solution

To disable the use of any SQL plan baselines within the database, set the OPTIMIZER_USE_SQL_PLAN_BASELINES initialization parameter to FALSE:

```
SQL> alter system set optimizer_use_sql_plan_baselines=false scope=memory;
```

The prior line disables the use of the plan baselines at the SYSTEM level and records the value in memory (but not in the server parameter file). To re-enable the use of plan baselines, set the value back to TRUE.

You can also set the OPTIMIZER_USE_SQL_PLAN_BASELINES at the session level. This disables the use of plan baselines for the duration of the session for the currently connected user:

```
SQL> alter session set optimizer_use_sql_plan_baselines=false;
```

How It Works

The default value for OPTIMIZER_USE_SQL_PLAN_BASELINES is TRUE, which means by default, if plan baselines are available, they will be used. When enabled, the optimizer will look for a valid plan baseline execution plan for the given SQL query and choose the one with the lowest cost. This gives you a quick and easy way to disable/enable the use of plan baselines within your entire database or specific to a session.

If you want to disable the use of one specific plan baseline, then alter its state to DISABLED (by setting the ENABLED attribute to a value of NO):

```
DECLARE
 pf PLS_INTEGER;
BEGIN
  pf := dbms_spm.alter_sql_plan_baseline(
    plan_name => 'SQL_PLAN_4ayzkz0kr3g9s6afbe2b3'
   ,attribute_name => 'ENABLED'
   ,attribute_value => 'NO');
END;
/
```

12-19. Removing Plan Baseline Information
Problem

You have several plan baselines that you no longer want to use and therefore want to remove them.

Solution

First, determine which plan baselines exist for your database:

```
SQL> select plan_name, sql_handle, optimizer_cost from dba_sql_plan_baselines;
```

Once you have either the PLAN_NAME or the SQL_HANDLE, you can drop a single plan baseline. This removes a single execution plan from the plan baseline using the PLAN_NAME parameter:

```
DECLARE
  plan_name1 PLS_INTEGER;
BEGIN
  plan_name1 := DBMS_SPM.DROP_SQL_PLAN_BASELINE(
                          plan_name => 'SQL_PLAN_bm39aw8a5xv1x519fc7bf');
END;
/
```

You can also drop all plans associated with a SQL statement. This example removes all plans associated with a SQL statement using the SQL_HANDLE parameter:

```
DECLARE
  sql_handle1 PLS_INTEGER;
BEGIN
  sql_handle1 := DBMS_SPM.DROP_SQL_PLAN_BASELINE(
                          sql_handle => 'SQL_b98d2ae2145eec3d');
END;
/
```

How It Works

You may occasionally want to remove SQL plan baselines for the following reasons:

- You have old plans that aren't used anymore because more efficient plans (evolved) are available for a SQL statement (see Recipe 12-14 for determining if a query is using a plan baseline).

- You have plans that were never accepted and now want to remove them.

- You have plans that were created for testing environments that are no longer needed.

As shown in the "Solution" section, you can remove a specific plan baseline via the PLAN_NAME parameter. This will remove one specific plan. If you have several plans associated with one SQL statement, you can remove all plan baselines for that SQL statement via the SQL_HANDLE parameter.

If you have a database where you want to clear out all plans, then you can encapsulate the call DBMS_SPM.DROP_SQL_PLAN_BASELINE within a PL/SQL block that drops all plans by looping through any plan found in DBA_SQL_PLAN_BASELINES:

```
SET SERVEROUT ON SIZE 1000000
DECLARE
  sql_handle1 PLS_INTEGER;
  CURSOR c1 IS
    SELECT sql_handle
    FROM dba_sql_plan_baselines;
BEGIN
  FOR r1 IN c1 LOOP
    sql_handle1 := DBMS_SPM.DROP_SQL_PLAN_BASELINE(sql_handle => r1.sql_handle);
    DBMS_OUTPUT.PUT_LINE('PB dropped for SH: ' || r1.sql_handle);
  END LOOP;
END;
/
```

12-20. Transporting Plan Baselines

Problem

You have a test environment, and you want to ensure that all of the plan baselines in the test system are moved to a production database.

Solution

Follow these steps to transport plan baselines:

1. Create a table using the DBMS_SPM package and CREATE_STGTAB_BASELINE procedure.

2. Populate the table with plan baselines using the DBMS_SPM.PACK_STGTAB_BASELINE function.

3. Copy the staging table to the destination database using a database link or Data Pump.

4. Import the plan baseline information using the DBMS_SPM.UNPACK_STGTAB_BASELINE function.

This example first uses the DBMS_SPM package to create a table named EXP_PB:

```
BEGIN
  DBMS_SPM.CREATE_STGTAB_BASELINE(table_name => 'exp_pb');
END;
/
```

■ **Note**   You cannot create the staging table in the SYS user.

Next the EXP_PB table is populated with plan baselines created by the database user MV_MAINT:

```
DECLARE
  pbs NUMBER;
BEGIN
  pbs := DBMS_SPM.PACK_STGTAB_BASELINE(
           table_name => 'exp_pb',
           enabled => 'yes',
           creator => 'MV_MAINT');
END;
/
```

The prior code populates the table with all plan baselines created by a user. You can also populate the table by PLAN_NAME, SQL_HANDLE, SQL_TEXT, or various other criteria. The only mandatory parameter is the name of the table to be populated.

Now copy the staging table to the destination database. You can use a database link or Data Pump to accomplish this.

Lastly, on the destination database, use the DBMS_SPM.UNPACK_STGTAB_BASELINE function to take the contents of the EXP_PB table and create plan baselines:

```
DECLARE
  pbs NUMBER;
BEGIN
  pbs := DBMS_SPM.UNPACK_STGTAB_BASELINE(
          table_name => 'exp_pb',
          enabled => 'yes');
END;
/
```

You should now have all of the plan baselines transferred to your target database. You can query DBA_SQL_PLAN_BASELINES to verify this.

How It Works

It's a fairly easy process to create a table, populate it with plan baseline information, copy the table, and the import its contents into the destination database. As shown in step 2 of the "Solution" section of this recipe, the PACK_STGTAB_BASELINE function is used (see Table 12-9) for details on parameters to this function). This function allows quite a bit of flexibility in what types of plan baselines you want exported. You can limit the plan baselines extracted to a specific user, or enabled, or accepted, and so on.

Table 12-9. *Parameters for the PACK_STGTAB_BASELINE Function*

Parameter Name	Description
TABLE_NAME	Mandatory name of table to be populated with plan baseline information
TABLE_OWNER	Staging table owner; NULL specifies current user.
SQL_HANDLE	Uniquely identifies a SQL statement
PLAN_NAME	Uniquely identifies a specific plan baseline; % wildcards valid as input
SQL_TEXT	Identifies SQL queries by text; % wildcards valid as input
CREATOR	User who created plan baseline
ORIGIN	Origin of plan baseline; valid values are: MANUAL-LOAD, AUTO_CAPTURE, MANUAL_SQLTUNE, or AUTO_SQLTUNE.
ENABLED	Specifies enabled plan baselines; YES and NO are valid values.
ACCEPTED	Specifies accepted plan baselines; YES and NO are valid values.
FIXED	Specifies fixed plan baselines; YES and NO are valid values.
MODULE	Module name
ACTION	Action name

Likewise, the DBMS_SPM.UNPACK_STGTAB_BASELINE function allows you a great deal of flexibility on what types of plan baselines are extracted from the staging table and loaded into the destination database. The input parameters for UNPACK_STGTAB_BASELINE are the same as the parameters used for PACK_STGTAB_BASELINE (described in Table 12-9).

CHAPTER 13

Configuring the Optimizer

The cost optimizer determines the most efficient execution plan for a SQL statement. The optimizer depends heavily on the statistics that you (or the database) gather. This chapter explains how to set the optimizer goal and how to control the behavior of the optimizer. You'll learn how to enable and disable automatic statistics collection by the database and when to collect statistics manually. You'll learn how to set preferences for statistics collection as well as how to validate new statistics before making them available to the optimizer. The chapter explains how to lock statistics, export statistics, gather system statistics, restore older versions of statistics, and handle missing statistics.

Bind peeking behavior, wherein the optimizer looks at the bind variable values when parsing a SQL statement, can have unpredictable effects on execution plans. The chapter explains adaptive cursor sharing, which is designed to produce execution plans based on the specific values of bind variables.

Collecting statistics on large tables is always problematic, so the chapter shows how to use the incremental statistics gathering feature to speed up statistics collection for large partitioned tables. You'll also learn how to use the new concurrent statistics collection feature to optimize statistics collection for large tables.

Collecting extension statistics for expressions and column groups improves optimizer performance, and you'll learn how to collect these types of statistics. The chapter also explains how to let the database tell you which columns in a table are candidates for creating a column group.

13-1. Choosing an Optimizer Goal
Problem

You want to set the cost optimizer goal for your database.

Solution

You can influence the behavior of the cost optimizer by setting an optimizer goal. The optimizer will collect appropriate statistics based on the goal you set. You set the optimizer goal with the optimizer_mode initialization parameter. You can set the parameter to the value ALL_ROWS or FIRST_ROWS_n, as shown here:

```
optimizer_mode=all_rows
optimizer_mode=first_rows_n          /* n can be 1,10,100 or 1000 */
```

The default value for the optimizer_mode parameter is ALL_ROWS.

How It Works

The default value for the optimizer_mode parameter, ALL_ROWS, has the goal of maximizing throughput—it minimizes resource use to complete the processing of the entire statement and get all the requested rows. The alternate value of FIRST_ROWS_*n* uses the goal of response time, which is the time it takes to return the first *n* number of rows.

If you set the optimizer_mode parameter to FIRST_ROWS_*n*, all sessions will use the optimizer goal of best response time. However, you can change the optimizer goal just at the session level by executing a SQL statement such as the following:

```
SQL> alter session set optimizer_mode=first_rows_1;
```

Note that the ALL_ROWS optimizer mode setting has built-in bias toward full table scans because its goal is to minimize resource usage. The FIRST_ROWS_*n* setting, on the other hand, favors index accesses because its goal is minimizing response time and thus returns the requested number of rows as fast as possible.

In addition to the optimizer_mode parameter, you can also set the following parameters to influence the behavior of the optimizer:

- optimizer_index_caching

- optimizer_index_cost_adj

- db_file_multiblock_read_count

In general, changing these parameters at the database level can lead to unexpected optimizer behavior, including potential performance deterioration for some queries. The recommended practice is to leave these parameters at their default levels. We, however, do show (Recipe 13-11) how to use one of these parameters (optimizer_index_cost_adj) at the session level to improve the performance of a long-running query by forcing the optimizer to use an index.

13-2. Enabling Automatic Statistics Gathering

Problem

You want to enable automatic statistics gathering in your database.

■ **Tip**　Oracle recommends enabling automatic optimizer statistics collection.

Solution

You enable automatic statistics collection by using the enable procedure in the DBMS_AUTO_TASK_ADMIN package. Check the status of the auto optimizer stats collection task in the following way:

```
SQL> select client_name,status from dba_autotask_client;

CLIENT_NAME                          STATUS
------------------------------       --------
auto optimizer stats collection      DISABLED
auto space advisor                    ENABLED
sql tuning advisor                    ENABLED
SQL>
```

Execute the dbms_auto_task_admin.enable procedure to enable the automatic statistics collection task:

```
SQL> begin dbms_auto_task_admin.enable(
  2   client_name=>'auto optimizer stats collection',
  3   operation=>NULL,
  4   window_name=>NULL);
  5   end;
  6   /

PL/SQL procedure successfully completed.
```

Check the status of the auto optimizer stats collection task:

```
SQL>  SELECT client_name,status from dba_autotask_client;

CLIENT_NAME                        STATUS
--------------------------------   --------
auto optimizer stats collection    ENABLED
auto space advisor                 ENABLED
sql tuning advisor                 ENABLED

SQL>
```

You can disable the statistics collection task by using the dbms_auto_task_admin.disable procedure:

```
SQL> begin
  2   dbms_auto_task_admin.disable(
  3   client_name=> 'auto optimizer stats collection',
  4   operation=> NULL,
  5   window_name=> NULL);
  6   end;
  7   /

PL/SQL procedure successfully completed.

SQL>
```

How It Works

Automatic optimizer statistics collection is enabled by default when you create a database with the DBCA. If you've disabled automatic statistics collection, you can enable it by executing the procedure shown in the "Solution" section. Once you enable automatic statistics collection, the database collects statistics whenever they get stale; the database determines this based on the changes made to the tables and indexes. Automating statistics collection eliminates all the work involved in collecting statistics yourself.

When you enable automatic optimizer statistics collection, the auto optimizer stats collection task calls the DBMS_STATS.GATHER_DATABASE_STATS_JOB_PROC procedure. This procedure is virtually identical to the DBMS_STATS.GATHER_DATABASE_STATS procedure—the big difference is that the database will collect the statistics only during the maintenance window you specify. If you don't specify a maintenance window, the database uses the default maintenance window, which opens every night from 10 p.m. to 6 a.m. and all day on weekends. The "auto optimizer stats collection auto optimizer stats job collects statistics first for those objects that need the new statistics the most. Thus, the auto statistics collection job will first collect statistics for objects that don't have any statistics or objects that underwent substantial modifications (usually about 10 percent of the rows). This way, if the statistics collection job doesn't complete before the end of the maintenance window, the database ensures that objects with the stalest statistics are refreshed.

You can query the DBA_OPTSTAT_OPERATIONS view to find out the beginning and ending times for the automatic statistics collection job, as shown here:

```
SQL> select operation,target,start_time,end_time from dba_optstat_operations
2*   where operation='gather_database_stats(auto)';


OPERATION                     START_TIME                    END_TIME
--------------------  ----------------------------  ---------------------------
gather_database_stats  26-APR-13 10.00.02.970000 PM   26-APR-13 10.03.13.671000 PM
...
SQL>
```

■ **Tip** Automatic statistics collection works very well with OLTP databases whose data changes moderately on a day-to-day basis but not for most data warehouses that perform nightly data loading from ETL jobs.

The DBA_TAB_MODIFICATIONS view stores information about the inserts, deletes, and updates to a table. By default, the OPTIONS parameter for the GATHER_DATABASE_STATS procedure is set to the value GATHER AUTO. This means that once you enable automatic statistics collection, the database will collect statistics for all tables where more than 10 percent of the rows have been affected by insert, delete, and update operations.

Automatic statistics collection by the database works well for most OLTP databases. However, in a data warehouse environment, you may run into issues because the automatic statistics collection job runs during the nightly maintenance window. If your ETL or ELT jobs load data into a table after the auto job has already collected statistics for that table, you could end up with unrepresentative statistics for that table. In a data warehouse environment, it's a good idea to collect statistics manually right after the load process completes and disable the default automatic statistics collection job.

■ **Note** In Oracle Database 12c, the automatic statistics gathering job uses concurrency when gathering statistics.

13-3. Setting Preferences for Statistics Collection
Problem

You want to set default values for the parameters used by the DBMS_STATS procedures that gather various types of statistics.

Solution

Use the appropriate DBMS_STATS.SET_*_PREFS procedure to change the default values for parameters that control statistics collection. Use the following procedures for changing the default values of the parameters used at various levels of statistics collection:

- SET_TABLE_PREFS: Lets you specify default parameters to be used by the DBMS_STATS. GATHER_*_STATS procedures for a specific table.

- SET_SCHEMA_PREFS: Lets you change the default parameters to be used by the DBMS_STATS. GATHER_*_STATS procedures for all objects in a specific schema.

- SET_DATABASE_PREFS: Lets you change the default parameters to be used by the DBMS_STATS. GATHER_*_STATS procedures for the entire database, including all user schemas and system schemas such as SYS and SYSTEM.

- SET_GLOBAL_PREFS: Sets global statistics preferences; this procedure lets you change the default statistic collection parameters for any object in the database that doesn't have an existing preference at the table level. If you don't set table-level preferences or you don't set any parameter explicitly in the DBMS_STATS.GATHER_*_STATS procedure, the parameters default to their global settings.

Here's an example that shows how to set default preferences at the database level by invoking the SET_DATABASE_PREFS procedure:

```
SQL> execute dbms_stats.set_database_prefs('ESTIMATE_PERCENT','20');
```

Once you set a preference for a parameter at the database level, it applies to all tables in the database. Note that the SET_*_PREFS procedures accept three parameters:

- pname refers to the name of the preference, such as the ESTIMATE_PERCENT preference used in the previous example.

- pvalue lets you specify a value for the preference. If you specify NULL as the value for the pvalue parameter, the preference's value will be set to the Oracle default values.

- add_sys is an optional parameter that, if set to TRUE, will also include all Oracle-owned tables in the statistics collection process.

How It Works

All DBMS_STATS.GATHER_*_STATS procedures use default values for the various parameters. There are two ways you can handle the specification of values for the various parameters that are part of the procedures in the DBMS_STATS package such as the GATHER_TABLE_STATS procedure. You can specify the preference values when you execute a procedure such as GATHER_TABLE_STATS to collect statistics. Alternatively, you can change the default values of the preferences at the table, schema, database, or global level with the appropriate DBMS_STATS.SET_*_PREFS procedure, as shown in the "Solution" section. If you don't specify a value for any of the statistics gathering parameters, the database uses the default value for that parameter.

You can find the default value of any preference by executing the DBMS_STATS.GET_PREFS procedure. The following example shows how to find the value of the current setting of the STALE_PERCENT parameter:

```
SQL> select dbms_stats.get_prefs ('STALE_PERCENT','SH') stale_percent from dual;
```

```
STALE_PERCENT
-------------

10

SQL>
```

You specify similar preferences when you collect statistics at the table, schema, or database level. Here is a description of the various preferences you can specify to control the way the database gathers statistics.

CASCADE

This specifies whether the database should collect index statistics along with the table statistics. If you set CASCADE=TRUE, this is the same as executing the GATHER_INDEX_STATS procedure on all the indexes in the database, besides collecting table and column statistics. The default is the constant DBMS_STATS.AUTO_CASCADE, which means that Oracle will determine whether to collect any index statistics.

DEGREE

This specifies the degree of parallelism the database must use when gathering statistics. Oracle recommends using the default setting of the constant DBMS_STATS.AUTO_DEGREE. Oracle chooses the correct degree of parallelism based on the object and the parallelism-related initialization parameters. When you use the default DBMS_STATS.AUTO_DEGREE setting, Oracle determines the degree of parallelism based on the size of the object. If the object is small enough, Oracle collects statistics serially, and if the object is large, Oracle uses the default degree of parallelism based on the number of CPUs. Note that the default degree is NULL, which means that the database collects statistics using parallelism only if you set the degree of parallelism at the table level with the DEGREE clause.

ESTIMATE_PERCENT

This specifies the percentage of rows the database must use to estimate the statistics. For large tables, estimation is the only way to complete the statistics collection process within a reasonable time. Statistics collection is not a trivial process—it's resource-intensive and consumes a lot of time for large tables. You can set a value between 0 and 100 for the estimate_percent parameter. A rule of thumb here is that the more uniform a table's data, the smaller the sample size can be. On the other hand, if a table's data is highly skewed, you should use a higher sample size to capture the variations in the data distribution. Of course, setting this parameter to 100 means that the database isn't doing an estimation—it will collect statistics for each row in a table. Often, DBAs set the estimate_percent parameter too high because they've had bad experiences with a table when they set a small sample size. If you think the data is uniformly distributed, even a 1 or 2 percent sample will get you very accurate statistics and save you a bunch of time and processing overhead.

■ **Tip** In Oracle Database 11g, the NDV (number of distinct values) count, which is a key statistic calculated by setting the estimate_percent parameter to DBMS_STATS.AUTO_SAMPLE_SIZE, is statistically identical to the NDV count calculated by a 100 percent complete statistics collection. The best practice is to start with the AUTO_SAMPLE_SIZE and set your own sample size only if you must.

It's not easy to select the best size for the estimate_percent parameter. If you set it too high, it'll take a long time to collect statistics. If you set it too low, you can gather the statistics quickly all right, but those statistics can very well be inaccurate. By default, the database uses the constant DBMS_STATS.AUTO_SAMPLE_SIZE to determine the best sample size. You specify the AUTO value for the estimate_percent parameter in the following way:

```
SQL> exec dbms_stats.gather_table_stats(NULL, 'MASSIVE_TABLE', estimate_percent=>
dbms_stats.auto_sample_size)
```

When you set the AUTO value for the estimate_percent parameter, not only does the database automatically determine the sampling size, but it also adjusts the size of the sample as the data distribution changes. NDV is a good criterion to calculate the accuracy of the statistics collected with varying samples sizes. The NDV of a column is defined as follows:

```
accuracy rate = 1 - (estimated NDV - actual NDV) /actual NDV
```

The accuracy rate can range from 0 to 100 percent. A 100 percent sample size will always give you a 100 percent accuracy rate. What is significant is that in Oracle 11g, auto sampling provides accuracy rates that are very close to 100 percent and take a fraction of the time it takes to collect complete statistics for a large table.

METHOD_OPT

You can specify two things with the METHOD_OPT parameter: the columns for which the database will collect statistics and the columns on which the database will create histograms. You can also specify the number of buckets in the histograms. You can specify one of the following options, or both options in combination, for this parameter:

```
FOR ALL [INDEXED | HIDDEN] COLUMNS [size_clause]
FOR COLUMNS [size_clause] column [size_clause]
```

Note that the HIDDEN option is available only in Oracle Database 12c and not in earlier releases. The FOR ALL option lets you specify that the database must collect statistics for all columns or only for the indexed columns. If you specify the INDEXED COLUMNS option, the database will collect statistics only for those columns that have an index on them. Be careful with this option because the database will not collect statistics on the table's columns, instead using basic default statistics for the columns. Using FOR ALL INDEXED COLUMNS in a data warehouse environment could be especially problematic because indexes aren't heavily used in that environment.

The FOR COLUMNS option lets you specify one or more columns on which the database must gather statistics instead of on all columns in a table, which is the default behavior. Here's how to specify the column clause in this context:

```
column:= column_name | extension name | extension
```

The column_name clause refers to the name of the column, and extension can be either a column group (in the format column_name, column_name [,...]) or an expression.

The key clause for both the FOR ALL and FOR COLUMNS options is size_clause. The clause size_clause determines whether the database should collect histograms for a column and under what conditions. One option is to supply an integer value indicating the number of histogram buckets—in the range 1 through 254—that you would like. Here's an example:

```
SQL> exec dbms_stats.gather_table_stats('HR','EMPLOYEES',method_opt=> 'for columns size 254 job_id')

PL/SQL procedure successfully completed.
SQL>
```

When you execute this procedure, the database collects histograms, and there will be 254 histogram buckets.

> ■ **Note** A value of 1 for the integer clause (for example, 'FOR ALL COLUMNS SIZE 1') won't really create any histograms on the columns because all the data is placed into a single bucket. Also, if there's already a histogram on a table, setting the value 1 for the integer clause will remove it.

Another option for the clause size_clause is to specify one of the following three values:

- REPEAT: Specifies that the database must collect histograms on only those columns that already have histograms collected for them; setting the value repeat instead of the integer 1 value ensures that you retain any useful histograms

- AUTO: Lets the database determine for which columns it should collect histograms, based on each column's data distribution (whether it's uniform or skewed) and the actual column usage statistics

- SKEWONLY: Lets the database determine for which columns it should collect histograms, based on each column's data distribution

Here is an example that specifies SKEWONLY:

```
SQL> exec dbms_stats.gather_table_stats('HR','EMPLOYEES',method_opt=> 'for all columns size
skewonly')
PL/SQL procedure successfully completed.
SQL>
```

When you specify SKEWONLY, the database will look at the data distribution for each column to determine whether the data is skewed enough to warrant the creation of a histogram.

The default value for the METHOD_OPT parameter is FOR ALL COLUMNS SIZE AUTO. That is, the database will collect statistics for all columns in a table, and it automatically selects the columns for which it should create histograms. Oracle uses the column usage metrics to determine which size to collect.

NO_INVALIDATE

You can set three different values for this parameter. The value TRUE means that the database doesn't invalidate the dependent cursors of the table for which it's collecting statistics. The value FALSE means that the database immediately invalidates the dependent cursors. Finally, you can set this parameter to the value DBMS_STATS.AUTO_INVALIDATE to let Oracle decide to invalidate the cursors—this is also the default value for the NO_INVALIDATE parameter.

GRANULARITY

This parameter determines how the database handles statistics gathering for partitioned tables. Here are the various options you can specify for the GRANULARITY parameter:

- ALL: Gathers subpartition-, partition-, and global-level statistics; this setting provides an accurate set of table statistics but is extremely resource-intensive and takes much longer to complete than a statistics collection job with the other options.

- GLOBAL: Gathers just global statistics for a table.

- PARTITION: Gathers only partition-level statistics. The partition-level statistics are rolled up at the table level and may not be very accurate at the table level.

- GLOBAL AND PARTITION: Gathers the global- and partition-level statistics but not the subpartition-level statistics.

- SUBPARTITION: Gathers only subpartition statistics.

- AUTO: This is the default value for the GRANULARITY parameter and determines the granularity based on the partitioning type.

Note that the ALL setting could take a long time to complete besides using up a lot of resources. It's not really necessary to gather statistics at the subpartition level for composite partitioned tables. In most cases, the default setting of AUTO works well. Before specifying the ALL setting, consider whether the subpartition level statistics are really useful, since they aren't used by the optimizer unless you specify the subpartition columns in the predicate. Consider using the INCREMENTAL option instead, which may be a better strategy when dealing with partitioned and subpartitioned tables.

PUBLISH

By default, the database publishes all statistics right after it completes the statistics gathering process. You can specify that the database keep newly collected statistics as pending statistics by setting the PUBLISH parameter to FALSE.

INCREMENTAL

The INCREMENTAL preference determines whether the database maintains a partitioned table's statistics without having to perform a full table scan. The default value of this parameter is FALSE, meaning the database does a full table scan to maintain global statistics. Recipe 13-19 discusses incremental statistics collection in detail.

STALE_PERCENT

The STALE_PERCENT preference determines the proportion of a table's rows that must change before the database considers the table's statistics as "stale" and starts gathering fresh statistics. By default, the STALE_PERCENT parameter is set to 10 percent. Don't collect statistics on tables that haven't changed at all, or have changed very little, because you'd be collecting unnecessary statistics.

AUTOSTATS_TARGET

This preference is valid only for auto stats collection, and you specify it when setting global statistics preferences with the SET_GLOBAL_STATS procedure. You can set the following values for this preference:

- ALL: This collects statistics for all objects in the database.

- ORACLE: This collects statistics for all Oracle-owned objects (for example, the SYSMAN user).

- AUTO: The database determines for which objects it should collect statistics.

The default value for the AUTOSTATS_TARGET parameter is AUTO. Note that currently the ALL and AUTO (default) settings work the same way. We've incorporated several Oracle best practices for statistics collection in this recipe. Try to stick with the default settings for the preferences unless you have strong reasons to do otherwise. Remember that if you're creating a new table, you can load the data first and collect statistics just for the table. Create the indexes afterward because the database automatically computes statistics for the indexes during index creation time.

13-4. Manually Generating Statistics

Problem

You're trying to determine whether you should let the database automatically collect the optimizer statistics or whether you must manually collect the statistics.

Solution

In most cases, the automatic statistics collection task is good enough to collect the optimizer statistics. In fact, there are many production databases that automate statistics collection as shown in Recipe 13-2 and never use a manual statistic collection process. However, there are cases where manual statistic collection may be necessary. Here are two cases when you must manually collect statistics.

Volatile Tables

If your database contains volatile tables that experience numerous deletes (or even truncates) throughout the day, then an automatic stats collection job that runs during the nightly maintenance window isn't adequate. There are a couple of strategies you can use in this type of situation, where a table's data keeps fluctuating throughout the day:

- Collect the statistics when the table has the number of rows that represent its "typical" state. Once you do this, lock the statistics to prevent the automatic statistics collection job from collecting fresh statistics for this table during the nightly maintenance window.

- The other option is to make the statistics of the table null.

You make the statistics of a table null by deleting the statistics first and then locking the table's statistics right after that, as shown in the following example:

```
SQL> execute dbms_stats.delete_table_stats('OE','ORDERS');

PL/SQL procedure successfully completed.

SQL> execute dbms_stats.lock_table_stats('OE','ORDERS');

PL/SQL procedure successfully completed.

SQL>
```

Bulk Loaded Tables

For tables that you bulk load data into, you must collect statistics immediately after loading the data. If you don't collect statistics right after bulk loading data into a table, the database can still use dynamic statistics to estimate the statistics, but these statistics aren't as comprehensive as the statistics that you collect.

In releases prior to Oracle Database 12c, you'd use the capability to lock statistics when a large table's data was frequently refreshed, so you'd have statistics available immediately after data loading. Locking statistics in this case prevents new statistics from being collected. The optimizer uses the old statistics once the data is loaded and available. In Oracle Database 12c, the database automatically gathers table statistics during the following two types of bulk data loads:

- `Create table as select` to create a table and load it

- `Insert into ...select` into an empty table by using the direct path insert technique

In both of these cases, there's no need to collect any table statistics because the database automatically collects them during the load. This new feature is especially useful in cases where a large table such as data warehouse's SALES table is loaded nightly.

It's important to understand that the online statistics feature gathers only table statistics and not index statistics. You can therefore run DBMS_STATS.GATHER_INDEX_STATS after the bulk load is completed to gather the index statistics and histograms, if you need them.

By default the database always gathers statistics for a table when you bulk load the table. You can disable the stats gathering by specifying the NO GATHER OPTIMZIER STATISTICS hint, as shown here:

```
CREATE TABLE employees2 AS
  SELECT /*+NO_GATHER_OPTIMIZER_STATISTICS */* FROM employees
```

You can also enable the stats gathering at the statement level by specifying the GATHER OPTIMIZER STATISICS hint. Automatic statistics gathering during bulk loads doesn't happen when a table has the following characteristics:

- The table is in an Oracle-owned schema such as SYS.

- It's a nested table.

- It's an index-organized table (IOT).

- It's an external table.

- It's a global temporary table defined as ON COMMIT DELETE ROWS.

- It's a table with virtual columns.

- It's a table whose PUBLISH preference is set to FALSE.

- It's a partitioned table where INCREMENTAL is set to true and extended syntax is not used.

How It Works

Before Oracle introduced the automatic optimizer statistics collection feature in the Oracle Database 10g release, every DBA collected scripts using the recommended DBMS_STATS package (or even the older analyze table command). With automatic statistics collection, DBAs don't have to collect optimizer statistics by scheduling DBMS_STATS jobs. However, you may still run into situations where automatic statistics collection isn't appropriate. The "Solution" section describes two such cases and how to handle them by manually collecting the statistics.

You can manually collect statistics at the table, schema, or database level by using the appropriate DBMS_STATS.GATHER_*_STATS procedure.

When you're manually gathering the optimizer statistics, it's a good idea to stick with the default settings for the various parameters that control how the database collects the statistics. Often, performance of the statistics gathering job (how fast) and the quality of the statistics itself improve when you revert to the default settings. For example, many DBAs set too high a sample size with the estimate_percent parameter, rather than letting the database use the appropriate sample size based on the DBMS_STATS.AUTO_SAMPLE_SIZE constant.

13-5. Locking Statistics
Problem

You want to lock the statistics for a table or a schema to freeze the statistics.

Solution

You can lock a table or a schema's statistics by executing the appropriate DBMS_STATS.LOCK_* procedures. For example, you can lock a table's statistics with the LOCK_TABLE_STATS procedure in the DBMS_STATS package, as shown here:

```
SQL> execute dbms_stats.lock_table_stats(ownname=>'SH',tabname=>'SALES');

PL/SQL procedure successfully completed.
SQL>
```

You can unlock the table's statistics by executing the following procedure:

```
SQL> execute dbms_stats.unlock_table_stats(ownname=>'SH',tabname=>'SALES');

PL/SQL procedure successfully completed.

SQL>
```

You can lock a schema's statistics with the DBMS_STATS.LOCK_SCHEMA_STATS procedure, as shown here:

```
SQL> execute dbms_stats.lock_schema_stats('SH');

PL/SQL procedure successfully completed.
SQL>
```

Unlock the statistics with the UNLOCK_SCHEMA_STATS procedure:

```
SQL> execute dbms_stats.unlock_schema_stats('SH');

PL/SQL procedure successfully completed.

SQL>
```

How It Works

You may want to lock a table's statistics to freeze the current set of statistics. You may also lock the statistics after you delete the existing statistics first; in this case, you are forcing the database to use dynamic statistics to estimate the table's statistics. Deleting a table's statistics and then locking the statistics is in effect the same as setting the statistics on a table to null. You have the option of setting the force argument with the GATHER_TABLE_STATS procedure to override a table's lock on its statistics.

■ **Note** Locking a table also locks all statistics that depend on that table, such as index, histogram, and column statistics.

13-6. Handling Missing Statistics

Problem

Certain tables in your database are missing statistics because the tables have had data loaded into them outside the nightly batch window. You can't collect statistics on the table during the day when the database is handling other workload.

Solution

Oracle uses dynamic statistics to compensate for missing statistics. In earlier releases, the databases always gathered dynamic statistics by default when it was confronted by a table with missing optimizer statistics. In Oracle Database 12c, the optimizer determines whether dynamic statistics collection is useful in a particular case, as well as the statistics level to use. In Oracle Database 12c, not only missing statistics but also insufficient statistics can trigger dynamic statistics collection by the optimizer. By default, when optimizer statistics are either missing or not sufficient, the database automatically collects dynamic statistics.

The database will scan a random sample of data blocks in a table when you enable dynamic sampling. You enable/disable dynamic sampling in the database by setting the `optimizer_dynamic_sampling` initialization parameter. Dynamic sampling is enabled by default, as you can see from the following:

```
SQL> show parameter dynamic

NAME                          TYPE      VALUE
----------------------------- --------- -----
optimizer_dynamic_sampling    integer       2
SQL>
```

The default level of dynamic sampling is 2; setting it to 0 disables dynamic sampling. You can modify the default value by setting a different sampling level as shown here:

```
SQL> alter system set optimizer_dynamic_sampling=4 scope=both;
System altered.

SQL>
```

How It Works

Ideally, you should gather optimizer statistics with the `DBMS_STATS` package (manually or through automatic statistics collection). In cases where you don't have a chance to collect statistics for a newly created or newly loaded table, the table won't have any statistics until the database automatically generates the statistics through its automatic stats collection job or when you schedule a manual statistics collection job. Even if you don't collect any statistics, the database uses some basic statistics, such as table and index block counts, estimated number of rows, join column, and `GROUP BY` statistics, to estimate the selectivity of the predicates in a query. Dynamic statistics go a step further, augmenting these basic statistics by dynamically gathering additional statistics at compile time. Dynamic sampling is of particular help when dealing with frequently executed queries that involve tables with no statistics.

■ **Note**   Oracle doesn't collect dynamic statistics for external tables.

There's a cost to collecting dynamic statistics because the database uses resources to gather statistics during query compilation. If you don't execute these queries many times, the database incurs an overhead each time it executes a query involving table(s) for which it must dynamically collect statistics. For dynamic sampling to really pay off, it must help queries that are executed frequently.

It's important to understand the significance of the dynamic statistics levels, which can range from 0 to 11. The dynamic statistics level controls when Oracle collects dynamic statistics as well as the size of the sample. You can set the dynamic statistics level with the OPTIMIZER_DYNAMIC_SAMPLING initialization parameter or with a SQL hint.

Unlike in previous releases when the database collected dynamic statistics only when tables had no statistics, in Oracle Database 12c the optimizer decides automatically whether dynamic statistics are useful and which statistics level to use. So, the main determinant of whether the database collects dynamic statistics isn't the presence or absence of statistics; it is whether the available statistics are sufficient to generate optimal execution plans. Whenever the optimizer deems that the existing statistics are insufficient, it collects and uses dynamic statistics.

Automatic dynamic statistics are enabled when any of the following is true:

- The OPTIMIZER_DYNAMIC_SAMPLING initialization parameter is set to its default value.

- You set the OPTIMIZER_DYNAMIC_SAMPLING initialization parameter to 11.

- You invoke the gathering of dynamic statistics through a SQL hint.

The optimizer automatically collects dynamic statistics when there are missing statistics, stale statistics, or insufficient statistics. The optimizer decides whether to use dynamic statistics based on factors such as the following:

- SQL statements use parallel execution.

- You've created a SQL plan directive.

- The SQL statement was captured in SQL Plan Management or Automatic Workload Repository or is currently in the shared SQL area.

Note that the sample size used for dynamic statistics at various sampling levels is in terms of data blocks, not rows. Here is a brief description of the various dynamic statistics levels:

- *Level 0*: Doesn't use dynamic statistics.

- *Level 1*: Uses dynamic statistics for all tables that don't have statistics, provided there's at least one nonpartitioned table without statistics in the query; the table must also not have any indexes, and it must be larger than 32 blocks, which is the sample size for this level.

- *Level 2*: Uses dynamic statistics if at least one table in the query has no statistics; the sample size is 64 blocks.

- *Level 3*: Uses dynamic statistics if the query meets the level 2 criteria and it has one or more expressions in a WHERE clause predicate; a sample size is 64 blocks.

- *Level 4*: Uses dynamic statistics if the query meets all level 3 criteria, and in addition, it uses complex predicates such as an OR/AND operator between multiple predicates; the sample size is 64 blocks.

- *Levels 5-9*: Use dynamic statistics if the statement meets the level 4 criteria; each of these levels differs only in the sample size, which ranges from 128 to 4,086 blocks.

- *Level 10*: This level uses dynamic statistics for all statements, and the sample it uses isn't really a sample because it checks all data blocks to get the statistics.

- *Level 11*: Uses dynamic statistics automatically when the optimizer deems it necessary. The statistics collected by setting this level are stored and made available to other queries.

You can disable dynamic statistics collection by setting the dynamic statistics level to 0:

```
SQL> alter session set optimizer_dynamic_sampling=0;
```

Dynamic statistics are a complement to the statistics collected by the DBMS_STATS package's procedures. Oracle doesn't expect you to use this in general because of the additional overhead for gathering optimizer statistics during the generation of an execution plan. Dynamic statistics do help in getting better cardinality estimates but are more suitable for longer-running queries in a data warehouse or a decision support system, rather than for queries in an OLTP database, because of the overhead involved. You must also keep in mind that the statistics collected through dynamic sampling are by no means the same as the statistics collected through the DBMS_STATS procedures. Dynamic statistics merely collect rudimentary statistics such as the number of data blocks and the high and low values of columns. If you must set a dynamic statistics level, do so at the session level with an `alter session` statement, rather than setting it database-wide.

13-7. Exporting Statistics

Problem

You want to export a set of statistics from your production database to a much smaller test database.

Solution

You can export optimizer statistics from one database to another by using the DBMS_STATS.EXPORT_*_STATS procedures. These procedures let you export optimizer statistics from a source table, schema, or database. Once you complete the export of the statistics, you must execute one of the DBMS_STATS.IMPORT_*_STATS procedures to import the statistics into a different database. You can export statistics at the table, schema, or database level. Here's an example that explains how to export statistics from a table:

1. Create a table to hold the exported statistics:

    ```
    SQL> execute dbms_stats.create_stat_table(ownname=>'SH',stattab=>'mytab',
                                                 tblspace=>'USERS')

    PL/SQL procedure successfully completed.

    SQL>
    ```

2. Export the statistics for the table SH.SALES from the data dictionary into the mytab table, using the DBMS_STATS.EXPORT_*STATS procedure:

    ```
    SQL> exec dbms_stats.export_table_stats(ownname=> 'SH',tabname=>'SALES',stattab=
    >'mytab')

    PL/SQL procedure successfully completed.

    SQL>
    ```

3. Export and import the table mytab to the other database.

4. In a different database, import the statistics using the DBMS_STATS.IMPORT_*STATS procedure:

```
SQL> exec dbms_stats.import_table_stats(ownname=>'SH',tabname=>'SALES',stattab=>
'MyTab',no_invalidate=>true);

PL/SQL procedure successfully completed.

SQL>
```

How It Works

The EXPORT_TABLE_STATS procedure exports the current statistics for a table from the data dictionary and stores them in a table that you create. Note that this procedure doesn't generate fresh statistics, and the database will continue to use the current statistics for the table (SH.SALES in our example). By default, the cascade option is true, meaning the procedure will export statistics for all indexes in the SH.SALES table along with the column statistics.

You can make the optimizer use the exported statistics only after you import them into the data dictionary, in the same or a different database. The IMPORT_TABLE_STATS procedure imports the statistics you've exported earlier into the data dictionary. Setting the no_invalidate parameter to true (the default is false) ensures that any dependent cursors aren't invalidated. By default, you can't import a table's statistics when the statistics are locked. You can override this property by setting the force parameter to true. If you're importing the statistics into a different database from the one from which you exported the statistics, you must export the table in which you stored the statistics to the target database. You must then import the table into the target database before you can execute the IMPORT_TABLE_STATS procedure.

Exporting and importing statistics is an ideal way to present the same statistics to the optimizer in a test system as those in a production system to ensure consistent explain plans. It's also a good strategy when you want to preserve a known set of good statistics for a longer period than what is allowed by the "restore statistics" feature explained in Recipe 13-8. The ability to export and import statistics enables you to test different sets of statistics before deciding which set of parameters is the best for your database.

In this recipe, we showed you how to export and import table-level statistics. The DBMS_STATS package also contains procedures to export and import statistics at the column, index, schema, and database levels. In addition, there are procedures for exporting and importing dictionary statistics, statistics for fixed objects, and system statistics.

13-8. Restoring Previous Versions of Statistics
Problem

The performance of certain queries has deteriorated suddenly after collecting fresh statistics. You want to see whether you can use an older set of statistics that you know worked well.

Solution

Use the DBMS_STATS.RESTORE_STATS procedure to revert to an older set of optimizer statistics. Before you restore older statistics, check how far back you can go to restore older statistics:

```
SQL> select dbms_stats.get_stats_history_availability from dual;

GET_STATS_HISTORY_AVAILABILITY
-----------------------------------------
19-APR-OCT13 07.49.26.718000000 AM -04:00

SQL>
```

The output of this query shows that you can restore statistics to a timestamp that's more recent than the timestamp shown, which is 19-APR-11 07.49.26.718000000 AM -04:00.

Execute the RESTORE_*_STATS procedures of the DBMS_STATS package to revert to statistics from an earlier period. The following example shows how to restore statistics at the schema level:

```
SQL> exec dbms_stats.restore_schema_stats(ownname=>'SH',as_of_timestamp=>'19-OCT-13
01.30.31.323000 PM -04:00',no_invalidate=>false)

PL/SQL procedure successfully completed.

SQL>
```

How It Works

When the database collects fresh statistics, it doesn't get rid of the previous set of statistics. Instead, it retains the older versions for a set number of days. You have the ability to restore older statistics by executing the DBMS_STATS. RESTORE_*_STATS procedures, which replace the current statistics with the statistics from the time you specify. Restore statistics when you want the optimizer to use the same execution plans as it did when it had access to an older set of statistics. By default, the database manages the retention and purging of historical statistics. Here's how to find out how many days of statistics the database retains by default:

```
SQL> select dbms_stats.get_stats_history_retention from dual;

GET_STATS_HISTORY_RETENTION
---------------------------
                         31
SQL>
```

The database automatically purges statistics it has collected more than 31 days ago (provided newer statistics exist!). You can manually purge all old versions of statistics by executing the DBMS_STATS.PURGE_STATS procedure. You can change the number of days the database retains statistics by executing the following command:

```
SQL> exec dbms_stats.alter_stats_history_retention(retention=>60);

PL/SQL procedure successfully completed.

SQL>
```

The command tells the database to save historical statistics for a period of 60 days.

In the example shown in the "Solution" section, we showed how to restore statistics for a schema. You can similarly restore statistics for a database with the RESTORE_DATABASE_STATS procedure or for a table with the RESTORE_TABLE_STATS procedure. You can also restore dictionary stats with the RESTORE_DICTIONARY_STATS procedure and system stats with the RESTORE_SYSTEM_STATS procedure.

13-9. Gathering System Statistics
Problem

You know the optimizer uses I/O and CPU characteristics of a system during the selection of an execution plan. You want to ensure that the optimizer is using accurate system statistics.

Solution

You can collect two types of system statistics to capture your system's I/O and CPU characteristics. You can collect *workload statistics* or *noworkload statistics* to enable the optimizer to better estimate the true I/O and CPU costs, which are a critical part of query optimization.

When the database gathers noworkload statistics, it simulates a workload. Here's how you collect noworkload statistics, using the DBMS_STATS.GATHER_SYSTEM_STATS procedure:

```
SQL> execute dbms_stats.gather_system_stats()

PL/SQL procedure successfully completed.

SQL>
```

You can also gather system statistics while the database is processing a typical workload. These system statistics, called *workload statistics*, are more representative of actual system I/O and CPU characteristics and present a more accurate system hardware picture to the optimizer. You can collect workload system statistics by executing the DBMS_STATS.GATHER_SYSTEM_STATS procedure with the start and stop options:

```
SQL> execute dbms_stats.gather_system_stats('start')

PL/SQL procedure successfully completed.
SQL>
```

You can execute the previous command before the beginning of the workload window. Once the workload window ends, stop the system statistics gathering by executing the following command:

```
SQL> execute dbms_stats.gather_system_stats('stop')

PL/SQL procedure successfully completed.

SQL>
```

You can also execute the GATHER_SYSTEM_STATS procedure with an interval parameter to instruct the database to collect workload system statistics over a period of time that you specify and automatically stop the statistics gathering process at the end of the period. Here's an example:

```
SQL> execute dbms_stats.gather_system_stats('interval',90);
PL/SQL procedure successfully completed.
SQL>
```

The previous command collects workload statistics for 90 minutes.

Once you collect noworkload or workload system statistics, you can check the values captured for the various system statistics in the sys.aux_stats$ view, shown in the next section.

■ **Tip** Oracle highly recommends the gathering of system statistics in order to provide more accurate CPU and I/O cost estimates to the optimizer.

How It Works

Accurate system statistics are critical for the optimizer's evaluation of alternative execution plans. It's through its estimates of various system performance characteristics such as I/O speed and CPU speed that the optimizer calculates the cost of, say, a full table scan versus an indexed read.

You can pass up to nine optimizer system statistics to the optimizer by collecting system statistics. The database gathers the first three statistics during a noworkload simulated statistics gathering process. It gathers all nine system statistics during a workload mode system statistics collection. Here's a summary of the nine system statistics:

- cpuspeedNW: This shows the noworkload CPU speed, in terms of the average number of CPU cycles per second.

- ioseektim: This is the sum of seek time, latency time, and OS overhead time.

- iotfrspeed: This stands for I/O transfer speed and tells the optimizer how fast the database can read data in a single read request.

- cpuspeed: This stands for CPU speed during a workload statistics collection.

- maxthr: This shows the maximum I/O throughput.

- slavethr: This shows the average parallel slave I/O throughput.

- sreadtim: The Single Block Read Time statistic shows the average time for a random single-block read.

- mreadtim: The Multiblock Read Time statistic shows the average time (in milliseconds) for a sequential multiblock read.

- mbrc: The Multi Block Read Count statistic shows the average multiblock read count in blocks.

When you collect the noworkload system statistics, the database captures only the cpuspeedNW, ioseektim, and iotfrspeed system statistics. Here's a query that shows the default system statistics in an Oracle 11g database (on a Windows system):

```
SQL> select pname, pval1 from sys.aux_stats$ where sname = 'SYSSTATS_MAIN';

PNAME                          PVAL1
-----------------         ----------
CPUSPEED
CPUSPEEDNW                 1183.90219
IOSEEKTIM                          10
IOTFRSPEED                       4096
MAXTHR
MBRC
MREADTIM
SLAVETHR
SREADTIM

9 rows selected.

SQL>
```

The database uses noworkload systems statistics by default, with the values of the three noworkload statistics—I/O transfer speed (IOTFRSPEED), I/O seek time (IOSEEKTIM), and CPU speed (CPUSPEEDNW)—initialized to default values when you start the instance. Once you collect the noworkload statistics as shown in the "Solution" section, some or all of the three noworkload system statistics may change. In our case, once we collected the noworkload statistics, the value of CPUSPEEDNW changed to 2039.06 and the value of the IOSEEKTIM statistic changed to 14.756. However, the value of the IOTFRSPEED statistic remained constant at 4096.

■ **Caution** You must ensure that you collect the system statistics during a relatively busy time in your database, a time that's representative of peak workloads for your database.

If you notice that the sys.aux_stats$ view continues to show the default values for noworkload statistics even after you manually gather the statistics a few times, you can manually set the statistics values to known specifications of your I/O or CPU system by using the DBMS_STATS.SET_SYSTEM_STATS procedure. You can use this procedure to set values for any of the nine system statistics.

When you gather system statistics in the workload mode, you'll see values for some or all of the remaining six system statistics. In our example, these are the system statistics collected by running the GATHER_SYSTEM_STATS procedure in the workload mode.

```
SQL>  select pname, pval1 from sys.aux_stats$ where sname = 'SYSSTATS_MAIN';

PNAME                             PVAL1
------------------           ----------
CPUSPEED                           2040
CPUSPEEDNW                      2039.06
IOSEEKTIM                        14.756
IOTFRSPEED                         4096
MAXTHR
MBRC                                  7
MREADTIM                      46605.947
SLAVETHR
SREADTIM                      51471.538

9 rows selected.

SQL>
```

If the database performs any full table scans during the workload statistics collection period, Oracle uses the value of the mbrc and the mreadtim statistics to estimate the cost of a full table scan. In the absence of these two statistics, the database uses the value of the db_file_multiblock_read_count parameter to estimate the cost of full table scans.

You can delete all system statistics by executing the DELETE_SYSTEM_STATS procedure:

```
SQL> execute dbms_stats.delete_system_stats()

PL/SQL procedure successfully completed.

SQL>
```

According to Oracle, collecting workload statistics doesn't impose an additional overhead on your system. However, ensure that you specify a specific interval or stop the statistics collection after a brief period to avoid potential overhead.

13-10. Validating New Statistics

Problem

You're collecting new statistics, but you don't want the database to automatically use those statistics until you confirm that they will not bring in worse performance than what you have now.

Solution

In this example, we'll show how to keep the database from automatically publishing new statistics for a table. Here are the procedures you must follow to do this:

1. Execute the following statement to keep the database from automatically publishing new statistics it collects for the SH.SALES table:

   ```
   SQL> execute dbms_stats.set_table_prefs('SH','SALES','PUBLISH','false');

   PL/SQL procedure successfully completed.

   SQL>
   ```

   The statement sets the preference for the PUBLISH parameter to false (default=true) for the SH.SALES table. From here on, the database won't automatically publish the statistics you collect for the SH.SALES table. Rather, it keeps those statistics in abeyance, pending your approval. These statistics are called *pending statistics*, because the database hasn't made them available to the optimizer yet.

2. Collect new statistics for the SH.SALES table:

   ```
   SQL> exec dbms_stats.gather_table_stats('sh','sales');

   PL/SQL procedure successfully completed.
   SQL>
   ```

3. Tell the optimizer to use the newly collected pending statistics so you can test your queries with those statistics:

   ```
   SQL>  alter session set optimizer_use_pending_statistics=true;

   Session altered.

   SQL>
   ```

4. Perform your tests by running a workload against the SH.SALES table and checking the performance and the execution plans.

5. If you're happy with the new set of (pending) statistics, make them public by executing this statement:

```
SQL> execute dbms_stats.publish_pending_stats('SH','SALES');

PL/SQL procedure successfully completed.

SQL>
```

6. If you want to delete the new statistics instead, execute the following command:

```
SQL> exec dbms_stats.delete_pending_stats('SH','SALES');

PL/SQL procedure successfully completed.

SQL>
```

How It Works

Cursors are invalidated in a rolling fashion since the Oracle Database 10g release. Before that release, Oracle used to mark a cursor invalid immediately after you collected new statistics. Starting with the Oracle Database 10g release, Oracle marks a cursor for a "rolling cursor invalidation" instead of marking it invalid right away. When you next execute the query behind the cursor, Oracle generates a random number that takes a value between 0 and the value of the undocumented initialization parameter _optimizer_invalidation_period (the default value is 18,000 seconds, which is 5 minutes). Oracle will then keep the cursor valid for the same number of seconds as the value of the random number. Oracle will hard-parse the query only after the random timeout expires. This means that after this timeout period is completed, Oracle will hard-parse the query using the new statistics that you've collected.

However, you can specify that the database not automatically use the new statistics it collects until you decide that the statistics are going to improve or at least don't degrade current execution plans. You do this by keeping the new statistics in a *pending* state. Making the statistics available to the optimizer so it can use them in figuring out execution plans is called *publishing* the statistics. The database stores published statistics in its data dictionary. If you aren't sure about the efficacy of a new set of statistics, you can keep the database from automatically publishing statistics until you complete testing them first. When you keep statistics in the pending state, the database won't store them in the data dictionary; instead, it stores them in a private area and makes those statistics available to the optimizer only if you set the optimizer_use_pending_statistics parameter to true.

After specifying that the database must keep newly collected statistics in the pending status, you can choose to either publish the new statistics or delete them. Use the publish_pending_stats procedure to publish the statistics and the delete_pending_stats procedure to delete the statistics. If you delete the pending statistics for an object, the database will use existing statistics for that object.

In this example, we showed how to change the PUBLISH setting for statistics at the table level. You can also do this at the schema level but not at the database level. If working at the schema level, you need to run the following statements instead (the schema name is SH):

```
SQL> execute dbms_stats.set_schema_prefs('SH','PUBLISH','false');
SQL> execute dbms_stats.publish_pending_stats(null,null);
SQL> execute dbms_stats.delete_pending_stats('SH');
```

13-11. Forcing the Optimizer to Use an Index

Problem

You know that using a certain index on a column is going to speed up a query, but the optimizer doesn't use the index in its execution plans. You want to force the optimizer to use the index.

Solution

You can force the optimizer to use an index when it isn't doing so by adjusting the `optimizer_index_cost_adj` initialization parameter. You can set this parameter at the system or session level. Here's an example that shows how to set this parameter at the session level:

```
SQL> alter session set optimizer_index_cost_adj=50;

Session altered.
SQL>
```

The default value for the `optimizer_index_cost_adj` parameter is 100, and you can set the parameter to a value between 0 and 10000. The lower the value of the parameter, the more likely it is for the optimizer to use an index.

How It Works

The `optimizer_index_cost_adj` parameter lets you adjust the cost of an index access. The optimizer uses a default value of 100 for this parameter, which means that it evaluates an indexed access path based on the normal costing model. Based on the optimizer's estimate of the cost of performing an indexed read, it makes the decision of whether to use the index. Usually this works fine. However, in some cases, the optimizer doesn't use an index even if it leads to a better execution plan because the optimizer's estimates of the cost of the indexed access path may be off. Since it uses a default value of 100 for the `optimizer_index_cost_adj` parameter, you make the index cost seem lower to the optimizer by setting this parameter to a smaller value. Any value less than 100 makes the use of an index look cheaper (in terms of the cost of an indexed read) to the optimizer. Often, when you do this, the optimizer starts using the index you want it to use. In our example, we set the `optimizer_index_cost_adj` parameter to 50, making the cost of an index access path appear half as expensive as its normal cost (100). The lower you set the value of this parameter, the cheaper an index cost access path appears to the optimizer, and the more likely it will be to prefer an index access path to a full table scan.

We recommend that you set the `optimizer_index_cost_adj` parameter only at the session level for a specific query because it has the potential to change the execution plans for many queries if you set it at the database level. By default, if you set the ALL_ROWS optimizer goal, there's a built-in preference for full table scans by the optimizer. By setting the `optimizer_index_cost_adj` parameter to a value less than 100, you're inducing the optimizer to prefer an index scan over a full table scan. Use the `optimizer_index_cost_adj` parameter with confidence, especially in an OLTP environment, where you can experiment with low values such as 5 or 10 for the parameter to force the optimizer to use an index.

By default, the optimizer assumes that the cost of a multiblock read I/O associated with a full table scan and the single-block read cost associated with an indexed read are identical. However, a single-block read is likely to be less expensive than a multiblock read. The `optimizer_index_cost_adj` parameter lets you adjust the cost of a single-block read associated with an index read more accurately to reflect the true cost of an index read vis-à-vis the cost of a full table scan. The default value of 100 means that a single-block read is 100 percent of a multiblock read, so it's telling the optimizer to treat the cost of an indexed read as identical to the cost of a multiblock I/O full table scan. When you set the parameter to a value of 50, you're telling the optimizer that the cost of a single-block I/O (index read) is only half the cost of a multiblock I/O. This makes the optimizer choose the indexed read over a full table scan.

Note that accurate system statistics (mbrc, mreadtim, sreadtim, and so on) have a bearing on the use of indexes versus full table scans. Ideally, you should collect workload system statistics and leave the optimizer_index_cost_adj parameter alone. You can also calculate the relative costs of a single-block read and a multiblock read and set the optimizer_index_cost_adj parameter value based on those calculations. However, the best strategy is to simply use the parameter at the session level for a specific statement and not at the database level. Simply experiment with various levels of the parameter until the optimizer starts using the index.

You can also use a more "scientific" way to figure out the correct setting for the optimizer_index_cost_adj parameter by setting it to a value that reflects the "true" difference between single and multiblock reads. You can simply compare the average wait times for the db file sequential read wait event (represents a single-block I/O) and the db file scattered read wait event (represents multiblock I/O) to arrive at an approximate value for the optimizer_index_cost_adj parameter. Issue the following query to view the average wait times for both of the wait events:

```
SQL> select event, average_wait from v$system_event
        where event like 'db file s%read';
EVENT                           AVERAGE_WAIT
----------------------          ------------
db file sequential read                  .91
db file scattered read                  1.41

SQL>
```

Based on the output of this query, single-block sequential reads take roughly 75 percent of the time it takes to perform a multiblock (scattered) read. This indicates that the optimizer_cost_index_adj parameter should be set to somewhere around 75. However, as we mentioned earlier, setting the parameter at the database level isn't recommended; instead, use this parameter sparingly for specific statements where you want to force the use of an index.

13-12. Enabling Query Optimizer Features
Problem

You've upgraded your database, but you want to ensure the query plans don't change because of new optimizer features in the new release.

Solution

By default, the database enables all query optimizer features in the current database version. You can control the set of optimizer features enabled in a database by setting the optimizer_features_enable initialization parameter. For example, if you're running an Oracle Database 11g Release 2 database, the optimizer features are set to the 11.2 release, as shown here:

```
SQL> show parameter optimizer_features_enable;

NAME                            TYPE      VALUE
------------------------        ------    --------
optimizer_features_enable       string    12.1.0.1
SQL>
```

You can set the optimizer features of a database to an earlier release by setting the `optimizer_features_enable` parameter to a different value from its default value (same as the database release). For example, in a 12.1 release, you can do this:

```
SQL> alter system set optimizer_features_enable='11.2.0.4';

System altered.

SQL>
```

You can now check the current value of the parameter:

```
SQL> show parameter optimizer_features_enable;

NAME                         TYPE      VALUE
-------------------------    ------    --------
optimizer_features_enable    string    11.2.0.4
SQL>
```

You can set the `optimizer_features_enable` parameter to any past major release or a point release, all the way back to the Oracle Database 8.0 release.

How It Works

Setting the `optimizer_features_enable` parameter to the value of the previous database release ensures that when you upgrade the database, the optimizer will behave similarly to the way it did before the upgrade. We say "similarly" and not "exactly the same way" because often some bug fixes and changes in the ways statistics are collected (especially changes in the collection of system statistics) may make the old release perform somewhat differently from how it did earlier. This is a strategy that DBAs commonly use to ensure that query plans don't suddenly deteriorate following an upgrade. Once you understand the new optimizer features better, you can set the value of the `optimizer_features_enable` parameter to the same value as the upgraded database release.

Of course, you won't be able to take advantage of any of the new optimizer features when you set the `optimizer_features_enable` parameter to a lower value than the current release, but you aren't going to be surprised by any sudden changes in the execution plans either. Optimizer features don't change drastically between releases, but it all depends on the database release. For example, there are six major new optimizer features in the 11.1.0.6 release that weren't in the 10.2.0.2 release. These include the enhanced bind peeking feature and the ability to use extended statistics to estimate selectivity. Different applications will behave differently following the introduction of a new optimizer feature—that's where the ability to retain the current optimizer feature set during an upgrade provides you a safety net. You get the opportunity to fully test and understand the implications of the new optimizer features before enabling them in a production database.

The example shown in the "Solution" section shows how to set the optimizer features level for an entire database. You can, however, enable it just at the session level (`alter session ...`) to test for regressions in execution plans following an upgrade. You can also specify the release number with a hint so you can test a query with optimizer features from a specific release, as shown here in an 11.2 release database:

```
SQL>  select /*+ optimizer_features_enable ('11.1.0.6')  */ sum(sales)
      from sales
      order by product_id;
```

This SELECT statement was executed in an 11.2 release database but uses optimizer features from the 11.1 release.

13-13. Keeping the Database from Creating Histograms

Problem

You think that the presence of a histogram on a particular column is leading to suboptimal execution plans. You want the database not to use any histograms on that column.

Solution

You need to do two things if you want to keep Oracle from using the histogram it's automatically collecting on a column:

1. Drop the histogram by executing the DELETE_COLUMN_STATS procedure:

    ```
    SQL> begin
      2  dbms_stats.delete_column_stats(ownname=>'SH',tabname=>'SALES',
      3  colname=>'PROD_ID',col_stat_type=>'HISTOGRAM');
      4  end;
      5  /

    PL/SQL procedure successfully completed.

    SQL>
    ```

2. Once you drop the histogram, tell Oracle not to create a histogram on the PROD_ID column by executing the following SET_TABLE_PREFS procedure:

    ```
    SQL> begin
      2  dbms_stats.set_table_prefs('SH','SALES','METHOD_OPT','FOR  ALL COLUMNS SIZE
         AUTO,
         FOR COLUMNS  SIZE 1 PROD_ID');
      3  end;
      4  /

    PL/SQL procedure successfully completed.

    SQL>
    ```

How It Works

For various reasons, DBAs sometimes want to keep the optimizer from using a histogram on a column. If there's already a histogram on a column, you must first get rid of it and then use the dbms_stats.set_table_prefs procedure to keep the database from creating a histogram on that column. In the Oracle Database 10g release, you drop the histogram first, freeze the statistics (with the lock_table_stats procedure), and then manually collect statistics on the table, specifying that the database must not collect statistics for the column for which you dropped the histogram. Because you locked the statistics, you must also specify the force=true option when executing the dbms_stats.gather_table_stats procedure to manually collect statistics on a table. As you can see, the dbms_stats. set_table_prefs procedure in the 11g release makes things a lot simpler.

In the command shown in the "Solution" section, the FOR ALL COLUMNS SIZE AUTO option tells the database to create histograms on any column that Oracle deems skewed. However, FOR COLUMNS SIZE 1 PROD_ID tells the database not to create a histogram for the column PROD_ID in the SH.SALES table. The SIZE column accepts values from 1 to 254, with the integer number you specify representing the number of buckets in the histogram. Telling the database to use just a single bucket (N=1) means that all data will be in a single bucket; in other words, the database won't create a histogram on that column.

13-14. Improving Performance When Not Using Bind Variables

Problem

For various reasons, your developers didn't specify bind variables in the code. You notice heavy latch contention and poor response times because of the nonuse of bind variables. You want to improve the performance of the database in a situation like this, where you can't change existing code.

Solution

If your applications aren't using bind variables, there will be an increase in expensive hard-parsing in the database. To avoid this, you need to set the cursor_sharing initialization parameter to a nondefault value. The default value for this parameter is EXACT. You can set the cursor_sharing parameter to FORCE to determine which SQL statements can share the same cursors.

Here's how you can set the cursor_sharing parameter to force:

```
SQL> alter system set cursor_sharing=force;
```

Setting the cursor_sharing parameter to a nondefault value has several implications, as the next section explains.

How It Works

The best practice in writing SQL code is to use bind variables so the SQL statements are shareable. During the parse stage, the optimizer will compare a SQL statement's text with the texts of existing statements that are stored in the shared pool. The database considers the current statement *identical* to another statement only if it matches the other statement in all respects, including each character, space, and even case. When you leave the cursor_sharing parameter at its default value of EXACT, Oracle will reuse the shared SQL area when it reexecutes a SQL statement that uses bind variables. There's no need for hard-parsing the new statement because a parsed version already exists in the shared pool. The new statement can use an existing cursor (it's called a *shared cursor*) and not create its own parent cursor.

If the code doesn't use bind variables but the new SQL statement the database is parsing is the same in all respects to a previously parsed statement in the shared pool, the statement is considered *similar* to the previous statement.

By default, the database shares cursors when SQL statements are identical but not when they are similar. The database will perform a heavy amount of hard-parsing if applications use literal values instead of bind variables, and in a busy system, it could put enormous pressure on the shared pool and the cursor cache. You can make the database share cursors when the new statement is similar (but not identical) to an existing parsed statement by setting the cursor_sharing parameter to FORCE. Setting the cursor_sharing parameter to FORCE lets the database replace the literal values with system-generated bind variables. The goal here is to reduce the number of parent cursors in the shared pool. Sharing cursors even when the application doesn't use bind variables relieves the pressure on the shared pool by reducing the number of parent cursors in the cursor cache (in the shared pool). Leaving the cursor_sharing parameter at its default value will make the database perform a hard parse if the statement it's parsing isn't identical to an existing statement in the shared pool. However, if you set the parameter to FORCE, the database will perform the much cheaper soft parse when it finds a similar statement in the shared pool.

When to Set CURSOR_SHARING to a Nondefault Value

Ideally, you should leave the cursor_sharing parameter at its default value of EXACT. However, if your response time is suffering because of a heavy amount of library cache misses and the SQL statements aren't using bind variables, consider setting the cursor_sharing parameter to FORCE. If the application doesn't use bind variables, your hands are tied—the fixes will be long in coming, and meanwhile, you have a slow-performing database on your hands. Go ahead and change the cursor_sharing parameter from its default setting under these circumstances. There are really no issues with setting the cursor_sharing parameter to a nondefault value, except minor drawbacks such as the nonsupport for star transformation, for example.

■ **Tip** Oracle recommends using the FORCE setting for the CURSOR_SHARING parameter in an OLTP environment.

Oracle recommends that, if possible, you should leave the cursor_sharing parameter at its default value of EXACT and use shareable SQL by employing bind variables in your code instead of literal values. If you do decide to change the default setting to FORCE because of pressure in the shared pool and latch contention, be aware that there are some performance implications in doing so. If you set the cursor_sharing parameter to FORCE, the database uses system-generated bind values, uses the same execution plan for each execution of a statement, and uses one parent cursor and one child cursor for each distinct SQL statement.

Implications of Setting CURSOR_SHARING to a Nondefault Value

The FORCE setting can help you get around the nonuse of bind variables in an application by letting the database generate bind values (system-generated bind values, as opposed to user-specified)). However, you should be aware of the differences in the behavior of the optimizer when you set the cursor_sharing parameter to FORCE as opposed to the EXACT setting. The key thing to understand here is that there's a conflict between query performance and the space used in the shared pool by multiple executions of a query. Here is a summary of the performance implications of setting the cursor_sharing parameter to EXACT and FORCE. Let's assume the following query, which contains a literal:

```
select * from employees where job = 'Clerk'
```

Note that if the query were to use bind variables instead of literals, it would be of the following form:

```
select * from employees where job=:b
```

EXACT: The database doesn't replace any literals, and the optimizer sees the query as it's presented to the optimizer. The optimizer generates a different plan for each execution of the statement, based on the literal values in the statement. The plan would thus be an optimal one, but each statement has its own parent cursor, and therefore a statement that's executed numerous times can use a considerable amount of space in the shared pool. This could potentially lead to latch contention and a slowdown in performance.

FORCE: Regardless of whether there's a histogram, the optimizer will replace the literal values with a bind value and optimize this query as if it were in the following form:

```
select * from employees where job=:b
```

The optimizer uses a single plan for each SQL statement, regardless of the literal values. Thus, the execution plan won't be optimal, as the plan is generic and not based on the literal values. If a query uses literal values, the optimizer will use those values to find the most efficient execution plan. If there are no literals in the SQL statement, it's hard for the optimizer to figure out the best execution plan. By "peeking" at the value of the bind variables, the optimizer can get a better idea of the selectivity of the where clause condition—it is almost as if literals had been used in the SQL statement. The optimizer peeks at the bind values during the hard-parse state. Since the execution plan is based on the specific value of the bind variable that the optimizer happened to peek at, the execution plan may not be optimal for all possible values of the bind variable.

In this example, the optimizer uses bind peeking based on the specific value of the JOB column it sees. In this case, the optimizer uses the value Clerk to estimate the cardinality for the query. When it executes the same statement (with a different value in the JOB column, say, Manager), the optimizer will use the same plan that it generated the first time (JOB=Clerk). Since there is only one parent cursor and just child cursors for the distinct statements, there's less pressure on the shared pool. Note that a child cursor uses far less space in the shared pool than a parent cursor. Often, setting the cursor_sharing parameter to FORCE immediately resolves serious latch contention in the database, making this one of the few magic bullets that can help you quickly reduce latch contention.

The choice among the various settings of the cursor_sharing parameter really boils down to an assessment of what's more critical to database performance: using the default EXACT setting does provide better query performance but leads to the generation of numerous parent cursors. If there's a severe pressure in the shared pool and consequent latch contention, the entire database will perform poorly. Under these circumstances, you're better off implementing a system-wide solution by setting the cursor_sharing parameter to FORCE because this guarantees that there's only a single child cursor for each SQL statement. If you're concerned about the impact of a single SQL statement, just drop the histogram on the relevant columns used in the SQL statement and set the cursor_sharing parameter to FORCE; this will ensure that the optimizer uses system-generated bind values for the column(s) and will ensure that the SQL statement uses much less space in the shared pool. As you'll see in the next section, Oracle Database 11g's adaptive cursor sharing offers an even better solution if you set the cursor_sharing parameter to FORCE and keep the histograms on the columns.

Oracle recommends as a best practice that you write shareable SQL and use the default setting OF EXACT for the cursor_sharing parameter. However, if you're beset with numerous similar SQL statements, you may find that setting the CUSOR_SHARING parameter to FORCE significantly improves performance by improving cursor sharing, reducing memory usage, and reducing latch contention in the database. If you find that response time is poor because of a high number of misses in the library cache, you can consider changing the setting of the CURSOR_SHARING parameter to EXACT. As mentioned earlier, setting this value will make the optimizer act as if the SQL statement did contain a bind variable and it uses bind peeking to estimate cardinality. All this means that statements that differ just in the bind variables can and will share the same execution plan.

Don't ignore the following drawbacks that result from setting the cursor_sharing parameter to EXACT:

- The database performs more work during the soft parse to find a similar statement in the shared pool.

- There is an increase in the maximum lengths of any selected expression that contains literals in a SELECT statement.

- Star transformation is not supported.

13-15. Understanding Adaptive Cursor Sharing
Problem

Your database uses user-defined bind variables. You want to know whether there's anything you can do to optimize database behavior so it doesn't "blindly" use the same execution plan for all bind variable values.

Solution

In prior releases, Oracle used a single execution plan for each execution of a SQL statement, regardless of the values of the bind variables. In Oracle Database 11g, the database feature called *adaptive cursor sharing* enables a SQL statement with bind variables to use multiple execution plans, with each execution plan based on the values of the bind variables. Adaptive cursor sharing is enabled by default, and you can't disable it.

How It Works

The adaptive cursor sharing feature is designed to improve the execution plans for SQL queries that contain bind variables. To understand how adaptive cursor sharing helps, it's important to understand how Oracle's bind peeking feature works. Bind peeking (introduced in Oracle 9i) lets the optimizer peek at the value of a bind variable when the database invokes the cursor for the first time. The optimizer uses the "peeked value" to determine the selectivity of the WHERE clause.

The problem with using user-defined bind variables is that the execution plan doesn't have an accurate measure of the selectivity of the WHERE clause. Bind peeking helps improve matters by letting the optimizer act as if it were actually using a literal value instead of the bind variable, thus helping it generate better execution plans for SQL statements with bind variables. Bind peeking works well when the values of the column in the WHERE clause have a uniform distribution. If the column values are skewed, the plan the optimizer chooses by peeking at the value of the user-defined bind variable may not necessarily be good for all possible values of the bind variable. You thus end up with a situation where the execution plan will be very efficient if the SQL statement has the bind variable value that the optimizer has peeked at—and inefficient execution plans for all other possible values of the bind variable.

Let's learn how adaptive cursor sharing works, with the help of an example that involves a column with skewed data.

Our test table, DEMO, has 78,681 rows. The data has three columns, which are all skewed. Thus, when we gathered statistics for this table, we created histograms on the three columns, as shown here:

```
SQL> select column_name,table_name,histogram from user_TAB_COLUMNS
     where table_name='DEMO';

COLUMN_NAME          TABLE_NAME        HISTOGRAM
-------------\-      -----------       ---------------
RNUM                 DEMO              HEIGHT BALANCED
RNAME                DEMO              HEIGHT BALANCED
STATUS               DEMO              FREQUENCY
```

Note that when the optimizer notices that there's a histogram on a table, it marks the data in that column as skewed. The column STATUS has two values: Coarse and Fine. Only 157 rows have the value of Coarse, and 78,524 rows have the value Fine, making the data extremely skewed.

Let's perform a sequence of operations to illustrate how adaptive cursor sharing works. Issue a query with the bind variable set to the value Coarse. Since very few rows in the DEMO table have this value, we expect the database to use an index range scan, which is exactly what the optimizer does. Here is our query and its execution:

```
SQL> var b varchar2(6)
SQL> exec :b:='Coarse';

PL/SQL procedure successfully completed.

SQL> select /*+ ACS */ count(*) from demo where status = :b;
  COUNT(*)
----------
       157

SQL> select * from table(dbms_xplan.display_cursor);
```

```
PLAN_TABLE_OUTPUT
---------------------------------------------------------
SQL_ID  cxau3vvabpzd0, child number 0
---------------------------------------
select /*+ ACS */ count(*) from demo where status = :b

Plan hash value: 3478245284

-------------------------------------------------------------------------
| Id  | Operation        | Name     | Rows  | Bytes | Cost (%CPU)| Time     |
-------------------------------------------------------------------------
|   0 | SELECT STATEMENT |          |       |       |   1 (100)|          |
|   1 |  SORT AGGREGATE  |          |     1 |     6 |          |          |
```

```
PLAN_TABLE_OUTPUT
-------------------------------------------------------------------------
|*  2 |   INDEX RANGE SCAN| IDX01_DEMO |   157 |   942 |     1    (0)| 00:00:52 |
-------------------------------------------------------------------------
Predicate Information (identified by operation id):
---------------------------------------------------
   2 - access("STATUS"=:B)
19 rows selected.
```

Next issue the following statement to check whether the database has marked the STATUS column as bind-sensitive or bind-aware or both:

```
SQL> select child_number, executions, buffer_gets, is_bind_sensitive as
  2   "BIND_SENSI", is_bind_aware as "BIND_AWARE", is_shareable as "BIND_SHARE"
  3   from v$SQL
  4*  where sql_text like 'select /*+ ACS */%'
SQL> /
CHILD_NUMBER  EXECUTIONS  BUFFER_GETS  BIND_SENSI  BIND_AWARE  BIND_SHARE
------------  ----------  -----------  ----------  ----------  -----------
           0           1           43           Y           N           Y

SQL>
```

Note that the database marks the STATUS column as bind-sensitive, because there's a histogram on the column STATUS. Each time you execute the query with a different value for the bind variable, the database compares the execution statistics with those from the prior execution. If the execution statistics differ significantly, it marks the column as bind-aware. One of the inputs the database uses in deciding whether to mark a statement as bind-aware is the number of rows processed. Once a cursor is marked bind-aware, the optimizer will choose an execution plan based on the value of the bind variable. Here, the IS_BIND_AWARE column is marked N because there are no prior execution statistics to compare. The BIND_SHAREABLE column is marked Y.

Issue the query again, with the bind variable set to the value Fine. Since almost all of the rows have the STATUS column set to the value Fine, we expect the optimizer to prefer a full table scan. However, the optimizer picks the same plan as before (INDEX RANGE SCAN). The reason for this is that the database is using the same execution plan from the first execution. Here's an example:

```
SQL> exec :b := 'Fine';

PL/SQL procedure successfully completed.
```

```
SQL> select /*+ ACS */ count(*) from demo where status = :b;

  COUNT(*)
----------
     78524

SQL> select * from table(dbms_xplan.display_cursor);

PLAN_TABLE_OUTPUT
------------------------------------------------------------
SQL_ID  cxau3vvabpzd0, child number 0
------------------------------------
select /*+ ACS */ count(*) from demo where status = :b

Plan hash value: 3478245284

-----------------------------------------------------------------------------
| Id  | Operation         | Name        | Rows  | Bytes | Cost (%CPU)| Time     |
-----------------------------------------------------------------------------
|   0 | SELECT STATEMENT  |             |       |       |   1 (100)|          |
|   1 |  SORT AGGREGATE   |             |     1 |     6 |          |          |

PLAN_TABLE_OUTPUT
-----------------------------------------------------------------------------
|*  2 |   INDEX RANGE SCAN| IDX01_DEMO |   157 |   942 |   1   (0)| 00:00:52 |

-----------------------------------------------------------------------------

Predicate Information (identified by operation id):
---------------------------------------------------
   2 - access("STATUS"=:B)

19 rows selected.
```

Since the cursor for the SQL statement is marked bind-sensitive, the optimizer uses the same execution plan (INDEX RANGE SCAN) as before. Note in the following example that the BIND_AWARE column is still marked N. The optimizer is using the same cursor as before (child_number 0).

```
SQL> select child_number, executions, buffer_gets, is_bind_sensitive as
  2  "BIND_SENSI", is_bind_aware as "BIND_AWARE", is_shareable as "BIND_SHARE"
  3  from v$sql
  4  WHERE sql_text like 'select /*+ ACS */%';

CHILD_NUMBER EXECUTIONS BUFFER_GETS BIND_SENSI  BIND_AWARE BIND_SHARE
------------ ---------- ----------- ----------- ---------- ----------
           0          2         220 Y                    N          Y

SQL>
```

Execute the query again, with the same value for the STATUS column as in the previous query ('Fine'). *Voila!* The optimizer now uses an INDEX FAST FULL SCAN, instead of the INDEX RANGE SCAN. The change in execution plans is automatic; it is as if the optimizer is learning as it goes along and modifies the plan when it's certain that the new plan is more efficient. Here is the execution and the new plan:

```
SQL>  exec :b := 'Fine';
PL/SQL procedure successfully completed.

SQL> select /*+ ACS */ count(*) from demo where status = :b;
  COUNT(*)
----------
     78524

SQL> select * from table(dbms_xplan.display_cursor);
PLAN_TABLE_OUTPUT
-------------------------------------------------------
SQL_ID  cxau3vvabpzd0, child number 1
-------------------------------------
select /*+ ACS */ count(*) from demo where status = :b

Plan hash value: 2683512795
-------------------------------------------------------------------------------
| Id  | Operation              | Name       | Rows  | Bytes | Cost (%CPU)| Time  |

PLAN_TABLE_OUTPUT
-------------------------------------------------------------------------------
|   0 | SELECT STATEMENT       |            |       |       |    45 (100)|
   |
|   1 |  SORT AGGREGATE        |            |     1 |     6 |            |
   |
|*  2 |   INDEX FAST FULL SCAN| IDX01_DEMO | 78524 |  460K|    45   (0)| 00:38:
PLAN_TABLE_OUTPUT
-------------------------------------------------------------------------------
37 |
-------------------------------------------------------------------------------
Predicate Information (identified by operation id):
---------------------------------------------------
   2 - filter("STATUS"=:B)
19 rows selected.
```

Note that the BIND_AWARE column now shows the value Y. When we execute the query with the same bind variable value (Fine) the second time, since the query is marked as bind-sensitive, the database evaluates the execution statistics from the previous execution. Since the statistics are different, it marks the cursor as bind-aware. The optimizer then decides a new plan is more optimal and thus performs a hard parse and generates a new execution plan that uses an INDEX FAST FULL SCAN instead of an INDEX RANGE SCAN. The following query shows details about the child cursors as well as whether the query is bind-sensitive or bind-aware:

```
SQL> select child_number, executions, buffer_gets, is_bind_sensitive as
  2  "BIND_SENSI", is_bind_aware as "BIND_AWARE", is_shareable as "BIND_SHARE"
  3  from v$sql
  4  WHERE sql_text like 'select /*+ ACS */%';
```

CHILD_NUMBER	EXECUTIONS	BUFFER_GETS	BIND_SENSI	BIND_AWARE	BIND_SHARE
0	2	220	Y	N	Y
1	1	184	Y	Y	Y

SQL>

Note that the IS_BIND_AWARE column shows the value Y now. Notice also that there is a new child cursor (child_number 1) that represents the new execution plan containing the INDEX FAST FULL SCAN—this new cursor is marked bind-aware.

We execute the query again, but this time with the original bind variable value Coarse. The optimizer will choose the correct execution plan by performing an INDEX RANGE SCAN. Here's the information about the child cursors, as well as whether the query is bind-sensitive or bind-aware:

```
SQL> select child_number, executions, buffer_gets, is_bind_sensitive as
  2  "BIND_SENSI", is_bind_aware as "BIND_AWARE", is_shareable as "BIND_SHARE"
  3  from v$sql
  4  where sql_text like 'select /*+ ACS */%';
```

CHILD_NUMBER	EXECUTIONS	BUFFER_GETS	BIND_SENSI	BIND_AWARE	BIND_SHARE
0	2	220	Y	N	N
1	1	184	Y	Y	Y
2	1	2	Y	Y	Y

SQL>

The database creates a new child cursor (child_number=2) for this query and marks the original cursor (child_cursor=0) as not being bind-aware. Eventually the database will remove this cursor from the shared pool.

In our example, we used only two values for the bind variable in our tests. What happens if there are dozens of different bind variable values? Oracle doesn't always perform a hard parse for each distinct bind variable value. Initially it performs a hard parse for some values of the bind variable, during which it determines the relationships between various bind variables and the associated execution plan. After the initial mapping of the bind variable values and the associated execution plans, Oracle is smart enough to simply pick the optimal child cursor from the cache without performing a hard parse for other bind values.

Adaptive cursor sharing is a new feature introduced in the Oracle Database 11g release. In earlier releases, DBAs often flushed the shared pool (and worse, sometimes restarted the database) when confronted with situations where the database apparently started using an inappropriate execution plan for a SQL statement because of the bind peeking effect. In the 11g release, you don't have to do anything—the optimizer automatically changes execution plans when it encounters skewed data. With adaptive cursor sharing, the database uses multiple execution plans for a statement that uses bind variables, ensuring that the best execution plan is always used, depending on the value of the bind variable. Adaptive cursor sharing means that when different bind variable values indicate different amounts of data to be handled by the query, Oracle adapts its behavior by using different execution plans for the query instead of sticking to the same plan for all bind values. Since adaptive cursor sharing works only where literal values are replaced with binds, Oracle encourages you to use the FORCE setting for the cursor_sharing parameter. If you set the parameter to SIMILAR and you have a histogram on a column, the optimizer doesn't perform a literal replacement with bind variables, and thus adaptive cursor sharing won't take place. You must set the cursor_sharing parameter to FORCE for adaptive cursor sharing to work, thus letting the optimizer select the optimal execution plan for different values of the bind variable.

13-16. Creating Statistics on Expressions

Problem

You want to create statistics on an expression such as a user-created function.

Solution

Execute the GATHER_TABLE_STATS procedure of the DBMS_STATS package in the following way to gather statistics on an expression. In this example, we're gathering statistics for the lower function, which transforms the cust_state_province column.

```
SQL> execute dbms_stats.gather_table_stats('sh','customers',-
  > method_opt =>'for all columns size skewonly -
  > for columns(lower(cust_state_province)) size skewonly');

PL/SQL procedure successfully completed.

SQL>
```

Alternatively, you can collect expression statistics by invoking the create_extended_stats function. Here's an example:

```
SQL> select
     dbms_stats.create_extended_stats(null,'customers',
     '(lower(cust_state_province))')
     from dual;
```

Note that (lower (cust_state_province)) is called an *extension* because collecting statistics on functions is a type of Oracle extended statistic. Any statistics you collect for expressions and column groups (see Recipe 13-17) are called *extended statistics*.

How It Works

The optimizer knows the selectivity of a table's column and uses the selectivity estimates for creating optimal execution plans. However, applying a function to a column in the WHERE clause of a query throws off the optimizer because it can't estimate the selectivity of the underlying column. Here's an example of a function that makes the optimizer's job harder:

```
SQL> select count(*) from customers
     where lower(cust_state_province) = 'CA';
```

Expression statistics on functions enable the optimizer to obtain a vastly more accurate selectivity value for predicates that involve expressions.

You can issue the following query to find details about expression statistics on a table's columns:

```
SQL> select extension_name, extension
     from user_stat_extensions
     where table_name='CUSTOMERS';
```

```
EXTENSION_NAME                              EXTENSION
----------------------------               ----------------------------
SYS_STUBPHJSBRKOIK9O2YV3W8HOUE             (LOWER("CUST_STATE_PROVINCE"))
SQL>
```

You can delete expression statistics you've collected on a table by using the drop_extended_stats function:

```
SQL> exec dbms_stats.drop_extended_stats(null,'customers','(lower(cust_state_pro
vince))');

PL/SQL procedure successfully completed.

SQL>
```

Note that extended statistics include both statistics on expressions such as a function and statistics gathered for a column group that consists of two or more related columns. Recipe 13-17 shows how to collect statistics on column groups.

13-17. Creating Statistics for Related Columns
Problem

You're aware that certain columns from a table that are part of a join condition are correlated. You want to make the optimizer aware of this relationship.

Solution

To generate statistics for two or more related columns, you must first create a *column group* and then collect fresh statistics for the table so the optimizer can use the newly generated "extended statistics." Use the DBMS_STATS.CREATE_EXTENDED_STATS function to define a column group that consists of two or more columns from a table. Here's how you execute this function to create a column group that consists of the COUNTRY_ID and CUST_STATE_PROVINCE columns in the table SH.CUSTOMERS:

```
SQL> select dbms_stats.create_extended_stats(null,'CUSTOMERS',
'(country_id,cust_state_province)') from dual;

DBMS_STATS.CREATE_EXTENDED_STATS(NULL,'CUSTOMERS','(COUNTRY_ID,CUST_STATE_PROVI
----------------------------------------------------------------------------

SYS_STUJGVLRVH5USVDU$XNV4_IR#4
SQL>
```

Once you create the column group, gather fresh statistics for the CUSTOMERS table to generate statistics for the new column group.

```
SQL> exec dbms_stats.gather_table_stats(null,'customers');

PL/SQL procedure successfully completed.

SQL>
```

How It Works

Often, values in one column of a table influence the values of another column in that table because of natural relationships that exist between the data stored in the two columns. For example, the values of the CUST_STATE_PROVINCE column in the SH.CUSTOMERS table are influenced by the values of the COUNTRY_ID column. You can find a CUST_STATE_PROVINCE value of Florida only in the United States. The optimizer doesn't know about real-life relationships and thus tends to produce wrong estimates of the all-important cardinality statistic when multiple related columns appear in the WHERE clause of a query or in a group_by key. Column group statistics help the optimizer capture the correlation among a table's columns. If a query includes the predicates CUST_STATE_PROVINCE ='Florida' and COUNTRY_ID='U.S.', Oracle can derive a better estimate of the combined selectivity of these two predicates by looking up the statistics for the column group instead of using separate statistics for the two columns.

The statistics the database gathers on the column groups that you create are called *extended statistics*. These statistics provide much more accurate cardinality estimates to the optimizer, which helps the optimizer produce more efficient execution plans. When you create extended statistics, Oracle maintains a subset of statistics for the column groups you create, including the number of distinct values, nulls, and histograms for the group. Even if a query contains columns in addition to the columns that are part of a column group, the optimizer takes advantage of the extended stats that are available to it. For example, suppose you've created a column group as shown in this recipe using the CUST_STATE_PROVINCE and COUNTRY_ID columns. If the WHERE clause for a query includes these two columns as well as the CUST_CITY column, Oracle will still take advantage of the extended statistics on the CUST_STATE_PROVINCE and COUNTRY_ID columns.

13-18. Automatically Creating Column Groups
Problem

You know that creating extended statistics by generating statistics on correlated table columns helps generate better execution plans. You want to find out how to select candidate column groups for creating extended statistics.

Solution

In Oracle Database 11.2.0.2 and newer releases, you can use the Auto Column Group Creation feature to let the database tell you which column groups you must create. You can use this feature for creating column groups but not for collecting extended statistics for columns with expressions (see Recipe 13-16).

To use the Auto Column Group Creation capability and let the database provide advice on which column groups to create in the database, you must let the database monitor the workload in the database. Begin by executing the DBMS_STATS.SEED_COL_USAGE procedure to determine the appropriate column groups that you must create:

```
SQl> begin
    dbms_stats.seed_col_usage(null,null,900);
    end;
    /
```

By executing this procedure, you're telling the database to monitor the workload for 15 minutes (900 seconds) to determine whether you need to create any column groups. The procedure captures the column usage information and stores it in the sys.col_group_usage$ view.

Next run some queries to create the workload. If the queries are long-running, you can just run explain plan statements for the queries so the database can capture the column group information. Once the monitoring period (15 minutes) ends, review the captured column usage information by using the following query:

```
SQL> select dbms_stats.report_col_usage(user,'customers') from dual;
```

The REPORT_COL_USAGE procedure shows a column usage report for the CUSTOMERS table, based on the queries you've executed and the explain plans that you ran. The column usage shows how the database used each column of the CUSTOMERS table and lists column usage in the following format:

- Equality predicates (EQ): If a column was used in an equality predicate such as in the clause where COUNTRY_ID='US', that column was used independently. No extension statistics are called for in this case.

- FILTER: If a set of columns was used in a SELECT statement that contained one or more of those columns in a GROUP BY clause, all columns in the SELECT statement are recorded as a column group filter.

- GROUP_BY: Shows all the columns used together in a GROUP_BY clause.

Once you view the column usage report, you can let Oracle automatically create the column groups for the columns used in the filter predicates and the columns used in the GROUP_BY clause. Do that by executing the following procedure:

```
SQL>select dbms_stats.create_extended_stats(user,'customers') from dual;
```

Alternatively, you can create column groups only for columns that you specify by issuing the following command:

```
SQL> select dbms_stats.create_extended_stats(null,'CUSTOMERS',
'(cust_city,cust_state_province,country_id)') from dual
SQL> /
DBMS_STATS.CREATE_EXTENDED_STATS(NULL,'CUSTOMERS','(CUST_CITY,CUST_STATE_PROVIN
--------------------------------------------------------------------------
SYS_STUMZ$C3AIHLPBROI#SKA58H_N
SQL>
```

At this point, you've created the column group, but there are no statistics on the column group. Regather statistics for the CUSTOMERS table to generate statistics for the new column group. Here's an example:

```
SQL> exec dbms_stats.gather_table_stats(user,'customers')
PL/SQL procedure successfully completed.
SQL>
```

How It Works

Letting Oracle point out potential column groups based on the actual column usage during a workload is far more efficient than trying to figure out the appropriate column groups for each table. Once you run the workload, you can view the column usage report and ask the database to create all proposed column groups for an entire schema at the same time, by executing the dbms_stats.create_extended_stats function and passing the value NULL for the table_name parameter.

13-19. Maintaining Statistics on Partitioned Tables
Problem

You load data into one or more partitions frequently, and the maintenance of global statistics is a problem. You want to collect new global statistics without having to go through a time- and resource-consuming process.

Solution

You can use the *incremental statistics maintenance* feature in the Oracle 11g release to maintain global statistics after each load into a new partition. For example, if you want to maintain global statistics for the SH.SALES table, here are the steps to follow:

1. Turn on incremental statistics collection for the SH.SALES table:

   ```
   SQL> exec dbms_stats.set_table_prefs('SH','SALES','INCREMENTAL','TRUE');

   PL/SQL procedure successfully completed.

   SQL>
   ```

2. After each load into a partition, gather global table-level statistics as shown here:

   ```
   SQL> exec dbms_stats.gather_table_stats('SH','SALES');

   PL/SQL procedure successfully completed.

   SQL>
   ```

To set the incremental statistics collection feature for partitioned tables, you must specify the AUTO_SAMPLE_SIZE value for the ESTIMATE_PERCENT parameter and the AUTO value for the GRANULARITY parameter.

How It Works

The incremental statistics collection feature is disabled by default. You enable the feature by setting the INCREMENTAL preference. In our example, we showed how to set the INCREMENTAL preference at the table level, but you can also set it at the schema or database level.

When dealing with a partitioned table, the optimizer uses both global statistics (statistics for the entire table) and statistics for the individual partitions to select the optimal execution plan. By default, following a change in a partition's data, the database uses a two-pass scanning technique to maintain accurate table statistics. Under this two-pass technique, the database will do the following:

- Scan the entire table to gather the global statistics during the first pass

- Scan the changed partitions in the second pass to gather the partition statistics

When you load data into (or delete data from) a partition as part of a nightly batch job, for example, the database will scan the partition to gather the partition-level statistics. In addition, it scans the entire table to gather the table-level global statistics. The database scans not only the changed partitions but also all the other partitions in the table. As you can tell, this full scan of the table each time a partition's data changes is an expensive process, especially when dealing with large tables.

Once you turn on the incremental statistics collection feature, Oracle uses a far more efficient technique to maintain a partitioned table's statistics. When a partition's data changes, the database gathers just the statistics for that partition and derives the global table statistics without scanning any of the other partitions. How does the database maintain the global statistics without scanning the entire table? Oracle can derive some global statistics from partition-level statistics; for example, it derives the total number of rows by just adding up the rows in each partition. For deriving the number of distinct values (NDVs), Oracle makes use of a structure called a *synopsis*, which is something like a sample of the NDVs in a column. Oracle derives the global NDV by merging all partition synopses. In summary, when you implement incremental statistics collection, Oracle skips the default full table scan to gather the table's statistics and instead does the following:

1. Gathers statistics for the partition you loaded and creates synopses for that partition

2. Creates a global synopsis by merging all the partition-level synopses

3. Computes the global statistics from the partition-level statistics and the global synopses

Incremental statistics collection is extremely efficient and something you must consider using when dealing with large partitioned tables, especially when you're loading data into one or more empty partitions frequently, as is the case in many data warehouses.

13-20. Concurrent Statistics Collection for Large Tables
Problem

You want to minimize the amount of time it takes to gather statistics by taking advantage of your multiprocessor environment.

Solution

You can specify the *concurrent statistics gathering mode* to gather statistics on multiple tables and multiple partitions (and subpartitions) within a table concurrently. By doing this, you can take advantage of your multiprocessor environment and complete the statistics collection process much faster.

By default, concurrent statistics gathering is disabled. You enable it by executing the SET_GLOBAL_PREFS procedure. Follow these steps to enable concurrent statistics gathering:

1. Set the job_queue_processes parameter to at least 4.

    ```
    SQL>alter system set job_queue_processes=4;
    ```

    If you don't plan on using parallel execution for gathering statistics (see the following section) but want to fully utilize your system resources, you must set the job_queue_processes parameter to two times the number of CPU cores on the server.

2. Enable concurrent statistics gathering.

    ```
    SQL> begin
        dbms_stats.set_global_prefs('CONCURRENT','TRUE');
        end;
        /
    ```

Make sure the user executing this command has the CREATE JOB, MANAGE SCHEDULER, and MANAGE ANY QUEUE privileges.

How It Works

The goal of concurrent statistics gathering is to reduce the statistics gathering time for large tables and partitions. When you enable concurrent statistics gathering, Oracle uses the job scheduler and advanced queuing capabilities of the database to create multiple concurrent statistics gathering jobs. The job_queue_processes parameter determines the maximum number of concurrent statistics gathering jobs. In a RAC environment, you must set this parameter on each node. Concurrent statistics gathering works somewhat differently depending on the level of statistics gathering (table level or not), as explained here.

If you execute the DBMS_STATS.GATHER_TABLE_STATS procedure to collect statistics on a partitioned table, Oracle will create a separate statistics collection job for each partition (and subpartition) in the table. The scheduler determines how many jobs to run concurrently, and how many jobs it must queue, based on the system capacity.

■ **Note**   The value of the job_queue_processes parameter determines the maximum number of concurrent statistics collection jobs.

If you execute the GATHER_DATABASE_STATS, GATHER_SCHEMA_STATS, or GATHER_DICTIONARY_STATS procedure, Oracle creates a separate statistics collection job for each table and each partition in a partitioned table. To prevent potential deadlocking issues, Oracle won't process multiple partitioned tables concurrently. Oracle creates a coordinator job for each partitioned table to manage the partition statistics collection jobs. Each job either is a coordinator for a table's partition-level jobs (if the table is partitioned) or is an actual statistics gathering job. If you have multiple partitioned tables, the database queues all partitioned tables except one; as it finishes gathering statistics for each partitioned table, it dequeues and starts another job for a partitioned table. This queuing behavior doesn't apply to nonpartitioned tables.

Using a Parallel Execution Strategy

If you're gathering statistics for very large tables, you can enable parallel execution of the individual statistics gathering jobs. To do this, you must disable the parallel_adaptive_multi_user initialization parameter as shown here:

```
SQL> alter system set parallel_adaptive_multi_user=false;
```

Although not necessary, Oracle also recommends that you enable parallel statement queuing by activating the resource manager, creating a temporary resource plan, and enabling queuing for the consumer group OTHER _GROUPS. Here's a simple example that shows how to create a temporary resource plan and enable the resource manager:

```
begin
  dbms_resource_manager.create_pending_area();
  dbms_resource_manager.create_plan('parallel_test', 'parallel_test');
  dbms_resource_manager.create_plan_directive(
        'parallel_test',
        'OTHER_GROUPS',
        'OTHER_GROUPS directive for parallel test',
        parallel_target_percentage => 90);
  dbms_resource_manager.submit_pending_area();
end;
/
ALTER SYSTEM SET RESOURCE_MANAGER_PLAN = 'parallel_test' SID='*';
```

Monitoring Concurrent Stats Collection Jobs

Use the DBA_SCHEDULER_JOBS view to monitor the concurrent statistics gathering jobs. You can view all the concurrent statistics collection jobs in your database by issuing the following statement:

```
SQL> select job_name,state,comments
     from dba_scheduler_jobs
     where job_class like 'CONC%';
```

If you want to limit the output to currently executing jobs, add the line and state='RUNNING' to the previous query. Similarly, you can add the line and state='SCHEDULED' to view only the scheduled jobs that are waiting to run. You can check the elapsed time for the currently executing statistics gathering jobs by issuing the following query:

```
SQL> select job_name,elapsed_time
     from dba_scheduler_running_jobs
     where job_name like 'ST$%';
```

13-21. Determining When Statistics Are Stale

Problem

You want to identify which statistics are stale statistics.

Solution

You can query the DBA_TAB_STATISTICS and DBA_IND_STATISTICS views to determine whether statistics are stale for any object. The STALE_STATS view in these two views tells you whether the statistics are stale.

The STALE_STATS view can take one of the following values:

- YES: The statistics are stale.

- NO: The statistics aren't stale.

- NULL: No statistics were collected for the object.

For the stale/fresh information to be recorded in these two view, table monitoring must be enabled for the object. However, you don't have to set this explicitly if you've already set the STATISTICS_LEVEL initialization parameter to TYPICAL or ALL.

How It Works

The database uses its table monitoring facility to determine whether a database object's statistics are fresh or stale. Monitoring tracks the DML operations on a table.

If you want to ensure that the two views DBA_TAB_STATISTICS and DBA_IND_STATISTICS have the most up-to-date information, you can execute the following first:

```
SQL> BEGIN
     DBMS_STATS.FLUSH_DATABASE_MONITORING_INFO;
     END;
/
```

Once you flush the database monitoring information as shown here, you can query the STALE_STATS column in the views DBA_TAB_STATISTICS and DBA_IND_STATISTICS to determine whether the statistics are stale.

Here's an example that shows how to query the DBA_TAB_STASTISTICS view to determine whether the statistics for the SH.SALES table are stale:

```
SQL> SELECT PARTITION_NAME, STALE_STATS
     FROM   DBA_TAB_STATISTICS
     WHERE  TABLE_NAME = 'SALES'
     AND    OWNER = 'SH'
     ORDER BY PARTITION_NAME;
 hasan
PARTITION_NAME   STALE_STATS
---------------  -----------
SALES_2010       NO
SALES_2011       NO
SALES_H1_2012    NO
SALES_H2_2012    NO
SALES_Q1_2013    NO
SALES_Q1_2014    NO
.
.
SQL>
```

13-22. Previewing Statistics Gathering Targets
Problem

You want to preview the objects for which the database will gather statistics when you execute a specific statistics gathering function.

Solution

Execute the DBMS_STATS statistics gathering functions in the reporting mode to get a report of the objects that the statistics gathering function will process. The optimizer doesn't actually gather any statistics when you do this.

Here are the DBMS_STATS.REPORT_GATHER_*_STATS functions that you can use to get a report on statistics collection by the corresponding statistics gathering function:

- REPORT_GATHER_TABLE_STATS: Runs the GATHER_TABLE_STATS function in reporting mode

- REPORT_GATHER_SCHEMA_STATS: Runs the GATHER_SCHEMA_STATS function in reporting mode

- REPORT_GATHER_DICTIONARY_STATS: Runs the GATHER_DICTIONARY_STATS function in reporting mode

- REPORT_GATHER_DATABASE_STATS: Runs the GATHER_DATABASE_STATS function in reporting mode

- REPORT_GATHER_FIXED_OBJ_STATS: Runs the GATHER_FIXED_OBJ_STATS function in reporting mode

- REPORT_GATHER_AUTO_STATS: Runs the automatic statistics gathering job in reporting mode

Here's an example that shows how to execute the DBMS_STATS.REPORT_GATHER_SCHEMA_STATS function:

```
VARIABLE my_report CLOB;
BEGIN
  :my_report :=DBMS_STATS.REPORT_GATHER_SCHEMA_STATS(
    ownname      => 'OE'      ,
    detail_level => 'TYPICAL' ,
    format       => 'HTML'    );
END;
/
```

You can also use the DBMS_STATS functions to get a report on statistics gathering operations that occurred in the past, during a specific period of time. Here are the functions you can use to get a report on operations that occurred between two points in time:

- REPORT_STATS_OPERATIONS: Generates a report of all statistics gathering operations performed between two points in time

- REPORT_SINGLE_STATS_OPERATIONS: Generates a report of a specific operation

The following example shows how to get a report on all statistics gathering operations in the past day:

```
VARIABLE my_report CLOB;
BEGIN
  :my_report := DBMS_STATS.REPORT_STATS_OPERATIONS (
    since        => SYSDATE-1
,   until        => SYSDATE
,   detail_level => 'TYPICAL'
,   format       => 'HTML'
);
END;
/
```

The following example shows how to generate a report for an individual operation:

```
BEGIN
  :my_report :=DBMS_STATS.REPORT_SINGLE_STATS_OPERATION (
    OPID   => 999
,   FORMAT => 'HTML'
);
END;
```

How It Works

Often, when you're in the process of collecting optimizer statistics, you want to know exactly for which objects you'll be collecting statistics for. The new reporting functions provide you with a convenient way to know ahead of time what a particular statistics gathering option will do. Using the DBMS_STATS functions, you can get useful reports on past statistics gathering operations in your database. These reports are definitely superior to reports you can create without using the DBMS_STATS reporting functions.

You can use the statistics gathering reporting functions in a multitenent environment for specific PDBs by providing a set of pluggable database (PDB) IDs.

Implementing Query Hints

Placing hints in SQL is a common and simple approach to improve performance. Hints influence Oracle's optimizer to take a specific path to accomplish a given task, overriding the default path the optimizer may have chosen. Hints can also be viewed as a double-edged sword. If not implemented and maintained properly, they can hurt performance in the long run.

The initial goal of any application should be to implement SQL without hints because over time an application and its data can change, the database can be upgraded, hardware can change, and other factors can affect performance. Hints help an application at a specific point in time, but over time the usefulness of hints is unpredictable. All that said, they can be a useful tool if used in the right way to gain performance benefits for an application.

The most popular reason to use hints is simply to get data out of the database faster, and many of the available hints are geared for that purpose. The Oracle 12c version of the database supports more than 80 documented hints plus many undocumented hints. Hints can be placed in SQL for a multitude of reasons. The purpose of this chapter is to categorize these hints into subsets and then to show specific examples of some of the popular and most performance-impacting hints.

Some of the reasons to place hints in SQL are to change the access path to the database, change the join order or join type for queries that are doing joins, enhance performance for DML, and enhance performance for data warehouse-specific operations, to name a few. In addition, there are a few new hints to take advantage of some of the new features of Oracle 12c.

14-1. Writing a Hint
Problem

You want to place a hint into a SQL statement.

Solution

Place your hint into the statement using the /*+ hint */ syntax. Here's an example:

```
SELECT /*+ full(emp) */ * FROM emp;
```

Be sure to leave a space following the plus sign. The /*+ sequence is exactly three characters long, with no spaces. Generally, you want to place your hint immediately following the SQL verb beginning the statement. While it is not required to place this sequence of characters after the SQL verb, it is customary to do this.

How It Works

Hints are delimited by special characters placed within your SQL statement. Each hint starts with a forward slash, followed by the star and plus characters. They end with a star and forward slash:

```
SELECT /*+ full(emp) */ * FROM emp;
```

Table 14-1 breaks down many of the most popular hints into specific categories. This table is meant to make it easier to zero in on a hint based on your specific need, so keep in mind that some of these hints actually can fit into multiple categories. Another thing to remember about hints is that for many of them, you can enable a particular feature or aspect, and you can disable that same feature or aspect. For example, there is an INDEX hint to enable the use of an index. There is also a NO_INDEX hint, which disables the use of an index. This is true for many of the available hints within the Oracle database.

Table 14-1. *Hints by Category*

Access path (table)	FULL
	HASH
	CLUSTER
Access path (index)	INDEX / NO_INDEX
	INDEX_ASC / INDEX_DESC
	INDEX_FFS / NO_INDEX_FFS
	INDEX_SS / NO_INDEX_SS
	INDEX_SS_ASC / INDEX_SS_DESC
	INDEX_COMBINE / INDEX_JOIN
Join order	ORDERED
	LEADING
Join method	USE_HASH
	USE_NL
	USE_MERGE
	USE_CUBE
Data warehousing	STAR_TRANSFORMATION
	FACT
	REWRITE
Optimizer hints	FIRST_ROWS
	ALL_ROWS
	OPTIMIZER_FEATURES_ENABLE
	GATHER_OPTIMIZER_STATISTICS
	GATHER_PLAN_STATISTICS
Parallelism	PARALLEL / NO_PARALLEL
	PARALLEL_INDEX / NO_PARALLEL_INDEX
	PQ_DISTRIBUTE
	PQ_CONCURRENT_UNION
	PQ_FILTER
	PQ_SKEW
	STATEMENT_QUEUING

(continued)

Table 14-1. (*continued*)

Access path (table)	FULL
	HASH
	CLUSTER
DML-related hints	APPEND
	APPEND_VALUES
Miscellaneous hints	CACHE
	RESULT_CACHE
	DRIVING_SITE
	DYNAMIC_SAMPLING
	CURSOR_SHARING_EXACT

For a complete listing of hints, refer to the Oracle Database Performance Tuning Guide for your version of the database.

14-2. Changing the Access Path
Problem

You have a query that you have determined is not taking the access path you desire.

Solution

You can change the access path of your SQL statement by placing an access path hint in your query. The two most common access path hints to place in a query tell the Oracle optimizer to do a full table scan or use an index. Often, the optimizer does a good job of choosing the best or at least a reasonable path to the data needed for a query. Sometimes, though, because of the specific makeup of data in a table, the statistics for the objects, or the specific configuration of a given database, the optimizer doesn't necessarily make the best choice. In these cases, you can influence the optimizer by placing a hint in your query.

By the time you decide to place a hint in a query, you should already know that the optimizer isn't making the choice you want. Let's say you want to place a hint in your query to tell the optimizer to modify the access path to either perform a full table scan or change how the optimizer will access the data from the table. Full table scans are appropriate if your query will be returning a large number of rows. For example, if you want to perform a full table scan on your table, your hint will appear as follows:

```
SELECT /*+ full(emp) */ empno, ename
FROM emp
WHERE DEPTNO = 20;
```

The foregoing hint instructs the optimizer to bypass the use of any possible indexes on the EMP table and simply scan the entire table in order to retrieve the data for the query.

Conversely, let's say you are retrieving a much smaller subset of data from the EMP table, and you want to get the average salary for those employees in department 20. You can tell the optimizer to use an index on a given table in the query:

```
SELECT /*+ index(emp emp_i2) */ avg(sal)
FROM emp
WHERE deptno = 20;
```

■ **Tip**   Hints with incorrect or improper syntax are ignored by the optimizer. Hints with index names that have been dropped or renamed will also be ignored or produce unpredictable execution plans.

How It Works

Access path hints, like many hints, are placed in your query because you already know what access path the optimizer is going to take for your query, and you believe it will be more efficient using the method you specify with the hint. It is important that before you use a hint, you validate that you are not getting the access path you desire or think you should be getting. You can also gauge the potential performance gain by analyzing the optimizer's cost of the query with and without the hint.

For example, you want to compare your salary to other jobs in your company, so you write the following query to get, by job title, the minimum, average, and maximum salaries:

```
SELECT job, min(sal), avg(sal), max(sal)
FROM emp
WHERE deptno=20
GROUP BY job;
```

```
-------------------------------------------------
| Id  | Operation                   | Name  |
-------------------------------------------------
|   0 | SELECT STATEMENT            |       |
|   1 |  HASH GROUP BY              |       |
|   2 |   TABLE ACCESS BY INDEX ROWID| EMP  |
|   3 |    INDEX RANGE SCAN         | EMP_I2 |
-------------------------------------------------
```

If you want to bypass the use of the index in the query, placing the FULL hint in the query will instruct the optimizer to bypass the use of the index:

```
SELECT /*+ full(emp) */ job, min(sal), avg(sal), max(sal)
FROM emp
WHERE deptno=20
GROUP BY job;
```

```
------------------------------------
| Id | Operation          | Name |
------------------------------------
|  0 | SELECT STATEMENT   |      |
|  1 |  HASH GROUP BY     |      |
|  2 |   TABLE ACCESS FULL| EMP  |
------------------------------------
```

Another way you can tell the optimizer to bypass the use of an index is by telling the optimizer to not use indexes to retrieve the data for a given query. In this particular case, it has the same effect as the FULL hint:

```
SELECT /*+ no_index(emp) */ job, min(sal), avg(sal), max(sal)
FROM emp
WHERE deptno=20
GROUP BY job;
```

You can also explicitly state the name of the index you want to bypass:

```
SELECT /*+ no_index(emp emp_i2) */ job, min(sal), avg(sal), max(sal)
FROM emp
WHERE deptno=20
GROUP BY job;
```

In both of the foregoing cases, the result is a full table scan. In a different case, you may have a query that could possibly use different indexes. For instance, on our EMP table, we have an index on the DEPTNO column, and we also have an index on the HIREDATE column. If we wanted to execute a query to get the employees who started in 1980 for department 20, our query would look like this:

```
SELECT empno, ename
FROM emp
WHERE DEPTNO = 20
AND hiredate
BETWEEN to_date('1980-01-01','yyyy-mm-dd')
AND to_date('1980-12-31','yyyy-mm-dd');
```

```
-----------------------------------------------
| Id | Operation                   | Name    |
-----------------------------------------------
|  0 | SELECT STATEMENT            |         |
|  1 |  TABLE ACCESS BY INDEX ROWID| EMP     |
|  2 |   INDEX RANGE SCAN          | EMP_I1  |
-----------------------------------------------
```

In this case, the optimizer chose the EMP_I1 index, which is the index on the HIREDATE column. We can instruct the optimizer to bypass the use of that index:

```
SELECT /*+ no_index(emp emp_i1) */ job, min(sal), avg(sal), max(sal)
FROM emp
WHERE deptno=20
GROUP BY job;
```

In this case, we don't necessarily know what the optimizer is going to do next. It may decide to use our other index on the DEPTNO column, or it could choose to perform a full table scan. When using index hints, it is good practice to be as specific as possible when instructing the optimizer what to do. Therefore, if we place an index hint to tell the optimizer to use the index on the DEPTNO column, we can see that the optimizer now uses that index:

```
SELECT /*+ index(emp emp_i2) */ empno, ename
FROM emp
WHERE DEPTNO = 20
AND hiredate
BETWEEN to_date('1980-01-01','yyyy-mm-dd')
AND to_date('1980-12-31','yyyy-mm-dd');
```

```
---------------------------------------------
| Id | Operation                 | Name    |
---------------------------------------------
|  0 | SELECT STATEMENT          |         |
|  1 |  TABLE ACCESS BY INDEX ROWID| EMP   |
|  2 |   INDEX RANGE SCAN        | EMP_I2  |
---------------------------------------------
```

Other examples of index hints are the INDEX_FFS hint for an index fast full scan and the INDEX SS hint for an index skip scan. The INDEX_SS hint is appropriate if you have a table with composite, multicolumn indexes. It is possible to have Oracle use the index, even if the query does not use the leading column of the index. At times, the INDEX_SS hint can be beneficial to retrieve data fast, even if the column noted in the WHERE clause isn't the leading column of an index. For example, if we want to get the names of all employees who received a commission, our query would look like this:

```
SELECT ename, comm FROM emp
WHERE comm > 0;
```

```
----------------------------------------
| Id | Operation          | Name |
----------------------------------------
|  0 | SELECT STATEMENT    |      |
|  1 |  TABLE ACCESS FULL| EMP   |
----------------------------------------
```

As noted in the explain plan, no index is used. We happen to know there is a composite index on the SAL and COMM columns of our EMP table. We can add a hint to use this index to gain the benefit of having an index on the COMM column, even though it is not the leading column of the index:

```
SELECT /*+ index_ss(emp emp_i3) */ ename, comm FROM emp
WHERE comm > 0;
```

```
---------------------------------------------
| Id | Operation                 | Name    |
---------------------------------------------
|  0 | SELECT STATEMENT          |         |
|  1 |  TABLE ACCESS BY INDEX ROWID| EMP   |
|  2 |   INDEX SKIP SCAN         | EMP_I3  |
---------------------------------------------
```

■ **Note** Historically within Oracle documentation, hints are stated as instructions to the optimizer. In the Oracle 12c Performance Tuning Guide, the documentation implies that hints may be ignored. The guide states that hints only *influence* the optimizer. If you are not seeing the behavior you expect from a hint, contact Oracle support for direction.

14-3. Changing the Join Order

Problem

You have a performance issue with a query where you are joining multiple tables, and the Oracle optimizer is not choosing the join order you desire.

Solution

There are two hints—the ORDERED hint and the LEADING hint—that can be used to influence the join order used within a query.

Using the ORDERED Hint

You are running a query to join two tables, EMP and DEPT, because you want to get the department names for each employee. By placing an ORDERED hint into the query, you can see how the hint alters the execution access path. Here's an example:

```
SELECT ename, dname
FROM emp JOIN dept USING(deptno);
```

```
-------------------------------------------------
| Id  | Operation                    | Name    |
-------------------------------------------------
|   0 | SELECT STATEMENT             |         |
|   1 |  MERGE JOIN                  |         |
|   2 |   TABLE ACCESS BY INDEX ROWID| DEPT    |
|   3 |    INDEX FULL SCAN           | PK_DEPT |
|   4 |   SORT JOIN                  |         |
|   5 |    TABLE ACCESS FULL         | EMP     |
-------------------------------------------------
```

```
SELECT /*+ ordered */ ename, dname
FROM emp JOIN dept USING(deptno);
```

```
------------------------------------
| Id  | Operation       | Name |
------------------------------------
|   0 | SELECT STATEMENT |     |
|   1 |  HASH JOIN       |     |
|   2 |   TABLE ACCESS FULL| EMP  |
|   3 |   TABLE ACCESS FULL| DEPT |
------------------------------------
```

Using the LEADING Hint

As with the example using the ORDERED hint, you have the same control to specify the join order of the query. The difference with the LEADING hint is that you specify the join order from within the hint itself, while with the ORDERED hint, it is specified in the FROM clause of the query. Here's an example:

```
SELECT /*+ leading(emp dept) */ ename, dname
FROM emp JOIN dept USING(deptno);
```

```
------------------------------------
| Id  | Operation       | Name |
------------------------------------
|   0 | SELECT STATEMENT |     |
|   1 |  HASH JOIN       |     |
|   2 |   TABLE ACCESS FULL| EMP  |
|   3 |   TABLE ACCESS FULL| DEPT |
------------------------------------
```

From the foregoing query, we can see that the table order specified in the FROM clause is irrelevant because the order specified in the LEADING hint specifies the join order for the query.

How It Works

The main purpose of specifying either of these hints is for multitable joins where the optimal join order is known. This is usually known from past experience with a given query, based on the makeup of the data and the tables. In these cases, specifying either of these hints will save the optimizer the time of having to process all of the possible join orders in determining the optimal join order. This can improve query performance, especially as the number of tables to join within a query increases.

When using either of these hints, you instruct the optimizer about the join order of the tables. Because of this, it is critically important that you know that the hint will improve the query's performance. Oracle recommends, where possible, to use the LEADING hint over the ORDERED hint because the LEADING hint has more versatility built in. When specifying the ORDERED hint, you specify the join order from the list of tables in the FROM clause, while with the LEADING hint, you specify the join order within the hint.

14-4. Changing the Join Method
Problem

You have a query where the optimizer is choosing a nonoptimal join type for your query, and you want to override the join type by placing the appropriate hint in the query.

Solution

There are three possible types of joins: nested loops, hash, and sort merge. Depending on the size of your tables, certain join types perform better than others. You can use hints to specify the join order that you prefer.

Nested Loops Join Hint

To invoke a nested loops join, use the USE_NL hint, and place both tables needing the join within parentheses inside the USE_NL hint:

```
SELECT /*+ use_nl(emp dept)  */ ename, dname
FROM emp JOIN dept USING (deptno);
```

```
-------------------------------------------------
| Id | Operation                  | Name   |
-------------------------------------------------
|  0 | SELECT STATEMENT           |        |
|  1 |  NESTED LOOPS              |        |
|  2 |   NESTED LOOPS            |        |
|  3 |    TABLE ACCESS FULL      | DEPT   |
|  4 |    INDEX RANGE SCAN       | EMP_I2 |
|  5 |   TABLE ACCESS BY INDEX ROWID| EMP  |
-------------------------------------------------
```

The nested loops join is usually best when joining smaller tables. In a nested loops join, one table is considered the "driving" table. This is the outer table in the join. For each row in the outer, driving table, each row in the inner table is searched for matching rows. In the execution plan for the foregoing statement, the EMP table is the driving, outer table, and it is seen in the execution plan as the outermost part of the plan. The DEPT table is the inner table and is shown as the innermost part of the execution plan.

Hash Join Hint

To invoke a hash join, use the USE_HASH hint, and place both tables needing the join within parentheses inside the USE_HASH hint:

```
SELECT /*+ use_hash(emp_all dept)  */ ename, dname
FROM emp_all JOIN dept USING (deptno);
```

```
-------------------------------------------------
| Id | Operation            | Name    | Rows  |
-------------------------------------------------
|  0 | SELECT STATEMENT     |         | 1037K|
|  1 |  HASH JOIN          |         | 1037K|
|  2 |   TABLE ACCESS FULL| DEPT    |     4 |
|  3 |   TABLE ACCESS FULL| EMP_ALL |  1037K|
-------------------------------------------------
```

For the optimizer to use a hash join, it must be an equijoin condition. Hash joins are best used when joining large amounts of data or where a large percentage of rows from a table is needed. The smaller of the two tables is used by the optimizer to build a hash table on the join key between the two tables. In the foregoing example, the DEPT table is the smaller table and will be used to build the hash table. For best performance, the hash table completely resides in memory.

Sort Merge Join Hint

To invoke a sort merge join, use the USE_MERGE hint, and place both tables needing the join within parentheses inside the USE_MERGE hint:

```
SELECT /*+ use_merge(emp dept)  */ ename, dname
FROM emp JOIN dept USING (deptno)
WHERE deptno != 20;
```

```
-------------------------------------------------
| Id | Operation                   | Name    |
-------------------------------------------------
|  0 | SELECT STATEMENT            |         |
|  1 |  MERGE JOIN                 |         |
|  2 |   TABLE ACCESS BY INDEX ROWID| DEPT   |
|  3 |    INDEX FULL SCAN          | PK_DEPT |
|  4 |   SORT JOIN                 |         |
|  5 |    TABLE ACCESS FULL        | EMP     |
-------------------------------------------------
```

Sort merge joins, like hash joins, are used to join a large volume of data. Unlike the hash join, the sort merge join is used when the join condition between the tables is not an equijoin. The hash join will generally perform better than the sort merge join, unless the data is already sorted on the two tables. During this operation, the input data from both tables is sorted on the join key and then merged.

Join Hints When Querying Multiple Tables

If you are joining several tables and want to invoke a specific join method between all of the associated tables in the query, you must add a hint for each join condition. Here's an example:

```
SELECT /*+ use_hash(employees department) use_hash(departments locations)  */
last_name, first_name, department_name,  city, state_province
FROM employees JOIN departments USING (department_id)
JOIN locations USING (location_id);
```

```
----------------------------------------------------------
| Id | Operation              | Name                |
----------------------------------------------------------
|  0 | SELECT STATEMENT       |                     |
|  1 |  HASH JOIN             |                     |
|  2 |   HASH JOIN            |                     |
|  3 |    TABLE ACCESS FULL   | LOCATIONS           |
|  4 |    TABLE ACCESS FULL   | DEPARTMENTS         |
|  5 |   VIEW                 | index$_join$_001    |
|  6 |    HASH JOIN           |                     |
|  7 |     INDEX FAST FULL SCAN| EMP_NAME_IX        |
|  8 |     INDEX FAST FULL SCAN| EMP_DEPARTMENT_IX  |
----------------------------------------------------------
```

How It Works

Table 14-2 summarizes the hints available for each of the different join methods. Hints to instruct the optimizer to choose a join method are sometimes necessary because of several factors:

- Status of statistics on the table

- Size of the PGA

- If the data is sorted at join time

- An unexplained choice of the optimizer

Table 14-2. *Join Methods and Their Hints*

Method	Hint	Description
Nested loops	USE_NL / NO_USE_NL / USE_NL_WITH_INDEX	Nested loops joins are efficient when processing a small number of rows. The optimizer chooses a driving table, which is the "outer" table in the join. For each row in the outer table, each row in the inner table is searched.
Hash	USE_HASH / NO_USE_HASH	Hash joins are efficient when processing a large number of rows. Hash joins are used only for equijoins.
Sort merge	USE_MERGE / NO_USE_MERGE	A sort merge join is ideal for presorted rows and full table scans. The sort merge join is used for nonequality joins. Both tables are sorted on the join key and then merged. It outperforms nested loops joins for large sets of rows.
Cube	USE_CUBE NO_USE_CUBE	This is a new hint as of Oracle 12c. As stated in the Oracle 12c SQL Language reference, when the right side of a join operation is a cube, this hint instructs the optimizer to join each specified table with another row source using a cube join.

Oracle advises against using hints as much as possible because over time what was optimal at one moment under one circumstance and one version of the database software may not be optimal the next time. However, sometimes these hints can simply be helpful in fulfilling the short-term need or simply may be the only way to get the optimizer to do what you want it to do.

■ **Tip**   The size of your PGA can affect which join method the optimizer uses for your query.

14-5. Changing the Optimizer Version
Problem

You have upgraded to a newer version of Oracle, and you are having query performance problems related to the newer version of Oracle. The problem is isolated to a small number of queries, so you want to place a hint in these queries to use the previous version of the optimizer's rules and features.

Solution

To specify a version of the optimizer for a given query, you specify the version of the optimizer you desire within the optimizer_features_enable hint. Within parentheses, place the desired version of the database within single quotes.

```
SELECT /*+ optimizer_features_enable('11.2.0.4') */ *
FROM EMP JOIN DEPT USING(DEPTNO);
```

This method is mostly used as an interim measure to improve performance immediately following an upgrade, until analysis can be done and a resolution is found with the query and the upgraded version of the database.

How It Works

You can modify the version of the optimizer for a given query. This can be done via the optimizer_features_enable hint and will be in effect only for a given query. The primary reason this hint is used is that a query that performed well under one specific version of Oracle has seen performance degrade immediately following an Oracle database version upgrade.

There is an Oracle initialization parameter, optimizer_features_enable, that can be changed for the entire database instance, and it is an option when widespread performance problems occur within queries immediately after you've upgraded your database. Often, however, changing this parameter at the database instance level is not feasible, nor even desired, because the primary reason for upgrading is to take advantage of new features. So, unless there are significant and widespread performance issues, it is not recommended to change the optimizer_features_ enable parameter for an entire database instance.

You can, however, change this parameter at the session level as well, which may be much more feasible for a given application. See the following example of changing the parameter at the session level:

```
alter session set optimizer_features_enable='11.2.0.4';
```

If you enter an invalid value for the parameter, the resulting error message will display all the valid values, which is helpful, especially because there are so many intermediate patch set levels for a given database version:

```
alter session set optimizer_features_enable='7';
```

```
ERROR:
ORA-00096: invalid value 7 for parameter optimizer_features_enable, must be from
among 12.1.0.1.1, 12.1.0.1, 11.2.0.4,
11.2.0.3, 11.2.0.2, 11.2.0.1, 11.1.0.7, 11.1.0.6, 10.2.0.5, 10.2.0.4, 10.2.0.3,
10.2.0.2, 10.2.0.1, 10.1.0.5, 10.1.0.4,
10.1.0.3, 10.1.0, 9.2.0.8, 9.2.0, 9.0.1, 9.0.0, 8.1.7, 8.1.6, 8.1.5, 8.1.4,
8.1.3, 8.1.0, 8.0.7, 8.0.6, 8.0.5, 8.0.4, 8.0.3, 8.0.0
```

If you have a given query or a small subset of critical queries that are performing at a substandard performance level after an upgrade, a quick method to return to the preupgrade performance is to use the optimizer_features_enable hint to point to a specific version of the optimizer for a given query.

14-6. Choosing Between a Fast Response and Overall Optimization

Problem

When you execute a query, you can choose between two goals:

- *Fast, initial response*: Get to the point of returning some rows as quickly as possible.

- *Overall optimization*: Minimize overall cost at the expense of up-front processing time.

Your instance will have a default goal configured for it. You can specify hints on a query-by-query basis to override the default goal and get the behavior you want for a given query.

Solution

There are hints that can be used to override the optimization goal of your database instance. Before using any of the hints related to the `optimizer_mode` parameter, you first want to validate what your database instance is currently set to. If you have the `SELECT ANY DICTIONARY` system privilege, you can see what value is set for the `optimizer_mode` parameter.

```
SQL> show parameter optimizer_mode
```

```
NAME               TYPE      VALUE
--------------     ------    --------
optimizer_mode     string    ALL_ROWS
```

If we run an explain plan for an example query, we can see what the execution plan is by using the default `optimizer_mode` setting for our database instance.

```
SELECT *
FROM employees NATURAL JOIN departments;
```

```
-------------------------------------------
| Id | Operation          | Name          |
-------------------------------------------
|  0 | SELECT STATEMENT   |               |
|  1 |  HASH JOIN         |               |
|  2 |   TABLE ACCESS FULL| DEPARTMENTS   |
|  3 |   TABLE ACCESS FULL| EMPLOYEES     |
-------------------------------------------
```

Since the foregoing query is doing full table scans against the tables and we want to see some rows as soon as possible but not necessarily the full result set, we can pass in a `FIRST_ROWS` hint to accomplish this task. It is apparent that this changes the optimizer's execution plan in order to provide results as soon as possible. You also have to pass in an integer value within the hint, specifying how many rows you want to see. The following example demonstrates the use of the `FIRST_ROWS` hint:

```
SELECT /*+ first_rows(10) */ *
FROM employees NATURAL JOIN departments;
```

```
---------------------------------------------------------
| Id  | Operation                    | Name        |
---------------------------------------------------------
|   0 | SELECT STATEMENT             |             |
|   1 |  NESTED LOOPS                |             |
|   2 |   NESTED LOOPS               |             |
|   3 |    TABLE ACCESS FULL         | EMPLOYEES   |
|   4 |    INDEX UNIQUE SCAN         | DEPT_ID_PK  |
|   5 |   TABLE ACCESS BY INDEX ROWID| DEPARTMENTS |
---------------------------------------------------------
```

The integer value supplied within the hint will influence the optimizer's decision on determining the execution plan for the query. For instance, for the following query, if we increase the number of rows we want to see quickly, it can change the execution plan for the query:

```
SELECT /*+ first_rows(100) */ *
FROM employees NATURAL JOIN departments;
```

```
-------------------------------------------
| Id  | Operation          | Name         |
-------------------------------------------
|   0 | SELECT STATEMENT   |              |
|   1 |  HASH JOIN         |              |
|   2 |   TABLE ACCESS FULL| DEPARTMENTS  |
|   3 |   TABLE ACCESS FULL| EMPLOYEES    |
-------------------------------------------
```

Therefore, be as precise as possible when determining how many rows you want to see using the FIRST_ROWS hint.

If we needed the reverse situation and the database's default optimizer_mode was set to FIRST_ROWS, we can supply an ALL_ROWS hint to tell the optimizer to use that mode when determining the execution plan:

```
SQL> alter system set optimizer_mode=first_rows scope=both;

System altered.

SQL> show parameter optimizer_mode

NAME                TYPE       VALUE
--------------      ------     ----------
optimizer_mode      string     FIRST_ROWS

SELECT /*+ all_rows */ *
FROM employees NATURAL JOIN departments;
```

```
-------------------------------------------
| Id  | Operation          | Name         |
-------------------------------------------
|   0 | SELECT STATEMENT   |              |
|   1 |  HASH JOIN         |              |
|   2 |   TABLE ACCESS FULL| DEPARTMENTS  |
|   3 |   TABLE ACCESS FULL| EMPLOYEES    |
-------------------------------------------
```

As with many Oracle parameters, you can also change the value at the session level, which is also true for optimizer_mode:

```
alter session set optimizer_mode=first_rows;

SELECT *
FROM employees NATURAL JOIN departments;
```

```
-----------------------------------------------------
| Id | Operation                    | Name        |
-----------------------------------------------------
|  0 | SELECT STATEMENT             |             |
|  1 |  NESTED LOOPS                |             |
|  2 |   NESTED LOOPS               |             |
|  3 |    TABLE ACCESS FULL         | EMPLOYEES   |
|  4 |    INDEX UNIQUE SCAN         | DEPT_ID_PK  |
|  5 |   TABLE ACCESS BY INDEX ROWID| DEPARTMENTS |
-----------------------------------------------------
```

The valid values for optimizer_mode at the session level are FIRST_ROWS, FIRST_ROWS_1, FIRST_ROWS_10, FIRST_ROWS_100, FIRST_ROWS_1000, ALL_ROWS, CHOOSE, and RULE.

How It Works

The fast, initial response goal is often a good choice for queries when a user is awaiting results. It causes the database engine to make choices that allow rows to begin coming back from the query almost immediately. For example, optimizing for initial response often results in a nested loops join because such a join can begin returning rows from the beginning. The trade-off is possibly a longer overall execution time.

The goal of reducing overall query cost is usually a good choice for batch processes. No live, human user is awaiting results, so it is acceptable to spend more time on up-front processing in order to reduce overall query cost. An example might be to execute a hash join, which can't begin returning rows until the join is done but which might execute in less overall time than a nested loops join.

You can use either the FIRST_ROWS or ALL_ROWS hint in your query to change the optimizer mode, which controls which of the preceding two goals applies to a given query.

To check what the current optimizer mode is for your database instance, check the value of the optimizer_mode initialization parameter. By specifying an optimizer goal hint, you override the optimizer mode set at the database instance level, as well as any settings at the session level.

The FIRST_ROWS hint is popular because it can quickly return the first possible rows back from a query. The FIRST_ROWS hint is also common because ALL_ROWS is the default value for the optimizer_mode parameter. It's thus unusual to need to specify ALL_ROWS.

14-7. Performing a Direct-Path Insert
Problem

You are doing a DML INSERT statement, and it is performing slower than needed. You want to optimize the INSERT statement to use a direct-path insert technique.

Solution

By using the APPEND or APPEND_VALUES hint, you can significantly speed up the process of performing an insert operation on the database. Here is an example of the performance savings using the APPEND hint. First, we have a query that does a conventional insert between two tables:

```
INSERT INTO emp_dept
SELECT * FROM emp_ctas_new;

19753072 rows created.
```

Elapsed: 00:01:17.86

```
--------------------------------------------------
| Id  | Operation               | Name          |
--------------------------------------------------
|  0  | INSERT STATEMENT        |               |
|  1  |  LOAD TABLE CONVENTIONAL | EMP_DEPT      |
|  2  |   TABLE ACCESS FULL      | EMP_CTAS_NEW  |
--------------------------------------------------
```

Then, if we place the APPEND hint inside the same INSERT statement, we see a considerable gain in performance:

```
INSERT /*+ append */ INTO emp_dept
SELECT * FROM emp_ctas_new;

19753072 rows created.
```

Elapsed: 00:00:12.15

```
-------------------------------------------
| Id  | Operation          | Name         |
-------------------------------------------
|  0  | INSERT STATEMENT   |              |
|  1  |  LOAD AS SELECT     | EMP_DEPT     |
|  2  |   TABLE ACCESS FULL | EMP_CTAS_NEW |
-------------------------------------------
```

The APPEND hint works with an INSERT statement only with a subquery; it does not work with an INSERT statement with a VALUES clause. For that, you need to use the APPEND_VALUES hint. Here are two examples of an INSERT statement with a VALUES clause, and we can see the effect the hint has on the execution plan:

```
INSERT INTO emp_dept
VALUES (15867234,'Smith, JR','Sales',1359,'2010-01-01',200,5,20);
```

```
--------------------------------------------------
| Id  | Operation               | Name          |
--------------------------------------------------
|  0  | INSERT STATEMENT        |               |
|  1  |  LOAD TABLE CONVENTIONAL | EMP_DEPT      |
--------------------------------------------------
```

```
INSERT /*+ append_values */ INTO emp_dept
VALUES (15867234,'Smith, JR','Sales',1359,'2010-01-01',200,5,20);
```

```
-------------------------------------
| Id | Operation          | Name     |
-------------------------------------
|  0 | INSERT STATEMENT   |          |
|  1 |  LOAD AS SELECT    | EMP_DEPT |
|  2 |   BULK BINDS GET   |          |
-------------------------------------
```

How It Works

The APPEND hint works within statements performing DML insert operations from another table, that is, using a subquery from within an INSERT SQL statement. This is appropriate for when you need to copy a large volume of rows between tables. By bypassing the Oracle database buffer cache blocks and appending the data directly to the segment above the high-water mark, you save significant overhead. This is a popular method for inserting rows into a table very quickly.

When you specify one of these hints, Oracle will perform a direct-path insert. In a direct-path insert, the data is appended at the end of a table, rather than using free space that is found within current allocated blocks for that table. The APPEND and APPEND_VALUES hints, when used, automatically convert a conventional insert operation into a direct-path insert operation. In addition, if you are using parallel operations during an insert, the default mode of operation is to use the direct-path mode. If you want to bypass performing direct-path operations, you can use the NOAPPEND hint.

Keep in mind that if you are running with either of these hints, there is a risk of contention if you have multiple application processes inserting rows into the same table. If two append operations are inserting rows at the same time, performance will suffer: since the insert append operation appends the data above the high water mark for a segment, only one operation should be done at one time. However, if you have partitioned objects, you can still run several concurrent append operations, as long as each insert operates on separate partitions for a given table.

There are trade-offs in using either append hint. First, direct-path inserts require more space than normal insert operations because they are applied above the high-water mark of the table. This is even more true when running direct-path operations in parallel because then an extent is needed for each parallel insert process. Second, append hints will be ignored if performing them on tables with referential integrity constraints or on tables with triggers.

Starting with Oracle 12.1, statistics are automatically gathered when doing certain direct-path operations. If using either the CREATE TABLE ... AS SELECT or INSERT operation using direct-path operations, statistics are automatically gathered. The following example of a CREATE TABLE ... AS SELECT demonstrates that statistics are gathered automatically:

```
create table cre_test as select * from dual;

SQL> select owner, table_name, last_analyzed from dba_tables
  2  where table_name = 'CRE_TEST';
```

```
OWNER    TABLE_NAME    LAST_ANALY
-----    ----------    ----------
HR       CRE_TEST      2013-10-21
```

In the following example, we show two tables to be used to demonstrate statistics gathering for insert statements. Note that the table must be loaded in direct-path mode and be empty for statistics to be gathered. Here is the same query used in the CREATE TABLE example, but in this case used for two empty tables that will be used for INSERT operations:

```
SQL> select owner, table_name, last_analyzed from dba_tables
  2  where table_name in ('INS_CONV_TEST','INS_BULK_TEST');

OWNER      TABLE_NAME       LAST_ANALY
-----      -------------    ----------
HR         INS_BULK_TEST
HR         INS_CONV_TEST

2 rows selected.
```

Let's insert a row into a table using a conventional INSERT statement:

```
SQL>
SQL> insert into ins_conv_test select * from dual;

1 row created.
```

Then, we will do the same for a table using the APPEND hint, which is a direct-path load operation:

```
SQL> insert /*+ append */ into ins_bulk_test select * from dual;

1 row created.

SQL> commit;

Commit complete.
```

If we then rerun our query against the data dictionary to check the statistics for our two tables, we can see that statistics have been gathered for our table on which we performed a direct-path insert using APPEND:

```
SQL>
SQL> select owner, table_name, last_analyzed from dba_tables
  2  where table_name in ('INS_CONV_TEST','INS_BULK_TEST');

OWNER      TABLE_NAME       LAST_ANALY
-----      -------------    ----------
HR         INS_BULK_TEST    2013-10-21
HR         INS_CONV_TEST

2 rows selected.
```

If, for whatever reason, you want to defer statistics gathering when using these operations, you can use the NO_GATHER_OPTIMIZER_STATISTICS hint:, which will prevent statistics gathering on the affected table. See the following example:

```
SQL> insert /*+ append no_gather_optimizer_statistics */ into ins_nostat_test
  2   select * from dual;

1 row created.
```

```
SQL> commit;

Commit complete.

SQL>
SQL> select owner, table_name, last_analyzed from dba_tables
  2  where table_name = 'INS_NOSTAT_TEST';

OWNER       TABLE_NAME         LAST_ANALY
-----       ---------------    ----------
HR          INS_NOSTAT_TEST
```

14-8. Placing Hints in Views
Problem

You are creating a view and want to place a hint in the view's query in order to improve performance on any queries that access the view.

Solution

Hints can be placed in views because a view is simply a stored query in the database. Depending on the type of hint used, as well as the type of view that is being queried, you can determine whether your hint will be used. It is important to understand what type of view you have so you can determine what impact hints will have on that view. To understand this, you first need to determine which of the following describes your view:

- Mergeable or nonmergeable view
- Simple or complex view

A simple view is a view that references only one table, and there are not any grouping functions or expressions:

```
CREATE view emp_high_sal
AS SELECT /*+ use_index(employees) */ employee_id, first_name, last_name, salary
FROM employees
WHERE salary > 10000;
```

A complex view can reference multiple tables, or it will have grouping clauses or use functions and expressions:

```
CREATE or replace view dept_sal
AS SELECT /*+ full(employees) */ department_id, department_name,
departments.manager_id, SUM(salary) total_salary, AVG(salary) avg_salary
FROM employees JOIN departments USING(department_id)
GROUP BY department_id, department_name, departments.manager_id;
```

A mergeable view is simply one in which the optimizer can replace the query calling the view with the query within the view definition. For example, we simply want to query all the rows from our EMP_HIGH_SAL view. The optimizer simply has to go directly to the EMPLOYEES table:

```
SELECT * FROM emp_high_sal;
```

```
-------------------------------------
| Id | Operation          | Name     |
-------------------------------------
|  0 | SELECT STATEMENT   |          |
|  1 |  TABLE ACCESS FULL | EMPLOYEES |
-------------------------------------
```

The optimizer has simply replaced the query with the query that defined the view:

```
SELECT /*+ full(employees) */ department_id, department_name,
departments.manager_id, SUM(salary) total_salary, AVG(salary) avg_salary
FROM employees JOIN departments USING(department_id)
GROUP BY department_id, department_name, departments.manager_id;
```

With a mergeable view, the hint inside the view is preserved because the essential structure of the view definition is intact based on the query calling the view. See Table 14-3 for the guidelines for hints regarding mergeable views.

Table 14-3. Rules for Using Hints in Mergeable Views

Hint Category	Placing Hints Inside Views	Placing Hints in Queries Accessing a View
Access path/join	Used only if the query referencing the view does not reference any other tables or views	Ignored unless single-table view; if so, hint applied to the single table inside the view
Optimizer mode hints	Used unless there are conflicting hints inside the view, in which case they are all ignored	Hints used regardless of hints inside the views

For a nonmergeable view, the optimizer must break up the work into two pieces. It first must execute the query that defines the view and then must execute the top-level query. Because of this, the hints defined within the view are preserved. For instance, we are querying our DEPT_SAL view. We can see from the explain plan that the query is broken up into pieces:

```
SELECT manager_id, sum(total_salary)
FROM dept_sal
GROUP BY manager_id;
```

```
---------------------------------------------------------
| Id | Operation                     | Name         |
---------------------------------------------------------
|  0 | SELECT STATEMENT              |              |
|  1 |  HASH GROUP BY                |              |
|  2 |   VIEW                        | DEPT_SAL     |
|  3 |    HASH GROUP BY              |              |
|  4 |     MERGE JOIN               |              |
|  5 |      TABLE ACCESS BY INDEX ROWID| DEPARTMENTS |
|  6 |       INDEX FULL SCAN         | DEPT_ID_PK   |
|  7 |      SORT JOIN                |              |
|  8 |       TABLE ACCESS FULL       | EMPLOYEES    |
---------------------------------------------------------
```

See Table 14-4 for the guidelines for hints regarding nonmergeable views.

Table 14-4. *Rules for Using Hints in Nonmergeable Views*

Hint Category	Placing Hints Inside Views	Placing Hints in Queries Accessing a View
Access path	Preserved	Ignored
Join	Preserved	Preserved
Optimizer mode hints	Ignored	Used, if present

It can be confusing to understand all the possible scenarios with hints and views, so they need to be used sparingly and only when other means of tuning have not met the needed requirements.

How It Works

Since a view, as mentioned, is simply a stored query, hints can be placed easily inside the view as they would be inside any query. The type of hint placed in the view will determine how and if a hint can be used within the view. Much like performing DML on a view, there are limitations on when hints are used or ignored.

As a rule of thumb, the simpler a view is, the more likely hints can be effective. Because of the uniqueness of each application, query, and view, the only true way to know whether a hint will be used is to simply try the hint and perform an explain plan to validate whether a given hint is used.

Oracle does not recommend placing hints in views; because the underlying objects can change over time, you can expect unpredictable execution plans. Also, views can be created for one specific use but could be used for other purposes later, and any hints in the views may not help every scenario. In addition, hints placed within views are managed differently than if you were simply executing the query itself. Before any hint placed inside a view is used, the optimizer needs to determine whether the view can be merged with the query calling the view.

You can also consider placing hints within queries that access views. It is important to understand the rules of precedence when hints are placed within queries that access the views that have hints within themselves. This especially underlines the need for caution before placing a hint within a view.

■ **Tip** Hints placed in queries that select against complex views are ignored.

14-9. Caching Query Results
Problem

You want to improve the performance on a given set of often-used queries and want to use Oracle's result cache to store the query results so they can be retrieved quickly for future use when the same query has been executed.

Solution

The result cache was created in order to store results from often-used queries in memory for quick and easy retrieval. If you run an explain plan on a given query, you can see whether the results will be stored in the result cache:

```
SELECT /*+ result_cache */
job_id, min_salary, avg(salary) avg_salary, max_salary
FROM employees JOIN jobs USING (job_id)
GROUP BY job_id, min_salary, max_salary;
```

```
-------------------------------------------------------------
| Id | Operation                     | Name                  |
-------------------------------------------------------------
|  0 | SELECT STATEMENT              |                       |
|  1 |  RESULT CACHE                 | 1kvbu5w68ng3y8x745w5k2bap6 |
|  2 |   HASH GROUP BY               |                       |
|  3 |    MERGE JOIN                 |                       |
|  4 |     TABLE ACCESS BY INDEX ROWID| JOBS                 |
|  5 |      INDEX FULL SCAN          | JOB_ID_PK             |
|  6 |     SORT JOIN                 |                       |
|  7 |      TABLE ACCESS FULL        | EMPLOYEES             |
-------------------------------------------------------------
```

```
Result Cache Information (identified by operation id):
------------------------------------------------------
   1 -
```

If you then query the V$RESULT_CACHE_OBJECTS view, you can validate whether the results of a query are stored in the result cache by looking at the cache ID value from the explain plan.

```
SELECT ID, TYPE, to_char(CREATION_TIMESTAMP,'yyyy-mm-dd:hh24:mi:ss') cr_date,
BLOCK_COUNT blocks, COLUMN_COUNT columns, PIN_COUNT pins, ROW_COUNT "ROWS"
FROM   V$RESULT_CACHE_OBJECTS

WHERE  CACHE_ID = '1kvbu5w68ng3y8x745w5k2bap6';
```

```
ID  TYPE       CR_DATE               BLOCKS  COLUMNS  PINS  ROWS
--- ---------- -------------------   ------  -------  ----  ----
 5  Result     2013-10-22:23:19:12        1        4     0    19
```

If for some reason the RESULT_CACHE_MODE parameter in your database is set with a default mode of FORCE at the database or table level, you can use the NO_RESULT_CACHE hint to bypass the result cache. If we run our previous query with the result cache mode set to FORCE, it is evident that the result cache is used automatically.

```
SQL> show parameter result_cache_mode
```

```
NAME                TYPE     VALUE
----------------    ------   -----
result_cache_mode   string   FORCE
```

```
select job_id, min_salary, avg(salary) avg_salary, max_salary
from employees join jobs using (job_id)
group by job_id, min_salary, max_salary;
```

```
-------------------------------------------------------------------------
| Id  | Operation                     | Name                            |
-------------------------------------------------------------------------
|  0  | SELECT STATEMENT              |                                 |
|  1  |  RESULT CACHE                 | 1kvbu5w68ng3y8x745w5k2bap6      |
|  2  |   HASH GROUP BY               |                                 |
|  3  |    MERGE JOIN                 |                                 |
|  4  |     TABLE ACCESS BY INDEX ROWID| JOBS                           |
|  5  |      INDEX FULL SCAN          | JOB_ID_PK                       |
|  6  |     SORT JOIN                 |                                 |
|  7  |      TABLE ACCESS FULL        | EMPLOYEES                       |
-------------------------------------------------------------------------
```

If we then rerun with the NO_RESULT_CACHE hint, the result cache is not used, and the statement is executed:

```
SELECT /*+ no_result_cache */ job_id, min_salary, avg(salary) avg_salary, max_salary
FROM employees JOIN jobs USING (job_id)
GROUP BY job_id, min_salary, max_salary;
```

```
----------------------------------------------------
| Id  | Operation                     | Name        |
----------------------------------------------------
|  0  | SELECT STATEMENT              |             |
|  1  |  HASH GROUP BY                |             |
|  2  |   MERGE JOIN                  |             |
|  3  |    TABLE ACCESS BY INDEX ROWID| JOBS        |
|  4  |     INDEX FULL SCAN           | JOB_ID_PK   |
|  5  |    SORT JOIN                  |             |
|  6  |     TABLE ACCESS FULL         | EMPLOYEES   |
----------------------------------------------------
```

The following query was run twice in order to show consistent results of not using the result cache (results were suppressed for the second run):

```
SELECT /*+ no_result_cache */
j.job_id, min_salary, avg(salary) avg_salary, max_salary, department_name
FROM employees_big e, jobs j, departments d
WHERE e.department_id = d.department_id
AND e.job_id = j.job_id
AND salary BETWEEN 5000 AND 9000
GROUP BY j.job_id, min_salary, max_salary, department_name;
```

```
JOB_ID   MIN_SALARY  AVG_SALARY  MAX_SALARY  DEPARTMENT_NAME
-------  ----------  ----------  ----------  ---------------
HR_REP         4000        6500        9000  Human Resources
ST_MAN         5500        8000        8500  Shipping
IT_PROG        4000        9000       10000  IT
MK_REP         4000        6000        9000  Marketing
```

4 rows selected.

Elapsed: 00:00:07.42

SQL> /
Elapsed: 00:00:07.36

Then, the same query with a `result_cache` hint was run three times for comparison:

```
SELECT /*+ result_cache */
j.job_id, min_salary, avg(salary) avg_salary, max_salary, department_name
FROM employees_big e, jobs j, departments d
WHERE e.department_id = d.department_id
AND e.job_id = j.job_id
AND salary BETWEEN 5000 AND 9000
GROUP BY j.job_id, min_salary, max_salary, department_name;
```

Elapsed: 00:00:07.56

SQL> /
Elapsed: 00:00:00.01

SQL> /
Elapsed: 00:00:00.00

By using the `result_cache` hint, you can see that the first time running with the hint showed no improvement in the run time. This can be explained because the results have not yet been placed in the result cache. With each subsequent execution, however, we can see that the results are returned immediately because they are now stored in memory within the result cache.

How It Works

The result cache hint, if placed in a query, will override any database-level, table-level, or session-level result cache settings. Before using hints in your queries, you need to determine the configuration of the result cache on your database. There are two separate result caches to look at: the server-side result cache and the client-side result cache. The server-side result cache is part of the shared pool of the SGA and stores SQL query results and PL/SQL function results. Query time can be improved significantly because query results are checked within the result cache first, and if the results exist, they are simply pulled from memory, and the query is not executed. The result cache is most appropriately used for often-run queries that produce the same results.

The result cache can be configured at several levels. As Table 14-5 indicates, it can be configured at the database level, the session level, the table level, or the statement level. The statement level is where hints are specified. If you decide to configure the result cache in your database, there are several initialization parameters that need to be configured. Table 14-6 reviews these parameters. Some are specific parameters for the result cache, while the remaining memory-related PL/SQL package parameters need to be analyzed to see whether they need to be changed to accommodate the result cache. The DBMS_RESULT CACHE can also be used to configure, flush, and retrieve information for the result cache.

Table 14-5. *Result Cache Configuration Hierarchy*

Configuration Level	How to Configure Result Cache
Database level	Configured via initialization parameters (see Table 14-6)
Table level	Configured with the CREATE TABLE or ALTER TABLE statement—for example, ALTER TABLE EMPLOYEES RESULT_CACHE (MODE FORCE)
Session level	Configured via the ALTER SESSION statement—for example, ALTER SESSION SET RESULT_CACHE_MODE=FORCE
Statement level	Configured via the RESULT_CACHE or NO_RESULT_CACHE hint

Table 14-6. *Result Cache Initialization Parameters*

Key Result Cache Initialization Parameters	Description
RESULT_CACHE_MODE	Indicates whether the result cache is active for all activity or only for manually run activities; MANUAL is the default, which means the result cache is not used unless specified at the table, session, or statement level. FORCE means it will be enabled for all queries for a database instance.
RESULT_CACHE_MAX_SIZE	Determines memory allocated for server-side result cache for database.
RESULT_CACHE_MAX_RESULT	Determines maximum size for single result for server-side result cache. The default is 5 percent.
CLIENT_RESULT_CACHE_SIZE	Determines maximum size for each client-side session result cache.
MEMORY_TARGET	By default, 0.25 percent of total is allocated for result cache if this parameter is configured.
SGA_TARGET	By default, 0.5 percent of total is allocated for result cache if this parameter is configured.
SHARED_POOL_SIZE	By default, 1 percent of total is allocated for result cache if this parameter is configured.
RESULT_CACHE_REMOTE_EXPIRATION	Number of minutes that a result dependent on remote database objects will remain valid. The default is 0, which means results dependent on remote objects will not be stored in the result cache. In most circumstances, the default is recommended because remote results can become stale.

14-10. Directing a Distributed Query to a Specific Database
Problem

You are joining two or more tables that exist on different databases and want to direct the work to take place on a particular database because the remote database is where most of the data resides.

Solution

By default, when you are joining tables that exist on different databases, the database where the query originated is where the majority of the work takes place. You can change this behavior and tell the optimizer which database will do the work:

```
SELECT /*+ driving_site(employees) */ first_name, last_name, department_name
FROM employees@to_emp_link JOIN departments USING(department_id);
```

Specifying the remote site as the driver is most appropriate if the volume on the remote site is large or if you are querying many tables on the remote site. To process a distributed query, the optimizer first has to bring rows from remote tables over to the local site, before processing the overall query. This can be very resource-intensive on the temporary tablespaces on the local database. Therefore, by instructing the optimizer to perform the work at the site where the biggest percentage of the data resides, you can drastically improve your query performance.

When specifying the hint, you simply need to specify the remote table or table alias within your hint to direct the optimizer to the site that will do the work. There is no need to specify any hint if you want the optimizer to do the work on the local database; the hint needs to be specified when you want to direct the work to a remote database.

How It Works

Distributed queries can be a blessing and a curse. By being able to join tables from remote databases, it gives users the impression of data transparency (that is, that the data they need to retrieve appears to be in one place because they can assemble a single query to retrieve data when in fact the data may reside on two or more databases). This simplicity in assembling queries is a key advantage of being able to perform distributed queries. The key disadvantage is optimizing distributed queries is difficult. Essentially, the originating or local database where the query is initiated becomes the "driver" database by default. The optimizer at the local site has no knowledge of the makeup or volume of data at the remote site, and therefore the work is split up into pieces, and the query is not, by default, optimized as a single unit. Therefore, it is important to understand the makeup of the data on each database in order to attempt to best optimize the query. The key decision you need to make with a distributed query is which database you want to be the "driving" site. The biggest factors in determining which site should be the driving site are as follows:

- How many tables are in the distributed query?

- How many databases are involved in the distributed query?

- Which database contains the most tables involved in the query?

- Which database contains the greatest volume of data needed by the query?

In essence, if a majority of tables or a large volume of data resides remotely, it may be beneficial to use a remote database as the driving site. Let's say we are joining three tables together, and we want to get employee information along with the department they work in and their work address. In this scenario, the employee table, being the largest, resides on one database, while two smaller tables, the department and location tables, reside on our local database:

```
SELECT first_name, last_name, department_name, street_address, city
FROM employees@to_emp_link JOIN departments USING(department_id)
JOIN locations USING (location_id);
```

```
-------------------------------------------
| Id | Operation          | Name          |
-------------------------------------------
|  0 | SELECT STATEMENT   |               |
|  1 |  HASH JOIN         |               |
|  2 |   HASH JOIN        |               |
|  3 |    TABLE ACCESS FULL| LOCATIONS    |
|  4 |    TABLE ACCESS FULL| DEPARTMENTS  |
|  5 |   REMOTE           | EMPLOYEES     |
-------------------------------------------
```

From the execution plan, we can see that the EMPLOYEES table is the remote table. What this means is before the join to the employee data can occur, all of that employee data must be brought over to the local database before the query can be completed. In this case, the employee data is by far the largest table of the three. There are far more employees than there are departments or locations, and therefore a large volume of data will be brought over to the local database before the remainder of the query can be processed. So, in this case, performance many improve by having the work done on the database where the employee data resides:

```
SELECT /*+ driving_site(employees) */
first_name, last_name, department_name, street_address, city
FROM employees@to_emp_link JOIN departments USING(department_id)
JOIN locations USING (location_id);
```

```
----------------------------------------------------------------
| Id | Operation             | Name                            |
----------------------------------------------------------------
|  0 | SELECT STATEMENT REMOTE |                               |
|  1 |  HASH JOIN            |                                 |
|  2 |   VIEW                | index$_join$_001                |
|  3 |    HASH JOIN          |                                 |
|  4 |     INDEX FAST FULL SCAN| EMP_DEPARTMENT_IX             |
|  5 |     INDEX FAST FULL SCAN| EMP_NAME_IX                   |
|  6 |   HASH JOIN           |                                 |
|  7 |    REMOTE             | DEPARTMENTS                     |
|  8 |    REMOTE             | LOCATIONS                       |
----------------------------------------------------------------
```

Now the explain plan shows the two smaller tables as remote tables, since the database where the EMPLOYEES table resides is now the driving site for the query. Sometimes you may simply need to determine this by trial and error when it is not obvious which site should be the driving site.

Another easy way to determine this is simply by determining which query returns faster. If we want to get the average salary for each department and location, the query would look like the following:

```
SELECT department_name, city, avg(salary)
FROM employees_big@to_emp_link JOIN departments USING(department_id)
JOIN locations USING (location_id)
GROUP BY department_name, city
ORDER BY 2,1;
```

DEPARTMENT_NAME	CITY	AVG(SALARY)
Human Resources	London	6500
Public Relations	Munich	10000
Sales	Oxford	8955.88235
Accounting	Seattle	10150
Administration	Seattle	4400
Executive	Seattle	19333.3333
Finance	Seattle	8600
Purchasing	Seattle	4150
Shipping	South San Francisco	3475.55556
IT	Southlake	5760
Marketing	Toronto	9500

11 rows selected.

Elapsed: 00:00:42.87

Since no driving site hint is specified, the local site is the driving site. If we issue the same query specifying the remote and larger table to be the driving site, we see a benefit simply from the time the query takes to execute:

```
SELECT /*+ driving_site(employees_big) */ department_name, city, avg(salary)
FROM employees_big@to_emp_link JOIN departments USING(department_id)
JOIN locations USING (location_id)
GROUP BY department_name, city
ORDER BY 2,1;
```

Elapsed: 00:00:22.24

One more way you can try to determine which site should be the driving site is by figuring out exactly what work is being performed on each site. For example, using the foregoing query as an example, if we do not use the hint, perform the following:

1. Retrieve an explain plan for the query.

2. On the remote database, determine what part of the query is running remotely.

First, we can see the execution plan of our query. Again, we are not using the driving_site hint.

```
-----------------------------------------------
| Id | Operation          | Name          |
-----------------------------------------------
|  0 | SELECT STATEMENT   |               |
|  1 |  SORT GROUP BY     |               |
|  2 |   HASH JOIN        |               |
|  3 |    HASH JOIN       |               |
|  4 |     TABLE ACCESS FULL| LOCATIONS   |
|  5 |     TABLE ACCESS FULL| DEPARTMENTS |
|  6 |     REMOTE         | EMPLOYEES_BIG |
-----------------------------------------------
```

Second, we can determine that the operation occurring on the remote database is the SELECT statement returning columns from the remote EMPLOYEES_BIG table. You can retrieve this information directly from the data dictionary on the remote database or from a tool such as Enterprise Manager.

```
SELECT "SALARY","DEPARTMENT_ID"
FROM "EMPLOYEES_BIG" "EMPLOYEES_BIG"
```

If we repeat the foregoing two steps with the same query but this time we insert a driving_site hint for the EMPLOYEES table, we get the following results. First, we can get the execution plan of our query with the driving_site hint:

```
----------------------------------------------------------------
| Id | Operation              | Name                           |
----------------------------------------------------------------
|  0 | SELECT STATEMENT REMOTE|                                |
|  1 |  RESULT CACHE          | 326m75n1yb5kt2qysx7f37cy2y     |
|  2 |   SORT GROUP BY        |                                |
|  3 |    HASH JOIN           |                                |
|  4 |     HASH JOIN          |                                |
|  5 |      REMOTE            | LOCATIONS                      |
|  6 |      REMOTE            | DEPARTMENTS                    |
|  7 |      TABLE ACCESS FULL | EMPLOYEES_BIG                  |
----------------------------------------------------------------
```

Second, we can see which part of the query is being performed on the remote site. In this case, the data was retrieved from Enterprise Manager:

```
SELECT "A2"."DEPARTMENT_NAME","A1"."CITY",AVG("A3"."SALARY")
FROM "EMPLOYEES_BIG" "A3","DEPARTMENTS"@! "A2","LOCATIONS"@! "A1"
WHERE "A2"."LOCATION_ID"="A1"."LOCATION_ID" AND "A3"."DEPARTMENT_ID"="A2"."DEPARTMENT_ID"
GROUP BY "A2"."DEPARTMENT_NAME","A1"."CITY" ORDER BY "A1"."CITY","A2"."DEPARTMENT_NAME"
```

Without the driving site hint, we had to move all rows for the EMPLOYEES_BIG table for the SALARY and DEPARTMENT_ID columns. After transporting this data, the query results could be processed.

With the driving_site hint, we had to move all rows for all columns of the DEPARTMENTS and LOCATIONS table to the remote database. Then, the query results could be processed. And, because we used the driving_site hint, after the query results were compiled, the complete result set had to be transported to the local database. Therefore, you need to factor in not only the data moving between databases for the query itself but also, if you are using the driving_site hint, the results themselves being transported back to the local database where the query originated.

14-11. Gathering Extended Query Execution Statistics
Problem

You don't know whether the cardinality estimates in your explain plan are accurate for a specific query, and you want to gather extended explain plan statistics to validate those estimates.

Solution

You can use the GATHER_PLAN_STATISTICS hint, which, if placed within a query at runtime, will generate extended runtime statistics. It is a two-step process:

1. Execute the query with the gather_plan_statistics hint.

2. Use dbms_xplan.display_cursor to display the results.

See the following example:

```
SELECT /*+ gather_plan_statistics */
city, round(avg(salary)) avg, min(salary) min, max(salary) max
FROM employees JOIN departments USING (department_id)
JOIN locations USING (location_id)
GROUP BY city;
```

CITY	AVG	MIN	MAX
London	6500	6500	6500
Seattle	8844	2500	24000
Munich	10000	10000	10000
South San Francisco	3476	2100	8200
Toronto	9500	6000	13000
Southlake	5760	4200	9000
Oxford	8956	6100	14000

Then, you can use dbms_xplan to display the extended query statistics. Ensure that the SQL Plus setting SERVEROUTPUT is set to OFF, or else the results will not be properly displayed.

```
SELECT * FROM table(dbms_xplan.display_cursor(format=>'ALLSTATS LAST'));
```

Id	Operation	Name	Starts	E-Rows	A-Rows
0	SELECT STATEMENT		1		7
1	HASH GROUP BY		1	7	7
* 2	HASH JOIN		1	106	107
* 3	HASH JOIN		1	27	27
4	VIEW	index$_join$_004	1	23	23
* 5	HASH JOIN		1		23
6	INDEX FAST FULL SCAN	LOC_CITY_IX	1	23	23
7	INDEX FAST FULL SCAN	LOC_ID_PK	1	23	23
8	VIEW	index$_join$_002	1	27	27
* 9	HASH JOIN		1		27
10	INDEX FAST FULL SCAN	DEPT_ID_PK	1	27	27
11	INDEX FAST FULL SCAN	DEPT_LOCATION_IX	1	27	27
12	TABLE ACCESS FULL	EMPLOYEES	1	107	111

```
Predicate Information (identified by operation id):
---------------------------------------------------
   2 - access("EMPLOYEES"."DEPARTMENT_ID"="DEPARTMENTS"."DEPARTMENT_ID")
   3 - access("DEPARTMENTS"."LOCATION_ID"="LOCATIONS"."LOCATION_ID")
   5 - access(ROWID=ROWID)
   9 - access(ROWID=ROWID)

Note
-----
   - statistics feedback used for this statement
   - this is an adaptive plan
```

Many other options are available using the DISPLAY_CURSOR procedure; ,refer to the Oracle PL/SQL Packages and Types Reference Guide for a more complete listing of these options.

How It Works

The GATHER_PLAN_STATISTICS hint gathers runtime statistics; therefore, the query needs to be executed in order to gather these statistics. If you already have a query that is performing at a substandard optimization level, it may be useful to run your query with the GATHER_PLAN_STATISTICS hint. This can quickly give you information that you simply do not have with a normal explain plan because it shows you estimated and actual information regarding query statistics. From this, you can determine whether the optimizer is optimally executing the SQL, and you can determine whether any optimization is needed.

Keep in mind that it does take some resources in order to gather these extra runtime statistics, so use this option with care. It may even be worthwhile to test the runtime differences in some cases. One key benefit of this hint is that the extra statistics are gathered only for the specific query. That way, the scope is limited and has little effect on other processes in the database, or even a particular session. If you wanted a more global setting to gather extended statistics, you can set STATISTICS_LEVEL=ALL at the session or instance level. One quick set of columns to review are the E-Rows and A-Rows columns. The E-Rows column shows the original optimizer estimates, and the A-Rows column shows the actual statistics gathered during execution. By looking at these columns, you can quickly tell whether the optimizer is executing the query based on accurate statistics. If there is a large discrepancy between these columns, it is a sign of an inefficient execution plan. The one needed calculation for an accurate analysis is for the E-Rows column. You need to multiply the Starts column with E-Rows to accurately compare the total with A-Rows.

14-12. Enabling Query Rewrite
Problem

You have materialized views in your database environment and want to have queries that access the source tables that make up the materialized views go against the materialized views directly to retrieve the results.

Solution

You can use the REWRITE hint to direct the optimizer to use a materialized view. The materialized view must have query rewrite enabled, and statistics for the materialized view and the associated objects should be current to increase the likelihood for a query to be rewritten.

To demonstrate how this works, first observe the following materialized view DDL. This materialized view calculates the total compensation for each department for a company. Let's say the base query embedded in this materialized view is often used by executives of this company to determine how their particular department is doing in terms of distributing compensation to its employees:

```
CREATE MATERIALIZED VIEW DEPT_SAL_MV
ENABLE QUERY REWRITE
AS
SELECT department_id,
sum(nvl(salary+(salary*commission_pct),salary)) total_compensation
FROM employees
GROUP BY department_id;
```

Then, let's see an example of a query that does the same calculation as that in the materialized view, for which the results are already stored:

```
SELECT /*+ rewrite(dept_sal_mv) */ department_id,
sum(nvl(salary+(salary*commission_pct),salary)) total_compensation
FROM employees
GROUP BY department_id
having sum(nvl(salary+(salary*commission_pct),salary)) > 10000
ORDER by 2;
```

In the following explain plan we can see that the optimizer used the materialized view in the execution plan, rather than processing the entire query and recalculating the summary:

```
-------------------------------------------------------
| Id  | Operation                   | Name         |
-------------------------------------------------------
|   0 | SELECT STATEMENT            |              |
|   1 |  SORT ORDER BY              |              |
|   2 |   MAT_VIEW REWRITE ACCESS FULL| DEPT_SAL_MV |
-------------------------------------------------------
```

How It Works

Materialized views are commonly used to store the result set for often-executed queries. While regular views are simply stored queries in the data dictionary, materialized views are essentially tables that store the result for these queries. Usually, they are created when there are complex joins, summaries, or aggregations occurring within a query. Since the results are stored in the database, there is no need for the optimizer to reprocess the query to retrieve the data. The end-user community does not have to execute a complex join or aggregation over and over, so it is a considerable performance benefit. Some users may not be aware of the materialized views in your environment and may be executing the raw queries against the star schema or other tables. It is here that the REWRITE hint may help in improving performance on queries that could use a materialized view.

If you enable query rewrite for a materialized view and if a query executes where the results can be found in that materialized view, the optimizer may choose to "rewrite" the query to go directly against the materialized view, rather than process the query itself. In these cases, no hint is usually required because the optimizer will automatically attempt to rewrite the query. However, it's possible the optimizer may not choose to rewrite the query to use the materialized view, even though that is the desired outcome. In those instances, you can place a hint within your query to have the optimizer use the materialized view, regardless of the execution cost. You can place the actual view name within the hint or place the hint without the view name:

```
SELECT /*+ rewrite */ department_id,
sum(nvl(salary+(salary*commission_pct),salary)) total_compensation
FROM employees
GROUP BY department_id
having sum(nvl(salary+(salary*commission_pct),salary)) > 10000
ORDER by 2;
```

Conversely, you can also use a NOREWRITE hint if, for some reason, you do not want the optimizer to use the materialized view. One possible reason is that the data in the materialized view is stale compared to the source tables, and you want to ensure you are getting the most current data. Here we can see that the optimizer bypassed the use of the materialized view and resummarized the data directly from the EMPLOYEES table:

```
SELECT /*+ norewrite */ department_id,
sum(nvl(salary+(salary*commission_pct),salary)) total_compensation
FROM employees
GROUP BY department_id
having sum(nvl(salary+(salary*commission_pct),salary)) > 10000
ORDER by 2;
```

```
-------------------------------------------
| Id  | Operation            | Name       |
-------------------------------------------
|   0 | SELECT STATEMENT     |            |
|   1 |  SORT ORDER BY       |            |
|   2 |   FILTER             |            |
|   3 |    HASH GROUP BY     |            |
|   4 |     TABLE ACCESS FULL| EMPLOYEES  |
-------------------------------------------
```

14-13. Improving Star Schema Query Performance

Problem

You work in a data warehouse environment that contains star schemas, and you want to improve the performance of queries.

Solution

Oracle has a specific solution called *star transformation*, which was designed to help improve performance against star schemas in the data warehouse environment. Oracle has the STAR_TRANSFORMATION and FACT hints to help improve query performance using star schemas. In your queries, you can use the STAR_TRANSFORMATION or FACT hint, or you can use both. The following query is an example of how to use these hints:

```
SELECT /*+ star_transformation */ pr.prod_category, c.country_id,
t.calendar_year, sum(s.quantity_sold), SUM(s.amount_sold)
FROM sales s, times t, customers c, products pr
WHERE s.time_id = t.time_id
```

```
AND    s.cust_id = c.cust_id
AND    pr.prod_id = s.prod_id
AND    t.calendar_year = '2011'
GROUP BY pr.prod_category, c.country_id, t.calendar_year;
```

To use just the FACT hint, simply place the fact table name or alias within parentheses in the hint:

```
SELECT /*+ fact(s) */ pr.prod_category, c.country_id,
```

At times, the optimizer will be more likely to perform star transformation when both hints are present:

```
SELECT /*+ star_transformation fact(s) */ pr.prod_category, c.country_id,
```

Here is a typical explain plan that has undergone star transformation:

```
-----------------------------------------------------------------
| Id  | Operation                              | Name                  |
-----------------------------------------------------------------
|  0  | SELECT STATEMENT                       |                       |
|  1  |  HASH GROUP BY                         |                       |
|  2  |   HASH JOIN                            |                       |
|  3  |    HASH JOIN                           |                       |
|  4  |     HASH JOIN                          |                       |
|  5  |      PARTITION RANGE ALL               |                       |
|  6  |       TABLE ACCESS BY LOCAL INDEX ROWID| SALES                 |
|  7  |        BITMAP CONVERSION TO ROWIDS     |                       |
|  8  |         BITMAP AND                     |                       |
|  9  |          BITMAP MERGE                  |                       |
| 10  |           BITMAP KEY ITERATION         |                       |
| 11  |            BUFFER SORT                 |                       |
| 12  |             TABLE ACCESS FULL          | CUSTOMERS             |
| 13  |            BITMAP INDEX RANGE SCAN      | SALES_CUST_BIX        |
| 14  |          BITMAP MERGE                  |                       |
| 15  |           BITMAP KEY ITERATION         |                       |
| 16  |            BUFFER SORT                 |                       |
| 17  |             VIEW                       | index$_join$_016      |
| 18  |              HASH JOIN                 |                       |
| 19  |               INDEX FAST FULL SCAN     | PRODUCTS_PK           |
| 20  |               INDEX FAST FULL SCAN     | PRODUCTS_PROD_CAT_IX  |
| 21  |             BITMAP INDEX RANGE SCAN     | SALES_PROD_BIX        |
| 22  |      TABLE ACCESS FULL                 | TIMES                 |
| 23  |     TABLE ACCESS FULL                  | CUSTOMERS             |
| 24  |    VIEW                                | index$_join$_004      |
| 25  |     HASH JOIN                          |                       |
| 26  |      INDEX FAST FULL SCAN              | PRODUCTS_PK           |
| 27  |      INDEX FAST FULL SCAN              | PRODUCTS_PROD_CAT_IX  |
-----------------------------------------------------------------
```

Note

  - **star transformation used for this statement**

How It Works

Before you start running star queries, there are two key configuration elements that need to be taken care of before star transformation can occur:

- Ensure the `star_transformation_enabled` parameter is set to TRUE.

- Ensure that on the fact table there is a bitmap index on every dimension foreign key column.

If you are at a point to want to use a hint within a star schema, be it the FACT hint or the STAR_TRANSFORMATION hint, it is assumed you have a properly configured environment, or else these hints will not be used by the optimizer. These hints are not required for star transformation, but by using either of these hints, the optimizer will look to do transformation. Even with the hint, however, the optimizer may choose to ignore the request, based on what it thinks the best execution plan will be for the query. Star queries are efficient and perform well because the transformation is designed to operate specifically with star schemas.

If, for some reason, you want to avoid the use of star transformation for your query, simply use the `no_star_transformation` hint, and the optimizer will bypass the use of star transformation:

```
SELECT /*+ no_star_transformation */ pr.prod_category, c.country_id,
t.calendar_year, sum(s.quantity_sold), SUM(s.amount_sold)
FROM sales s, times t, customers c, products pr
WHERE s.time_id = t.time_id
AND    s.cust_id = c.cust_id
AND    pr.prod_id = s.prod_id
AND    t.calendar_year = '2011'
GROUP BY pr.prod_category, c.country_id, t.calendar_year;
```

From the explain plan, we can see that the optimizer did not transform our query:

```
-----------------------------------------------------------
| Id  | Operation                      | Name         |
-----------------------------------------------------------
|   0 | SELECT STATEMENT               |              |
|   1 |  HASH GROUP BY                 |              |
|   2 |   NESTED LOOPS                 |              |
|   3 |    NESTED LOOPS                |              |
|   4 |     NESTED LOOPS               |              |
|   5 |      NESTED LOOPS              |              |
|   6 |       PARTITION RANGE ALL      |              |
|   7 |        TABLE ACCESS FULL       | SALES        |
|   8 |       TABLE ACCESS BY INDEX ROWID| PRODUCTS   |
|   9 |        INDEX UNIQUE SCAN       | PRODUCTS_PK  |
|  10 |       TABLE ACCESS BY INDEX ROWID | CUSTOMERS |
|  11 |        INDEX UNIQUE SCAN       | CUSTOMERS_PK |
|  12 |      INDEX UNIQUE SCAN         | TIMES_PK     |
|  13 |     TABLE ACCESS BY INDEX ROWID | TIMES       |
-----------------------------------------------------------
```

At times, it can be tricky to get the star transformation to take place. It is critically important that you have properly configured the star schema with all the appropriate bitmap indexes. Even having one missing bitmap index can affect the ability to have star transformation occur for your queries, so it is important to be thorough and validate the configuration, especially regarding the bitmap indexes. Some star schemas also employ the use of bitmap join indexes between the fact and dimension tables to aid in achieving star transformation.

CHAPTER 15

■ ■ ■

Executing SQL in Parallel

Parallelism can help improve performance on particular operations simply by assigning multiple resources to a task. Parallelism is best used on systems with multiple CPUs because the multiple processes used (that is, the parallel processes) will use those extra system resources to more quickly complete a given task.

As a general rule, parallelism is also best used on large tables or indexes and on databases with large volumes of data. It is ideal for use in data warehouse environments, which are large by their nature. Parallelism is not well suited for OLTP environments just because of the transactional nature of those systems.

To use parallelism properly, there are several important factors to understand:

- The number of CPUs on your system

- Proper configuration of the related initialization parameters

- The key SQL statements that you want to tune for parallelization

- The degree of parallelism (DOP) configured on your database

- The actual performance vs. expected performance of targeted SQL operations

One of the most common pitfalls of parallelism is overuse. It is sometimes seen as a magic bullet to tune and speed up SQL operations. In turn, parallelism can actually lead to poorer rather than better performance. Therefore, it is critically important for the DBA to understand the physical configuration of a system and configure parallelism-related parameters to best suit the system. Educating developers and users of your database about basic questions will increase the success rate of parallel operations. When is it appropriate to use parallelism? How do you properly enable parallelism in SQL operations? What type of operations can be parallelized? Parallelism is a powerful tool to aid in drastically improving the performance of database operations, but with that power comes responsibility.

This chapter focuses on the methods to properly configure your database for parallelism, key operations that can be parallelized, how to induce parallelism in your SQL, and some tools to use to see whether parallel operations are running optimally.

15-1. Enabling Parallelism for a Specific Query
Problem

You have a slow-running query accessing data from a large table. You want to see whether you can speed up the query by instructing Oracle to use multiple processes to retrieve the data.

Solution

There are two distinct types of hints to place in your SQL to try to speed up your query by using multiple processes, or parallelism. One type of hint is for data retrieval itself, and the other is to help speed the process of reading the indexes on a table.

Parallel Hints for Tables

First, you need to determine the degree of parallelism (DOP) desired for the query. This instructs Oracle how many processes it will use to retrieve the data. Second, place a parallel hint inside the query specifying the table(s) on which to execute parallel SQL, as well the degree of parallelism to use for the query. Here's an example:

```
SELECT /*+ parallel(emp,4) */  empno, ename
FROM emp;
```

If you use a table alias in your query, you must use it in your hint, or else the Oracle optimizer will ignore the hint.

```
SELECT/*+ parallel(e,4) */  empno, ename
FROM emp e;
```

The hints in the preceding two queries result in four processes dividing the work of reading rows from the EMP table. Four processes working together will get the job done faster in terms of wall-clock time than one process doing all the work by itself.

Optionally, you can omit specifying a degree of parallelism within the hint. If you specify only the table name or alias in the hint, Oracle will derive the degree of parallelism based on the database initialization parameters, which may or may not give you the desired degree of parallelism:

```
SELECT/*+ parallel(e) */  empno, ename
FROM emp e;
```

Parallel Hints for Indexes

Specify the parallel_index hint to control parallel access to indexes. You can generally access an index in parallel only when the index is a locally partitioned index. In that case, you can apply the parallel_index hint. Here's an example:

```
SELECT /*+ parallel_index(emp, emp_i4 ,4) */ empno, ename
FROM emp
WHERE deptno = 10;
```

There are two arguments to the parallel_index hint: table name and index name. As with specifying the degree of parallelism on tables, if you omit the degree of parallelism from within an index hint, the database itself will compute the degree of parallelism for the query.

If you alias your tables, then you must use the alias names in your hints. See the preceding section, "Parallel Hints for Tables," for an example.

How It Works

To effectively use parallel hints, you need to take the following items into consideration:

- The number of tables in your query
- The size of table(s) in your query
- The number of CPUs on your system
- The filtering columns in your WHERE clause
- What columns are indexed, if any

You also must analyze and understand three key components of your system prior to using parallel hints in queries:

- System configuration, such as amount of memory and CPUs and even disk configuration

- Database configuration parameters related to parallelism

- The DOP specified on the objects themselves (tables and indexes)

Parallel SQL must be used with caution because it is common to overuse and can cause an overutilization of both CPU and I/O resources, which ultimately results in *slower* rather than faster performance. Overuse is a common mistake in the use of parallelism.

Depending on the number of tables in your query, you may want to place parallelism on one or more of the tables, depending on their size. A general rule of thumb is that if a table contains more than 10 million rows, or is at least 2 GB in size, it may be a viable candidate for using parallelism.

The degree of parallelism (DOP) should be directly related to the number of CPUs on your system. If you have a single-CPU system, there is little, if any, benefit of using parallel SQL, and the result could very well be returned slower than if no parallelism was used at all.

To help determine whether you can use parallelism on any indexes, you need to first determine whether any of the filtering columns in your WHERE clause are indexed. If so, check to see whether the table is partitioned. Typically, then, for a query on a large table, a parallel_index hint may help the speed of your query. Overall, when trying to determine whether to use parallelism for your query, it's helpful to perform an explain plan to determine whether parallelism will be used. Also, there may be parallelism already specified for an object within your query, so it is also a good idea to check the DEGREE column in the USER_TABLES or USER_INDEXES view prior to checking the degree of parallelism within a hint.

Table 15-1 shows the different parallel hints that can be used.

Table 15-1. *Types of Parallel Hints*

Table Head	Parameters
PARALLEL	Table name, DOP
PARALLEL_INDEX	Table name, index name, DOP
NO_PARALLEL	--
NO_PARALLEL_INDEX	--
PQ_DISTRIBUTE	Table name, distribution value
PQ_CONCURRENT_UNION	For concurrent processing of UNION and UNION ALL operations
NO_PQ_CONCURRENT_UNION	Inhibits concurrent processing of UNION and UNION ALL operations
PQ_FILTER	Enables special instructions to the optimizer for correlated subqueries
PQ_SKEW	Advises the optimizer that data distribution of join keys for a parallel join operation is highly skewed
NO_PQ_SKEW	Asserts the lack of skew

Oracle gives you many options to help you determine a proper DOP and whether you want to specify it yourself or you want Oracle to determine the DOP for your query. Table 15-2 briefly describes these options.

Table 15-2. *Degree of Parallelism Options*

Hint Name	Description
PARALLEL	Statement always runs in parallel.
PARALLEL (DEFAULT)	Same as PARALLEL.
PARALLEL (AUTO)	Optimizer computes DOP to be used.
PARALLEL (MANUAL)	Parallelism is based on object parallelism.
PARALLEL (integer)	The DOP used is specified by the integer.

Parallel Hints for Tables

To determine whether parallelism is being used in your query, first perform an explain plan on your query. The following are a simple query and its associated execution plan:

```
select * from emp;
```

```
-------------------------------------------------------------------
| Id | Operation        | Name | Rows | Bytes | Cost (%CPU)| Time     |
-------------------------------------------------------------------
|  0 | SELECT STATEMENT |      |   14 | 1218  |    3   (0)| 00:00:01 |
|  1 |  TABLE ACCESS FULL| EMP  |   14 | 1218  |    3   (0)| 00:00:01 |
-------------------------------------------------------------------
```

If parallelism isn't being used, you can insert the parallel hint and then rerun the explain plan to verify that the optimizer will use parallelism in the execution plan. Here's an example:

```
select /*+ parallel(emp,4) */ * from emp;
```

```
-------------------------------------------------------------------
| Id | Operation            | Name     | TQ    |IN-OUT| PQ Distrib |
-------------------------------------------------------------------
|  0 | SELECT STATEMENT     |          |       |      |            |
|  1 |  PX COORDINATOR      |          |       |      |            |
|  2 |   PX SEND QC (RANDOM)| :TQ10000 | Q1,00 | P->S | QC (RAND)  |
|  3 |    PX BLOCK ITERATOR |          | Q1,00 | PCWC |            |
|  4 |     TABLE ACCESS FULL| EMP      | Q1,00 | PCWP |            |
-------------------------------------------------------------------
```

■ **Note** The proper database initialization parameters need to be properly set in order for parallelism to be enabled and used via the use of hints.

Parallel Hints for Indexes

Although it is far less common to parallelize index-based queries, it may be of benefit in certain circumstances. For example, you may want to parallelize the query against a local index that is part of a partitioned table. The following is an example query and the resulting execution plan:

```
SELECT /*+ parallel_index(emp, emp_i3) */ empno, ename
FROM emp
WHERE hiredate between '2010-01-01' and '2010-12-31';
```

```
-------------------------------------------------------------------
|Id|Operation                          |Name    |  TQ |IN-OUT| PQ Dist|
-------------------------------------------------------------------
|  0|SELECT STATEMENT                  |        |     |      |        |
|  1|  PX COORDINATOR                  |        |     |      |        |
|  2|   PX SEND QC (RANDOM)            |:TQ10000|Q1,00| P->S |        |
|  3|    PX PARTITION RANGE ITERATOR   |        |Q1,00| PCWC |        |
|  4|     TABLE ACCESS BY LOCAL INDEX ROWID|EMP |Q1,00| PCWP |        |
|  5|      INDEX RANGE SCAN            |EMP_I3  |Q1,00| PCWP |        |
-------------------------------------------------------------------
```

When formatting the hint, you can specify all the parameters that tell the optimizer exactly which index to use and what DOP you desire. In the following query, we're telling the optimizer that we want to use the EMP_I3 index, with a DOP of 4.

```
SELECT /*+ parallel_index(emp, emp_i3, 4) */ empno, ename
FROM emp
WHERE hiredate between '2010-01-01' and '2010-12-31';
```

If you omit the DOP from the hint, the optimizer determines the DOP based on the initialization parameter settings. For instance, in the following example, the table name and index name are specified in the hint, but the DOP is not specified. Oracle will compute the DOP for us in these cases.

```
SELECT /*+ parallel_index(emp, emp_i3) */ empno, ename
FROM emp
WHERE hiredate between '2010-01-01' and '2010-12-31';
```

You can also simply place the table name in the hint, and the optimizer will determine which index, if any, can be used. If the optimizer determines that no index is suitable, then no index will be used. In the following example, only the table name is used in the hint:

```
SELECT /*+ parallel_index(emp) */ empno, ename
FROM emp
WHERE hiredate between '2010-01-01' and '2010-12-31';
```

15-2. Enabling Parallelism at Object Creation
Problem

You have new tables to create in your database that will be growing to a very large size, and you want to speed up the queries against those tables.

Solution

Having a higher than default DOP on a table or index is an easy way to set a more consistent and fixed method of enabling multiple processes on tables and indexes. Enabling parallelism on tables or indexes is done within DDL commands. You can enable parallelism within the CREATE statement when creating a table or an index.

For a new table, if you are expecting to have consistent queries that can take advantage of multiple processes, it may be easier to set a fixed DOP on your object, rather than having to place hints in your SQL or let Oracle set the DOP for you. In the following example, we've specified a DOP of 4 on the EMP table:

```
CREATE TABLE EMP
(
 EMPNO NUMBER(4) CONSTRAINT PK_EMP PRIMARY KEY,
 ENAME VARCHAR2(10),
 JOB VARCHAR2(9),
 MGR NUMBER(4),
 HIREDATE DATE,
 SAL NUMBER(7,2),
 COMM NUMBER(7,2),
 DEPTNO NUMBER(2) CONSTRAINT FK_DEPTNO REFERENCES DEPT
)
PARALLEL(DEGREE 4);
```

By placing a static DOP of 4 on the table, any user accessing the EMP table will get a DOP of 4 for each query executed.

```
select * from emp;
```

```
-------------------------------------------------------------------
| Id | Operation            | Name     |   TQ |IN-OUT| PQ Distrib |
-------------------------------------------------------------------
|  0 | SELECT STATEMENT     |          |      |      |            |
|  1 |  PX COORDINATOR      |          |      |      |            |
|  2 |   PX SEND QC (RANDOM)| :TQ10000 | Q1,00| P->S | QC (RAND)  |
|  3 |    PX BLOCK ITERATOR |          | Q1,00| PCWC |            |
|  4 |     TABLE ACCESS FULL| EMP      | Q1,00| PCWP |            |
-------------------------------------------------------------------
```

You can also specify a default DOP when creating an index. There are circumstances where it may be beneficial to create an index with a higher DOP. With large partitioned tables, it is common to have secondary locally partitioned indexes on often-used columns in the WHERE clause. Some queries that use these indexes may benefit from increasing the DOP. In the following DDL, we've created this index with a DOP of 4:

```
CREATE INDEX EMP_I1
ON EMP (HIREDATE)
LOCAL
PARALLEL(DEGREE 4);
```

How It Works

Placing parallelism on objects themselves helps multiple processes complete the task at hand sooner—whether it be to speed up queries or to help speed up the creation of an index. To be able to assess the proper DOP to place on an object, you should know the access patterns of the data. If less information is known about the objects, the more conservative the DOP should be. Placing a high DOP on a series of objects can hurt performance just as easily as it can help, so enabling DOP on objects needs to be done with careful planning and consideration.

■ **Tip**   If automatic DOP is enabled and configured properly (PARALLEL_DEGREE_POLICY=AUTO), then the parallelism that you set on objects is ignored, and the optimizer chooses the degree of parallelism to be used. See Recipe 15-10 for details on enabling automatic DOP.

15-3. Enabling Parallelism for an Existing Object
Problem

You have a series of slow-running queries accessing a set of existing database tables, and you want to take steps to reduce the execution time of the queries.

Solution

Setting a higher DOP on an existing table or index is an easy way to have a more consistent and fixed method of enabling multiple processes on tables and indexes. Setting the DOP for tables or indexes is done within DDL commands. You can change the DOP on a table or index by using the ALTER statement. For instance, if you have an existing table that needs to have the DOP changed to accommodate user queries that want to take advantage of multiple processes, they can be added easily to the table, which takes effect immediately. The following example alters the default DOP for a table:

```
ALTER TABLE EMP
PARALLEL(DEGREE 4);
```

If, after a time, you want to reset the DOP on your table, you can also do that with the ALTER statement. See the following two examples on how to reset the DOP for a table:

```
ALTER TABLE EMP
PARALLEL(DEGREE 1);

ALTER TABLE EMP
NOPARALLEL;
```

If you have an already existing index that you think will benefit from a higher DOP, it can also easily be changed. As with tables, the change takes effect immediately. The following example shows how to change the default DOP for an index:

```
ALTER INDEX EMP_I1
PARALLEL(DEGREE 4);
```

As with tables, you can reset the DOP on an index in either of the following two ways:

```
ALTER INDEX EMP_I4
PARALLEL(DEGREE 1);

ALTER INDEX EMP_I4
NOPARALLEL;
```

How It Works

Increasing the DOP on an existing object is a sign that you already have a performance issue for queries accessing tables within your database. Monitoring parallelism performance is a key factor in knowing whether the DOP set for an object or set of objects is appropriate. Examine data in V$PQ_TQSTAT to assist in determining the DOP that has been used, or examine data in V$SYSSTAT to assist in determining the extent that parallelism is being used on your database. Refer to Recipe 15-12 for some examples of using these data dictionary views.

15-4. Implementing Parallel DML
Problem

You want to induce parallelism when performing DML operations (INSERT, UPDATE, MERGE, DELETE) in order to speed performance and reduce transaction time.

Solution

If operating within a data warehouse environment or an environment with large tables that require a high volume of bulk transactions, parallel DML can help speed up processing and reduce the time it takes to perform these operations. Parallel DML is disabled by default on a database and must be explicitly enabled with the following statement:

```
ALTER SESSION ENABLE PARALLEL DML;
```

By specifying the foregoing statement, it truly *enables* parallel DML to be possible in a session but does not guarantee it. Parallel DML operations will occur only under certain conditions:

- Hints are specified in a DML statement.

- Tables with a parallel attribute are part of a DML statement.

- The DML operations meet the appropriate rules for a statement to run in parallel. Key restrictions for using parallel DML are noted later in the recipe.

You may desire, in certain circumstances, to force parallel behavior, regardless of the parallel degree you have placed on an object or regardless of any hints you've placed in your DML. So, alternatively, you can force parallel DML with one of the following statements:

```
ALTER SESSION FORCE PARALLEL DML;
```

```
ALTER SESSION FORCE PARALLEL DML PARALLEL 4;
```

From the foregoing examples, it is worth noting that it is always best to specify an explicit DOP. You can see in the first example that no DOP is shown, while the second one shows a DOP of 4. If you omit DOP, Oracle automatically calculates the DOP and, often, can consume a large amount of system resources, without regard to other processes running on the database. Because of the unpredictability of the DOP Oracle automatically derives, it is best to always specify the DOP to be used.

As a general rule, use the FORCE option for exception-based DML processing. It is really an override and should not be regarded as a best practice to use for regularly scheduled processing. It is best used sparingly and can help with occasional large DML operations.

How It Works

Parallel DML can work for any DML operation—INSERT, UPDATE, MERGE, and DELETE. The rules vary slightly depending on which DML operation you are running. If you want to run an INSERT statement in parallel, for instance, first enable parallelism for your session and then execute your INSERT statement with the appropriate mechanism in order for the DML to run in parallel:

```
ALTER SESSION ENABLE PARALLEL DML;

INSERT /*+ PARALLEL(DEPT,4) */ INTO DEPT
SELECT /*+ PARALLEL(DEPT_COPY,4) */ * FROM DEPT_COPY;
```

With the foregoing statement, we put a parallel hint into the INSERT statement and also put a parallel HINT into the SELECT portion of the statement. It's important to remember that even if parallelism is in effect for your DML statement, it does not directly impact any parallelism on a related query within the same statement. For instance, the following statement's DML operation can run in parallel, but the corresponding SELECT statement will run in serial mode because no parallelism is specified on the query itself.

```
ALTER SESSION ENABLE PARALLEL DML;

INSERT /*+ PARALLEL(DEPT,4) */ INTO DEPT
SELECT * FROM DEPT_COPY;
```

To take full advantage of parallel capabilities, try to parallelize all portions of a statement. If you parallelize the INSERT but not the SELECT, the SELECT portion becomes a bottleneck for the INSERT, and the INSERT performance suffers.

Parallel DML operations can also occur on UPDATE, MERGE, and DELETE statements. Let's say your company was generous and decided to give everyone in the accounting department a 1 percent raise:

```
UPDATE /*+ PARALLEL(EMP,4) */ EMP
SET SAL = SAL*1.01
WHERE DEPTNO=10;
```

Then, after a period of months, your company decides to lay off those employees they gave raises to in accounting:

```
DELETE /*+ PARALLEL(EMP,4) */ FROM EMP
WHERE DEPTNO=10;
```

Another way to parallelize a DML transaction within your database is to use the DBMS_PARALLEL_EXECUTE PL/SQL package. Although more complex to configure, there are some key advantages of using this package to run your parallelized transactions:

- The overall transaction is split into pieces, each of which has its own commit point.

- Transactions are restartable.

- Locks are done only on affected rows.

- Undo utilization is reduced.

- You have more control over how the work is divided. You can divide the work in several ways:

  - By column

  - By ROWID

  - By SQL statement

The obvious benefits of using the DBMS_PARALLEL_EXECUTE package are greater control over how large transactions are run, increased functionality, and more efficient use of database resources. The key trade-off with using this package is it is simply more complex to configure, set up, and run—but may be well worth it when processing large volumes of data.

■ **Tip**   You must execute the ALTER SESSION ENABLE | FORCE PARALLEL DML statement in order for parallel DML to occur for your transaction.

Restrictions on Parallel DML

There are plenty of restrictions in using parallel DML, and you need to understand that even if dealing with a large volume of data, parallel DML may not be possible in certain circumstances:

- Individual inserts of rows (using the VALUES clause) cannot be run in parallel.
- You can modify a table only one time within a transaction.
- It cannot be run for tables with triggers.
- Tables with certain constraints may not be eligible.
- There is limited parallel DML functionality on tables with objects or LOB columns.
- There is limited parallel DML functionality on temporary tables.
- Distributed transactions cannot be parallelized.

Degree of Parallelism

Once you submit a parallelized DML operation for execution, Oracle determines, based on a set of precedence rules, what DOP will be used for the entire statement being submitted. It is important to understand these rules so you get the desired DOP you are expecting for your transaction.

For DML transactions, Oracle applies the following base rules of precedence to determine DOP:

1. Checks to see whether a hint is specified on INSERT, UPDATE, MERGE, or DELETE statements
2. Checks to see whether there are any session-level instructions
3. Checks the object-level parallelism on the target object
4. Chooses maximum DOP specified between the queried table or any associated indexes for the query portion of the statement (insert only)

After choosing the appropriate DOP for the insert and query portions of the statement, the query is executed. Note that the DOP chosen for each portion of the statement can be different.

Other Considerations

Using parallel DML can be complex because there are many permutations of possibilities of the type of objects involved: whether they are partitioned, the DOP specified on the objects, the hints specified in statements, and the parallel parameter settings, just to name a few.

Here are some other factors that need to be considered when using parallel DML:

- For parallelized insert transactions, direct-path loads are performed unless the NOAPPEND hint is used.

- When deciding whether to use parallel DML, you must weigh the performance gain you will achieve with the space usage for that operation. Parallelized INSERT statements are fast but cost you more space. If you have specified a DOP of 4 for an insert transaction, four extents will be allocated for that operation. You must determine based on your requirements what is more important.

- If objects are partitioned, it can affect how a parallel DML transaction runs.

15-5. Creating Tables in Parallel
Problem

You need to quickly create a table from an existing large table and want to employ the use of multiple processes to help speed up the creation of the table.

Solution

If you are administering very large databases (VLDBs) or have to rebuild a large table, parallel DDL is fast and has advantages over running parallel DML. Speed is the biggest factor in choosing to use parallel DDL to create a table from an existing large table. Within your specific DDL command, there is a PARALLEL clause that determines whether operations are to be performed in parallel. This is done by using the CREATE TABLE ... AS SELECT operation:

```
CREATE TABLE EMP_COPY
PARALLEL(DEGREE 4)
AS
SELECT * FROM EMP;
```

```
---------------------------------------------------------------------
| Id | Operation               | Name     |  TQ  |IN-OUT| PQ Distrib |
---------------------------------------------------------------------
|  0 | CREATE TABLE STATEMENT  |          |      |      |            |
|  1 |  PX COORDINATOR         |          |      |      |            |
|  2 |   PX SEND QC (RANDOM)    | :TQ10000 | Q1,00| P->S | QC (RAND)  |
|  3 |    LOAD AS SELECT        | EMP_COPY | Q1,00| PCWP |            |
|  4 |     PX BLOCK ITERATOR    |          | Q1,00| PCWC |            |
|  5 |      TABLE ACCESS FULL   | EMP      | Q1,00| PCWP |            |
---------------------------------------------------------------------
```

How It Works

The reason parallel DDL is popular is that it is a fast way to perform operations on a large amount of data. The work is divided up in several pieces and done concurrently. Let's say you just bought a new house and are in the process of moving. If you are loading a large moving truck with boxes, it will simply be faster with four people loading rather than one. Moreover, parallel DDL is an attractive way to perform DML-type operations under the covers of DDL commands.

The most common reasons to use CREATE TABLE ... AS SELECT include the following:

- The table structure has changed and you need to rebuild the table.
- You are creating a like structure for some specific application purpose.
- You are deleting a large number of rows from the table.
- You need to drop multiple columns from a large table.

Some of the foregoing operations could also be strictly handled with parallel DML, but using parallel DDL has a distinct advantage over parallel DML. Since DDL operations cannot be rolled back, normal transaction undo is not generated for these operations, and it is simply a more efficient operation.

The DOP for a parallel DDL operation is determined by the object DOP. This also includes the query portion of the statement. If you choose, you can override the DOP of the objects by issuing one of the following commands:

```
ALTER SESSION FORCE PARALLEL DDL;

ALTER SESSION FORCE PARALLEL DDL PARALLEL 4;
```

As with parallel DML, it is always best to explicitly set DOP; otherwise, it is unpredictable how much system resources your statement will consume.

If you have a large table from which you need to delete many rows, consider using CREATE TABLE ... AS SELECT rather than using a DML DELETE statement. Deleting rows is an expensive operation. In large data warehouse environments, in scenarios where a large volume of rows needs to be deleted, the cost and time of doing the delete can quickly become unmanageable. Because of the nature of delete, it is very resource-intensive for the database as far as the amount of redo and undo generation it takes to perform the operation. One good rule of thumb to use is that if you are deleting as little as 5-10 percent of the rows of a large table, it can be simply faster to create a new table with all the rows you want to keep.

Here is an example where we are deleting about 20 percent of the rows from our EMP table of 1,234,568 rows:

```
delete /*+ parallel(emp,4) */ from emp
where empno > 1000000
SQL> /

234568 rows deleted.

Elapsed: 00:00:09.94
```

```
--------------------------------------------------------------------------
| Id  | Operation                | Name      |  TQ   |IN-OUT| PQ Distrib |
--------------------------------------------------------------------------
|  0  | DELETE STATEMENT         |           |       |      |            |
|  1  |  PX COORDINATOR          |           |       |      |            |
|  2  |   PX SEND QC (RANDOM)    | :TQ10001  | Q1,01 | P->S | QC (RAND)  |
|  3  |    INDEX MAINTENANCE     | EMP       | Q1,01 | PCWP |            |
|  4  |     PX RECEIVE           |           | Q1,01 | PCWP |            |
|  5  |      PX SEND RANGE       | :TQ10000  | Q1,00 | P->P | RANGE      |
|  6  |       DELETE             | EMP       | Q1,00 | PCWP |            |
|  7  |        PX BLOCK ITERATOR |           | Q1,00 | PCWC |            |
|  8  |         TABLE ACCESS FULL| EMP       | Q1,00 | PCWP |            |
--------------------------------------------------------------------------
```

This delete took 9.94 seconds to run. If we now run a CREATE TABLE ... AS SELECT statement to achieve the same result, we can see the difference in performance.

```
create table emp_ctas_new2
parallel(degree 4)
nologging
as select /*+ parallel(a,4) */ * from emp_ctas
where empno <= 1000000
SQL> /
Elapsed: 00:00:01.70
```

```
-------------------------------------------------------------------------------
|Id  |Operation                        |Name          |  TQ |IN-OUT|PQ Distrib|
-------------------------------------------------------------------------------
|  0 |CREATE TABLE STATEMENT           |              |     |      |          |
|  1 | PX COORDINATOR                  |              |     |      |          |
|  2 |  PX SEND QC (RANDOM)            |:TQ10001      |Q1,01| P->S |QC (RAND) |
|  3 |   LOAD AS SELECT                |EMP_CTAS_NEW  |Q1,01| PCWP |          |
|  4 |    PX RECEIVE                   |              |Q1,01| PCWP |          |
|  5 |     PX SEND ROUND-ROBIN         |:TQ10000      |     | S->P |RND-ROBIN |
|  6 |      TABLE ACCESS BY INDEX ROWID|EMP_CTAS      |     |      |          |
|  7 |       INDEX RANGE SCAN          |EMP_CTAS_PK   |     |      |          |
-------------------------------------------------------------------------------
```

Creating the table took 1.7 seconds, which is more than five times faster than performing the same operation with a DELETE statement. If you have indexes on the table, however, you need to consider that as a factor before choosing this method because if you re-create a table, you must also re-create the associated indexes for that table. It's still likely to be faster, however, because you can re-create any indexes in parallel as well.

Keep in mind that, even though the foregoing example uses parallel DDL on these statements, this concept holds true even if you are running in serial mode. When you need to delete a large number of rows from a table, the CREATE TABLE ... AS SELECT can be compared favorably to DELETE with parallel-executed DDL or nonparallel, serial-executed DDL.

One potential drawback of creating tables in parallel is that the space allocations for these operations may leave the table more fragmented than if you created the table serially. This is a trade-off that should be considered when creating tables in parallel. The DOP that is specified in the operation spawns that number of parallel threads, and one extent is allocated for each thread. So, if you have specified a DOP of 4 for your parallel operation, there will be a minimum of four extents allocated for the operation. Depending on the MINIMUM EXTENT size for the tablespace, Oracle does attempt to trim unused space at the end of the operation. You should expect, though, that parallel create table operations are simply less space-efficient than operations run serially.

15-6. Creating Indexes in Parallel
Problem

You need to create indexes for a large table as quickly as possible and want to employ the use of multiple processes to help speed up the index creation.

Solution

Any time you have a large table, it is a good idea to always create any associated index for that table using parallel DDL, even if you want the DOP on the index to be nonparallelized for queries. The major benefit of creating an index in parallel is that it simply takes much less time to create the index. It always makes sense to create an index for a large table in parallel and then optionally choose to reset the DOP used for queries after the create operation is complete. In the following example, we are creating the index with a DOP of 4, which will be used during the process of creating the index:

```
CREATE INDEX EMP_COPY_I1
ON EMP_COPY (HIREDATE)
PARALLEL(DEGREE 4);
```

Then, after the index has been created, we can choose to reset the DOP to a different value for use by queries, using either of the following examples:

```
ALTER INDEX EMP_COPY_I1 NOPARALLEL;
ALTER INDEX EMP_COPY_I1 PARALLEL(DEGREE 1);
```

How It Works

The primary reason you want to run parallel DDL on an index is to either create or rebuild a large, existing index. Some of the reasons you may have to do this include the following:

- You want to add an index to an already existing large table.

- You want to rebuild an index that has become fragmented over time.

- You want to rebuild an index after a large, direct-path load of data.

- You want to move an index to a different tablespace.

- The index is in an unusable state because of a partition-level operation on the associated table.

As with tables, if you want to bypass the parallelism specified on the index, you can "force" the issue by running one of the following commands:

```
ALTER SESSION FORCE PARALLEL DDL;
```

```
ALTER SESSION FORCE PARALLEL DDL PARALLEL 4;
```

15-7. Rebuilding Indexes in Parallel
Problem

You have an existing index that needs to be rebuilt quickly, and you want to use multiple processes to speed up the index rebuild process.

Solution

At some point you may need to rebuild an index, for many of the same reasons as when you want to re-create an index. To rebuild an index in parallel, use the ALTER INDEX command:

```
ALTER INDEX EMP_NAME_IX
REBUILD
PARALLEL(DEGREE 4);
```

```
---------------------------------------------------------------
|Id |Operation                 |Name       |  TQ |IN-OUT|PQ Distrib|
---------------------------------------------------------------
|  0|ALTER INDEX STATEMENT      |           |     |      |          |
|  1| PX COORDINATOR            |           |     |      |          |
|  2|  PX SEND QC (ORDER)       |:TQ10001   |Q1,01| P->S |QC (ORDER)|
|  3|   INDEX BUILD NON UNIQUE  |EMP_NAME_IX|Q1,01| PCWP |          |
|  4|    SORT CREATE INDEX      |           |Q1,01| PCWP |          |
|  5|     PX RECEIVE            |           |Q1,01| PCWP |          |
|  6|      PX SEND RANGE        |:TQ10000   |Q1,00| P->P |RANGE     |
|  7|       PX BLOCK ITERATOR   |           |Q1,00| PCWC |          |
|  8|        TABLE ACCESS FULL  |EMPLOYEES  |Q1,00| PCWP |          |
---------------------------------------------------------------
```

If you need to rebuild a partition of a large local index, you can also use parallelism to perform this operation. See the following example:

```
ALTER INDEX emppart_i1
REBUILD PARTITION emppart2001_p
PARALLEL(DEGREE 4);
```

```
-----------------------------------------------------------------------
|Id|Operation                  |Name      |Pstart|Pstop |IN-OUT|PQ Distrib|
-----------------------------------------------------------------------
|  0|ALTER INDEX STATEMENT      |          |      |      |      |          |
|  1| PX COORDINATOR            |          |      |      |      |          |
|  2|  PX SEND QC (ORDER)       |:TQ10001  |      |      | P->S |QC ORDER) |
|  3|   INDEX BUILD NON UNIQUE  |EMPPART_I1|      |      | PCWP |          |
|  4|    SORT CREATE INDEX      |          |      |      | PCWP |          |
|  5|     PX RECEIVE            |          |      |      | PCWP |          |
|  6|      PX SEND RANGE        |:TQ10000  |      |      | P->P |RANGE     |
|  7|       PX BLOCK ITERATOR   |          |  2   |   2  | PCWC |          |
|  8|        INDEX FAST FULL SCAN|EMPPART_I1|  2   |   2  | PCWP |          |
-----------------------------------------------------------------------
```

How It Works

Rebuilding an index has a key advantage, as well as a key disadvantage, over re-creating an index from scratch. The advantage of rebuilding an index is that the existing index is in place until the rebuild operation is complete, so it can therefore be used by queries that are run concurrently with the rebuild process. The main disadvantage of the index rebuild process is that you will need space for both indexes, which is required during the rebuild process. Some of the key reasons to rebuild an index include the following:

- You want to rebuild an index that has become fragmented over time.

- You want to rebuild an index after a large, direct-path load of data.

- You want to move an index to a different tablespace.

- The index is in an unusable state because of a partition-level operation on the associated table.

When indexes are created or re-created in parallel, keep in mind that the degree of parallelism stays on the index after the creation is complete. For instance, in the foregoing example of rebuilding the EMP_NAME_IX index, we can see that when looking at the data dictionary before and after the rebuild, the degree of parallelism stays on the index. The impact of this is when users issue queries that use the index, it can spawn parallel query slaves, which may not be desirable. Usually, you will want to reset the degree of parallelism to its original value on the index after creating it. To demonstrate, see the following example, which does the following:

- Checks the degree of parallelism before rebuilding the index

- Rebuilds the index in parallel

- Checks the degree of parallelism to validate it has been modified to the value specified in the PARALLEL clause of the ALTER INDEX statement

- Resets the index to the original degree of parallelism

- Validates the degree of parallelism to ensure it is set to the original value

Here is the example that does all of the foregoing:

```
select table_name, index_name , degree
from user_indexes
where index_name = 'EMP_NAME_IX';

TABLE_NAME INDEX_NAME   DEGREE
---------- ------------ ---------
EMPLOYEES  EMP_NAME_IX  1

ALTER INDEX EMP_NAME_IX
REBUILD
PARALLEL(DEGREE 4);

Index altered.

select table_name, index_name , degree
from user_indexes
where index_name = 'EMP_NAME_IX';

TABLE_NAME INDEX_NAME   DEGREE
---------- ------------ ---------
EMPLOYEES  EMP_NAME_IX  4

ALTER INDEX EMP_NAME_IX PARALLEL 1;

Index altered.
```

```
select table_name, index_name , degree
from user_indexes
where index_name = 'EMP_NAME_IX';

TABLE_NAME INDEX_NAME   DEGREE
---------- ------------ ---------
EMPLOYEES  EMP_NAME_IX  1
```

15-8. Moving Partitions in Parallel
Problem
You need to move a table partition to a different tablespace and want to employ the use of multiple processes to accomplish this task.

Solution
Let's say you want to move a table partition to another tablespace. For instance, you've created a tablespace on slower, cheaper storage and you want to move older data there in order to reduce the overall cost of storage on your database. To alter a table to rebuild a partition in parallel, you would issue a command such as the one here:

```
ALTER TABLE EMPPART
MOVE PARTITION SYS_P820
TABLESPACE USERS
PARALLEL(DEGREE 4);
```

If there are indexes associated with the partition you are moving, you can also add the UPDATE INDEXES clause, in which case all indexes will be rebuilt as well:

```
ALTER TABLE EMPPART
MOVE PARTITION SYS_P820
TABLESPACE USERS
PARALLEL(DEGREE 4)
UPDATE INDEXES;
```

How It Works
The ALTER TABLE statement to move a partition is an easy, efficient way to move data around for a partitioned table. As with some of the other parallel DDL operations shown within this chapter, there are several reasons to move a table partition to a different tablespace:

- You are moving older data to cheaper, slower storage.

- You are consolidating a series of partitions to a single tablespace.

- You are moving certain partitions to separate tablespaces to logically group types of data.

Table partitioning is often done to store historical data. Over time, partition maintenance often needs to occur for partitioned tables. By enabling the use of parallelism when moving partitions for a table within your database, it can simply be done faster. With maintenance windows shrinking and data access needs growing, this helps perform necessary partition movements faster, while reducing downtime for your database tables.

If there are indexes on the table and you omit the UPDATE INDEXES clause, any affected indexes or index partitions will be left in an unusable state. If the underlying indexes are local partitioned indexes, you only have to rebuild the index partitions that correspond to the table partitions that were moved. If the underlying indexes are either globally partitioned or nonpartitioned, you will have to rebuild all indexes on the table, even if the majority of the partitions are unaffected by the partition move. Because of this impact, it is recommended, where possible, to always use local indexes on partitioned tables.

For our foregoing example with omitting the UPDATE INDEXES clause, the EMPPART table had three indexes. We can see from the data dictionary that the index partitions are now unusable:

```
SELECT index_name, partition_name, status
FROM dba_ind_partitions
WHERE index_owner = 'HR'
AND status = 'UNUSABLE';
```

```
INDEX_NAME       PARTITION_NAME   STATUS
---------------  ---------------  --------
EMPPART_I3       SYS_P804         UNUSABLE
EMPPART_I1       SYS_P1100        UNUSABLE
EMPPART_I2       SYS_P1042        UNUSABLE
```

We then can issue an index rebuild statement to rebuild each index. An example of rebuilding one of the indexes is shown here:

```
ALTER INDEX EMPPART_I1 REBUILD PARTITION SYS_P1100
PARALLEL(DEGREE 4);
```

```
Index altered.
```

Then, we can validate that the index is again in a usable state by rerunning the foregoing SELECT statement from DBA_IND_PARTITIONS:

```
INDEX_NAME       PARTITION_NAME   STATUS
---------------  ---------------  --------
EMPPART_I3       SYS_P804         USABLE
EMPPART_I1       SYS_P1100        USABLE
EMPPART_I2       SYS_P1042        USABLE
```

Keep in mind that table partition names and index partition names may not match and correspond to each other, and you may have to check the data dictionary to obtain the correct index partition names. This is especially true if you are using interval partitioning.

Yet another way to rebuild any locally partitioned indexes if you omitted the UPDATE INDEXES clause is to rebuild all index partitions using one command. See the following example:

```
ALTER TABLE EMPPART
MODIFY PARTITION SYS_P820
REBUILD UNUSABLE LOCAL INDEXES;
```

There may be valid reasons to defer rebuilding indexes. You may simply want to split the work into individual pieces to more easily track where you are in completing the entire operation. For very large partitions with many indexes, it may be more prudent to move the data in one operation and then rebuild each index in separate operations.

Keep in mind that the UPDATE INDEXES clause rebuilds each index serially, one at a time. There may be a performance boost by simply running separate, concurrent ALTER INDEX REBUILD statements when rebuilding all the indexes. Each environment is different, the volume is different, and the number and characteristics of the indexes are different, so test the alternatives and implement what is best for your environment.

15-9. Splitting Partitions in Parallel
Problem

You have a partition with a large amount of data and want to split that larger partition into two or more smaller partitions.

Solution

As a DBA, at times the need arises to split partitions, and this operation can also be done in parallel. For instance, let's say you have a partitioned table that has a default high-end partition with a large amount of data and you want to split that data into multiple partitions. In cases such as these, you can split that default partition in parallel to speed up the partition split process. Here is an example of splitting a partition using parallelism:

```
ALTER TABLE EMP
SPLIT PARTITION PMAX at ('2011-04-01') INTO
(PARTITION P4 TABLESPACE EMP_S,
PARTITION PMAX TABLESPACE EMP_S)
PARALLEL(DEGREE 4);
```

How It Works

Adding parallelism can speed up the process of splitting a partition with a large amount of data. Here is an example of a partition with more than 16 million rows, and enabling parallelism for the split operation reduced the time of the split operation. First, the split was performed in parallel:

```
ALTER TABLE EMPPART SPLIT PARTITION emppart2000_p AT ('2000-01-01')
INTO (PARTITION emppart1990_p, PARTITION emppart2000_p)
PARALLEL(DEGREE 4);
```

Table altered.

Elapsed: 00:00:53.61

The same split was then performed on a similar table to see the performance impact of doing the split serially:

```
ALTER TABLE EMPPART2 SPLIT PARTITION emppart2000_p AT ('2000-01-01')
INTO (PARTITION emppart1990_p, PARTITION emppart2000_p);
```

Table altered.

Elapsed: 00:01:05.36

Again, keep in mind that for parallel operations, an extent needs to be allocated for each parallel operation. For the foregoing partition split operation, the table that used parallelism has a significantly higher number of extents allocated:

```
SELECT segment_name, partition_name, extents
FROM dba_segments
WHERE segment_name LIKE '%EMP%'
AND owner = 'SCOTT'
ORDER BY 2,1;
```

```
SEGMENT_NAME          PARTITION_NAME         EXTENTS
--------------------  --------------------  ----------
EMPPART               EMPPART1990_P              335
EMPPART2              EMPPART1990_P              121
EMPPART               EMPPART2000_P              338
EMPPART2              EMPPART2000_P              125
```

Remember that splitting partitions, like moving partitions, will render affected indexes or partitions of indexes on the associated table unusable. See Recipe 15-8 for an example on checking and rebuilding an index after a partition-level operation.

15-10. Enabling Automatic Degree of Parallelism

Problem

You want to allow Oracle to automatically determine whether a SQL statement should execute in parallel and what DOP it should use.

Solution

Set PARALLEL_DEGREE_POLICY to AUTO to allow Oracle to determine whether a statement runs in parallel. You can set this either at the system level or at the session level. To set it for all SQL statements, run the following command:

```
alter system set parallel_degree_policy=auto scope=both;
```

To set it for a single SQL statement, you can alter your session to enable automatic DOP:

```
alter session set parallel_degree_policy=auto;
```

One prerequisite of using automatic DOP is to run the DBMS_RESOURCE_MANAGER.CALIBRATE_IO procedure. This procedure needs to be run only once and gathers information on the hardware characteristics of your system. Before running this procedure, ensure that the parameter disk_asynch_io is set to true. You can also run the following query to ensure that asynchronous I/O is enabled appropriately:

```
SELECT name,asynch_io
FROM v$datafile f,v$iostat_file i
WHERE f.file#=i.file_no
AND (filetype_name='Data File' or filetype_name='Temp File');
```

```
NAME                                            ASYNCH_IO
----------------------------------------------- ----------
+DATA/orcl1/datafile/system.3522.827962061      ASYNC_ON
+DATA/orcl1/datafile/system.3522.827962061      ASYNC_ON
+DATA/orcl1/datafile/sysaux.3521.827962063      ASYNC_ON
+DATA/orcl1/datafile/undotbs1.3520.827962063    ASYNC_ON
+DATA/orcl1/datafile/users.3514.827962063       ASYNC_ON
+DATA/orcl1/datafile/example.3571.827962145     ASYNC_ON
+DATA/orcl1/datafile/undotbs2.3570.827962239    ASYNC_ON
```

The DBMS_RESOURCE_MANAGER.CALIBRATE_IO procedure has two input parameters and three output parameters. The input parameters are as follows:

- NUM_DISKS: This represents the number of physical disks (not LUNs) on your system. You may have to obtain this from your system administrator.

- MAX_LATENCY: This represents the maximum tolerable latency in milliseconds for I/O requests. This may vary, and you may need to determine the appropriate value for your system.

After verifying the proper values for the input parameters for the DBMS_RESOURCE_MANAGER.CALIBRATE_IO procedure, you can run it, as shown in the following example. Note that the three output parameters can be displayed by creating variables within a PL/SQL block when running the procedure:

```
  1* SET SERVEROUTPUT ON
  2  DECLARE
  3     latc INTEGER;
  4     iops INTEGER;
  5     mbps INTEGER;
  6  BEGIN
  7     DBMS_RESOURCE_MANAGER.CALIBRATE_IO (64, 10, iops, mbps, latc);
  8     DBMS_OUTPUT.PUT_LINE ('max_iops = ' || iops);
  9     DBMS_OUTPUT.PUT_LINE ('latency = ' || latc);
 10     dbms_output.put_line('max_mbps = ' || mbps);
 11* END;
23:51:58 SQL> /
max_iops = 62165
latency = 0
max_mbps = 3368

PL/SQL procedure successfully completed.

Elapsed: 00:15:59.32
```

How It Works

By default, Oracle executes a statement in parallel only when the DOP is set for the table or the parallel hint is used. You can instruct Oracle to automatically consider using parallelism for a statement via the PARALLEL_DEGREE_POLICY initialization parameter. Oracle takes the following steps when a SQL statement is issued when PARALLEL_DEGREE_POLICY is set to AUTO:

1. The statement is parsed.

2. The PARALLEL_MIN_TIME_THRESHOLD parameter is checked:

   • If execution time is less than the threshold set, then the statement runs without parallelism.

   • If execution time is greater than the threshold set, then the statement runs in parallel depending on the automatic DOP that is calculated by the optimizer.

The PARALLEL_DEGREE_POLICY parameter can be set to three different values: AUTO, LIMITED, and MANUAL. MANUAL is the default and turns off the automatic degree of parallelism. LIMITED instructs Oracle to use automatic DOP only on those objects with parallelism explicitly set. The AUTO setting gives Oracle full control over setting automatic DOP.

Once all configuration is complete, you can validate whether automatic DOP is being derived by running a query against a table in your database. The following example shows an explain plan for a query where DOP has been automatically derived:

```
select /*+ parallel */ count(*) from employees_big;
```

```
-----------------------------------------------------------------------
|Id|Operation              |Name          |    TQ |IN-OUT|PQ Distrib|
-----------------------------------------------------------------------
| 0|SELECT STATEMENT       |              |       |      |          |
| 1| SORT AGGREGATE        |              |       |      |          |
| 2|  PX COORDINATOR       |              |       |      |          |
| 3|   PX SEND QC (RANDOM) |:TQ10000      | Q1,00| P->S |QC (RAND) |
| 4|    SORT AGGREGATE     |              | Q1,00| PCWP |          |
| 5|     PX BLOCK ITERATOR |              | Q1,00| PCWC |          |
| 6|      TABLE ACCESS FULL|EMPLOYEES_BIG | Q1,00| PCWP |          |
-----------------------------------------------------------------------
```

Note

   - automatic DOP: Computed Degree of Parallelism is 10
   - parallel scans affinitized

If you have omitted running the DBMS_RESOURCE_MANAGER.CALIBRATE_IO procedure, you will see the following in the note section of the explain plan:

Note

   - automatic DOP: skipped because of IO calibrate statistics are missing

With automatic DOP, there is a shift away from downgrading parallel operations based on available parallel slaves to using a new feature in Oracle 11g R2 called *statement queuing*. With statement queuing, statements will not be downgraded and will always be run with the query's specified DOP. If there are not enough slaves to meet that DOP, the statement will be queued until that DOP is available. While it may appear that queuing could actually degrade the performance of queries in your database because some statements may have to wait for the specified DOP to be available, it is designed to improve the overall parallelism performance on the database because running fewer statements with the specified DOP will outperform running more statements, some with a downgraded DOP. There are many other parameters that can be set related to parallelism. Table 15-3 lists other parallel parameters you may want to consider for your application.

Table 15-3. *Oracle Parallelism-Related Initialization Parameters*

Parameter	Description
parallel_degree_limit	Automatic DOP is determined either by the number of CPUs on the system, by the I/O requirements of a given query, or by a set integer value. To use the IO value, you must run the DBMS_RESOURCE_MANAGER.CALIBRATE_IO procedure.
parallel_degree_policy	Determines whether automatic DOP, statement queuing, and in-memory query execution are enabled. The MANUAL setting disables automatic DOP. The AUTO setting gives Oracle full control over setting automatic DOP. The LIMITED value exercises automatic DOP only on those objects with parallelism explicitly set.
parallel_max_servers	This specifies the maximum number of parallel processes (from 0 to 3600) for a database instance.
parallel_min_servers	This specifies the minimum number of parallel processes for a database instance. Setting to a nonzero value keeps that minimum number of parallel processes alive and ready to accept new requests. This saves start-up costs of these processes but costs more in memory utilization.
parallel_servers_target	Setting this parameter tells the database how many parallel processes can run at one time before query statements requiring parallel execution begin to be queued for execution.

Another benefit of setting automatic DOP is something called *in-memory parallel execution* or *in-memory parallel query*. If you've set PARALLEL_DEGREE_POLICY to AUTO, this is automatically in effect for your database. In the past, parallel processing reads directly from disk and bypasses the buffer cache during processing. With in-memory parallel execution, Oracle may decide to load data blocks into the buffer cache for processing. By doing this, processing a parallel query may simply be much faster. The decision to store blocks in memory is internal to Oracle and is based on such factors as the size of the object, the frequency of change for the object, the frequency of access, and the size of the buffer cache. In-memory parallel execution can occur for blocks of tables, indexes, and partitioned objects.

Also, if you are running on a Real Application Cluster (RAC) environment, the data blocks and the resulting parallel processing load are spread across the instances of your RAC environment. Furthermore, Oracle implements the notion of node affinity when splitting up the blocks between instances, and the blocks are not shared with other processes occurring within your RAC environment. This makes the parallel processing very efficient.

15-11. Examining Parallel Explain Plans
Problem

You want to understand how to read parallel explain plans.

Solution

When reading your explain plan, interpret it from the innermost to outermost levels and from the bottom going up. For instance, here again is our parallel execution plan from using a parallel hint against the EMP table:

```
select /*+ parallel(emp,4) */ * from emp;
```

```
-----------------------------------------------------------------
| Id  | Operation             | Name    |   TQ  |IN-OUT| PQ Distrib |
-----------------------------------------------------------------
|   0 | SELECT STATEMENT      |         |       |      |            |
|   1 |  PX COORDINATOR       |         |       |      |            |
|   2 |   PX SEND QC (RANDOM) | :TQ10000|  Q1,00| P->S | QC (RAND)  |
|   3 |    PX BLOCK ITERATOR  |         |  Q1,00| PCWC |            |
|   4 |     TABLE ACCESS FULL | EMP     |  Q1,00| PCWP |            |
-----------------------------------------------------------------
```

Looking at the foregoing plan starting at the bottom, we are doing a full table scan of the EMP table. The PX BLOCK INTERATOR just above the table scan is responsible for taking that request for a full table scan and breaking it up into chunks based on the DOP specified. The PX SEND processes pass the data to the consuming processes. Finally, the PX COORDINATOR is the process used by the query coordinator to receive the data from a given parallel process and return to the SELECT statement.

If you look at the IN-OUT column of your explain plan, you can see the execution flow of the operation and determine whether there are any bottlenecks or any parts of the plan that are not parallelized, which may cause a decrease in the expected performance. As shown in Table 15-5, the operation that normally shows that there may be a bottleneck is the PARALLEL_FROM_SERIAL operation because it means parallel processes are being spawned from a serial operation, which denotes an inefficiency in the process.

For instance, say you have a series of employee tables by region of the country, and a user is performing a query to get information from several of these tables. However, the makeup of the query is such that a bottleneck occurs.

```
select /*+ parallel(e,4) */ e.ename, d.dname
from emp e join dept d using (deptno);
```

```
-----------------------------------------------------------------
|Id |Operation                |Name    |   TQ |IN-OUT|PQ Distrib  |
-----------------------------------------------------------------
|  0|SELECT STATEMENT         |        |      |      |            |
|  1| PX COORDINATOR          |        |      |      |            |
|  2|  PX SEND QC (RANDOM)    |:TQ10002|Q1,02| P->S |QC (RAND)   |
|  3|   MERGE JOIN            |        |Q1,02| PCWP |            |
|  4|    SORT JOIN            |        |Q1,02| PCWP |            |
|  5|     BUFFER SORT         |        |Q1,02| PCWC |            |
|  6|      PX RECEIVE         |        |Q1,02| PCWP |            |
|  7|       PX SEND HYBRID HASH|:TQ10000|    | S->P |HYBRID HASH|
|  8|        STATISTICS COLLECTOR|     |      |      |            |
|  9|         TABLE ACCESS BY INDEX|DEPT|    |      |            |
|   |           ROWID BATCHED  |        |      |      |            |
| 10|          INDEX FULL SCAN |PK_DEPT |      |      |            |
| 11|    SORT JOIN            |        |Q1,02| PCWP |            |
| 12|     PX RECEIVE          |        |Q1,02| PCWP |            |
| 13|      PX SEND HYBRID HASH|:TQ10001|Q1,01| P->P |HYBRID HASH|
| 14|       PX BLOCK ITERATOR |        |Q1,01| PCWC |            |
| 15|        TABLE ACCESS FULL |EMP     |Q1,01| PCWP |            |
-----------------------------------------------------------------
```

You can tell from the foregoing explain plan output that the PX SEND process from the DEPT table is serial and is sending data back to be fed into a parallel process. This represents a bottleneck in this query. If we change all aspects of the query to run in parallel, we see an improvement in the execution plan and that both PX SEND processes are parallelized:

```
select /*+ parallel(e,4) parallel(d,4) */ e.ename, d.dname
from emp e join dept d using (deptno);
```

```
--------------------------------------------------------------------
|Id |Operation              |Name     |  TQ |IN-OUT|PQ Distrib  |
--------------------------------------------------------------------
|  0|SELECT STATEMENT       |         |     |      |            |
|  1| PX COORDINATOR        |         |     |      |            |
|  2|  PX SEND QC (RANDOM)  |:TQ10002|Q1,02| P->S |QC (RAND)   |
|  3|   HASH JOIN BUFFERED  |         |Q1,02| PCWP |            |
|  4|    PX RECEIVE         |         |Q1,02| PCWP |            |
|  5|     PX SEND HYBRID HASH|:TQ10000|Q1,00| P->P |HYBRID HASH|
|  6|      STATISTICS COLLECTOR|     |Q1,00| PCWC |            |
|  7|       PX BLOCK ITERATOR|        |Q1,00| PCWC |            |
|  8|        TABLE ACCESS FULL|DEPT    |Q1,00| PCWP |            |
|  9|    PX RECEIVE         |         |Q1,02| PCWP |            |
| 10|     PX SEND HYBRID HASH|:TQ10001|Q1,01| P->P |HYBRID HASH|
| 11|      PX BLOCK ITERATOR|         |Q1,01| PCWC |            |
| 12|       TABLE ACCESS FULL|EMP_BIG |Q1,01| PCWP |            |
--------------------------------------------------------------------
```

How It Works

Tables 15-4 and 15-5 delineate the fundamental information that can be used to determine the execution plan for a parallel operation. To understand the basics of interpreting your explain plan output, you should be aware of two aspects:

- The fundamental parallel execution steps (Table 15-4)

Table 15-4. *Parallel Execution Steps*

Operation	Description
PX BLOCK ITERATOR	In this step, the work to be done is split into pieces, which in turn will be done by the parallel slaves specified.
PX COORDINATOR	Much like a project manager, this process coordinates and schedules the parallel slaves' work, as well as being responsible for getting data back from the parallel slaves once they complete their tasks.
PX RECEIVE	These processes are consumer slaves of the data written via the producers of the PX SEND processes.
PX SEND	These processes are the producer slaves of getting a portion of the data and writing to areas to be read by the consumers.

- The parallel operations that occur within each step (Table 15-5)

Table 15-5. *Parallel Operations*

PLAN_TABLE Operation (Other_Tag Column)	Explain Plan In/Out Tag	Description
PARALLEL_FROM_SERIAL	S->P	This denotes that a serial process with the operation is passing information to a parallel process. This is a sign of a bottleneck and an area of potential improvement.
PARALLEL_TO_PARALLEL	P->P	This means that both the producer and the consumer are parallelized. This is the most desired execution flow.
PARALLEL_TO_SERIAL	P->S	This step, although hinting at a bottleneck, is fairly normal. It is toward the top (that is, the end) of an operation and denotes that results from a parallel process are being fed to the query coordinator at the end of the process.
PARALLEL_COMBINED_WITH PARENT	PCWP	This means a step is being combined with its parent step and run simultaneously (for example, a sort/merge operation).
PARALLEL_COMBINED_WITH CHILD	PCWC	This is the same as PCWP, except it means that a child step/slave process is being run simultaneously with the child process from the execution plan.

The execution steps are the aspects of a parallelized plan, while the operations that occur within your parallel execution plan can help you determine whether you have an optimized plan or one that needs tuning and improvement.

As with nonparallel operations, the explain plan utility is a useful tool in determining what the optimizer is planning to do to complete the task at hand. When executing operations in parallel, there are specific aspects of the explain plan related to parallelism. These are important to understand so you can determine whether the operation is running as optimized as possible. One of the key aspects of analyzing a parallel explain plan is to determine whether there are any aspects of the plan that are being run serially because this bottleneck can reduce the overall performance of a given operation. That it is why it is critical to understand aspects of the explain plan that relate to parallel operations, with the end goal being that all aspects of the operation are parallelized.

15-12. Monitoring Parallel Operations
Problem

You want to quickly get information regarding the performance of your parallel operations from the database.

Solution

If you look at the V$SYSSTAT view, which gives information on system-level statistics in your database, including parallelism-related statistics, you can see, at a quick glance, if the DOP requested was actually used and if any of those operations were downgraded:

```
SELECT name , value
FROM v$sysstat
WHERE name LIKE '%Parallel%';
```

```
------------------------------------------------------------ ----------
NAME                                                              VALUE
------------------------------------------------------------ ----------
Parallel operations not downgraded                              1069711
Parallel operations downgraded to serial                            249
Parallel operations downgraded 75 to 99 pct                           0
Parallel operations downgraded 50 to 75 pct                           0
Parallel operations downgraded 25 to 50 pct                           8
Parallel operations downgraded 1 to 25 pct                            0
```

6 rows selected.

If you look at the V$PQ_SYSSTAT view, you can see parallel slave activity on your database. From looking at these statistics, you can quickly see whether parallelism is properly configured on your database just by looking at the parallel slave activity. For instance, if you see that the Servers Shutdown and Servers Started values are high, it can be an indication that the PARALLEL_MIN_SERVERS parameter is set too low because there is overhead occurring to consistently start and stop parallel processes.

```
SELECT * FROM v$pq_sysstat
WHERE statistic LIKE 'Server%';
```

```
STATISTIC                      VALUE
-----------------------------  ----------
Servers Busy                       0
Servers Idle                      36
Servers Highwater                218
Server Sessions              4965880
Servers Started                33573
Servers Shutdown               33497
Servers Cleaned Up                72
```

7 rows selected.

If you are looking for session-level statistics regarding a parallel operation, looking at the V$PQ_TQSTAT view is useful in determining exactly how the work was split up among the parallel slaves, as well as giving you information about the actual DOP used based on the information within V$PQ_TQSTAT. Let's rerun our parallel query against the EMP table with a hint specifying a DOP of 4.

```
SELECT /*+ parallel(emp,4) */ * FROM emp;
```

After completion of the query but also within the same session, we can query the V$PQ_TQSTAT view to get information about the parallel operations used for that query:

```
SELECT dfo_number, tq_id, server_type, process, num_rows, bytes
FROM v$pq_tqstat
ORDER BY dfo_number DESC, tq_id, server_type DESC , process;
```

DFO_NUMBER	TQ_ID	SERVER_TYPE	PROCESS	NUM_ROWS	BYTES
1	0	Producer	P000	309399	23665153
1	0	Producer	P001	308763	23616810
1	0	Producer	P002	309602	23681189
1	0	Producer	P003	309189	23648954
1	0	Consumer	QC	1234567	94434916

We can see that between the four producer parallel slaves, the work was divided fairly evenly between them. We can also validate that the actual DOP used for this query was 4, as specified in the query hint.

How It Works

One of the quickest methods to analyze the performance of parallel operations within your database is to analyze the dynamic performance views. These views give you a glimpse of how parallelism is performing overall within your database, which can indicate how well-tuned or badly tuned your database is for parallelism. It can also give you very session-specific details, such as how the work was split up between slaves and information on the actual DOP used for a given operation. Table 15-6 gives you an overview of the parallelism-related dynamic performance views.

Table 15-6. *Key Dynamic Performance Views Related to Parallel Operations*

View Name	Description
V$PQ_SESSTAT	Shows parallelism-related session-level statistics, including number of parallel slaves used
V$PQ_SYSSTAT	Shows parallelism-related statistics for the database instance, including number of parallel slaves used
V$PQ_TQSTAT	Contains statistics on parallel operations across the database instance, including the DOP used and rows processed for each slave of a given operation
V$SYSSTAT	Contains at-a-glance statistics on downgraded parallel-related operations
V$PX_SESSION	Contains information about sessions running parallel operations and information about the DOP requested and used
V$PQ_SLAVE	Contains information about the current parallel slaves being used by a database instance
V$PX_PROCESS	Contains information about parallel processes and status

15-13. Finding Bottlenecks in Parallel Processes
Problem

You have some parallel processes that are underperforming, and you want to do analysis to find the bottlenecks.

Solution

There are many wait events related to parallelism. Many of these events are considered "idle" wait events—that is, they don't usually indicate a problem. If you query the V$SYSTEM_EVENT view, you can get an idea of the parallelism-related waits that have occurred in your database instance. The following query results show some of the common wait events that can occur:

```
SELECT event, wait_class, total_waits
FROM v$session_event
WHERE event LIKE 'PX%';

EVENT                        WAIT_CLASS   TOTAL_WAITS
---------------------------  -----------  -----------
PX Deq Credit: need buffer   Idle            6667936
PX Deq Credit: send blkd     Other           8161247
PX Deq: Execute Reply        Idle             490827
PX Deq: Execution Msg        Idle             685175
PX Deq: Join ACK             Idle              26312
PX Deq: Msg Fragment         Idle                 67
PX Deq: Parse Reply          Idle              20891
PX Deq: Signal ACK           Other             25729
PX Deq: Table Q Get Keys     Other              3141
PX Deq: Table Q Normal       Idle           25120970
PX Deq: Table Q Sample       Idle              11124
PX Deq: Table Q qref         Other           1705216
PX Idle Wait                 Idle             241116
PX qref latch                Other           1208472
```

How It Works

Table 15-7 describes some of the key parallelism-related wait events. If you are having significant performance issues, it may be worthwhile to browse these wait events to see whether you have excessive waits or wait times. If so, it may indicate an issue with the processing occurring with the parallel slaves. Again, events that are "idle" *generally* do not indicate a problem.

Table 15-7. Key Parallelism Wait Events That Could Signify a Tuning Issue

View Name	Description
PX Deq: Execute Reply	Denotes that the query coordinator (QC) is waiting for results from parallel slaves; this can be a sign of badly tuned SQL. If high waits, analyze the execution plan for efficiency.
PX Deq: Parse Reply	Denotes that parallel slaves are parsing SQL statements; high wait times may point to library cache contention.
PX Deq: qref latch	This wait can indicate that the producer slaves are processing too fast, and the consumer slaves cannot keep up. Consider increasing the parallel_execution_message_size parameter or reducing the degree of parallelism at the database, session, or statement level as appropriate for your system.
PX Deq: Table Q Normal	This is usually just an idle wait event, but extremely high values may indicate that some producer slaves are slow and that the consumer slaves are waiting.

Parallelism-related wait events can be grouped into the following categories:

- Parallel query

- Parallel recovery

- OLAP operations

- Index operations

- Statement queuing

- General parallelism-related wait events

See My Oracle Support note 1097154.1 for a complete description of all parallelism-related wait events.

15-14. Getting Detailed Information on Parallel Sessions
Problem

You have some underperforming parallel processes and need more detailed information on the sessions.

Solution

By turning on session tracing, you can get detailed trace information on your parallel sessions. This is essentially a four-step process:

1. Set the event in your session.

2. Execute your SQL statement.

3. Turn off your session tracing.

4. Analyze your trace file output.

For example, you are again executing a parallel query against the EMP table. To gather trace information, you would do the following:

```
alter session set events '10391 trace name context forever, level 128';

select /*+ parallel(emp,4) */ * from emp;

alter session set events '10391 trace name context off';
```

In Oracle 12c, there appears to be a trace file generated per parallel slave, along with one general trace file. Some of the contents you can see with the trace files look similar to the following excerpt:

```
PARSING IN CURSOR #47940292534688 len=40 dep=0 uid=102 oct=3 lid=102 tim=1383019215069949
hv=3986116938 ad='3c8882230' sqlid='6cy2sfzqtfnaa'
select /*+ parallel(emp,4) */ * from emp
END OF STMT
PARSE #47940292534688:c=0,e=178,p=0,cr=0,cu=0,mis=0,r=0,dep=0,og=1,plh=2873591275,
tim=1383019215069948
EXEC #47940292534688:c=1000,e=120786,p=0,cr=3,cu=0,mis=0,r=0,dep=0,og=1,plh=2873591275,
tim=1383019215190784
```

```
FETCH #47940292534688:c=1000,e=232,p=0,cr=0,cu=0,mis=0,r=1,dep=0,og=1,plh=2873591275,
tim=1383019215191208
FETCH #47940292534688:c=1000,e=1074,p=0,cr=0,cu=0,mis=0,r=14,dep=0,og=1,plh=2873591275,
tim=1383019215192766
STAT #47940292534688 id=1 cnt=15 pid=0 pos=1 obj=0 op='PX COORDINATOR
(cr=3 pr=0 pw=0 time=120732 us)'
STAT #47940292534688 id=2 cnt=0 pid=1 pos=1 obj=0 op='PX SEND QC (RANDOM) :TQ10000 (cr=0 pr=0 pw=0
time=0 us cost=2 size=570 card=15)
```

How It Works

As with other session tracing, the trace file can be found in the destination specified under the diagnostic_dest parameter. The user_dump_dest parameter can still be used, although it has been deprecated. The trace file shows granular information for the parallel processes. If you are experiencing significant performance issues with parallelism and you want to delve further into investigating the results of the trace files generated by this event, it may be beneficial to simply create a service request with Oracle in order to get the most detailed information. Reading and understanding these trace files can be difficult and cumbersome, and it may be more expedient to simply send the files to Oracle Support for analysis. Yet another way to validate the DOP used for a parallel operation is to use the _px_trace facility, which also generates a trace file. The base syntax for using the _px_trace is as follows:

```
alter session set "_px_trace"=[[Verbosity,]area],[[Verbosity,]area],..,[time];
```

For Verbosity, the possible values are as follows:

- High
- Medium
- Low

For the Area parameter, the possible values are as follows:

- Scheduling
- Execution
- Granule
- Messaging
- Buffer
- Compilation
- All
- None

For the Time parameter, the only possible value is time.

The following basic example shows how to use this facility with a query you want to analyze:

```
alter session set "_px_trace"="compilation","execution","messaging";

select /*+ parallel(emp,4) */ * from emp;
```

567

Then, within the trace files, you can evaluate the DOP requested and used:

```
2013-10-28 22:10:51.901117*:PX_Messaging:kxfp.c@12057:kxfpg1srv():
        trying to get server 1.0 for q=0x3d3ee5270
        slave is local
        found dp=0x3d852ac90 flg=18
        local slave 1.0 already started..
        Got It. 1 so far.
2013-10-28 22:10:51.901117*:PX_Messaging:kxfp.c@12057:kxfpg1srv():
        trying to get server 1.1 for q=0x3d3ee5270
        slave is local
        found dp=0x3d852ade8 flg=18
        local slave 1.1 already started..
        Got It. 2 so far.
2013-10-28 22:10:51.901117*:PX_Messaging:kxfp.c@12057:kxfpg1srv():
        trying to get server 1.2 for q=0x3d3ee5270
        slave is local
        found dp=0x3d852af40 flg=18
        local slave 1.2 already started..
        Got It. 3 so far.
2013-10-28 22:10:51.901117*:PX_Messaging:kxfp.c@12057:kxfpg1srv():
        trying to get server 1.3 for q=0x3d3ee5270
        slave is local
        found dp=0x3d852b098 flg=18
        local slave 1.3 already started..
        Got It. 4 so far.
        Acquired 4 slaves on 1 instances avg height=4 #set=1 qser=14337
                P000 inst 1 spid 14290
                P001 inst 1 spid 14292
                P002 inst 1 spid 14294
                P003 inst 1 spid 14296
```

Again, while you may be able to extract helpful information from the trace files, the best source to analyze these files is Oracle Support. More information regarding this utility also can be found on the My Oracle Support note 444164.1.

Index

▪ A

Active Session History (ASH), 125, 129, 147, 151
    ashrpt.sql script, 147
    awrrpt.sql script, 147
    background events, 148
    blocking sessions, 149
    circular buffer, 151
    data dictionary
        DBA_HIST_ACTIVE_SESS_HISTORY
          view, 154–155
        query, 154–155
        SESSION_STATE column, 155
        time frame, 155–156
        V$ACTIVE_SESSION_HISTORY view, 154–155
    DBA_HIST_ACTIVE_SESS_HISTORY view, 151
    DB files, 150
    enterprise manager
        DBA_HIST_EVENT_NAME view, 153
        Filter drop-down menu, 153
        filter option, 153
        performance tuning activities, 152
        sample report, 152
        SQL_ID, 153
        time frames, 152
    P1/P2/P3 values, 148
    real-time/near real-time session
        information, 147
    report section information, 150
    snapshots, 147
    SQL command types, 148
    SQL statements, 149
    user events, 147
ashrpt.sql script, 152
Automated SQL tuning, 375
    ADDM, 376
    automatic SQL tuning advisor, 375

    in AWR
        begin and end AWR snapshot IDs, 393
        creating SQL tuning set object, 393
        DBMS_SQLTUNE.SELECT_WORKLOAD_
          REPOSITORY funcion, 394
    DBMS_AUTO_TASK_ADMIN.ENABLE/DISABLE
        procedure, 386, 388
    DBMS_SQLTUNE.CREATE_SQLSET
        procedure, 390
    DBMS_SQLTUNE.CREATE_TUNING_TASK
        procedure, 404
        SQL_ID and AWR snapshot IDs, 406
        SQL ID, Cursor Cache, 405
        SQL tuning set name, 407
        text of SQL statement, 405
    diagrammatic representation, 377
    job details, 377
    maintenance task view
        descriptions, 378–379
    in Memory
        CAPTURE_CURSOR_CACHE_SQLSET parameter
        descriptions, 399
        DBMS_SQLTUNE.CAPTURE_CURSOR_CACHE
        procedure, 398
        DBMS_SQLTUNE.SELECT_CURSOR_CACHE
        funcion, 396–397
    modifying maintenance window, 388
        Automatic SQL Tuning, 389
        segment advice, 389
        statistics gathering, 389
    SQL performance problems, 376
    SQL tuning advisor, 376
        from ADDM, 412–414
        from Enterprise Manager, 409
        from SQL Developer, 409
        optimizer tuning modes, 411
        steps to run manually, 407

Automated SQL tuning (*cont.*)
  SQL tuning sets, 375
    deleting statements, 401–402
    displaying contents, 399–400
    transporting to another database, 402
  tuning advice, 379
    DBMS_AUTO_SQLTUNE.SET_AUTO_TUNING_
      TASK parameter, 384–385
    detail section, 381
    e-mailing output, 380
    error section, 382
    findings section, 382
    general information section, 381
    REPORT_AUTO_TUNING_TASK function, 382
    SCRIPT_TUNING_TASK function, 383–384
    summary section, 381
  tuning task, 375
  viewing resource-intensive
    in AWR, 391
    in Memory, 395
  with Enterprise Manager, 386
Automatic Database Diagnostic Monitor (ADDM), 104, 376
  DBMS_ADDM Package, 412
  performance recommendations, 414
  SQL*plus script, 411
Automatic Diagnostic Repository Command Interpreter
    (ADRCI), 236
  ADR base, 238
  alert log, 240, 242
  in batch mode, 237
  diagnostic tasks, 238
  HELP command, 237
  homepath command, 239–240
  in interactive mode, 236
  V$DIAG_INFO view, 238
  view incidents, 242–243
Automatic memory management, 95
  buffer pool, 98
    KEEP, 99
    RECYCLE, 99
  caching client result sets, 115
    advantages, 116
    CLIENT_RESULT_CACHE_LAG, 115
    CLIENT_RESULT_CACHE_SIZE, 115
    OCIStmtExecute(), 116
    OCIStmtFetch(), 116
    optional client-side configuration file, 116
  caching PL/SQL function, 117
    considerations, 119
    requirements, 120
  caching SQL query result, 112
    read consistency requirements, 114
    RESULT_CACHE_MODE initialization
      parameter, 112
    table annotations and query hints, 113–114

configuring server query cache
  DBMS_RESULT_CACHE.FLUSH procedure, 108
  initialization parameters, 107
  materialized views, 108
  PL/SQL collection, 108
  RESULT_CACHE_MAX_RESULT, 108
  RESULT_CACHE_MAX_SIZE, 108
  RESULT_CACHE_REMOTE_EXPIRATION, 108
DBCA, 96
implementing steps, 95
managing server result cache, 109
  DBMS_RESULT_CACHE.STATUS(), 109
  shared pool percentage, 111
MEMORY_MAX_TARGET PARAMETER, 97–98
memory resizing operations
  V$MEMORY_RESIZE_OPS, 102
  V$MEMORY_TARGET_ADVICE, 101
memory structures
  PGA, 97
  SGA, 97
MEMORY_TARGET parameter, 96–97
optimizing memory usage, 103
  ADDM reports, 104
  tuning steps, 103
Oracle Database Smart Flash Cache, 120
  DB_FLASH_CACHE_FILE, 120
  DB_FLASH_CACHE_SIZE, 121
PGA memory allocation
  AWR, 107
  PGA_AGGREGATE_TARGET parameter, 104–105
  steps, 104
  V$SQL_WORKAREA_HISTOGRAM, 106
  V$SYSSTAT and V$SESSTAT, 107
pga_memory_target, 96
redo log buffer tuning, 123
SCOPE parameter, 96
setting minimum values, 100
Automatic Segment Space Management (ASSM), 1, 8
Automatic SQL Tuning Advisor, 375
Automatic workload repository (AWR), 24, 107, 125
  active session information (*see* Active Session
    History (ASH))
  baseline statistics
    adaptive metrics, 139
    awrextr.sql script, 143
    awrload.sql script, 143
    AWR_REPORT_TEXT function, 143
    awrrpt.sql script, 143
    configuration, 138
    CREATE_BASELINE_TEMPLATE procedure, 144
    DBA_HIST_BASELINE_TEMPLATE view, 145
    DROP_BASELINE procedure, 142
    DROP_BASELINE_TEMPLATE procedure, 145
    Dropping, 142
    enterprise manager, 140

fixed baselines, 137
moving baselines, 137
performance statistics, 136
RENAME_BASELINE procedure, 142
renaming, 142
retention period, 138–139
snapshot range, 142
template, 144
categories, 127
DBA, 125
historical database performance statistics, 125
interval and retention periods, 128–129
interval-based historical statistics, 126
output, 145
report
awrrpt.sql script, 129, 132
database instance, 131
data dictionary, 131
DBA_HIST views, 132
enterprise manager, 133
name, 131
single SQL statement, 135–136
snapshot ids, 131
type, 130
snapshots, 333
statistical components, 126
STATISTICS_LEVEL parameter, 126
time frame, 125
type of information, 127
UTLBSTAT/UTLESTAT and Statspack, 125
AUTOSTATS_TARGET parameter, 465

■ B

Baseline statistics
adaptive metrics, 139
awrextr.sql script, 143
awrload.sql script, 143
AWR_REPORT_TEXT function, 143
awrrpt.sql script, 143
configuration, 138
CREATE_BASELINE_TEMPLATE procedure, 144
DBA_HIST_BASELINE_TEMPLATE view, 145
DROP_BASELINE procedure, 142
DROP_BASELINE_TEMPLATE procedure, 145
Dropping, 142
enterprise manager, 140
fixed baselines, 137
moving baselines, 137
RENAME_BASELINE procedure, 142
renaming, 142
retention period, 138–139
snapshot range, 142
template, 144

BFILE command, 16
Bitmap index, star schema
B-tree indexes, 84
data warehouse environments, 83
filtering data, fact table, 84
WHERE clause, 83
Bitmap join index, 85
BLOB command, 16
Bottlenecks
CPU, 202
database network connectivity
troubleshooting, 209–210
input/output, 205
AWR report, 208
data dictionary, 208
I/O rates, 206
iostat column descriptions, 207
iostat command, 205
I/O statistics, 205, 208
iostat output examination, 206
problem, 205
Statspack, 208
V$ views, 208
iostat, AWR, 208
network-intensive processes
detection
diagnosing sources, 209
nctstat command, 208
OS process ID, 209
problem, 208
Send-Q column, 209
Solaris, prstat utility, 205
virtual memory statistics (vmstat), 198–199
CPU section, 200
IO section, 200
memory area, 199
OS components, 199
output interpretation, 199
processing jobs section, 199
swap section, 199
swpd column, 199
system area, 200
B-tree indexes, 59, 84
DBMS_SPACE CREATE_INDEX
procedure, 59
index blocks, 56
CUST table, 57
Index fast full scan, 56
Index range scan, 56
Oracle's Autotrace utility, 56
ROWID, 54
table blocks, 58
table layout, 55
technical aspects, 53

■ C

Cartesian join, 268
Center of Expertise (CoE), 350
Check the Flash Recovery Area (FRA), 232
CLOB command, 16
COALESCE function, 288
column_name clause, 463
Concatenated index, 73
    skip-scan feature, 73
    WHERE clause, 72–73
Contention, 157
    analyzing Oracle wait events, 161
    blocking locks, 174–175
        DML locks, 178
        enqueue wait event, 176–177
        exclusive locks, 175
        long-term strategy, 178
        shared locks, 175
        short-term strategy, 177–178
        transaction locks, 178
        V$LOCK view, 176
        V$SESSION view, 176
    buffer busy waits, 167
        data block, 168
        segment header, 167
        undo header and undo block, 168
    identifying locked object, 179
    indentifying SQL statements, 159
    latch contention, 188
        cache buffer chains, 190
        cache buffers LRU chain, 190
        CURSOR_SHARING parameter, 191
        shared pool and library latches, 190
    log file sync wait events, 169
    Oracle waiting interface, 157
    read by other session wait event, 170
    recently locked sessions, database, 182–184
    recent wait events, database, 185–186
    reducing direct path read wait events, 171, 173
    RVWR, 173
    simultaneous requests, SGA, 157
    time spent waiting, locking, 186–188
    TM lock contention, 180–181
    transaction locks, 157
    understanding response time, 157
        detailed information, wait event, 158
        processing time, 157
        time model statistics, 159
        wait time, 157
    understanding wait class events, 162
        application wait class, 162–163
        user I/O wait class, 162
    V$SESSION_WAIT view, 163–164
    wait classes, 164
        concurrency issues, 167
        types, 165
CONTROL_MANAGEMENT_PACK_ACCESS
    parameter, 127
Correlated subqueries, 274
    EXISTS clause, 274
    NOT EXISTS, 275
Cost-based optimizer (CBO), 343, 366
CPU, bottlenecks, 202
CPU-consuming processes, 204
cpuspeedNW system statistics, 475
CREATE DATABASE script
    automatic UNDO tablespace, 6
    default tablespace, USERS, 4
    default temporary tablespace, TEMP, 4
    in directories, 6
    online redo logs, 6
    passwords, DBA-related users, 6
    SYSTEM tablespace, 4
Cross join, 268
Cursor leak, 231
cursor_sharing parameter, 483–485

■ D

Database Configuration Assistant (DBCA), 96
Database network connectivity troubleshooting, 209–210
DATE data type, 15
DBA/ALL/USER_EXTENTS, 38
DBA/FS/ALL/FS/USER_CONSTRAINTS view, 68
dbca utility, 4
    advanced mode option, 4
    database creation, 4
    find command, 5
    in Linux/Unix environments, 4
    mydb.rsp file, 5
    rman utility, 6
    in silent mode, 4–5
db file scattered read wait event, 166
db file sequential read wait event, 166
DBMS_AUTO_TASK_ADMIN package, 458
DBMS_MONITOR package, 335
DBMS_WORKLOAD_REPOSITORY package, 137, 139, 142–143
DBMS_WORKLOAD_REPOSITORY PL/SQL package, 128
Degree of parallelism (DOP), 462, 538–539
Diag Trace, 337
Direct path loading
    maximizing speed of insert statements, 18–20
Disk space issues, 195
    df command, 195
    du, sort and head commands, 196
    filesp.bsh, 198

find, Is, sort and head commands, 196
mount point, 196
problem, 195
shell script, monitoring, 196–198
usedSpc variable, 198
Dropping, 142

■ E

Estimate_percent parameter, 462–463, 467
Execution plan, SQL
AUTOTRACE feature, 308–310
DBMS_SQLPA package, 329, 333
DBMS_XPLAN.DISPLAY function, 311–312
ALL, 312
BASIC, 312
cost information, 313
format options, 312
SERIAL, 312
TYPICAL, 312
DISPLAY function, 311
execution statistics
aggregation, 322
V$SQL_MONITOR view, 320–322
GUI view, 314
identifying resource-consuming
DBA_HIST_SQL_PLAN view, 328
DBA_HIST_SQLSTAT view, 327
DBA_HIST_SQLTEXT view, 327
monitoring
DBMS_SQLTUNE.REPORT_SQL_MONITOR
function, 324–326
HASH JOIN, 324
long running query, 317
MERGE JOIN, 324
V$SQL_PLAN_MONITOR view, 323, 325
optimization, 415
formulating steps, 419
hints, 417, 419
initialization parameters, 417, 419
out-of-the-box settings, 417
plan baselines, 420
skep-shaped diagram, 418–419
SQL profiles (see SQL profiles)
statistics, 419
stored outlines, 420
reading
AUTOTRACE, 315
DEPT and EMP tables, 317
factors, 316
Join methods, 317
query processing, steps, 316
resource-consuming SQL statements, 318
V$SQLSTATS to V$SQL, join, 319
V$SQLSTATS view, 319

SQL performance Analyzer, 328, 333
AWR snapshots, 333
considerations, 333
creating analysis task, 329
DBA_ADVISOR, 334
executing analysis task, 329
REPORT_ANALYSIS_TASK function, 330
reporting analysis task function, 333

■ F

Foreign key columns, 69
leading-edge, 69
LISTAGG analytical function, 70
many-to-many intersection table, 69
WHERE clause, 68
Function-based index, 76–77
issues, 76
UPPER function, 76

■ G

GRANULARITY parameter, 464–465

■ H

HASH JOIN, 324
Hybrid columnar compression, 48–49

■ I

INCREMENTAL preference, 465
Index, 51
bitmap index, star schema, 82
B-tree indexes, 84
data warehouse environments, 83
filtering data, fact table, 84
WHERE clause, 83
bitmap join, 85
B-tree, 53 (see also B-tree indexes)
B-tree cluster, 52–53
compression, 74
advantages, 75
COMPRESS N clause, 75
concatenated index, 72–74
skip-scan feature, 73
WHERE clause, 72–73
creating aspects, 51
deciding which columns to index
foreign key columns, 60
index creation and maintenance guidelines, 62
index creation standards, 60
index with NOSEGMENT clause, 63
primary key constraint, 60
unique key constraint, 60

Index (*cont.*)

Domain, 53

foreign key columns

B-tree index creation, 68

leading-edge, 69

LISTAGG analytical function, 70

many-to-many intersection table, 69

WHERE clause, 68

freeing up unused space, 91

rebuilding the index, 92

shrinking the index, 92–93

function-based index, 52

issue, 76

UPPER function, 76

Global partitioned, 52

Hash cluster, 52–53

Indexed virtual column, 52

index-organized table, 86

DBA/ALL/USER_TABLES, 87

INCLUDING clause, 87

ORGANIZATION INDEX, 86

invisible indexes

creation, 81

OPTIMIZER_USE_INVISIBLE_INDEXES, 81

performance, 81

key-compressed, 52

local partitioned, 53

maximizing index creation speed, 89

advantage of NOLOGGING, 90

disadvantage of NOLOGGING, 90

increasing degree of parallelism, 90

turning off redo generation, 89

monitoring usage, 88–89

ALTER INDEX…MONITORING USAGE, 88

Oracle Index types, 52

primary key constraint, 63

ALTER TABLE…AND CONSTRAINT

statement, 63

constraint inline creation, 64

index creation, 64

out of line creation, 65

reverse-key, 52

REBUILD NOREVERSE clause, 80

REBUILD REVERSE clause, 80

REVERSE clause, 79

reverse-key (*see also* B-tree indexes)

unique index

adding constraint, 66

CREATE TABLE statement, 67

creation, 67

techniques, 66

virtual column, 78

cautions, 79

definition, 79

vs. function-based indexes, 78

improving performance, 78

Index creation standards, 60

Index Fast Full Scan (IndexFFS), 368

Index-organized tables (IOTs), 86–87

Inner join

advantages, 264

filtering criteria, 264

ISO syntax, 263–264

advantages, 264

JOIN …ON clause, 264

JOIN…USING clause, 264

NATURAL JOIN clause, 264

traditional Oracle

SQL, 263–264

Inner query, 270

Input/output (I/O) bottlenecks, 205

AWR report, 208

data dictionary, 208

I/O rates, 206

iostat column descriptions, 207

iostat command, 205

I/O statistics, 205, 208

iostat output examination, 206

problem, 205

Statspack, 208

V$ views, 208

ioseektim system statistics, 475

iotfrspeed system statistics, 475

ISO syntax, 259

■ J

Join condition

cross join, 268

full outer join, 268

inner join, 268

inner join (*see* Inner join)

left outer join, 268

outer join (*see* Outer join)

right outer join, 268

■ K

KEEP buffer pool, 99

■ L

LOB data type, 16

Locally managed tablespaces, 1, 8

Low cardinality indexes, 168

■ M

Memory-consuming processes, 204

MERGE JOIN, 324

METHOD_OPT parameter, 463–464

MMON background process, 151

Monitoring
DBMS_SQLTUNE.REPORT_SQL_MONITOR
function, 324–326
HASH JOIN, 324
MERGE JOIN, 324
V$SQL_PLAN_MONITOR view, 323, 325
Multicolumn indexes, 73
Multiple-column subqueries, 273
Multiple-row subqueries, 272
ALL operator, 272
ANY and SOME operators, 272
IN operator, 272

■ N

NCLOB command, 16
Netstat command, 208
Network-intensive processes detection
diagnosing sources, 209
netstat command, 208
OS process ID, 209
problem, 208
Send-Q column, 209
NO_INVALIDATE parameter, 464
NOLOGGING
maximizing speed of insert statements, 18–20
Numeric data type, 14

■ O

Operating system performance analysis, 193
bottlenecks, 198
CPU, 202
CPU and memory (ps), 204
database network connectivity
troubleshooting, 209–210
input/output, 205
network-intensive processes detection, 208
problem, 198
virtual memory statistics (vmstat), 199
vmstat, 198–199
CPU and memory-consuming processes, 204
database performance problem isolation, 193
decision-making process, 193
disk space issues, 195
df command, 195
du, sort and head commands, 196
filesp.bsh, 198
find, ls, sort and head commands, 196
mount point, 196
problem, 195
shell script, monitoring, 196–198
usedSpc variable, 198
OS watcher, 200
oradebug, 213
ps command, 194

resource-intensive process
and database process mapping, 210
termination, 213
top server-resource consuming
processes, 200
column descriptions of top Output, 202
commands to change top output, 201–202
problem, 200
process ID, 201
Task Manager utility, 201
top command, 200
w command, 201
troubleshooting poor performance, 194–195
Operating System (OS) watcher, 200
Optimizer, 457
adaptive cursor sharing
BIND_AWARE column, 488–489
bind peeking, 486
BIND_SHAREABLE column, 487
child cursor, 490
INDEX FAST FULL SCAN, 489
INDEX RANGE SCAN, 489
IS_BIND_AWARE column, 487
Oracle Database 11g, 485, 490
STATUS column, 487
automatic statistics gathering
dbms_auto_task_admin.disable procedure, 459
dbms_auto_task_admin.enable procedure, 459
DBMS_STATS.GATHER_DATABASE_STATS_
JOB_PROC procedure, 459
DBMS_STATS.GATHER_DATABASE_STATS
procedure, 459
enable procedure, 458
GATHER_DATABASE_STATS procedure, 460
bind peeking behavior, 457
bulk loaded tables, 466
column groups, 493–494
concurrent statistics collection
DBMS_STATS.GATHER_TABLES_STATS
procedure, 497
job_queue_processes parameter, 496
monitoring concurrent stats collection jobs, 498
multi-processor environment, 496
parallel execution strategy, 497
SET_GLOBAL_PREFS procedure, 496
exporting statistics, 471–472
goal, 457–458
histograms, 482
index, 479–480
locking statistics, 467–468
missing statistics, 469, 471
new statistics, 477–478
non-use of bind variables, 483–485
partitioned tables, 494–496
query optimizer features, 480–481
related columns, 492–493

Optimizer (*cont.*)
  restoring previous versions, 472–473
  statistics on expressions, 491–492
  system statistics
    interval parameter, 474
    I/O and CPU characteristics, 473
    IOTFRSPEED, IOSEEKTIM, and
      CPUSPEEDNW, 475
    mbrc and mreadtim statistics, 476
    noworkload statistics, 474
    Oracle 11g database, 475
    workload mode, 475
    workload statistics, 474
  types of statistics
    add_sys parameter, 461
    AUTOSTATS_TARGET parameter, 465
    CASCADE parameter, 462
    DEGREE parameter, 462
    ESTIMATE_PERCENT parameter, 462
    GRANULARITY parameter, 464
    INCREMENTAL preference, 465
    METHOD_OPT parameter, 463–464
    NO_INVALIDATE parameter, 464
    pname, 461
    PUBLISH parameter, 465
    pvalue, 461
    SET_DATABASE_PREFS, 461
    SET_GLOBAL_PREFS, 461
    SET_SCHEMA_PREFS, 461
    SET_TABLE_PREFS, 461
    STALE_PERCENT preference, 465
  volatile tables, 466
optimizer_dynamic_sampling initialization parameter, 469
optimizer_features_enable parameter, 481
optimizer_index_cost_adj parameter, 479–480
optimizer_use_pending_statistics parameter, 478
Oracle Database 11g, 340
Oracle Database 11g R2, 16–17
Oracle Diagnostics Pack, 127
Oracle Enterprise Manager, 339
$ORACLE_HOME/rdbms/admin directory, 129
Oracle listener, 371–372
Oracle locks, 174
Oracle Process ID (ORAPID), 359
Oracle's Autotrace utility, 56–57
Oracle's basic compression
  column level
    hybrid columnar compression, 48–49
  direct path loading, 44
    advantage, 45
    ALTER statemment, 45
    COMPRESS clause, 46
    CREATE TABLE…AS SELECT statement, 44
    DBA/ALL/USER_TABLES view, 44
    DML statements, 45
    MOVE COMPRES clause, 45

DML
  ALTER TABLE statement, 47
  COMPRESS FOR OLTP clause, 46–47
  I/O performance, 46
  OLTP compression, 46
Oracle Trace Analyzer, 335, 352
  CoE, 350
  individual SQL, 351
  installation and running steps, 349
  non-default initialization parameters, 351
  non-recursive tome and totals, 351
  self-time, totals, waits, binds and row source
    plan, 351
  tables and indexes, 351
  tacreate.sql script, 349
  top SQL, 351
  /trca/install/trcreate.sql script, 349
  trca_instructions HTML document, 351
  ZIP file, 350
Oradebug, 213
OS Kill command, 214
Outer join
  cross join, 268
  FULL OUTER JOIN, 267
  ISO SQL syntax, 267
  ISO syntax, 268
  left outer join, 267
  Oracle SQL, 268
  right outer join, 267
  syntax, 266
  traditional Oracle SQL, 266

■ P

Parallelism, 537
  ALTER statement, 543
  creating indexes, 549–550
  creating tables, 547
    DDL advantages, 548
    deleting rows, 548
    drawbacks, 549
    reasons, 547
  degree of parallelism, 538, 540
  DML operations, 544
    ALTER SESSION ENABLE PARALLEL DML, 544
    ALTER SESSION FORCE PARALLEL DML, 544
    considerations, 547
    DBMS_PARALLEL_EXECUTE PL/SQL
      package, 545
    DOP, 546
    INSERT statement, 545
    restrictions, 546
    UPDATE, MERGE and DELETE statements, 545
  DOP, 556, 558–559
  EMP table, 542
  existing object, 543

explain plans, 560–561
  execution steps, 562
  operations, 562
finding bottlenecks, 564–565
general rule, 537
indexes, 538, 541
monitoring operations, 562, 564
moving partitions, 553
object creation, 542
pitfalls, 537
rebuilding indexes, 550–551
sessions, detailed information, 566–567
splitting partitions, 555–556
system components, 539
tables, 538, 540
types, 539
understanding factors, 537
PGA histogram, 257
Plan baselines
  altering
    ALTER_SQL_PLAN_BASELINE function, 442
    ATTRIBUTE_NAME and ATTRIBUTE_VALUE, 443
    DBMS_SPM package, 442
  benefits, 416
  disabling, 452
  DISPLAY_SQL_PLAN_BASELINE function, 447–448
  EVOLVE_SQL_PLAN_BASELINE function, 448, 450
  managing tasks, 445
  OPTIMIZER_CAPTURE_SQL_PLAN_BASELINES, 441
  PACK_STGTAB_BASELINE function, 455
  removing, 453
  for SQL statements
    AWR baseline, 438
    DBMS_SPM.LOAD_PLANS_FROM_CURSOR_
      CACHE function, 436
    LOAD_PLANS_CURSOR_CACHE function, 437
    resource-intensive queries, 440
    tuning set object, 439
  transporting, 454
Primary key constraint
  ALTER TABLE…AND CONSTRAINT statement, 63
  constraint inline creation, 64
  index creation, 64
  out of line creation, 65
Primary key index, 63–65
Program global area (PGA), 97
ps command, 194
PUBLISH parameter, 465, 477

NO_RESULT_CACHE hint, 523
PL/SQL package, 524
result_cache hint, 524
server-side result cache, 524
V$RESULT_CACHE_OBJECTS, 522
changing the access path
  analyzing optimizer's cost, 504
  index, 503–504, 506
  INDEX_FFS hint, 506
  index hint, 506
  INDEX_SS hint, 506
  optimizer, 503
  table scan, 503, 505
changing the join method
  cube hint, 511
  hash join, 509, 511
  necessary factors, 511
  nested loops, 509, 511
  querying multiple tables, 510
  sort merge, 510–511
  sort merge joins, 510
changing the join order
  LEADING hint, 508
  optimal join, 508
  ORDERED hint, 507–508
changing the optimizer version, 511
data warehouse performance, 501
directing a distributed query
  disadvantages, 526
  driving site, 526–529
  resource-intensive, 526
direct-path insert technique
  APPEND hint works, 517
  APPEND_VALUES hint, 516
  direct-path load operation, 518
  INSERT operations, 517
  multiple application process, 517
  NO_GATHER_OPTIMIZER_STATISTICS
    hint, 518
  trade-offs, 517
DML performance, 501
enabling query rewrite
  materialized view, 532
  NOREWRITE hint, 533
  REWRITE hint, 532
fast response and overall optimization, 513, 515
  optimizer_mode, 514
  session level, 515
GATHER_PLAN_STATISTICS hint
  A-Rows column, 531
  dbms_xplan, 530
  DISPLAY_CURSOR procedure, 531
  E-Rows column, 531
  gather extended statistics, 531
hint categories, 502
hint writing, 501–502

■ Q

Query coordinator (QC) controls, 353
Query hints
  caching query results
    configuration hierarchy, 525
    initialization parameters, 525

Query hints (*cont.*)
 star information/fact hint
  bitmap index, 535
  configuration elements, 535
 in views
  complex view, 519
  execution plan, 521
  mergeable view, 519
  non-mergeable view, 520
  rules, mergeable view, 520
  simple view, 519

■ R

RAC system, 354–355
RAW data type, 15
Real Application Cluster (RAC) environment, 559
Recovery writer process (RVWR), 173
RECYCLE buffer pool, 99
Resource-intensive process
 and database process mapping, 210
 termination, 213
  problem, 213
  using OS Kill command, 214
  using SQL kill session, 214
  working principle, 215
Reverse-key index, 79–80

■ S

Segment Advisor Advice
 display table information
  advice and recommendations, 24
  ASA_RECOMMENDATIONS, 25
  AWR, 24
  DBMS_SCHEDULER, 24
  DBMS_SPACE package, 23
  Enterprise Manager, 25
  findings, 24
  retrieving tools, 24
 e-mailing advice automatically
  shell script, 29–30
 freeing unused space, 42
  ALTER TABLE…SHRINK SPACE statement, 42–43
  enable row movement, 42
 generating advice manually
  DBMS_ADVISOR.CREATE_TASK procedure, object types, 28
  DBMS_ADVISOR package, 26, 28
  DBMS_ADVISOR.SET_TASK_PARAMETER procedure, 29
  DBMS_SPACE package, 27
 rebuild spanned rows, 31
  MOVE statement, 32
  row chaining, 33–34
  row migration, 35

SELECT_BASELINE_DETAILS function, 139
SELECT statement, 260
 FROM clause, 261
 SELECT clause, 260
 subqueries (*see* Subqueries)
Single-row subqueries, 271
Skip-scan feature, 73
SQL, 259, 307
 avoiding full table scan, 297–298
 avoiding NOT clause, 301
  comparison operators, 302
  drawbacks, 301
  NOT IN, 302
  NOT LIKE, 302
 BETWEEN clause, 281
  Oracle optimizer, 284
  pitfalls, 282
 comparing tables
  INTERSECT set operator, 278
  MINUS set operator, 276–277
 controlling transaction sizes, 303–305
 execution plan, 308 (*see also* Execution plan, SQL)
 inline view, 298–299
  BILLING_INFO view, 300
  PRODUCT_INFO view, 300
  SERVICE_INFO view, 300
 ISO syntax, 259
 joining tables, outer join (*see* Outer join)
 null values, 285
  in SELECT clause, 285–286
  in WHERE clause, 286–288
 partial column values
  benefits, 291
  considerations, 289
  LIKE operator, 288
  TO_CHAR function, 289
 plan baselines (*see* Plan baselines)
 re-using SQL statements, 292–293
  bind variables, 292–293
  execute immediate statement, bind variables, 296
  hard-parsing, 293–294
  PL/SQL block, 292
  soft-parsing, 293
  steps, 293
  TKPROF utility, 294
 SAVEPOINT command, 305
 SELECT statement (*see* SELECT statement)
 UNION/UNION ALL, 279–280
 WHERE clause, 261
SQL kill session, 214
SQL performance Analyzer
 AWR snapshots, 333
 considerations, 333
 creating analysis task, 329
 DBA_ADVISOR, 334

executing analysis task, 329
REPORT_ANALYSIS_TASK function, 330
reporting analysis task function, 333
SQL plan management
plan baselines (*see* Plan baselines)
plan history, 416
SQL profiles, 416
automatic acceptance, 425
vs. database profiles, 424
disabling, 433
manage features, 434
parameters
CATEGORY, 423
DESCRIPTION, 423
FORCE_MATCH, 423–424
NAME, 423
OBJECT_ID, 423
PROFILE_TYPE, 423
REPLACE, 423
TASK_NAME, 423
TASK_OWNER, 423
transporting database, 430
copy the staging table, 432
DBMS_SQLTUNE.CREATE_STGTAB_SQLPROF
procedure, 431
DBMS_SQLTUNE.PACK STGTAB SQLPROF
procedure, 432
DBMS_SQLTUNE.PACK_STGTAB_SQLPROF
procedure, 431
DBMS_SQLTUNE.UNPACK STGTAB SQLPROF
procedure, 432
Tuning Advisor (*see* SQL Tuning Advisor)
SQL Test Case Builder (TCB), 249
SQL tracing, 335
<ADR Home>/trace subdirectory, 337
archive logs, Data Guard environment, 373
automatic Oracle error traces, 369–370 ·
background process, 370–371
correct session, 356
$DIAG_INFO view, 337
diagnostic_dest initialization parameter, 337
Diag Trace, 337
event 10046 trace
instance, 363–364
session, 361, 363
instance/database, 361
login, 365–366
max_dump_file_size parameter, 336, 338
multiple sessions, 360
multiple trace files, 355
optimizer's execution path
access path analysis for SALES, 368
CBO, 366–367
IndexFFS, 368
Oracle event 10053, 366–367
types of information, 367

Oracle Database 11g, 337
Oracle listener, 371–372
own session, 340
parallel query
alter system set events command, 353
MyTrace1, 352
Oracle Database 11g, 353
query coordinator, 353
RAC system, 354–355
show tracefile-t command, 353
trcsess utility, 352–353
process ID, 358–359
running session, 364–365
specific SQL statement, 338
SQL session, 357–358
timed_statistics parameter, 335–336
TKPROF utility, 335
trace dump file, 335
trace files
analysis, 343–344
examination, 342–343
execution plan, 348
execution statistics, 346
finding, 340–341
formatting with TKPROF, 344
header, 346
Oracle Trace Analyzer (*see* Oracle Trace Analyzer)
row source operations, 347
tkprof command, 345
wait events, 348
SQL Tuning Advisor, 376
from ADDM
DBMS_ADDM Package, 412
Enterprise Manager, 413
SQL*plus script, 411
types of recommendations, 414
create and accept SQL profile, 422
DBMS_SQLTUNE, 421
from Enterprise Manager, 409
executing the task, 421
optimizer tuning modes, 411
recommendations, 422
from SQL Developer, 409
steps to run manually, 408
SQL tuning set (STS), 375
in AWR, high-resource consuming
statements, 393
creating object, 390
deleting statements, 401
displaying contents, 399
in Memory, resource-consuming statements, 396
transporting to another database
copy the staging table, 403
create staging table, 402
populate staging table, 403
unpack the staging table, 404

STALE_PERCENT preference, 465
Statement queuing, 558
Statspack, 125–126, 145
Subqueries, 270–271
    correlated subqueries, 274–275
    inline view, 270
    multiple-column subqueries, 273
    multiple-row subqueries, 272
    single-row subqueries, 271
System global area (SGA), 97
Systemstate dump, 233–234
System statistics
    interval parameter, 474
    I/O and CPU characteristics, 473
    IOTFRSPEED, IOSEEKTIM, and CPUSPEEDNW, 475
    mbrc and mreadtim statistics, 476
    noworkload statistics, 474
    Oracle 11g database, 475
    workload mode, 475
    workload statistics, 474

■ T

Table performance, 1
    building database
        CREATE DATABASE script, 3–4, 6
        dbca utility, 4
        default permanent tablespaces, 2, 6
        default temporary tablespaces, 2, 7
        locally managed tablespaces, 2
    compressing data
        column level, 48
        direct path loading, 44–46
        DML, 46
    creating table
        avoiding extent allocation delays, 16–17
        character data types, 13
        data types, 13
        DATE/TIMESTAMP data types, 15
        LOB data type, 16
        numeric data types, 14
        performance and sustainability issues, 10, 12
        RAW data type, 15
        ROWID data type, 15
        scalability and maintainability, 10–12
        SEGMENT CREATION DEFERRED, 18
        SEGMENT CREATION IMMEDIATE, 18
    creating tablespaces
        AUTOEXTEND ON clause, 8
        storage attributes, tables and indexes, 7
    maximizing data loading speeds
        direct path loading, 18–19
        NOLOGGING, 19
    Oracle database, 1

removing table data
    COMMIT/ROLLBACK, 22
    DELETE vs. TRUNCATE statement, 22
    high-water mark, 21
    TRUNCATE statement, 20–21
row chaining and migration, 35
    CHAINED_ROWS tables, 37
    COMPUTE STATISTICS statement, 35
    PCTFREE, 37
    querying V$SYSSTAT, 36
    row length calculation, 37
    table re-organizing, 37
ROWID pseudo-column, 33
Segment Advisor Advice (see Segment
    Advisor Advice)
table, 2
tablespace, 1
table types, 8
    clustered, 9
    external, 9
    heap-organized, 9
    materialized view, 9–10
    nested, 9
    object, 9
    partitioned, 9
    temporary, 9
unused space detection, 38
Task Manager utility, 201
TIMESTAMP data type, 15
TKPROF utility, 294
TM lock contention wait events, 180–181
Top command, 200
tracefile_identifier parameter, 342
Troubleshooting Database
    AWR report
        awrrpt.sql script, 250–251
        Compare Periods report, 253–254
        DBMS_WORKLOAD_REPOSITORY
          package, 252
        instance efficiency percentages, 256
        load profile section, 255–256
        PGA histogram, 257
        session information, 255
        SQL statements, 257
        Time Model Statistics, 257
        Top 5 Foreground Events, 256
    hung database
        oradebug hanganalyze command, 233, 235
        prelim option, 235
        resolving steps, 232
        systemstate dump, 233–234
        true database hang, 234
    invoke ADRCI (see Automatic Diagnostic Repository
        Command Interpreter (ADRCI))

optimal undo retention
parameter, 217
criteria, 220
statistics, 220
V$UNDOSTAT view, 220–221
ORA-01555 error, 223
guaranteed undo retain
feature, 224
snapshot too old error, 224
undo extents, 225
Packaging Incidents, Oracle
Support, 244–245
resolving open cursor errors, 230–231
running health check, 245, 247
SQL test case
creation process information, 250
DBMS_SQLDIAG package, 249
exporting data, 247–248
EXPORT_SQL_TESTCASE
procedure, 250
temporary tablespace
identifying the user, 226
monitoring the usage, 225
one-pass/multi-pass
operations, 227
unable to extend TEMP segment
error, 228–229
UNDO_TABLESPACE initialization
parameter, 219–220
Undo usage
V$SESSION, 222
V$TRANSACTION, 222
Tuning task, 375

■ U

Unique index, 66–67
adding constraint, 66
CREATE TABLE statement, 67
creation, 67
techniques, 66
UTLBSTAT/UTLESTAT, 125, 145

■ V

V$SESSION_LONGOPS view, 317–318
Very large databases (VLDBs), 547
Virtual column
cautions, 79
definition, 79
vs. function-based indexes, 78
improving performance, 78
Virtual memory statistics (vmstat), 198–199
CPU section, 200
IO section, 200
memory area, 199
OS components, 199
swap section, 199
swpd column, 199
system area, 200

■ W, X, Y, Z

Wait events, 348
analyzing Oracle wait events, 161
application class, 162
buffer busy waits, 167
data block, 168
segment header, 168
undo header and undo block, 168
class, 165
commit class, 162
db file scattered read wait event, 166
db file sequential read wait event, 166
examining session waits, 163–164
indentifying SQL statements, 159
log file sync waits, 169–170
Network class, 162
read by other session, 170
reducing direct path read, 172
RVWR wait events, 173
User I/O class, 162
V$ACTIVE_SESSION_HISTORY view, 185–186
W command, 201
WHERE clause, 83

Get the eBook for only $10!

Now you can take the weightless companion with you anywhere, anytime. Your purchase of this book entitles you to 3 electronic versions for only $10.

This Apress title will prove so indispensible that you'll want to carry it with you everywhere, which is why we are offering the eBook in 3 formats for only $10 if you have already purchased the print book.

Convenient and fully searchable, the PDF version enables you to easily find and copy code—or perform examples by quickly toggling between instructions and applications. The MOBI format is ideal for your Kindle, while the ePUB can be utilized on a variety of mobile devices.

Go to www.apress.com/promo/tendollars to purchase your companion eBook.

CPSIA information can be obtained at www.ICGtesting.com
Printed in the USA
BVOW09s1138280615

406498BV00007B/82/P